BUSINESS ESSENTIALS

Second Edition

Ronald J. Ebert

University of Missouri-Columbia

Ricky W. Griffin

Texas A&M University

Prentice-Hall, Upper Saddle River, New Jersey 07458

FOR JACK AND FRAN—WHO HAVE SHOWN THAT
COMMITMENT, LOYALTY, AND SERVICE ARE
COMPANIONS OF LOVE AND HONOR

R.J.E.

FOR GLENN AND NORA LEE MAY—
MY "OTHER" PARENTS

R.W.G.

Senior Acquisitions Editor: Donald J. Hull
Assistant Editor: John Larkin
Vice President/Editorial Director: James Boyd
Marketing Manager: John Chillingworth
Managing Editor: Dee Josephson
Manufacturing Supervisor: Arnold Vila
Designer Manager: Pat Smythe
Cover Design: Pat Smythe
Photo Research: Melinda Alexander
Composition/Editorial: Monotype Comp. Co. Inc.

Senior Development Editor: Ronald Librach
Editorial Assistant: Jim Campbell
Director of Development: Steve Deitmer
Production Editor: Aileen Mason
Associate Managing Editor: Linda DeLorenzo
Manufacturing Manager: Vincent Scelta
Interior Design: Lorraine Castellano
Illustrator (Interior): Electra Graphics, Inc.
Cover Art: Marjory Dressler

Ebert, Ronald J.
  Business essentials / Ronald J. Ebert, Ricky W. Griffin.
    p. cm.
  Includes bibliographical references and index.
  ISBN 0-13-751710-6 (pbk.)
  1. Industrial management—United States. 2. Business enterprises—
United States. I. Griffin, Ricky W. II. Title.
HD70.U5E2 1998
658—dc21   97-19714
                                CIP

Printed in the United States of America
10 9 8 7 6 5 4 3

Prentice-Hall International (UK) Limited, London
Prentice-Hall of Australia Pty. Limited, Sydney
Prentice-Hall Canada, Inc., Toronto
Prentice-Hall Hispanoamericana, S.A., Mexico
Prentice-Hall of India Private Limited, New Delhi
Prentice-Hall of Japan, Inc., Tokyo
Simon & Schuster Asia Pte. Ltd., Singapore
Editora Prentice-Hall do Brasil, Ltda., Rio de Janeiro

■ OVERVIEW

■ CONTENTS

v

■ PREFACE

We didn't foresee that developing a new product could be so exciting! Indeed, following its introduction just three years ago, the enthusiastic reception for *Business Essentials* among instructors and students has stimulated this second edition of the book. For this revision, as with the first edition, we have conceived *Business Essentials* as a new product with a unique purpose. The book reflects more than just changes that are occurring in the practice of business. It also reflects the changing needs of students and teachers of business.

■ MEETING THE CUSTOMER'S NEEDS

Business Essentials is an alternative for those who want a no-nonsense approach for the introduction to business course. It contains the "no-frills" essentials of business for those instructors who want focused coverage in a low-priced book.

In creating this second edition of *Business Essentials*, we drew upon our experiences in developing the first edition and upon even earlier experiences in developing four successful editions of *Business*. Much of the core material in this new edition of *Business Essentials* is adapted from *Business*. It has been thoroughly updated, and the organization and format of the two books are completely different. We have retained or adapted the most valuable features of *Business*. In this revision, for example, we have retained the *Business Field Trip* feature that chronicles the activities and fortunes of Chaparral Steel Co., a world-class mini-mill located in Midlothian, Texas. This feature has proved popular because it provides a running account of how a particular company handles all facets of its operations. In all other major respects, however, *Business Essentials* is a different product intended for a specific audience. We encourage you to compare the books, side-by-side, for a convincing demonstration of their distinctly different orientations.

We are most proud of *Business Essentials* because its development enabled us to practice what we preach by addressing the significant but previously unmet needs of an important market segment. Prentice Hall, the authors, and the panel of advisors who teach business listened closely to our customers, both students and instructors, in creating a successful new product. Not surprisingly, the twofold mandate of *Business Essentials*—brevity and high quality—involved sometimes challenging, often difficult decisions about content and orientation. Very early in the project, we learned to appreciate the difficulties of being selective; deciding upon which subject matter to emphasize and which materials to exclude was painful (you can't have a shorter book of high quality without cutting). Ultimately, our decisions for this second edition, as for the first, were guided by suggestions from teachers and students, as well as by our own experiences with the practice of business.

■ THE OBJECTIVES OF *BUSINESS ESSENTIALS*

This second edition of *Business Essentials* was guided by the same fundamental objectives that we established for the book at the outset:

- ■ We wanted it to be an *affordable, lower-price* alternative for students in the introductory course.
- ■ We wanted it to be *reduced in length* while retaining high quality in its coverage of the essential facets of business.
- ■ We wanted it to be *accurate*, with all statements of fact based on scientific research and/or managerial practice.
- ■ We wanted it to be *current*, with illustrative examples and cases drawn from business stories that are still unfolding.
- ■ We wanted it to be *readable* so that students could appreciate the experience of encountering and thinking about life in the world of business.

We believe that we have met all of these objectives. The price of *Business Essentials* is lower than that of most major, high-quality books designed for the introductory course. The book offers significant coverage of business essentials, including both traditional topics and newer ideas. All of our examples are drawn from today's business world, and we added and updated information and examples right up to the moment we went to press in the spring of 1997.

■ THE THEMES OF *BUSINESS ESSENTIALS*

The 1990s have been a particularly exciting time in which to do business. But to be fully prepared for business in the third millennium, students need to be aware of the trends that will affect them as they start their careers. For this reason, we have concentrated on bringing several important themes to their attention.

- ■ **The Growth of International Business.** Many businesspeople and observers of the business world see globalization of the economy as the great challenge in the coming century. To keep students aware of this challenge, we have based many of the examples, vignettes, boxes, and cases in this book on the experiences of global companies. Chapter 5, "Understanding the Global Context of Business," provides full coverage of this important topic.

- ■ **The Significance of Small Business.** Because we recognize that most students will not go to work for large corporations, we have provided balanced coverage of both small and large companies throughout the text. Chapter 8, "Understanding Entrepreneurship and the Small Business," is comprehensive. In addition, examples throughout the book deal with small businesses, and many chapters contain sections on how specific practices and issues apply to the special concerns of small businesses.

- ■ **The Growth of the Service Sector.** The 1990s have witnessed the continued growth of the service sector around the globe. We stress the importance of this sector by giving it equal billing with manufacturing in Chapter 11, "Managing Production and Improving Quality." Throughout, the book also provides prominent coverage of service businesses in the examples, cases, visuals, and end-of-chapter exercises.

- ■ **The Need to Manage Information and Communications Technology.** In our information-based society, the people and organizations that learn how to obtain and use information will be the ones that succeed. The explosive growth in information systems stems from the emergence of communications technologies such as multimedia communications systems. We cover this important topic in detail in Chapter 12, "Understanding Accounting and Information Systems," where the discussion has been completely reworked for accuracy and currency.

■ **The Role of Ethics and Social Responsibility.** Because business ethics and social responsibility have been generating much discussion in recent years, we devote a full chapter to them (Chapter 4, "Conducting Business Ethically and Responsibly"). And we treat issues of business ethics and social responsibility in our examples, cases, and other features.

■ **The Quality Imperative.** Quality improvement continues to be of special interest as we approach the year 2000. Its coverage in Chapter 11, "Managing Production and Improving Quality," was initiated in response to requests and suggestions of instructors. We also present quality considerations where they relate to other materials throughout the book.

■ **The Importance of Career Preparation.** Most business students are naturally quite concerned about their careers. In response to these concerns, we have developed a special appendix, "Business Careers and the Job Search," which has been significantly revised and updated from the first edition. Sections on employment trends, guidelines for preparing cover letters and résumés and attending job interviews, and methods for assessing job offers provide practical guidance for seeking employment and understanding the process.

■ FEATURES OF *BUSINESS ESSENTIALS*

A textbook must be packaged effectively and engagingly if it is to accomplish its objectives. We have designed a number of devices to make this book as user-friendly as possible.

■ Every chapter begins with the first part of a **two-part case** that introduces a current real-world business situation by engaging student interest in the content and issues that follow in the chapter. Next comes a list of **learning objectives** for the chapter—a simple blueprint to alert students to the key subjects of study in the chapter.

■ Within each chapter are **figures, tables,** and **photographs** to illustrate a point or convey a message. The selective inclusion of these visuals increases the reader's involvement in the text. All photos are inspired by the text material; captions expand upon the text content.

■ Each chapter includes two **thematic boxes** designed to provide additional perspectives on the material. Various topics include reports on high-interest topics, analyses of newly emerging problems, and examinations of controversial issues in today's business environment. In one chapter of each part, one of the two boxes is devoted to our *Business Field Trip* to Chaparral Steel, introducing and describing in detail the various facets of Chaparral's operations.

■ To emphasize fundamental concepts, each **key term** is printed in boldface in the text and defined in the margin of the page where it is introduced. A comprehensive **glossary** at the end of the book provides readily accessible definitions as well as a reference to the text page where the word first occurs.

■ Selected **cartoons** and **quotation callouts** are used occasionally to stimulate interest and enhance understanding of certain key points.

- At the conclusion of each chapter, we wrap up the **two-part case** with which we opened the chapter. Here we incorporate questions for discussion so that students can analyze the case, either on their own or in class as a group activity.

- Several other useful features are found toward the end of each chapter. A concise *Summary of Learning Objectives* is followed by pedagogical features that both review what's been learned and ask students to apply what they've learned. *Study Questions and Exercises* are divided into three categories: **review** (which tests recall of material), **analysis** (which tests understanding), and **application exercises** (which ask students to apply concepts to basic problems).

- *Building Your Business Skills* exercises give students an opportunity to apply both their knowledge and their critical-thinking skills to extended problems drawn from a wide range of realistic business experiences. Each exercise begins with a list of specific goals. A business situation is then described, and a step-by-step method for proceeding is outlined. Follow-up questions help students focus on the topic at hand.

  All of the *Building Your Business Skills* exercises are brand-new to this edition and have been specifically designed to satisfy the pedagogical criteria laid out in the Secretary of Labor's Commission on Achieving Necessary Skills (SCANS). SCANS was developed to identify the competencies that will be needed by students preparing to assume their roles in the workplace, and the exercises in this feature have been designed to foster in-depth involvement and problem solving in a format suitable for both out-of-class preparation and in-class discussion. To help students apply classroom and textbook lessons to the real world of business, *Building Your Business Skills* exercises emphasize the following areas in which students are encouraged to practice their skills: resources, interpersonal skills, information, systems, and technology.

- The growing prominence of the Internet as an information medium has stimulated the introduction of a new feature—*Exploring the Net*—at the end of each chapter. Students are directed toward Internet information sources and hands-on network activities that enhance and reinforce understanding of important topics in each chapter. As in *Building Your Business Skills*, the *Exploring the Net* exercises are specifically designed to foster in-depth involvement and problem solving. The format is hands-on, and activities are designed to accommodate both out-of-class preparation and in-class discussion.

  Finally, although we waited until the last possible minute to finalize the installments in this feature, we understand that users will undoubtedly encounter problems in accessing the same home pages and subdirectories that we used in creating these exercises. The reason will almost always be the same: a content provider has exercised his or her option to make changes in material without incurring the costs of reworking printed material. Change and flexibility, in other words, are integral features of the Internet, and so we urge everyone to be flexible and creative. There are numerous sources for most types of information, and both we and our colleagues have found that when faced with glitches, determined students not only find what they want but gain valuable experience in working with search engines. We are convinced that inventive students will not only locate alternative solutions to most exercise problems but will gain in enthusiasm in the process.

- Each of the book's seven parts concludes with two **video exercises.** These exercises are designed to cover a range of issues raised in the part as a whole and are drawn from two different resources:

- **Video Exercises 1.1 through 7.1** are coordinated with video segments gleaned from the on-air files of ABC News. These exercises provide a glimpse into those occasions when business and business-related activities are literally newsworthy.
- The segments in **Video Exercises 1.2 through 6.2** were produced specifically for Prentice Hall. Each 8- to 10-minute segment focuses on a relevant aspect of operations at Lands' End Inc., a major catalog retailer located in Dodgeville, Wisconsin. ▼ The purpose of these videos, which were shot on location and include interviews with managers and employees at Lands' End, is to anchor exercises focusing on the operations of a successful American company that deals with both goods and services on a global scale. Both authors and publisher wish to thank Coordinator of Public Relations Lisa Mullens and the other individuals at Lands' End who extended courtesy, cooperation, and resources in helping to create the *On Location* video exercises.

Note that the video exercises in this edition of *Business Essentials*, like the *Building Your Business Skills* and *Exploring the Net* exercises, have been redesigned for pedagogical effectiveness. The videos themselves *are* now the part-ending "cases," and the material placed in the text itself is designed to *direct or focus student activities:*

- *Learning Objectives* tell students what information to look for and what concepts to focus on as they watch the video
- *Background Information* provides context and supplements facts where needed
- A description of *The Video* previews the content of the segment
- *Discussion Questions* help students organize their thoughts on the material shown
- *Follow-Up Assignments* furnish an opportunity for further study about the video topic
- Where applicable, a section designed *For Further Exploration* encourages supplemental activities, many of which are geared to further research on the Internet

In 1981, Lands' End coined the term "direct merchant" to describe its approach to the retailing business. Since 1994, Lands' End has been the biggest specialty-catalog company in the United States, with more than 8 million customers in 75 countries. "One thing we have learned over the years," says Managing Director Phil Young, "is that change is constant." **Lands' End is the subject of the** *On Location* **video exercises integrated into this edition of** *Business Essentials.*

■ THE *BUSINESS FIELD TRIP*

Finally, we would like to return briefly to the feature that we have called the *Business Field Trip*. Accompanied by Senior Acquisitions Editor Don Hull, the authors journeyed to Midlothian, Texas, for guided tours, education, and interviews with the top managers of Chaparral Steel Co. The seven installments in the *Business Field Trip* integrated in this edition were compiled from the tapes, notes, and photos that we brought back, as well as from follow-up interviews. These elements appear in the second edition of *Business Essentials* as follows:

- PART 1/CHAPTER 1: "A Business Field Trip to Chaparral Steel"
- PART 2/CHAPTER 5: "International Markets Are Our Elastic Band"
- PART 3/CHAPTER 7: "You Have to Encourage Creativity Just to Stay in Place"
- PART 4/CHAPTER 10: "We Want Employees to Think Like Owners"
- PART 5/CHAPTER 11: "Keep the Mill Running or Lose $10,000 an Hour"
- PART 5/CHAPTER 12: "Who Needs Paper Anyway?"
- PART 6/CHAPTER 14: "Our Customers Know Us and We Know Them"

Chaparral has also provided a video to introduce its operations and its employees. That video is the "text" for Video Exercise 1.1, "Best Practices at Chaparral Steel: 'If It Ain't Broke, We Break It,'" immediately following Chapter 2.

Why Chaparral Steel? Chaparral Steel is a medium-sized company that has found new ways of doing business in an old industry—an industry in which some traditional giants have struggled or declined in productivity. We believe that our material on Chaparral provides a fully integrated—and highly detailed—approach to understanding the realities of business in today's world. ▼

■ SUPPLEMENTS

Because we recognize both the excitement and the challenge of teaching, we have endeavored to provide you with a text that will make your work more enjoyable. Toward this end, we have assembled what we believe is the best total instructional system avail-

The landscape of the U.S. steel industry has changed dramatically since Chaparral Steel was incorporated as a so-called "mini-mill" in 1973. CEO Gordon E. Forward emphasizes that Chaparral has thrived by nurturing a corporate culture which reflects the needs of a changing industry in the last quarter of the 20th century. The key, he says, is "reinvesting in our people."

able for a business text. Each component of the teaching and learning package has been carefully crafted to ensure that this first course in business is a rewarding experience for both instructors and students.

- *Instructor's Manual*
- *Study Guide*
- Test Item File
- *Prentice Hall Custom Test*
- Powerpoint Transparencies
- Color Transparencies
- Prentice Hall/ABC News and Prentice Hall *On Location* Video Libraries
- Stock Market and Investment Practice Set
- *The Prentice Hall Career Guide*
- *Beginning Your Career Search*
- Prentice Hall/*New York Times* "Themes of the Times" for Business
- *Threshold Competitor: A Management Simulation*
- PHLIP: Prentice Hall's excellent Website
- *Enterprise: The CD-ROM for Business*
- *The Business Student Writer's Manual*

Further, we would like to highlight the following elements in the new package for the second edition of *Business Essentials:*

- **Prentice Hall Custom Test** (Windows version) is based on the number-one bestselling test-generating software program developed by Engineering Software Associates. This state-of-the-art test-creation program is not only suitable for established courses but is customizable according to individual needs. It is userfriendly, and this powerful program permits instructors to originate error-free tailor-made tests quickly and easily. Exams can be administered either on-line or traditionally, and *Custom Test* also tracks students' results and analyzes the success of specific tests.

- **Threshold Competitor: A Management Simulation** (Second Edition) is the only Windows-based introduction to business simulation currently available. Using *Threshold*, students work in groups to manage small manufacturing companies competing in the same marketplace. They decide on company missions, goals, policies, and strategies in areas ranging from marketing to finance and manufacturing. They practice skills in planning, organizing, directing, and controlling and get responses to both questions and decisions.

- **PHLIP Website** is a Web-based learning environment that contains numerous links to discipline-specific Websites. In addition to download areas and bulletin board capacity, PHLIP features current events articles that are updated about every two weeks and a faculty support section that provides instructors with access to textual and media material in the Prentice Hall Business Publishing archive. The purpose of PHLIP is to furnish up-to-date classroom support through state-of-the-art technology and resources. Instructors and students can access PHLIP from the PH Business Publishing home page at

http://www.prenhall.com/ph business

- **Enterprise: The CD-ROM for Business** is an innovative encyclopedia that allows students to study material by focusing on selected topics rather than by retracing their steps through fixed, preexisting chapters. The encyclopedia format (which is constructed from the text and features of the fourth edition of *Business*) permits students to construct their own courses of study with each session, interacting with the text and an array of audio and visual features not only to strengthen the conceptual connections that they need to understand for class but also to explore areas of personal interest. The special capabilities of the CD-ROM format make interactive study both challenging and speedy.

■ *Beginning Your Career Search,* prepared by James S. O'Rourke, IV, Director, Fanning Center for Business Communication at the University of Notre Dame, is a concise book that discusses all of the essentials for career planning. Chapters cover résumé preparation, introductory and follow-up letters, researchig companies, interviews, handling job offers, and sample letters.

■ *The Business Student Writer's Manual,* by Tom Bergman, Greg Scott, and Steve Garrison, all of the University of Central Oklahoma, is a separate book from Prentice Hall that teaches writing skills in the context of regular classes.

■ ACKNOWLEDGEMENTS

Although only two names appear on the cover of this book, we could never have completed it without the participation of many fine individuals. First, we would like to thank the professionals who took time from their busy schedules to review materials for us:

Michael Baldigo
Sonoma State University

Harvey Bronstein
Oakland Community College

Gary Christiansen
North Iowa Area Community College

Pat Ellebracht
Northeast Missouri State University

John Gubbay
Moraine Valley Community College

Edward M. Henn
Broward Community College

Betty Ann Kirk
Tallahassee Community College

Sofia B. Klopp
Palm Beach Community College

Kenneth J. Lacho
University of New Orleans

Keith Leibham
Columbia Gorge Community College

John F. Mastriani
El Paso Community College

William E. Matthews
William Paterson College of New Jersey

Thomas J. Morrisey
Buffalo State College

David William Murphy
Madisonville Community College

Scott Norwood
San Jose State University

Joseph R. Novak
Blinn College

Constantine Petrides
Borough of Manhattan Community College

Roy R. Pipitone
Erie Community College

William D. Raffield
University of St. Thomas

Richard Randall
Nassau Community College

Betsy Ray
Indiana Business College

Richard Reed
Washington State University

Lewis Schlossinger
Community College of Aurora

Robert N. Stern
Cornell University

Arlene Strawn
Tallahassee Community College

Philip A. Weatherford
Embry-Riddle Aeronautical University

Jane A. Treptow
Broward Community College

Jerry E. Wheat
Indiana University Southeast

Janna P. Vice
Eastern Kentucky University

Pamela J. Winslow
Berkeley College of Business

Joseph Hecht of Montclair State University prepared the *Study Guide*, and Athena Miklos of Charles County Community College developed 100 acetate and 125 PowerPoint transparencies. Judy Block, president of JRB Communications Inc. of Westport, Connecticut, prepared both the *Prentice Hall Career Guide* and Appendix II, "Business Careers and the Job Search." We are also greatly indebted to Judy's substantive contributions to the text, ranging from resource materials to draft material on specialized topics and finished cases, boxes, and exercises. As always, she was inventive and indefatigible in her capacity as professional researcher and writer.

Authors, of course, typically get the credit when a book is successful, but the success of this book must be shared with an outstanding group of people at Prentice Hall, where a superb team of professionals made this book a pleasure to write. Our editor, Don Hull, initiated this project and has contributed to the package in more ways than we can list. We are engaged in ongoing discussions with Don about the best possible positioning of *Business* and *Business Essentials* and their future in both traditional and electronic formats. Lyn Camire and Rachel Stadden of Monotype Editorial Services oversaw the production of the text, which was beautifully designed by Lorraine Castellano. Assistant Editor John Larkin managed the development of all the supplements. Melinda Reo and Melinda Alexander handled photo research. Marketing Manager John Chillingworth made numerous contributions to the product itself and has since been tireless in getting out the message about the result. Ron Librach, our development editor, inspired the overall tone for the revision, pored over the manuscript at every step of the process, provided truly innovative design ideas, and continually encouraged us to add value here, to update there, to clarify the discussion, and to meet our deadlines.

Also at Prentice Hall we would like to acknowledge the expertise and support of Director of Development Steve Deitmer, Director of Production and Manufacturing Joanne Jay, Design Manager Pat Smythe, Production Editor Aileen Mason, Monotype copy editor Barbara Karni and compositor Lori Atwell, and Editorial Assistant Jim Campbell. On campus, Phyllis Washburn furnished timely and professional secretarial services.

We owe a great deal of thanks to the professionals at Chaparral Steel Co. in Midlothian, Texas, who opened their doors to us and worked with us every step of the way to ensure that our *Business Field Trip* feature would be as informative as possible to our readers. Specifically, we would like to thank Gordon E. Forward, Dennis Beach, Jeff Roesler, Jeff Werner, Tom Harrington, Jack Loteryman, Larry Clark, H. Duff Hunt III, and Gary Shirley, not to mention the many other employees of Chaparral Steel to whom we spoke during our visits.

Our colleagues at the University of Missouri and Texas A&M University also deserve recognition. We both have the good fortune to be a part of a community of scholars who enrich our lives and challenge our ideas. Without their intellectual stimulation and support, our work would suffer greatly.

Finally, our families . . . . We take pride in the accomplishments of our wives, Mary and Glenda, and draw strength from the knowledge that they are there for us to lean on. And we take great joy from our children, Matt, Kristen, Doug, Ashley, and Dustin. Sometimes in the late hours when we're ready for sleep but have to get one or two more pages written, looking at your pictures keeps us going. Thanks to all of you for making us what we are.

■ ABOUT THE AUTHORS

Ronald J. Ebert is Professor of Management at the University of Missouri–Columbia. He received his B.S. in Industrial Engineering from Ohio State University, his M.B.A. from the University of Dayton, and his D.B.A. from Indiana University, where he was a U.S. Steel Fellow. A member of and an active participant in the Academy of Management, the Institute of Management Sciences, the American Production and Inventory Control Society, and the Operations Management Association, Dr. Ebert has also served as the editor of the *Journal of Operations Management* and as Chair of the Production and Operations Management Division of the Academy of Management. In addition to *Business*, he is the co-author of three books: *Organizational Decision Processes*, *Production and Operations Management* (published in English, Spanish, and Chinese), and *Management*.

Dr. Ebert has held engineering and supervisory positions in quality management with the Frigidaire Division of General Motors Corporation. He has also done TQM and operations strategy consulting for the National Science Foundation, the United States Savings and Loan League, Kraft Foods, Oscar Mayer, Sola Optical USA, Inc., the City of Columbia, and the American Public Power Association. His research interests include manufacturing policy and strategy, engineering design processes in product development, statistical quality control, and subjective managerial judgments in strategy formulation.

Ricky W. Griffin was born and raised in Corsicana, Texas. He received his B.A. from North Texas State University and his M.B.A. and Ph.D. from the University of Houston. He served on the faculty of the University of Missouri–Columbia from 1978 until 1981, when he joined the faculty at Texas A&M. In 1990, he was named the university's Lawrence E. Fouraker Professor of Business Administration.

Dr. Griffin's research interests include leadership, workplace violence, and international management. He has done consulting in the areas of task design, employee motivation, and quality circles for such organizations as Baker-Hughes, Texas Instruments, Six Flags Corporation, Texas Commerce Bank, and AT&T. His research has won two Academy of Management Research Awards (both in the Organizational Behavior division) and one Texas A&M University Research Award.

Dr. Griffin currently serves as the Director of the Center for Human Resource Management at Texas A&M. In addition to *Business*, he is the author or co-author of five books and more than 40 journal articles and book chapters.

BUSINESS ESSENTIALS

1

CHAPTER

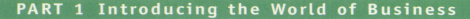
UNDERSTANDING THE U.S. BUSINESS SYSTEM

Tired of Mickey Mouse Vacations?

TRY DISNEY'S VERSION OF CHINESE COOKING, SEAWEED FACIALS, AND SPIRITUAL INQUIRY

There's no getting around it: the baby boom generation is aging. The oldest of the 76 million baby boomers turned 50 in 1996, and in the next decade, the number of Americans over 50 will increase by 50 percent, to nearly 38 million. Most are so-called "empty nesters"—couples whose children have left home. Many thrive on personal and even physical challenge, but—perhaps predictably—most have absolutely no interest in taking another Disney World vacation. To borrow an expression from Generation X, they've "been there, done that."

Creative minds at the Walt Disney Co. saw these demographic and mood shifts as a commercial challenge requiring a tailor-made solution: They had to find a way to attract 40- and 50-year-olds who were no longer as active or child-oriented as they once were and who wanted to return from their vacations with something more than a suntan. In other words, asks Orlando-based marketing researcher Peter Yesawich, "What do you do if you're 48 and your kids are grown up?"

Disney's answer is the Disney Institute, a 75-acre resort within a resort. Located at Orlando's Disney

> ### "What do you do if you're 48 and your kids are grown up?"
>
> —Peter Yesawich
> *Orlando-based marketing researcher*

World, the resort allows guests to try their hands at bird watching, cartoon animation, rock climbing, gourmet cooking, spiritual inquiry, and more. This $35 million solution—billed by Disney as "smart fun"—is pretty much like a summer camp for adults. Described in the official guide as "a unique resort with 80 different programs to expand your mind and challenge your body," the Disney Institute required that Disney build the equivalent of a new business from scratch.

The vision for the Disney Institute began to take shape when Disney CEO Michael Eisner visited the Chautauqua Institution, an adult-learning community located in upstate New York that holds classes on politics, philosophy, and the performing arts. Eisner's 1985 visit convinced him that Disney could create a similar

environment "to enhance and improve quality of life in the Disney fashion." But unlike Chautauqua, Disney's version would be designed for mainstream Americans. Marketing research revealed that this type of vacation alternative was particularly attractive to baby boomers. It also showed that baby boomers had money to spend and the willingness to spend it on themselves: according to government data, adults between 45 and 54 years of age—Disney's target market—have higher incomes than any other U.S. age group.

Eleven years after Eisner's visit to Chautauqua, the Disney Institute opened its doors. Not surprisingly, visitors found elements of the Disney they knew, including perky, uniformed staff and immaculate grounds. Missing, however, were Goofy, Mickey, Donald, and Pluto. Gone, too, were endless lines for rides and stores filled with stuffed animals. In their place were feel-good classes, like the one on "Culinary Technique" taken by Greg Dawson, a columnist for the *Orlando Sentinel*. Dawson described his instructors as "two Disney chefs with comedy-club ambitions" who advised students to "never cook bacon in your bathing suit." The Institute is also a recreational resort, with nightly entertainment and such features as a golf program created by legendary pro Gary Player.

The greatest challenge for Disney was to convince the public to try a venture that was so far afield from Disney's traditional mass-market resorts. It had to build a new market by slowly creating demand. Disney responded to this need in several ways:

- By catering to the trend toward shorter vacations (the Disney Institute offers three-, four-, and seven-night packages)
- By striking a balance between education and entertainment (although it offers a variety of unique "challenges," no one would ever accuse the Institute of being a grind)
- By offering special introductory rates as part of its "First 100 Days of Discovery"
- By relying on word of mouth as well as traditional advertising to build a base of support
- By deciding that the Institute would be a long-term investment

Underlying all of these efforts was an appeal to the needs and wants of each individual customer in the target market. "Experience a vacation," beckons one ad, "where every day is different and every day is yours to design."

The challenge of sustaining a business despite changing market forces is as common to a corporate Goliath like Disney as it is to a small business. A changing marketplace creates the need for the kind of innovative responses that have long defined business in the United States. These responses require vision, careful attention to quality and customer service, substantial financial commitment, and a well-defined marketing strategy that helps a business grow over time. These and a host of other forces are the main themes in stories of success and failure that are told over and over again in the annals of enterprise in the United States. As you will see in this chapter, those forces are also the key factors in the U.S. market economy. You will also see that although the world's economic systems differ markedly, standards for evaluating success or failure are linked to a system's capacity to achieve certain basic goals.

By focusing on the learning objectives of this chapter, you will better understand the U.S. business system and the mechanisms by which it not only pursues its goals but permits businesses large and small to pursue theirs.

After reading this chapter, you should be able to

1. Define the nature of U.S. *business* and identify its main goals

2. Describe different types of *economic systems* according to the means by which they control the *factors of production*

3. Show how *demand* and *supply* affect resource distribution in the United States

4. Identify the elements of *private enterprise* and explain the various *degrees of competition* in the U.S. economic system

5. Explain the criteria for evaluating the success of an economic system in meeting its goals and show how the federal government attempts to manage the U.S. economy

Continued on page 21

1

The Concept of Business and the Concept of Profit

What do you think of when you hear the word *business?* Does it conjure up images of huge corporations like General Motors and IBM? Are you reminded of smaller companies, like your local supermarket? Or do you think of even smaller one-person operations, like the barbershop around the corner? Each of these organizations is a **business**—an organization that provides goods or services in order to earn profits. Indeed, the prospect of earning **profits**—the difference between a business's revenues and its expenses—is what encourages people to open and to expand businesses. Profits reward owners for taking the risks involved in investing their money and time.

Today businesses produce most of the goods and services that we consume. They also employ most of the working people in the United States. Moreover, new forms of technology, service businesses, and international opportunities promise to keep production, consumption, and employment growing indefinitely.[1] In turn, profits from businesses are paid to millions of owners and stockholders. Taxes on businesses help support governments at all levels. In many cases, businesses also support charitable causes and provide community leadership.

In this chapter, we begin our introduction to business by looking at its role in both the U.S. economy and U.S. society. There are, of course, a variety of economic systems around the world. Once you understand something about the systems of most developed countries, you will better appreciate the workings of the U.S. system. As we will see, the effects of economic forces on businesses and the effects of businesses on the economy are dynamic—and, indeed, sometimes volatile.

business
An organization that provides goods or services in order to earn profits

profits
The difference between a business's revenues and its expenses

■ ECONOMIC SYSTEMS AROUND THE WORLD

Not surprisingly, a U.S. business operates differently from a business in, say, France or China. And businesses in these countries are different from businesses in Japan or Brazil. A major factor in these differences is the economic system of a firm's "home" country—the country in which it conducts most of its business. An **economic system** is a nation's system for allocating its resources among its citizens—both individuals and organizations. In this section, we will show how economic systems differ according to the ownership and/or control of these resources, often called *factors of production*. We will also describe several kinds of economic systems.

economic system
A nation's system for allocating its resources among its citizens

Factors of Production

The key difference in economic systems lies in the different ways in which they manage the **factors of production**—that is, the basic resources a country's businesses use to produce goods and services. These resources include *labor, capital, entrepreneurs,* and *natural resources.*[2]

factors of production
Resources used in the production of goods and services—natural resources, labor, capital, and entrepreneurs

labor (or human resources)
The physical and mental capabilities of people as they contribute to economic production

Labor   The people who work for businesses represent labor. Sometimes called **human resources, labor** includes both the physical and mental contributions of people as they are engaged in economic production. For example, Philip Morris Companies Inc. employs about 165,000 people worldwide. Not surprisingly, the operations of such a huge company require a widely skilled labor force, ranging from financial planners to taste testers to truck drivers.

capital
The funds needed to create and operate a business enterprise

Capital   **Capital** refers to the financial resources needed to first start and then to operate an enterprise, and the machines, tools, equipment, and facilities those resources can buy. Capital is the lifeblood of any organization. Managers also use capital to buy inventory, to pay wages and salaries, and to keep the enterprise in operation. Philip Morris requires millions of dollars every year just to buy ingredients for various food products.

Entrepreneurs　In 1847, a businessman named Philip Morris opened a small tobacco store in London. After his death, another businessman, William Thomson, bought the firm from Morris's widow and began to export cigarettes to the United States. American investors eventually bought the company and turned it into one of this country's largest tobacco companies. Recent acquisitions, including Miller Brewing Co., General Foods, and Kraft, have turned the firm—still bearing the name of its founder—into the largest packaged-goods company in the world. Many economic systems need and encourage entrepreneurs like Philip Morris and William Thomson, people who start new businesses and who make the decisions that expand small businesses into larger ones.

Natural Resources　**Natural resources** are materials supplied by nature. The most common natural resources are land, water, mineral deposits, and trees. For example, Philip Morris, maker of such products as Marlboro cigarettes, Breyers ice cream, Jell-O, Oscar Mayer hot dogs, Miller beer, Maxwell House coffee, and Toblerone chocolates, uses a wide variety of natural resources, including the land on which its manufacturing and administrative facilities are located. It also needs tobacco (for cigarettes), grains (for beer), coffee beans, and a host of other ingredients for its numerous food products.

> **natural resources**
> Materials supplied by nature—for example, land, water, mineral deposits, and trees

Types of Economic Systems

Different types of economic systems manage the factors of production in different ways. In some systems, ownership is private; in others, the factors of production are owned by the government. Economic systems also differ in the ways decisions are made about production and allocation. A **planned economy,** for example, relies on a centralized government to control all or most factors of production and to make all or most production and allocation decisions. In **market economies,** individuals—producers and consumers—control production and allocation decisions through supply and demand. We will describe each of these economic types and then discuss the reality of the *mixed market economy.* We will also look closely at *privatization*—an important process in the development of the mixed market economy in more and more countries.

> **planned economy**
> Economy that relies on a centralized government to control all or most factors of production and to make all or most production and allocation decisions
>
> **market economy**
> Economy in which individuals control production and allocation decisions through supply and demand

Planned Economies　Most planned economies are found in countries that still adhere to the principles of *communism* or *socialism.* As originally proposed by the nineteenth-century German economist Karl Marx, *communism* is a system in which the government owns and operates all sources of production. Marx envisioned a society in which individuals would ultimately contribute according to their abilities and receive economic benefits according to their needs. He expected government ownership of production factors to be only temporary: once society had matured, government would "wither away" and the workers would own the factors of production.

As we know, most Eastern European countries and the former Soviet Union operated under communist systems until very recently. During the early 1990s, however, one country after another renounced communism as both an economic and a political system. Today Cuba, North Korea, Vietnam, and China are among the few nations with communist systems. Even in these countries, however, planned economic systems are making room for features of the free enterprise system, from the lowest to the highest levels.

market
Mechanism for exchange between buyers and sellers of a particular good or service

capitalism
Market economy that provides for private ownership of production and encourages entrepreneurship by offering profits as an incentive

mixed market economy
Economic system featuring characteristics of both planned and market economies

privatization
Process of converting government enterprises into privately owned companies

socialism
Planned economic system in which the government owns and operates only selected major sources of production

Market Economies A **market** is a mechanism for exchange between the buyers and sellers of a particular good or service. To understand how a *market economy* works, consider what happens when a customer goes to a fruit market to buy apples. Let's say that one vendor is selling apples for $1 a pound, and another is charging $1.50 a pound. Both vendors are free to charge what they want, and customers are free to buy what they choose. If both vendors' apples are of the same quality, the customer will buy the cheaper ones. But if the $1.50 apples are fresher, the customer may buy them instead. In short, both buyers and sellers enjoy freedom of choice.

Capitalism. Market economies, which are based on the principles of capitalism, rely on markets, not governments, to decide what, when, and for whom to produce. **Capitalism** provides for the private ownership of the factors of production. It also encourages entrepreneurship by offering profits as an incentive. Businesses can provide whatever goods and services and charge whatever prices they choose. Similarly, customers can choose how and where they spend their money.

Mixed Market Economies In their theoretical forms, planned and market economies are often seen as two extremes or opposites. In reality, however, most countries rely on some form of **mixed market economy**—that is, a system featuring characteristics of both planned and market economies. For example, most of the countries of the former Eastern bloc are now adopting market mechanisms through a process called **privatization**—the process of converting government enterprises into privately owned companies.

In Hungary, for instance, privatization is being used to help reduce the country's $22 billion national debt. Among the industries now being privatized are the state-owned oil and telephone companies, all major banks, and the entire electricity- and gas-distribution industry. Successful privatization often requires the ingenuity of a creative capitalist like Peter Rona, a Hungarian who is a major financial backer of North American Bus Industries Ltd., a Hungarian company that manufacturers buses for U.S. mass-transit fleets in Miami, Baltimore, Buffalo, and Washington. After privatizing part of the state-owned bus company, Rona developed a plan to manufacture buses in both Hungary and Alabama, thereby meeting U.S. government requirements that 60 percent of the value of federally financed urban buses come from the United States. Although parts and partially assembled vehicle bodies are shipped back and forth from Budapest to Alabama, the company is more competitive than its American business rivals, largely because of the low cost of Hungarian labor ($4 per hour) and Rona's perseverence. "I wanted to take a dying socialist company and save it," says Rona, who left his native Hungary after the Soviet-crushed uprising of 1956 and did not return until 1989.[3]

"I wanted to take a dying socialist company and save it."

—Peter Rona
Repatriated Hungarian capitalist

In the partially planned system often called **socialism,** the government owns and operates *selected* major industries. In such mixed market economies, the government may control banking, communications, transportation, and industries that produce such basic goods as oil and steel. Smaller businesses, such as clothing stores and restaurants, are privately owned. For example, many Western European countries, including Great Britain and France, allow free market operations in most economic areas but maintain government control in others, such as health care. Government planners in

Japan give special centrally planned assistance to new industries that are expected to grow.

■ THE U.S. ECONOMIC SYSTEM

Understanding the complex nature of the U.S. economic system is essential to understanding the environment in which U.S. businesses operate. In this section we describe the workings of the U.S. market economy. Specifically, we examine markets, the nature of demand and supply, private enterprise, and degrees of competition.

Markets, Demand, and Supply

A market economy consists of many different markets. Virtually every good and service has its own market. In each market, businesses decide what products to make, what quantities to produce, and what price to charge. Customers, too, make decisions: they decide what to buy and how much they are willing to pay. Billions of exchanges take place every day between businesses and individuals; between different businesses; and between individuals, businesses, and governments. Moreover, exchanges conducted in one place often have an impact on exchanges elsewhere.

The following events, for example, are not unrelated:

1. In early April 1994, South Africa held the first all-race elections in the country's history.

2. On April 28, 1994, the Ford Motor Co. joined General Motors and Chrysler in announcing first-quarter earnings that pointed to the automakers' best year since 1989.

3. On April 29, 1994, the price of platinum futures—agreements to buy platinum at a future date—jumped by $7.70 per ounce on the New York Mercantile Exchange.

How are these events connected? Investors on the New York exchange were unsure about the future policies of the new government in South Africa, which (with Russia) produces most of the world's platinum. In other words, they were concerned about the platinum supply. In addition, automakers require platinum to manufacture catalytic converters. Increased car sales—like those reported by America's Big Three—generate greater demand for platinum.

According to the basic rules of demand and supply, therefore, the value—and the price—of platinum were bound to rise. Indeed, as you can see from Figure 1.1, the price of platinum rose between mid-1993 and August 1994, when it reached $410 per ounce. But note, too, that with the stabilization of the South African government, the price dropped back to $389 per ounce in June 1996.[4]

The Laws of Demand and Supply On all economic levels, decisions about what to buy and what to sell are determined primarily by the forces of demand and supply. **Demand** is the willingness and ability of buyers to purchase a product (a good or a service). **Supply** is the willingness and ability of producers to offer a good or service for sale. Generally speaking, demand and supply follow basic "laws":

- The **law of demand:** Buyers will purchase (*demand*) more of a product as its price drops and less of a product as its price increases.
- The **law of supply:** Producers will offer (*supply*) more of a product for sale as its price rises and less as its price drops.

demand
The willingness and ability of buyers to purchase a good or service

supply
The willingness and ability of producers to offer a good or service for sale

law of demand
Principle that buyers will purchase (demand) more of a product as its price drops and less as its price increases

law of supply
Principle that producers will offer (supply) more of a product for sale as its price rises and less as its price drops

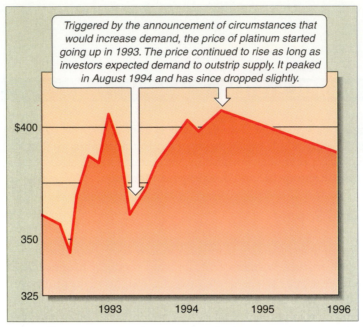

> Triggered by the announcement of circumstances that would increase demand, the price of platinum started going up in 1993. The price continued to rise as long as investors expected demand to outstrip supply. It peaked in August 1994 and has since dropped slightly.

FIGURE 1.1 ◆ **Price of Platinum, 1993–1996**

demand and supply schedule
Assessment of the relationships between different levels of demand and supply at different price levels

demand curve
Graph showing how many units of a product will be demanded (bought) at different prices

supply curve
Graph showing how many units of a product will be supplied (offered for sale) at different prices

market price
(or **equilibrium price**)
Profit-maximizing price at which the quantity of goods demanded and the quantity of goods supplied are equal

Demand and Supply Schedule. To appreciate these laws in action, consider the market for pizza in your town. If everyone in town is willing to pay $25 for a pizza (a relatively high price), the town's only pizzeria will produce a large supply. But if everyone is willing to pay only $5 (a relatively low price), the restaurant will make fewer pizzas. Through careful analysis, we can in fact determine how many pizzas will be sold at different prices. These results, called a **demand and supply schedule,** are obtained from marketing research and other systematic studies of the market. Properly applied, they help managers better understand the relationships among different levels of demand and supply at different price levels.

Demand and Supply Curves. The demand and supply schedule can be used to construct demand and supply curves for pizza in your town. A **demand curve** shows how many products—in this case, pizzas—will be *demanded* (bought) at different prices. A **supply curve** shows how many pizzas will be *supplied* (cooked) at different prices.

Figure 1.2 shows the hypothetical demand and supply curves for pizzas in our illustration. As you can see, demand increases as price decreases; supply increases as price increases. When the demand and supply curves are plotted on the same graph, the point at which they intersect is the **market price,** or **equilibrium price**—the price at which the quantity of goods demanded and the quantity of goods supplied are equal. Note in Figure 1.2 that the equilibrium price for pizzas in our example is $10. At this point, the quantity of pizzas demanded and the quantity of pizzas supplied are the same—1,000 pizzas per week.

Surpluses and Shortages. But what if the restaurant chooses to make some other number of pizzas? For example, what would happen if the owner tried to increase profits by making more pizzas to sell? Or what if the owner wanted to reduce overhead, cut back on store hours, and reduce the number of pizzas offered for sale? In either case, the result would be an inefficient use of resources—and perhaps lower profits. For example, if the restaurant supplies 1,200 pizzas and tries to sell them for $10 each, 200 pizzas will not be purchased. The demand schedule clearly shows that only 1,000

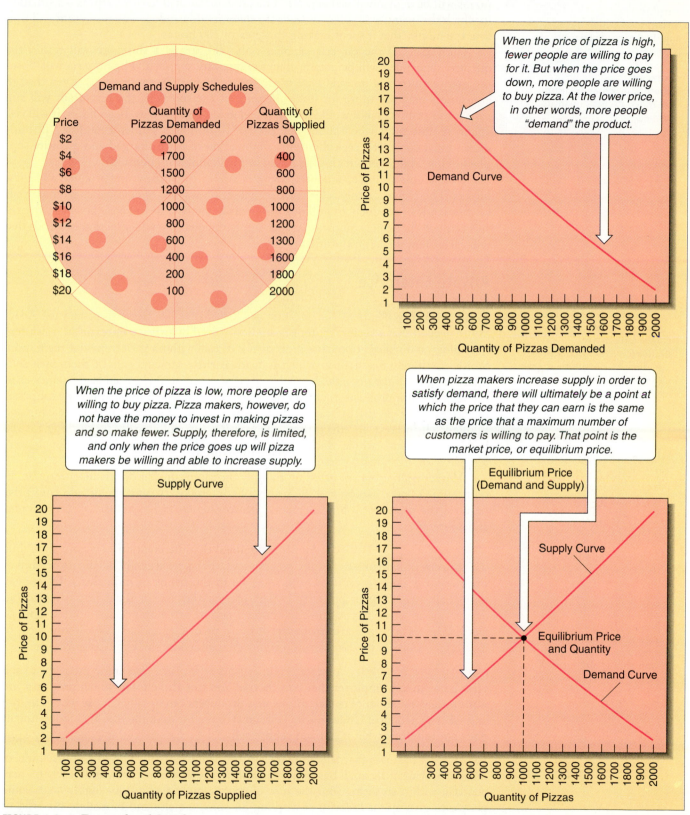

FIGURE 1.2 ◆ **Demand and Supply**

surplus
Situation in which quantity supplied exceeds quantity demanded

shortage
Situation in which quantity demanded exceeds quantity supplied

pizzas will be demanded at this price. The pizza maker will have a **surplus**—a situation in which the quantity supplied exceeds the quantity demanded. The restaurant will thus lose the money that it spent making those extra 200 pizzas.

Conversely, if the pizzeria supplies only 800 pizzas, a **shortage** will result: the quantity demanded will be greater than the quantity supplied. The pizzeria will "lose" the extra money that it could have made by producing 200 more pizzas. Even though consumers may pay more for pizzas because of the shortage, the restaurant will still earn lower profits than it would have if it had made 1,000 pizzas. In addition, it will risk angering customers who cannot buy pizzas. To optimize profits, therefore, all businesses must constantly seek the right combination of price charged and quantity supplied. This "right combination" is found at the equilibrium point.

This simple example, of course, involves only one company, one product, and a few buyers. The U.S. economy is far more complex. Thousands of companies sell hundreds of thousands of products to millions of buyers every day. In the end, however, the result is much the same: companies try to supply the quantity and selection of goods that will earn them the largest profits.

Private Enterprise

private enterprise
Economic system that allows individuals to pursue their own interests without undue governmental restriction

In his book *The Wealth of Nations*, first published in 1776, Scottish economist Adam Smith argued that a society's interests are best served by **private enterprise**—a system that allows individuals to pursue their own interests without governmental restriction. Smith envisioned a system in which individual entrepreneurs sought their own self-interest. At the same time, the "invisible hand of competition" would lead businesses to produce the best products as efficiently as possible and to sell them at the lowest possible prices. After all, that strategy was the clearest route to successful profit making and fulfilled self-interest. In effect, then, each business would actually be working for the good of society as a whole. Society, therefore, would benefit most from minimal interference with individuals' pursuit of economic self-interest.

Market economies are based on roughly the same concept of private enterprise. In both Smith's "pure" vision and the reality of contemporary practice, private enterprise requires the presence of four elements: *private property rights*, *freedom of choice*, *profits*, and *competition*.

private property rights
The right to buy, own, use, and sell almost any form of property

Private Property Rights Smith maintained that the creation of wealth should be the concern of individuals, not the government. Thus, he argued that the ownership of the resources used to create wealth must be in the hands of individuals. Of course, individual ownership of property is part of everyday life in the United States. No doubt you or someone you know has bought and owned automobiles, homes, land, or stock. The right to **private property**—to buy, own, use, and sell almost any form of property—is one of the fundamental rights guaranteed by the U.S. Constitution.

Freedom of Choice A related right is *freedom of choice*. You enjoy the right to sell your labor to any employer that you choose. You can also choose which products you want to buy. Freedom of choice means that producers can usually choose whom to hire and what to produce. Under normal circumstances, for example, the U.S. government does not tell Sears what it can and cannot sell.

Profits A business that fails to make a profit will eventually close its doors. Indeed, more than half of all small businesses fail within the first four years, and nearly 65 percent fail within six years.[5] But the lure of profits (and freedom) inevitably leads some people to give up the security of working for someone else and to assume the risks of entrepreneurship. Anticipated profits also play a large part in individuals' choices of the goods or services that they will produce.

Competition   If profits motivate individuals to start businesses, competition motivates them to operate their businesses efficiently. **Competition** occurs when two or more businesses vie for the same resources or customers. For example, if you decide to buy a new pair of athletic shoes, you have a choice of several different stores in which to shop. After selecting a store, you may then choose between brands—say, Nike, Reebok, or Adidas. If you intend to buy only one pair of shoes, all these manufacturers are in competition with one another, as are all the shoe retailers in your area, from mass marketers like Kmart to specialty outlets like Foot Locker.

To gain an advantage over its competitors, a business must produce its goods or services efficiently and must be able to sell them for prices that generate reasonable profits. To achieve these goals, it must convince customers that its products are either better or less expensive than those of competitors. In this sense, competition benefits society by forcing all competitive businesses to make their products better and/or cheaper. A company that produces inferior, expensive products is sure to be forced out of business.

> **competition**
> Vying among businesses for the same resources or customers

Degrees of Competition

Not all industries are equally competitive. Economists have identified four basic degrees of competition within a private enterprise system: *pure competition, monopolistic competition, oligopoly,* and *monopoly.* Table 1.1 summarizes the features of these four degrees of competition.

Pure Competition   For **pure competition** to exist, two conditions must prevail:

1. All firms in a given industry must be small.
2. The number of firms in the industry must be large.

Under such conditions, no single firm is powerful enough to influence the price of its product or service in the marketplace.

These conditions reflect four important principles:

1. The products offered by each firm are so similar that buyers view them as identical to those offered by other firms.
2. Both buyers and sellers know the prices that others are paying and receiving in the marketplace.

> **pure competition**
> Market or industry characterized by a large number of small firms producing an identical product

TABLE 1.1 ◆ Degrees of Competition

Characteristics	Pure Competition	Monopolistic Competition	Oligopoly	Monopoly
Example	Local farmer	Stationery store	Steel industry	Public utility
Number of competitors	Many	Many, but fewer than in pure competition	Few	None
Ease of entry into industry	Easy	Relatively easy	Difficult	Regulated by government
Similarity of goods or services offered by competing firms	Identical	Similar	Can be similar or different	No directly competing goods or services
Level of control over price by individual firms	None	Some	Some	Considerable

3. Because each firm is small, it is relatively easy for any single firm to enter or leave the market.

4. Prices are set exclusively by supply and demand and are accepted by both sellers and buyers.

Despite certain government price-support programs agriculture is a good example of pure competition in the U.S. economy. The wheat produced on one farm is essentially the same as that produced on another. Both producers and buyers are well aware of prevailing market prices. Moreover, it is relatively easy to start producing wheat and relatively easy to stop producing when doing so is no longer profitable.

monopolistic competition
Market or industry characterized by a large number of buyers and a relatively large number of sellers trying to differentiate their products from those of competitors

Monopolistic Competition   In **monopolistic competition,** there are fewer sellers than in pure competition. However, because there are still many buyers, sellers try to make their products at least appear to be different from those of competitors. Differentiating strategies include establishing brand names (Tide and Cheer), creating a different design or style (Ralph Lauren and Guess? jeans), and advertising (Coke and Pepsi). For example, in an effort to attract health-conscious consumers, the Kraft and General Foods divisions of Philip Morris are actively promoting such differentiated products as low-fat Breyers ice cream and Cool Whip, low-calorie Jell-O, and sugar-free Kool-Aid.

Monopolistically competitive businesses may be large or small. It is still relatively easy, however, for firms to enter or leave the market. For example, many small clothing stores compete successfully with large apparel retailers like Liz Claiborne and The Limited. Product differentiation also gives sellers some control over the prices they charge. For instance, although Sears and Ralph Lauren Polo shirts may have similar styling and other features, Ralph Lauren Polo shirts can be priced with little regard for the lower price of Sears shirts.

oligopoly
Market or industry characterized by a handful of (generally large) sellers with the power to influence the prices of their products

Oligopoly   When an industry has only a handful of sellers, an **oligopoly** exists. As a general rule, these sellers are very large. The entry of new competitors is difficult because large capital investment is necessary. Consequently, oligopolistic industries—for instance, the automobile, rubber, airline, and steel industries—tend to stay that way. Only two companies, both among the biggest in the world, manufacture large commercial aircraft—Boeing and Airbus.

Not surprisingly, individual oligopolists have more control over their own strategies than do monopolistically competitive firms. At the same time, however, the actions of any one firm can significantly affect the sales of every other firm. For example, when one firm reduces prices or offers incentives to increase sales, the others usually protect their sales by doing the same. Likewise, when one firm raises prices, the others generally follow suit. The prices of comparable products, therefore, are usually quite similar. Thus, whenever a major airline announces a new program of fare discounts, the other airlines generally follow suit almost immediately. And just as quickly, when the fare discounts end for one airline, they usually end for all the others at the same time.

monopoly
Market or industry in which there is only one producer, which can therefore set the prices of its products

natural monopoly
Industry in which one company can most efficiently supply all needed goods or services

Monopoly   A **monopoly** exists when an industry or market has only one producer. A sole supplier enjoys complete control over the prices of its products. Its only constraint is the fall of consumer demand in response to increased prices. In the United States, laws like the Sherman Antitrust Act (1890) and the Clayton Act (1914) forbid many monopolies and regulate the prices charged by so-called **natural monopolies**—industries in which one company can most efficiently supply all the needed goods or services. Most utilities, for example, are natural monopolies because they can supply all the power needed in an area, and duplicate facilities—such as two power plants, two sets of power lines, and so forth—would be wasteful.

■ EVALUATING ECONOMIC SYSTEMS

Figures 1.3 through 1.7 display a variety of current economic indicators that can be used to highlight some key facts about the U.S. economy. Using these data for reference points, we will explain more fully the key goals of the U.S. economic system and measure the success of that system in achieving its goals. We will conclude by describing government attempts to manage the U.S. economy in the interest of meeting national economic goals.[6]

Economic Goals

Nearly every economic system has three broad goals: *stability*, *full employment*, and *growth*. Naturally, different systems place different emphasis on each of these goals and take different approaches to achieving them.

Stability   In economic terms, **stability** is the condition in which the money available in an economy and the goods produced in that economy are growing at about the same rate. In other words, there are enough desirable products to satisfy consumer demand, and consumers have enough money, in the aggregate, to buy what they need and want. When conditions are stable, therefore, prices for consumer goods, interest rates, and wages paid to workers change very little. Stability helps maintain predictable conditions in which managers, consumers, and workers can analyze the business environment, project goals, and assess performance.

stability
Condition in which the balance between the money available in an economy and the goods produced in it are growing at about the same rate

Inflation.   The biggest threat to stability is **inflation,** the phenomenon of widespread price increases throughout an economic system. Typically, inflation has an impact on virtually all goods and services the system produces. For example, inflation explains why a pair of Levi's jeans that costs $35 today cost only $29 ten years ago and only $18 twenty years ago. For the last several years, inflation rates in the United States have hovered around 4 percent per year, finally dropping below 3 percent in 1994.

inflation
Phenomenon of widespread price increases throughout an economic system

Over the course of this century, inflation in the United States has varied dramatically. Prices rose sharply before the Great Depression and then plummeted. Immediately after the Depression, prices began to rise steadily again, punctuated by brief periods of deflation. This same pattern characterized economic activity throughout the entire industrialized world in the years just before World War II. Immediately after the war, the United States experienced several decades of constant inflation, with steep increases often exceeding 10 percent per year in the late 1970s and early 1980s. Since then, however, inflation rates have declined.

Figure 1.3 shows inflation rates in the United States since 1960 by tracing the average annual increase in producer prices. At current levels, prices double approximately every 19 years. What does this figure mean in real terms for consumers like you? Among other things, it means that when your children enter college, they will pay twice what you are now paying for tuition, fees, textbooks, clothing, and housing. In theory, your income would also be about twice as high.

Inflation, however, is not necessarily or entirely bad. Stability, for example, can actually degenerate into stagnation and contribute to a decline in the development and marketing of new products. After all, when there are enough products to buy at reasonable prices and enough money with which to buy them, innovation and growth in new areas are not as urgent as business priorities. For the same reason, the onset of inflation is often a sign of economic growth. For one thing, when businesses see that they can charge higher prices, they provide higher wages for workers, invest more dollars in advertising, and introduce new products. In addition, new businesses may open to take

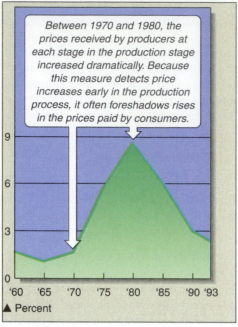

Between 1970 and 1980, the prices received by producers at each stage in the production stage increased dramatically. Because this measure detects price increases early in the production process, it often foreshadows rises in the prices paid by consumers.

FIGURE 1.3 ◆ **Inflation Trends in the United States**

advantage of perceived prosperity. At this point, of course, a damaging inflationary trend may set in: workers may start demanding higher wages to pay for more expensive products, and because higher wages mean lower profits, sellers may raise prices even more. Inflation can be curtailed both "naturally" and "artificially." For example, rates of increase may slow either because of an economic slump, such as the recession that hit the United States in the late 1980s, or through government intervention (see Chapter 16).

Recession and Depression. Inflation is not the only threat to economic stability. Suppose that a major factory in your hometown closes. Hundreds or even thousands of workers would lose their jobs. If other companies in the area do not have jobs for them, these unemployed people will reduce their spending. As a result other local businesses will suffer drops in sales—and perhaps cut their own work forces. The resulting **recession,** characterized by decreases in employment, income, and production, may spread across the city, the state, the nation, and even the world. A particularly severe and long-lasting recession, like the one that affected much of the world in the 1930s, is called a **depression.**

Full Employment   Although there is some disagreement about the meaning of the term *full employment*, the concept remains a goal of most economic systems. Strictly speaking, full employment means that everyone who wants to work has an opportunity to do so. In reality, full employment is impossible: there will always be people looking for work.

Unemployment. **Unemployment** can be defined as the level of joblessness among people actively seeking work. Employment rates are an important element in understanding the health of a nation's economy. High unemployment, for example, suggests that businesses are performing poorly, low unemployment that business is performing well. The rate of unemployment in the United States has varied widely during the twentieth century. As with inflation, major fluctuations occurred during the Great Depression, which began in 1929 and lasted through most of the 1930s. Since the end of World War II, unemployment has generally varied between 5 and 10 percent.

Growth   Perhaps the most fundamental goal of most economic systems is **growth**—an increase in the amount of goods and services produced by a nation's resources. In theory, we all want the whole system to expand and provide more businesses, more jobs, and more wealth for everyone. In practice, however, it is difficult to achieve growth without triggering inflation or other elements of instability. An extended period without growth may eventually result in economic decline: business shutdowns, lost jobs, a decrease in overall wealth, and a lower standard of living for everyone.

Currently, many major U.S. companies are emphasizing growth rather than layoffs and "downsizing"—a shift that began shortly after AT&T announced in 1996 that it

recession
Period characterized by decreases in employment, income, and production

depression
Particularly severe and long-lasting recession

unemployment
Level of joblessness among people actively seeking work

growth
Increase in the amount of goods and services produced by a nation's resources

TRENDS & CHALLENGES

HOW HOLLYWOOD BLOWS ITSELF OUT OF PROPORTION

"If you fail to account for inflation, your numbers are gibberish."
—David R. Henderson
Research fellow at Stanford University's Hoover Institution

Is the cost of movie making in Hollywood out of control? Why, of course it is. At least that's what the conventional wisdom—and Hollywood reporters—tell us. Typically, they use bottom-line budget costs to prove their point. In 1960, for example, Stanley Kubrick's gladiator epic *Spartacus* cost $12 million and was considered the most expensive movie ever made. Granted, there were good reasons for such a huge budget, including a cast and crew of more than 10,000 people, 100 major sets, 5,000 costumes, 27 tons of statues rented from museums, and the salaries of big-name stars. But all this aside, the idea of pouring $12 million into a single motion picture made the public gasp in disbelief. If they gasped then, some commentators choked in 1995, when they learned that *Waterworld*, Kevin Costner's epic adventure, cost Universal Studios more than $175 million. Conventional wisdom reckoned that *Waterworld* was now the most expensive movie ever made.

Not so fast, says David R. Henderson, a research fellow at the Hoover Institution at Stanford University. Henderson points out that conventional wisdom has neglected to consider the effects of inflation on actual movie-making costs. "If you fail to account for inflation when you compare dollar amounts in different years," he says, "your numbers are gibberish." If we calculate the effects of inflation, we find that *Cleopatra*, a movie epic made in 1963, actually holds the record as the most expensive motion picture ever made. In 1995 dollars, *Cleopatra's* production costs exceeded $219 million—a full 25 percent more than the $175 million spent on *Waterworld*.

So what Hollywood movie has *made* the most money? Not surprisingly, Henderson points out that historians who compare revenues without accounting for inflation are making a serious error on this side of the ledger as well. *E.T.*, Steven Spielberg's 1982 sci-fi adventure movie, was the highest-grossing movie in Hollywood history. In financial reality, however, *E.T.*'s revenues pale in comparison to those generated by the favorite from 1939, *Gone with the Wind*. Translating the gross revenues of both movies into 1995 dollars, Henderson found that *E.T.* earned $632 million dollars—a handsome sum, but relatively modest compared with the $2.11 billion earned by *GWTW*. "In other words," Henderson reminds would-be Hollywood moguls, "*GWTW* outgrossed *E.T.* by more than 3 to 1."

Henderson also notes that inflation often takes it toll in subtle, even silent ways. After all, since 1939, inflation has averaged only 4.4 percent per year—an erosion in the value of the dollar that we can easily live with. Before you breathe a sigh of monetary relief, however, remember that inflation *compounds*. In other words, the 1941 inflation rate of 4.4 percent went to work on a 1939 dollar that had already been inflated by 4.4 percent in 1940. And so on and so on. The result: between 1939 and 1995, the price of everything—including Hollywood movie-making—increased by a whopping 998 percent.

would eliminate 40,000 jobs. Although the ultimate goal of the downsizing trend, which began in the early 1980s, was always growth, the focus on cost-cutting and layoffs overshadowed growth-oriented strategies—namely, attempts to create new markets, improve production, increase profits, and boost hiring. According to many observers, this incomplete picture probably contributed to the backlash of criticism of AT&T. "There was too much emphasis," argues William Matassoni, a partner in the consulting firm McKinsey & Company, "on let's cut back, let's get rid of people and not enough on how to grow once companies become leaner and more efficient." Allied Signal Inc. learned from AT&T's mistakes when it announced that for every layoff in its shrinking auto parts division, there would usually be a worker hired in a growing division, such as chemicals and plastics.[7]

**"There was too much emphasis on let's get rid of people
and not enough on how to grow once companies
became leaner and more efficient."**

—William Matassoni
Partner in the consulting firm McKinsey & Company

For many decades, the United States grew at a faster rate than most other nations. More recently, however, other countries have grown more rapidly. During the 1980s, South Korea, Taiwan, Japan, and Germany all grew faster than the United States. In the 1990s, India, Chile, Venezuela, Brazil, and Mexico have posted impressive growth rates.[8] Still, the United States continues to have the largest and strongest economy in the world.

Measuring Economic Performance

To judge the success of an economic system in meeting its goals, economists use one or more of the following five measures: *gross national* and *gross domestic product*, *productivity*, *balance of trade*, and *national debt*.

Gross National Product and Gross Domestic Product

If we add the total value of all the goods and services produced by an economic system in a one-year period, the sum is that country's **gross national product,** or **GNP.** Note that GNP includes a nation's output *regardless of where the factors of production are located.*

GNP is a useful indicator of economic growth because it allows us to track an economy's performance over time. The measure of an economy, however, can be affected by inflation as well as other factors affecting the value of its currency. For example, if an economic system has a 5-percent decline in goods produced but experiences a 10-percent increase in inflation, its GNP will actually go up 5 percent. Changes in the value of a nation's currency relative to that of other countries will distort the value of imports and exports, and thus GNP. To control for the effects of such factors, we must compare economies according to an adjusted figure called **real gross national product:** the GNP adjusted for inflation and changes in the value of a country's currency.

The United States has the highest real GNP of any industrial nation in the world. For example, real GNP per capita in the United States is currently almost $21,000. By comparison, real GNP per capita in Japan is only slightly over $14,000. Other countries with relatively high real GNP per capita include Canada (almost $19,000), Norway (almost $17,000), and Germany (almost $15,000).

Gross domestic product (GDP) is another calculation of the value of all goods and services produced in the economy during a given period of time (usually a year). Like GNP, GDP measures a nation's annual output. There are, however, important differences between GNP and GDP. The profits earned by a U.S. company abroad are included in *GNP* but *not* in *GDP.* Why? Because the output is not produced *domestically*—that is, *in the United States.* Conversely, however, goods and services produced by foreign workers in the United States, as well as profits earned by foreign firms operating here, *are* counted in U.S. GDP because they are produced domestically.[9] ▶ Currently, U.S. GDP is $6.7 trillion (about $12 billion more than GNP).

Productivity

As a measure of economic growth, **productivity** compares what a system produces with the resources needed to produce it. The principle may be easier to

gross national product (GNP)
The value of all goods and services produced by an economic system in one year regardless of where the factors of production are located

real gross national product
Gross national product adjusted for inflation and changes in the value of a country's currency

gross domestic product (GDP)
The value of all goods and services produced in a year by a nation's economy through domestic factors of production

productivity
Measure of economic growth that compares how much a system produces with the resources needed to produce it

This Subaru-Isuzu plant in Lay-fayette, Indiana, employs 1,700 local residents to make 60,000 cars and 60,000 trucks annually. The local payroll is $39 million per year. The plant's payroll, the value of the 120,000 vehicles manufactured there, and the prof-its earned by its Japanese owners are produced domestically and therefore counted in the U.S. gross domestic product.

understand if we apply the same measure on a smaller scale: if Xerox can produce a copier for $1,000 but Canon needs $1,200 to make a comparable product, Xerox is more productive.

U.S. workers are among the most productive in the world. Figure 1.4 shows man-ufacturing productivity growth since 1960 in terms of annual average percentage of in-crease. As you can see, productivity growth slumped during the 1970s but began to rise again in the mid-1980s. In recent years, however, other countries have made even greater strides in productivity growth. For example, annual increases in productivity in Taiwan were almost twice as high as in the United States over the past ten years.

Figures 1.5 and 1.6 show two other aspects of the U.S. economy that affect pro-ductivity. First, if we calculate output per dollar of equipment and plants, we see that U.S. businesses are investing their capital more and more ef-ficiently—they are buying new equipment and using it wisely (Figure 1.5). Second, if we cal-culate spending as a share of growth in real gross domestic product—that is, GDP ad-justed for inflation—we see that both businesses and in-dividuals have dramatically increased spending on infor-mation and multimedia equip-ment and technology (Figure 1.6). As the information revolu-tion picks up steam, this invest-

© 1998 Robert Mankoff *from* The Cartoon Bank,™ Inc.

"The Net National Product—the total output of all the goods and services minus the total output of all the bads and disservices—rose slightly last month."

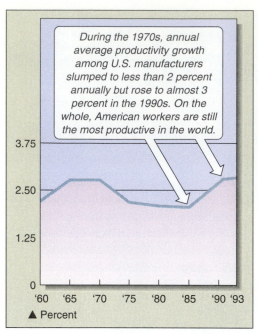

During the 1970s, annual average productivity growth among U.S. manufacturers slumped to less than 2 percent annually but rose to almost 3 percent in the 1990s. On the whole, American workers are still the most productive in the world.

3.75

2.50

1.25

0

'60 '65 '70 '75 '80 '85 '90 '93

▲ Percent

FIGURE 1.4 ◆ **Manufacturing Productivity in the United States**

ment should also begin to pay big dividends in productivity. ▼ We will take a more detailed look at the importance—and specific features—of productivity in Chapter 11.

Balance of Trade The *balance of trade* refers to the difference between a country's *exports to* and *imports from* other countries. A *positive* balance of trade is generally considered favorable because new money flows into a country from the sales of its exports. A *negative* balance, however, means that money is flowing out to pay for imports. During the 1980s, the United States suffered a large negative balance of trade. Things improved during the 1990s, however, and the annual growth rate of the trade deficit has dropped to under $100 million a year. Citing the increased competitiveness of U.S. business, experts expect continued improvement in the U.S. balance of trade, which currently totals about $11 billion. As Figure 1.7 shows, we can see that international trade is becoming an increasingly important part of the U.S. economy if we measure exports plus imports as a share of GDP. Thus, makers of economic and public policy pay correspondingly closer attention to such economic indicators as balance of trade.

National Debt Like a business, the government takes in revenues (primarily in the form of taxes) and has expenses (military spending, social programs, and so forth). For

The Information Superhighway is actually constructed of vast fiber-optic networks like those being built at AT&T Bell Laboratories. "Information technologies," says Bell Labs president John S. Mayor, "are the most powerful forces ever generated to make things cost-effective."

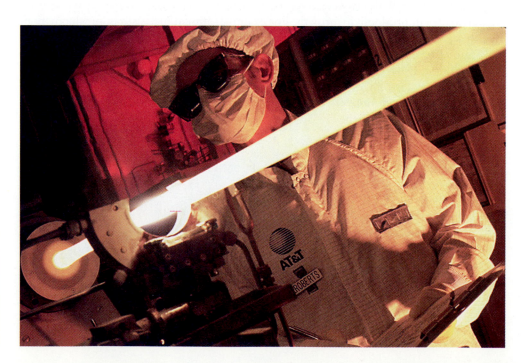

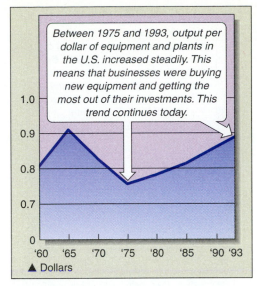

FIGURE 1.5 ◆ Capital Investment in the United States

the last several years, the United States has been running a **budget deficit:** it has been spending more money than it has been taking in. This deficit has created a huge **national debt**—the amount of money that the United States owes its creditors.

The current national debt exceeds $4 *trillion.* Because this high level of debt results in higher interest rates throughout the economy, it limits growth. One of the campaign promises that first propelled President Bill Clinton to the White House was a commitment to reduce the size of the national debt. Unfortunately, despite some progress, actually doing so has proved difficult. To reduce the budget deficit, the United States will have to raise taxes and/or reduce spending. Unfortunately, neither of these is a popular option. No one is happy about the prospect of paying more taxes, and the prospect of spending cuts in virtually any area—the military, social programs, environmental protection, the prison system, education, or transportation—calls forth objections from so many special interest groups that policymakers have long been reluctant to take the political risks involved in cutting spending.

budget deficit
Situation in which a government body spends more money than it takes in

national debt
Total amount that a nation owes its creditors

FIGURE 1.6 ◆ Technology Spending in the United States

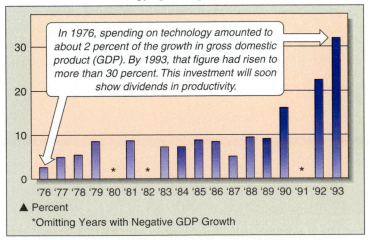

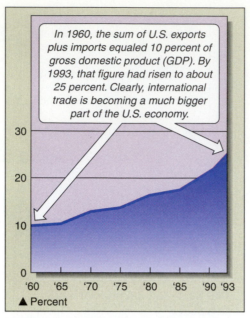

In 1960, the sum of U.S. exports plus imports equaled 10 percent of gross domestic product (GDP). By 1993, that figure had risen to about 25 percent. Clearly, international trade is becoming a much bigger part of the U.S. economy.

▲ Percent

FIGURE 1.7 ◆ **Expanding International Trade in the United States**

Managing the U.S. Economy

fiscal policies
Government economic policies that determine how the government collects and spends its revenues

monetary policies
Government economic policies that determine the size of a nation's money supply

The government manages the collection and spending of its revenues through **fiscal policies.** Tax increases, for instance, can function as fiscal policy to increase revenues. The 1993 income tax increase generated an estimated $50 billion in additional revenues. As part of his 1996 campaign platform, Robert Dole proposed a significant tax cut. According to his logic, based on so-called *supply-side economic theory*, lower tax rates would induce people to work harder, discourage tax avoidance, and increase savings. Dole believed that, in turn, these events would lead to lower interest rates, greater business investment, and long-term economic growth. Similarly, budget cuts (for example, closing military bases) function as fiscal policy when spending is decreased. Changes in such policies can have a direct impact on inflation, growth, and employment.[10]

The government also acts to manage the U.S. economic system through two sets of policies. **Monetary policies** focus on controlling the size of the nation's money supply. Working primarily through the Federal Reserve System (the nation's central bank), the government can influence the ability and willingness of banks throughout the country to lend money. It can also influence the supply of money by prompting interest rates to go up or down. A primary goal of the Federal Reserve in recent years has been to adjust interest rates so that inflation is kept at a manageable level.

BUSINESS FIELD TRIP
CHAPARRAL STEEL

Drive anywhere near Midlothian, Texas, and you are likely to see a tractor trailer hauling a load of flattened automobiles. Chances are that truck is headed in the direction of Chaparral Steel Corp., the twelfth-largest steel producer in the United States, with $460 million in annual sales. Chaparral's two giant electric-arc furnaces consume approximately 500,000 scrap vehicles a year, as well as appliances and other recycled metal products. Chaparral, explains Dr. Gordon E. Forward, President and CEO, is "a recycling company with the highest-capacity auto shredder in the world. A car is shredded every 15 seconds. We produce nearly 1.5 million tons of steel a year."

Forward hastens to add that this feat is accomplished "with no virgin raw materials—a fact that keeps our production costs down." Indeed, recycling is crucial to Chaparral's competitive vision.▶ The company defines itself as "an international producer of low-cost, quality products." Its success, says Forward, depends on both controlling materials costs and keeping labor costs below $30 a ton. Forward points out that this is precisely what it costs Korean steelmakers—Chaparral's main competitors—to transport a ton of steel to the United States.

A MINIMILL IS BORN. Chaparral has operated in this competitive, cost-driven environment since it was incorporated in 1973 as a joint venture of Texas Industries Inc. and Co-Steel Inc. (Texas Industries

acquired Co-Steel's 50-percent interest in 1985 and currently owns nearly 81 percent of Chaparral's common stock.) As Chaparral's first president, Forward understood that the huge, integrated mills that had long been the backbone of the U.S. steel industry were too costly to build and operate. A more efficient solution, he reasoned, was needed. That solution took shape in the form of the steel "minimill," a mill with a small geographic reach, a limited number of products, and a relatively limited steel-tonnage output. "When we opened in 1975," explains Forward, "minimills were a different concept. The steel industry of the 1950s and 1960s was accustomed to huge bureaucracies" that employed many more people than we have today. "In 1975," Forward observes, "there were 750,000 people in the U.S. steel industry; today 125,000 employees produce the same capacity.[11]▶ "Minimills," he emphasizes, "operate without the layers of bureaucracy that exist in traditional mills. Our engineers are managers on the floor, and we buy and refurbish used equipment. We're scavengers," boasts Forward, emphasizing once again that the ultimate goal is cost savings.

> **"Minimills operate without the layers of bureaucracy that exist in traditional mills. Our engineers are managers on the floor, and we buy and refurbish used equipment. We're scavengers."**
>
> —Dr. Gordon E. Forward
> *CEO of Chaparral Steel Co.*

In part, Chaparral manages to remain a low-cost producer with reach into international markets because it uses no virgin raw materials. It makes steel entirely out of recycled metal products.

One cost-saving practice at Chaparral is a bureaucracy-free work force trained to perform multiple tasks. Engineers, for example, join with production workers to manage manufacturing operations with computerized efficiency.

In fact, traditional mills cannot compete with Chaparral's labor costs. Most mills produce an average of one ton of steel with 3 to 5 man-hours, and Chaparral produces a ton with less than 1.4 man-hours. This productivity advantage reflects not only a high-technology operation but also a management philosophy that emphasizes teamwork and continuing education for a majority of the company's 1,000 employees.

A VARIED PRODUCT LINE.   Today, Chaparral produces a variety of steel products for all types of jobs.▶ Included in its product line are concrete reinforcing bars, known as "rebars"—the long steel rods that strengthen concrete in highways and building foundations by giving it load-carrying capacity. SBQ bars (for special bar quality) include both flat bars and smooth round bars that can be reshaped by customers for use in springs, gears, spindles, and shafts. Chaparral also manufactures structural products, including the large I-beams and H-beams that provide strength and stability in buildings, large ships, and other structures, as well as in heavy equipment and machinery.

To meet market demand, the company produces eighty-five different sizes of H-beams alone and adjusts its product line to keep pace with industry trends. For example, Chaparral's innovative multigrade structural steel makes building more efficient because one kind of steel can be used for a variety of jobs. The flexibility of this innovative product also results in less waste.

Chaparral products have been used to build everything from the Texas Rangers baseball park in Arlington, Texas, to motor shafts manufactured by Emerson Electric. Whatever the purpose of the products, how-

ever, customer requirements play a large part in determining manufacturing specifications. The manufacture of SBQ bars, for instance, reflects some critical interplay between the customer and the company. Explains Jeff Werner, Senior Vice President for Structural Sales: "SBQ products contain the exact combination of chemical and physical properties the customer requires. We do this through complex engineering processes that mix different amounts of carbon and alloys."

THE BUSINESS FIELD TRIP: WHAT'S AHEAD. This brief introduction is the first of six text features about Chaparral Steel Co. As you will see in the six remaining features, Chaparral prides itself on being in the forefront of change through innovation. In management, human resources, production, marketing, management information systems, and finance, the company lives by corporate values that embrace change rather than run from it. "If it ain't broke, we break it," boasts Dennis Beach. "We constantly try to create an environment for change and reward that change with recognition."

> **"If it ain't broke, we break it. We constantly try to create an environment for change and reward that change with recognition."**
>
> **—Dennis Beach**
> *Vice President for Administration at Chaparral Steel Corp.*

Both to keep pace with industry trends and to meet a broad range of customer demands, Chaparral produces and keeps on hand a wide inventory of steel products.

Continued from page 1

Been There, Done That

Not If You're Headed to the Disney Institute

The Disney Institute is Disney's first attempt to enter the adult education market. As such, it is part of a much broader diversification strategy that includes theme parks, movie studios, a sports complex, the Mighty Ducks professional hockey team, cruise lines, and the City of Celebration, near its Disney World hub. The Disney Institute expects to attract about 100,000 visitors a year, far fewer than the 33 million people who visit Disney World each year. Disney disagrees, preferring to keep its focus on the changing needs of its changing customer base. Not surprisingly, Disney is also eyeing Institute programs as the possible content for future television and direct-to-video programming.

Case Questions

1. How is the Disney Institute a good example of capitalism at work?
2. What role did changing market forces play in Disney's decision to create the Disney Institute?
3. Disney's strategy is to be patient in building the demand for spaces at the Disney Institute. As demand increases, are prices likely to drop, increase, or remain the same? What factors might affect Disney's pricing decisions?
4. If Warner Brothers, which owns Universal Studios, decides to open a competing institute in Orlando, how might the competition affect the operation and marketing of the Disney Institute?
5. Do you agree or disagree with the following statement: *The Disney Institute would never have been created in a communist or socialist economy.* Support your answer with specific reasons.

SUMMARY OF LEARNING OBJECTIVES

1. **Define the nature of *business* and identify its main goals.** *Businesses* are organizations that produce or sell goods or services to make a profit. *Profits* are the difference between a business's revenues and expenses. The prospect of earning profits encourages individuals and organizations to open and to expand businesses. The benefits of business activities also extend to wages paid to workers and to taxes that support government functions.

2. **Describe different types of *economic systems* according to the means by which they control the *factors of production*.** An *economic system* is a nation's system for allocating its resources among its citizens. Economic systems differ in terms of who owns and/or controls the four basic *factors of production*: labor, capital, entrepreneurs, and natural resources. In *planned economies*, the government controls all or most factors of production. In *market economies*, which are based on the principles of capitalism, individuals control the factors of production. Most countries today have *mixed market economies* that are dominated by one of these systems but include elements of the other. The process of *privatization* is an important means by which many of the world's planned economies are moving toward mixed market systems.

3. **Show how *demand* and *supply* affect resource distribution in the United States.** The U.S. economy is strongly influenced by markets, demand, and supply. *Demand* is the willingness and ability of buyers to purchase a good or service. *Supply* is the willingness and ability of producers to offer goods or services for sale. Demand and supply work together to set a *market*, or *equilibrium*

price—the price at which the quantity of goods demanded and the quantity of goods supplied are equal.

4. **Identify the elements of *private enterprise* and explain the various *degrees of competition* in the U.S. economic system.**   The U.S. economy is founded on the principles of *private enterprise: private property rights, freedom of choice, profits,* and *competition.* Degrees of competition vary because not all industries are equally competitive. Under conditions of *pure competition*, a large number of small firms compete in a market governed entirely by demand and supply. In an *oligopoly*, only a handful of sellers compete. A *monopoly* exists when there is only one seller.

5. **Explain the criteria for evaluating the success of an economic system in meeting its goals and show how the federal government attempts to manage the U.S. economy.**   The basic goals of an economic system are stability, *full employment,* and *growth.* Measures of how well an economy has accomplished these goals include *gross national and gross domestic product, productivity, the balance of trade,* and *the national debt.* The U.S. government uses *fiscal policies* to manage the effects of its spending and revenue collection and *monetary policies* to control the size of the nation's money supply.

STUDY QUESTIONS AND EXERCISES

Review

1. What are the factors of production? Is one more important than the others? If so, which one? Why?
2. What are the major characteristics of a market economy? How does a market economy differ from a planned economy?
3. Explain the differences in the four degrees of competition and give an example of each. (Do not use the examples given in the text.)
4. Why is productivity important? Why is inflation both good and bad?

Analysis

5. Select a local business and show how it uses the basic factors of production. Show how the factors of production are used by your college or university. What are the similarities and differences?
6. In recent years many countries have moved from planned economies to market economies. Why do you think this has occurred? Can you envision a situation that would cause a resurgence of planned economies?
7. Identify a situation in which excess supply of a product led to decreased prices. Identify a situation in which a shortage led to increased prices. What eventually happened in each case? Why?

Application Exercises

8. Choose a locally owned and operated business. Interview the owner to find out how it uses the factors of production, and identify its sources for acquiring them.

9. Visit a local shopping mall or shopping area. List each store that you see and determine what degree of competition it faces in that environment. For example, if there is only one store in the mall that sells shoes, that store represents a monopoly. How do other businesses compete to market their goods or services?

10. Go to the library and read about ten different industries. Classify each according to degree of competition.

BUILDING YOUR BUSINESS SKILLS

This exercise is designed to enhance the following SCANS workplace competencies: demonstrating basic skills, demonstrating thinking skills, and working with information.

Goal

To encourage students to understand how pricing changes announced by one company in an oligopoly affect other companies in the oligopoly

Situation

Suppose that you are the CEO of Yummie Cereal Co., one of the nation's largest cereal manufacturers. You must decide whether or not to decrease the price of your company's breakfast products. You have watched Kellogg, General Mills, and the Post and Nabisco cereals produced by Philip Morris announce price cuts as deep as 20 percent. But you are worried that if you follow suit, you will reduce annual company revenues by hundreds of millions of dollars—without increasing demand. You are concerned about getting into a price war that may destroy your business.

Method

In order to make the best decision for your company, you must first research and analyze

1. The marketing environment for breakfast foods

2. The effects that price reductions have had on other cereal manufacturers

The following information and accompanying questions will help guide your analysis:

■ *Cereal consumption is a price-sensitive behavior.* Do you agree or disagree with this statement? Support your position with evidence from your own breakfast-eating habits.

■ After 40 years of 3-percent annual sales growth, the volume of cereal shipments fell 1 percent in the year ending June 1995. In addition to price, what other factors may have contributed to this drop? In your answer, consider the increasing popularity of other breakfast foods, including muffins and bagels, as well as lifestyle changes that have created a demand for faster, more convenient breakfasts.

■ Kellogg did not cut prices on its most popular cereals, including Kellogg's Corn Flakes and Rice Krispies. Why do you think the company refused to make across-the-board price cuts? How do you think this pricing strategy affected consumers?

Based on your answers to the above questions, what should you, as Yummie's CEO, do in order to remain competitive with other cereal manufacturers?

Follow-Up

1. If the company chooses to maintain its cereal prices, suggest other methods that it can use to compete with other cereal makers.

2. If Yummie drops its prices and demand for its products increases, should the CEO assume a cause-and-effect relationship? That is, should he or she assume that no other factors contributed to the sales increase? (As you will see later in the text, other factors that might affect sales include improved advertising, new packaging, an expanded distribution system, or even an improved cereal formula.)

3. Is it always in a company's best interest to offer the lowest prices?

4. How often do you think Yummie's CEO should reassess his company's pricing decision? Why is regular reassessment especially important to oligopolistic firms? How does the need for reassessment differ according to different degrees of competition?

http://www.disney.com/disneyworld/disneyinstitute/welcome.html

Read the posted material about the Disney Institute and then consider the following questions:

1. How much interest do you have in attending the Disney Institute?
2. Do you see the Institute as a program having real value in and of itself, or is it simply a marketing ploy to get more visitors to Disney World?
3. Which Institute programs do you think are likely to be the most popular? The least popular?
4. Are there other programs that you think Disney could offer at the Institute?
5. Construct a basic profile of the kind of person you think is most likely to attend the Institute.
6. Do you think Disney's Website itself is a good marketing tool?

CONDUCTING BUSINESS IN THE UNITED STATES

Avis Tries Harder, Succeeds in Selling Out

WHY IS GUILLERMO ENCISO A VERY HAPPY MAN?

It's been no drive in the country for the employees of Avis Inc., the nation's second-largest rental car company. Since the company was founded in 1946, employees have endured eleven different owners. And now there's a twelfth. In July 1996, a hotel and real estate conglomerate named HFS Inc. announced that it would buy Avis for $800 million.

This deal is worth noting because HFS purchased Avis from Avis' own *employees*. In 1987, Avis' 13,500 employees became the company's eleventh owner by virtue of their *employee stock ownership plan*, or *ESOP*. In selling their company to HFS, therefore, Avis' employee/owners were now "firing" themselves as their own bosses and opting instead to become ordinary employees of a major corporation.

Nine years earlier, forming the Avis ESOP had made good business sense. Tired of being palmed off from one corporate owner to another, Avis employees borrowed enough money to buy control of Avis and take it private—that is, to control the company's stock, which was no longer for sale to the public. Avis was thus re-

> **"We saw this company being sold from one person to another for 20 years and we never got any money."**
>
> —Guillermo Enciso
> *Avis employee*

born as a worker-owned company in which employees controlled 71 percent of the corporation's stock. The remaining 29 percent was owned by General Motors.

Ownership was originally transferred to employees through a formula that awarded six shares annually for every $1,000 of an employee's salary. Allocations were also based on the percentage of salary diverted to each employee's retirement plan. When HFS purchased Avis employees' stake in the company, it agreed to pay $35 a share—three times the per-share value at the end of 1995. Employee-owners, therefore, reaped a sweet reward. "We saw this company being sold from one person to another for 20 years and we never got any money," explains Guillermo En-

ciso, who works at Avis' Maspeth, New York, facility. "Now a lot of us will get a good sum." In fact, Enciso walked away from the deal with about $90,000 for his retirement nest egg.

Financial gains aside, Avis' employees had other reasons to relinquish ownership. With the ESOP approaching its tenth anniversary, for instance, employees would be eligible to withdraw some of the value of their shares for cash. Workers nearing retirement would also be eligible to cash in their shares. Paying off employees in these categories would have caught the ESOP in a cash crunch that might have forced it to raise money by issuing shares for sale to the public. This prospect was unappealing because the issuing of more shares would have diluted the value of shares already held by employees. It was at this point that Avis' employee/owners decided to find a buyer who would transform the company back into a traditionally owned corporation. Sale proceeds, of course, would then be distributed to employee/owners.

Did Avis employees "sell out" the ESOP concept? Not in the opinion of Michael Keeling of the Washington

D.C.–based ESOP Association. According to Keeling, the primary objective of an ESOP is to provide workers with financial security. If an ESOP fails to take advantage of a significant financial opportunity—even one that means its own demise—workers would have every reason to question the ESOP's mission. Even so, some employees regretted giving up their status as owners. After all, it was employee ownership that gave meaning to the "We" to Avis' celebrated "We Try Harder" motto. On the other hand, says Enciso, "We always had the 'We Try Harder' spirit even before we were owners, and I don't think that's going to change."

Before the HFS sale, many Avis employees had known firsthand what it was like to work for different corporations and what it was like to own their own company. In large part, this knowledge gave them the ability to assess the HFS offer. Their decision to return to major corporate ownership was based partly on experience with two very different forms of business ownership—traditional corpora-

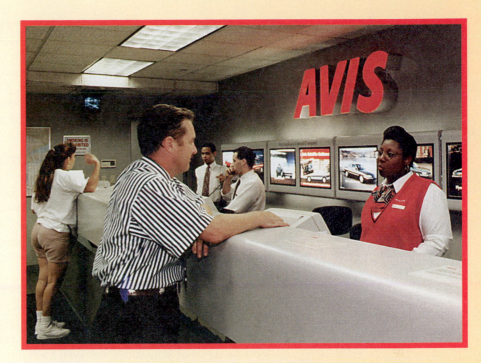

tions and ESOPs. Avis employees knew how each form of ownership affected the company's management and finances, and their decision to sell was based on the financial certainty that relinquishing ownership would transform their ownership shares into a financial windfall.

In this chapter, we examine the business structures that are open to both large and small businesses. By focusing on the learning objectives of this chapter, you will better understand the structural options open to U.S. businesses.

After reading this chapter, you should be able to

1. Trace the history of business in the United States

2. Identify the major *forms of business ownership*

3. Describe *sole proprietorships* and *partnerships*, and explain the advantages and disadvantages of each

4. Describe *corporations* and explain their advantages and disadvantages

5. Describe the basic issues involved in creating and managing a corporation

6. Identify recent trends and issues in corporate ownership

Continued on page 43

■ A SHORT HISTORY OF BUSINESS IN THE UNITED STATES

The contemporary landscape of U.S. business ownership has evolved over the course of many decades. A look at the history of U.S. business shows a steady development from sole proprietorships to today's intricate corporate structures. We can gain a more detailed understanding of this development by tracing its history.

The Factory System and the Industrial Revolution

Industrial Revolution
Major mid-eighteenth-century change in production characterized by a shift to the factory system, mass production, and the specialization of labor

With the coming of the **Industrial Revolution** in the middle of the eighteenth century, a manufacturing revolution was made possible by advances in technology and by the development of the factory system. Replacing hundreds of cottage workers who had turned out one item at a time, the factory system brought together in one place both the materials and the workers required to produce items in large quantities and the new machines needed for mass production.

In turn, mass production reduced duplication of equipment and allowed firms to purchase raw materials at better prices by buying in large lots. Even more important, it encouraged specialization of labor. Mass production replaced a system of highly skilled craftspeople who performed all the different tasks required to make a single item. Instead, a series of semiskilled workers, each trained to perform only one task and supported by specialized machines and tools, greatly increased output.

Laissez Faire and the Entrepreneurial Era

Despite early problems during the nineteenth century, the U.S. banking system began providing American business with some independence from European capital markets. In addition, improvements in transportation—the opening of the Erie Canal in the 1820s, steamboat navigation on major rivers, and the development of the railroads—soon made it not only possible but economical to move products to distant markets.

Another significant feature of the times was the rise of the entrepreneur on a grand scale. Like businesses in many other nations in the nineteenth century, U.S. business embraced the philosophy of *laissez faire*—the principle that the government should not interfere in the economy but should instead let business function without regulation and according to its own "natural" laws. Risk taking and entrepreneurship became hallmarks of aggressive practices that created some of the biggest companies in the world. During the last half of the 1800s, for instance, Andrew Carnegie founded U.S. Steel and Andrew Mellon created the Aluminum Company of America (Alcoa). At the same time, J. P. Morgan's Morgan Guarantee and Trust came to dominate the U.S. financial system, and John D. Rockefeller's Standard Oil took over—in fact, monopolized—the petroleum industry. ▶

The rise of such giant enterprises increased the national standard of living and made the United States a world power. But the size and economic power of such firms made it difficult, if not impossible, for competitors to enter their markets. Complete market control became a watchword in many industries, with many major corporations opting to collude rather than compete. Price fixing and other forms of market manipulation became common business practices, with captains of industry often behaving as so-called "robber barons." Reacting against unethical practices and the unregulated struggle for dominance, critics in many quarters began calling for corrective action and, ultimately, for antitrust laws and the breakup of monopolies.

The Sherman Antitrust Act of 1890 and the Clayton Act of 1914 were passed specifically to limit the control that a single business could gain in any given market.

Other laws passed during this era sought to regulate a variety of employment, advertising, and financial practices. (Chapter 3 provides more information about the legal environment of business, much of which has its roots in this era.)

The Production Era

The concepts of specialization and mass production that originated in the Industrial Revolution were further refined at the outset of the twentieth century. At this time, many analysts of business organizations sought to focus management attention on the production process. Especially among the theorists of so-called scientific management, increased efficiency through the "one best way" to accomplish production tasks became a major goal of management. Developed during the early 1900s, scientific management focused on maximizing output by developing the most efficient and productive ways for workers to perform carefully designed tasks.

A contemporary caricature suggests the power wielded by John D. Rockefeller and Standard Oil Co. over the U.S. oil-refining industry. By 1880, a mere ten years after its founding, Standard controlled almost 95 percent of the nation's oil-refining capacity. In 1911, the U.S. Supreme Court finally declared Standard a trust *and ordered it dissolved into competing business units.*

Scientific management was given further impetus when, in 1913, Henry Ford introduced the moving assembly line and ushered in the **production era.** The focus was largely on manufacturing efficiency: by adopting fixed workstations, increasing task specialization, and moving the work to the worker, Ford increased productivity and lowered prices. In so doing, he also made the automobile affordable for the average person.

Both the growth of corporations and improved assembly-line output, however, came partially at the expense of worker freedom. The dominance of large firms made it harder for individuals to go into business for themselves. In some cases, employer-run company towns gave people little freedom of choice, either in selecting an employer or in choosing what products to buy. If some balance were to be restored in the overall system, two elements within it had to grow in power: government and organized labor. The production era thus saw the rise of labor unions and the practice of collective bargaining (see Chapter 9). In addition, the Great Depression of the 1930s and World War II prompted the government to intervene in the economic system on a previously unforeseen scale. Today, business, government, and labor are frequently referred to by economists and politicians as the three countervailing powers in society. Although all are big and all are strong, none completely dominates the others.

production era
Period during the early twentieth century in which U.S. business focused primarily on improving productivity and manufacturing efficiency

The Marketing Era

After World War II, the demand for consumer goods that had been frustrated by wartime shortages fueled the U.S. economy for some time. Despite brief periodic recessions, the 1950s and 1960s were relatively prosperous times. Production continued to increase, technology advanced, and the standard of living rose. During this era, a new philosophy of business came of age—the *marketing concept.* Previously, business had been essentially production- and sales-oriented: businesses tended to produce what other businesses produced, what they thought customers wanted, or simply what owners wanted to produce. Henry Ford, for example, is supposed to have said that his customers could buy his cars in whatever color they wanted—as long as it was black.

According to the **marketing concept,** business starts with the customer. Producers of goods and services begin by determining what customers want and then provide it. The most successful practitioners of the marketing concept are companies like Procter & Gamble and Anheuser-Busch. Such firms allow consumers to choose what best suits their needs by offering an array of products within a given market (toothpaste or beer, for example).

marketing concept
Idea that a business must focus on identifying and satisfying consumer wants in order to be profitable

The Global Era

The 1980s saw the continuation of technological advances in production, computer technology, information systems, and communications capabilities. It also saw the emergence of a truly global economy. American consumers now drive cars made in Japan, wear sweaters made in Italy, and listen to CD players made in Taiwan. Elsewhere around the world, people drive Fords, drink Pepsi, wear Levi's jeans, use IBM computers, and watch Paramount movies and television shows.

How fast is the global economy growing? Figure 2.1 shows the dramatic increase in the number of overseas telephone calls billed in the United States between 1970 and 1992. This increase reflects much more than the need of businesspeople in one place to talk to other businesspeople in faraway places. In addition to highlighting the profound importance of technology, it shows that U.S. firms are actively seeking—and finding—opportunities to transact exchanges in new markets. In other words, technology makes exchanges easier. One key result is the willingness of companies to buy what they need instead of making it in-house. Thus companies can focus on a narrower range of activ-

FIGURE 2.1 ◆ **Overseas Phone Calls from the United States**

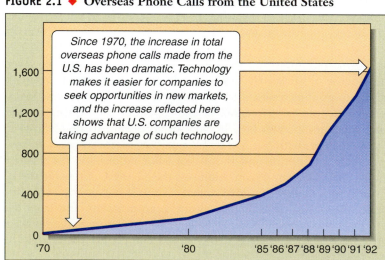

Since 1970, the increase in total overseas phone calls made from the U.S. has been dramatic. Technology makes it easier for companies to seek opportunities in new markets, and the increase reflected here shows that U.S. companies are taking advantage of such technology.

ities. Companies are getting smaller, and such strategies as outsourcing are on the up-swing.[1]

Admittedly, many U.S. businesses have been hurt by foreign competition. Many others, however, have profited from exploring new foreign markets. In addition, international competition has forced many U.S. businesses to work harder than ever to cut costs, increase efficiency, and improve quality. A variety of important trends, opportunities, and challenges in the new global era are explored throughout this book.

■ TYPES OF BUSINESS ORGANIZATIONS

Whether they run small agricultural enterprises or large manufacturing concerns, all business owners must decide which form of legal organization best suits their goals: *sole proprietorship*, *partnership*, *cooperative*, or *corporation*. Because this choice affects a host of managerial and financial issues, few decisions are more critical. In choosing a form of organization, entrepreneurs must consider their own preferences, their immediate and long-range needs, and the advantages and disadvantages of each form.

Sole Proprietorships

The very first legal form of business organization, the **sole proprietorship** is owned—and usually operated—by one person, who is responsible for its debts. About 74 percent of all businesses in the United States are sole proprietorships. However, they account for only about 6 percent of the country's total business revenues.[2]

Although a sole proprietorship is usually small, it may be as large as a steel mill or a department store. Moreover, many of today's largest companies started out as sole proprietorships. Sears, Roebuck and Co., for example, was originally a one-man enterprise owned and operated by Richard Sears, who founded the R. W. Sears Watch Co. in 1886. (Alvah Roebuck, who had answered an advertisement for a watchmaker in 1887, joined Sears to form a partnership in 1893.)

Advantages of Sole Proprietorships   Freedom is perhaps the most important benefit of sole proprietorships. Because they own their businesses completely, sole proprietors answer to no one but themselves. Moreover, they enjoy a certain degree of privacy because they need not report information about their operations to shareholders or partners. Finally, they alone reap the rewards of success (or, of course, suffer the penalties of failure).

Sole proprietorships are also simple to form. Sometimes a proprietor can go into business simply by putting a sign on the door. Naturally, the simplicity of legal set-up procedures makes this form of organization appealing to self-starters and independent spirits. Sole proprietorships are also easy to dissolve. In fact, many proprietorships are organized for short life spans. For example, rock concerts and one-time athletic events are often organized as sole proprietorships and then dissolved when the events are over.

Low start-up costs also make sole proprietorships attractive. Because some sole proprietorships must register only with state governments (to ensure that no other business bears the same name), legal fees are usually low. However, some proprietorships—for example, restaurants, beauty salons, florist shops, and pet shops—must be licensed.

Finally, a particularly appealing feature of sole proprietorships is the tax benefits extended to new businesses that are likely to suffer losses in their early years. Tax laws generally permit sole proprietors to treat sales revenues and operating expenses as part

sole proprietorship
Business owned and usually operated by one person who is responsible for all of its debts

of their personal finances. They can thus cut their taxes by deducting business losses from income earned elsewhere—that is, from personal sources other than the business. Because most new businesses lose money in the early stages of operation, tax incentives are helpful to entrepreneurs.[3]

Disadvantages of Sole Proprietorships   A major drawback of sole proprietorships is **unlimited liability**: a sole proprietor is personally liable for all debts incurred by the business. In other words, if the business fails to generate enough cash, bills must be paid out of the proprietor's own pocket. If bills are not paid, creditors can claim many of the proprietor's personal possessions, including home, furniture, and automobiles. Another disadvantage is lack of continuity: a sole proprietorship legally dissolves when the owner dies. Although the business can be reorganized if a successor is prepared to take over, executors or heirs must otherwise sell the assets of the business.

Finally, a sole proprietorship is dependent upon the resources of a single individual. If the proprietor is a skillful manager with ample resources, this limitation may not be a problem. In many cases, however, owners' managerial and financial limitations also put limits on their organizations as well. Sole proprietors, for example, often find it hard to borrow money, not only to start up but also to expand. Many commercial bankers fear that they will not be able to recover loans when sole proprietors become disabled or insolvent. Often, therefore, would-be proprietors must rely for start-up funds on personal savings or family loans.

Partnerships

The most common type of partnership, the **general partnership,** is simply a sole proprietorship multiplied by the number of partner-owners. There is no legal limit to the number of parties who may form a general partnership. Moreover, partners may invest equal or unequal sums of money and may earn profits that bear no relation to their investments. A partner with no financial investment in a two-person partnership could, for example, receive 50 percent or more of the profits. Bill Trainer and Harvey Woodman, for example, opened an automatic car wash in Houston called Shinin' Bright. Woodman put up most of the funds, and Trainer provided the expertise needed to manage the business. They agreed to split the profits equally for the first three years. Trainer has the option to invest some of his profits in return for a larger share in the business.

Partnerships are often extensions of sole proprietorships. The original owner may want to expand, or the business may have grown too big for one person to handle.

Richard Sears, for instance, sold his watch business and formed a mail-order catalog business two years later. When his new business grew so large that he could no longer run it by himself, he invited former business associate Alvah Roebuck to join him as a partner. ◀ Many professional organizations, such as legal, architectural, and accounting firms, are also organized as partnerships.

---

unlimited liability
Legal principle holding owners responsible for paying off all debts of a business

general partnership
Business with two or more owners who share in both the operation of the firm and in financial responsibility for its debts

The "Big Store" actually began as a sole proprietorship in a railroad station in North Redwood, Minnesota, from which the Sears Watch Co. began operations in 1886. In 1893, founder Richard Sears joined with fellow entrepeneur Alvah Roebuck to create Sears, Roebuck and Co. Roebuck sold out his one-third interest in 1897 for $25,000, and Sears took on a new partner named Julius Rosenwald. In 1900, gross sales under Sears and Rosenwald reached $10 million and topped $50 million in 1907. The company issued common and preferred stock on the open market for the first time in 1905 and has been publicly owned ever since.

Advantages of Partnerships   The most striking advantage of general partnerships is their ability to grow with the addition of new talent and money. Because lending institutions prefer to make loans to enterprises that are not dependent on single individuals, partnerships also find it easier to borrow money than do sole proprietorships. Moreover, most partnerships have access to the resources of more than one individual. Thus when they needed money to fund an expansion program, Sears and Roebuck invited new partners to join them by investing in the company.

Like a sole proprietorship, a partnership can be organized by meeting only a few legal requirements. Even so, all partnerships must begin with an agreement of some kind. All but two states subscribe to the Revised Uniform Limited Partnership Act, which describes a written certificate that requires the filing of specific information about the business and its partners. Partners may also agree to bind themselves in ways not specified by the certificate.[4]

A partnership agreement should answer questions like the following:

- Who invested what sums of money?
- Who will receive what share of the profits?
- Who does what and who reports to whom?
- How may the partnership be dissolved? In the event of dissolution, how will assets be distributed?
- How will surviving partners be protected from claims made by a deceased partner's heirs?

Although it helps to clarify matters for the partners themselves, the partnership agreement is strictly a private document. No laws require partners to file their agreements with any government agency. Nor are partnerships regarded as legal entities: in the eyes of the law, a partnership is just two or more people working together. Because partnerships have no independent legal standing, the Internal Revenue Service taxes partners as individuals.

Disadvantages of Partnerships   For general partnerships, as for sole proprietorships, unlimited liability is the greatest drawback. By law, each partner may be liable for all debts incurred in the name of the partnership. If any partner incurs a business debt (with or without the knowledge of the other partners), all partners may still be held liable.

For example, shortly after Trainer and Woodman's car wash opened, their equipment severely damaged a customized van. The owner sued for damages. Because the business was just getting started and had no financial reserves, Trainer and Woodman were faced with the prospect of covering the costs out of their own pockets. Unfortunately, Trainer lacked the personal funds to cover his share. To keep the business afloat, Woodman agreed to lend Trainer the money for his half of the business expense.

Partnerships also share with sole proprietorships the potential lack of continuity. When one partner dies or leaves it, the original partnership dissolves, even if one or more of the other partners wants it to continue. The dissolving of a partnership, however, need not cause a loss of sales revenues. Surviving partners may form a new partnership to retain the old firm's business.

A related disadvantage of partnerships is the difficulty of transferring ownership. No partner, for example, may sell out without the consent of the others. Moreover, a partner who wants to retire or to transfer interest to a son or daughter must have the other partners' consent. Thus, the life of a partnership depends on the ability of retiring partners to find buyers who are compatible with current partners. Failure to do so may end a partnership. Remaining partners, of course, may also buy out a retiring partner.

Finally, a partnership provides little or no guidance for resolving internal conflicts. Suppose, for example, that one partner wants to expand the business rapidly while the

TRENDS & CHALLENGES

THE TRAUMA OF LEGAL SEPARATION

Leonard D. Jacoby and Stephen Z. Meyers were visionaries who helped change the way law is practiced in the United States. After forming a business partnership in 1972, they opened the first Jacoby & Meyers legal clinic in Los Angeles. Based on the simple idea that middle-class people would buy legal services if they could afford them, Jacoby & Meyers targeted middle-class clients. Perhaps more important, they also used marketing methods that were tried-and-true in retailing but not in law. For example, they charged fixed fees (as low as $100 for an uncontested divorce) and sought high client volume instead of high prices. They accepted credit cards, and after battling with state legal establishments that prohibited the advertising of legal services, they created a visible brand name through mass-market ad campaigns. With a third partner, Gail Koff, Jacoby and Meyers ultimately operated 150 legal clinics in New York, New Jersey, Connecticut, Arizona, Pennsylvania, and California. Their business arrangement made them wealthy, famous, and—it turns out—miserable.

A combination of personal and business problems ultimately destroyed Jacoby and Meyers' partnership. Eventually, it fell victim to too little money, sometimes bitter personal disagreements, soured business deals, geographic separation, divergent goals, and mistrust. Richard Neimand, the firm's creative director between 1979 and 1992, watched from the sidelines as the partnership self-destructed. "I felt," he recalls, "like the chorus of a Greek tragedy in which the very things that made everyone heroic were the things that eventually drove all of them apart."

Problems began to surface in the mid-1980s. In order to establish a solid base on the East Coast, Meyers moved to New York in 1984, leaving Jacoby to run the West Coast offices. The relationship between the partners became increasingly strained because Meyers felt that he was making a greater contribution to the firm. "In retrospect," says former advertising director Evelyn Goldstein, "[Meyers's move to New York] could be marked as the beginning of the end." After the New York expansion, cash, too, became a problem. By the mid-1980s, Jacoby & Meyers was already strapped for cash because of the cost of operating so many offices, a $4-million annual advertising budget, and new competition for the firm's core businesses. "Suddenly," says Gary Rose, a former company manager in New York, "everybody was doing divorces and bankruptcies and wills at the same prices."

> ## "I felt like the chorus of a Greek tragedy in which the very things that made everyone heroic were the things that eventually drove all of them apart."
>
> —Richard Neimand
> *Former creative director of Jacoby & Meyers*

By April 1995, the partnership had deteriorated beyond repair. Tired of maintaining the mere appearance of a viable operation, Meyers and Koff actually stopped paying rent on Jacoby's California office and reduced his pay. In response, Jacoby sued his ex-partners, charging them with fraud, breach of the partnership agreement, and intentional infliction of emotional distress. Shortly thereafter, the partnership was dissolved and replaced by two separate legal-services companies. Jacoby ran one, and Meyers ran the other. In April 1996, Stephen Meyers was killed in an auto accident in Connecticut. "I've known Steve for 30 years," said Leonard Jacoby. "We've been partners for 22 years. . . . We had a business disagreement at the end, but we have the same friends. It's a real tragedy."

other wants it to grow cautiously. If the partnership agreement grants equal power, it may be difficult for the two partners to resolve the dispute. Conflicts can involve disagreements ranging from the company smoking policy to key managerial practices. Quite simply, it is sometimes impossible to resolve disagreements.

Corporations

There are almost 3.5 million corporations in the United States. As you can see from Figure 2.2, corporations account for nearly 20 percent of all U.S. businesses and gen-

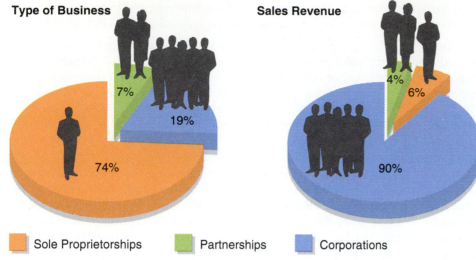

Type of Business

7%
19%
74%

Sales Revenue

4%
6%
90%

■ Sole Proprietorships   ■ Partnerships   ■ Corporations

FIGURE 2.2 ◆ Corporations: Business and Revenues

erate about 90 percent of all sales revenues.[5] Almost all large businesses use this form, and corporations dominate the global business landscape. At the top of the Fortune 500 list, General Motors generated 1995 earnings of $6.9 billion. According to *Fortune*, Coca-Cola—at $60.8 billion—had the greatest market value of any U.S. company at the end of 1995. Even "smaller" large corporations post impressive figures. For example, Advanced Micro Devices of Sunnyvale, California, the 500th-largest corporation in the United States, posted a profit of $300 million on sales of more than $2.4 billion in 1995.[6] Given the size and influence of this form of ownership, we will devote a great deal of attention to various aspects of corporations.

The Corporate Entity   When you think of corporations, you probably think of giant businesses like General Motors and IBM. Indeed, the very word *corporation* inspires images of size and power. In reality, however, the tiny corner newsstand has as much right to incorporate as a giant automaker. Moreover, the incorporated newsstand and GM would share the characteristics of all **corporations**: legal status as separate entities, property rights and obligations, and indefinite life spans.

In 1819, the U.S. Supreme Court defined a corporation as "an artificial being, invisible, intangible, and existing only in contemplation of the law." By these words, the Court defined the corporation as a legal entity. Thus corporations may perform the following activities:

- Sue and be sued
- Buy, hold, and sell property
- Make and sell products to consumers
- Commit crimes and be tried and punished for them

Public and Private Corporations   Corporations may be either public or private. The stock of a **public corporation** is widely held and available for sale to the general public. For example, anyone who has the money can buy shares of Caterpillar, Digital Equipment, or Time Warner. In contrast, the stock of a **private corporation** is held by only a few people and is not available for sale to the general public. The controlling group of stockholders may be a family, a management group, or even the firm's employees. Gallo Wine, Levi Strauss, and United Parcel Service are all private corporations. Because few investors will buy unknown stocks, most new corporations start out

corporation
Business that is legally considered an entity separate from its owners and is liable for its own debts; owners' liability extends to the limits of their investments

public corporation
Corporation whose stock is widely held and available for sale to the general public

private corporation
Corporation whose stock is held by only a few people and is not available for sale to the general public

as private corporations. As the corporation grows, however, and investors see evidence of success, it may issue shares to the public as a way to raise additional money.

Advantages of Incorporation   The biggest advantage of regular corporations is **limited liability:** the liability of investors is limited to their personal investments in the corporation. In the event of failure, the courts may seize and sell a corporation's assets but cannot touch the personal possessions of investors. For example, if you invest $1,000 in a corporation that goes bankrupt, you may lose your $1,000—but you cannot lose more. Your $1,000 is the extent of your liability.

limited liability
Legal principle holding investors liable for a firm's debts only to the limits of their personal investments in it

Another corporate advantage is continuity. Because it has a legal life independent of its founders and owners, a corporation can, at least in theory, go on forever. Shares of stock, for example, may be sold or passed on from generation to generation. Moreover, most corporations also benefit from the continuity provided by professional management.

Finally, corporations have advantages in raising money. By selling more stock, for instance, they can expand the number of investors and the amount of available funds. Continuity and the legal protections afforded to corporations also tend to make lenders more willing to grant loans.

Disadvantages of Incorporation   One of the corporation's chief attractions is ease of transferring ownership. However, as top executives at Chase Manhattan Bank found out in 1994, this same feature can also complicate the lives of corporate managers. Chase Manhattan Bank's problems started when money manager Michael Price began acquiring shares of Chase Manhattan Corp. until he owned 11.1 million shares, or 6.1 percent of the company. Unhappy with both Chase's poor performance and its undervalued stock, Price pressured Chase to take drastic actions to boost its stock price. Chase CEO Thomas Labrecque cut 9,000 staff positions, wrote off $490 million in bad commercial real estate loans, and sold off several nonessential businesses. Nevertheless, Chase's stock price stayed low, forcing the bank to merge with Chemical Banking Corp. in 1995. Although the new bank would be the nation's largest and be known as Chase Manhattan, top corporate leadership was transferred to Chemical CEO Walter Shipley.[7]

Among other disadvantages of incorporation is the cost. Not surprisingly, forming a corporation is more expensive than forming a sole proprietorship or a partnership. Corporations are heavily regulated, and incorporation entails meeting the complex legal requirements of the state in which the firm is chartered. Nonetheless, some states provide much better environments in which to charter corporations than others. For this reason, businesses often take out charters and maintain small headquarters facilities in one state while conducting most of their business in others. Because of its low corporate tax rate, for instance, Delaware is home to more corporations than any other state.

Double Taxation.   The greatest potential drawback to corporate organization, however, is **double taxation.** A regular corporation must pay income taxes on company profits. In addition, stockholders must pay taxes on income returned by their investments in the corporation. In contrast, because profits are treated as owners' personal income, sole proprietorships and partnerships are taxed only once.

double taxation
Situation in which taxes may be payable both by a corporation on its profits and by shareholders on dividend incomes

Table 2.1 summarizes and compares the most important differences among the three major business forms.

■ CREATING AND MANAGING A CORPORATION

corporate governance
Roles of shareholders, directors, and other managers in corporate decision making

Not surprisingly, creating a corporation can be complicated. In addition, once the corporate entity has come into existence, it must be managed by individuals who understand the complex principles of **corporate governance**—the roles of shareholders, directors, and other managers in corporate decision making.

TABLE 2.1 ◆ Comparative Summary: Three Forms of Business

Business Form	Liability	Continuity	Management	Sources of Investment
Proprietorship	Personal, unlimited	Ends with death or decision of owner	Personal, unrestricted	Personal
General Partnership	Personal, unlimited	Ends with death or decision of any partner	Unrestricted or depends on partnership agreement	Personal by partner(s)
Corporation	Capital invested	As stated in charter, perpetual or for specified period of years	Under control of board of directors, which is selected by stockholders	Purchase of stocks

In this section, we describe the steps involved in creating a corporation. We then discuss the principles of *stock ownership* and *stockholders' rights* and describe the role of *boards of directors*. Finally, we will examine some of the most important trends in corporate ownership.

Creating a Corporation

In its simplest form, the process of creating a corporation consists of three basic steps:

1. *Consult an attorney.* Although it is possible to establish a corporation without legal guidance, most people soon realize that the process involves, among other things, satisfying various governmental rules and regulations.

2. *Select a state in which to incorporate.* As we noted earlier, many companies choose Delaware for tax purposes. However, it usually makes sense for a smaller company to incorporate in the state in which it will conduct most of its business.

3. *File articles of incorporation and corporate bylaws.* **Articles of incorporation** specify such information as the firm's name and address, its purpose, the amount of stock it intends to issue, and other legally required information. **Bylaws** detail methods for electing directors and define terms and basic responsibilities. They also describe the process of issuing new stock and address such issues as stock ownership and stockholders' rights.

Corporate Governance

Corporate governance, which is specified for each firm by its bylaws, involves three distinct bodies. *Stockholders* are the real owners of a corporation—investors who buy shares of ownership. The *board of directors* is a group of individuals elected by stockholders to oversee the management of the corporation. Corporate *officers* are top managers hired by the board to run the corporation on a day-to-day basis.

Stock Ownership and Stockholders' Rights Corporations sell shares in the business—**stock**—to investors, who then become **stockholders,** or **shareholders.** Profits are distributed among stockholders in the form of dividends. Corporate managers serve at the discretion of the stockholders. Stockholders, then, are the owners of a corporation.

articles of incorporation
Document detailing the corporate governance of a company, including its name and address, its purpose, and the amount of stock it intends to issue

bylaws
Document detailing corporate rules and regulations, including election and responsibilities of directors and procedures for issuing new stock

stock
A share of ownership in a corporation

stockholder (or shareholder)
An owner of shares of stock in a corporation

preferred stock
Stock that guarantees its holders fixed dividends and priority claims over assets but no corporate voting rights

common stock
Stock that pays dividends and guarantees corporate voting rights but offers last claims over assets

proxy
Authorization granted by a shareholder for someone else to vote his or her shares

board of directors
Governing body of a corporation, which reports to its shareholders and delegates power to run its day-to-day operations but remains responsible for sustaining its assets

A contemporary cartoon shows financial speculator Jay Gould at the reins of the railroads that he controlled in the late 1860s and 1870s. In 1867, Gould "watered" the stock of the Erie Railroad by issuing huge amounts of new securities unjustified by any increase in the company's profitability. Unsuspecting investors were thus seduced into thinking that they could gain greater ownership of a highly profitable business by buying more and more stock. They were, of course, merely spinning their wheels.

Preferred and Common Stock. Corporate stock may be either preferred or common. **Preferred stock** guarantees holders fixed dividends, much like the interest paid on savings accounts. Preferred stockholders have preference, or priority, over common stockholders when dividends are distributed and, if a business liquidates, when the value of assets is distributed. Although many major corporations issue preferred stock, few small corporations do.

Common stock, however, must be issued by every corporation, big or small. Usually common stock pays dividends only if the corporation makes a profit. Dividends on both common and preferred stock are paid on a per-share basis. Thus, a stockholder with ten shares receives ten times the dividend paid to a stockholder with one share. Holders of common stock have the last claims to any of the company's assets if the company folds.

Another difference involves voting rights. Preferred stockholders generally have no voting rights. Common stockholders, however, always have voting rights, with each share of stock carrying one vote. Investors who cannot attend a stockholders' meeting may delegate their voting shares to someone who will attend. This procedure, called voting by **proxy,** is the way almost all individual investors vote.

Ownership of common stock, however, does not automatically give an individual the right to act for the corporation or to share in its management. The only way that most stockholders can influence the running of a corporation is by casting their annual votes for the board of directors. In reality, however, any one individual usually has very little influence over the affairs of a large corporation. ▼ For example, while General Motors boasts more than 1 million stockholders, only a handful have enough votes to affect the way GM is actually run.

Boards of Directors By law, the governing body of a corporation is its **board of directors.** Boards communicate with stockholders and other potential investors through such channels as the annual report, a summary of the company's financial health. Directors also set policy on dividends, major spending, and executive salaries and benefits. They are legally responsible for corporate actions and are, in fact, increasingly being held liable for their actions.

Board Makeup. Although requirements differ, most states require that there be at least three directors and one board meeting per year. Large corporations tend to have as many as 20 or 30 directors. Smaller corporations often have no more than five directors. Usually directors are people with personal or professional ties to the corporation, such as family members, lawyers, and accountants.

"*Gentlemen, when I consider the mess we've made of this company, I can only commend our foresight in not investing any of our own money in it.*"

© 1998 Robert Mankoff *from* The Cartoon Bank,™ Inc.

Many boards have both outside and inside directors. *Inside directors* are top managers who have primary responsibility for the corporation. *Outside directors* are typically attorneys, accountants, university officials, and executives from other firms. All directors share the same basic responsibility: to ensure that the corporation is managed in the best interests of the stockholders.

Officers   Although board members oversee the corporation's operation, most of them do not participate in day-to-day management. Instead, they hire a team of top managers to run the firm. As we have already seen, this team, called *officers*, is usually headed by the firm's **chief executive officer,** or **CEO,** who is responsible for the firm's overall performance. Other officers typically include a *president*, who is responsible for internal management, and *vice presidents*, who oversee various functional areas, such as marketing or operations. Some officers may also be elected to serve on the board, and in some cases, a single individual plays multiple roles. For example, one person might serve as board chairperson, CEO, and president. In most cases, however, a different person fills each slot.

chief executive officer (CEO)
Top manager hired by the board of directors to run a corporation

Special Issues in Corporate Ownership

In recent years, several special issues have arisen or grown in importance in corporate ownership. The most important of these trends are *mergers* and *acquisitions* (including *corporate alliances*), *multinational corporations*, *joint ventures*, *employee stock ownership plans*, and *institutional ownership*.

Mergers and Acquisitions   A **merger** occurs when two firms combine to create a new company. In an **acquisition,** one firm buys another outright. While mergers and acquisitions are not new, they increased in both frequency and importance in the United States during the 1980s. In the 1990s, they remain an important form of corporate strategy. They allow firms to increase product lines, expand operations, go international, and create new enterprises in conjunction with other organizations.[8]

Mergers usually take one of three forms:

merger
The union of two corporations to form a new corporation

acquisition
The purchase of one company by another

■ A *horizontal merger* occurs between two companies in the same industry. For example, the Walt Disney Co. and Capital Cities/ABC Inc. announced in July 1995 that Disney would take over Capital Cities to form an entertainment and media Goliath unequaled in the industry. The combined company, known as the

When Walt Disney CEO Michael Eisner (standing left) completed a horizontal merger with Capital Cities/ABC Inc. in July 1995, he transformed his company into a $19.3 billion entertainment industry behemoth. He doubled not only its assets but its opportunities for future growth. "We're not sure what the world will look like in five years," admitted Disney's chief operating officer, Sanford Litvak, "but having a broad array of assets certainly positions you better."

Walt Disney Co., has revenues in excess of $19 billion and enormous growth potential. For example, sports programs from ESPN, the ABC-owned cable channel, and children's programs from the Disney cable channel can be packaged together for sale to international broadcasters, who are actively seeking both sports and children's programming.[9] ▲

■ When one of the companies is a supplier to or customer of the other, the venture is called a *vertical merger*. In 1995, for example, computer maker IBM acquired software developer Lotus Development Corp., whose most successful product was a program that would enable IBM to compete with Microsoft in the market for operating systems.[10]

■ When the companies are unrelated, the acquisition is called a *conglomerate merger*. In August 1994, ITT Corp., which already had interests in insurance, financial services, hotels, and other areas, joined with Cablevision Systems Inc. to purchase Madison Square Garden, a sports entertainment company that includes two professional sports franchises among its holdings.

Takeover Tactics.   A merger or acquisition can take place in one of several different ways. The process usually starts when one firm announces that it wants to buy another for a specified price. After some negotiation, the owners or board of the second company agree to the sale and the firm is soon taken over by the buyer. Sometimes a firm may realize that it is a likely takeover target and cannot forestall the inevitable. In this case, a firm may seek out a favorable buyer and, in effect, ask to be acquired. In both of these scenarios, the acquisition is called a *friendly takeover* because the acquired company welcomes the merger.

Sometimes, however, takeover target companies resist. In such a case, a firm may wish to remain independent, or it may regard a purchase offer as too low or a potential buyer as a poor match. The would-be buyer, however, may persist. It may offer to buy the target firm's stock on the open market, usually at a premium price. If it can acquire a sufficient quantity of stock, it will gain control of the target company despite the resistance of the target firm's management. In this case, the acquisition is called a *hostile takeover*. IBM's takeover of Lotus was generous—it paid $64 a share for stock trading at $30—but hostile nonetheless.

Corporate Alliances. Although merger and acquisition activity has leveled off in recent years, the number of corporate alliances has skyrocketed. Alliances offer the advantage of allowing each firm to remain independent while sharing the risk of a new venture. Japan's Mitsubishi Motors Corp., for instance, has raised its brand recognition in the United States by means of a marketing agreement with Chrysler Corp., for which it also makes several car models.[11]

Multinational Corporations

A multinational corporation conducts operations and marketing activities on an international scale. For example, British Petroleum, although incorporated in Great Britain, maintains various operations in the United States, where each of its U.S. subsidiaries is incorporated. One subsidiary runs a chemical business, one runs a fertilizer business, and still another runs a petroleum business. (Multinational corporations are discussed more fully in Chapter 5.)

Joint Ventures

In a *strategic alliance*, two or more organizations collaborate on an enterprise. When the partners share ownership stakes in the enterprise, it is called a **joint venture.** The number of joint ventures has increased rapidly in recent years on both the domestic and international fronts. In 1995, for example, the U.S. telecommunications firm MCI Communications Corp. entered a joint venture with News Corp., a British-based media giant. The new venture intends to produce and distribute various communications products internationally, including movies "on demand" to consumers' TV sets and high-speed information services to the PCs of business clients. MCI and News Corp. suggest that the new joint venture company will ultimately be in a position to deliver home shopping by satellite and *The Simpsons* over the Internet.[12]

joint venture (or strategic alliance) Collaboration between two or more organizations on an enterprise

Employee Stock Ownership Plans

As we saw in the opening vignette, another trend in corporate ownership is the **employee stock ownership plan,** or **ESOP.** There is a trend today for significant portions of large corporations to be bought by their employees through ESOPs, which are essentially trusts established on behalf of employees. The company first secures a loan with which it buys shares of its own stock on the open market. A portion of future corporate profits is used to guarantee and eventually repay the loan. Employees gradually receive ownership of the stock, usually on the basis of seniority. Because the stock is being used to secure the original loan, employees do not take immediate possession of the stock. They do, however, immediately gain voting rights. Current estimates suggest that there are now almost 10,000 ESOPs in the United States.

employee stock ownership plan (ESOP) Arrangement in which a corporation holds its own stock in trust for its employees, who gradually receive ownership of the stock and control its voting rights

ESOPs do not always ensure stability for the firms that establish them. Nor do they necessarily ensure permanence. If the deal is advantageous, for example, an ESOP (like the one at Avis) may be willing to accept a buyout from a traditional corporation. Understandably, ESOPs are under the same competitive pressures as ordinary corporations and, like more traditional employers, may be forced to lay off employee-owners to cut costs. For example, Cranston Print Works, a Rhode Island textile company owned by its 1,400 workers, laid off 100 workers and closed a plant in 1996 after losing customers to Asian rivals with lower wage scales and lower overhead.[13]

Institutional Ownership

Most individual investors do not own enough stock to exert any influence on the management of large corporations. In recent years, however, more and more stock has been purchased by **institutional investors.** Because they control enormous resources, these investors—especially mutual and pension funds—can buy huge blocks of stock. For example, the national teachers' retirement system (TIAA-CREF) has assets of more than $95 billion, more than a third of which is invested in stocks.

institutional investors Large investors, such as mutual funds and pension funds, that purchase large blocks of corporate stock

Indeed, institutional investors now own almost 40 percent of all the stock in the United States. An important trend in recent years is increased involvement by such investors in the companies they partially own. TIAA-CREF, for example, now recommends standards for the makeup of company boards. According to these standards, boards should have a majority of independent directors, and committees should be composed entirely of unaffiliated outsiders. Occasionally, institutional investors may expect to be consulted on major management decisions.

TRENDS & CHALLENGES

CalPERS Pressures Little Guys to Measure Up

Since the 1980s, large corporations have learned to live with the shareholder activism of institutional investors. The CEOs of General Motors, IBM, Sears, Time Warner, and other large publicly traded companies now realize that unhappy institutional shareholders are as likely to flex their muscles as to sell their stock. Thus, it was no surprise to the Philip Morris Corp. when the California Public Employees' Retirement System (CalPERS) decided at the company's 1995 annual meeting to "just vote no" against management's slate of candidates for the board of directors. CalPERS' gripe: Philip Morris' independent directors had refused to meet with them to discuss critical company issues. Ultimately, because the pension plan owned 5,395,000 shares of Philip Morris stock, the company was forced to listen when CalPERS spoke.

With assets of more than $97 billion, CalPERS is now flexing its muscles in the direction of some of the nation's publicly traded small- and medium-sized companies. Specifically, it has targeted 8 firms from its portfolio of more than 1,500 companies with less than $2 billion in annual sales. The weakest performers in the small-company category, these firms include Applied Bioscience, Bassett Furniture, Charming Shoppes, Edison Brothers Stores, Rollins Environmental Services, Stride Rite Shoes, United States Surgical, and Venture Stores.

As one of the largest institutional investors in the country, CalPERS expected that the chief executives and directors of these companies would agree to discuss corporate performance with them. Instead, seven out of eight ignored plan representatives before finally agreeing to meetings. Speculates Richard H. Koppes, CalPERS' deputy executive officer and head of its corporate governance program: "The corporate governance movement hasn't reached these smaller com-

panies. They don't understand that shareholders have a right to talk with them."

> **"The corporate governance movement hasn't reached smaller companies. They don't understand that shareholders have a right to talk with them."**
>
> —Richard H. Koppes
> *CalPERS' deputy executive officer in charge of corporate governance*

Given CalPERS' track record with large companies, these companies *should* have understood. As a leading institutional force in the shareholder activism movement, CalPERS has pushed for numerous changes, including independent directors, the linking of executive pay to corporate performance, and confidential voting at shareholders' meetings. Many companies have voluntarily complied. Others, like Philip Morris, have responded to the kind of pressure that CalPERS can exert, such as a blocs of "no" votes and flurries of shareholder resolutions.

CalPERS' meeting with Stride Rite, one of its targeted mid-sized companies, came after it filed a shareholder proposal calling for the meeting. "We basically had to be nasty," said Koppes. But considering Stride Rite's performance in fiscal 1995, CalPERS believed that its determination was justified. After all, Stride Rite's sales had dropped 5 percent and the company had lost $8.4 million. Even after the meeting, however, CalPERS considered Stride Rite's response inadequate. To continue the pressure, it supported a shareholder proposal calling for the annual election of company directors.

Such resistance from small- and mid-sized companies does not surprise expert observers, including Stephen J. Friedman, a former member of the Securities and Exchange Commission. "Most of these companies," explains Friedman, "don't have a full-time shareholder relations officer, so there's no one to focus on these issues. They think it's someone else's issue."

Continued from page 27

Taking Stock of the Situation

Romantic Visions Aside, Avis Employee-Owners Are a Proud Bunch

According to an editorial in the *New York Times*, those people with the romantic notion that ESOPs would somehow change the "power relationship" of capitalism, which pits workers on one side of the table against owners on the other, were disappointed in the decision of Avis' employee-owners to sell their company to a traditional corporation. Most employees did not share this philosophical disappointment. When the sale was announced, many stood outside the company's Long Island, New York, headquarters and talked among themselves about the changes about to take place. Granted, they were anxious about the future. Would there be layoffs? Would the company move to New Jersey? At the same time, however, they were pleased that HFS was willing to pay $800 million for *their* company—the company that they had helped to nurture and build.

Case Questions

1. By the time of the sale, most Avis employees had already worked for several major corporate owners. How valuable was this experience to employees as they assessed the HFS offer?
2. Would being part owner of a company make you work harder or smarter than if you were an employee without an ownership stake? Explain your answer.
3. Do you agree with Michael Keeling that the Avis ESOP did the right thing when it agreed to the sale?
4. What effect might the value of Avis' stock have had on the decision to sell? Should stock value be the primary determinant in a decision of this kind?
5. What differences do you think employees will experience as they make the transition from an ESOP back to traditional corporation?

SUMMARY OF LEARNING OBJECTIVES

1. **Trace the history of business in the United States.** Modern U.S. business structures reflect a pattern of development over centuries. The rise of the factory system during the *Industrial Revolution* brought with it *mass production* and *specialization of labor*. During the *entrepreneurial era* in the nineteenth century, huge corporations—and monopolies—emerged. During the *production era* of the early twentieth century, companies grew by emphasizing output and production. During the *marketing era* of the mid-1900s, businesses began focusing on sales staff, advertising, and the need to produce what consumers wanted. The most recent development has been toward a global perspective.

2. **Identify the major forms of business ownership.** The most common forms of business ownership are the *sole proprietorship*, the *partnership*, and the regular *corporation*. Each form has several advantages and disadvantages. The form under which a business chooses to organize is crucial because it affects both long-term strategy and day-to-day decision making. In addition to weighing the advantages and disadvantages of each form of ownership, entrepreneurs must consider their preferences and long-range requirements.

3. **Describe *sole proprietorships* and *partnerships* and explain the advantages and disadvantages of each.** *Sole proprietorships*, the most common form of business, consist of one person doing business. Although sole proprietorships offer freedom and privacy and are easy to form, they lack continuity and present

certain financial risks. For one thing, they feature *unlimited liability*—the sole proprietor is liable for all debts incurred by the business. *General partnerships* are proprietorships with multiple owners. *Limited partnerships* allow for limited partners who can invest without being liable for debts incurred by general or active partners.

4. **Describe *corporations* and explain their advantages and disadvantages.** *Corporations* are independent legal entities that are usually run by professional managers. The corporate form is used by most large businesses because it offers continuity and opportunities for raising money. It also offers financial protection through *limited liability:* the liability of investors is limited to their personal investments in the business. However, the corporation is a complex legal entity subject to *double taxation:* in addition to taxes paid on corporate profits, investors must pay taxes on earned income. The stock of *public corporations* is sold widely to the general public. The stock of *private corporations* is held by a few investors and is not available to the public.

5. **Describe the basic issues involved in creating and managing a corporation.** Creating a corporation generally requires legal assistance to file *articles of incorporation* and corporate *bylaws* and to comply with government regulations. Managers must understand stockholders' rights as well as the rights and duties of the *board of directors*.

6. **Identify recent trends and issues in corporate ownership.** Recent trends in corporate ownership include *mergers* (when two companies combine to create a new one) and *acquisitions* (when one company buys another outright); *multinational corporations* (which conduct activities on an international scale); *joint ventures* or *strategic alliances* (in which two or more organizations collaborate on an enterprise); *employee stock ownership plans (ESOPs)* (by which employees buy large shares of their company); and *institutional ownership* of corporations (by groups such as mutual and pension funds).

STUDY QUESTIONS AND EXERCISES

Review

1. Why is it important to understand the history of U.S. business?
2. Compare and contrast the advantages and disadvantages of the major forms of business ownership.
3. Why might a corporation choose to remain private? Why might a private corporation choose to go public?
4. Why have joint ventures become more common in recent years?
5. Why have institutional investors become more powerful in recent years?

Analysis

6. How can you, as a prospective manager, better prepare yourself for the challenges you will face in the next 20 years?
7. What steps must be taken to incorporate a business in your state?
8. Go to the library and research a recent merger or acquisition. What factors led to the arrangement? What circumstances characterized the process of completing the arrangement? Were the circumstances friendly or unfriendly?

Application Exercises

9. Interview the owner-manager of a sole proprietorship or a general partnership. What characteristics of that business form led the owner to choose it? Does the owner contemplate ever changing the form of the business?

10. Interview the owner of or principal stockholder in a corporation. What characteristics of that business form led the individual to choose it?

BUILDING YOUR BUSINESS SKILLS

This exercise enhances the following SCANS workplace competencies: demonstrating basic skills, demonstrating thinking skills, working with information, and applying systems knowledge.

Goal

To encourage students to evaluate the advantages and pitfalls of meeting potential business partners via the Internet

Situation

According to the *Wall Street Journal*, a handful of entrepreneurs are meeting potential business partners on the Internet. Typically, these business relationships begin with an electronic conversation that determines whether the potential partners have interests and skills in common. If the chemistry is right, the initial conversation may lead to face-to-face meetings and joint projects. Meetings are essential to determine if long-term partnerships are feasible.

Jim Whitehead and Carol Krugman met through a forum conducted on Compu-Serve and soon realized how much their conference-planning businesses had in common. They communicated electronically for eight months before they finally met face to face. By that time, however, they had already made up their minds to form a partnership. White had relocated from Huntington Beach, California, joining Krugman in Fort Lauderdale, Florida, to form Whitehead & Krugman International Conference Consultants.

Method

Working in groups of four or five, choose a product commonly produced by small businesses. Then consider how the following factors might influence your decision to form a business partnership with someone you met via the Internet:

- The nature of your company's product and how it differs from that of your potential partner

- The location of each potential partner and the differences, if any, between marketplaces in different geographic areas

- The compatibility of business operations

- Your company's financial situation (is your company in debt or making a profit?)

Follow-Up

1. How can the nature of a company's product, market, business operation, and finances affect the likelihood of finding a business partner on the Internet?

2. If you owned a small business, would you consider using the Internet to find a business partner? Why or why not?

3. Management consultants believe that partnership decisions should never be made on the basis of electronic communications alone. Decisions should be made only after potential partners have engaged in lengthy face-to-face meetings. Do you agree or disagree with this position? Are face-to-face meetings necessary if the principals are thousands of miles apart and meetings would be costly?

4. Why do you think that "virtual" partnerships involving principals who live in different cities are rare? Why might such a partnership tend to be a problem?

Exploring the Net

TO LEARN MORE ABOUT EMPLOYEE STOCK OWNERSHIP PLANS, LOG ON TO THE WEBSITE MAINTAINED BY THE NATIONAL CENTER FOR EMPLOYEE OWNERSHIP (NCEO) AT:

http://www.nceo.org:80

Examine several sections of this site, especially those under "Library," "Training," "Columns," and "International." Then consider the following questions:

1. How effectively does the material in this Website characterize the advantages and disadvantages of ESOPs?

2. What parts of the Website do you find most informative? Least informative?

3. Note that you can perform your own searches from within this Website. What, for example, can you find out about ESOPs in other countries? What sort of "Publications" does the NCEO offer? What sort of "Internet Resources" does it make available? What sort of ESOP-related "Events" are held, and what purposes are they designed to serve?

4. Do you think that you would want to work for a firm that offered an ESOP? Why or why not?

5. What factors do you think probably led to the creation of the National Center for Employee Ownership?

6. Specifically, what value can this Website have for employees and managers at companies that already have ESOPs? At companies that do not?

Best Practices at Chaparral Steel
"If It Ain't Broke, We Break It"

Learning Objectives

The purpose of this video exercise is to help students

1. Become better acquainted with a specific company currently conducting manufacturing operations in the United States.
2. Appreciate the extent to which technology is changing manufacturing operations in today's business environment.
3. Appreciate changes in the management of human resources among innovative U.S. companies.

Background Information

Chaparral Steel Corp., founded in 1975, is the twelfth-largest steel producer in the United States. It was created as a "minimill"—a steel-manufacturing firm with a small geographic reach, a limited product line, and relatively limited output. Today it is widely recognized as a medium-sized company that has found new ways of doing things in an old industry. In particular, Chaparral has been successful in finding ways to reduce costs and increase productivity by encouraging innovation and a bureaucracy-free workforce.

The Video

Video Source. "Chaparral Steel" was produced by the company as a general introduction to its goals, policies, and practices. Among the interviewees, CEO Gordon E. Forward, Dennis Beach (Vice President for Administration), and Jeff Werner (Senior Vice President for Structural Sales) describe the environment in which the company operates, its competitive challenges and advantages, and a wide range of the firm's operations, including management, production, human resources, marketing, and information control. In explaining the company's goals—"to be the easiest steel company for our customers to do business with"—they emphasize the following:

- Technology and innovation
- Employee empowerment, training, and teamwork
- Responsiveness to the marketplace
- Responsiveness to customer needs

> **"Whenever possible, we want people to do the thinking and technology to do the making."**
>
> —Lloyd Schmelzle
> *Vice President of Operations at Chaparral Steel*

Discussion Questions

1. Consider Chaparral's goal of being "the easiest steel company for our customers to do business with." Judging from the video, what would you characterize as the company's key strategies for meeting this goal?

2. Describe Chaparral Steel in terms of its management of the factors of production (labor, capital, entrepreneurship, and natural resources).

3. To what degree is Chaparral Steel engaged in monopolistic competition? In oligopolistic competition?

4. In what ways does the video indicate that Chaparral Steel is operating in the marketing and global eras?

Follow-Up Assignment

"In 1975," recalls CEO Gordon Forward, "there were 750,000 people in the U.S. steel industry. Today 125,000 employees produce the same capacity." The U.S. steel industry has undergone some major changes in the nearly quarter century since Chaparral was founded. To get a better idea of the environment in which Chaparral now operates, go to the library and research these changes. What are the key measures of productivity in the steel industry today? What has been the long-term effect of the minimill? What kinds of technology have been introduced in the last 25 years? Specifically, what changes has technology brought about, and what benefits have resulted from them? With employment down so far from the peak levels of two, three, and four decades ago, what is the status of labor relations in most steel mills today? How are American steel companies faring against competitors in other countries?

For Further Exploration

On the Internet, contact the Office of the American Workplace (OAW) at

http://www.fed.org/uscompanies/labor

Between 1993 and 1996, the OAW singled out several U.S. companies, including Chaparral, because of their "best practices" in the areas of human resources and labor management. Scroll down to and click on the directory labeled "A-M." Then click on the link to Chaparral Steel. To get a more detailed look at Chaparral's policies, practices, activities, and goals, examine this report.

VIDEO EXERCISE 1.2

Lands' End, Inc.: A Brief History

"We Are Able to Sell at Lower Prices Because . . ."

Learning Objectives

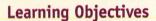

The purpose of this video exercise is to help students

1. Become better acquainted with a specific company currently conducting business as a public corporation in the United States.
2. Understand the path to growth taken by a U.S. company that has been in existence for less than four decades.
3. Understand more about the operations of a U.S. company that deals in both consumer goods and services.

Background Information

Lands' End is a *mail order* (or *catalog marketing*) retailer based in Dodgeville, Wisconsin. From its headquarters, the company mails out catalogs featuring high-quality merchandise that is competitively priced and backed by an unconditional guarantee. Lands' End catalogs specialize in casual and tailored clothing but include a variety of other products, including shoes, accessories, luggage, and items for the bed and bath.

Founded in Chicago in 1963, Lands' End originally specialized in sailing equipment; the first black-and-white catalog featured no clothing at all. By 1977, clothing and luggage dominated the catalog, and by 1979—the year of the move to Dodgeville—Lands' End had already recruited personnel in such areas as fabrics and clothing manufacture. The company now works directly with fabric mills and clothing manufacturers who are contracted to make products according to Lands' End's own specifications.

"We are able to sell at lower prices because we support no fancy emporiums with their high overhead. Our main location is in the middle of a 40-acre cornfield in rural Wisconsin."

—Principle 8
"Lands' End Principles of Doing Business"

Lands' End introduced the term "direct merchant" to describe itself in 1981. In 1994, when sales surpassed those of L.L. Bean, it became the largest specialty catalog retailer in the country. Today more than 1,000 phone lines handle 50,000 calls a day (about 100,000 calls a day in the weeks just before Christmas). Toll-free lines (both to sales and customer service operators) are open 24 hours a day. In-stock orders are usually shipped from the distribution center the day after they are received. Within the continental United States, standard delivery usually requires two business days.

The Video

Video Source. "Lands' End, Inc.: A Brief History," *Prentice Hall Presents: On Location at Lands' End.* This video introduces Lands' End by tracing the company's history from its origins in a small Chicago outlet in 1963 to its current position as the largest specialty catalog company in the United States. In describing the firm's current operations, the video focuses on the emphasis Lands' End places on customer service and distribution efficiency.

Discussion Questions

1. In general terms, describe the effect on Lands' End's past, present, and/or future operations of each of the four factors of production (labor, capital, entrepreneurs, and natural resources).

2. In what ways do Lands' End's operations reflect patterns of demand and supply in its particular industry?

3. Lands' End operates in an industry characterized by pure competition. Which facets of the company's operations most clearly reflect conditions of pure competition? Which facets reflect the position currently enjoyed by Lands' End in its particular industry?

4. Lands' End became a public corporation in October 1986. In August 1987 and again in May 1994, shares were split two-for-one. If you were presented *today* with an opportunity to buy stock in Lands' End, would you buy some stock? Why or why not?

Follow-Up Assignment

To better understand the nature of Lands' End's industry and operations, familiarize yourself with the following concepts:

- Operations processes (Chap. 11)
- Service operations (Chap. 11)
- Quality control (Chap. 11)
- The marketing mix (Chap. 13)
- Pricing products (Chap. 14)
- Promoting products (Chap. 14)
- Direct mail (Chap. 14)
- Nonstore retailing (Chap. 15)
- Mail order marketing (Chap. 15)
- Physical distribution (Chap. 15)
- Distribution center (Chap. 15)

For Further Exploration

Lands' End can be contacted on the Internet at

http://www.landsend.com

On the Web page, you will find an icon for the company's home page. From the home page, click on the link to "The Company Inside and Out." Examine "The Lands' End Principles of Doing Business." On what aspects of competition in its industry does Lands' End place the greatest emphasis? How does the company place that emphasis? What do phrases like "branded merchandise with high protected mark-ups" and "fancy emporiums with their high overhead" mean to you? As a potential customer, what value do you place on the fact that Lands' End "add[s] back features and construction details" to its clothing and other products?

UNDERSTANDING THE LEGAL CONTEXT OF BUSINESS

The Fine Line between Overseeing and Oversight

SECOND LOOK IS TOO LATE FOR VICTIMS OF VALUJET FLIGHT 592

Before May 11, 1996—the day that ValuJet Flight 592 crashed into the Florida Everglades, killing all 110 people on board—the Federal Aviation Administration (FAA) experienced some serious difficulty in carrying out two conflicting objectives. On the one hand, the FAA is mandated to certify that every U.S. airliner is fit to fly—a mandate that requires rigorous rules and even more rigorous inspection practices to root out safety and maintenance violations. On the other hand, the agency felt growing pressure to provide the public with a hands-off regulatory environment that encouraged the growth of low-fare, low-cost start-up airlines.

The FAA dealt with this dilemma by following a policy of regulatory flexibility that encouraged growth—a "go-easy" approach that allowed start-ups to enter the marketplace and

> **"ValuJet has not demonstrated that it has an effective maintenance-control system."**
>
> David R. Hinson
> *FAA Administrator*

stay there by cutting costs on everything from customer service to airplane maintenance. When ValuJet requested the right to farm out nearly all of its maintenance work to outside companies—a move that would save the small carrier millions of dollars annually—the FAA said yes.

Investigators now believe that poor communication between ValuJet and Sabretech, one of its maintenance contractors, may have played a major role in the May 11 crash. Improperly sealed oxygen generators were placed

in the plane's cargo hold, where they are believed to have set fire to tires also stored in the hold. After the crash, the FAA suggested that ValuJet bore primary responsibility for the mistake and the resulting disaster.

In response to both public criticism and its own sense that it had failed in its regulatory role, the FAA grounded ValuJet indefinitely. The agency based its decision on the results of an intense post-crash evaluation. According to FAA administrator David R. Hinson, ValuJet was no longer considered "airworthy" because of "multiple shortcomings" in the supervision of maintenance contractors. The airline, announced Hinton, "has not demonstrated that it has an effective maintenance-control system" to oversee contract work.

The ValuJet crash also demonstrated the flawed relationship between the FAA and the airlines it regulates. While encouraging Valu-

Jet's rapid growth—including the acquisition of 48 aircraft in just 31 months—the FAA ignored a documented history of safety violations dating back to 1993. According to some industry observers, ValuJet was an accident waiting to happen. Included in ValuJet's expanding fleet, for instance, were no fewer than 11 different types of aircraft. How could so many different planes be serviced? Who was responsible for maintaining safety standards?

The ValuJet disaster throws some light on the complex legal and regulatory environment in which many U.S. industries operate. In this case, an airline was forced to shut down and meet new requirements laid down by the FAA. Like ValuJet, firms face serious financial penalties and may even fail when managers misunderstand—or ignore or violate—the law. A practical understanding of the law is thus essential for all businesspeople. In this chapter, we will describe the basic tenets of U.S. law and show how

these principles work through the court system. We will also survey a few major areas of business-related law. By focusing on the learning objectives of this chapter, you will see that laws may create opportunities for business activity just as readily as they set limits on them.

After reading this chapter, you should be able to

1. Explain the meaning and basic forms of *law*

2. Describe the *U.S. judicial system*

3. Identify and discuss the six major areas of *business law*

4. Describe the *international framework of business law*

Continued on page 70

■ THE U.S. LEGAL AND JUDICIAL SYSTEMS

laws
Codified rules of behavior enforced by a society

If people could ignore contracts or drive down city streets at any speed, it would be unsafe to do business on Main Street—or even to set foot in public. Without law, people would be free to act "at will," and life and property would constantly be at risk. **Laws** are the codified rules of behavior enforced by a society. In the United States, laws fall into three broad categories according to their origins: *common*, *statutory*, and *regulatory*.[1] After discussing each of these types of laws, we will briefly describe the three-tier system of courts through which the judicial system administers the law in the United States.

Types of Law

Law in the United States originates primarily with English common law.[2] Its sources include the U.S. Constitution, state constitutions, federal and state statutes, municipal ordinances, administrative agency rules and regulations, executive orders, and court decisions.

common law
Body of decisions handed down by courts ruling on individual cases

Common Law   Court decisions follow *precedents*, or the decisions of earlier cases.[3] Following precedent lends stability to the law by basing judicial decisions on cases anchored in similar facts. This principle is the keystone of **common law:** the body of decisions handed down by courts ruling on individual cases. Although some facets of common law predate the American Revolution (and even hearken back to medieval Europe), common law continues to evolve in the courts today.

statutory law
Law created by constitutions or by federal, state, or local legislative acts

Statutory Law   Laws created by constitutions or by federal, state, or local legislative acts constitute **statutory law.** For example, Article I of the U.S. Constitution is a statutory law that empowers Congress to pass laws on corporate taxation, the zoning authority of municipalities, and the rights and privileges of businesses operating in the United States.

State legislatures and city councils also pass statutory laws. Some state laws, for example, prohibit the production or sale of detergents containing phosphates, which are believed to be pollutants. Nearly every town has ordinances specifying sites for certain types of industries or designating areas where cars cannot be parked during certain hours.

regulatory (or administrative) law
Law made by the authority of administrative agencies

Regulatory Law   Statutory and common law have long histories. Relatively new, is **regulatory** (or **administrative**) **law:** law made by the authority of administrative agencies. By and large, the expansion of U.S. regulatory law has paralleled the nation's economic and technological development. Lacking the technical expertise to develop specialized legislation for specialized business activities, Congress established the first administrative agencies to create and administer the needed laws in the late 1800s. Before the early 1960s, most agencies concerned themselves with the *economic* regulation of specific areas of business—say, transportation or securities. Since then many agencies have been established to pursue narrower *social* objectives. They focus on issues that cut across different sectors of the economy—clean air, for example, or product testing.[4]

Today a host of agencies, including the Equal Employment Opportunity Commission (EEOC), the Environmental Protection Agency (EPA), the Food and Drug Administration (FDA), the Federal Trade Commission (FTC), and the Occupational Safety and Health Administration (OSHA) regulate U.S. business practices. Figure 3.1 shows the growth in the number of federal agencies from 1900 to 1979, when the dramatic growth spurt of new agencies, begun in the 1960s, peaked.

In this section, we look briefly at the nature of regulatory agencies and describe some of the key legislation that makes up administrative law in this country. We also discuss an area of increasing importance in the relationship between government and business; *regulation*—or, more accurately, *deregulation.*

Agencies and Legislation.

Although Congress retain control over the scope of agency action, once passed regulations have the force of statutory law. Government regulatory agencies act as a secondary judicial system, determining whether or not regulations have been violated and imposing penalties. A firm that violates OSHA rules, for example may receive a citation, a hearing, and perhaps a heavy fine. Much agency activity consists of setting standards

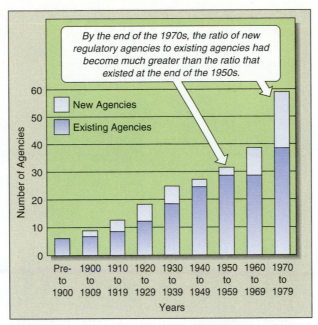

By the end of the 1970s, the ratio of new regulatory agencies to existing agencies had become much greater than the ratio that existed at the end of the 1950s.

FIGURE 3.1 ◆ **The Growth of Federal Regulatory Agencies**

for safety or quality and monitoring the compliance of businesses. The FDA, for example, is responsible for ensuring that food, medicines, and even cosmetics are safe and effective.

Regulatory laws have been on the books for nearly a century. As early as 1906, for example, the Pure Food and Drug Act mandated minimum levels of cleanliness and sanitation for food and drug companies. More recently, the Children's Television Act of 1990 requires that broadcasters meet the educational and informational needs of younger viewers and limit the amount of advertising broadcast during children's programs. In 1996, a sweeping new law to increase competition in the communications industry required television makers to install a "V-chip," which allows parents to block undesirable programming.

Congress has created many new agencies in response to pressure to address social issues. In some cases, agencies were established in response to public concern about corporate behavior. The activities of these agencies have sometimes forced U.S. firms to consider the public interest almost as routinely as they consider their own financial performance.[5] ▶

The Move toward Deregulation.

Although government regulation has benefited U.S. business in many ways, it is not without its drawbacks. Businesspeople complain—with some justification—that government regulations require too much paperwork. In order to comply with just one OSHA regulation for one year, Goodyear once generated 345,000 pages of computer reports weighing 3,200 pounds. It now costs Goodyear $35.5 million each year to comply with the regulations of six government agencies, and it takes 36 employee-years annually (the equivalent of one employee working full-time for 36 years) to fill out the required reports.

Not surprisingly, many people in both business and government support broader **deregulation:** the elimination of rules that restrict business activity. Advocates of both regulation and deregulation claim that each acts to control business expansion and prices, increase government efficiency, and right wrongs that the marketplace cannot or does not handle itself. Regulations such as those enforced by the EEOC, for example,

deregulation
Elimination of administrative laws and rules that restrict business activity

In August 1996, the Clinton Administration announced a long list of new restrictions designed to regulate cigarette advertising which, according to the Food and Drug Administration, reaches children. The FDA now considers nicotine an addictive drug and according to the new guidelines can limit billboard advertising and brand-name sporting events sponsorships. The tobacco and advertising industries have fought a legal war against the restrictions, partly on the grounds that they violate freedom of speech.

are supposed to control undesirable business practices in the interest of social equity. In contrast, the court-ordered breakup of AT&T was prompted by a perceived need for greater market efficiency. For these and other reasons, the federal government began deregulating certain industries in the 1970s.

It is important to note that the United States is the only industrialized nation that has deregulated key industries—financial services, transportation, telecommunications, and host of others. Most recently, for instance, a 1996 law allowed the seven "Baby Bells"—regional phone companies created when AT&T was broken up—to compete for long-distance business. It also allowed cable television and telephone companies to enter each other's markets by offering any combination of video, telephone, and high-speed data communications services.[6] Many analysts contend that such deregulation is now and will become an even greater advantage in an era of global competition. Deregulation, they argue, is a primary incentive to innovation.

According to this view, deregulated industries are forced to innovate in order to survive in fiercely competitive industries. Those firms that are already conditioned to compete by being more creative will outperform firms that have been protected by regulatory climates in their home countries. "What's important," says one economist, "is that competition energizes new ways of doing things." The U.S. telecommunications industry, proponents of this view say, is twice as productive as its European counterparts because it is the only such industry forced to come out from under a protective regulatory umbrella.[7]

> ## "What's important is that competition energizes new ways of doing things."
> —Donald McCloskey
> *Economist*

TRENDS & CHALLENGES

HOOKED ON TELECOMMUNICATIONS

Both *Fortune* magazine and the *Wall Street Journal* referred to the 1996 passage of federal legislation to overhaul the nation's telecommunications industry as the beginning of a battle for survival and dominance among corporate Goliaths. "Let the telecom wars begin," proclaimed the *Journal*.

This legislation deregulated the telecommunications industry and set the stage for a new era of competition (and mergers). Coming at a time when new technologies are creating dramatically different communication services, Congress' mandate will fundamentally change both the companies that deliver these services and the way in which customers receive them. Among the services affected by the legislation are long-distance, local, and cellular-phone services; broadcasting (including both television and radio); cable service; and computer-based Internet technology.

To survive in this deregulated environment, companies must learn to compete in the $500 billion integrated telecommunications market, not just in one market segment. Thus, Sourthern New England Telephone (SNET), long the supplier of local telephone service in Connecticut, is now entering the long-distance and cellular phone markets and has plans to become involved in broadcast services, including television and movie rentals. SNET also intends to deliver Internet services and even video games via phone lines. Why the change in direction? With the average Connecticut family spending $200 a month on communication and entertainment—four times as much as it does on phone service alone—the company sees the potential for enormous profits.

Indeed, the goal of every telecommunications company competing in this deregulated market is to sell a variety of wired and wireless communications services to every customer. "We want to get as many hooks into

each of our customers as possible," explains MCI CEO Bert C. Roberts, Jr. MCI's own studies show that the greater the number of "hooks," the greater the customer loyalty. Customers who are linked to a company through more than one communication and/or entertainment service switch carriers at a 40-percent lower rate than those who buy only single services.

> ## "We want to get as many hooks into each of our customers as possible."
>
> —Bert C. Roberts Jr.
> *MCI Chairman and CEO*

The 1996 telecommunications bill included the following provisions (among others):

- *Long-distance telephone service.* The seven regional Bell phone companies can enter the long-distance market. Increased competition will probably result in lower rates.
- *Local telephone service.* New competitors, including AT&T, MCI, and local cable television companies, can provide local telephone service. Despite increased competition, this change may cause rates to rise, since in the short-run, new carriers will be forced to pay local phone companies for the privilege of connecting into existing local lines.
- *Broadcasting.* Broadcasters can own an unlimited number of television and radio stations. Mergers between Westinghouse Electric and CBS (television and radio) and Westinghouse and Infinity Broadcasting (radio) have already changed the face of the broadcasting industry.
- *Cable television.* The new law deregulates the rates that cable companies charge for their services. Cable TV rates may rise, but extra earnings from cable TV operations may give cable companies the boost they need to begin competing in local phone service markets.

The U.S. Judicial System

Laws are of little use unless they are enforced. Much of the responsibility for law enforcement falls to the courts. Although few people would claim that the courts are capable of resolving every dispute, there often seem to be more than enough lawyers to handle them all: Indeed, there are 140 lawyers for every 100,000 people in the United

States. Litigation is a significant part of contemporary life, and we have given our courts a voice in a wide range of issues, some touching profoundly personal concerns, some ruling on matters of public policy that affect all our lives. In this section, we look at the operations of the U.S. judicial system.

The Court System   As Figure 3.2 shows, there are three levels in the U.S. judicial system—*federal*, *state*, and *local*. These levels reflect the *federalist* structure of a system in which a central government shares power with state or local governments. Federal courts were created by the U.S. Constitution. They hear cases on questions of constitutional law, disputes relating to maritime laws, and violations of federal statutes. They also rule on regulatory actions and on such issues as bankruptcy, postal law, and copyright or patent violation. Both the federal and most state systems embody a three-tiered system of *trial*, *appellate*, and *supreme courts*.

Trial Courts.   At the lowest level of the federal court system are the **trial courts,** general courts that hear cases not specifically assigned to another court. A case involving contract violation would go before a trial court. Every state has at least one federal trial court, called a *district court*.

trial court
General court that hears cases not specifically assigned to another court

Trial courts also include special courts and administrative agencies. *Special courts* hear specific types of cases, such as cases involving tax evasion, fraud, international disputes, or claims against the U.S. government. Within their areas of jurisdiction, administrative agencies also make judgments much like those of courts.

Courts in each state system deal with the same issues as their federal counterparts. However, they may rule only in areas governed by state law. For example, a case involving state income tax laws would be heard by a state special court. Local courts in each state system also hear cases on municipal ordinances, local traffic violations, and similar issues.

appellate court
Court that reviews case records of trials whose findings have been appealed

Appellate Courts.   A losing party may disagree with a trial court ruling. If that party can show grounds for review, the case may go before a federal or state **appellate court.** These

FIGURE 3.2 ◆ The U.S. Judicial System

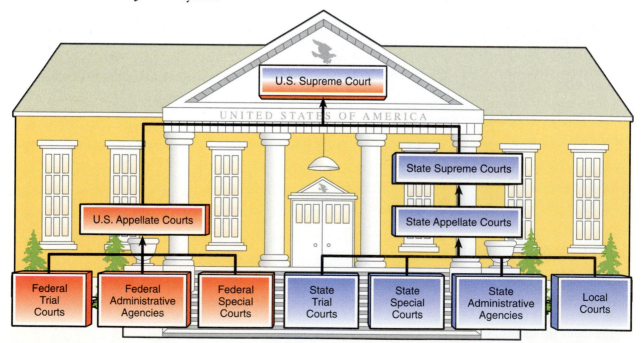

courts consider questions of law, such as possible errors of legal interpretation made by lower courts. They do not examine questions of fact. There are now 13 federal courts of appeal, each with 3 to 15 judges. Cases are normally heard by three-judge panels.

Supreme Courts. Cases still not resolved at the appellate level can be appealed to the appropriate state supreme courts or to the U.S. Supreme Court. If it believes that an appeal is warranted or that the outcome will set an important precedent, the U.S. Supreme Court also hears cases appealed from state supreme courts. Each year, the U.S. Supreme Court receives about 5,000 appeals but typically agrees to hear fewer than 200.

■ BUSINESS LAW

Most legal issues confronted by businesses fall into one of six basic areas: *contract, tort, property, agency, commercial,* or *bankruptcy law.* These areas cover a wide range of business activity.

Contract Law

A **contract** is any agreement between two or more parties that is enforceable in court. As such, it must meet six conditions. If all these conditions are met, one party can seek legal recourse from another if the other party breaches (that is, violates) the terms of the agreement.[8]

1. *Agreement.* Agreement is the serious, definite, and communicated offer and acceptance of the same terms. Let us say that an auto parts supplier offers in writing to sell rebuilt engines to a repair shop for $500 each. If the repair shop accepts the offer, the two parties have reached an agreement.

2. *Consent.* A contract is not enforceable if any of the parties has been affected by an honest mistake, fraud, or pressure. For example, a restaurant manager orders a painted sign, but the sign company delivers a neon sign instead.

3. *Capacity.* To give real consent, both parties must demonstrate legal **capacity** (competence). A person under legal age (usually 18 or 21) cannot enter into a binding contract.

4. *Consideration.* An agreement is binding only if it exchanges **considerations,** that is, items of value. If your brother offers to paint your room for free, you cannot sue him if he changes his mind. Note that "items of value" do not necessarily entail money. For example, a tax accountant might agree to prepare a homebuilder's tax return in exchange for a new patio. Both services are items of value. Contracts need not be "rational," nor must they provide the "best" possible bargain for both sides. They need only include "legally sufficient" consideration. The terms are met if both parties receive what the contract details.

5. *Legality.* A contract must be for a lawful purpose and must comply with federal, state, and local laws and regulations. For example, an agreement between two competitors to engage in price fixing—that is, to set a mutually acceptable price—is not legal.

6. *Proper form.* A contract may be written, oral, or implied from conduct. It must be written, however, if it involves the sale of land or goods worth more than $500. It must be written if the agreement requires more than a year to fulfill—say, a contract for employment as an engineer on a 14-month construction project. All changes to written contracts must also be in writing.

contract
Any agreement between two or more parties that is enforceable in court

capacity
Competence required of individuals entering into a binding contract

consideration
Any item of value exchanged between parties to create a valid contract

© 1998 Charles Barsotti *from* The Cartoon Bank,™ Inc.

"BY GOLLY, EDGAR, YOU'VE DONE IT. IT'S NOT ILLEGAL, BUT IT SHOULD BE."

Breach of Contract   What can one party do if the other fails to live up to the terms of a valid contract? Contract law offers a variety of remedies designed to protect the reasonable expectations of the parties and, in some cases, to compensate them for actions taken to enforce the agreement.

As the injured party to a breached contract, any of the following actions might occur:

- You might cancel the contract and refuse to live up to your part of the bargain. For example, you might simply cancel a contract for carpet shampooing if the company fails to show up.
- You might sue for damages up to the amount that you lost as a result of the breach. Thus, you might sue the original caterer if you must hire a more expensive caterer for your wedding reception because the original company canceled at the last minute.
- If money cannot repay the damage you suffered, you might demand specific performance—that is, require the other party to fulfill the original contract. For example, you might demand that a dealer in classic cars sell you the antique Stutz Bearcat he agreed to sell you and not a classic Jaguar instead.

Tort Law

tort
Civil injury to people, property, or reputation for which compensation must be paid

Tort law applies to most business relationships *not governed by contracts*. A **tort** is a *civil*—that is, noncriminal—injury to people, property, or reputation for which compensation must be paid. For example, if a person violates zoning laws by opening a convenience store in a residential area, he or she cannot be sent to jail as if the act were a criminal violation. But a variety of other legal measures can be pursued, such as fines or seizure of property. Trespass, fraud, defamation, invasion of privacy, and even assault can be torts, as can interference with contractual relations and wrongful use of trade secrets. In this section, we explain three classifications of torts: *intentional, negligence,* and *product liability.*

intentional tort
Tort resulting from the deliberate actions of a party

Intentional Torts   **Intentional torts** result from the deliberate actions of another person or organization—for instance, a manufacturer knowingly fails to install a relatively inexpensive safety device on a product. Similarly, refusing to rectify a product design flaw—as in the case of the space shuttle *Challenger* disaster—can render a firm liable for an intentional tort. The actions of employees on the job may also constitute intentional torts—say, an overzealous security guard who wrongly accuses a customer of shoplifting. To remedy torts, courts will usually impose **compensatory damages:** payments intended to redress an injury actually suffered. They may also impose **punitive damages:** fines that exceed actual losses suffered by plaintiffs and that are intended to punish defendants.

In 1992, for example, a jury awarded $300,000 in compensatory damages plus $4 million in punitive damages to a couple who alleged that a two-way mirror in their penthouse suite had allowed strangers to spy on them at a local hotel. The compensatory damages were awarded because the jury agreed that the couple's privacy had been invaded. The large punitive award cited the plaintiffs's emotional distress in the aftermath of the incident. (The case was later settled for $1 million in total damages.)[9]

Negligence Torts   Ninety percent of tort suits involve charges of **negligence,** conduct falling below legal standards for protecting others against unreasonable risk. If a company installs a pollution-control system that fails to protect a community's water supply, it may later be sued by an individual who gets sick from drinking the water.

Negligence torts may also result from employee actions. For example, if the captain of a supertanker runs aground and spills 11 million gallons of crude oil into coastal fishing waters, the oil company may be liable for potentially astronomical damages. ▼ Thus in September 1994, a jury in Alaska ordered Exxon Corp. to pay $5 billion in punitive damages to 34,000 fishermen and other plaintiffs as a consequence of the *Exxon Valdez* disaster of 1989. (Plaintiffs had asked for $15 billion.) A month earlier, the jury had awarded plaintiffs $287 million in compensatory damages. In 1993, the firm responsible for pipeline operations at the Valdez, Alaska, terminal (which is partially owned by Exxon) agreed to pay plaintiffs in the same case $98 million in damages. In a separate case, Exxon paid $20 million in damages to villagers whose food supply had been destroyed. A separate state jury will consider another $120 million in claims by Alaskan corporations and municipalities. Even before any of these awards was handed down, Exxon had spent $2.1 billion on the cleanup effort and paid $1.3 billion in civil and criminal penalties.[10]

compensatory damages
Monetary payments intended to redress injury actually suffered because of a tort

punitive damages
Fines imposed over and above any actual losses suffered by a plaintiff

negligence
Conduct falling below legal standards for protecting others against unreasonable risk

After the Exxon Valdez *spilled 11 million gallons of oil into Alaska's Prince William Sound in 1989, Exxon spent $3.4 billion cleaning up the mess and offering compensation to victims—some 15,000 fishermen and other natives who claimed that their livelihoods had been destroyed. Minneapolis lawyer Brian O'Neill led the legal team supporting plaintiffs who refused to accept Exxon's offers. "Multinational corporations," charges O'Neill, "get a franchise to be rich and wealthy and respected beyond people's dreams. And with that franchise comes responsibility to behave. This case will teach people that they are responsible."*

product liability tort
Tort in which a company is responsible for injuries caused by its products

Product Liability Torts   In cases of **product liability,** a company may be held responsible for injuries caused by its products. Product liability is an issue in each of the following situations:

- In a raft of recent lawsuits, plaintiffs have charged that certain three-wheel all-terrain vehicles are unsafe; they contend that they are unstable and too easily overturned. They argue that manufacturers are liable for injuries suffered by drivers operating those vehicles.
- In early 1997, suits were filed against Mattel. During the preceding Christmas season, the toymaker had sold thousands of Cabbage Patch dolls with a brand-new feature: the dolls could "chew" play food. Unfortunately, they were also prone to gnaw on the hair of young children.

According to a special government panel on product liability, about 33 million people are injured and 28,000 killed by consumer products each year. Even so, U.S. courts seem to be taking a harder look at many product liability claims, especially when they are based on "soft" science:

- An appeals court overturned a $1 million award to a psychic who claimed that a CAT scan destroyed her special abilities.
- A federal judge barred as "unreliable" medical testimony linking carpal tunnel syndrome to a computer keyboard made by Unisys.
- Another federal judge dismissed a case claiming that cellular phone use caused a woman's brain tumor.[11]

strict product liability
Principle that liability can result not from a producer's negligence but from a defect in the product itself

Strict Product Liability.   Since the early 1960s, businesses have faced a number of legal actions based on the relatively new principle of **strict product liability:** the principle that liability can result not from a producer's negligence but from a defect in the product itself. An injured party need show only that

1. The product was defective.
2. The defect was the cause of injury.
3. The defect caused the product to be unreasonably dangerous.

Many recent cases in strict product liability have focused on injuries or illnesses attributable to toxic wastes or other hazardous substances that were legally disposed of. Because plaintiffs need not demonstrate negligence or fault, these suits frequently succeed. Not surprisingly, the number of such suits promises to increase.[12]▶

Property Law

As the name implies, *property law* concerns property rights. But what exactly is "property"? Is it the land under a house? The house itself? A car in the driveway? A dress in the closet? The answer in each case is yes: in the legal sense, **property** is anything of value to which a person or business has sole right of ownership. Indeed, property is technically those *rights.*

property
Anything of value to which a person or business has sole right of ownership

Within this broad general definition, we can divide property into four categories. In this section, we define these categories and then examine more fully the legal protection of a certain kind of property—intellectual property.

tangible real property
Land and anything attached to it

- **Tangible real property** is land and anything attached to it. A house and a factory are both tangible real property, as are built-in appliances or the machines inside the buildings.

- **Tangible personal property** is any movable item that can be owned, bought, sold, or leased. Examples are automobiles, clothing, stereos, and cameras.
- **Intangible personal property** cannot be seen but exists by virtue of written documentation. Examples are insurance policies, bank accounts, stocks and bonds, and trade secrets.
- **Intellectual property** is created through a person's creative activities. Books, articles, songs, paintings, screenplays, and computer software are all intellectual property.

Protection of Intellectual Rights The U.S. Constitution grants protection to intellectual property by means of copyrights, trademarks, and patents. Copyrights and patents apply to the tangible expressions of an idea—not to the ideas themselves. Thus, you could not copyright the idea of cloning dinosaurs from fossil DNA. Michael Crichton, could copyright his novel *Jurassic Park*, which is a tangible result of that idea, and sell the film rights to producer-director Steven Spielberg. Both creators are entitled to the profits, if any, that may be generated by their tangible creative expressions.

Copyrights. **Copyrights** give exclusive ownership rights to the creators of books, articles, designs, illustrations, photos, films, and music. Computer programs and even semiconductor chips are also protected. Copyrights extend to creators for their entire lives and to their estates for 50 years thereafter. All items are automatically copyrighted from the moment of creation.

Trademarks. Because the development of products is expensive, companies must prevent other firms from using their brand names. Often they must act to keep competitors from seducing consumers with similar or substitute products. A producer can apply to the U.S. government for a **trademark**—the exclusive legal right to use a brand name.[13] ▶

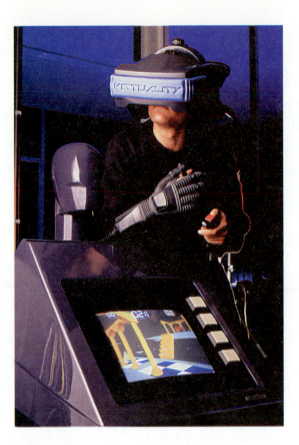

tangible personal property
Any movable item that can be owned, bought, sold, or leased

intangible personal property
Property that cannot be seen but that exists by virtue of written documentation

intellectual property
Property created through a person's creative activities

Experiments with virtual reality (VR) systems conducted by such organizations as Sega Enterprises Ltd. and the U.S. military have shown that many users are subject to what the VR community calls "cybersickness." Symptoms include eyestrain, nausea and confusion, and even LSD-style "flashbacks." Although there is as yet little hard evidence on causes, many manufacturers of VR equipment admit to being concerned about the potential for product liability lawsuits.

copyright
Exclusive ownership right belonging to the creator of a book, article, design, illustration, photo, film, or musical work

trademark
Exclusive legal right to use a brand name or symbol

According to Heublein Inc., it purchased the rights to the Smirnoff name (as in vodka) in 1939 for $14,000. Today the Smirnoff brand, which is outsold worldwide only by Bacardi rum, is worth $1.4 billion. Back in Russa, however, Boris Smirnoff, a great grandson of the original founder, is trying to reclaim the family name, which was lost when the Bolsheviks stripped Russians of all private property nearly 80 years ago. The Smirnoff dispute is just one of a growing number of trademark battles between U.S. and Russian organizations.

TRENDS & CHALLENGES
SCIENTISTS SEARCH FOR THE MISSING LINKAGE

Dr. Marcia Angell is an editor of the *New England Journal of Medicine*, one of the most prestigious medical journals in the country, and she followed the development of the mass tort case over silicone breast implants. On one side were women who charged that leaking implants caused a variety of ailments, including autoimmune diseases. On the other side was Dow Corning Corp., the leading implant manufacturer, which claimed that there was no proven link between the implants and the onset of medical problems. The plaintiffs were part of a *class action lawsuit* in which a select few sued on behalf of thousands.

After reviewing a major study conducted by the Mayo Clinic, Dr. Angell concluded that evidence was lacking to support claims of a cause-and-effect relationship. The results of a second breast implant study conducted at the Harvard Medical School confirmed her conclusion. Nevertheless, Dr. Angell's scientific evidence failed to convince juries hearing implant cases. According to Dr. Angell, courts awarded plaintiffs millions of dollars in settlements by "avoiding the issue of causation altogether." Juries, she contends, sidestepped the causation issue by listening to a parade of "experts"—witnesses called by plaintiffs' lawyers who (in exchange for consulting fees) testified that breast implants were responsible for such debilitating illnesses as rheumatoid arthritis. When scientific studies like Angell's questioned claims of a cause-and-effect linkage, lawyers responded by claiming that implants caused "atypical" diseases. What is an "atypical" disease? To plaintiffs' lawyers, explains Angell, "the best diseases are those that can't be defined, because they can't be studied systematically."

In 1992, Dow Corning voluntarily stopped producing silicone implants at the request of the Food and Drug Administration, which raised questions about implant safety and, specifically, about leakage. In 1994,

Dow Corning and other companies involved in implant litigation offered $4.25 billion to settle the claims of 440,000 women involved in the class action suit. Although manufacturers continued to argue the lack of evidence linking implants and certain diseases, they felt compelled to settle because of the large number of lawsuits they faced. Under the terms of the settlement, women with serious, proven symptoms would receive multimillion-dollar payments. Those with such vague complaints as aches and chronic fatigue could receive payments as high as $200,000. Eventually, when 19,000 additional lawsuits were initiated and the cost of settling the original class action suit proved higher than expected, Dow Corning sought financial protection under the U.S. bankruptcy code.

> **"To lawyers, the best diseases are those that can't be defined, because they can't be studied systematically."**
>
> —Dr. Marcia Angell
> *Editor,* New England Journal of Medicine

Although this maneuver does not protect Dow Corning from litigation, the company hopes that future juries, armed with new medical evidence, will dismiss what it calls "junk science" claims. Specifically, Dow Corning hopes that the courts will allow a high-profile trial that decides the case on the basis of disease causation. Meanwhile, plaintiffs attack Dow Corning's position by pointing to the words of Mayo Clinic researchers who have cautioned that "our results . . . cannot be considered proof of the absence of an association between breast implants and connective-tissue disease." They also focus on Dow Corning's behavior after implant problems first surfaced in the 1980s—the company's failure to acknowledge complaints and investigate them in a timely manner. In the plaintiffs' view, these failures make Dow Corning legally responsible for their medical problems.

Trademarks are granted for 20 years and may be renewed indefinitely if a firm continues to protect its brand name. If a firm allows the brand name to lapse into *common usage*, it may lose protection. Common usage takes effect when a company fails to use the ® symbol to indicate that its brand name is a registered trademark. It also takes effect if a company seeks no action against those who fail to acknowledge its trademark. Recently, for example, the popular brand-name sailboard Windsurfer lost its trademark. Like *trampoline*, *yo-yo*, and *thermos*, *windsurfer* has become the common term for the product and can now be used by any sailboard company. In contrast, Formica Corp. successfully spent the better part of a decade in court to protect the name *Formica* as a trademark. The Federal Trade Commission had contended that the word had entered the language as a generic name for any similar laminate material.

Patents. **Patents** provide legal monopolies for the use and licensing of manufactured items, manufacturing processes, substances, and designs for objects. A patentable invention must be *novel, useful,* and *nonobvious.* Since June 1995, U.S. patent law has been in harmony with that of most developed nations. For example, patents are now valid for 20 years rather than 17 years. In addition, the term now runs from the date on which the application was *filed*, not the date on which the patent itself was *issued*.[14]

Although the U.S. Patent Office issues about 1,200 patents a week, requirements are stringent, and U.S. patents actually tend to be issued at a slow pace. While Japan and most European countries have installed systems to speed up patent filing and research, the U.S. system can extend the process to years. Other observers argue that American firms trail their foreign counterparts in patents because of the sluggishness with which U.S. companies move products through their own research and development programs.

About 50 percent of all U.S. patents granted each year are awarded to foreign companies. However, the percentage of patents awarded to U.S. companies is increasing as U.S. companies become more aggressive. In 1992, for example, Digital Equipment Corp. won 223 U.S. patents, up from a mere 20 in 1985. Intel Corp. increased the number of its filings from 100 in 1990 to 400 in 1993.[15]

Restrictions on Property Rights   Property rights are not always absolute. For example, rights may be compromised under any of the following circumstances:

- Owners of shorefront property may be required to permit anglers, clam diggers, and other interested parties to walk near the water.
- Utility companies typically have rights called easements, such as the right to run wire over private property or to lay cable or pipe under it.
- Under the principle of **eminent domain,** the government may, upon paying owners fair prices, claim private land to expand roads or erect public buildings.

Agency Law

The transfer of property—whether the deeding of real estate or the transfer of automobile title—often involves agents. An **agent** is a person who acts for, and in the name of, another party, called the **principal.** The most visible agents are those in real estate, sports, and entertainment. Many businesses, however, use agents to secure insurance coverage and handle investments. Every partner in a partnership and every officer and director in a corporation is an agent of that business. Courts have also ruled that both a firm's employees and its outside contractors may be regarded as its agents.

Authority of Agents   Agents have the authority to bind principals to agreements. They receive that authority, however, from the principals themselves; they cannot

patent
Exclusive legal right to use and license a manufactured item or substance, manufacturing process, or object design

eminant domain
Governmental right to claim private land for public use after paying owners fair prices

agent
Individual or organization acting for, and in the name of, another party

principal
Individual or organization authorizing an agent to act on its behalf

create their own authority. An agent's authority to bind a principal can be express, implied, or apparent. The following illustration involves all three forms of agent authority:

> Ellen is a salesperson in Honest Sam's Used Car Lot. Her written employment contract gives her **express authority** to sell cars, to provide information to prospective buyers, and to approve trade-ins up to $2,000. Derived from the custom of used-car dealers, she also has **implied authority** to give reasonable discounts on prices and to make reasonable adjustments to written warranties. Furthermore, Ellen may—in the presence of Honest Sam—promise a customer that she will match the price offered by another local dealer. If Honest Sam assents—perhaps merely nods and smiles—Ellen may be construed to have the **apparent authority** to make this deal.

Responsibilities of Principals   Principals have several responsibilities to their agents. They owe agents reasonable compensation, must reimburse them for related business expenses, and should inform them of risks associated with their business activities. Principals are liable for actions performed by agents *within the scope of their employment.* Thus, if agents make untrue claims about products or services, the principal is liable for making amends. Employers are similarly responsible for the actions of employees. In fact, firms are often liable in tort suits because the courts treat employees as agents.

Businesses are increasingly being held accountable for *criminal* acts by employees. Court findings, for example, have argued that firms are expected to be aware of workers' propensities for violence, to check on their employees' pasts, and to train and supervise employees properly. Suppose, for instance, that a delivery service hires a driver with a history of driving while intoxicated. If the driver has an accident with a company vehicle while under the influence of alcohol, the company may be liable for criminal actions.

Commercial Law

Managers must be well acquainted with the most general laws affecting commerce. Specifically, they need to be familiar with the provisions of the *Uniform Commercial Code*, which sets down rules regarding *warranties*.

The Uniform Commercial Code   For many years, companies doing business in more than one state faced a special problem: laws governing commerce varied, sometimes widely, from state to state. In 1952, however, the National Conference of Commissioners on Uniform State Laws and the American Law Institute drew up the **Uniform Commercial Code (UCC).** Subsequently accepted by every state except Louisiana, the UCC describes the rights of buyers and sellers in transactions.

For example, buyers who believe that they have been wronged in agreements with sellers have several options. They can cancel contracts, refuse deliveries, and demand the return of any deposits. In some cases, they can buy the same products elsewhere and sue the original contractors to recover any losses incurred. Sellers, too, have several options. They can cancel contracts, withhold deliveries, and sell goods to other buyers. If goods have already been delivered, sellers can repossess them or sue the buyers for purchase prices.

Warranties.   A **warranty** is a seller's promise to stand by its products or services if a problem occurs after the sale. Warranties may be express or *implied.* The terms of an **express warranty** are specifically stated by the seller. For example, many stereo systems are expressly warranted for 90 days. If they malfunction within that period, they can be returned for full refunds.

express authority
Agent's authority, derived from written agreement, to bind a principal to a certain course of action

implied authority
Agent's authority, derived from business custom, to bind a principal to a certain course of action

apparent authority
Agent's authority, based on the principal's compliance, to bind a principal to a certain course of action

Uniform Commercial Code (UCC)
Body of standardized laws governing the rights of buyers and sellers in transactions

warranty
Seller's promise to stand by its products or services if a problem occurs after the sale

express warranty
Warranty whose terms are specifically stated by the seller

An **implied warranty** is dictated by law. Implied warranties embody the principle that a product should (1) fulfill the promises made by advertisements and (2) serve the purpose for which it was manufactured and sold. If you buy an advertised frost-free refrigerator, the seller implies that the refrigerator will keep your food cold and that you will not have to defrost it. It is important to note, however, that warranties, unlike most contracts, are easily limited, waived, or disclaimed. Consequently, they are the source of more and more tort action, as dissatisfied customers seek redress from producers.

Bankruptcy Law

At one time, individuals who could not pay their debts were jailed. Today, however, both organizations and individuals can seek relief by filing for **bankruptcy**—the court-granted permission not to pay some or all debts.

Hundreds of thousands of individuals and tens of thousands of businesses file for bankruptcy each year, and their numbers continue to increase. Filings have doubled since 1985, peaking in 1996 at 1.1 million (a 25-percent increase over 1995).[16] Why do individuals and businesses file for bankruptcy? Cash-flow problems and drops in farm prices caused many farmers, banks, and small businesses to go bankrupt. In recent years, large enterprises such as Continental Airlines and R. H. Macy have sought the protection of bankruptcy laws as part of strategies to streamline operations, cut costs, and regain profitability.

Three main factors account for the increase in bankruptcy filings:

1. The increased availability of credit
2. The "fresh-start" provisions in current bankruptcy laws
3. The growing acceptance of bankruptcy as a financial tactic

In some cases, creditors force an individual or firm into **involuntary bankruptcy** and press the courts to award them payment of at least part of what they are owed. Far more often, however, a person or business chooses to file for court protection against creditors. In general, individuals and firms whose debts exceed total assets by at least $1,000 may file for **voluntary bankruptcy.**

Business Bankruptcy   A business bankruptcy may be resolved by one of three plans:

- Under a *liquidation plan*, the business ceases to exist. Its assets are sold and the proceeds used to pay creditors.
- Under a *repayment plan*, the bankrupt company simply works out a new payment schedule to meet its obligations. The time frame is usually extended, and payments are collected and distributed by a court-appointed trustee.
- *Reorganization* is the most complex form of business bankruptcy. The company must explain the sources of its financial difficulties and propose a new plan for remaining in business. Reorganization may include a new slate of managers and a new financial strategy. A judge may also reduce the firm's debts to ensure its survival. Although creditors naturally dislike debt reduction, they may agree to the proposal, since 50 percent of one's due is better than nothing at all.

New legislation passed in 1994 has made some major revisions in bankruptcy laws. For example, it is now easier for individuals with up to $1 million in debt to make payments under installment plans instead of liquidating assets immediately. In contrast, the new law restricts how long a company can protect itself in bankruptcy while continuing to do business. Critics have charged, for instance, that many firms have succeeded in operating for many months under bankruptcy protection. During that time, they were able to cut costs and prices, not only competing with an unfair advantage but

implied warranty
Warranty, dictated by law, based on the principle that products should fulfill advertised promises and serve the purposes for which they are manufactured and sold

bankruptcy
Permission granted by the courts to individuals and organizations not to pay some or all of their debts

involuntary bankruptcy
Bankruptcy proceedings initiated by the creditors of an indebted individual or organization

voluntary bankruptcy
Backruptcy proceedings initiated by an indebted individual or organization

dragging down overall industry profits. The new laws place time limits on various steps in the filing process. The intended effect is to speed up the process and prevent assets from being lost to legal fees.

■ THE INTERNATIONAL FRAMEWORK OF BUSINESS LAW

Laws can vary dramatically from country to country, and as we will see in Chapter 5, many businesses today have international markets, suppliers, and competitors. It follows that managers need a basic understanding of the international framework of business law that affects the ways in which they can do business.

National laws are created and enforced by countries. The creation and enforcement of international law is more complicated. For example, if a company shipping merchandise between the United States and Mexico breaks an environmental protection law, to whom is that company accountable? The answer depends on several factors. Which country enacted the law in question? Where did the violation occur? In which country is the alleged violator incorporated?

international law
Set of cooperative agreements and guidelines established by countries to govern actions of individuals, businesses, and nations

Issues such as pollution across borders are matters of **international law:** the very general set of cooperative agreements and guidelines established by countries to govern the actions of individuals, businesses, and nations themselves. In this section, we examine the various sources of international law. We then discuss some of the important ways in which international trade is regulated and place some key U.S. trade laws in the international context in which they are designed to work.

Sources of International Law

International law has several sources. One source is custom and tradition. Among countries that have been trading with each other for centuries, many customs and traditions governing exchanges have gradually evolved into practice. Although some trading practices still follow ancient unwritten agreements, there has been a clear trend in more recent times to approach international trade within more formal legal framework. Key features of that framework include a variety of formal trade agreements.

Trade Agreements   In addition to subscribing to international rules, virtually every nation has formal trade treaties with other nations. A *bilateral agreement* is one involving two countries; a *multilateral agreement* involves several nations.

General Agreement on Tariffs and Trade (GATT)
International trade agreement to encourage the multilateral reduction or elimination of trade barriers

General Agreement on Tariffs and Trade.   The **General Agreement on Tariffs and Trade (GATT)** was first signed shortly after the end of World War II. Its purpose is to reduce or eliminate trade barriers, such as tariffs and quotas. It does so by encouraging nations to protect domestic industries within internationally agreed-upon limits and to engage in multilateral negotiations.

In December 1994, the U.S. Congress ratified a revision of GATT that had been worked out by 124 nations over a 12-year period. Still, many issues remain unresolved—for example, the opening of foreign markets to most financial services. Governments may still provide subsidies to manufacturers of civil aircraft, and no agreement was reached on limiting the distribution of American cultural exports—movies, music, and the like—in Europe. With those agreements that have been reached, however, one international economic group predicts that world commerce will have increased by $270 billion by 2002.[17]

North American Free Trade Agreement (NAFTA)
Agreement to gradually eliminate tariffs and other trade barriers between the United States, Canada, and Mexico

North American Free Trade Agreement.   The **North American Free Trade Agreement (NAFTA)** was negotiated to remove tariffs and other trade barriers among the United States, Canada, and Mexico. NAFTA also included agreements to monitor environmental and labor abuses. It took effect on January 1, 1994, and immediately eliminated some tariffs; others will disappear after 5-, 10-, or 15-year intervals.

In the first year after its passage, observers agreed that, by and large, NAFTA achieved what it was supposed to: a much more active North American market. The following were among the results after one year:[18]

- Direct foreign investment increased. U.S. and Canadian firms, for example, accounted for 55 percent of all foreign investment in Mexico, investing $2.4 billion. Companies from other nations—for instance, Toyota Motor Corp.—also made new investments, such as expanding production facilities, to take advantage of the freer movement of goods in the new market.
- U.S. exports to Mexico increased by about 20 percent. Procter & Gamble, for example, enjoyed an increase of nearly 75 percent, and the giant agribusiness firm of Archer Daniels Midland reported a tripling of its exports to Mexico. Mexico passed Japan as the second-largest buyer of U.S. goods, and trade with Canada rose 10 percent (twice the gain in Europe and Asia).
- U.S. imports from Mexico and Canada rose even faster than rates in the opposite direction, setting records of $48 billion and $120 billion, respectively. In particular, electronics, computers, and communications products came into the United States twice as fast as they went out. "We pointed out," says one NAFTA opponent, "that there was a fairly sophisticated manufacturing base in Mexico that pays peanuts, and the numbers bear that out."

"We pointed out that there was a fairly sophisticated manufacturing base in Mexico that pays peanuts, and the numbers bear that out."

—Anti-NAFTA economist Jeff Faux
on the record number of 1994 U.S. imports from Mexico

- NAFTA created fewer jobs than proponents had hoped. Although the U.S. economy added 1.7 million new jobs in 1994, the Labor Department estimates that only 100,000 jobs were NAFTA-related. At the same time, however, the flood of U.S. jobs to Mexico predicted by Ross Perot and other NAFTA critics, especially by labor union officials, did not occur. In fact, the president of Ford Motor Co.'s Mexico operations has boasted that his activities "have created jobs here and in the U.S." His reasoning: Ford's exports of Mexican-made vehicles to the United States are up 30 percent, and 80 percent of all components in those cars are made in the United States. Ford also reports that its exports of American-made cars to Mexico rose from 1,200 to 30,000 in NAFTA's first year.

European Union. Originally called the Common Market, the **European Union (EU)** includes the principal Western European nations. These countries have eliminated most quotas and have set uniform tariff levels on products imported and exported within their group. In 1992, virtually all internal trade barriers were eliminated, making the European Union the largest free marketplace in the world.

European Union (EU)
Agreement among major Western European nations to eliminate or make uniform most trade barriers affecting group members

Continued from page 53

"It's Not My Job to Sell Tickets on ValuJet"

Debating the Cost of Bargain Basement Fares

In the aftermath of the crash of ValuJet Flight 592, the Federal Aviation Administration asked Congress to resolve its conflicting roles of watchdog and cheerleader for the aviation industry. The agency has sought a single mandate—namely, to *promote aviation safety*—and believes that it cannot promote the aviation industry at the same time. Mary Fackler Schiavo, Inspector General of the Department of Transportation, had been critical of the FAA's twofold role for some time. Alluding both to the conflicting demands on the FAA and her own responsibility for checking on the agency, she said on ABC's *Nightline* that "It's not my job to sell tickets on ValuJet."

Yet it is naive to assume that resolving the conflicts in the FAA's mandate will ease the pressurized environment in which the airlines themselves operate. Says one industry observer: "Demanding 100-percent risk protection from regulators . . . is insane. The public wants bargain basement air fares, but no crashes. It demands speedy approval of drugs to care for our children, but is horrified when deaths occur from their effects. Regulators and politicians walk a fine line. . . . Perhaps the lesson of ValuJet is this: neither safety nor economic efficiency comes without a price."

Case Questions

1. Has deregulation of the airline industry made the FAA's job easier or harder?
2. Argue for or against the FAA's policy of regulatory flexibility.
3. What role do you think public and political pressure play in the policies of regulatory agencies?
4. Was it a mistake to give the FAA the dual missions of promoting aviation and ensuring aviation safety? Explain your answer.
5. The FAA gave ValuJet the right to outsource its maintenance work. How did this decision affect the agency's ability to regulate the airline industry?

SUMMARY OF LEARNING OBJECTIVES

1. **Explain the meaning and basic forms of *law*.** *Laws* are the rules of behavior enforced by a society. In the United States, *common law* is the body of decisions handed down by courts ruling on individual cases. *Statutory laws*, such as criminal, tax, and environmental laws, are created by federal, state, and local legislative bodies. Both statutory and common law have long histories. Administrative agencies like the Environmental Protection Agency, the Federal Communications Commission, and the Federal Trade Commission have the power to create and enforce regulatory law. U.S. *regulatory law* has expanded in proportion to the nation's economic and technological development.

2. **Describe the *U.S. judicial system*.** The U.S. judicial system is based on the federalist structure. Courts function at the *federal*, *state*, and *local* levels. At the federal level and in most state systems, there are *trial courts*, intermediate *courts of appeal*, and a *supreme court*. Most cases begin their journey through the judicial system at the trial court level. Parties have the right to appeal the decision of a trial court to the appellate courts, which provide a forum in which to revisit rulings from trial court cases. The U.S. Supreme Court is the highest court of appeal.

3. **Identify and discuss the six major areas of business *law*.** Most legal issues concern *contracts*, *torts*, *property*, *agency*, *commercial*, or *bankruptcy law*. An enforceable *contract* meets six conditions: agreement, consent, capacity, consideration, legality, and proper form. *Tort law* applies to most business relationships

not governed by contracts. Torts concern injury to people, property, or reputation for which compensation must be paid. These actions may be classified as intentional, negligence, and strict liability torts.

Property law concerns anything of value to which a person or business has right of ownership. The four categories are tangible real property, tangible personal property, intangible personal property, and intellectual property. The last category includes copyrights, trademarks, and patents. *Agency law* concerns the legal relationship among parties known as agents (for example, lawyers and accountants) and principals (clients) in the transfer of property. *Commercial law*, including the Uniform Commercial Code, pertains to the sale of goods and other commercial transactions. *Bankruptcy law* allows individuals and businesses to ask courts to relieve them of their debt obligations and to distribute their assets among creditors.

4. **Describe the *international framework of business law.*** Much of international law depends on international trade agreements. The *General Agreement on Tariffs and Trade (GATT)* is a multilateral agreement that commits 124 nations to reduce such trade barriers as tariffs and quotas. The *North American Free Trade Agreement (NAFTA)*, which took effect in 1994, removed trade barriers between the United States, Canada, and Mexico. The *European Union (EU)* eliminated virtually all trade barriers between the principal Western European nations.

STUDY QUESTIONS AND EXERCISES

Review

1. Compare and contrast statutory, common, and regulatory law.
2. Define the three different kinds of torts and give examples of each.
3. What are the major categories of protected intellectual property?
4. What is the difference between implied and express warranties?
5. What are the two major international trade agreements to which the United States is a party?

Analysis

6. Scan the advertising in a magazine or newspaper. Which trademarks or logos attract your attention? Which ones have been updated or redesigned? Why do you suppose they have been changed? What are the possible advantages of a given change? The potential disadvantages?
7. Obtain a copy of a product warranty—such as for a stereo system or a car. Examine it closely and summarize both the rights of the holder and the responsibilities of the issuer.
8. Give an example of a situation in which either you or a relative has dealt with an agent. Was the experience satisfactory? Why or why not?

Application Exercises

9. Some instructors run their college classes on a contractual basis. Develop a contract for this class: That is, draw up a document that specifies exactly what students need to do in order to earn a particular grade.
10. Assess past and present presidential administrations in terms of their attitudes toward business. What have been some of the cases and issues investigated by the Justice Department during each administration?

BUILDING YOUR BUSINESS SKILLS

This exercise enhances the following SCANS workplace competencies: demonstrating basic skills, demonstrating thinking skills, exhibiting interpersonal skills, and working with information.

Goal

To encourage students to understand why many faculty members of a large university objected to a business contract which, in their opinion, infringed on their right to free speech

Situation

As a faculty member of a major university, you are perplexed when you read about a contract that the university recently signed with Reebok International, the sports equipment manufacturer. The bulk of the contract is a standard cross-promotional deal under which Reebok will provide shoes to the university's intercollegiate teams and the university will allow the manufacturer to place the Reebok name and logo on university athletic clothing. The university will also receive $7.9 million over the five-year term of the contract.

As you continue to read the contract, you discover that it also includes a clause that bars the university from criticizing Reebok. You find that other faculty members agree with your interpretration of this clause: It infringes on your freedom of speech. In particular, the free-speech restriction bothers you because of questions you have about Reebok's foreign labor practices and, more specifically, about whether the company is meeting acceptable human rights standards in its treatment of contract workers in its foreign factories.

Method

Step 1: Join with groups of three or four students to analyze the implications of the contract language. First address the offending clause, which states the following:

■ the "university will not issue any official statement that disparages Reebok."

■ the "university will promptly take all reasonable steps necessary to address any remark by any university employee . . . that disparages Reebok."

The clause also states that "nothing herein is intended to abridge anyone's First Amendment rights."

Each group should then attempt to answer the following questions:

■ Considering the language of the contract, do you agree with Reebok that it does not restrict free speech as long as the person criticizing Reebok is not presented as a spokesperson for the university?

■ Do you agree with faculty members who believe that the contract would muzzle free speech?

Step 2: Based on the group's conclusions, write a letter to the university president or chancellor stating your position.

Follow-Up

1. Can a business contract legitimately take away personal freedom of speech?

2. What legal mechanisms can faculty members use to challenge the contract?

3. Would the university be guilty of breach of contract if faculty members spoke out about Reebok's foreign labor practices?

4. Ultimately, Reebok decided to drop the controversial clause. Do you agree with the company's decision?

 **Exploring the Net**

TO FIND OUT MORE ABOUT THE AGENCIES THAT ADMINISTER REGULATORY LAW IN THE UNITED STATES, VISIT EACH OF THE FOLLOWING GOVERNMENT ORGANIZATIONS ON THE INTERNET:

♦ **ENVIRONMENTAL PROTECTION AGENCY AT**
http://www.epa.gov

♦ **OCCUPATIONAL SAFETY AND HEALTH ADMINISTRATION AT**
http://www.osha.gov

♦ **SECURITIES AND EXCHANGE COMMISSION AT**
http://www.sec.gov

♦ **EQUAL EMPLOYMENT OPPORTUNITY COMMISSION AT**
http://www.eeoc.gov

Review each Website, and then consider the following questions:

1. Compare and contrast these sites in terms of their stated and apparent objectives. Identify what you think to be the intended audience for each site. More specifically:

   ■ Examine the EPA's postings under "Programs and Initiatives." Why is the EPA "Reinventing EPA"? What are the stated objectives of the "EPA's Five-Year Strategic Plan"? What are the top priorities for the EPA in today's business environment?

   ■ Examine OSHA's postings under "Programs and Services." Describe the kinds of programs offered as part of "The OSHA Consultation Service." What is the major purpose of the courses offered by OSHA's "Office of Training & Education"? What are OSHA's underlying objectives in establishing its "Programs and Outreach Assistance for Small Business"?

   ■ Examine the SEC's postings under "Enforcement Actions" and "Investor Assistance and Complaints." In describing its operations, what does the "SEC Division of Enforcement Complaint Center" tell the layman about the basic functions and objectives of the SEC? What about the description of operations at the "Office of Investor Education and Assistance"? What sort of "Investor Protection" does the SEC offer over the Internet?

   ■ Examine the EEOC's postings under "Fact Sheets and Related Information." What does the description of "Federal Sector Equal Employment Opportunity Complaint Processing" tell the layman about the basic functions and objectives of the EEOC? What do the EEOC's "Fact Sheets" tell you about "Sexual Harassment," "Race/Color Discrimination," "Age Discrimination," and other illegal activities that you might not learn from less official descriptions?

2. What features do these Websites have in common? Are there any major differences in the user-friendliness of these four Websites?

CONDUCTING BUSINESS ETHICALLY AND RESPONSIBLY

Mending Imperfections in the System

MALDEN MILLS RISES FROM THE ASHES

Aaron Feuerstein was the 70-year-old CEO of Malden Mills Industries, a privately owned textile company in Methuen, Massachusetts. Three days after a boiler explosion destroyed two of the factory's century-old buildings on December 11, 1995, Feuerstein stood before 1,000 of his employees who had gathered in the local high school gym to learn whether they would ever work for the company again.

"I will get right to my announcement," said Feuerstein to the anxious crowd. "For the next 30 days—and it might be more—all our [3,200] employees will be paid their full salaries. But over and above the money, the most important thing Malden Mills can do for our workers is to get you back to work. By January 2, we will restart operations, and within 90 days we will be fully operational."

When Feuerstein pledged to preserve the jobs of all company employees, the crowd cheered. Even hardened union members were moved to tears by Feuerstein's social conscience. Feuerstein's act of corporate generosity also catapulted him onto center stage as the nation grappled with the issue of just what companies owe their workers. At a time of

> **"I feel that I am a symbol of the movement against downsizing and layoffs that will ultimately produce an answer. People see me as a turning of the tide."**
>
> —Aaron Feuerstein
> *CEO of Malden Mills Industries*

massive corporate layoffs by AT&T and other companies, Feuerstein was invited by President Clinton to sit in the balcony during the 1996 State of the Union address, and he was acknowleged by visits from Labor Secretary Robert Reich and Massachusetts Senator John Kerry. For his own part, Feurstein implied that trying to save the jobs of the hardworking men and women who had contributed so much to his company was the decent and ethical thing to do. But he also argued that his actions might be a model for other chief executives. "I feel that I am a symbol," he said, "of the movement against downsizing and layoffs that will ultimately produce an answer. People see me as a turning of the tide."

Symbolism aside, Feuerstein's decision to rebuild his plant, pay displaced workers full wages for up to 90 days, and preserve jobs placed his company in a financial vise. Rebuilding costs, including the installation of sophisticated equipment and payments to laid-off workers, totalled more than $300 million. Although Feuerstein expects his fire insurance to cover the bill, so far it has paid only a fraction of the cost, with the difference coming from borrowed funds. If the insurance company fails to reimburse Feuerstein, or if company profits slide, Malden Mills may become a victim of its own generosity. Despite these risks, Feuerstein remains committed to doing what he regards as the right thing. "For Aaron, I don't think there really was a choice," says his wife, Louise. "It would never have occurred to him not to rebuild."

In part, Feuerstein's actions were motivated by loyalty. He credits his workers with saving the company in the early 1980s, when it was forced into bankruptcy. When consumers no longer wanted its specialty textile, fake fur, Malden had to develop a replacement product. The answer was an innovative textile product created by Malden Mills workers themselves. Polartec, an artificial yarn with the softness and warmth of wool, was responsible for the company's success from the mid-1980s until the 1995 fire. It is featured in outerwear sold by Patagonia, Lands' End, and L.L. Bean and accounts for half of Malden's $400 million annual sales.

The Polartec manufacturing process depends on just the right environmental conditions—the slightest variations in temperature and humidity cause imperfections. The key to quality control is the role played by workers on the line. Operators like Adelina Santiago stop the mill when conditions are unfavorable. "I give to catching imperfections the same importance that I would give if this were my own business," says Santiago. The commitment of his employees helped fuel Feuerstein's insistence that Malden Mills would operate again. "Aaron did not have an obligation to reopen here, but he did," says Santiago, who understands that Feuerstein could have collected millions in insurance money and closed his company. "We felt pleased that he paid us while we were out," she adds, "but that was not as important as knowing we would get our jobs back."

In fact, Santiago was back within a week of the fire—thanks to her union, which agreed to bypass seniority rules and allow Feuerstein to call workers back according to skills rather

than length of service. Less than a month after the fire, Malden Mills was producing Polartec textile at 80 percent of capacity. Within six months, all but 500 of the company's workers had been recalled.

In an age in which ethics and responsibility toward workers often take a back seat to profits and self-interest, Aaron Feuerstein showed how a company can treat employees fairly and ethically during a crisis. Ethics in the workplace are becoming increasingly important as we move

into an era of intense competition not only for public and consumer support but also for the support of employees and stockholders. By focusing on the learning objectives of this chapter, you will see that many companies establish policies on business ethics and social responsibility in order to define exactly how managers and employees should act with regard to the environment, customers, fellow employees, and investors.

After reading this chapter, you should be able to

1. Explain how individuals develop their personal *codes of ethics* and why ethics are important in the workplace

2. Distinguish *social responsibility* from *ethics* and trace the evolution of social responsibility in U.S. business

3. Show how the concept of social responsibility applies both to environmental issues and to a firm's relationships with customers, employees, and investors

4. Identify three general *approaches to social responsibility*

and describe the four steps that a firm must take to implement a social responsibility program

5. Explain how issues of social responsibility and ethics affect small business

Continued on page 92

In this chapter, we look at the issues of individual ethics in business and the social responsibility of business as a whole. Remember that these issues were not always considered important in business philosophy or practice. Today, however, the ethical implications of business practices are very much in the spotlight. Managers must confront a variety of ethical problems, and companies must address many issues of social responsibility.

■ ETHICS IN THE WORKPLACE

Just what is *ethical behavior?* For one thing, it is behavior that affects both internal and external relationships. On the most basic level, *business ethics* is a matter of making decisions that affect *others*—other individuals or other organizations.

Consider the recent behavior of one U.S. company. A few years ago, Los Angeles–based Erly Industries, the parent company of Comet Rice, sent a cable to the Iraqi Grain Board, a large buyer of imported rice. Responding to the Board's call for bids, Erly guaranteed that it could supply rice for at least $30 less per ton than any other bidder. The attractive offer, said Erly, was made possible by the company's brand-new plant in Aqaba, Jordan, where rice could be unloaded, processed, and shipped to Iraq at considerable savings to the buyer.

The explanation was accurate: Erly did in fact maintain such a plant in Jordan. It had been built with a low-cost loan of $4 million from the United States Agency for International Development (AID), from which Erly had also claimed $134 million for consulting work. AID's mandate, however, is to aid needy nations by investing in development—not to finance a U.S. firm's monopolization of one of the world's most lucrative rice markets. Erly had never revealed to the government the true purpose of its Aqaba project—namely, competitive advantage in the Mideast rice market.

Moreover, the firm had let AID assume that its Jordanian partner was in charge of a project designed to benefit all U.S. rice exporters. Figure 4.1, however, shows quite clearly that the real beneficiary was Erly and its Comet Rice subsidiary. Although the U.S. government subsidized less in rice sales to Iraq between 1987 and 1990, Comet's share of those sales skyrocketed from 17.5 percent to 81.5 percent. In addition, Erly reinvested proceeds from its low-cost government loan back in the United States and earned higher interest rates. Finally, according to critics, Erly had also routinely exploited political connections and loosely managed government programs.

Richard L. McCall, who took over AID in 1993, sees Erly's re-

FIGURE 4.1 ◆ Erly Industries: Sales and Subsidies, 1987–1990

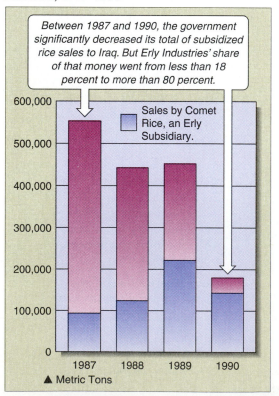

Between 1987 and 1990, the government significantly decreased its total of subsidized rice sales to Iraq. But Erly Industries' share of that money went from less than 18 percent to more than 80 percent.

Sales by Comet Rice, an Erly Subsidiary.

▲ Metric Tons

lationship with the agency as a clear-cut matter: "It's an ethical question. For us to be used in any shape, form, or fashion for anything but to help needy nations is wrong." Erly CEO Gerald D. Murphy disagrees, seeing his tactics as an innovative way of "solving my customers' problems. . . . Those are the rules. I've never understood people who sit back and play a game and don't understand the rules. How the hell are you going to win if you do that?"[1]

> ### "Those are the rules. I've never understood people who sit back and play a game and don't understand the rules. How the hell are you going to win if you do that?"
>
> —Gerald D. Murphy
> *CEO of Erly Industries*

Although Erly Industries has not been charged with any criminal activity, the ethics of its activities have come under close scrutiny. One question is this: How can the actions in this case be unethical but not illegal? And, to return to the more basic question: just what is ethical behavior? **Ethics** are beliefs about what is right and wrong or good and bad in actions that affect others. **Ethical behavior** conforms to generally accepted *social* norms concerning beneficial and harmful actions.

Because ethics are based on both social concepts and individual beliefs, they vary from person to person, from situation to situation, and from culture to culture. Social standards, for example, tend to be broad enough to support certain differences in beliefs. Without violating the general standards of the culture, therefore, individuals may develop personal codes of ethics that reflect a wide range of attitudes and beliefs. Thus, what constitutes ethical and unethical behavior is determined partly by the individual and partly by culture.

ethics
Beliefs about what is right and wrong or good and bad in actions that affect others

ethical behavior
Behavior conforming to generally accepted social norms concerning beneficial and harmful actions

Company Policies and Business Ethics

Within the work place, the company itself influences individual ethical behavior. As unethical and even illegal activities by both managers and employees have plagued more and more companies, many firms have taken steps to encourage ethical behavior in the work place.[2] Many firms, for example, establish codes of conduct and develop clear ethical positions on how the firm and its employees will conduct its business.

Perhaps the single most effective step that a company can take is to demonstrate top management support. When United Technologies, a Connecticut-based industrial conglomerate, published its 21-page code of ethics, it also named a vice president for business practices. In contrast, the management of Rockwell International, an industrial manufacturer based in California, has been criticized for providing unethical leadership. In 1992, Rockwell pleaded guilty to five felonies and five misdemeanors involving the improper discharge of hazardous nuclear waste and chemicals into creeks near its Colorado plant. The cost: $18.5 million in fines. In 1993, residents in Russellville, Kentucky, sued Rockwell for illegally discharging industrial pollutants into their air and water. The company will bear the brunt of the $12 million cleanup. In 1995, federal agents investigated an explosion at a Rockwell facility in California that might have been caused by the improper—and illegal—disposal of rocket propellants and other hazardous materials.[3] ▶

Demonstrating Commitment   The power of ethical commitment was revealed by Johnson & Johnson (J&J) in 1982, when capsules of the company's Tylenol pain reliever were found to be laced with cyanide. The episode threatened disaster in both the

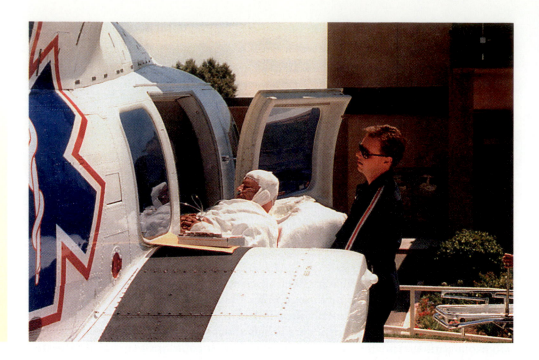

One of five scientists is airlifted to a hospital after being injured in a 1994 chemical explosion at a Rockwell International Corp. facility in California. The Rocket-dyne test facility north of Los Angeles already had a troubled environmental record, and California authorities suggest that the injured researchers—and the two who died in the blast—were actually engaged in the illegal disposal of rocket fuel. At the same site in 1989, the U.S. Energy Department had found evidence of widespread nuclear contamination, and in 1990 the California Environmental Protection Agency fined the plant $280,000 for hazardous waste violations.

marketplace and the workplace. Managers at J&J quickly recalled all Tylenol bottles still on retailers' shelves and then went public with candid information throughout the crisis. Its ethical choices proved to be a crucial factor in J&J's campaign to rescue its product. Both the firm and the brand bounced back much more quickly than most observers had thought possible. In addition to demonstrating an attitude of honesty and openness, firms can take specific steps to formalize the commitment to ethical practices. Two options are *adopting written codes* and *instituting ethics programs.*

Adopting Written Codes. Many companies, including J&J, have adopted written codes of ethics that formally acknowledge their intent to do business in an ethical manner. Indeed, the number of such companies has risen dramatically in the last three decades. In 1968, 32 percent of companies surveyed maintained ethical codes. A mere two years later, the number was 75 percent. Today more than 90 percent of all Fortune 500 firms have such codes.[4]

Many experts attribute J&J's successful response to the Tylenol-tampering scare to the ethical anchor provided by its written code. Called "Our Credo," J&J's written code was first published in 1948. The code is revised as new issues arise, but its explicit purpose is to furnish a set of *core* values that is as consistent as possible over time.[5] Most such codes are designed to perform one or more of these four functions:

- To increase public confidence in a firm or its industry
- To stem the tide of government regulation—that is, to aid in self-regulation
- To improve internal operations by providing consistent standards of both ethical and legal conduct
- To respond to problems that arise as a result of unethical or illegal behavior[6]

Instituting Ethics Programs. Cases like the Tylenol case suggest that ethical responses can be learned through experience. But can business ethics be "taught," either in the workplace or in schools? Not surprisingly, business schools have become important players in the debate about ethics education. Most analysts agree that even though business schools must address the issue of ethics in the work place, companies must take the chief responsibility for educating employees. In fact, more and more firms are doing so.

It is not hard to figure out where Levi Strauss & Co. stands with regard to ethical issues—just check the company's "Aspiration Statement." Forged by top management and printed on recycled denim, the Statement is a real document that hangs on office and factory walls. It spells out Levi's unusual values-based formula for simultaneously earning profits and making the world a better place. It addresses a number of issues, including workforce diversity, employee empowerment and recognition, honest communication, and ethical management practices. It declares, for example, that management will set an example for ethical behavior that others in the company must follow. "We must," says the Statement, "provide clarity about our expectations and must enforce these standards throughout the corporation." In addition to encouraging teamwork and open communication, top management works to see that Levi's offers attractive career opportunities for minorities and women.

In 1992, Levi Straus got serious about child-labor laws in countries where it contracted for work. In Bangladesh, for example, contractors admitted that they hired children and agreed to fire them in accord with local regulations. Unfortunately, many young workers were also the sole support for their families. Levi's thus struck a deal: the company would pay to send the children to school if contractors would continue to pay wages and hire the children back at age fourteen. The deal has cost Levi's only a few thousand dollars and preserved its reputation as a conscientious Third World employer.

Management also believes that special responsibilities go hand in hand with the image that Levi's wants to project, both in the United States and elsewhere. For example, about half of the apparel sold by the company is manufactured in low-wage countries like Bangladesh, Indonesia, and Malaysia. Throughout the world, Levi's is strict about enforcing International Labor Organization standards on child labor. In Bangladesh, for instance, Levi's learned that many underage employees were the sole breadwinners in their families. Instead of firing the children, Levi's agreed to pay their wages while the children returned to school and to hire back the youths when they come of age.▲ Says marketing executive David Schmidt: "When ethical issues collide with commercial appeal, we try to ensure ethics as the trump card."[7]

> ### "When ethical issues collide with commercial appeal, we try to ensure ethics as the trump card."
> —David Schmidt
> *Vice President for Corporate Marketing, Levi Strauss & Co.*

■ SOCIAL RESPONSIBILITY

Ethics affect individual behavior in the workplace. **Social responsibility,** however, refers to the way in which a business tries to balance its commitments to groups and individuals in its social environment: customers, other businesses, employees, and investors. In effect, social responsibility is an attempt to balance different commitments. For example, to behave responsibly toward investors, a company must try to maximize profits. But it also has a responsibility toward its customers to market safe products—a commitment that may raise production costs and lower profits. Not surprisingly, then, firms sometimes act irresponsibly toward customers because of their zeal to please

social responsibility
The attempt of a business to balance its commitments to groups and individuals in its environment, including customers, other businesses, employees, and investors

investors. Jacques Robinson, CEO of cordless phone maker Cincinnati Microwave Inc., announced that substantial losses in 1994 were attributable to a worldwide parts shortage—a one-time problem, contended Robinson, that was beyond management control. Critics, however, suggest that the real reason for the losses was poor relations with the firm's primary supplier of the parts. They also claimed that Robinson had focused on the parts-supply problem to deflect attention from extensive problems in a greater range of company operations, including the design and manufacture of products. They also charged that Robinson made bold sales projections that were substantially higher than those developed by internal analysts.[8]

Like an individual's personal code of ethics, an organization's sense of social responsibility is influenced by many factors. To a large extent, of course, social responsibility reflects the ethics of the individuals employed by a firm—especially its top management. But social responsibility can also be encouraged—even enforced—from outside, whether by government agencies or by consumers. A firm's behavior is also shaped by the demands of investors and by the behavior of other firms in the same country and same industry.

Contemporary Social Consciousness

Social consciousness and views toward social responsibility continue to evolve. Today's views seem to be moving toward an enlightened view stressing the need for a greater social role for business. Some observers suggest that an increased awareness of the global economy and heightened campaigning on the part of environmentalists and other activists have combined to make many businesses more sensitive to their social responsibilities.

In 1996, for example, when Marge Schott, owner of the Cincinnati Reds baseball team, made offensive remarks—including racial slurs and at least one comment that apparently defended Adolf Hitler—fellow major league baseball owners suspended her and barred her from taking an active role in running the team. Retailers like Sears and Target have policies against selling handguns and other weapons. Likewise, national toy retailers KayBee and Toys "Я" Us refuse to sell toy guns that look too realistic.

Firms in numerous other industries have also integrated socially conscious thinking into their production plans and marketing efforts. The production of environmentally safe products, for example, has become a potential boom area, as many companies introduce products designed to be "environmentally friendly." Sales of vegetable-based cleaning products, recycled-paper products, and all-natural toiletries are on the rise. Procter & Gamble's Downy fabric softener concentrate is sold in paper packages and reconstituted in plastic bottles already owned by consumers. Paper maker Union Camp Corp. now removes the ink from discarded paper so that recycled fibers can go into new paper; the company has also replaced chlorine (a toxic water pollutant) with ozone in the bleaching line at its riverside plant in Franklin, Virginia.[9] Volkswagen and BMW are designing cars whose parts will be completely recyclable.

■ AREAS OF SOCIAL RESPONSIBILITY

When defining its sense of social responsibility, a firm typically confronts four areas of concern: responsibilities toward the *environment*, its *customers*, its *employees*, and its *investors*.

Responsibility toward the Environment

Controlling pollution—the injection of harmful substances into the environment—is a significant challenge to contemporary business. Although noise pollution is now attracting increased concern, air, water, and land pollution remain the greatest problems in need of solutions from both governments and businesses. In the following sections, we will focus on the nature of the problems in these areas as well as some of the current efforts to address them.

Air Pollution   Air pollution results when several factors combine to lower air quality. Carbon monoxide emitted by automobiles contributes to air pollution, as do smoke and other chemicals from manufacturing plants. Air quality is usually worst in certain geographic locations, such as the Denver area and the Los Angeles basin, where pollutants tend to get trapped in the atmosphere.[10]

Legislation has gone a long way toward controlling air pollution. Under new laws, for example, many companies must now install special devices to limit the pollutants they expel into the air. Such efforts are costly. Air pollution is compounded by problems like *acid rain*, which occurs when sulphur is pumped into the atmosphere, mixes with natural moisture, and falls to the ground as rain. Much of the damage to forests and streams in the eastern United States and Canada has been attributed to acid rain originating in sulphur from manufacturing and power plants in the midwestern United States.

Water Pollution   Water becomes polluted primarily from chemical and waste dumping. For years, businesses and cities dumped waste into rivers, streams, and lakes with little regard for the consequences. Cleveland's Cuyahoga River was once so polluted that it literally burst into flames one hot summer day. After an oil spill in 1994, a Houston ship channel burned for days.

Thanks to new legislation and increased awareness, water quality in many areas of the United States is improving. The Cuyahoga River now boasts fish and is even used for recreation. Laws forbidding phosphates (an ingredient found in many detergents) in New York and Florida have helped to make Lake Erie and other major waters safe for fishing and swimming again. Both the Passaic River in New Jersey and the Hudson River in New York are much cleaner now than they were just a few years ago.

Land Pollution   There are two key issues in land pollution. The first is how to restore the quality of land that has already been damaged. Land and water damaged by toxic waste, for example, must be cleaned up for the simple reason that people still need to use them. The second problem, of course, concerns how to prevent future contamination. New forms of solid waste disposal constitute one response to these problems. Combustible wastes, can be separated and used as fuels in industrial boilers, and decomposition can be accelerated by exposing waste matter to certain microorganisms.

Toxic Waste Disposal.   An especially controversial problem in land pollution is toxic waste disposal. *Toxic wastes* are dangerous chemical and/or radioactive byproducts of manufacturing processes. U.S. manufacturers produce between 40 and 60 *million tons of* such material each year. As a rule, toxic waste must be stored; it cannot be destroyed or processed into harmless material. However, very few people want toxic waste storage sites in their backyards. ▶

Recycling.   At least one new industry has arisen from increased consciousness about land pollution. *Recycling*, the reconversion of waste materials into useful products, has become a priority not only for municipal and state governments but also for many companies engaged in high-waste activities. At Union Camp's Virginia paper plant, for

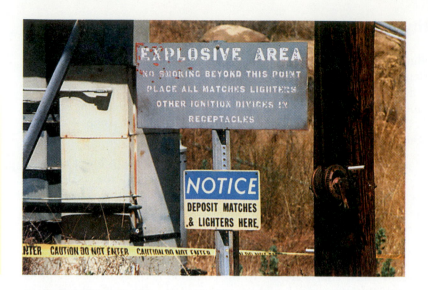

In 1992, the State of California fined Rockwell International Corp. $650,000 for burning toxic solvents in open barrels at its jet engine plant in Santa Susana. In the same year, Rockwell paid $18.5 million in federal fines for illegally storing nuclear waste at its nuclear weapons plant in Rocky Flats, Colorado. Rockwell contends that its record has improved, and in fact it won an Environmental Protection Agency award for reducing toxic emissions in 1995.

example, one executive explains the firm's commitment to recycling as a market-oriented strategy: "Customers," he says, "want recycled products. There is a growing awareness that waste is a form of pollution and that will keep demand for recycled paper high."

"There is a growing awareness that waste is a form of pollution."

—Charles H. Greiner, Jr.
Vice president of Union Camp Corp.

Over the past 25 years, recycling enterprises have established a solid industry. First, commitments by manufacturers to build plants using recycled products has increased the capacity of waste that can be handled. Figure 4.2, for example, shows the announced *additional* capacity of recycled paper mills in the United States through 1996: for office paper alone, there was an increase of nearly 4 million tons in 1995–1996, compared with an increase of just 700,000 tons in 1993–1994.

In addition, economic recovery has increased the demand for—and the price of—raw materials. Old corrugated boxes, which sold for $35 a ton in September 1993, sold for $110 a ton in September 1994. International events have also affected demand for recycled raw material in the United States. Because China had a poor cotton harvest in mid-1994, Chinese textile makers are offering top dollar for old soda bottles, which can be recycled into synthetic fibers.[11]

FIGURE 4.2 ◆ Capacity of Recycled Paper Mills, 1993–1996

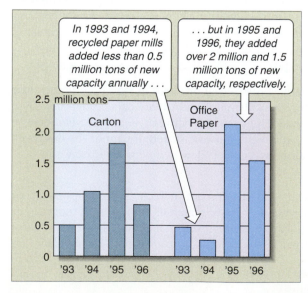

Responsibility toward Customers

A company that does not act responsibly toward its customers will ultimately lose their business. Moreover, the government controls what businesses can and cannot do regarding consumers. The Federal Trade Commission (FTC), for example, regulates advertising and pricing practices. The Food and Drug Administration (FDA) enforces guidelines for labeling food products.

Unethical and irresponsible business practices toward customers can result in government-imposed penalties and expensive civil litigation. For example, SmithKline Beecham PLC, the maker of Orafix denture adhesive, has been charged with using benzine, a proven carcinogen, in the product. The FDA forced a recall of the product in 1990, and by 1996, several lawsuits—including one for $30 million—had been filed against the company. If found guilty of negligence, SmithKline Beecham could face whopping civil damages and fines of several millions of dollars.[12]

Social responsibility toward customers generally falls into two categories:

- Providing quality products
- Pricing products fairly

Naturally, firms differ as much in their level of concern about customer responsibility as in their approaches to environmental responsibility. Yet unlike environmental problems, many customer problems do not require expensive solutions. In fact, most problems can be avoided if companies simply heed laws regarding consumer rights and regulated practices.

Consumer Rights   Much of the current interest in business responsibility toward customers can be traced to the rise of **consumerism:** social activism dedicated to protecting the rights of consumers in their dealings with businesses. The first formal declaration of consumer rights protection came in the early 1960s, when President John F. Kennedy identified four basic consumer rights. These rights are now backed by numerous federal and state laws:

1. Consumers have a right to safe products.
2. Consumers have a right to be informed about all relevant aspects of a product.
3. Consumers have a right to be heard.
4. Consumers have a right to choose what they buy.

consumerism
Form of social activism dedicated to protecting the rights of consumers in their dealings with businesses

Unfair Pricing   Interfering with competition can take the form of illegal pricing practices. **Collusion** occurs when two or more firms agree to collaborate on such wrongful acts as price fixing. The U.S. Department of Justice recently charged several hospitals in Danbury, Connecticut, and St. Joseph, Missouri, with *price fixing*. In both cases, the charges involved illegal agreements between hospitals and local physicians as to what prices physicians would charge for various hospital services. There were also agreements by which doctors would perform a specified percentage of their outpatient services—such as radiology and minor surgery—in the hospitals. As a result of this practice, managed care companies were unable to enter the market because virtually all of the local doctors were affiliated with the hospitals.[13]

Under some circumstances, firms can also come under attack for *price gouging*—responding to increased demand with overly steep (and often unwarranted) price increases. For example, BMW produces only a small quantity of its new Z3 Roadsters each year and demand for the car is strong. Consequently, some dealers will sell Z3s only to customers willing to pay thousands of dollars over sticker prices.

collusion
Illegal agreement between two or more companies to commit a wrongful act

Ethics in Advertising   In recent years, increased attention has been given to ethics in advertising and product information. In the early 1970s, for example, many firms

TRENDS & CHALLENGES

WHAT TO DO IN A MAD COW CRISIS

The British public was jittery, and top executives at McDonald's and Burger King knew why. On March 21, 1996, the British government announced a possible link between bovine spongiform encephalopathy (BSE), or "mad cow disease," and Creutzfeld-Jakob disease, a fatal brain condition in humans. Fifty-five people in England had died from Creutzfeld-Jakob in 1994, including 10 people who had probably contracted the disease from beef contaminated with BSE. Coinciding with the increase in human deaths was a mad cow disease epidemic that had affected more than 162,000 animals since 1986.

To American fast food restaurants doing business in Great Britain, the government announcement translated immediately into a business crisis. Customers' concerns about product safety and the need to maintain consumer confidence were uppermost on executives' minds. McDonald's was the first to act. Three days after the government announcement, the British division of the American fast food giant suspended the sale of all British beef products. "Our customers expect us to take a lead and we have," declared Paul Preston, president of McDonald's United Kingdom division. "We believe that British beef is safe. However, we cannot ignore the fact that recent announcements have led to a growing loss of consumer confidence in British beef." McDonald's served nonburger selections for four days until its restaurants began receiving beef products from continental Europe.

Burger King acted seven days later to pull all British beef from its 382 restaurants. In making this decision, the firm cited the need to maintain consumer confidence in the safety of its products and the concern that it would be forced to close restaurants if it continued to use British beef. Burger King also announced that its burgers would be made from Italian, German, and French beef. The decision was well received. Burger King, confirmed company official Alan Randall, "has advertised extensively since this thing started and has been informing people that it imports all its meat. Because of that, our sales have not been hurt at all. People trust Burger King."

Many British food companies also took swift action. Bass Taverns, a chain of 2,700 restaurants and pubs, withdrew all British beef and beef products from its menus four days after the crisis began. Monte's, an expensive private dining club in London, yielded to the concerns of diners who "can well afford the price of fine, imported cuts of meat." However, other British food companies took a different tack. Less concerned with consumer confidence than their U.S. counterparts, they continued to sell domestic beef and let customers make their own decisions about what not to eat. Many British firms seemed satisfied that the decision would not result in long-term sales drops. In fact, the first news of mad cow disease caused burger sales to decrease by half at restaurants, theme parks, and other food and beverage sellers. But, reports Maxine Donne, a food-service manager in Blackpool, "things quickly went back to normal. Everyone's aware of it now. I don't think anyone really cares." Colin Dawson, the managing director of a seaside resort park in Margate, agreed. "It's not that big a deal," argued Dawson. "The media has blown it out of proportion."

What influenced most the rapid decision of U.S. firms to pull British beef off their shelves? Was it an American culture that emphasizes health concerns? Or was it an equally American anxiety about litigation? No one can say for sure. It is certain, however, American fast food chains placed great value on maintaining consumer confidence and trust. Perhaps the best indicator of whether these companies did the right thing is the collective reaction of their own consumers. If 20-year-old David Baker is typical, the choice to emphasize safety was on the mark: "I'm pretty wary of beefburgers now," volunteers Baker.

"I'm pretty wary of beefburgers right now."

—A British fast food consumer

---

began promoting food products touted as "light"—suggesting that the products were low in calories and/or saturated fat. The FDA confirmed that although many such products were in fact lower in fat than the same products in their regular versions; often they still contained fairly high levels of fat and calories and certainly did not qualify as health food. As a result, many products were forced to drop "light" labeling; others added notices to the consumer that they were not truly low-fat products. Food producers are now required to use a standardized format for listing ingredients on product packages.

Another issue concerns advertising that some consumers consider morally objectionable. Recent examples have involved controversial ads by Calvin Klein showing scantily clad teenagers and Victoria's Secret television ads showing models wearing skimpy underwear and exchanging banter with popular figures like Chicago Bulls basketball star Dennis Rodman. Under renewed attack are also comprehensive advertising campaigns by tobacco companies that apparently target young people (such as R.J. Reynolds' Joe Camel ads).

Responsibility toward Employees

In Chapter 9, we will see how a number of human resource management activities are essential to a smoothly functioning business. These activities—recruiting, hiring, training, promoting, and compensating—are also the basis for social responsibility toward employees. A company that provides its employees with equal opportunities for rewards and advancement without regard to race, sex, or other irrelevant factors is meeting its social responsibilities. Firms that ignore these responsibilities run the risk of losing productive, highly motivated employees. They also leave themselves open to lawsuits.

In addition to their responsibility to employees as company resources, firms have a responsibility to employees as people who are more productive when their needs are met. Firms that accept this responsibility ensure that the workplace is safe, both physically and socially.

Ethical Commitments: The Case of Whistleblowers
Respecting employees as people means respecting their behavior as ethically responsible individuals. Too often, however, individuals who try to act ethically on the job find themselves in trouble with their employers. This problem is especially true for **whistleblowers**: employees who detect and try to put an end to a company's unethical, illegal, and/or socially irresponsible actions by publicizing them.

In a socially responsible company, whistleblowers can confidently report findings to higher-level managers who can be expected to take action. In fact, many whistleblowers find management unwilling to listen—or worse. Whistleblowers at Beech-Nut, Citicorp, Prudential Insurance, General Dynamics, and Archer-Daniels Midland have all reported a lack of interest by managers about charges of company misconduct.

In extreme circumstances, whistleblowers may find themselves demoted or fired. The law does offer some recourse to employees who take action. The current whistleblower law stems from the False Claims Act of 1863, which was designed to prevent contractors from selling defective supplies to the Union Army during the Civil War. With 1986 revisions to the law, the government can recover triple damages from fraudulent contractors. Since 1986, some 700 suits have been filed. The government has intervened to prosecute in about 100 of those and collected $750 million in damages. With more cases being filed and larger amounts of fraudulent funds coming to light, that figure will soon top $1 billion. Whistleblowers receive 15–25 percent of what the government collects. If the Justice Department does not intervene, a whistleblower can proceed with a civil suit. In that case, the whistleblower receives 25–30 percent of any money recovered. More than 700 civil suits were filed by whistleblowers between 1986 and 1994. In one, a former vice president for finance at United Technologies received 15 percent of a $150 million settlement ($22.5 million).[14]

whistleblower
Employee who detects and tries to put an end to a company's unethical, illegal, or socially irresponsible actions by publicizing them

TRENDS & CHALLENGES

KATHIE LEE'S LABOR PAINS

When Charles Kernaghan, executive director of the National Labor Committee Education Fund in Support of Worker and Human Rights in Central America, turned the media spotlight on America's Sweetheart, Kathie Lee Gifford, he knew exactly what he was doing. He wanted media attention for the struggle to end the deplorable working conditions endured by 13- and 14-year-old children in Honduran factories. And what better way than to report to Congress that Gifford's Wal-Mart clothing line was manufactured by Honduran children working 20-hour days under sweatshop conditions?

The strategy amounted to an unprecedented attack on a celebrity who had licensed her name to a clothing line but who played no part in manufacturing decisions. Instead of pulling out of the business, however, Gifford decided to join the fight against sweatshops. "My first reaction," she announced, "was 'I don't need this.' But they told me that I had a unique opportunity to make a difference by using what happened to me to stop the horrible practices of some of these manufacturers." To her dismay, Gifford soon learned that her clothing line was also connected to sweatshops in New York City. A rush order for 50,000 blouses had been subcontracted to Seo Fashions in New York's garment district. There, workers endured sweatshop conditions, and, in fact, many were not paid. ▶ Kathie Lee sent her husband, Frank, to hand each worker $300 in cash and to inspect the deplorable conditions.

In the minds of many people, however, a key question remained largely unanswered: was Kathie Lee Gifford in some way responsible for workplace abuses in New York and Honduras? In her contract to produce clothing for Wal-Mart, specific contractors and subcontractors were mentioned. All provided acceptable workplace conditions. What the contract did not disclose, however, was the standard practice in the garment industry of calling in "sub-sub-subcontractors" when rush orders must be filled. The prevalence of subcontracting often makes it all but impossible to monitor work and pay conditions in U.S. and developing world factories.

Gifford also learned that it is difficult to impose U.S. standards on developing countries. Indeed, what might seem like exploitation in the United States may represent an opportunity for a better life in Honduras, where annual per capita income is $600 and the unemployment rate is 40 percent. Children work because they have to, and child labor is legal, as Evangelina Argueta, a labor organizer in Honduras explains: "This country is not the United States. Very few Honduran mothers can afford the luxury of feeding children until they are 18 years old without putting them to work."

> ### "Very few Honduran mothers can afford the luxury of feeding children until they are 18 years old without putting them to work."
> —Evangelina Argueta
> *Honduran labor organizer*

Nevertheless, human rights activist Charles Kernaghan believes that U.S. companies have a moral obligation to pay fair wages, not merely wages that local markets will bear. He also believes that U.S. companies have the moral obligation to demand humane working conditions. As a result of human rights complaints, like those filed by organizations like Kernaghan's, many Honduran apparel plants have stopped hiring minors and are dismissing workers younger than 16. Unfortunately, rather than return to school, most of these children will search elsewhere for work and, say many observers, find even lower-paying, more arduous jobs. "Obviously," admits Kernaghan, "this is not what we wanted to happen."

For her part, Kathie Lee Gifford has acknowledged that she can do little to change labor practices in the developing world. She did, however, join with former Labor Secretary Robert Reich to speak out against exploitation in the U.S. garment industry. The controversy also convinced Wal-Mart to review its own inspection process, and the retailer may hire an independent group to monitor the contractors and subcontractors who produce its private-label clothing.

Responsibility toward Investors

Because shareholders are the owners of a company, it may sound odd to say that a firm can act irresponsibly toward its investors. Managers can abuse their responsibilities to investors in a number of ways. As a rule, irresponsible behavior toward shareholders means abuse of a firm's financial resources. In such cases, the ultimate losers are indeed the shareholder-owners who do not receive their due earnings or dividends. Companies can also act irresponsibly toward shareholder-owners by misrepresenting company resources.

In May 1996, three weeks after it was disclosed that her Wal-Mart clothing line was manufactured by children laboring in sweatshops, Kathie Lee Gifford joined with New York Governor George Pataki to announce legislation that would prohibit the sale or distribution of clothing made under such conditions. "I'm a talk-show hostess, but I'm learning," said Gifford, who added, "we want to shine the light on the cockroaches."

Improper Financial Management   Occasionally, organizations or their officers are guilty of blatant financial mismanagement—offenses that are unethical but not necessarily illegal. In 1993, for example, CEO Ronald Moskowitz retired from Ferrofluidics Corp., a manufacturer of high-tech industrial products located in Nashua, New Hampshire. Moskowitz's departure followed closely on an internal investigation conducted by the firm's board. According to the board, the CEO had treated the company as a personal checking account. Between 1988 and 1993, for instance, Moskowitz and his family trusts took more than $16 million in pay, bonuses, and profits from stock prerogatives. During the same period, Ferrofluidics lost $17.7 million. Meanwhile, the company continued to loan millions of dollars to Moskowitz and to guarantee personal bank loans. It also took out a hefty life insurance policy on Moskowitz and his wife, for which their son received a $6 million broker's commission. From a high of $44 in 1983, Ferrofluidics stock plummeted to $8. The firm is now under investigation for publishing a 1992 report contending that sales would go up fivefold and profits tenfold by 1996. Says one employee who has remained with the company, "You probably could teach six months of business and corporate ethics at Harvard on this story."[15]

> ## "You probably could teach six months of business and corporate ethics at Harvard on this story."
> —Employee at Ferrofluidics Corp.

In situations like this, creditors can often do little, and stockholders have few options. Trying to force a management changeover, for example, is a difficult process that can drive down stock prices, a penalty that shareholders are usually unwilling to impose on themselves.

© 1998 Robert Mankoff *from*
The Cartoon Bank,™ Inc.

*"But won't absconding with the company's funds
cast the board in a bad light?"*

check kiting
Illegal practice of writing
checks against money that has
not yet been credited at the
bank on which the checks are
drawn

Check Kiting   Other unethical practices are illegal. **Check kiting,** for instance, involves writing a check against money that has not yet arrived at the bank on which it is drawn. In 1994, E. F. Hutton and Co. was convicted of violating kiting laws on a massive scale. In a carefully planned scheme, company managers were able to use as much as $250 million every day that did not belong to the firm. How did the scheme work? Managers would deposit customer checks totaling $1 million, for example, into the company account. Knowing that the bank would not collect all of the total deposit for several days, they nevertheless wrote checks against the total amount deposited.

Insider Trading   *Insider trading* occurs when someone uses confidential information to gain from the purchase or sale of stocks. One highly publicized case featured Wall Street trader Ivan Boesky. An acquaintance of Boesky's, Dennis Levine, worked for Drexel Burnham Lambert, an investment banking firm. When Levine heard of an upcoming merger or acquisition, he passed the information along to Boesky. Boesky then bought and sold the appropriate stocks at times calculated to generate huge profits, which he split with Levine. In one especially profitable instance, Boesky used Levine's information about Nestlé's plans to buy Carnation stock to earn more than $28 million in profits.[16]

Misrepresentation of Finances   Certain behavior regarding financial representation is also illegal. In maintaining and reporting its financial status, every corporation must conform to *generally accepted accounting practices (GAAP)* (see Chapter 12). Sometimes, however, managers project profits far in excess of what they actually expect to earn. When the truth comes out, investors are disappointed. Cincinnati Microwave CEO Jacques Robinson is charged with having overstated his firm's profit projections and making misleading statements about losses, actions that boosted the share price to $18 during an August 1995 offering of the company's stock. As the facts became known just two months later, investors were left holding shares valued at only $7.

■ IMPLEMENTING SOCIAL RESPONSIBILITY PROGRAMS

Thus far, we have discussed social responsibility as if there were some agreement on how organizations should behave. In fact, there are dramatic differences of opinion concerning the role of social responsibility as a business goal. Some people oppose any business activity that threatens profits. Others argue that social responsibility must take precedence over profits.

Even businesspeople who agree on the importance of social responsibility will cite different reasons for their views. Some skeptics of business-sponsored social projects fear that if businesses become too active, they will gain too much control over the ways in which those projects are addressed by society as a whole. These critics point to the influence that many businesses have been able to exert on the government agencies that are supposed to regulate their industries. Other critics claim that business organizations lack the expertise needed to address social issues. They argue, for instance, that technical experts, not businesses, should decide how to clean up polluted rivers.

Proponents of socially responsible business believe that corporations are citizens and should therefore help to improve the lives of fellow citizens. Still others point to the vast resources controlled by businesses and note that they help to create many of the problems social programs are designed to alleviate.

Approaches to Social Responsibility

Given these differences of opinion, it is little wonder that corporations have adopted a variety of approaches to social responsibility. In this section, we describe the three most common approaches: the *social obligation*, *social reaction*, and *social response approaches*.

Social Obligation Approach   The **social obligation approach,** a fairly conservative concept, is consistent with the argument that profits should not be spent on social programs. Companies adopting this approach tend to meet the minimum requirements of government regulation and standard business practices.

Tobacco companies can be said to exemplify this approach. They attached health warnings on cigarette packages and stopped advertising on television in the United States only when forced to do so by the government. In countries that lack such controls, U.S. tobacco companies advertise heavily and make no mention of the negative effects of smoking.

Social Reaction Approach   An intermediate level of social responsibility is found in the **social reaction approach.** Firms taking this stance go beyond the bare minimum if they are specifically asked to do so. Many companies, for example, match employee contributions to company-approved causes. Others sponsor community activities. As a rule, however, someone must first ask for this support.

Social Response Approach   Firms that adopt the most liberal approach to social responsibility, the **social response approach,** actively seek opportunities to contribute to social projects. McDonald's, for example, established Ronald McDonald Houses to provide lodging for families of children hospitalized away from home. Sears and General Electric support artists and performers. Such efforts go beyond the normal response to requests for contributions.

Managing Social Responsibility Programs

Making a company socially responsible in the full sense of the social response approach takes a carefully organized and managed program. In particular, managers must take steps to foster a companywide sense of social responsibility. Figure 4.3 summarizes those steps.

1. *Social responsibility must start at the top.* Without the support of top management, no program can succeed. Thus, top management must embrace a strong stand on social responsibility and develop a policy statement outlining that commitment.

social obligation approach
Approach to social responsibility by which a company meets only minimum legal requirements in its commitments to groups and individuals in its social environment

social reaction approach
Approach to social responsibility by which a company, if specifically asked to do so, exceeds legal minimums in its commitments to groups and individuals in its social environment

social response approach
Approach to social responsibility by which a company actively seeks opportunities to contribute to the well-being of groups and individuals in its social environment

FIGURE 4.3 ◆ Establishing a Social Responsibility Program

2. *A committee of top managers must develop a plan detailing the level of management support.* Some companies set aside percentages of profits for social programs. Levi Strauss, for example, earmarks 2.4 percent of pretax earnings for worthy projects. Managers must also set specific priorities. For instance, should the firm train the hard-core unemployed or support the arts?

3. *One executive must be put in charge of the firm's agenda.* Whether the role is created as a separate job or added to an existing one, the selected individual must monitor the program and ensure that its implementation is consistent with the firm's policy statement and strategic plan.

4. *The organization must conduct occasional **social audits**: systematic analyses of its success in using funds earmarked for its social responsibility goals.* Consider the case of a company whose strategic plan calls for spending $100,000 to train 200 hard-core unemployed people and to place 180 of them in jobs. If at the end of one year the firm has spent $98,000, trained 210 people, and filled 175 jobs, a social audit will confirm the program's success. But if the program has cost $150,000, trained only 90 people, and placed only 10 of them, the audit will reveal the program's failure. Such failure should prompt a rethinking of the program's implementation and/or its priorities.

social audit
Systematic analysis of a firm's success in using funds earmarked for meeting its social responsibility goals

Social Responsibility and the Small Business

As the owner of a garden supply store, how would you respond to a building inspector's suggestion that a cash payment will speed up your application for a building permit? As the manager of a liquor store, would you call the police, refuse to sell, or sell to a customer whose identification card looks forged? As the owner of a small laboratory, would you call the state board of health to make sure that it has licensed the company with which you want to contract to dispose of medical waste? Who will really be harmed if a small firm pads its income statement to help it get a much-needed bank loan?

Most of the examples in this chapter illustrate big business responses to ethical and social responsibility issues. Examples like these, however, show quite clearly that small businesses must answer many of the same questions. Differences are primarily differences of scale.

At the same time, these are largely questions of *individual* ethics. What about questions of *social* responsibility? Can a small business, for example, afford a social agenda?

Should it sponsor Little League baseball teams, make donations to the United Fund, and buy light bulbs from the Lion's Club? Do joining the Chamber of Commerce and supporting the Better Business Bureau cost too much? Clearly, ethics and social responsibility are decisions faced by all managers in all organizations, regardless of rank or size. One key to business success is to decide in advance how to respond to the issues that underlie all questions of ethical and social responsibility.▼

The small business can demonstrate its responsibility toward the local community in a variety of ways, such as sponsoring a Little League baseball team. In fact, one recent study concluded that "companies that increased their community involvement were more likely to show an improved financial picture than those that did not increase their community involvement."

Continued from page 75

The Socially Conscious CEO

What's the Norm in Corporate America?

Aaron Feuerstein's decision—to pay his workforce full wages for up to 90 days and to preserve jobs after a fire destroyed Malden Mills's main factory—may not be a fair model for every business gripped by crisis. Malden had some advantages—rapid sales growth and expected future profits of between $40 million and $60 million a year. The company also expected to rebuild rapidly. Companies with limited growth prospects may have no choice but to lay off workers without pay.

Seven months after the fire, even Feuerstein was forced to accept the fact that his model of a socially responsible employer represented too great a financial burden: he was forced to lay off 450 employees. However, Feuerstein was able to promise these workers that they would get first crack at new jobs when the factory was ready for operation in 18–24 months.

Despite this setback, Feuerstein still has a hard time believing that corporations cannot do more to support loyal employees at a time of crisis. "I haven't really done anything," he says. "Corporate America has made it so that when you behave the way I did, it's abnormal."

Case Questions

1. What responsibility do you think a CEO has to a workforce during a business crisis? What factors should influence this determination?
2. If Feuerstein loses his company because of lower-than-expected sales and/or unreimbursed debt, did he do the right thing?
3. Feuerstein pays his workers $12.50 an hour—one of the highest textile wages in the world. How do you think this wage influenced workers' willingness to help the company?
4. Malden Mills is a private company. Could the CEO of a public corporation make similar decisions to keep workers on the payroll? How would such a decision be affected by responsibilities to stockholders?
5. Feuerstein wanted to pay his skilled workers for up to 90 days so that they would be available when the company needed them. He then asked his insurance company to reimburse Malden Mills for these wages. If you were an insurance examiner, how would you respond to this request?
6. At 70 years of age, Feuerstein could have taken his money out of the business and retired after the fire. What do you think motivated him to rebuild his family business?

SUMMARY OF LEARNING OBJECTIVES

1. **Explain how individuals develop their personal *codes of ethics* and why ethics are important in the workplace.** Individual *codes of ethics* are derived from social standards of right and wrong. *Ethical behavior* is behavior that conforms to generally accepted social norms concerning beneficial and harmful actions. Because ethics affect the behavior of individuals on behalf of the companies that employ them, many firms are adopting formal statements of ethics. Unethical behavior can result in loss of business, fines, and even imprisonment.

2. **Distinguish *social responsibility* from *ethics* and trace the evolution of social responsibility in U.S. business.** *Social responsibility* refers to an organization's response to social needs. Until the second half of the nineteenth century, businesses often paid little attention to these needs. Since then, however, both public pressure and government regulation, especially as a result of the Great Depression of the 1930s and the social activism of the 1960s and 1970s, have forced businesses to consider the public welfare, at least to some degree. A trend toward increased social consciousness, including a heightened sense of environmental activism, has recently emerged.

3. **Show how the concept of social responsibility applies both to environmental issues and to a firm's relationships with customers, employees, and investors.** Social responsibility toward the environment requires firms to

minimize pollution of air, water, and land. Social responsibility toward customers requires firms to provide products of acceptable quality, to price products fairly, and to respect consumers' rights. Social responsibility toward employees requires firms to respect workers both as resources and as people who are more productive when their needs are met. Social responsibility toward investors requires firms to manage their resources and to represent their financial status honestly.

4. **Identify three general *approaches to social responsibility* and describe the four steps a firm must take to implement a *social responsibility program*.** The *social obligation approach* emphasizes compliance with legal minimum requirements. Companies adopting the *social reaction approach* go beyond minimum activities, if asked. The *social response approach* commits a company to actively seeking to contribute to social projects. Implementing a social responsibility program entails four steps: (1) drafting a policy statement with the support of top management, (2) developing a detailed plan, (3) appointing a director to implement the plan, and (4) conducting *social audits* to monitor results.

5. **Explain how issues of social responsibility and ethics affect small businesses.** Managers and employees of small businesses face many of the same ethical questions as their counterparts at larger firms. Small businesses face the same issues of social responsibility and the same need to decide on an approach to social responsibility. The differences are primarily differences of scale.

STUDY QUESTIONS AND EXERCISES

Review

1. What basic factors should be considered in any ethical decision?
2. What are the major areas of social responsibility with which businesses should be concerned?
3. List the four rights of consumers that were proposed during the Kennedy Administration and eventually formalized by state and federal law.
4. What are the three basic approaches to social responsibility?
5. In what ways do you think your personal code of ethics might clash with the operations of some companies? How might you try to resolve these differences?

Analysis

6. What kind of wrongdoing would most likely prompt you to be a whistle-blower? What kind of wrongdoing would be least likely? Why?
7. In your opinion, which area of social responsibility is most important? Why? Are there areas other than those noted in the chapter that you consider important?
8. Identify some specific ethical or social responsibility issues that might be faced by small business managers and employees in each of the following areas: environment, customers, employees, and investors.

Application Exercises

9. Develop and put in writing a code of ethics for use in the classroom. Your document should include guidelines for students, instructors, and administrators.
10. Using newspapers, magazines, and other business references, identify and describe at least three companies that take a social obligation approach to social responsibility, three that take a social reaction approach, and three that take a social response approach.

BUILDING YOUR BUSINESS SKILLS

This exercise enhances the following SCANS workplace competencies: demonstrating basic skills, demonstrating thinking skills, exhibiting personal qualities, exhibiting interpersonal skills, and working with information.

Goal

To encourage students to apply general concepts of business ethics to specific business situations

Situation

As the head of human resources of a large bank, you are in the process of developing a corporate code of ethics that will be issued to every bank employee. Among the major sections in the document are those that deal with the following sensitive topics:

- Discrimination against minority employees
- Discrimination against minority customers
- Sexual harrassment
- Conflicts of interest
- Accepting gifts from clients
- Privacy and confidentiality
- Accounting irregularities
- Lying to clients and fellow employees

Method

Step 1: Working with four other students, determine your company's ethical stance on each of the topics listed above. This part of the project may require additional research. In your analysis, be certain to distinguish between your company's *ethical* and *legal* responsibilities. For example, while discriminating against black mortgage applicants on the basis of race is clearly illegal, lying to fellow employees may violate ethical, rather than legal, rules.

Step 2: Using the information gathered in your research, draft a corporate code of ethics that explains the bank's position in each area. The code should define what the bank will do in each of the following situations:

- A white supervisor has been systematically bypassing qualified black employees for promotion.
- A mortgage officer refuses to grant mortgages to qualified Hispanic-American clients.
- A female employee is sexually harrassed by a male supervisor.
- A lending officer grants a million-dollar loan to his wife's business associate even though the associate fails to meet appropriate qualifications.
- A supplier of computer equipment receives special treatment after he gives gifts to bank employees in charge of computer purchases.
- False data are included in accounting reports to stockholders.
- Employees are regularly caught lying to clients and fellow employees in order to enhance their own positions in the company.

Follow-Up

1. Do your responses to the seven ethics situations presented here have a common thread? If so, does this thread represent a values-based approach to corporate ethics? Explain.

2. What measures would you suggest for making your written code of ethics a living document that influences the way in which every employee conducts business?

3. In your opinion, is the need for corporate codes of ethics greater than it was five years ago? Explain your answer.

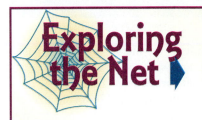

Exploring the Net

IN THIS CHAPTER, WE NOTE THAT SOME ORGANIZATIONS DEVELOP CODES OF CONDUCT OR WRITTEN STATEMENTS THAT CONVEY TO EMPLOYEES AND OTHER INTERESTED PARTIES HOW THE FIRM VIEWS ETHICS AND SOCIAL RESPONSIBILITY. ONE OF THE FIRST FIRMS TO DRAW UP A WRITTEN STATEMENT OF SUCH PRINCIPLES WAS TEXAS INSTRUMENTS (TI). FOR A SUMMARY OF THE COMPANY'S VIEWS ON ETHICS AND RELATED ACTIVITIES, VISIT TI'S WEBSITE AT

http://www.ti.com/recruit/docs/working.htm

Read the material posted here, especially the statement entitled "Ethics: The Cornerstone of TI's Success," and then consider the following questions:

1. TI seems to place a strong emphasis on ethics. Does this emphasis seem to be too much, too little, or about right?

2. TI's actual ethics statement is printed in a small booklet of about 20 pages. Do you think TI should put the entire statement on its Website, or does the current summary suffice?

3. Note that TI groups its Web discussion of ethics with related topics, such as its companywide commitment to an "Open Environment," to "Diversity," and to a "Smoke-Free Workplace/Drug-Free Workplace." Visit each of these sites as well. What is the common theme in the various statements contained in these features? What overall ethics theme does the TI Website seem to be stressing? Why?

4. Visit this related TI Website:

http://www.ti.com/corp/docs/community/community.html

The two features included here—"Building the Future through Education" and "Diversity at TI"—address a different constituency than most of the features posted at the previous Website. To what groups is a social responsibility commitment being announced here? What is the common thread running through the social responsibility messages contained in the two TI Websites that you have visited?

5. Visit one more TI Website:

http://www.ti.com

Under "Company Information," click on "Company Profile." How do TI's statements of "Principles" and "Values" support its statements about commitment to ethical and socially responsible corporate behavior?

6. Identify some parties who would be interested in TI's Website material about ethics and social responsibility (for example, potential employees and competitors). In what ways would each group find this Website material useful?

CHAPTER

UNDERSTANDING THE GLOBAL CONTEXT OF BUSINESS

For a Few Dollars More

MICROSOFT HEADS FOR THE WILD, WILD EAST

There's a lot that Microsoft founder and CEO Bill Gates doesn't like about doing business in China—piracy, for example. Every year, factories in the People's Republic manufacture 54 million illegally copied software packages, robbing Microsoft and other U.S. firms of revenue that is rightfully theirs. So severe is the problem that a pirated version of Windows 95 was available months before the product's official launch—at just $5 a package.

Nevertheless, Microsoft views China as a huge marketing opportunity (and a 1996 U.S.–Chinese agreement banning the reproduction and sale of pirated intellectual property undoubtedly is helping to ease the company's concerns). With a population of 1.2 billion people, China is on the verge of mass computerization. Only 1 million computers were sold in 1995, but sales of 5 million are projected for the year 2000. Not surprisingly, Bill Gates is doing everything he can to make sure that these computers use Microsoft software.

Other multinational companies share Gates' view of China as an

> **"Software pirates are actually helping Microsoft by creating a huge installed base of Chinese customers."**
>
> —Software industry analyst in Hong Kong

emerging consumer giant. "Any international company that's not planning to do something in China," predicts J. Tracy O'Rourke, CEO of a California-based manufacturer of medical equipment, "is probably missing a bet. It's like the frontier of days past."

Priming the Chinese computerization pump are government purchases. In Beijing, for example, officals are planning to levy new taxes and monitor their collection through a computerized network connected to a central database. The success of the plan depends on the purchase of 20,000 computers to link 3,200 tax offices via Microsoft servers, Windows NT, and Windows 95. In another deal, the central bank of China is

planning to install Windows-based PCs and servers in every one of its 10,000 branches. Thanks to purchases like these, Microsoft expects its annual sales in China of $20 million to skyrocket. "We're looking at 100-percent growth every year as far as we can see," beams Bryan Nelson, Microsoft's director for Greater China.

With its sights set on such a lucrative market, Microsoft is using various strategies to bolster its Chinese position. It has set up facilities to train thousands of technicians and programmers to use Microsoft products. Working with government officials, it is developing a Chinese-language Windows operating system, and it is collaborating with Chinese researchers to develop speech recognition and handwriting analysis software—products that are critical because of the difficulty in entering Chinese characters through a keyboard.

Ironically, pirated Microsoft software may help rather than hurt longterm sales. Thanks in large part to software pirates, about 8 out of 10 computers in China currently rely on Microsoft products—compared with only about 3 out of 100 computers running on Apple operating systems. "Software pirates," observes industry analyst Darwin P. Singson of Dataquest Inc. in Hong Kong, "are actually helping Microsoft by creating a huge installed base of customers."

Selling software to Chinese consumers is not the same thing as selling it here in the United States, but it is an increasingly important facet of Microsoft's business strategy. Indeed, many companies, both American and foreign based, produce goods at facilities and market finished products to consumers around the world. Toys 'Я' Us, which runs more than 500 stores in the United States, has opened nearly 150 outlets in France, Italy, Japan, Singapore, and elsewhere. Midwestern farmers sell wheat to Russia, and U.S. food processors buy cheese from Argentina and chocolate from Switzerland. Electronics stores in the United States feature VCRs and camcorders made in Japan, and IBM and Apple dominate the Japanese computer market.

Boeing sells aircraft to Delta and British Airways, both of which fly from Houston to London.

In a climate of growing international activity, the study and practice of basic business management has in many ways become the study and practice of international business. By focusing on the learning objectives of this chapter, you will better understand the dynamics of international business management.

After reading this chapter, you should be able to

1. Describe the rise of international business and identify the major world marketplaces

2. Explain how different forms of *competitive advantage*, *import-export balances*, *exchange rates*, and *foreign competition* determine the ways in which countries and businesses respond to the international environment

3. Discuss the factors involved in deciding to do business internationally and in selecting the appropriate levels of *international involvement* and *international organizational structure*

4. Describe some of the ways in which *social*, *cultural*, *economic*, *legal*, and *political differences* among nations affect international business

Continued on page 116

■ THE RISE OF INTERNATIONAL BUSINESS

The total volume of world trade today is immense—around $7 trillion each year. Foreign investment in the United States alone is approaching $1 trillion, and direct investment abroad by U.S. firms has already passed the $1 trillion mark. As more and more firms engage in international business, the world economy is fast becoming a single interdependent system—a process called **globalization.** We often take for granted the diversity of goods and services available today as a result of international trade. Your television set, your shoes, even your morning cup of coffee may be U.S. **imports**—that is, products made or grown abroad and sold in the United States. At the same time, the success of many U.S. firms depends in large part on **exports**—products made or grown here and shipped for sale abroad.

globalization
Process by which the world economy is becoming a single interdependent economic system

import
Product made or grown abroad but sold domestically

export
Product made or grown domestically but shipped and sold abroad

The Contemporary Global Economy

MIT professor Paul Krugman argues that what we now think of as an extremely active "global economy" is not as unprecedented as we might think. Recall, for instance, our discussion of *gross domestic product (GDP)*, which we defined in Chapter 1 as the value of all goods and services produced domestically by a nation each year. If an American firm imports foreign products to sell in this country, those imports are included in GDP. In 1880, Krugman points out, U.S. imports represented 8 percent of GDP. Today they are only 11 percent of GDP. Thus, actual trade of products is not much more active than it was in the nineteenth century. What about the movement of money from country to country—a phenomenon known as *capital mobility?* Except for some new forms of exchange, observes Krugman, capital mobility is about the same as it was in 1914. At that time, moreover, England's trade surplus—4 percent of GDP—was the same as the surplus enjoyed by Japan during the peak decade of the 1980s.

What factors, then, typify the "global economy" in the mid-1990s? Krugman points to vastly expanding growth in the exchange of information and the trade in services:

- In Cambridge, Massachusetts, for example, Montague Corp. designs a unique product—folding mountain bikes. Montague manufactures most of its bikes in Taiwan and sells them in Europe. A key facet of the company's operations is transmitting design specifications to three continents—sometimes on a daily basis. The process works—and the small firm survives—largely because fax machine technology is available.
- Molloy Electric is a small firm that services electric motors in Sioux Falls, South Dakota. Owner Garry Jacobson has observed that more and more customers are bringing in products powered by unreliable foreign-made motors. "Either they bring them in or they just throw them away, which costs us," says Jacobson, who thus acknowledges the impact of the global economy on his small part of the business world.

Note that Molloy Electric's service is not *tradable*—it cannot be directly exchanged for another product on the international market. In fact, this is the case with about 85 percent of all U.S. services—restaurants, retail sales, and the like. In effect, then, the shift to the service economy would seem to work against the development of a global economy. That situation, will change, predicts Krugman; note the experience of Molloy Electric, which has already made contact with the manufacturing operations of

China and other countries. These conclusions can be drawn from the experiences of firms like Molloy Electric and Montague Corp.: Information technology will be the centerpiece of the new global economy, and the growth in the service sector will help to fuel its development.[1]

In this section, we will examine some of the key factors that have shaped—and are shaping—the global business environment of the 1990s. First, we identify and describe the major world marketplaces. Then we discuss some important factors that determine the ways in which both nations and their businesses respond to the international environment: the roles of different forms of *competitive advantage*, of *import-export balances*, and *exchange rates*.[2]

Major World Marketplaces

The contemporary world economy revolves around three major marketplaces: North America, Western Europe, and the Pacific Rim. However, business is not conducted solely in these markets. The World Bank notes, for example, that about 77 percent of the world's people live in so-called "developing" areas. Economies in those areas are expanding 5 percent to 6 percent annually. There are 300 million consumers in Eastern Europe and another 300 million in South America. In India alone, estimates of the size of the middle class range from 100 million to 300 million.[3]

North America   The United States dominates the North American business region. It is the single largest marketplace and enjoys the most stable economy in the world. Many U.S. firms, such as General Motors and Procter & Gamble, have had successful Canadian operations for years, and Canadian firms such as Northern Telecom and Alcan Aluminum are major international competitors.

Mexico has also become a major manufacturing center, especially along the U.S. border, where cheap labor and low transportation costs have encouraged many firms, from the United States and other countries, to build plants in Mexico. Both Chrysler and General Motors, for instance, are building new assembly plants, as are suppliers like Rockwell International Corp. Nissan opened an engine and transmission plant in 1983 and an automobile manufacturing plant in 1992. In addition to suppliers, Nissan has also attracted non-auto companies to the area, including Xerox and Texas Instruments. Forecasters expect 200,000 workers to be employed in the Mexican automobile industry by 1998.

Europe   Europe is often thought of as two regions—Western and Eastern Europe. Western Europe, dominated by Germany, the United Kingdom, France, and Italy, has long been a mature but fragmented marketplace. The transformation of the European Union in 1992 into a unified marketplace has further increased the importance of this marketplace. Major international firms like Unilever, Renault, Royal Dutch Shell, Michelin, Siemens, and Nestlé are all headquartered in Western Europe.

Eastern Europe, which was primarily communist until recently, has also gained in importance, both as a marketplace and as a producer. In May 1994, for example, Albania became the 197th country in which Coca-Cola is produced—Coke opened a new $10 million bottling plant outside the capital city of Tirana. Foreign companies invested more than $8 billion in Poland in 1995–1996, including $500 million from PepsiCo Inc., which is expanding its soft drink, restaurant, and snack food operations. In 1995, the Korean automaker Daewoo chose Poland as the center of its new European operation, spending $1 billion for an existing auto plant near Warsaw.[4] ▶

The Pacific Rim   The Pacific Rim consists of Japan, China, Thailand, Malaysia, Singapore, Indonesia, South Korea, Taiwan, Hong Kong, the Philippines, and Australia. Fueled by strong entries in the automobile, electronics, and banking industries,

When the Korean automaker Daewoo Group purchased this truck-making plant in Lublin, Poland, in 1995, it was a ramshackle collection of 14 overstaffed buildings with broken windows and 20-year-old equipment. Even today, molten steel for molding parts is poured by hand, and there is no computer system for keeping track of parts. Daewoo intends to change this state of affairs. Whereas demand for new cars is slowing in Western Europe, it's jumping in Central Europe, where Poland enjoys the largest economy. Says Daewoo founder and CEO Kim Woo-Chong: "We have to move into big potential markets where few competitors have gone."

the economies of these countries grew rapidly in the 1970s and 1980s. Experts expect these countries to spend nearly $2 trillion on energy, transportation, telecommunications, and office space by the year 2000.

The Pacific Rim is already an important force in the world economy and a major source of competition for North American firms. Led by Toyota, Toshiba, and Nippon Steel, Japan dominates the region. In addition, South Korea (with such firms as Samsung and Hyundai), Taiwan (owner of Chinese Petroleum and manufacturing home of many foreign firms), and Hong Kong (a major financial center) are also successful players in the international economy. China, the most densely populated country in the world, continues to emerge as an important market in its own right. In fact, the International Monetary Fund concluded in 1993 that the Chinese economy is now the world's third largest, behind the United States and only slightly behind Japan.[5]

Forms of Competitive Advantage

No country can produce all the goods and services that its people need. Thus, countries tend to export products they can produce better or less expensively than other countries and to use the proceeds to import products they cannot produce effectively. This principle does not fully explain why nations export and import what they do. Such decisions hinge partly on whether a country enjoys an *absolute* or a *comparative advantage* in the production of different goods and services.[6]

absolute advantage
The ability to produce something more efficiently than any other country can

An **absolute advantage** exists when a country can produce something more cheaply than any other country can. Saudi oil and Canadian timber approximate absolute advantage, but examples of true absolute advantage are rare. In reality, "absolute" advantages are always relative. Brazil produces about a third of the world's coffee. However, because its high-quality coffees are preferred by American consumers, the impact of Brazil's production is widely felt. A severe frost in the winter of 1994 destroyed as much as 45 percent of the 1995–1996 harvest. First, commodities prices—prices paid by producers, roasters, and speculators—rose to their highest levels in ten years. Then the three largest U.S. coffee producers—Procter & Gamble, Kraft, and Nestlé—raised retail prices by 45 percent. With the threat to worldwide supplies, prices for lower-quality African coffees also went up.[7]

A country has a **comparative advantage** in goods that it can produce more efficiently or better than other goods. For example, if businesses in a country can make computers more efficiently than automobiles, then firms have a comparative advantage in computer manufacture. The United States has comparative advantages in the computer industry (because of technological sophistication) and in farming (because of fertile land and a temperate climate). South Korea has a comparative advantage in electronics manufacturing because of efficient operations and cheap labor. As a result, U.S. firms export computers and grain to South Korea, and U.S. firms import VCRs and stereos from South Korea.

Import-Export Balances

There are many advantages of international trade, but trading with other nations can pose problems if a country's imports and exports do not strike an acceptable balance. In deciding whether an overall balance exists, economists use two measures: *balance of trade* and *balance of payments*.

Balance of Trade   A nation's **balance of trade** is the total economic value of all products that it imports minus the total economic value of all products that it exports. Relatively small trade imbalances are common and are generally unimportant. Large imbalances, however, are another matter. In 1993, for example, the United States imported $589.4 billion worth of products while exporting only $456.9 billion. Thus, the U.S. had a negative trade balance in 1993 of $142.5 billion. But as we also noted in Chapter 1, the U.S. trade imbalance has been declining and is now only around $75 billion a year.

Trade Deficits and Surpluses.   When a country's imports exceed its exports—that is, when it has a negative balance of trade—it suffers a **trade deficit.** In short, more money is flowing out than flowing in. A positive balance of trade occurs when a country's exports exceed its imports and it enjoys a **trade surplus:** more money is flowing in than flowing out.

For years, Japan has enjoyed consistently large surpluses. Today Japan exports about 15 percent of everything it makes while importing goods and services equal to only about 5 percent of what it makes at home. The resulting surplus amounts to several billion dollars every year. In 1995, however, the Japanese trade surplus fell for the first time in five years. Higher domestic costs, shifts in foreign exchange rates, a worldwide economic slowdown, and greater international competition have combined to cut Japan's trade surplus by reducing the flow of its exports. The trade surplus with the United States fell by 10 percent, to $59 billion. By June 1996, however, the U.S. deficit with China had risen to $3.3 billion—to about 40 percent of the total U.S. trade imbalance. Largely because of American imports of toys, apparel, and footwear, China passed Japan as the largest source of the U.S. trade deficit.[8]

Balance of Payments   The **balance of payments** refers to the flow of money into or out of a country. The money that a nation pays for imports and receives for exports—that is, its balance of trade—makes up much of its balance of payments. But other financial exchanges also enter in. For example, money spent by tourists, money spent on foreign aid programs, and money spent and received in the buying and selling of currency in international money markets all affect the balance of payments.

For many years, the United States enjoyed a positive balance of payments (more inflows than outflows); more recently, the balance has been negative. That trend is gradually reversing itself, however, and many economists soon expect a positive balance of payments. Some U.S. industries have positive balances, while others have negative balances. U.S. firms like Dow Chemical and Monsanto, for example, are among the world leaders in chemical exports. The cigarette, truck, and industrial machinery

---

comparative advantage
The ability to produce some products more efficiently than others

balance of trade
Economic value of all products a country imports minus the economic value of all products it exports

trade deficit
Situation in which a country's imports exceed its exports, creating a negative balance of trade

trade surplus
Situation in which a country's exports exceed its imports, creating a positive balance of trade

balance of payments
Flow of all money into or out of a country

industries also enjoy positive balances. Conversely, the metalworking machinery, electrical generation, airplane parts, and auto industries are suffering negative balances because the United States is importing more than it is exporting.

Exchange Rates

exchange rate
Rate at which the currency of one nation can be exchanged for the currency of another country

The balance of imports and exports between two countries is affected by the rate of exchange between their currencies. An **exchange rate** is the rate at which the currency of one nation can be exchanged for that of another. Recently, for example, one U.S. dollar has been valued at about five French francs. The exchange rate, then, has been about 5 to 1.

At the end of World War II, the major nations of the world agreed to establish *fixed* exchange rates. Under fixed exchange rates, the value of any country's currency relative to that of another country remains constant. Today, however, *floating* exchange rates are the norm, and the value of one country's currency relative to that of another varies with market conditions. For example, when many French citizens want to spend francs to buy U.S. dollars (or goods), the value of the dollar relative to the franc goes up, or gets "stronger"; *demand* for the dollar is high. The value of the dollar thus rises with the demand for U.S. goods. In reality, exchange rates fluctuate by very small degrees on a daily basis. More significant variations usually occur over a longer period of time.

Fluctuation in exchange rates can have an important impact on the balance of trade. Suppose that you want to buy some French wines priced at 50 francs per bottle. At an exchange rate of 10 francs to the dollar, a bottle will cost you $5.00 (50 ÷ 10 = 5). But what if the franc is stronger? At an exchange rate of only 5 francs to the dollar, that same bottle of wine would cost you $10.00 (50 ÷ 5 = 10).

Rate changes, of course, would affect more than wine. If the dollar were stronger in relation to the franc, the prices of all American-made products would rise in France and the prices of all French-made products would fall in the United States. As a result, the French, would buy fewer American-made products, and Americans would be prompted to spend more on French-made products. The result could conceivably be a U.S. trade deficit with France.

Exchange Rates and Competition   Companies conducting international operations must watch exchange rate fluctuations closely because such changes affect overseas demand for their products. In the summer of 1993, for example, Oldsmobile began running television ads in the United States with the tag line, "It's the exchange rate, you simpleton." At the time, the Japanese yen was "strong": the American dollar purchased fewer yen and fewer of those products for which Japanese manufacturers paid in yen. The price of Japanese products, including Japanese cars, was higher, and Oldsmobile was capitalizing on that fact.

"It's the exchange rate, you simpleton."
—1993 Oldsmobile advertisement

During this period, Japanese automakers suffered their biggest loss of market share in more than a decade. Because of the exchange rate, the reason was largely price: models made by Toyota, Honda, and Nissan cost about $3,300 more than comparably equipped American-made cars. In Europe, meanwhile, several countries, including Sweden, had opted to make their products more price competitive by devaluing their currencies. In 1993, U.S. sales of Swedish-made Volvos increased, with Volvo passing Volkswagen as the year's biggest-selling European automaker in the United States.[9]

This trend continued through mid-1995, even as Japanese automakers took steps to deal with the crisis: they cut costs, moved production offshore, bought imported parts, and raised the prices of exported cars. And yet the yen continued its 20-year gain in strength. In the 1970s, for example—the heyday of Japanese car sales in the United States—it took 360 yen to buy a dollar. In 1985, the ratio had reached 264 to 1. A low point of 79 yen to 1 dollar was reached in April 1995.[10]

By the mid-1990s, the trend began to reverse itself, with the U.S. dollar growing in strength. By July 1996, the dollar was selling at 110.30 yen—an increase of 38 percent in about a year. How do these numbers translate into prospects for profits and losses by U.S. automakers? Here, according to Chrysler CEO Robert Eaton, is one set of figures: at an exchange rate of 80 yen to the dollar, Toyota's cost to produce its Previa minivan is $4,870 greater than Chrysler's cost to build its Plymouth Grand Voyager minivan. Under these conditions Chrysler enjoys a considerable competitive advantage. But at an exchange rate of 110 yen, Eaton contends, Chrysler suddenly finds itself spending $2,650 *more* to build each of its competing vehicles. The competitive advantage has shifted, and U.S. industry officials complain that the impact may be felt in both Chrysler's profit-and-loss statement and in the number of jobs it can support.[11]

Why did the dollar grow in strength? U.S. assets became more attractive to investors when U.S. businesses and policymakers succeeded in reducing inflation, the budget deficit, and unemployment while promoting steady growth and improving overall corporate efficiency.

The U.S. Economy and Foreign Trade   As you can see from Figure 5.1, there was a clear correlation between the exchange rate of the U.S. dollar and total U.S. exports in the period 1978–1993. As the graph shows, with the 1978 dollar indexed at a value of 100, the value of the dollar has declined and then leveled off since the mid-1980s. During that period, the volume of exports has climbed dramatically—121 percent since 1978. Note, too, that the rise in the dollar's value from the early to mid-1980s had a dampening effect on the growth in exports. It is important to remember, however, that the exchange rate is by no means the sole factor in the export boom: more precisely, it is a key factor in a set of advantageous economic conditions. Even more important has been the overall globalization of American business in the last two decades.[12]

Trade and the Deficit   The theoretical relationship between the exchange rate and the balance of trade does not always hold. As you can see from Figure 5.2, which traces

FIGURE 5.1 ◆ Exports and the Exchange Rate, 1978–1993

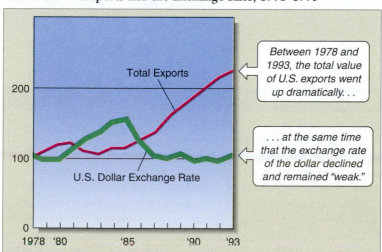

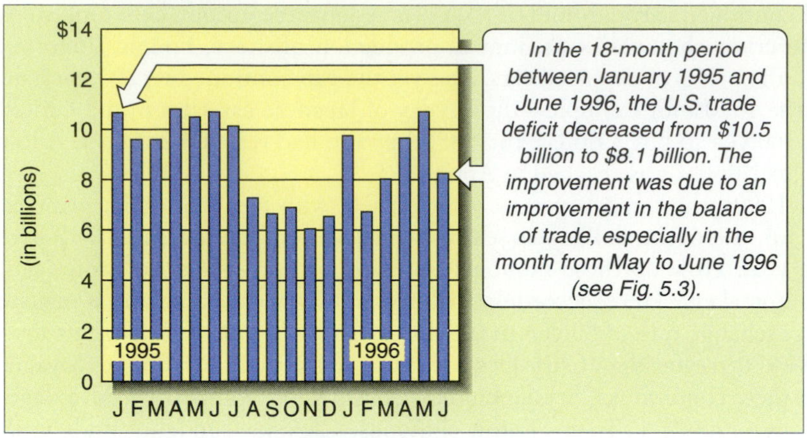

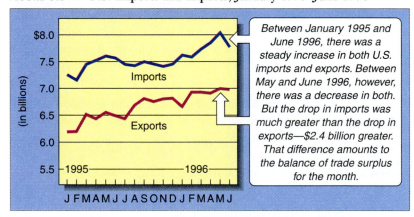

FIGURE 5.2 ◆ U.S. Trade Deficit, January 1995–June 1996

the deficit on a monthly basis for 18 months, the U.S. trade deficit decreased from $10.5 billion to $8.1 billion from January 1995 to June 1996. Also note the steep decline between May and June 1996—$2.4 billion. Why this dropoff? Part of the answer is revealed in Figure 5.3. While exports decreased, the decline was quite small—a mere $200 million (to $69.71 billion). At the same time, however, imports decreased by a whopping $2.6 billion (to $77.82 billion). The difference—$2.4 billion—is the balance-of-trade surplus for the month.[13]

FIGURE 5.3 ◆ U.S. Imports and Exports, January 1995–June 1996

■ INTERNATIONAL BUSINESS MANAGEMENT

Wherever a firm is located, its success depends largely on how well it is managed. International business is so challenging because the basic management responsibilities—planning, organizing, directing, and controlling—are much more difficult to carry out when a business operates in several markets scattered around the globe.

Managing, of course, means making decisions. In this section, we examine in some depth the three most basic decisions that a company's management must make when faced with the prospect of globalization. The first decision is whether to "go international" at all. Once that decision has been made, managers must decide on the company's level of international involvement and on the organizational structure that will best meet its global needs.

Going International

The world economy is becoming globalized, and more and more firms are conducting international operations. Blockbuster Entertainment, for example, has found its domestic market in the United States virtually saturated: officials estimate that there is a Blockbuster within a 10-minute drive of most American neighborhoods today. The firm's future growth must come almost completely from international expansion. Accordingly, Blockbuster plans to have 4,000 stores operating outside the United States by the year 2000.[14] This route, however, is not appropriate for every company. Companies that buy and sell fresh produce and fish may find it most profitable to confine their activities to limited geographic areas: storage and transport costs may be too high to make international operations worthwhile.

As Figure 5.4 shows, several factors enter into the decision to go international. One overriding factor is the business climate in other nations. Even experienced firms have encountered cultural, legal, and economic roadblocks. (These problems are discussed in more detail later in this chapter.) In considering international expansion, a company should also consider at least two other questions: Is there a demand for its products abroad? If so, must those products be adapted for international consumption?

Gauging International Demand   Products that are successful in one country may be useless in another. Snowmobiles, for example, are popular for transportation and recreation in Canada and the northern United States and actually revolutionized reindeer herding in Lapland. However, there is no demand for snowmobiles in Central America. Although this is an extreme example, the point is basic to the decision to go international: namely, that foreign demand for a company's product may be greater than, the same as, or weaker than domestic demand. Market research and/or the prior

FIGURE 5.4 ◆ Going International

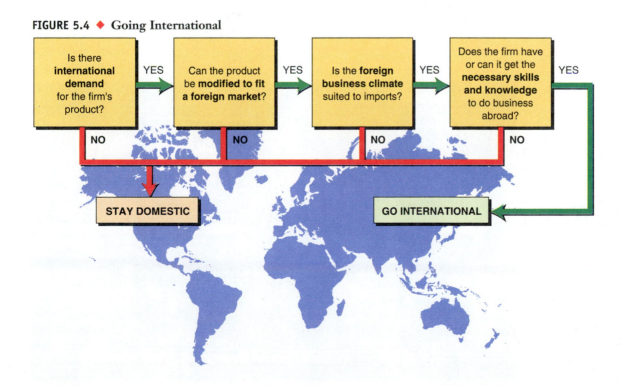

market entry of competitors may indicate that there is an international demand for a firm's products.

One very large category of U.S. products that travels well is American popular culture. In one recent 12-month period, for instance, 88 of the world's 100 most popular movies were American (no foreign film placed higher than 27th).▼ Billions of dollars are also involved in popular music, television shows, books, and even street fashions. Teenagers in Rome and Beirut, for instance, sport American baseball caps as part of their popular street dress; *Super Mario Brothers* is advertised on billboards in Bangkok, Thailand; and Bart Simpson piñatas are sold at bazaars in Mexico City. Vintage Levi's from the 1950s and 1960s sell for as much as $3,000 in countries like Finland and Australia.[15]

Adapting to Customer Needs   If there is international demand for its product, a firm must consider whether and how to adapt that product to meet the special demands of foreign customers. Consider the experience of General Motors in marketing the same product to buyers in two very different developing countries:

- In Mexico, GM's Chevrolet division sells a Spanish-made subcompact called the Joy. Chevy prices the Joy $1,500–$2,000 higher than Volkswagen's old-fashioned Beetle, which still sells well in Mexico. GM upped its price because it has found that in a country where 60 percent of the population is under 25, there is a huge market of younger buyers who will pay for stylish, more powerful vehicles.
- In the Czech Republic, however, GM markets the same car—known as the Opel Corsa—to potential buyers in their thirties. "Here," says GM's director of sales for Central Europe, "younger buyers can't even afford bicycles."[16]

"Here, younger buyers can't even afford bicycles."

—Andrej Barčak
GM director of sales for Central Europe

In October 1993, the appearance of the American hit movie Jurassic Park *in French theaters added fuel to a fire that was already raging in both cultural and economic forums. "There is less and less of France abroad and more and more that is foreign in France," complained one French cultural official. "One minute it's dinosaurs, the next North African immigrants, but it's the same basic anxiety." The concern over a disappearing culture and national identity issues largely from the French intellectual community, but it has spilled over into disputes over such trade negotiations as the GATT treaty on international trade (see Chapter 3).*

BUSINESS FIELD TRIP

"INTERNATIONAL MARKETS ARE OUR ELASTIC BAND"

Chaparral Steel does business in both local and global marketing arenas. Chaparral's largest market is in Texas, Oklahoma, Arkansas, and Louisiana, but it also has international clients in Mexico, Canada, Europe, and Asia. The extent of Chaparral's international business depends to a large extent on foreign-exchange rates and competitors' pricing. "International markets," says Vice President for Administration Dennis Beach, "are our elastic band. If it makes economic sense to ship overseas we do, and if it doesn't, we don't." With the broadening of its geographic reach, Chaparral is now considered a "market mill" rather than a minimill. Market mills manufacture more than a million tons of steel per year and ship outside a small geographic area.

> "If it makes economic sense to ship over-seas we do, and if it doesn't, we don't."
>
> —Dennis Beach
> *Vice President for Administration at Chaparral Steel Co.*

Chaparral also looks to international markets for cutting-edge technology as well as sales. "When we first opened," recalls Beach, "we purchased plant equipment manufactured in Japan, Canada, Europe, and the United States. Since then, we have maintained a reciprocal arrangement with steelmakers in Japan, because of their technological innovations, and Germany, because the Germans have some of the best steelmaking practices in the world. In fact, our employees have visited steel plants in Japan and Europe to study innovative steelmaking methods."

Although Chaparral sells internationally, it operates according to the environmental rules and regulations of the State of Texas. As protective regulations have become more stringent over the years, Chaparral officials admit that meeting state standards has become increasingly difficult. Vice President and Controller Larry Clark, for example, focuses on changing standards in just one environmental area—the gathering of dust. "In 1975," reports Clark, "we had a 'bagging plant'—essentially a huge vacuum cleaner—to gather dust, which we then buried in a hole in the ground. Later, we were required to bag then bury the dust. Now we send the residue to an extractor who removes the zinc. Then we dispose of the remaining material and use or sell the recovered zinc. These changes have meant more engineers, attorneys, monitoring equipment, and meeting time and have cost the company millions of dollars."

Chaparral has tried to deal with such problems as an integral part of its business planning. For example, in response to a state challenge to formulate environmental plans for the year 2000, in 1994 Chaparral earned a special citation from the State of Texas in recognition of its overall environmental strategy.

Levels of Involvement

After a firm decides to go international, it must decide on the level of its international involvement. At least three levels of involvement are possible. The firm may act as an exporter or importer, organize as an *international firm*, or operate as a *multinational firm*. Most of the world's largest industrial firms are multinationals.

Exporters and Importers   An **exporter** is a firm that makes products in one country and then distributes and sells them in others. An **importer** buys products in foreign markets and then imports them for resale in its home country. Exporters and importers tend to conduct most of their business in their home nations. Both enterprises entail the lowest level of involvement in international operations and are excellent ways to learn the fine points of global business. Many large firms began international operations as exporters. IBM and Coca-Cola, among others, exported to Europe for several years before building manufacturing facilities there.

The Exporting Boom.   In calendar year 1995, U.S. exports totaled $575 billion and grew at their fastest pace in seven years. Since 1986, U.S. exports have been growing

exporter
Firm that distributes and sells products to one or more foreign countries

importer
Firm that buys products in foreign markets and then imports them for resale in its home country

four times as fast as the gross domestic product. At that rate, exports in two decades would equal 37 percent of GDP. Says one Wall Street economist, "We are now—far more than we ever have been—an export economy."[17]

> ### "We are now—far more than we ever have been— an export economy."
>
> —H. Erich Heinemann
> *Chief economist at Ladenburg Thalmann & Co.*

The top 50 U.S. exporters—giant firms like General Motors, Boeing, Motorola, and Philip Morris—had export sales of almost $1.4 billion in 1993. The export boom is not limited to large companies however. Relatively small companies—so-called "mininationals"—are increasingly visible in the global market. They can compete through the latest long-distance communications technology and the flexibility to enter numerous new markets.

International Firms   As firms gain experience and success as exporters and importers, they may move to the next level of involvement. An **international firm** conducts a significant portion of its business abroad. International firms also maintain manufacturing facilities overseas. Kmart, for instance, is an international firm. Most of the retailer's stores are in the United States, but it has also opened stores in Canada, the Czech Republic, Slovakia, and Mexico. It has also bought an ownership interest in an Australian retailer and a department store chain in Prague. In addition, the company imports a substantial portion of its merchandise from other countries.

An international firm may be large and influential in the global economy, it remains basically a domestic firm with international operations: its central concern is the do-

international firm
Firm that conducts a significant portion of its business in foreign countries

© 1998 Robert Mankoff *from* The Cartoon Bank,™ Inc.

"You can't fool the American people—that's why I'm in exports."

mestic market in its home country. Kmart, for example, still earns over 90 percent of its revenues from U.S. sales. Product and manufacturing decisions typically reflect this concern. Burlington Industries, Toys "Я" Us, and BMW are also international firms.

Multinational Firms   **Multinational firms** do not ordinarily think of themselves as having domestic and international divisions. Instead, planning and decision making are geared to international markets. Headquarters locations are almost irrelevant. Royal Dutch Shell, Nestlé, IBM, and Ford are well-known multinationals.

The economic importance of multinationals cannot be underestimated. In 1995, for example, multinationals spearheaded $90 billion in investment by foreign companies in developing nations. China, India, and Vietnam are seen as especially important emerging markets, as are most Latin American countries. For example, in 1995, foreign firms invested $38 billion in China alone. East Asia and the Pacific Rim received another $53 billion, and Latin America received $17.8 billion. There are several reasons for such large outlays, including the need to move closer to customers and the rapid growth of emerging markets. World Bank officials expect emerging nations to provide a third of the growth in world trade between 1994 and 2005, and multinationals will account for a large part of that trade.[18]

International Organizational Structures

Different levels of involvement in international business require different kinds of organizational structure. For example, a structure that would help coordinate an exporter's activities would be inadequate for the activities of a multinational firm. In this section, we briefly consider the spectrum of international organizational strategies, including *independent agents, licensing arrangements, branch offices, strategic alliances,* and *direct investment.*

Independent Agents   An **independent agent** is a foreign individual or organization that agrees to represent an exporter's interests in foreign markets. Independent agents often act as sales representatives: they sell the exporter's products, collect payment, and make sure that customers are satisfied. Independent agents often represent several firms at once and usually do not specialize in a particular product or market. Levi Strauss uses agents to market clothing products in many small countries in Africa, Asia, and South America.

Licensing Arrangements   Companies seeking more substantial involvement in international business may opt for **licensing arrangements.** Firms give individuals or companies in a foreign country exclusive rights to manufacture or market their products in that market. In return, the exporter typically receives a fee plus ongoing payments called royalties. **Royalties** are usually calculated as a percentage of the license holder's sales.

Branch Offices   Instead of developing relationships with foreign companies or independent agents, a firm may simply send some of its own managers to overseas **branch offices.** A company has more direct control over branch managers than over agents or license holders. Branch offices also give a company a more visible public presence in foreign countries. Potential customers tend to feel more secure when a business has branch offices in their country.

Strategic Alliances   In a strategic alliance, a company finds a partner in the country in which it would like to conduct business. Each party agrees to invest roughly equal amounts of resources and capital into a new business. This new business—the alliance—is then owned by the partners, who divide its profits. Such alliances are sometimes called **joint ventures.** As we saw in Chapter 2, however, the term **strategic alliance** has arisen

multinational firm
Firm that designs, produces, and markets products in many nations

independent agent
Foreign individual or organization that agrees to represent an exporter's interests

licensing arrangement
Arrangement in which firms choose foreign individuals or organizations to manufacture or market their products in another country

royalty
Payment made to a license holder in return for the right to market the licenser's product

branch office
Foreign office set up by an international or multinational firm

strategic alliance
(or **joint venture**)
Arrangement in which a company finds a foreign partner to contribute approximately half of the resources needed to establish and operate a new business in the partner's country

because of the increasingly important role that such partnerships play in the larger organizational strategies of many major companies.

The number of strategic alliances among major companies has increased significantly over the last decade and is likely to grow even more. In many countries—Mexico, India, and China among them—laws make alliances virtually the only way to do international business within their borders. Mexico, for example, requires that all foreign firms investing there have local partners.

In addition to easing the way into new markets, alliances give firms greater control over their foreign activities than do independent agents and licensing arrangements. (At the same time, of course, all partners in an alliance retain some say in its decisions.) Perhaps most important, alliances allow firms to benefit from the knowledge and expertise of their foreign partners. The importance of such knowledge in Japan, for instance, has prompted all but a handful of U.S. companies to do business there through alliances. For example, Petrofsky's International, a St. Louis maker of frozen bagel dough, encountered trouble with health officials when it first tried to market its product in Japan. Food inspectors objected to the fact that yeast—an essential ingredient—was an "active bacteria." Petrofsky entered an alliance with Itochu, a giant Japanese importer, who managed to get the product certified.[19]

direct investment
Arrangement in which a firm buys or establishes tangible assets in another country

Direct Investment **Direct investment** means buying or establishing tangible assets in another country. For example, Toyota has already made significant investments in the United States by opening a major manufacturing plant in Georgetown, Kentucky, in 1988. Two German automakers, Mercedes-Benz and BMW, are making similar investments, BMW in Spartanburg, South Carolina, and Mercedes in Tuscaloosa, Alabama. Exxon has spent $1 billion to expand an oil refinery in Thailand, where it opens 40 new service stations every year. Texas Instruments recently invested $1.2 billion to build calculator and semiconductor plants in Italy. In China, drug maker Merck has opened a new factory to manufacture a vaccine for hepatitis B, and AT&T has entered a joint venture to make fiber optic cable with a Chinese partner. Allied-Lyons, the parent company of Baskin-Robbins, has opened China's first ice cream parlor.[20] Between 1989 and 1996, General Electric invested more than $10 billion in four European divisions—GE Plastics Europe (headquartered in the Netherlands), GE Aircraft Engines Group (a joint venture with a French firm), GE Medical Systems Europe (with plants in France, Portugal, and Spain), ▶ and GE Power Systems Europe (which operates in Italy, Russia, and Hungary).[21]

Matching Strategies and Opportunities Multinational firms often use whatever approach seems best suited to a particular situation in their search for worldwide business opportunities. In some cases, they opt for independent agents. In other cases, they prefer licensing arrangements, strategic alliances, or direct investments. For example, consider the case of ABB Asea Brown Boveri LTD, one of the world's most globally oriented businesses. Jointly owned by a Swedish firm and a Swiss firm, ABB is the world's largest electrical engineering company. It has 200,000 employees, of whom only 176 work at its headquarters in Zurich. ABB consists of 1,300 separate companies functioning in 140 countries. The CEO is Swedish, and other corporate officers are from Germany, France, Australia, and the United States.

■ BARRIERS TO INTERNATIONAL TRADE

Whether a business is truly multinational or sells to just a few foreign markets, a number of factors will affect its international operations. Its success in foreign markets

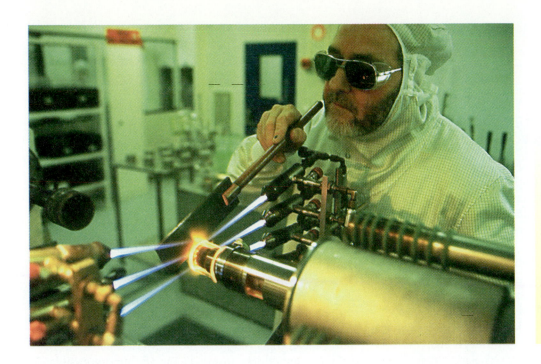

Since 1989, General Electric has invested more than $10 billion in Europe. Half of that money has been spent on acquisitions, and half has been spent on new facilities like this factory run by GE Medical Systems Europe in France. Here, GE uses skilled French labor to assemble what president Arno Bohn calls "low-cost components made in low-cost parts of Europe like Portugal and Spain." Its European operations currently supply about 15 percent of GE's total profit.

largely be determined by the ways in which it responds to social, economic, and political barriers to international trade.

Social and Cultural Differences

Any firm planning to conduct business in another country must understand the social and cultural differences between the host country and the home country. Some differences, of course, are fairly obvious. Companies must take language factors into account when making adjustments in packaging, signs, and logos. Pepsi-Cola is exactly the same product whether it is sold in Seattle or Moscow—except for the lettering on the bottle. Less "universal" products, however, face a variety of conditions that require them to adjust their practices. In Thailand, for example, Kentucky Fried Chicken adjusted its menus, ingredients, and hours of operation to suit Thai culture.

Sometimes even the physical stature of the host country's population must be considered. Average Japanese and French consumers are slimmer and shorter than their U.S. counterparts—an important consideration if you intend to sell clothes in these markets. Differences in the average ages in the local population can also have ramifications. Countries with growing populations (such as South Korea) tend to have a high percentage of young people. As a result, electronics and fashionable clothing sell well. Countries with stable or declining populations (such as Sweden) tend to have more older people. Generic pharmaceuticals are successful in such markets.

A wide range of more subtle value differences can also affect international operations. For example, many Europeans shop daily. To U.S. consumers accustomed to weekly supermarket trips, the European pattern may seem like a waste of time. For many Europeans, however, shopping is not just buying food. It is an outlet for meeting friends and exchanging political views. Consider the implications of this cultural difference for U.S. firms selling food products in European markets. First, large American supermarkets are not the norm in many parts of Europe. Second, people who shop daily do not need large refrigerators and freezers.

TRENDS & CHALLENGES

THE CAVALIER ATTITUDE TOWARD MURKY TEA

Quaker Oats and General Motors share a common set of woes. Recently, both companies introduced home-grown American products into the Japanese market, and both encountered cultural and business turbulence that turned the trip abroad into an unpleasantly bumpy ride.

For Quaker Oats, the global marketing debacle involved its Snapple Beverage division, which manufactures fruit and iced-tea flavored beverages. (As a result of marketing and distribution failures at home and abroad, Quaker sold Snapple in 1997—for $1.4 billion *less* than it had paid for it three years earlier.) Although Snapple's arrival in Japan was heralded by ads declaring that "The Snapple Phenomenon Has Landed," Japanese consumers disliked Snapple's sweet fruit juice flavorings and the trademark bits of fruit and granules of tea that Snapple likes to leave in its bottles. "The iced tea," volunteered at least one Japanese taster, "was murky looking."

Quaker's miscalculation of Japanese tastes, coupled with its refusal to adapt Snapple's formula and a poorly conceived marketing program, resulted in a dramatic drop in sales from 2.4 million bottles a month just after introduction in 1995 to a mere 120,000 bottles a month in 1996. Quaker decided to cut its losses in 1996 and stopped shipping Snapple to Japan. "Japan," eulogized the *Wall Street Journal*, "has given Snapple the raspberry."

General Motors also had high hopes when the Chevrolet Cavalier hit Japanese showrooms early in 1996—all decked out with a Toyota nameplate. The Cavalier was the first American car that Toyota had agreed to market on Japanese soil, and it was heralded by both companies as a model of U.S.–Japanese cooperation. The initial reaction of Japanese consumers was good, as it had been for Snapple. Within three months, sales reached the monthly goal of 1,667 vehicles. By May, however, sales had dropped to just 472 cars a month.

"Japan has given Snapple the raspberry."

The Wall Street Journal
April 1996

What went wrong? Problems began popping up when GM was forced to make 150 changes to meet the requirements of the Japanese market. Some changes—like moving the gas pedal forward—were needed because Japanese drivers are shorter than Americans. Other changes—like placing the steering column on the right—were obviously more fundamental. Still others—like covering the steering wheel and handbreak with leather—were merely attempts to satisfy finicky buyers. Whatever the reasons, costly redesigns left GM frustrated and complaining that unnecessary expenses were making competition inside Japan all but impossible. Meanwhile, Toyota regarded GM's stance as mere resistance to change.

Toyota also found the Cavalier to be plagued by an alarmingly high defect rate. According to some reports, as many as nine out of ten cars needed at least one repair before being accepted for sale in Japan. "Their vehicle defect rate is about 50 times that of Japanese vehicles," explained Naoki Yamaguchi, president of a regional Japanese dealer network. "If they would just put a little more effort into production control . . . ." GM denies the severity of Cavalier's quality problem and points instead to what it says is a well-known Japanese strategy, namely, keeping foreign goods out of the home market by finding excessive fault with them.

Clearly, both Quaker Oats and General Motors learned the hard way that marketing American goods in Japan is far from easy. Although both companies undoubtedly expected cultural and business problems, neither was prepared for what it got. Unfortunately, in the opinion of some analysts, both marketing ventures may have been doomed from the start.

Economic Differences

Although cultural differences are often subtle, economic differences can be fairly pronounced. In dealing with mixed economies like those of France and Sweden, for example, firms must be aware of when—and to what extent—the government is involved in a given industry. The French government, for instance, is heavily involved in all aspects of airplane design and manufacturing.

Legal and Political Differences

Governments can affect international business activities in many ways. They can, for example, set conditions for doing business within their borders or even prohibit doing business altogether. They can control the flow of capital and use tax legislation to either discourage or encourage international activity in a given industry. In the extreme, they can even confiscate the property of foreign-owned companies. In this section, we discuss some of the more common legal and political issues in international business: *quotas, tariffs,* and *subsidies; local content laws;* and *business practice laws.*

Quotas, Tariffs, and Subsidies   Even free market economies often establish some system of quotas and/or tariffs. Both quotas and tariffs affect the prices and quantities of foreign-made products. A **quota** restricts the number of products of a certain type that can be imported into a country. By reducing supply, the quota raises the prices of those imports. For example, Belgian ice cream makers can ship no more than 922,315 kilograms of ice cream to the United States each year. Quotas are often determined by treaties. Moreover, better terms are often given to friendly trading partners, and quotas are typically adjusted to protect domestic producers.

The ultimate form of quota is an **embargo:** a government order forbidding exportation and/or importation of a particular product—or even all the products—from a particular country. For example, many countries control bacteria and disease by banning certain agricultural products. The United States has embargoes against Cuba, Iraq, Libya, and Iran. Consequently, U.S. firms are forbidden from investing in these countries, and their products cannot be sold on American markets.[22] ▼

A **tariff** is a tax on imported products. Tariffs directly affect prices by raising the price of imports. Consumers pay not only for the products but also for tariff fees. Tariffs may take two forms. *Revenue tariffs* are imposed strictly to raise money for governments. Most tariffs, however, are *protectionist tariffs,* meant to discourage the import of particular products. For example, firms that import ironing board covers into the United States pay a tariff of 7 percent of the price of the product. Firms that import women's athletic shoes pay a flat rate of 90 cents per pair plus 20 percent of the price

quota
Restriction on the number of products of a certain type that can be imported into a country

embargo
Government order banning exportation and/or importation of a particular product or all products from a particular country

tariff
Tax levied on imported products

In their efforts to punish certain regimes of the Middle East— Iran, Iraq, and Libya—U.S. policy makers are encountering some cold, hard economic facts. Iraq's oil reserves, for example, are second only to those of Saudi Arabia; oil fields like this one in Iran make it the world's third-largest exporter. In addition, oil companies headquartered in other countries— notably Russia and France—are putting pressure on U.S. competitors by striking deals with Middle East producers. In 1995, for example, Conoco Inc. struck a $1 billion deal with Iran that it claims is legal despite the U.S. government embargo.

of the shoes. Each of these figures is set through a complicated process designed to put foreign and domestic firms on reasonably even competitive ground.

subsidy
Government payment to help a domestic business compete with foreign firms

A **subsidy** is a government payment to help a domestic business compete with foreign firms. Subsidies are really indirect tariffs: they lower prices of domestic goods rather than raise prices of foreign goods. Many European governments subsidize farmers to help them compete with U.S. grain imports.

Quotas and tariffs are imposed for a variety of reasons. For example, the U.S. government aids domestic automakers by restricting the number of Japanese automobiles that can be *imported* into this country. National security concerns have prompted the United States to limit the extent to which certain forms of technology can be *exported* to other countries—for example, computer and nuclear technology exports to China. The recent relaxation of controls on the licensing of technology has contributed to the export boom that we described earlier in this chapter. The United States is not the only country that uses tariffs and quotas. Italy, for example, imposes high tariffs on imported electronic goods to protect domestic firms. A Sony Walkman thus costs almost $150 in Italy, and CD players are prohibitively expensive.

The Protectionism Debate. In the United States as elsewhere, **protectionism**—the practice of protecting domestic business at the expense of free market competition—has long been controversial. Supporters argue, for example, that tariffs and quotas protect domestic firms and jobs and shelter new industries until they are able to compete internationally. They argue that the United States needs such measures to counter measures imposed by other nations. Other advocates justify protectionism in the name of national security. A nation, they argue, must be able to produce the goods needed for its survival in the event of war. Thus, the U.S. government requires the U.S. Air Force to buy all its planes from U.S. manufacturers.

protectionism
Practice of protecting domestic business against foreign competition

Critics cite protectionism as a source of friction between nations. They also charge that it drives up prices by reducing competition. In addition, they maintain that although jobs in some industries would be lost as a result of free trade, jobs in other industries—for example, electronics and automobiles—would be created if all nations abandoned protectionist tactics.

Local Content Laws   Many countries, including the United States, have **local content laws:** requirements that products sold in a particular country be at least partly made there. Typically, firms seeking to do business in a country must either invest there directly or take on a domestic partner. In this way, some of the profits from doing business in a foreign country stay there rather than flowing out to another nation. In some cases, the partnership arrangement is optional but wise. In Mexico, for instance, Radio Shack de Mexico is a joint venture owned by Tandy Corp. (49 percent) and Mexico's Grupo Gigante (51 percent).

local content law
Law requiring that products sold in a particular country be at least partly made there

Business Practice Laws   Even with this arrangement, however, Tandy reports problems, especially in importing merchandise across the Mexican border. Consider, too, the recent experience of Wal-Mart officials in Mexico City.

■ In June 1994, government inspectors swooped down on Wal-Mart's brand new Supercenter in Mexico City. Citing Mexican regulations, the inspectors reminded Wal-Mart managers that each of the store's 80,000 products must be labeled in Spanish. Labels must also indicate country of origin and provide instructions for use. Where necessary, they must display import permit numbers. Charging 11,700 violations, inspectors ordered the store closed for 72 hours while Wal-Mart rectified oversights. The store appealed to the U.S. ambassador, who managed to have the order lifted after only 24 hours.

Wal-Mart and other American companies that have recently entered Mexico have reported a host of problems in complying with stringent—and often changing—regulations and other bureaucratic obstacles.[23] Such practices fall under the heading of the host country's **business practice laws.** Sometimes, a legal—even an accepted—business practice in one country is illegal in another. For example, in some South American countries, it is sometimes legal to bribe other businesses and government officials. The formation of **cartels**—associations of producers that control supply and prices—has given tremendous power to some nations, such as those belonging to the Oil Producing and Exporting Countries (OPEC). U.S. law forbids both bribery and cartels.

Dumping. Many (but not all) countries forbid **dumping**—selling a product abroad for less than the cost of production. U.S. antidumping legislation is contained in the Trade Agreements Act of 1979. This statute sets tests for determining two conditions:

1. If products are being priced at "less than fair value"

2. If the result unfairly harms domestic industry

business practice laws
Laws or regulations governing business practices in given countries

cartel
Association of producers whose purpose is to control supply and prices

dumping
Practice of selling a product abroad for less than the cost of production

Continued from page 97

Opening Windows in the Great Wall of Chinese Business

Microsoft Miscalculates

Forty-five percent of China's 1.2 billion population is under the age of 26. This younger generation of consumers is spending more than its parents on all consumer goods, including such electronic products as color televisions, refrigerators, VCRs, telephones, and computers.

Tapping into this emerging consumer market requires that multinationals learn to deal effectively with local businesspeople and government officials, who often operate in distinctly non-Western ways. Microsoft learned the art of doing business in China the hard way when, in 1992, it contracted with a Taiwanese company to produce a Chinese-language version of Windows for use in mainland China. Government officials in Beijing rejected the product for various reasons. It was produced in Taiwan, which China does not recognize. The Chinese government also insisted that its officials, rather than outsiders, define the standards for translating Chinese character fonts into computer language.

Microsoft's miscalculations were serious enough for the Chinese electronics industry to threaten a ban on the Taiwanese version of Windows. Bill Gates was advised that if he wanted to do business in China, he had better spend time there and "learn something from 5,000 years of Chinese history." Gates did just that and, in the process, learned that Microsoft's success depends on a cooperative relationship with the Beijing government—one that sometimes places Microsoft in the back seat but which does ensure that it gets to go along for the ride.

Case Questions

1. To help control its exploding population, China enforces strict family planning. How do you think smaller families will affect consumer purchasing patterns in the emerging Chinese economy?
2. Because so many goods are manufactured in China and shipped to the United States, the U.S. is currently running a trade deficit with China that recently surpassed its deficit with Japan. How are Microsoft's strategies likely to affect the balance of payments between China and the United States?
3. After its 1992 business miscalculation, Microsoft replaced its Chinese management team. Do you think this was a wise decision? Explain your answer.
4. The national average annual household income in China was just $685 in 1994. However, per capita income is rising at about 20 percent per year and is expected to reach $4,000 by 2020. Why is Microsoft trying so hard to get a foothold in China if so few individuals and families can afford its products?
5. Why did the Chinese suggest that Microsoft's success depended on Bill Gates' firsthand knowledge of their country?

SUMMARY OF LEARNING OBJECTIVES

1. **Describe the rise of international business and identify the major world marketplaces.** More and more firms are engaged in international business. The term *globalization* refers to the process by which the world economy is fast becoming a single interdependent system. According to some experts, the global economy of the mid-1990s is best typified by the rapid growth in two areas: exchange of information and trade in services. The three major marketplaces for international business are *North America* (the United States, Canada, and Mexico), *Western Europe* (which is dominated by Germany, the United Kingdom, France, and Italy), and the *Pacific Rim* (where the dominant country, Japan, is surrounded by such rapidly advancing nations as South Korea, Taiwan, Hong Kong, and China).

2. **Explain how different forms of *competitive advantage, import export balances, exchange rates,* and *foreign competition* determine the ways in which countries and businesses respond to the international environment.** The different forms of *competitive advantage* are critical to international business. With an *absolute advantage*, a country engages in international trade because it can produce a product more efficiently than any other nation. But more often, countries trade because they enjoy *comparative advantages:* they can produce some items more efficiently than they can produce other items. The *import export balance*, including the *balance of trade* and the *balance of payments*, and *exchange rate differences* in national currencies affect the international economic environment and are important elements of international business.

3. **Discuss the factors involved in deciding to do business internationally and in selecting the appropriate *levels of international involvement* and *international organizational structure.*** In deciding whether to do business internationally, a firm must determine whether a market for its product exists abroad, and if so, whether the firm has the skills and knowledge to manage such a business. It must also assess the business climates of other nations to make sure that they are conducive to international operations.

   A firm must also decide on its level of international involvement. It can choose to be an *exporter* or *importer*, to organize as an *international firm*, or to operate as a *multinational firm*. The choice will influence the organizational structure of its international operations, specifically, its use of *independent agents*, *licensing arrangements*, *branch offices*, *strategic alliances*, and *direct investment*.

4. **Describe some of the ways in which *social, cultural, economic, legal,* and *political differences* among nations affect international business.** *Social* and *cultural differences* that can serve as barriers to trade include language, social values, and traditional buying patterns. Differences in economic systems may force businesses to establish close relationships with foreign governments before they are permitted to do business abroad. *Quotas, tariffs, subsidies,* and *local content laws* offer protection to local industries. Differences in *business practice laws* can make standard business practices in one nation illegal in another.

STUDY QUESTIONS AND EXERCISES

Review

1. How does the balance of trade differ from the balance of payments?
2. What are the three possible levels of involvement in international business? Give examples of each.
3. How does the economic system of a country affect the decisions of outside firms interested in doing business there?
4. What aspects of the culture in your state or region would be of particular interest to a foreign firm considering doing business there?

Analysis

5. Make a list of all the major items in your bedroom, including furnishings. Try to identify the country in which each item was made. Offer possible reasons why a given nation might have a comparative advantage in producing a given good.

6. Suppose that you are the manager of a small firm seeking to enter the international arena. What basic information would you need about the market that you are thinking of entering?

7. Do you support protectionist tariffs for the United States? If so, in what instances and for what reasons? If not, why not?

8. Do you think that a firm operating internationally is better advised to adopt a single standard of ethical conduct or to adapt to local conditions? Under what kinds of conditions might each approach be preferable?

Application Exercises

9. Interview the manager of a local firm that does at least some business internationally. Identify reasons why the company decided to "go international." Describe the level of the firm's international involvement and the organizational structure(s) it uses for its international operations.

10. Select a product familiar to you. Using library reference works to gain some insight into the culture of India, identify the problems that might arise in trying to market this product to Indian consumers.

BUILDING YOUR BUSINESS SKILLS

This exercise enhances the following SCANS workplace competencies: demonstrating basic skills, demonstrating thinking skills, exhibiting interpersonal skills, working with information, and applying systems knowledge.

Goal

To encourage students to appreciate the differences between high-context and low-context cultures and to understand how these differences affect global business communication

Background

One of the key factors influencing business communication is the cultural backdrop for the communication. This backdrop is often characterized as that of a low-context or high-context culture.

■ Members of *low-context cultures* use explicit written and verbal messages to communicate in both business and nonbusiness settings. Here, for example, written agreements and messages will probably determine business arrangements.

■ Members of *high-context cultures* communicate through both explicit messages and the implicit context in which they are communicated. Here such factors as interpersonal relationships and personal status will probably affect the success of the communication.

Among the contextual factors that affect communication in high-context cultures are the need to establish personal relationships before conducting business, the need to nurture these relationships (perhaps at the expense of schedules and other goals), and a high level of formality and etiquette in personal meetings and written documents.

Method

Step 1: A continuum of world cultures as defined by anthropologist Edward T. Hall is shown below. On the left are low-context cultures; on the right are high-context cultures. Use this information to develop a strategy for conducting meetings with businesspeople in Switzerland and Japan.

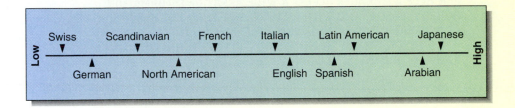

Step 2: Working in groups of four to five students, decide how you would approach the meeting in each country. Address the following specific questions:

- *Premeeting preparation:* Before you arrive at the meeting site in each country, what should you do to increase your chance of having a successful meeting? In your answer consider documents you could send, including letters of introduction written by you and others.

- *Time of arrival:* If your meeting is at 1:00 P.M. on Tuesday morning, when should you arrive to in order optimize the results you are likely to achieve in each country?

- *Formality:* If you are meeting with the company's executive vice president in charge of production, what title and position should you or another member of your business party hold in order to achieve your business goal in each country?

- *Getting down to business:* How would your business style differ in each country when it came time to introduce business issues? How would the pace of your business conversation differ?

Follow-Up

1. *Culture shock*—the inability to adapt to foreign cultures—is a problem that many American businesspeople face when they work abroad. Based on this exercise, why do you think this problem exists?

2. Many large companies conduct seminars for their employees on the cultural differences they are likely to encounter when doing business in the global marketplace. How can these seminars reduce the tendency toward *ethnocentrism*, the tendency to judge the cultures of foreign countries by U.S. standards? What are the chief dangers of the ethnocentric approach?

3. Japan, the Arab countries, and Latin American countries are all considered high-context cultures. Do some research to find out whether these countries share similar cultural patterns. How would you adapt your business style from country to country?

Exploring the Net

AS THIS CHAPTER SUGGESTS, SUCH FACTORS AS DISTANCE AND TIME DIFFERENCES, COMBINED WITH SOCIAL, ECONOMIC, AND OTHER DIFFERENCES, CAN MAKE THE STUDY OF INTERNATIONAL BUSINESS ESPECIALLY CHALLENGING. IN THIS RESPECT, THE INTERNET HAS IMMENSE POTENTIAL VALUE FOR ANYONE WHO IS INTERESTED IN THE GLOBAL ENVIRONMENT OF BUSINESS. FOR ONE THING, THE INTERNET CAN HELP A MANAGER ACCESS A WIDE ARRAY OF INFORMATION QUICKLY, EASILY, AND WITH LITTLE EXPENSE. AN EXCELLENT SOURCE OF GENERAL INFORMATION REGARDING INTERNATIONAL BUSINESS IS A WEBSITE CALLED "BUSINESS RESOURCES ON THE WEB: INTERNATIONAL BUSINESS." LOG ON TO THIS SITE AT

http://www.idbsu.edu/carol/busintl.htm

First, browse the site according to what interests you most. Then consider the following questions:

1. In what ways would a manager whose company conducts international business find this site useful? For example, among the wealth of data that can be accessed here, which information might be of practical use to a small manufacturer who is thinking about exporting his or her product to one or two selected overseas markets?

2. Select one country in each of the following areas:
   - Asia and the Pacific
   - Latin and South America
   - Russia and Eastern Europe

   Find out as much as you can about the following in all three countries:
   - social and cultural factors affecting business
   - economic factors affecting business
   - legal and political differences affecting business

3. Briefly review the textbook discussions of exporting and licensing. Identify two or three sites which might be especially relevant to someone considering these forms of international business.

4. Select one of the following sites:
   - "Go to Marketing, Finance, Small Business"
   - "Go to Economic Statistics, Government Statistics, Business Law"
   - "Go to Small Business"

   On the site that you explored, what further information is available to the American businessperson who is interested in learning more about the global environment of business today?

5. What are the limitations, if any, in a site such as this one?

"So Safe You Could Die"

The Agency That Wants to Be 100-Percent Sure

Learning Objectives

The purpose of this video exercise is to help students

1. Appreciate the role played by government regulation in certain areas of U.S. business activity
2. Understand some of the ways in which legal policies differ from country to country
3. Assess some of the ethical issues that face both U.S. businesspeople and policy makers

Background Information

Before a new medical product can be marketed in the United States, it must be approved by the Food and Drug Administration (FDA). Currently, the FDA has a backlog of 5,000 applications waiting for action; the average review lasts more than six months. The recent experiences of two manufacturing companies suggest that Yankee ingenuity may be suffering from an overdose of regulatory fervor. Both companies have run into obstacles in trying to gain approval for simple devices—devices that, according to many medical experts, have the potential to save lives:

- Ambu International, a Danish firm, manufactures a pump-like device developed by an American doctor that could increase revival rates among victims of cardiac arrest. Although the Ambu pump has been approved for use in numerous other countries, the FDA refuses to allow experimental testing of the device in the United States.
- Earl Wright Co. of Decatur, Illinois, has developed the Sensor Pad, a simple, inexpensive device designed to assist women detect early signs of breast cancer. The company has received permission to market the device in Canada and many countries in Southeast Asia and Western Europe. In the United States, however, the FDA has made numerous requests for additional information and has denied approval.

The Video

Video Source. "So Safe You Could Die: Overregulation by the FDA," *20/20*, August 12, 1994. This two-part segment focuses on the expensive (and sometimes outrageously long) testing procedures required by the FDA. Participants charge that FDA practice has resulted in loss of life by preventing the manufacture and distribution of several medical aids and devices.

Discussion Questions

1. Why do regulators in many countries outside the United States look more favorably on products like the Ambu pump and the Sensor Pad?

2. Do you agree with the Wrights' eventual decision to begin selling the Sensor Pad without FDA approval?

3. Would you have handled the Sensor Pad approval process differently had you been head of the FDA? Explain.

Follow-Up Assignment

Go to the library and investigate whether the FDA has made any significant changes in its approval process. Focus your research on changes in the approval process required for AIDS treatments. Given that a doctor's visit and a prescription are now required, what do you think about the FDA's final approval of the Sensor Pad?

> **"We as a society refuse to take risks and want 100-percent guarantees that our lives are going to be perfect."**
>
> —Dr. Mary Palmore
> *Expert on public health care policy*

VIDEO EXERCISE 2.2

Doing Business Abroad the Lands' End Way

Going International Means Knowing When to Say Nappy Bag

Learning Objectives

The purpose of this video exercise is to help students

1. Appreciate the difficulties experienced by an American company when it decides to go international
2. Understand how Lands' End responded to customer needs in markets as diverse as the United Kingdom and Japan
3. Understand how Lands' End dealt with social, cultural, and economic differences as it expanded into international markets

Background Information

International sales are nothing new to Lands' End, which first began selling to Canadian customers through regular mailings in 1987. But in the early 1990s, overseas expansion threatened to be a completely different matter:

- The company's first overseas venture—to the United Kingdom—was undertaken less than ten years ago. Surprisingly, one of the first challenges the company encountered was language. Lands' End's copywriters worked in American English, but its new British customers wanted to hear about products in British English—and said so. Adjustments were made to Lands' End copy, and by 1993, operations in the United Kingdom had been moved to a new home-based facility just outside London.
- In Japan, operations began in 1993, with the first Japanese catalog issued in August 1994. In Japan, the main challenge turned out to be advertising media and methods. Japanese customers are used to cluttered newspaper inserts; Lands' End has always worked to show individual products in the best possible light—a policy that doesn't lend itself to cluttered photography and advertising copy. Compromises were reached, and Lands' End discovered a formidable competitive tool in its iron-clad customer satisfaction guarantee.

The Video

Video Source. "Doing Business Abroad the Lands' End Way," *Prentice Hall Presents: On Location at Lands' End.* This video traces the history of Lands' End's forays into two overseas markets—the United Kingdom and Japan. Participants, including Vice

President for International Operations Frank Buettner, recount some of the key challenges that faced the company as it adapted its approach to catalog retailing to the demands of foreign customers.

Discussion Questions

1. How would you describe Lands' End's level of international involvement? Which type of international organizational structure best applies to the company's approach to business in the United Kingdom and Japan?

2. List and describe some of the specific barriers to international trade that Lands' End has encountered. With which kinds of differences—social and cultural, economic, legal and political—does Lands' End seem to be most concerned? Why? In what ways have some of these differences affected Lands' End's international operations?

3. Why did Lands' End move so quickly to establish headquarters for its British operations inside the United Kingdom? What kinds of problems should be solved more easily because the company now has a "creative team of nationals" working at its home-based British facility?

4. Every company that markets its products in several countries faces a basic choice: (1) use a *decentralized approach* with separate management for each country or (2) adopt a *global perspective* with a coordinated marketing program directed at one worldwide audience. Where would you place Lands' End on this spectrum? Is its approach primarily "decentralized"? Primarily "global"? If it reflects both options, why do you think this is so?

Follow-Up Assignment

At the conclusion of the video, Lands' End's three most important criteria for venturing into a foreign market are presented. All of these criteria concern a country's infrastructure: (1) the country must be economically stable, (2) it must have a good system for distributing goods, and (3) its telephone system must be dependable. You are also told that the company is now considering expansion into one of three countries—Germany, the Netherlands, or France. After your instructor has divided the class into groups of three to six people each, assign members to go to the library and gather current information on the infrastructure and economic conditions in these three countries. When each committee has collected its information, members should meet to compare notes and draw up a report that recommends that Lands' End select one country over the other two.

For Further Exploration

Lands' End can be contacted on the Internet at

http://www.landsend.com

On the Web page, you will find an icon for the company's "Home" page. From there, click on the link to "The Company Inside and Out" to find out what Lands' End has to say about "Our Guarantee," "The Lands' End Principles of Doing Business," and "The Company Facts."

"In all of our international ventures, we try to transplant what we believe has historically made Lands' End so successful—its culture, its principles, its customer focus, its way of doing business."

—Frank Buettner
Vice President for International Operations at Lands' End

6

CHAPTER

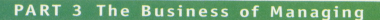

MANAGING THE BUSINESS ENTERPRISE

If the Shoe Virtually Fits

SHOE SALESMAN IS IN STEP WITH THE LATEST TECHNOLOGY

Jeffrey Silverman's first Custom Foot shoe store in Westport, Connecticut, is tiny in comparison to mega–shoe stores that hawk everything from Nike sneakers to satin slippers. In fact, the store is tiny even in comparison with the standard footwear store. With only 750 square feet of space, what's missing is the packed-with-inventory stockroom hidden from view at the back of the store. Instead, Custom Shoe is an "inventory-less" store that thrives on "mass-customization"—the process of using computers and flexible-manufacturing techniques to produce goods in large quantities, with certain elements of each product being customized according to the individual customer's specifications. Silverman sells his mass-customized shoes at off-the-shelf prices. "If customers are willing to wait a short period of time," he explains, "they can get the size, color, and style they want" at prices they can afford.

A thirtysomething entrepreneur, Silverman developed the Custom Foot concept while working as a shoe salesman (since the age of 16) and observing standard business practices.

> **"As a salesman, you're trained to sell customers what you have, not what they want."**
>
> —Jeffrey Silverman
> *Founder and CEO of Custom Foot*

"As a salesman," he says, "you're trained to sell customers what you have, not what they want. Customers should have a lot of choices, but stores don't want to carry the inventory." Tired of telling customers that their new shoes "will feel better later"—and sensing a business opportunity—Silverman decided to customize the process of matching shoes and customers.

His initial goal was to produce mass-customized men's shoes for the wholesale market. Soon, however, the positive response to mass-customization changed his direction. "I started out thinking that Custom Foot was a wholesale concept," he recalls, "but after talking to people at trade shows, I decided I wanted to control the entire product." To build his business,

Silverman approached investors, who put up $3.5 million for automated equipment, real estate, and salaries. Today, Measurably Better, the parent of Custom Foot, has a staff of fifteen in Westport, Connecticut, as well as three employees at a factory in Italy.

Customers first have their feet measured by an electronic scanner, which measures the foot in fourteen different ways. After the computer records subtle differences between the right and left foot, a salesperson helps the customer choose the style, color, grade of leather, lining, and so on from the store's "virtual inventory." (The 150 samples on display show customers how shoes look, but not how they feel on their feet.) Specially designed software then translates the customer's choices into an order, which is faxed, in Italian, to factories in Italy, where the shoes are mass-customized and delivered in two to three weeks. Ready-made prices, ranging from $99.95 to $249.95, are possible, says Silverman, because "we don't have any inventory, and there is no middleman."

How is Custom Foot doing? As chief executive of a private company, Jeffrey Silverman does not have to reveal revenues, but analysts estimate that his tiny Westport store alone took in $4–$7 million in its first year. With increased investor backing, Silverman has already opened stores in Short Hills, New Jersey, and at the Mall of America, near Minneapolis. His business plan calls for up to 100 stores nationwide by the end of 1997, followed shortly by a chain of sales outlets in podiatrists' offices. He plans to make a public stock offering by 1999.

Just like large corporations, small businesses like Custom Foot depend on effective management. In fact, starting a small business confronts key players with nearly every possible managerial decision. Jeffrey Silverman developed the Custom Foot concept and the goals and strategies necessary to grow his business. His work involves developing strategic and tactical plans. He must analyze his competitive environment, and he must organize, direct, and control day-to-day operations. In Jeffrey Silverman's case, we also have a manager who must function effectively in both global and technological environments.

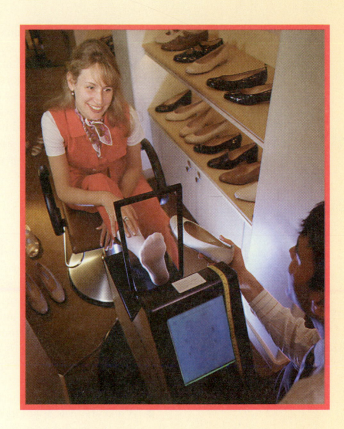

By focusing on the learning objectives of this chapter, you will better understand the nature of managing, the meaning of corporate culture, and the range of skills that managers like Jeffrey Silverman need if they are to work effectively.

After reading this chapter, you should be able to

1. Explain the importance of setting *goals* and formulating *strategies* as the starting points of effective management

2. Describe the four activities that constitute the *management process*

3. Identify *types of managers* by level and area

4. Describe the five basic *management skills*

5. Explain the importance of *corporate culture*

Continued on page 147

Although our focus here is on managers in *business* settings, remember that the principles of *management* apply to all kinds of organizations. Managers work in charities, churches, social organizations, educational institutions, and government agencies. The Prime Minister of Canada, curators at the Museum of Modern Art, the dean of your college, and the chief administrator of your local hospital are all managers. Remember, too, that managers bring to small organizations much the same kinds of skills—the ability to make decisions and respond to a variety of challenges—they bring to large ones.

Regardless of the nature and size of an organization, managers are among its most important resources. Consider, for example, recent events regarding three of the most visible managers in U.S. business:

■ After several years of phenomenal growth, Compaq Computer's sales stalled in 1991. The firm's board of directors ousted founder and CEO Rod Canion and replaced him with German-born and -educated Eckhard Pfeiffer. Pfeiffer had gone to work for Texas Instruments (TI) in 1964 and, at the age of 32, eventually became the firm's youngest vice president. Canion had hired Pfeiffer away from TI in 1983 to set up Compaq's European operation. After replacing his mentor in 1991, Pfeiffer quickly changed the firm from a bureaucratic, engineering-oriented operation into a flexible, sales-oriented company. By 1994, Compaq had regained its form and is now the largest PC maker in the world.[1]

■ When she was appointed CEO of Mattel in early 1997, Jill Barad became only the second woman to hold the top spot in a Fortune 500 firm. Barad had joined Mattel as a product manager in 1981. Over the next few years, she developed a reputation as a tough, no-nonsense manager. Her biggest contribution to the firm came when she took over the Barbie product line. Barad immediately began to identify new markets and product extensions, and today Barbie products account for more than 40 percent of Mattel's revenues. Barad was appointed to the firm's board of directors in 1991 and named president in 1992. Now that she's CEO, she plans to continue Mattel's aggressive international expansion, which she sees as the key to future growth.[2] ▶

■ In 1994, Continental Airlines was a firm headed nowhere. The company was saddled with enormous debt, high costs, declining revenues, low employee morale, and one of the poorest images in its industry. That's when Boeing executive Gordon Bethune was brought in to turn things around. Within months, Bethune had revamped the firm's reward system, overhauled its basic operational systems, and figured out dozens of ways to cut costs. As employees started to respond to companywide changes, Continental began to take off. Within a year, the firm was enjoying its highest profits ever, and the carrier was subsequently rated by J.D. Powers as having among the highest levels of customer satisfaction in the industry. Indeed, some experts see the results of Bethune's performance as one of the greatest corporate turnarounds in U.S. business history.[3]

Clearly, people like Eckhard Pfeiffer, Jill Barad, and Gordon Bethune are regarded highly in the business world. What can they do so well that their performance sets them apart so conspicuously? In this chapter, we describe the management process and the skills that managers must develop to perform their functions in organizations. You will then have a better feel for why organizations value managers so highly.

Jill Barad joined Mattel as a product manager in 1981. The next year, she took over Barbie—a dormant brand with $238 million in annual sales. Barad reincarnated her as Doctor Barbie, Business Executive Barbie, and a host of other career women. In 1996, sales of Barbie dolls and wardrobes reached $1.7 billion. When Barad became CEO of Mattel in 1997, she became one of only two women chief executives of a Fortune 500 company.

■ SETTING GOALS AND FORMULATING STRATEGY

The starting point in effective management is setting **goals**—objectives that a business hopes (and plans) to achieve. Every business needs goals. We begin by discussing the basic aspects of organizational goal setting. Remember, however, that deciding what it *intends* to do is only the first step for an organization. Managers must also make decisions about *actions* that will and will not achieve company goals. Decisions cannot be made on a problem-by-problem basis or merely to meet needs as they arise. At most companies, a broad program underlies those decisions. That program is called a *strategy*, and we will complete this section by detailing the basic steps in strategy formulation.

goal
Objective that a business hopes and plans to achieve

Setting Business Goals

Goals are performance targets—the means by which organizations and their managers measure success or failure at every level. In 1991, for example, Compaq Computer was perceived as "failing" not because it was losing money, but because it was falling short of goals for profit and growth. In this section, we identify the main purposes for which organizations establish goals, classify the basic levels of business goals, and describe the process by which goals are commonly set.

Purposes of Goal Setting   An organization functions systematically because it sets goals and plans accordingly. An organization commits its resources on all levels to achieving its goals. Specifically, we can identify four main purposes in organizational goal setting:

1. *Goal setting provides direction and guidance for managers at all levels.* If managers know precisely where the company is headed, there is less potential for error in the different units of the company. For example, 3M Corp. has a stated goal of earning 30 percent of its profits from sales of products less than four years old. 3M managers know that they must emphasize research and development and promote creativity and innovation.[4]

2. *Goal setting helps firms allocate resources.* Areas that are expected to grow, for example, will get first priority. The company allocates more resources to new projects with large sales potential than it allocates to mature products with established but stagnant sales potential. ▼

3. *Goal setting helps to define corporate culture.* General Electric's goal is to push each of its divisions to number one or number two in its industry. The result is a competitive (and often stressful) environment and a culture that rewards success and has little tolerance for failure.

4. *Goal setting helps managers assess performance.* If a unit sets a goal of increasing sales by 10 percent in a given year, managers in that unit who attain or exceed the goal can be rewarded. Units failing to reach the goal will also be compensated accordingly.

Kinds of Goals   Goals differ from company to company, depending on the firm's purpose and mission. Every enterprise has a *purpose*—a reason for being. Businesses seek profits, universities seek to discover and transmit new knowledge, government agencies seek to set and enforce public policy. Many enterprises also have missions and **mission statements**—statements of *how* they will achieve their purposes in the environments in which they conduct their business.

A company's purpose is usually easy to identify. Reebok, for example, attempts to make a profit by manufacturing and selling athletic shoes and related merchandise.

mission statement
Organization's statement of how it will achieve its purpose in the environment in which it conducts its business

The success of 3M Corp.'s Scotch-Brite Never Rust soap pads is an object lesson in setting goals and allocating resources. "We couldn't hit our growth targets without stepping up new products," explains CEO L.D. DeSimone, who demanded in 1991 that the company move much more quickly to bring new products from prototype to production. As a result, Never Rust (which won't rust or splinter because it's made from recycled plastic bottles) was the fastest product introduction in 3M history: ground was broken on a brand-new plant in March 1992, and the product was launched by March 1993.

IBM has the same purpose in selling computers and computer technology. The demands of change force many companies to rethink their missions—and thus to revise their statements of what they are and what they do. (We will discuss more fully the problems in—and some of the solutions to—managing change later in this chapter.)

At many companies, top management draws up and circulates detailed mission statements. Because such a statement reflects a company's understanding of its activities as a *marketer*, it is not easily described. For example, consider the similarities and differences between Timex and Rolex. Although both firms share a common purpose—to sell watches at a profit—they have very different missions. Timex sells low-cost, reliable watches in outlets ranging from department stores to corner drugstores. Rolex, sells high-quality, high-priced watches through selected jewelry stores.

Regardless of a company's purpose and mission, however, every firm has long-term, intermediate, and short-term goals:

- **Long-term goals** relate to extended periods of time—typically five years or more. For example, American Express might set a long-term goal of doubling the number of participating merchants during the next ten years. Kodak might adopt a long-term goal of increasing its share of the 35mm film market by 10 percent during the next eight years.

- **Intermediate goals** are set for a period of one to five years. Companies usually set intermediate goals in several areas. For example, the marketing department's goal might be to increase sales by 3 percent in two years. The production department might want to reduce expenses by 6 percent in four years. Human resources might seek to cut turnover by 10 percent in two years. Finance might aim for a 3-percent increase in return on investment in three years.

- **Short-term goals**—which are set for perhaps one year—are developed for several different areas. Increasing sales by 2 percent this year, cutting costs by 1 percent next quarter, and reducing turnover by 4 percent over the next six months are examples of short-term goals.

long-term goals
Goals set for extended periods of time, typically five years or more into the future

intermediate goals
Goals set for a period of one to five years into the future

short-term goals
Goals set for the very near future, typically less than one year

Formulating Strategy

Planning, then, is often concerned with the nuts and bolts of setting goals, choosing tactics, and establishing schedules. In contrast, strategy tends to have a wider scope. It is by definition a "broad program" that describes what an organization intends to do. It also includes the organization's responsiveness to new challenges and new needs.

For example, for years MCI Communications Corp. prospered by pursuing a straightforward strategy: taking long-distance telephone business away from AT&T. Relying on its marketing savvy and its image as a David challenging a Goliath, MCI grew into a $12 billion company. The firm's top managers then embarked on an ambitious change in strategy. MCI executives want to join the company's long-distance voice and data services businesses, local telephone operations, and new wireless digital technology into an integrated communications company unlike any other organization in the world. Strategically, MCI wants to be proactive, not reactive. Says CEO Bert C. Roberts, Jr.: "We really need to reposture this company into a leadership role, not a following role. You try to come up with a strategy based on what's *going* to happen—not what *is* happening."

> **"You try to come up with a strategy based on what's *going* to happen—not what *is* happening."**
> —Bert C. Roberts, Jr.
> *CEO of MCI Communications*

Among other things, therefore, MCI is expanding into foreign markets at a rapid pace. For example, it has launched major strategic alliances with firms in Canada, Mexico, and Europe. Because the U.S. long-distance market is growing at a pace of less than 5 percent a year, there are few domestic opportunities for significant growth. At the same time, overseas long-distance markets are growing at triple that pace.[5]

MCI's focus on integrated business operations and foreign expansion reflect its *strategy*. Like executives at MCI, most top managers must devote a great deal of attention (and creativity) to the formulation of business *strategies*—ways of meeting company goals at all levels. **Strategy formulation** involves three basic steps:[6]

1. Set strategic goals.
2. Analyze the organization and its environment.
3. Match the organization and its environment.

It is interesting to note at least one change in contemporary thinking about the role of strategy. Strategy was once the responsibility of top management and made its way into the everyday world of setting and implementing goals (planning) by means of a fairly rigid top-down process. Today, however, strategy formulation is often a much more "democratic" process.

Setting Strategic Goals

Strategic goals are long-term goals derived directly from a firm's mission statement. For example, when Eckhard Pfeiffer took over at Compaq, one of his first actions was to announce a new set of strategic goals. Most important was the decision to shift the company's focus away from engineering and toward marketing. As one longtime company engineer puts it, "We might do weird things if we were purely a technology-driven company. Eckhard Pfeiffer brought that sense of sanity back. Are we going to make money in it? How will customers respond?"

> ### "We might do weird things if we were purely a technology-driven company."
>
> —Compaq engineer Gary Stimac
> *on the company's strategic shift from engineering to marketing*

Pfeiffer's specific target was becoming the number-one PC maker in the world by 1996. Compaq achieved this goal by 1994—two years ahead of schedule. The two graphs in Figure 6.1 highlight the company's performance since Pfeiffer took over from Rod Canion. Although profits were off in 1994, sales grew by 36 percent. Pfeiffer would like to see $30 billion in annual sales by 2000, but at a yearly increase rate of 36 percent, Compaq would have sales of nearly $70 billion.[7]

Analyzing the Organization and Its Environment

Environmental analysis involves scanning the environment for threats and opportunities. Changing consumer tastes and hostile takeover offers are *threats*, as are new government regulations. Even more important threats come from new products and new competitors.

Consider the recent experience of American Express, the financial services company known for its green credit cards. Increased competition from rivals Visa and MasterCard combined with growing customers resistance to relatively high annual Amex fees had caused more than 2 million cardholders to cancel their accounts. To turn things around, CEO Harvey Golub set new goals and devised a new strategy. In analyzing the consequences of growing threats to his company, Golub realized that he had to attract new customers and encourage existing customers to spend more. The heart of Golub's strategy is a campaign to convince some of the company's 11 million U.S.

---

strategy formulation
Creation of a broad program for defining and meeting an organization's goals

strategic goals
Long-term goals derived directly from a firm's mission statement

environmental analysis
Process of scanning the business environment for threats and opportunities

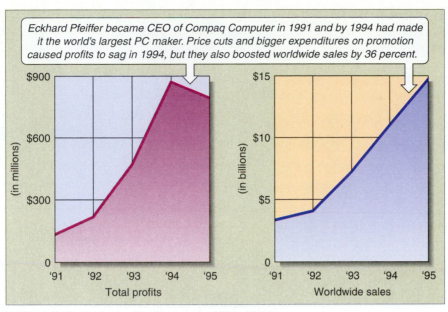

FIGURE 6.1 ◆ **Compaq: Performance, 1991–1995**

cardholders to start using a new family of Optima credit cards that offer different benefits to different users. Thus, while one card offers low interest rates, another requires no annual fee. Amex now hopes to attract about 1 million users to each of 15 different Optima cards.

According to Golub, the successful strategy is usually the one that enables a company to adapt. "The people that built buggies," he points out, "did not build cars." As for adapting, he adds that "you can do it yourself by shaping your business with new products. Or somebody else will do it for you. It's only a matter of time."[8]

> ## "You can [adapt] by shaping your business with new products. Or somebody else will do it for you. It's only a matter of time."
>
> —Harvey Golub
> *American Express CEO*

In addition to performing environmental analysis—that is, analysis of *external* factors—managers must also examine *internal* factors. The purpose of **organizational analysis** is to better understand a company's strengths and weaknesses. Strengths might include surplus cash, a dedicated work force, an ample supply of managerial talent, technical expertise, or little competition. The absence of any of these strengths could represent an important weakness.

When Gordon Bethune took over at Continental, he quickly saw a major weakness in a poorly motivated work force. Previous top managers had made promises to employees, but most of the promises went unmet. Bethune decided that one of his first priorities was to reestablish trust among his employees. Therefore, during the first month that Continental's on-time performance was in the top half of the industry, he mailed every employee in the company a check for $60. Along with the check was a letter promising that from that point forward, everyone would get another check for the same amount every time the airline was in the industrywide top five. When Continental

organizational analysis
Process of analyzing a firm's strengths and weaknesses

In addition to a poorly motivated work force, the organizational analysis conducted by Gordon Bethune, who became CEO of Continental Airlines Inc. in 1994, revealed the fact that "we had a crappy product and were trying to discount ourselves into profitability." Bethune thus turned his attention to improving operations. Between 1995 and 1996, Continental went from tenth to third in on-time service among the top-ten carriers. It went from tenth to second in baggage handling, and customer complaints were down 60 percent.

placed in the top three, every employee would receive a check for $100. This gesture told employees three things: (1) they were important, (2) they would be rewarded for their hard work, and (3) they had a CEO who was committed to winning as part of a team. Bethune's goal was to transform an organizational weakness into a strength. ▲

Matching the Organization and Its Environment   The final step in strategy formulation is matching environmental threats and opportunities against corporate strengths and weaknesses. The matching process is the heart of strategy formulation. More than any other facet of strategy, matching companies with their environments lays the foundation for successfully planning and conducting business. Mattel's Jill Barad, for example, recognizes that the U.S. domestic market for toys is not growing very quickly (an environmental threat), but that foreign growth is strong (an opportunity). Thus, she is working to match the firm's strengths with its opportunity to expand and grow in foreign markets.

Over the long term, this process may also determine whether a firm typically takes risks or behaves more conservatively. Either strategy can be successful. For example, Blue Bell is one of the most profitable ice cream makers in the world, even though it sells its products in only five states. Based in Brenham, Texas, Blue Bell controls more than 50 percent of the market in each state in which it does business. The firm has resisted the temptation to expand too quickly. Its success is based on product freshness and frequent deliveries—strengths that may suffer if the company grows too large.

A Hierarchy of Plans   Plans can be viewed on three levels: strategic, tactical, and operational. Managerial responsibilities are defined at each level. The levels constitute a hierarchy because implementing plans is practical only when there is a logical flow from one level to the next.

strategic plans
Plans reflecting decisions about resource allocations, company priorities, and steps needed to meet strategic goals

- ■ **Strategic plans** reflect decisions about resource allocations, company priorities, and the steps needed to meet strategic goals. They are usually determined by the board of directors and top management. Procter & Gamble's decision that viable products must be number one or number two within their respective categories is a matter of strategic planning.

TRENDS & CHALLENGES
BOOKSELLERS AT WAR

The bookselling business in the United States has long had one market leader: New York-based Barnes & Noble. Favoring the principle of strategic risk over that of safety, B&N chairman Leonard Riggio, a Brooklyn prizefighter's son, started with a single store in 1971 and now operates 400 superstores throughout the country. Riggio built an empire that poked holes in the tradition-bound world of bookselling. He offered books by the pound, shopping carts in which to carry them, deep discounts on bestsellers, couches on which to sit and read, and coffee bars—all tactics that gained the admiration of competitors. "Barnes & Noble," testifies the owner of a small chain in Austin, Texas, "understood the role of coffee, high ceilings, sofas, and chairs. They understood that a bookstore could be an extension of my living room. And no one knows like Riggio how to blow out a bestseller."

"Barnes & Noble understood the role of coffee, high ceilings, sofas, and chairs. They understood that a bookstore could be an extension of my living room."

—Gary Hoover
Owner of Bookstop, a small chain in Austin, Texas

Now, however, an unlikely competitor has emerged to challenge B&N for future control of the book superstore business. Borders Group Inc., a company founded in Ann Arbor, Michigan, is engaging in aggressive competition with B&N in cities across the country. The battle turned especially fierce when Borders opened its first superstore in New York City—turf long controlled by B&N and the heart of the publishing industry. The move into New York, says Borders CEO Robert DiRomualdo, is a sign of the future. "Almost every store we have is a direct Barnes & Noble competitor, often within sight of their stores. It's head-to-head competition in the future."

As Borders and B&N face off with each other in New York, Washington, D.C., Madison, Wisconsin, and other cities, they rely on powerful marketing tactics to capture customers' book-buying dollars. In its 38,000-square-foot New York City store (located in the World Trade Center), Borders offers books, periodicals, recordings, an "event" area, and a fifty-seat cafe that serves coffee imported from Africa and South America. "It's a media mall," commented one book lover who visited the store on opening day. Borders also differentiates itself from Barnes & Noble by marketing itself as a "cultural sanctuary" with salespeople who actually know something about books (and take a written exam to prove it). In contrast, B&N stores emphasize self-service—and, according to Borders, have the feel of a chain operation.

Although Leonard Riggio is prepared to defend the literary knowledge of his own staff, he also believes that B&N's greatest strength does not lie in its employees' ability to recite Shakespeare. Rather, he cites B&N's ability to apply the superstore concept to the bookselling business and its present leadership position. Meanwhile, Borders, having opened 80 of its 131 stores in a period of only two years, is moving at a breakneck pace to challenge its entrenched competitor. At stake are book sales that climbed 32 percent between 1990 and 1995 to more than $25 billion a year, as well as a book superstore market that promises to grow through the year 2000. Winning the battle of the books will undoubtedly depend on the ability of each company's management to analyze the changing competitive environment and to make thoughtful but rapid decisions.

■ **Tactical plans** are shorter-range plans for implementing specific aspects of the company's strategic plans. They typically involve upper and middle management. Coca-Cola's decision to increase sales in Europe by building European bottling facilities is an example of tactical planning.

■ **Operational plans,** which are developed by mid- and lower-level managers, set short-term targets for daily, weekly, or monthly performance. McDonald's, for example, establishes operational plans when it explains to franchisees precisely how Big Macs are to be cooked, warmed, and served.

tactical plans
Generally short-range plans concerned with implementing specific aspects of a company's strategic plans

operational plans
Plans setting short-term targets for daily, weekly, or monthly performance

■ THE MANAGEMENT PROCESS

management
Process of planning, organizing, directing, and controlling an organization's resources in order to achieve its goals

Management is the process of planning, organizing, directing, and controlling an organization's financial, physical, human, and information resources to achieve its goals. As managers, Eckhard Pfeiffer, Jill Barad, and Gordon Bethune oversee the use of all these resources. All aspects of a manager's job are interrelated. In fact, any given manager is likely to be engaged in each of these activities during the course of any given day.

Planning

planning
Management process of determining what an organization needs to do and how best to get it done

Determining what the organization needs to do and how best to get it done requires **planning.** Planning has three main components. As we have seen, it begins when managers determine the firm's goals. Next, they develop a comprehensive strategy for achieving those goals. After a strategy is developed, they design tactical and operational plans for implementing the strategy.

CEO Louis Gerstner had to determine how to cut costs at IBM while boosting sales and profits. His initial cost-cutting efforts focused primarily on reducing the work force and on closing less productive plants. At the same time, Gerstner committed IBM to the creation of new products and services that could generate additional revenues. Recently, growth in the Internet and networked computing have boosted sales of the firm's mainframe computers—products once almost written off as antiques.

As a result of these efforts, IBM saw profits in 1995, as it became more and more competitive. As you can see from Figure 6.2, investors have responded favorably: IBM's share price—which had plummeted to a mere $52 by the time Gerstner arrived in April 1993—topped $129 in March 1996.[9]

FIGURE 6.2 ◆ IBM: Stock Price, 1993–1996

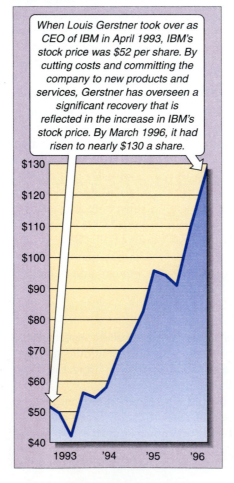

When Louis Gerstner took over as CEO of IBM in April 1993, IBM's stock price was $52 per share. By cutting costs and committing the company to new products and services, Gerstner has overseen a significant recovery that is reflected in the increase in IBM's stock price. By March 1996, it had risen to nearly $130 a share.

Organizing

As part of his efforts to change the way Compaq operated, Eckhard Pfeiffer sought to make the firm less bureaucratic and more responsive to changing technology and competition. Under former management, research and development, manufacturing, and marketing were all run as large, centralized groups. As the firm grew, these departments also grew—to the point at which it took too long to make decisions and take action. Pfeiffer broke the company down into several small units, each of which is now assigned responsibility for its own R&D, manufacturing, and marketing. As a result, each unit is now much more flexible and responsive. This process—determining the best way to arrange a business's resources and activities into a coherent structure—is called **organizing.** (We will explore this topic further in Chapter 7.)

Directing

Managers have the power to give orders and demand results. Directing, however, involves more complex activities. In **directing,** a manager works to guide and motivate employees to meet the firm's objectives. Shortly after reorganizing Compaq, for instance, Eckhard Pfeiffer informed his engineers that he wanted them to cut product costs, shorten the lead time required to get new products to market, and boost product quality—all at the same time. They were also informed that how they managed to meet these goals was up to them. They accepted his challenge and have so far exceeded the CEO's expectations.

Controlling

Controlling is the process of monitoring a firm's performance to make sure that it is meeting its goals. All CEOs must pay close attention to costs and performance. When a firm is small, monitoring costs is especially important. The same task, however, faces managers at the largest firms. After restoring employee morale at Continental, Gordon Bethune next focused his attention on costs. Two of the biggest variable costs in the airline industry are flight delays (refunding fares, paying for meals and lodging for delayed passengers) and misplaced luggage (replacing and rerouting luggage, buying replacement items). Bethune introduced major programs to bring both sets of costs down to acceptable levels.

Figure 6.3 illustrates the control process which begins when management establishes standards, often for financial performance. For example, if a company wants to

organizing
Management process of determining how best to arrange an organization's resources and activities into a coherent structure

directing
Management process of guiding and motivating employees to meet an organization's objectives

controlling
Management process of monitoring an organization's performance to ensure that it is meeting its goals

FIGURE 6.3 ◆ The Control Process

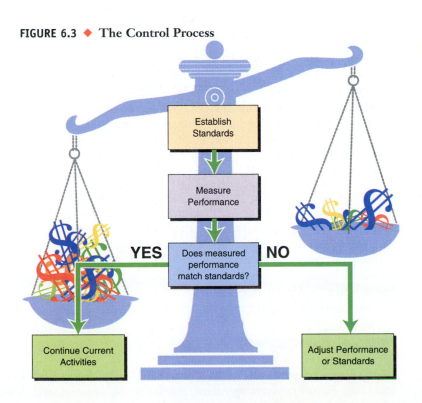

increase sales by 20 percent over the next ten years, an appropriate standard might be an increase of about 2 percent a year.

Managers then measure actual performance against standards. If the two figures agree, the organization continues along its present course. If they vary significantly, however, one or the other needs adjustment. For instance, if sales have increased 2.1 percent by the end of the first year, things are probably fine. If sales have dropped 1 percent, some revision in plans may be needed. Perhaps the original goal should be lowered or more money should be spent on advertising. (We will discuss the control process in more detail in Chapter 7.)

■ TYPES OF MANAGERS

Although all managers plan, organize, direct, and control, not all managers have the same degree of responsibility for these activities. Thus, it is helpful to classify managers according to levels and areas of responsibility.

Levels of Management

The three basic levels of management are *top*, *middle*, and *first-line*. Not surprisingly, most firms have more middle managers than top managers and more first-line managers than middle managers. Both the power of managers and the complexity of their duties increase as they move up the ladder.

top managers
Managers responsible to the board of directors and stockholders for a firm's overall performance and effectiveness

Top Managers   Like Eckhard Pfeiffer, Jill Barad, and Gordon Bethune, the fairly small number of executives who guide the fortunes of most companies are **top managers.** Common titles include *president*, *vice president*, *treasurer*, *chief executive officer (CEO)*, and *chief financial officer (CFO)*. Top managers are responsible for the overall performance and effectiveness of the firm. They set general policies, formulate strategies, approve all significant decisions, and represent the company in dealings with other firms and with government bodies.

middle managers
Managers responsible for implementing the strategies, policies, and decisions made by top managers

Middle Managers   Middle managers occupy positions of considerable autonomy and importance. Titles such as *plant manager*, *operations manager*, and *division manager* designate middle-management slots. In general, **middle managers** are responsible for implementing the strategies, policies, and decisions made by top managers. For example, if top management decides to bring out a new product in 12 months or to cut costs by 5 percent in the next quarter, middle management must decide how to meet these goals. The manager of a Compaq factory, Mattel warehouse, or Continental hub operation will likely be a middle manager.

first-line managers
Managers responsible for supervising the work of employees

First-Line Managers   **First-line managers** hold titles like *supervisor*, *office manager*, and *group leader*. Although they spend most of their time working with and supervising the employees who report to them, their activities are not limited to that arena. At a building site, for example, the *project manager* not only ensures that workers are carrying out construction as specified by the architect but also interacts extensively with materials suppliers, community officials, and middle- and upper-level managers at the home office. A district sales manager for Mattel and the flight services manager on a specific Continental flight are also first-line managers.

Areas of Management

In any large company, top, middle, and first-line managers work in a variety of areas, including *human resources*, *operations*, *marketing*, *information*, and *finance*. For the most

© 1998 Charles Barsotti *from* The Cartoon Bank,™ Inc.

part, these areas correspond to the types of managerial skills described later in this chapter and to the wide range of business principles and activities discussed in the rest of this book.

Human Resource Managers   Most companies have *human resource managers* to hire and train employees, to evaluate performance, and to determine compensation. At large firms, separate departments deal with recruiting and hiring, wage and salary levels, and labor relations. A smaller firm may have a single department—or a single person—responsible for all human resource activities. (Some key issues in human resource management are discussed in Part 4.)

Operations Managers   As we will see in Chapter 11, the term *operations* refers to the systems by which a firm produces goods and services. Among other duties, operations managers are responsible for production, inventory, and quality control. Manufacturing companies like Texas Instruments, Ford, and Caterpillar have a strong need for operations managers at many levels. Such firms typically have a *vice president for operations* (top), *plant managers* (middle), and *production supervisors* (first-line). In recent years, sound operations management practices have become increasingly important to a variety of service organizations. (Operations management is examined more fully in Part 5.)

Marketing Managers   As we will see in Chapter 13, *marketing* encompasses the development, pricing, promotion, and distribution of goods and services. *Marketing managers* are responsible for getting products from producers to consumers. Marketing is especially important for firms that manufacture consumer products, such as Procter & Gamble, Coca-Cola, and Levi Strauss. Such firms often have large numbers of marketing managers at several levels. For example, a large consumer-products firm is likely to have a *vice president for marketing* (top), several *regional marketing managers* (middle), and several *district sales managers* (first-line). (The different areas of marketing are discussed in Part 6.)

Information Managers   Occupying a fairly new managerial position in many firms, *information managers* design and implement systems to gather, organize, and distribute information. Huge increases in both the sheer volume of information and the ability to manage it have led to the emergence of this important function.

Although relatively few in number, the ranks of information managers are growing at all levels. Some firms have a top management position called a *chief information officer*. Middle managers help design information systems for divisions or plants. Computer systems managers within smaller businesses are usually first-line managers. (Information management is discussed in more detail in Chapter 12.)

According to Hilton Hotels Corp. CEO Stephen Bollenbach, the best chief financial officers are much more than bean counters who issue dry annual reports about other managers' ideas and deals. "The key to success as a CFO," he says, "is establishing the strategy for the entire company." When he was CFO at Walt Disney Co., Bollenbach's staff conceived and engineered Disney's 1995 merger with Capital Cities/ABC. Had the deal been handled by investment bankers and securities firms, the fees alone would have cost Disney at least $20 million.

Financial Managers   Nearly every company has *financial managers* to plan and oversee its accounting functions and financial resources. Levels of financial management may include *chief financial officer (CFO)*▲ or *vice president for finance* (top), a *division controller* (middle), and an *accounting supervisor* (first-line). Some institutions— NationsBank and Prudential for example—have even made effective financial management the company's reason for being. (Financial management is treated in more detail in Part 7.)[10]

Other Managers   Some firms also employ other specialized managers. Many companies, for example, have public relations managers. Chemical and pharmaceutical companies like Monsanto and Merck have research and development managers. The range of possibilities is very broad, and the areas of management are limited only by the needs and imagination of the firm.

■ BASIC MANAGEMENT SKILLS

While the range of managerial positions is almost limitless, the success that people enjoy in those positions is often limited by their skills and abilities. Effective managers must develop *technical, human relations, conceptual, decision-making,* and *time-management skills.*

Technical Skills

technical skills
Skills needed to perform specialized tasks

The skills needed to perform specialized tasks are called **technical skills.** A secretary's ability to type, an animator's ability to draw, and an accountant's ability to audit a company's records are all examples of technical skills. People develop technical skills through a combination of education and experience. Technical skills are especially important for first-line managers. Most of these managers spend considerable time helping employees solve work-related problems, training them in more efficient procedures, and monitoring performance.

Human Relations Skills

A few years ago, Hyatt Hotels checked 379 corporate employees into the chain's 98 hotels. They were not, however, treated as guests. Rather, they were asked to make beds, carry luggage, and perform the other tasks necessary to make a big hotel function. Top management at Hyatt believes that learning more about the work of lower-level employees will allow executives to understand them better as human beings (and co-workers).

The Hyatt experiment was designed to test and improve the **human relations skills** of upper-level managers—that is, skills in understanding and getting along with other people. A manager with poor human relations skills may have trouble getting along with subordinates, cause valuable employees to quit or transfer, and contribute to poor morale.

While human relations skills are important at all levels, they are probably most important for middle managers, who must often act as bridges between top managers, first-line managers, and managers from other areas of the organization. Managers should possess good communication skills. Many managers have found that being able to understand others—and to get them to understand—can go far toward maintaining good relations in an organization.

human relations skills
Skills in understanding and getting along with people

Conceptual Skills

Conceptual skills refer to a person's ability to think in the abstract, to diagnose and analyze different situations, and to see beyond the present situation. Conceptual skills help managers recognize new market opportunities (and threats). They can also help managers analyze the probable outcomes of their decisions. The need for conceptual skills differs at various management levels: top managers depend most on conceptual skills, first-line managers least. Although the purposes and everyday needs of various jobs differ, conceptual skills are needed in almost any job-related activity.

conceptual skills
Abilities to think in the abstract, diagnose and analyze different situations, and see beyond the present situation

Decision-Making Skills

Decision-making skills include the ability to define problems and select the best course of action. Figure 6.4 illustrates the basic steps in decision making.

1. *Define the problem, gather facts, and identify alternative solutions.* Current management at Schwinn recently realized that their predecessors had made some serious errors in assuming that mountain bikes were just a fad. The opposite proved to be true, and Schwinn's share of the bicycle market had dropped dramatically.

decision-making skills
Skills in defining problems and selecting the best courses of action

FIGURE 6.4 ◆ **The Decision-Making Process**

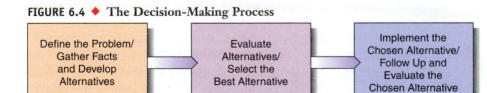

2. *Evaluate each alternative and select the best one.* Managers at Schwinn acknowledged that they had to take corrective action. They discussed such alternatives as buying a mountain bike maker, launching their own line of mountain bikes, or refocusing on other product lines. They chose to develop their own line of mountain bikes and did so in 1994.

3. *Implement the chosen alternative, periodically following up and evaluating the effectiveness of that choice.* Today Schwinn seems to be on track following its entry into the mountain bike market. Companywide sales and profits have begun to increase, and its new products are now attracting attention from the top mountain bike racers in the world.

Time Management Skills

time management skills
Skills associated with the productive use of time

Time management skills refer to the productive use that managers make of their time. In one recent year, for example, IBM CEO Louis Gerstner was paid $12.4 million in salary and bonuses. Assuming that he worked 50 hours a week and took two weeks' vacation, Gerstner earned $4,960 an hour—about $266 per minute. Any time that Gerstner wastes clearly represents a large cost to IBM and its stockholders. Most managers, of course, receive much smaller salaries than Gerstner. Their time, however, is valuable, and poor use of it still translates into costs and wasted productivity.

To manage time effectively, managers must address three leading causes of wasted time:

1. *Paperwork.* Some managers spend too much time deciding what to do with letters and or reports. Most documents of this sort are routine and can be handled quickly. Managers must learn to recognize those documents that require more attention.

2. *The telephone.* Experts estimate that managers get interrupted by the telephone every five minutes. To manage this time more effectively, they suggest having a secretary screen all calls and setting aside a certain block of time each day to return the important ones.

3. *Meetings.* Many managers spend as much as four hours a day in meetings. To help keep this time productive the person handling the meeting should specify a clear agenda, start on time, keep everyone focused on the agenda, and end on time.

Management Skills for the 1990s

Finally, we should note some of the major challenges that tomorrow's managers face as they prepare to enter the twenty-first century. We will touch upon two of the most significant challenges: *global management* and *technology.*

Global Management Skills   Tomorrow's managers must equip themselves with the special tools, techniques, and skills necessary to compete in a global environment. They will need to understand foreign markets, cultural differences, and the motives and practices of foreign rivals.

On a more practical level, businesses will need managers who are capable of understanding international operations. In the past, most U.S. businesses hired local managers to run their operations in the various countries in which they operated. More recently, however, the trend has been to transfer U.S. managers to foreign locations. This practice helps firms better transfer their corporate cultures to foreign operations. In addition, foreign assignments help managers become better prepared for international competition as they advance within the organization. General Motors now has almost 500 U.S. managers in foreign posts.[11]

Management and Technology Skills   Another significant issue facing tomorrow's managers is technology, especially as it relates to communication. Managers have always had to deal with information. In today's world, however, the amount of information has reached staggering proportions. In the United States alone, for example, there are already 28 million electronic mailboxes. New forms of technology have added to a manager's ability to process information while simultaneously making it even more important to organize and interpret an ever-increasing wealth of input.

Technology has also begun to change the way the interaction of managers shapes corporate structures. Computer networking, for example, exists because it is no longer too expensive to put a computer on virtually every desk in the company. In turn, this elaborate network controls the flow of the firm's lifeblood—information. Information no longer flows strictly up and down through hierarchies. It now flows to everyone at once. As a result, decisions are made more quickly—and more people are directly involved. With e-mail, teleconferencing, and other forms of communication, neither time nor distance—nor such corporate "boundaries" as departments and divisions—can prevent people from working more closely together. More than ever, bureaucracies are breaking down, while planning, decision making, and other activities are beginning to benefit from group building and teamwork.

This is why Bill Raduchel, chief information officer of Sun Microsystems, goes so far as to say that "e-mail is a major cultural event—it changes the way you run the organization."[12]

"E-mail is a major cultural event—
it changes the way you run the organization."

—Bill Raduchel
Chief information officer at Sun Microsystems

■ MANAGEMENT AND THE CORPORATE CULTURE

Consider the following story about the way in which one company set about creating a unique working environment for its employees:

■ Firms in the ultracompetitive software industry tend to rely on a different breed of worker than firms in more traditional arenas. Often, software developers ignore the traditional 9-to-5 mentality in favor of 80- to 100-hour work weeks. They seem to value their work for its own sake, not just for the income they receive, but they also value autonomy and workstyles that mesh with their lifestyles—casual, unfettered, and highly interactive. Hyperion Software Corp. has created a variety of employee "perks." For example, each wing of the firm's headquarters in Stamford, Connecticut, boasts kitchens stocked with snacks and drinks. There is also a gym on the premises, as well as a nature trail that rambles through the firm's 38-acre campus-like setting. Outside the cafeteria, a pool table awaits anyone who is suddenly in the mood for a game.[13] ▶

Not surprisingly, this setting contrasts starkly with that of, say, Exxon, the nation's largest oil company. Employees at Exxon work in relatively austere surroundings, wear formal business attire, and work fairly regimented work schedules. Both Hyperion and

The success of Hyperion Software Corp. depends on its ability to create new lines of financial management software. To do this, it must attract the best software designers to its Fairfield County, Connecticut, headquarters—which is a long way from such desirable locations as Boston and Silicon Valley. For Hyperion, the solution to this problem has been providing the right atmosphere in a relaxed workplace. "We don't care how you look or dress," says CFO Lucy Ricciardi. "We're looking for people who are geniuses at writing software."

corporate culture
The shared experiences, stories, beliefs, and norms that characterize an organization

Exxon are each quite successful in their respective industries, but they differ significantly in at least one obvious respect. Just as every individual has a unique personality, so every company has a unique identity, called **corporate culture:** the shared experiences, stories, beliefs, and norms that characterize an organization.

A strong corporate culture serves several purposes:

■ It directs employees' efforts and helps everyone work toward the same goals.
■ It helps newcomers learn accepted behaviors.
■ It gives each organization its own identity, much as personalities give identity to people.

Communicating the Culture and Managing Change

Corporate culture influences management philosophy, style, and behavior. Managers, therefore, must carefully consider the kind of culture they want for their organization, then work to nourish that culture by communicating with everyone who works there. Wal-Mart, for example, is acutely conscious of the need to spread the message of its culture as it opens new stores in new areas. One of the company's methods is to regularly assign veteran managers to lead employees in new territories.

Communicating the Culture   To use its culture to a firm's advantage, managers must accomplish several tasks, all of which hinge on effective communication:

■ Managers must have a clear understanding of the culture.
■ Managers must transmit the culture to others in the organization. Communication is thus one of the aims in training and orienting newcomers. A clear and meaningful statement of the organization's mission is also a valuable communication tool.
■ Managers can maintain the culture by rewarding and promoting those who understand it and work toward maintaining it.

Managing Change   Not surprisingly, organizations must sometimes change their cultures. In such cases, they must also communicate the nature of the change to both

TRENDS & CHALLENGES

CULTURE SHOCK AT SHONEY'S

There is a *before* and *after* version of the corporate culture at Shoney's Inc., the family-style restaurant chain based in Nashville, Tennessee. In the *before* version, chairman and co-founder Raymond Danner was known to order white managers to fire black employees when too many blacks staffed restaurants in white neighborhoods. When managers balked, their own jobs were threatened. In the *after* version, top management embraced racial diversity as a positive corporate value—one that was, in fact, crucial to corporate survival.

Although some critics trace Shoney's cultural rebirth solely to the loss of a class-action lawsuit brought by minority employees, other observers contend that the law suit cannot explain the depth of change that has transformed the organization. Nor can it explain the voluntary actions the company has taken to right past wrongs. These realities reflect management's determination that Shoney's represent the diversity of its job pool and customer base. According to one Florida attorney involved in the lawsuit, Shoney's radical shift reflects a genuine change of heart. "I've been in this business for 20 years," reports Thomas A. Warren, "and I've seen lots of whitewashes. But this is real. Black people know this is a company where they can get ahead."

More than 100 current and former employees filed suit against Shoney's in April 1989, charging the company with systematically discriminating against blacks in hiring and promotion. Ultimately, the suit was a catalyst for top management change. J. Mitchell Boyd replaced Danner as company chairman and took up the mission of making Shoney's more sensitive to the needs and rights of minorities. At first, he met resistance. At the time, for instance, the corporation had no affirmative action program. When Boyd suggested a monthly sensitivity workshop for top managers, the board of directors rejected the notion that the company needed any such help. "The average age of the board," recalls Boyd, "was 72, and those guys just couldn't comprehend how much the world had changed." In the board's view, Boyd adds, "Ray Danner had simply said that there were too many black people in a restaurant, and they couldn't see anything wrong with that."

Under Boyd, Shoney's nevertheless began the slow process of cultural change. The firm apologized for its affronts to the black community and, working with the Southern Christian Leadership Conference, voluntarily agreed to spend millions of dollars to hire minority workers and contract with minority firms. Black leaders at the SCLC were convinced that changes at the company were real.

> **"In the board's view, [former CEO] Ray Danner had simply said that there were too many black people in a restaurant, and they couldn't see anything wrong with that."**
>
> —Shoney's CEO J. Mitchell Boyd
> *on resistance to his new diversity policies*

Boyd, however, left Shoney's in December 1989 because the board remained unwilling to settle the lawsuit. Leonard H. Roberts, former president and CEO of Arby's Inc., succeeded Boyd and aggressively continued his policies, recruiting minorities and women for key positions and raising the salaries of black employees. "If Shoney's had to rely upon a white, male labor pool to grow its business," charged Roberts, "it was in trouble. Forget about the lawsuit. Even if it had never existed, the company still would have changed." (The suit was finally settled in 1993—for a whopping $134.5 million.) As the most visible signs of change in its employment practices, Shoney's now employs 83 black dining room supervisors, two black corporate vice presidents, and one black board member.

Between 1989 and 1993, Roberts also continued the program of targeting minority-owned companies as suppliers. By 1996, Shoney's had spent $194 million in contracts with minority-owned firms—26 percent more than it had pledged seven years earlier. Today C. Stephen Lynn, who succeeded Roberts as CEO in 1993, is committed to a corporate culture that values inclusion rather than discrimination. "Every great company," he believes, "has sins of the past. We learn more from our defeats and shortcomings."

employees and customers. According to the CEOs of several companies that have undergone radical change in the last decade or so, the process usually goes through three stages:[14]

1. *At the highest level, analysis of the company's environment highlights extensive change as the most effective response to its problems.* This period is typically characterized by conflict and resistance.

2. *Top management begins to formulate a vision of a new company.* Whatever that vision, it must include renewed focus on the activities of competitors and the needs of customers.

3. *The firm sets up new systems for appraising and compensating employees that enforce its new values.* The purpose is to give the new culture solid shape from within.

Continued from page 127

Targeting Well-Heeled Consumers Who Wait for Nothing

A Footnote on Customer Service

How do you convince consumers who are used to instant shopping gratification to wait up to three weeks for a new pair of shoes? That's the management challenge that Jeffrey Silverman faced in planning the operation of Custom Foot.

Silverman's answer was to combine a novel high-tech shopping experience with old-fashioned customer service. At Custom Foot, customers (who typically spend about half an hour in the store on their first visit) encounter a sales staff trained to build relationships. Although measurements are computerized, sales assis-

tants help customers through the shoe design process and ask questions about preferred style and fit and foot problems. "We want to know if someone actually prefers loafers even though they may have asked to see something else," explains director of marketing Lareen Kirsch. Information is then computerized so that it can be used for both target marketing and customer service. The computer enables store managers to alert customers to new styles in their preference categories and helps sales associates make purchase recommendations.

All of this is handled in a pleasant contemporary environment in which complimentary Pellegrino water, amaretto cookies, and biscotti are served. Anxious consumers who worry that their shoes won't fit or that they won't like the way they look are guaranteed their money back if their feet aren't completely satisfied. Time-conscious consumers realize that their personal data will be available the next time they shop, and as a little icing on the cake, every pair of shoes is delivered with a free shoe horn.

Case Questions

1. Describe the various aspects of goal setting and strategic planning involved in starting Custom Foot.
2. Explain why careful strategic planning was essential to the success of this business.
3. What were the key aspects of Silverman's environmental and organizational analysis?
4. A high level of customer service is a critical aspect of Custom Foot's strategic plans. These plans were developed by top management. However, it is up to first-line managers to carry them out. Discuss the potential opportunities and problems inherent in this situation.
5. As Custom Foot grows, what types of managers will become vital to the success of the operation?

SUMMARY OF LEARNING OBJECTIVES

1. **Explain the importance of setting *goals* and formulating *strategies* as the starting points of effective management.** *Goals*—the performance targets of an organization—can be *long-term*, *intermediate*, or *short-term*. They provide direction for managers, help managers decide how to allocate limited resources, define the corporate culture, and help managers assess performance. Strategies—the methods that a company uses to meet its stated goals—involve three major activities: setting strategic goals, analyzing the organization and its environment, and matching the organization and its environment. These strategies are translated into *strategic*, *tactical*, and *operational plans*.

2. **Describe the four activities that constitute the *management process*.** *Management* is the process of planning, organizing, directing, and controlling an organization's financial, physical, human, and information resources to achieve the

organization's goals. *Planning* means determining what the company needs to do and how best to get it done. *Organizing* means determining how best to arrange a business's resources and the necessary jobs into an overall structure. *Directing* means guiding and motivating employees to meet the firm's objectives. *Controlling* means monitoring the firm's performance to ensure that it is meeting its goals.

3. **Identify *types of managers* by level and area.**   Managers can be differentiated in two ways: by level and by area. By level, *top managers* set policies, formulate strategies, and approve decisions. *Middle managers* implement strategies, policies, and decisions. *First-line managers* usually work with and directly supervise employees. Areas of management include human resources, operations, marketing, information, and finance. Managers at all levels may be found in every area of a company.

4. **Describe the five basic *management skills*.**   Most managers agree that five basic management skills are necessary for success. *Technical skills* are associated with performing specialized tasks. *Human relations skills* are associated with understanding and getting along with other people. *Conceptual skills* are the abilities to think in the abstract, to diagnose and analyze different situations, and to see beyond present circumstances. *Decision-making skills* allow managers to define problems and to select the best course of action. *Time management skills* refer to the productive use that managers make of their time.

5. **Explain the importance of *corporate culture*.**   A strong, well-defined culture can help a business reach its goals and can influence management styles. In addition to having a clear understanding of *corporate culture*, managers must be able to communicate it effectively to others. Communication is especially important when organizations find it necessary to make changes in the culture. Top management must establish new values that reflect a vision of a new company, and these values must play a role in appraising and compensating employee performance.

STUDY QUESTIONS AND EXERCISES

Review

1. What are the four main purposes of setting goals in an organization?
2. Identify and explain the three basic steps in strategy formulation.
3. Relate the five basic management skills to the four activities in the management process. For example, which skills are most important in leading?
4. What is corporate culture? How is it formed? How is it sustained?

Analysis

5. Select any group of which you are a member (your company, your family, or a club or organization, for example). Explain how planning, organizing, directing, and controlling are practiced in that group.
6. Identify managers by level and area at your school, college, or university.

7. In what kind of company would the technical skills of top managers be more important than human relations or conceptual skills? Are there organizations in which conceptual skills are not important?

8. How well do you manage your own time? What activities or habits waste your time?

Application Exercises

9. Interview the manager at any level of a local company. Identify that manager's job according to level and area. Show how planning, organizing, directing, and controlling are part of this person's job. Inquire about the manager's education and work experience. Which management skills are most important for this manager's job?

10. Compare and contrast the corporate cultures of two companies that do business in most communities. Be sure to choose two companies in the same industry—for example, a Sears department store and a Wal-Mart discount store.

BUILDING YOUR BUSINESS SKILLS

This exercise enhances the following SCANS workplace competencies: demonstrating basic skills, demonstrating thinking skills, exhibiting interpersonal skills, and working with information.

Goal

To encourage students to think about the use—and overuse—of electronic mail

Situation

With more than 23 million workers now connected to electronic mail—and three times that number expected to be connected in the year 2000—learning to handle the billions of e-mail messages that are sent each year is becoming an urgent management issue for all workers. Workers must learn to evaluate when e-mail is appropriate and when it is not.

Method

Join with three or four other students to decide how you would handle the following e-mail–related situations. Discuss your analysis in terms of the nature of management and the specific effects of e-mail on the corporate culture:

■ You receive 80 to 100 e-mail messages a day. Many are from co-workers who send you copies of messages directed to other employees. What steps would you take to reduce this information overload?

- As a manager, you regularly send subordinates major work assignments that arrive late Friday afternoon, minutes before the end of the work week. Needless to say, your popularity has not risen as a result of this practice. How do you respond to your critics?

- You are under deadline pressure to issue peformance appraisals to your two-person staff. Should you send these documents via e-mail or find time for face-to-face meetings? Support your decision.

- You are one of four people involved in the decision to hire a top manager for your division. After your co-workers interview each job candidate, they e-mail you with comments about the candidate's strengths and weaknesses. As a result, you know what others think about the candidate before you conduct your interview. Do you see instant communication as an advantage or disadvantage in this situation?

Follow-Up

1. Electronic mail is changing not only the nature of corporate communication but the nature of management. Provide reasons why you agree or disagree with this statement.

2. Does e-mail fit into the category of an informal phone conversation or a written document? Explain why this distinction might make an important difference in the corporate culture of a given organization.

THE OPENING CASE FOR CHAPTER 6 DESCRIBES A SMALL BUT RAPIDLY GROWING BUSINESS CALLED CUSTOM FOOT, WHICH YOU CAN VISIT AT THE FOLLOWING WEBSITE:

http://www.thecustomfoot.com/

Browse the Custom Foot Website, and then consider the following questions:

1. Review each of the features in Custom Foot's Website. What new information and/or information about changes at the company supplement or update the material presented in the textbook?

2. By comparing the textbook case with the supplemental information that you have gathered from the Website, evaluate the apparent effectiveness of Custom Foot's overall strategy for marketing its product.

3. Evaluate the firm's performance in reaching its goals.

4. Judging from the company's description of its activities, which aspects of the management process play the most important role in Custom Foot's operations? Which management skills account most directly to its rapid growth?

5. What are the organizational strengths and weakness of Custom Foot? What environmental threats does it face? What opportunities does it enjoy?

6. What events in its industry will most likely shape the firm's culture in the future?

ORGANIZING THE BUSINESS ENTERPRISE

United Airlines Gives Managers the Power to Manage

FOR EMPLOYEES, UNITED'S SKIES ARE NOW FRIENDLIER

Are long ladders a sign of a successful corporate reorganization? At United Airlines they are. Long ladders symbolize the company's new approach to management—an approach that often depends on teamwork to solve problems. A case in point: a team made up of pilots, ramp workers, and managers sat down together—for the first time—to figure out how to power planes idling at the gate with electricity instead of jet fuel. Electricity would save money, but because their short working ladders prevented ramp workers from plugging electrical cables into the aircraft, using electricity was literally out of reach.

Not surprisingly, the solution—longer ladders—was a no-brainer for team members, and not simply because several of them actually knew the situation first hand. What *is* surprising, perhaps, was the failure of traditional managers to see that when the problem is short ladders, the solution is probably longer ladders. At United, it seems, managers far removed from the loading gates had no way of assessing even the simplest problem. Worse yet, a stringent top-down management style prevented them from consulting with the right people—in

> **"It wasn't uncommon to get a request for capital on my desk that had 13 to 14 signatures on it before it got to me."**
>
> —John A. Edwardson,
> *President and Chief Operating Officer of United Airlines*

this case, ramp workers at loading gates. According to Robert M. Sturtz, United's top fuel administrator, the company was able to identify the real problem only when management resorted to teamwork. In this instance, the result has been an annual savings of $20 million in fuel costs.

In 1994, United's 80,000 employees bought the carrier, creating one of the country's largest *employee stock ownership plans (ESOP)*. Since then, United has been transformed from a top-driven hierarchical organization into one that values teamwork, initiative, and creativity. Chairman and CEO Gerald Greenwald has also reduced the number of management layers and removed many functional divisions in favor of a horizontal integration of resources that focuses on

markets. "We are," he proclaims, "no longer a company that operates by command and control."

The key markets that now correspond to United's internal divisions are North America, international, cargo, shuttles, and new business development. Each division is headed by a senior vice president who reports directly to President and Chief Operating Officer John A. Edwardson. In addition, all operational groups, including on-board services and flight operations, report to the president. In short, authority has been decentralized, and divisional managers have the power to run their businesses.

Reorganization has also increased the authority of divisional and mid-level managers. Previously, such functional operations as airport services and reservations were worlds unto themselves, with their own organizational structures and chains of command. Because members of different areas rarely communicated, airline operations often suffered. According to James E. Goodwin, Senior Vice President for North America, United's Honolulu station nicely illustrated the poor coordination of the old system. "The sales organization," explains Goodwin, "reported to someone in Los Angeles, who then reported to someone in Chicago. The reservations function reported directly to Chicago. The airport manager reported to someone in San Francisco. In many cases, the people never even knew each other."

This arragement led to open conflicts among departments. "The sales organization," recalls Goodwin, "would go out and make commitments to the customer that they couldn't deliver at the airport. All they could do is say, 'I only sell it. I don't make it.'" Worse yet, customer service problems had to be transferred to headquarters for resolution. When the new management discarded this function-based organizational structure, managers received both greater power and the resources needed to use it. To further speed decision making, unnecessary managerial levels were eliminated, thus creating a "flatter" organizational structure (the old one resembled a pyramid). Before that, recalls Edwards, "it wasn't uncommon to get a request for capital on my desk that had thirteen to fourteen signatures on it before it got to me."

What effect have these changes had on United's performance? Thanks in large part to improved productivity, United is taking market share away from rivals American and Delta and has solidified its position as America's number one air carrier. In addition, operating margins are fatter, the stock price has climbed, and knowledgeable

outsiders have formed a favorable view of United's improved performance. Reports one industry analyst at Merrill Lynch, "United has hard statistics that show the company is working differently than in the past."

The reorganization of United Airlines shows the importance of effective organization to operations and profits. United's reorganization touches many of the topics that we explore in this chapter, including the decision-making hierarchy, the decentralization of authority, accountability, span of control, team authority, and the failure of a functional organizational structure.

The need to fit (or in United's case, to refit) structure to operations is common to all companies, large and small. Whether a company employs 5 people or 50,000, it needs organization to function. In this chapter, we consider the elements of business organization and the basic structures that firms typically use. By focusing on the learning objectives of this chapter, you will better understand the importance of business organization and the ways in which both formal and informal aspects of its structure affect the decisions that a business makes.

After reading this chapter, you should be able to

1. Discuss the elements that influence a firm's *organizational structure*

2. Describe *specialization* and *departmentalization* as the building blocks of organizational structure

3. Distinguish between *responsibility* and *authority* and explain the differences in decision making in *centralized* and *decentralized organizations*

4. Explain the differences between *functional, divisional, matrix,* and *international* organization structures

5. Describe the *informal organization* and discuss *intrapreneuring*

Continued on page 172

■ WHAT IS ORGANIZATIONAL STRUCTURE?

What do we mean by the term *organizational structure?* Consider a simple analogy. In some ways, a business is like an automobile. All cars have engines, four wheels, fenders, and other structural components. They all have passenger compartments, storage areas, and various operating systems (fuel, braking, climate control). Although each component has a distinct purpose, it must also work in accord with the others. In addition, although the ways they look and fit may vary widely, all automobiles have the same basic components. Similarly, all businesses have common structural and operating components, each composed of a series of *jobs to be done* and each with a *specific overall purpose.* From company to company, these components look different and fit together differently. But in every organization, components have the same fundamental purpose—each must perform its own function while working in concert with the others.

Although all organizations feature the same basic elements, each must develop the structure that is most appropriate for it. What works for Texas Instruments will not work for Exxon or the U.S. Department of Justice. The structure of the American Red Cross will probably not work for Union Carbide or the University of Minnesota. We define **organizational structure** as the specification of the jobs to be done within an organization and the ways in which those jobs relate to one another.

organizational structure
Specification of the jobs to be done within an organization and the ways in which they relate to one another

Determinants of Organizational Structure

How is an organization's structure determined? Does it happen by chance, or is there some logic that managers use to create structure? Does it develop by some combination of circumstance and strategy? Ideally, managers carefully assess a variety of important factors as they plan for and then create a structure that will allow their organization to function efficiently.

Indeed, many elements work together to determine an organization's structure. Chief among these are the organization's *purpose, mission,* and *strategy.* A dynamic and rapidly growing enterprise, for example, achieved that position because of its purpose and successful strategies for achieving it. Such a firm will need a structure that contributes to flexibility and growth. A stable organization with only modest growth will function best with a different structure.

Size, technology, and changes in environmental circumstances also affect structure. A large manufacturer operating in a strongly competitive environment—say, Boeing or Hewlett-Packard—requires a different structure than a local barbershop or video store. Moreover, even after a structure has been created, it is rarely free from tinkering—or even outright re-creation. Indeed, most organizations change their structures on an almost continuing basis.

For example, in addition to numerous ongoing changes, IBM has made major changes in its structure five times in the last ten years. Why such an apparently frantic struggle to reinvent a blue chip company over and over? IBM rose to dominance by building and selling computer hardware—the physical components, large and small, of computer systems. Its core customers were users of large computers and computer systems. By the mid-1980s, however, it was clear that IBM's biggest market consisted of customers looking for quite different products and services, namely, low-cost small computer items, like PCs and workstations, plus the know-how to deploy a seller's technology in sophisticated information systems. As IBM's former head of U.S. sales and marketing put it, "We were simply selling iron in a world that wanted help." IBM's latest goals, therefore, have been conceived in response to the changes in its environment. It now plans to sell more components to outside manufacturers, enter the field of client-server computing, and offer network services to large companies. With the purchase of developers like Lotus Development Corp. and Tivoli Systems Inc. in 1995, IBM is also committed to the development of cutting-edge business software.[1]

"We were simply selling iron in a world that wanted help."

—George Conrades
Former Head of U.S. Sales and Marketing at IBM

TRENDS & CHALLENGES
WHAT TO DO WHEN THE CORPORATION GOES INTO DENIAL

A company's organizational chart is only as strong as the people who fill key management positions. When something happens to these people—when they leave for other jobs, when they become disabled, when they die—the organizational integrity of the whole company may suffer short-term, and sometimes long-term, damage.

This vulnerability was brought into clear focus for several companies after the crash, in April 1996, of the plane carrying Commerce Secretary Ronald H. Brown. Brown was on a mission to encourage U.S. companies to do business in the Balkans. Brown and all twelve corporate executives aboard the plane died, including seven who played key operating roles at AT&T, ABB Asea Brown Boveri Ltd., Bechtel Corp., Parsons Corp., and other firms. Among the dead was P. Stuart Tholan, president of a unit at Bechtel covering Europe, Africa, the Middle East, and Southwest Asia. Asked a week after the crash who would succeed Tholan, a spokesman for the industrial construction firm replied, "I have no idea." The loss of Robert E. Donovan, president and CEO of ABB Inc., a Swiss-based maker of engineering products, left management empowered to appoint only an interim replacement, not a permanent successor. Inadequate plans like these are no surprise to experts in organizational succession. According to Robert Lefton, Chief Executive of Psychological Associates, between 60 and 70 percent of companies "don't have good plans below the CEO level."

Having gone through a succession crisis at his own company, Dana G. Mead, Chairman and CEO of Tenneco Inc., reacted strongly to the news of the crash. "This tragedy," he lamented, "has certainly caused a number of companies to . . . ask some very tough questions [about the adequacy of their succession planning]." Tenneco's succession crisis occurred after the cancer-related death, in 1994, of Mead's predecessor, Michael H. Walsh. When Mead took control of the company, a Fortune 500 maker of automotive parts, he instructed six key division heads to draw up succession plans to take effect if something happened to them. Initially, the division heads balked. Ironically, they feared that if they openly identified their divisional superstars, their counterparts in other areas of the company would lure them away. Ultimately, however, everyone agreed to Mead's plan.

"This tragedy has caused a number of companies to ask some very tough questions [about the adequacy of their succession planning]."

—Dana G. Mead
Chairman and CEO of Tenneco Inc.

At other companies, boards of directors have taken active roles in succession planning. The corporate board of General Motors, for example, demands that 65 key officers not only develop specific succession plans but appear annually to describe who among their heirs apparent is ready for succession and who needs more time to develop. Why is GM so insistent about succession planning? Board members are worried about personal tragedies, reports Gregory Lau, a GM executive in charge of global leadership development. But they are also concerned, admits Lau, "about all the headhunting that's going on at the highest levels."

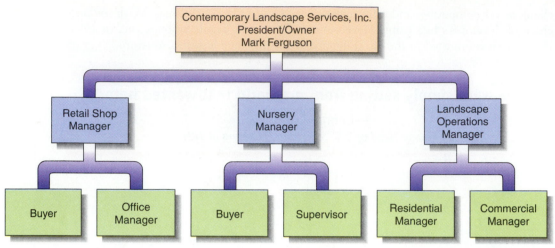

FIGURE 7.1 ◆ The Organization Chart: Contemporary Landscape Services Inc.

IBM's problems in meeting those goals are in large part internal. Longstanding, outmoded procedures have proved resistant to change, and IBM still depends heavily on its computer hardware business for revenue. As we saw in Chapter 6, organizing is a function of managerial planning. As such, it is conducted with an equal awareness of both a firm's external and internal environments.

Chain of Command

organization chart
Diagram depicting a company's structure and showing employees where they fit into its operations

chain of command
Reporting relationships within a company

Most businesses prepare **organization charts** to clarify structure and to show employees where they fit into a firm's operations. Figure 7.1 is an organization chart for Contemporary Landscape Services Inc., a small but thriving business in Bryan, Texas. Each box in the chart represents a job. The solid lines define the **chain of command**, or *reporting relationships*, within the company. For example, the retail shop, nursery, and landscape operations managers all report to the owner and president, Mark Ferguson. Within the landscape operation is one manager for residential accounts and another for commercial accounts. Similarly, there are other managers in the retail shop and the nursery.

The organization charts of large firms are far more complex and include individuals at many more levels than those shown in Figure 7.1. Indeed, size prevents many large firms from drawing charts that include all their managers. Typically, they create one organization chart showing overall corporate structure and separate charts for each division.

■ THE BUILDING BLOCKS OF ORGANIZATIONAL STRUCTURE

The first step in developing the structure of any business, large or small, is twofold:

- *Specialization:* determining who will do what
- *Departmentalization:* determining how people performing certain tasks can best be grouped together

These two tasks are the basic building blocks of all business organization.

Specialization

The process of identifying the specific jobs that need to be done and designating the people who will perform them leads to **job specialization.** In a sense, all organizations have only one major "job," such as making cars (like Ford), selling finished goods to consumers (like Wal-Mart), or providing telecommunications services (like AT&T). Usually, of course, the "job" is more complex in nature. For example, the "job" of Chaparral Steel is converting scrap steel, such as wrecked automobiles, into finished steel products like beams and reinforcement bars. But in order to perform this one overall "job," managers actually break it down, or *specialize* it, into several smaller jobs. Thus, some workers transport the scrap steel to the company's mill in Midlothian, Texas. Others operate shredding equipment before turning raw materials over to the workers who then melt them down into liquid form. Other specialists oversee the flow of the liquid into molding equipment in which it is transformed into new products. Finally, other workers are responsible for moving finished products to a holding area before they are shipped out to customers. When the overall "job" of the organization is thus broken down, each worker can develop real expertise in his or her job, and employees can better coordinate their work with that done by others.[2]

Specialization and Growth In a very small organization, the owner may perform every job. As the firm grows, however, so does the need to specialize jobs so that others can perform them. To see how specialization can evolve in an organization, consider the case of the Walt Disney Co. When Walt Disney first opened his studio, he and his brother Roy did everything. For example, when they created the very first animated feature, *Steamboat Willy,* they wrote the story, drew the pictures, transferred the pictures to film, provided the voices, and then went out and sold the cartoon to theater operators. Today, by sharp contrast, a Disney animated feature is made possible only through the efforts of hundreds and hundreds of creators. The job of a single cartoonist, for example, may be to draw the face of a single character throughout an entire feature. Another may be charged with erasing stray pencil marks inadvertently made by other illustrators. And artists have nothing to do with the subsequent operations that turn individual animated cells into a moving picture or with the marketing of the finished product. ▶

Job specialization, then, is a natural part of organizational growth. It also has certain advantages. For example, specialized jobs are learned more easily and can be performed more efficiently than nonspecialized jobs, and it is also easier to replace people who leave an organization. However, jobs at lower levels of the organization are especially susceptible to overspecialization. If such jobs become too narrowly defined, employees may become bored and careless, derive less satisfaction from their jobs, and lose sight of their roles in the organization.

Departmentalization

After jobs are specialized, they must be grouped into logical units. This process is called **departmentalization.** Departmentalized companies benefit from the division of activities. Control and coordination are narrowed and made easier, and top managers can see more easily how various units are performing.

For example, departmentalization allows the firm to treat a department as a **profit center**—a separate unit responsible for its own costs and profits. Thus, by assessing profits from sales in a particular area—say, men's clothing—Sears can decide whether to expand or curtail promotions in that area. Similarly, the profitability of Star Kist tuna will affect H. J. Heinz's decisions about whether to increase or decrease investment in the product.

job specialization
The process of identifying the specific jobs that need to be done and designating the people who will perform them

departmentalization
Process of grouping jobs into logical units

profit center
Separate company unit responsible for its own costs and profits

Whether they are produced manually or digitally, the drawings that comprise a full-length Walt Disney cartoon are the result of highly coordinated job specialization. A lead animator, for example, may provide a rough pencil sketch that is then refined by one or more artists. Other teams scan clean drawings into a computer and color them according to a plan devised by the art director. Finally, to achieve hand-drawn movement, a team of so-called "in-betweeners" completes all the drawings needed to give fluid motion to one or two key frames drawn by the lead animator.

Computer maker Hewlett-Packard Co. recently reorganized its structure to increase customer responsiveness and improve decision making. Most of the firm's operations are now handled by teams, each of which functions with a great degree of autonomy from the others. Indeed, individual teams are virtually business owners. In the network-server division, for instance, top managers are responsible for their unit's overall costs. "Our profit-and-loss statement," reports marketing manager Jim McDonnell, "is like any other small company." Similarly, managers have the authority to reinvest their profits back into their own operating units. As decision makers, they need not wait for budget requests to percolate to the top of the corporate hierarchy and then filter back down. At the same time, however, they are responsible for contributions to companywide operations—supporting the firm's general research unit, for example, and paying the CEO's salary.[3]

Managers do not group jobs randomly. They group them logically, according to some common thread or purpose. In general, departmentalization may occur along *customer*, *product*, *process*, *geographic*, or *functional* lines (or any combination of these).

Customer Departmentalization

customer departmentalization
Departmentalization according to types of customers likely to buy a given product

Stores like Sears and Macy's are divided into departments—a men's department, a women's department, a luggage department, and so on. Each department targets a specific customer category (men, women, people who want to buy luggage). **Customer departmentalization** makes shopping easier by providing identifiable store segments. Thus, a customer shopping for a baby's playpen can bypass Lawn and Garden Supplies and head straight for Children's Furniture. Stores can also group products in locations designated for deliveries, special sales, and other service-oriented purposes. In general, the store is more efficient and customers get better service—in part because salespeople tend to specialize and gain expertise in their departments.[4]

Product Departmentalization

product departmentalization
Departmentalization according to products being created

Both manufacturers and service providers often opt for **product departmentalization**—dividing an organization according to the specific product or service being created. A bank, for example, may handle consumer loans in one department and commercial loans in another. On a larger scale, 3M Corp., which makes both consumer and industrial products, operates different divisions for Post-it brand Tape Flags, Scotch-Brite scrub sponges, and the Sarns 9000 perfusion system for open-heart surgery.

Process Departmentalization

Other manufacturers favor **process departmentalization,** in which the organization is divided according to production processes. This principle, for example, is logical for the pickle maker Vlasic, which has separate departments to transform cucumbers into fresh-packed pickles, pickles cured in brine, and relishes. Cucumbers destined to become fresh-packed pickles must be packed into jars immediately, covered with a solution of water and vinegar, and prepared for sale. Those slated for brined pickles must be aged in brine solution before packing. Relish cucumbers must be minced and combined with a host of other ingredients. Each process requires different equipment and worker skills.

process departmentalization
Departmentalization according to production process used to create a good or service

Geographic Departmentalization

Some firms are divided according to the areas of the country—or the world—that they serve. Levi Strauss, for instance, has one division for the United States, one for Europe, and another for the rest of the world. Within the United States, **geographic departmentalization** is common among utilities. Thus, Pacific Power and Light is organized as four geographic departments, Southwestern, Columbia Basin, Mid-Oregon, and Wyoming.

geographic departmentalization
Departmentalization according to areas served by a business

Functional Departmentalization

Many service and manufacturing companies develop departments according to a group's functions or activities—a form of organization known as **functional departmentalization.** Such firms typically have production, marketing and sales, human resource, and accounting and finance departments. Departments may be further subdivided. For example, the marketing department might be divided geographically or into separate staffs for market research and advertising.

functional departmentalization
Departmentalization according to functions or activities

Because different forms of departmentalization have different advantages, larger companies tend to adopt different types of departmentalization for various levels. For example, the company illustrated in Figure 7.2 uses functional departmentalization at

FIGURE 7.2 ◆ Multiple Forms of Departmentalization

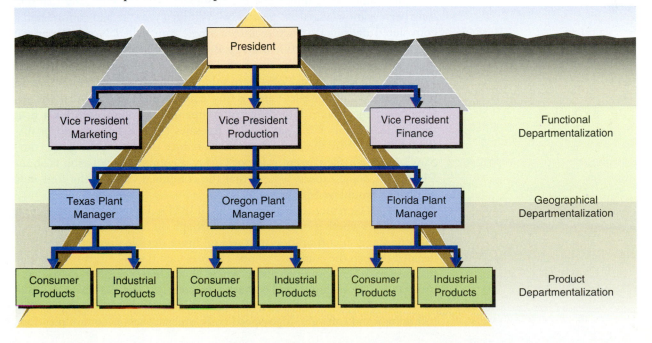

the top level. At the middle level, production is divided along geographic lines. At a lower level, marketing is departmentalized by product group.

Process Organization

In recent years, many companies have begun to realize that functional organization often lends itself to a sharper focus on customer needs. In May 1994, for example, CEO Lou Gerstner announced a sweeping organization of IBM's marketing and sales structure. The changes achieved a shift from geographic departmentalization to an organization based on customer industries. Previously, top sales managers reported to the heads of regional areas (say, New England) or countries (IBM Germany). Under the reorganization they report to the heads of fourteen newly formed industry groups—groups focused on customers engaged in banking, retailing, insurance, and so forth. Gerstner's foremost goal is to make top sales executives more customer-oriented by making them more knowledgeable about the industries they serve.[5]

IBM's reorganization plan has other advantages. Several management layers, for example, will be eliminated. Moreover, less power will be vested with top executives in far-flung countries and more power centralized at U.S. headquarters. In similar efforts to streamline decision making and to work more directly with customers, more and more companies have begun to use variations of functional organization. One variation is organizing according to units, or teams, responsible for *all* the various *processes* involved in getting products to consumers. The most important feature of this system is its marketing and customer orientation.

■ ESTABLISHING THE DECISION-MAKING HIERARCHY

■ When John F. (Jack) Smith, Jr., became CEO of General Motors in late 1992, he immediately undertook the reorganization of a company that had long been acknowledged as "unwieldy." Within a year, he had compressed a convoluted divisional structure into a single unit called North American Operations. A special NAO Strategy Board was formed to speed decision making. Corporate staff was cut from 13,500 to 2,500. Noncore businesses worth $2 billion in annual sales were sold, and businesses worth another $3 billion were put up for sale. Smith is now considering a plan to break the automobile giant up into four different companies—a radical step for a firm that, as recently as 1995, set records for sales ($168.8 billion) and profits ($6.9 billion). Why the decision, then, to reduce the size of the giant company? Although the current value of GM as a combined operation is about $40 billion, some experts believe that the combined value of the four new companies would be $58 billion.[6]

■ When Louis Gerstner took over as CEO of IBM in late 1992, one of his first decisions was whether or not to follow through on his predecessor's plan to split the sluggish corporation into several more flexible divisions. Gerstner decided to keep the company whole. He reasoned that a company with unified resources and communications would be in a better position to give customers unified technological systems. Currently Gerstner plans to take advantage of IBM's wide range of expertise, including custom networking technology and software; high-speed components, such as communications switches; and mainframes that can digitally store immense amounts of information. He believes that if he can integrate all of these product offerings, IBM will be in a position to offer large corporations "network-centric computing"—complete information technology resources that customers can either buy or lease. In short, he has reasoned that IBM's best chances for success depend upon its remaining a single integrated entity.[7]

We see here two companies with similar heritages—two long-established, long-dominant U.S. corporations. Each is considering change, but each has made a very different decision. While one may be broken down and split into four smaller companies, the other is likely to remain intact. This interesting state of affairs brings us to a major question that must be asked about any organization: *Who makes which decisions?* The answer almost never focuses on an individual or even a small group. The more accurate answer usually refers to the decision-making hierarchy. The development of this hierarchy generally results from a three-step process:

1. *Assigning tasks:* determining who can make decisions and specifying how they should be made
2. *Performing tasks:* implementing decisions that have been made
3. *Distributing authority:* determining whether the organization is to be centralized or decentralized

Assigning Tasks: Responsibility and Authority

The question of who is *supposed* to do what and who is *entitled* to do what in an organization is complex. In any company with more than one person, individuals must work out agreements about responsibilities and authority. **Responsibility** is the duty to perform an assigned task. **Authority** is the power to make the decisions necessary to complete the task.

For example, imagine a mid-level buyer for Macy's department store who encounters an unexpected opportunity to make a large purchase at an extremely good price.

responsibility
Duty to perform an assigned task

authority
Power to make the decisions necessary to complete a task

© 1998 Dean Vietor *from* The Cartoon Bank,™ Inc.

"I'll have the **Middle Management Lunch**.
Heavy on the **responsibility** and light on the the **authority**."

Let's assume that an immediate decision is absolutely necessary—a decision that this buyer has no authority to make without confirmation from above. The company's policies on delegation and authority are inconsistent, since the buyer is *responsible* for purchasing the clothes that will be sold in the upcoming season but lacks the *authority* to make the needed purchases.

Performing Tasks: Delegation and Accountability

delegation
Assignment of a task, a responsibility, or authority by a manager to a subordinate

accountability
Liability of subordinates for accomplishing tasks assigned by managers

Trouble occurs when appropriate levels of responsibility and authority are not clearly spelled out in the working relationships between managers and subordinates. Here, the issues become delegation and accountability. **Delegation** begins when a manager assigns a task to a subordinate. **Accountability** falls to the subordinate, who must then complete the task. If the subordinate does not perform the assigned task properly and promptly, he or she may be reprimanded or punished, possibly even dismissed.

Of course, subordinates sometimes fail to complete tasks because managers have not delegated the necessary authority. Employees may then face a dilemma: they cannot do what they are supposed to do because of a boss who will nevertheless hold them accountable. When Harold Geneen ran ITT Corp., his top managers frequently complained that he expected them to make important decisions but failed to give them the power to carry them out. Thus, they would on occasion launch new ventures or announce new programs only to discover later that Geneen would not approve the plan.

Distributing Authority: Centralization and Decentralization

centralized organization
Organization in which most decision-making authority is held by upper-level management

Delegation involves a specific relationship between managers and subordinates. Most businesses must also make decisions about general patterns of authority throughout the company. This pattern may be largely centralized or decentralized (or, usually, somewhere in between).

In a **centralized organization,** most decision-making authority is held by upper-level managers. Most lower-level decisions must be approved by upper management before they can be implemented. McDonald's, for example, practices centralization as a way to maintain standardization. At Dillard's Department Stores, a $2.7 billion family-run chain based in Little Rock, Arkansas, family management still insists on tight cost controls and the centralized administration of everything from payroll to buying. Indeed, owner-operated companies frequently have presidents or CEOs who make most of their decisions. Centralized authority is also typical of small businesses.[8] ▶

decentralized organization
Organization in which a great deal of decision-making authority is delegated to levels of management at points below the top

As a company gets larger, more and more decisions must be made. Thus, there is a tendency to adopt a more decentralized pattern. In a **decentralized organization,** much decision-making authority is delegated to levels of management at various points below the top. The purpose of decentralization is to make a company more responsive to its environment by breaking it into more manageable units, ranging from product lines to independent businesses. Reducing top-heavy bureaucracies is also a common goal.

span of control
Number of people supervised by one manager

Span of Control   The distribution of authority in an organization also affects the number of people who work for any individual manager. The number of people managed by one supervisor is called the manager's **span of control** and depends on many factors. Employees' abilities and the supervisor's managerial skills help determine whether span of control is wide or narrow. So do the similarity and simplicity of tasks performed under the manager's supervision and the extent to which they are interrelated.

At some companies—for example, General Electric—decentralization and reduced span of control have gone hand in hand in recent years. As a result of decentralization, GE plant managers now have the authority to make capital expenditures of up to

$100,000 without getting higher-level approval. The firm has become even more decentralized by shifting decision-making power to ever lower levels, and top managers' span of control is now ten to twelve subordinates—about twice as large as twenty years ago. Largely because of such changes, GE has lowered costs, shortened production times, and become more responsive to customers' needs.[9]

Other companies have gained the same benefits on lower levels of the decision-making hierarchy. When several employees perform either the same simple task or a group of interrelated tasks, a wide span of control is possible and often desirable. For instance, because all the jobs are routine, one supervisor may well control a whole assembly line. Moreover, each task depends on another. If one station stops, everyone stops. Having one supervisor ensures that all stations receive equal attention and function equally well.

In contrast, when jobs are more diversified or prone to change, a narrow span of control is preferable. For example, the fully automated Kellogg plant in Battle Creek, Michigan, produces breakfast cereals. Some machines process and mix ingredients, others sort and package. Although workers are highly skilled operators of their particular machines, each machine is different. In this kind of setup, the complexities of each machine and the advanced skills needed by each operator mean that one supervisor can oversee only a small number of employees.

Three Forms of Authority

Whatever type of structure a company develops it must decide who will have authority over whom. As individuals are delegated responsibility and authority in a firm, a complex web of interactions develops. These interactions may take one of three forms of authority: *line*, *staff*, or *committee and team*. In reality, like departmentalization, all three forms may be found in a given company, especially a large one.

Line Authority   **Line authority** is authority that flows up and down the chain of command, as shown in Figure 7.1. Most companies rely heavily on **line departments**—departments directly linked to the production and sales of specific products. For example, Clark Equipment Corp. has a division that produces forklifts and small earth

line authority
Organizational structure in which authority flows in a direct chain of command from the top of the company to the bottom

line department
Department directly linked to the production and sales of a specific product

movers. In this division, line departments include purchasing, materials handling, fabrication, painting, and assembly (all of which are directly linked to production) along with sales and distribution (both of which are directly linked to sales).

Each line department is essential to an organization's success. Line employees are the "doers" and producers in a company. If any line department fails to complete its task, the company cannot sell and deliver finished goods. Thus, the authority delegated to line departments is important. A bad decision by the manager in one department can hold up production for an entire plant. For example, say that the painting department manager at Clark Equipment changes a paint application on a batch of forklifts, which then show signs of peeling paint. The batch will have to be repainted (and perhaps partially reassembled) before the machines can be shipped.

staff authority
Authority that is based on expertise and that usually involves advising line managers

staff members
Advisers and counselors who aid line departments in making decisions but do not have the authority to make final decisions

Staff Authority   Most companies also rely on **staff authority.** Staff authority is based on special expertise and usually involves counseling and advising line managers. Common **staff members** include specialists in areas such as law, accounting, and human resource management. A corporate attorney, for example, may be asked to advise the marketing department as it prepares a new contract with the firm's advertising agency. Legal staff, however, do not actually make decisions that affect how the marketing department does its job. Staff members, therefore, aid line departments in making decisions but do not have the authority to make final decisions.

Suppose, for example, that the fabrication department at Clark Equipment has an employee with a drinking problem. The manager of the department could consult a human resource staff expert for advice on handling the situation. The staff expert might suggest that the worker stay on the job but enter a counseling program. But if the line manager decides that the job is too dangerous to be handled by a person whose judgment is often impaired by alcohol, that decision will most likely prevail.

Typically, the separation between line authority and staff responsibility is clearly delineated. As Figure 7.3 shows, this separation is usually shown in organization charts by solid lines (line authority) and dotted lines (staff responsibility). It may help to understand this separation by remembering that while staff members generally provide services to management, line managers are directly involved in producing the firm's products.

committee and team authority
Authority granted to committees or work teams involved in a firm's daily operations

Committee and Team Authority   Recently, more and more organizations have started to use **committee and team authority**—authority granted to committees or

FIGURE 7.3 ◆ Line-and-Staff Organization: Clark Equipment Corp.

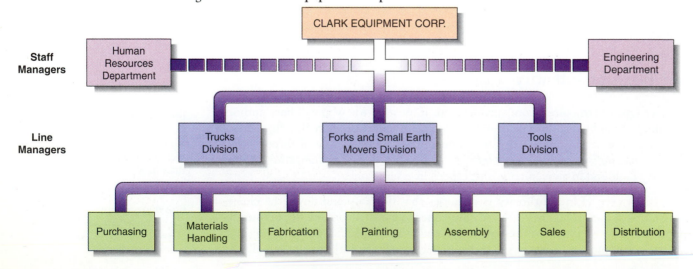

Westley Bingess works for BlueJacket Ship Crafters, a maker of mail-order model-ship kits located in Searsport, Maine. Bingess has only nine colleagues at BlueJacket, who are divided into five different teams that handle areas like production scheduling. Everyone serves on three or four teams. Since 1993, BlueJacket's owners have also introduced performance bonuses and self-scheduling and begun sharing financial information.

work teams that play central roles in the firm's daily operations. A committee, for example, may consist of top managers from several major areas. If the work of the committee is especially important, and if the committee will be working together for an extended time, the organization may even grant it special authority as a decision-making body that goes beyond the individual authority possessed by each of its members.

At the operating level, many firms today are also using *work teams*—groups of operating employees empowered to plan and organize their own work and to perform that work with a minimum of supervision. As with permanent committees, the organization will usually find it beneficial to grant special authority to work teams so that they may function more effectively.[10] ▲

■ BASIC FORMS OF ORGANIZATIONAL STRUCTURE

There is, of course, almost an infinite number of ways in which organizations can structure themselves—according to specialization, for example, or departmentalization or the decision-making hierarchy. Nevertheless, it is possible to identify four basic forms of organizational structure that reflect the general trends followed by most firms: *functional*, *divisional*, *matrix*, and *international*.

Functional Organizations

Functional organization is the approach to organizational structure used by most small to medium-sized firms. Such organizations are usually structured around basic business functions—marketing, operations, finance, and so forth. Thus, there is a marketing department, an operations department, and a finance department. The benefits of this approach include specialization within functional areas and smoother coordination among them. Experts with specialized training, for example, are hired to work in the marketing department, which handles all marketing for the firm.

functional organization
Form of business organization in which authority is determined by the relationships between group functions and activities

BUSINESS FIELD TRIP

"You Have to Encourage Creativity Just to Stay in Place"

There is no rest for the weary at Chaparral Steel—not if Dennis Beach has anything to say about it. "If you believe that change is constant and occurring at an increasingly rapid rate," says Beach, Vice President for Administration, "you have to encourage creativity just to stay in place, much less move ahead."

THE ATOMIC MODEL OF TEAMWORK. Encouragement at Chaparral is communicated up and down the organization through a corporate culture that focuses more on what an employee can do for the company than on where he or she is pegged on the organization chart. There are only four levels of management at Chaparral—executives, senior managers, first-line supervisors, and production, maintenance, and administrative personnel. The idea of "divisions," however, fails to reflect the way the company actually operates. "The best analogy of how we work is a model of an atom," explains Beach. "Depending on the expertise we need on a given project, we may assemble a team that includes people from finance, production, maintenance, engineering, purchasing, and human resources. We've had production workers at the center of the atom and senior managers as their advisors. Like electrons, protons, and neutrons, every team member rotates around the nucleus to get the job done." Adds Human Resources Head Jeff Roesler, "We involve not only management, but all personnel in the decision-making process. Our goal is across-the-board employee involvement on projects."

> "We've had production workers at the center of the atom and senior managers as their advisors. Like electrons, protons, and neutrons, every team member rotates around the nucleus to get the job done."
>
> —Dennis Beach
> *Vice President for Administration*
> *at Chaparral Steel Co.*

Here's a good illustration. When Chaparral needed a rolling mill lathe, it budgeted more than $1 million and put a machinist in charge of making the purchase. The machinist was chosen because of his hands-on experience with the equipment and the production process and because management believed that in this case, bottom-up decision making was more effective than relying solely on the results of an engineering study. "We told the machinist to research the kind of machine we should buy," recalls Beach. "He went to steel plants in Japan and Europe to look at different equipment. When he needed in-house engineering advice, he asked for it. In the end, he recommended a used lathe, which cut about $500,000 from our budgeted cost." The machine, adds Beach, is still working.

Admittedly, the atomic model requires managers with personalities who thrive on upsetting—and, of course, righting—the apple cart. Grooming such managers takes time and generally occurs from within the organization. "By the time managers become first-line supervisors," says Beach, "they are completely acculturated, especially since we give different group members the opportunity to 'practice' being managers when supervisors are on vacation. Everyone who is interested gets a shot at it, and we quickly learn who is suited for management and who is not."

STRATEGIC TIME FRAMES. Depending on their levels, Chaparral managers have different strategic time frames that determine their business focus. For example, executives, who make up the top 2 percent of the organization, look one to five years ahead. Senior managers—about 4 percent of the work force—focus on the company's position 1 year down the line. First-line supervisors—11 percent of the organization—work with weekly time frames. Production, maintenance, and administrative workers—who comprise the remaining 83 percent of the company's labor force—focus on the here and now as they operate the plant.

Beach adds, however, that "these strategic divisions have some flexibility. For example, even though an executive in accounting is supposed to be working on a one– to five–year time frame, he probably spends about 10 percent of his time on immediate issues. We think the 90/10 split is about right."

EFFECTIVE COMMUNICATION. A vital ingredient in the success of Chaparral's flexible structure is effective communication. Because Chaparral has an informal management style, communication is also informal. "We encourage people at all organizational levels to have face-to-face dialogues," explains Beach. He adds that this approach to communication implies a willingness on the part of management to listen to what production and maintenance workers tell them—and, when necessary, to act on what they learn. Similarly, managers listen to the communication grapevine. "I believe there are no secrets here or in any organization," says Jeff Roesler. "I would bet my last dollar on it."

Like all companies, of course, Chaparral suffers its share of garbled communications. Dennis Beach admits, for example, that management decisions are sometimes made with insufficient input. He also acknowledges that such decisions are very often wrong. "It happened to me," he recalls, "when I set holiday closing and opening times without consulting with people in production. Although I thought it made sense to shut everything down at 8 in the morning and open it back up at 8 the next morning, production and maintenance objected. They wanted everything shut twelve hours earlier. When the people who actually operate the equipment pointed out that my timing was off, I had to admit I was wrong.

"We manage chaos," Beach adds, but with a management group that has worked together for almost twenty years, Chaparral officials remain confident that their flexible, project-oriented approach is the best way to continue the company's winning ways.

In large firms, coordination across functional departments becomes more complicated. Functional organization also fosters centralization (which may or may not be desirable) and makes accountability more difficult. As organizations grow, therefore, they tend to shed this form and move toward one of the other three structures.

Divisional Organization

A **divisional organization** relies on product departmentalization. The firm creates product-based divisions, each of which may then be managed as a separate enterprise. Organizations using this approach are typically structured around several **divisions**—departments that resemble separate businesses in that they produce and market their own products. The head of each division may be a corporate vice president or, if the organization is large, a divisional president. In addition, each division usually has its own identity and operates as a relatively autonomous business under the larger corporate umbrella.

Consider United Technologies Corp., which is located in Hartford, Connecticut. Its divisions include Pratt & Whitney, an aircraft engine maker; Carrier Corp., which makes air conditioners; Otis Elevator Co.; and Flight Systems, which builds the Sikorsky helicopter. In the 1980s, UTC sold off such unrelated companies as a trout farm and a dumpster manufacturer. Since then, however, the company's largest division, Pratt & Whitney, has been hurt by airline and military cutbacks and currently represents the biggest drain on its profits. Smaller units, however, are performing well, largely because UTC has succeeded in developing new products, modernizing its manufacturing techniques, and finding new overseas markets. ▶ UTC is a good example of a divisionalized company that struggled into the 1980s but has begun to recover by focusing on the related businesses that it houses under a single organizational roof.[11]

Like UTC, divisionalized companies are free to

divisional organization
Organizational structure in which corporate divisions operate as relatively autonomous businesses under the larger corporate umbrella

division
Department that resembles a separate business in producing and marketing its own products

Aircraft engine maker Pratt & Whitney, United Technologies Corp.'s largest division, lost $1.3 billion and laid off 23,000 employees between 1991 and 1996. At the same time, the fortunes of UTC's smaller units—Carrier Air Conditioning, Otis Elevator, and Sikorsky helicopter—were revived by new manufacturing techniques and lighter payrolls. "This company is really two companies," observes CEO Robert F. Daniell. "The other part is doing quite well." At Sikorsky, for example, more efficient worker teams that now assemble products from start to finish are busy filling a $1 billion order for ninety-five helicopters from Turkey. UTC's smaller divisions have more than compensated for the losses by P&W.

buy, sell, create, and disband divisions without disrupting the rest of their operations. Divisions can maintain healthy competition among themselves by sponsoring separate advertising campaigns, fostering different corporate identities, and so forth. They can also share certain corporate-level resources (such as market-research data). Of course, if too much control is delegated to divisional managers, corporate managers may lose touch with daily operations. Competition between divisions has also been known to become disruptive, and efforts in one division may be duplicated by those of another.

Matrix Organization

matrix structure
Organizational structure in which teams are formed and team members report to two or more managers

In a **matrix structure,** teams are formed in which individuals report to two or more managers, usually including a line manager and a staff manager. This structure was pioneered by the National Aeronautics and Space Administration (NASA) for use in developing specific programs. It is a highly flexible form that is readily adaptable to changing circumstances. Matrix structures rely heavily on committee and team authority.

In some companies, matrix organization is a temporary measure, installed to complete a specific project and affecting only one part of the firm. In these firms, the end of the project usually means the end of the matrix—either a breakup of the team or a restructuring to fit it into the company's existing line-and-staff structure. For example, IBM used a matrix organization to put together the original PC but then disbanded the team and returned members to the line-and-staff structure once the PC was created. Elsewhere the matrix organization is a semipermanent fixture.

■ At Thermos, the well-known maker of insulated bottles, lunch boxes, and barbecue grills, interdisciplinary teams have largely replaced functions—marketing, engineering, and so forth—as the company's basic organizational principle. Japanese-owned Thermos now employs teams in all its product lines because of the success of its first experiment in matrix organization. Growth at Thermos had slowed because its products were becoming commodities—mass-produced lookalikes bought by consumers with little regard to differences in brand or quality. What the company needed most of all was new innovative products. A product-development team, therefore, was assembled comprising six managers from different disciplines, such as marketing, manufacturing, and finance. Team members abandoned their focus on separate functions in favor of a concentration on their target market—in this case, users of barbecue grills. Several additional team members came from the industrial design firm of Fitch Inc., adding outside perspectives on design and market research.

Most important, therefore, was the shift in focus from product to consumer, and the team spent much of its time in the field learning about customers' cookout needs. The result was the Thermos Thermal Electric Grill, which uses new technology to give food a barbecued taste while burning cleaner than gas or charcoal. The new grill, which also eliminates heavy propane tanks and messy cleanup, has already won numerous design awards and is expected to raise Thermos's market share for electric grills from 2 percent to 20 percent over the next few years. "We need to reinvent our product lines," admits Thermos CEO Monte Peterson, "and teamwork is doing it for us."[12] ▶

After an initial meeting in 1990, members of the Thermos Lifestyle team hit the road, holding focus groups, visiting homes, and video-taping family gatherings to find out what consumers wanted in a barbeque grill. Back at headquarters after field research was complete, team members hammered out a consensus on what the new grill should look like and do. Meanwhile, team members from engineering worked at improving electric grill technology and making sure that new designs were economically feasible. Designers worked out features that would add value and differentiate the new product. The first batch of grills rolled off the line in 1992 and grills were given to employees for testing. When tests proved successful, the new Thermos Thermal Electric Grill was rolled out nationally.

"We need to reinvent our product lines, and teamwork is doing it for us."

—Monte Peterson
CEO of Thermos

International Organization

As we saw in Chapter 5, many businesses today manufacture, purchase, and sell in the world market. Thus, a number of different **international organizational structures** have emerged. Moreover, as competition on a global scale becomes more complex, companies often find that they must experiment with the ways in which they respond:

international organizational structures
Approaches to organizational structure developed in response to the need to manufacture, purchase, and sell in global markets

■ In 1985, the German giant Daimler-Benz (best known for its Mercedes-Benz automobiles) embarked on a new strategy of acquisitions. In short order the firm bought several aerospace, electronic, and financial services businesses, some of which were German companies and some of which were international enterprises. At first, Daimler managers thought that they could simply fold all of the new companies into Daimler's existing organization and run the entire operation with their current management structure. It quickly became apparent, however, that a network of complex and far-flung international operations in diverse markets required a new form of organization structure. In 1994, therefore, the company reorganized into a holding company with four distinct—and autonomous—operating groups. Now a group called Debis handles financial services and insurance on a worldwide basis. Mercedes-Benz produces passenger cars and trucks. AEG handles Daimler's appliance and microelectronics businesses, and Deutsche Aerospace includes aircraft and jet propulsion businesses.

Other firms have developed a wide range of approaches to international organizational structure. Whirlpool, for example, purchased the appliance division of the Dutch electronics giant N.V. Philips and as part of its international organization structure now makes the cooling coils for its refrigerators at its new plant in Trento, Italy.[13] Other companies, such as Levi Strauss, handle all international operations through separate international divisions. Still others concentrate production in low-cost areas and then distribute and market globally. Some firms, such as Britain's Pearson PLC (which runs such diverse businesses as publishing, investment banking, and Madame Tussaud's Wax Museum), allow each of their businesses to function autonomously within local markets.[14]

Finally, some companies adopt a truly global structure in which they acquire resources (including capital), produce goods and services, engage in research and development, and sell products in whatever local market is appropriate, without any consideration of national boundaries. General Electric uses a global structure for many of its businesses and has also managed to graft other forms of organization onto its global operations. For its $3 billion lighting business, for example, GE has created a matrix-type team of nine to twelve senior managers. Team members have "multiple competencies" rather than narrow specialties, and the team itself is multidisciplinary—that is, it cuts across functions. From new product design to equipment redesign, the matrix team oversees about 100 programs and processes located all around the world.[15]

■ INFORMAL ORGANIZATION

Much of our discussion has focused on the organization's *formal* structure—its "official" arrangement of jobs and job relationships. In reality, however, all organizations also have another dimension—an *informal* organization within which people do their jobs in different ways and interact with other people in ways that do not follow formal lines of communication.

Formal versus Informal Organizational Systems

informal organization
Network, unrelated to the firm's formal authority structure, of everyday social interactions among company employees

The formal organization of a businesses is the part that can be seen and represented in chart form. The structure of a company, however, is by no means limited to the organization chart and the formal assignment of authority. Frequently, the **informal organization**—everyday social interactions among employees that transcend formal jobs and job interrelationships—effectively alters a company's formal structure. Indeed, this level of organization is sometimes just as powerful, if not more powerful, than the formal structure.

In their milestone book *In Search of Excellence*, Thomas Peters and Robert Waterman report that many successful companies support and encourage informal organization just as much as they support formal structure.[16] For example, 3M sponsors clubs for twelve or more employees to enhance communication and interaction across departments. Other companies have rearranged offices and other facilities to make them more conducive to informal interaction. Citibank, for instance, once moved two departments to the same floor to encourage intermingling of employees. MCI still has no doors on its offices—the better to grease the flow of ideas. These and other companies believe that informal interaction among employees stimulates the kind of discussions and group processes that can help solve organizational problems.

On the negative side, the informal organization can reinforce office politics that put the interests of individuals ahead of those of the firm. Likewise, a great deal of harm can be caused by distorted or inaccurate information communicated without management input or review. For example, if the informal organization is highlighting false information about impending layoffs, valuable employees may act quickly (and unnecessarily) to seek other employment.

Intrapreneuring

Sometimes organizations actually take steps to encourage the informal organization. They do so for a variety of reasons, two of which we have already touched on. First, most experienced managers recognize that the informal organization exists whether they want it or not. Second, many managers know how to use the informal organization to reinforce the formal organization. Perhaps more important, however, the energy of informal organization can be harnessed to improve productivity.

■ To stimulate innovation, for example, 3M Corp. maintains flat, decentralized organizational structure. As a rule, only a few levels of management bureaucracy are involved in approving new products. The corporate culture at 3M further supports innovation by encouraging researchers to spend 15 percent of their time exploring new ideas. Those who develop new products are rewarded both professionally and financially. As a result, 3M researchers usually develop about 200 new products each year. Among their most celebrated successes have been Post-it self-stick notes and a tape for mending broken bones.

■ Through Xerox Technology Ventures, Xerox Corp. allocates $30 million to fund companies like QuadMark Ltd., an electronics development firm in which Xerox has a 60-percent stake. The purpose of XTV is to nurture internal technological innovations that, for various reasons, do not receive adequate attention from the parent company's development center. For example, QuadMark developed a battery-operated copier that fits inside a briefcase next to a laptop computer. Another XTV-funded start-up invented an advanced circuit board that could be inserted into an inexpensive PC and made to do the work of a $10,000 Xerox office workstation. Xerox deemed it wise to buy out the potential new competitor (for $15 million). Since 1989, XTV has generated twelve start-ups and now offers as much as 20 percent of the new companies' shares to successful founders.[17]

Both 3M and Xerox are supporting a process called **intrapreneuring**—creating and maintaining the innovation and flexibility of a small business environment within the confines of a large, bureaucratic structure. The concept is sound. Historically, most innovations have come from individuals in small businesses (see Chapter 8). As businesses increase in size, however, innovation and creativity tend to become casualties in the battle for more sales and profits. In some large companies, new ideas are even discouraged, and champions of innovation have even been stalled in mid-career. In companies like 3M and Xerox, however, intrapreneuring is seen as an effective way of remaining as innovative as smaller firms that specialize in new products that the larger firms can bring to market quickly.

intrapreneuring
Process of creating and maintaining the innovation and flexibility of a small business environment within the confines of a large organization

Continued from page 153

"Is This a Joke, or Are You Testing Me?"

Or, Is This Any Way to Run a $12 Billion Company?

One of the most obvious signs of organizational change at United Airlines is the increased authority of mid-level managers to spend money. Before decentralization, vice presidents needed the president's approval for purchases over $4,999—a situation that undermined their autonomy and their ability to make decisions.

John A. Edwardson learned of the spending limit about a week after he took over as United's President and Chief Operating Officer: He received a purchase request from a vice president for $5,000 worth of typing paper. Edwardson relates what happened next. "I walked over to his office and said, 'Is this a joke, or are you testing me?' And he said, 'I never test

presidents, and I don't know you well enough to joke with you.'"

With the removal of United's rigid top-down organization, vice presidents can now spend up to $25,000 without seeking approval and have authority over about 95 percent of their budgets.

Case Questions

1. How have organizational changes at United affected the company's decision-making hierarchy?
2. Why did United's function-based organization fail?
3. How did reorganization affect managers' accountability and span of control?
4. Was increasing the spending authority of vice presidents a symbolic move, or did it have real organizational importance?
5. Why did a decentralized organizational structure work better at United than a top-down hierarchical structure?

SUMMARY OF LEARNING OBJECTIVES

1. **Discuss the elements that influence a firm's *organizational structure*.** Every business needs structure to operate. *Organizational structure* varies according to a firm's mission, purpose, and strategy. Size, technology, and changes in environmental circumstances also influence structure. In general, while all organizations have the same basic elements, each develops the structure that contributes to the most efficient operations.

2. **Describe *specialization* and *departmentalization* as the building blocks of organizational structures.** The building blocks of organizational structure are *job specialization* and *departmentalization*. As a firm grows, it usually has a greater need for people to perform specialized tasks (specialization). It also has a greater need to group types of work into logical units (departmentalization). Common forms of departmentalization are *customer*, *product*, *process*, *geographic*, and *functional*. Large businesses often use more than one form of departmentalization. *Process organization* (as opposed to process departmentalization) means organizing according to units or teams responsible for all the various processes involved in getting products to consumers.

3. **Distinguish between *responsibility* and *authority* and *delegation* and *accountability*, and explain the differences between decision making in *centralized organizations* and decision making in *decentralized organizations*.** *Responsibility* is the duty to perform a task; *authority* is the power to make the decisions necessary to complete tasks. *Delegation* begins when a manager assigns a task to a subordinate; *accountability* means that the subordinate must complete

the task. *Span of control* refers to the number of people who work for any individual manager. The more people supervised, the wider the span of control. Wide spans are usually desirable when employees perform simple or unrelated tasks. When jobs are diversified or prone to change, a narrower span is generally preferable.

In a *centralized organization*, only a few individuals in top management have real decision-making authority. In a *decentralized organization*, much authority is delegated to lower-level management. Where both *line* and *line-and-staff systems* are involved, *line departments* generally have authority to make decisions while *staff departments* have a responsibility to advise. A relatively new concept, *committee and team authority*, empowers committees or work teams involved in a firm's daily operations.

4. **Explain the differences between *functional, divisional, matrix,* and *international organization structures*.** In a *functional organization*, authority is usually distributed among such basic functions as marketing and finance. In a *divisional organization*, the various divisions of a larger company, which may be related or unrelated, operate in a relatively autonomous fashion. In *matrix organizations*, in which individuals report to more than one manager, a company creates teams to address specific problems or to conduct specific projects. A company that has divisions in many countries may require an additional level of *international organization* to coordinate those operations.

5. **Describe the *informal organization* and discuss *intrapreneuring*.** The informal organization consists of the everyday social interactions among employees that transcend formal jobs and job interrelationships. To foster the innovation and flexibility of a small business within the big-business environment, some large companies encourage *intrapreneuring*—creating and maintaining the innovation and flexibility of a small business environment within the confines of a large bureaucratic structure.

STUDY QUESTIONS AND EXERCISES

Review

1. What is an organization chart? What purpose does it serve?
2. Explain the significance of size as it relates to organizational structure. Describe the changes that are likely to occur as an organization grows.
3. What is the difference between responsibility and authority?
4. Why is process organization an innovative approach to organizational structure?
5. Why is a company's informal organization important?

Analysis

6. Draw up an organization chart for your college or university.
7. Describe a hypothetical organizational structure for a small printing firm. Describe changes that might be necessary as the business grows.
8. Compare and contrast the matrix and divisional approaches to organizational structure.

Application Exercises

9. Interview the manager of a local service business—say, a fast food restaurant. What types of tasks does this manager typically delegate? Is the appropriate authority also delegated in each case?

10. Using books, magazines, or personal interviews, identify an individual who has succeeded as an intrapreneur. In what ways did the structure of the intrapreneur's company help this individual succeed? In what ways did the structure pose problems?

BUILDING YOUR BUSINESS SKILLS

This exercise enhances the following SCANS workplace competencies: demonstrating basic skills, demonstrating thinking skills, exhibiting interpersonal skills, and working with information.

Goal

To encourage students to understand the roles that specialization and departmentalization play in the organization of a growing small business

Situation

As the owner of a small regional advertising agency doing business in Maine and New Hampshire, you have watched your business acquire new accounts and grow over the past three years. When you opened the agency, you had your hand in nearly every aspect of the business, including new business development, account management, copywriting, art direction, accounting, and even office maintenance. Today you define your job primarily in terms of landing new accounts and overseeing product quality and service.

With seventy people now on staff, you have decided to hire a director of human resources. His or her job will be to write specific job requirements for each position and to formalize the structure of your organization.

Method

Step 1: Working with three or four classmates, list twenty to thirty specific job categories you are likely to find in a growing advertising agency. Consult the latest *Occupational Outlook Handbook* in your library or write to a local advertising agency for job information.

Step 2: By grouping these jobs into logical units, create and name departments.

Step 3: Set up a chain of command in the form of an organizational chart to show how departments interrelate, both with one another and with senior management.

Follow-Up

1. Is there a point at which a small company must begin specializing its job functions? What signs might tell a small business owner that he or she has reached that point?

2. As the owner of a small but growing regional advertising agency, are you likely to departmentalize according to customer, product, process, geographic, or functional lines? Explain your answer.

Exploring the Net

CHAPTER 7 DESCRIBES THE INCREASING IMPORTANCE OF INTRAPRENEURSHIP IN MANY ORGANIZATIONS TODAY. THE FOLLOWING WEBSITE IS A USEFUL STARTING POINT IN LEARNING MORE ABOUT THIS CONCEPT:

http://www.pinchot.com:80/

Browse this site, and then consider the following questions:

1. Review "The Intrapreneur's Ten Commandments." Do these principles seem reasonable to you? Which would be the most difficult for you personally to adopt?
   - What is your first reaction to the advice that you should "come to work each day willing to be fired"? What is your reaction upon further reflection?
   - If there is one theme that is more insistent than the others in this list, what is it?

2. Take the quiz entitled "Are You an Intrapreneur?" Basing your ideas on these questions, draw up a brief "personality profile" of someone who would make a good intrapraneur. To what extent do you yourself fit this profile?

3. Review the feature entitled "Five People of Innovation" and draw up brief thumbnail sketches to characterize each of the five types described here. In what ways can people from these five groups be expected to work together successfully? In what ways might they encounter difficulties in working together?

4. Study the "Survey of the Climate for Innovation." Judging from the questions asked here, list five important characteristics of a climate that is conducive to innovation in an organization.

UNDERSTANDING ENTREPRENEURSHIP AND THE SMALL BUSINESS

Doll Maker Disarmed by Success

HOW TO FINANCE 80,000 LOOSE APPENDAGES

Hopes at the Georgetown Collection Inc. were high in the fall of 1995. The all-important Christmas selling season had arrived, and the company's 18-inch vinyl collectible dolls, each accompanied by an illustrated novel telling the doll's own story, held great promise. The Magic Attic Club dolls, as the collectibles were known, were targeted at girls aged 6 through 11, who were too old for Barbies but still loved playing with dolls.

Research had already shown that there was a market for these dolls. The Pleasant Co., Georgetown's chief competitor, had sold more than three million American Girl collectibles since 1986, and there was room in the market for a company with a different approach to marketing a competing product. And a different approach, according to Gretchen Springer, Georgetown's Vice President of Marketing, is precisely what Georgetown had. Whereas Pleasant dolls represent historical periods, Georgetown dolls are distinctly contemporary. "Pleasant Company," explains Springer, "has identified a whole new market, and we are trying to fill a gap in that mar-

> **"There is the point where companies grow or fail. We're at that point . . . where the company now has to *manage* its success and make the transition to the theoretical opportunity."**
>
> —Gretchen Springer
> *Vice President for Marketing
> at Georgetown Collection Inc.*

ket. Since out book characters and dolls are based on the present, we feel girls can relate to them more strongly. And the fantasy element of the books encourages girls to do more imaginative role-playing." Georgetown also enjoyed a major pricing advantage over Pleasant Co. While American Girl dolls sell for $82, their Magic Attic Club counterparts sells for only $59.

Georgetown's optimism, however, may have been premature. No sooner than it had bet its survival on the Magic Attic Club line, 40,000 dolls from a factory in China arrived

at the company's Westbrook, Maine, headquarters with their arms falling off. With only six weeks left before Christmas, Georgetown's staff of 100 employees worked late into the nights to repair 80,000 doll arms—a process that took 20 minutes per doll. Even so, the arm fiasco was financially devastating, in large part because of the company's history of poor capitalization. Because it was seated on a very thin financial cushion, 1995 was a make-or-break year for Georgetown. "If Magic Attic had failed miserably," admits Georgetown president Jeffrey H. McKinnon, "we'd have bankrupted the business."

Georgetown's emergency repairs succeeded and the company survived. But profits fell victim to the emergency as overtime costs ate away the company's financial base. Looking to the future, however, Georgetown sees itself as poised for success and hopes to double its sales in the coming year. Still, company executives can't help but feel a little uncertain about the shifting sands on which small businesses are so often built, and they worry about their ability to perform without a secure financial safety net. In particular, they understand the increasing importance of financing their own success. In just a few months in 1995, for instance, burgeoning demand forced Georgetown to expand both its telephone order center and its order-filling system. Moreover, in the midst of the bustling holiday season it was obliged to compete for qualified order takers with nearby L.L. Bean. "This is the point where companies grow or fail," says Springer. "We're at that point . . . where the company now has to *manage* its success and make the transition to the theoretical opportunity."

In many ways, Georgetown Collection is no different from thousands of small companies trying to succeed in a competitive marketplace. Like Georgetown, small companies face the problems associated with defining market niches and achieving enough sales to survive and thrive. And even if they are successful in creating demand for their products, they typically face obstacles associated with rapid expansion, including production, warehousing, distribution,

staffing, sales, and competitive pressures. Such obstacles are responsible for the failure of millions of small businesses a year. Nevertheless, small business ownership remains a prominent feature of the American dream. In this chapter, we consider what small businesses are and why they are so important to the U.S. economy.

After reading this chapter, you should be able to

1. Define *small business* and explain its importance to the U.S. economy

2. Explain which *types of small business* best lend themselves to success

3. Define *entrepreneurship* and describe some basic *entrepreneurial characteristics*

4. Describe the *start-up decisions* made by small businesses and identify sources

of *financial aid* and *management advice* available to such enterprises

5. Identify the advantages and disadvantages of *franchising*

Continued on page 196

■ WHAT IS A SMALL BUSINESS?

The term *small business* defies easy definition. Clearly, locally owned and operated groceries, video stores, and restaurants are small businesses, while giant corporations like Sony, Caterpillar, and Eastman Kodak are big businesses. Between these two extremes fall thousands of companies that cannot be easily categorized.

The U.S. Department of Commerce considers a business "small" if it has fewer than 500 employees. But the **U.S. Small Business Administration (SBA),** a government assistance agency for small businesses, regards some companies with 1,500 employees as "small." The SBA bases its definition on two factors: *number of employees* and *total annual sales.* For example, manufacturers are defined as "small" according to the first criterion and grocery stores according to the second. Thus, although an independent grocery store with $13 million in sales may sound large, the SBA still sees it as a small business because its revenues are small compared with those of large food retailers.

Because it is difficult to define a small business in numerical terms, we will define a **small business** as one that is independently owned and managed and that does not dominate its market.[1] A small business cannot be part of another business. Operators must be their own bosses, free to run their businesses as they please. In addition, the small business must have relatively little influence in its market. For example, from a single store in 1985, Blockbuster Entertainment now operates over 4,000 video stores and 500 music stores in 16 countries. Although a very small business only a little more than a decade ago, Blockbuster is now the dominant company in the home video-rental market.

The federal government plays a significant role in the formation and operation of small business in the United States. On the whole, this interest in the role and well-being of small business derives from the importance of such businesses to the overall economy. (As we will see later in this chapter, the U.S. government sponsors numerous assistance programs for small businesses.) In this section, we discuss the role and importance of small business in the U.S. economy and then describe the major types of small businesses in the United States.

The Importance of Small Business in the U.S. Economy

As Figure 8.1 shows, most U.S. businesses employ fewer than 100 people, and most U.S. workers are employed by small firms. For example, Figure 8.1(a) shows that approximately 87 percent of all U.S. businesses employ 20 or fewer people; another 11 percent employ between 20 and 99 people. Figure 8.1(b) shows that 27 percent of all U.S. workers are employed by firms with fewer than 20 people; another 29 percent work in firms that employ between 20 and 99 people. The vast majority of these companies are owner-operated.[2]

On the basis of numbers alone, then, small business is a strong presence in the economy. This is true in virtually all the world's mature economies. In Germany, for example, companies with fewer than 500 employees produce two-thirds of the nation's gross national product, train nine out of ten apprentices, and employ four out of every five workers. Small businesses also play major roles in the economies of Italy, France, and Brazil. In a recent five-year period, while large and mid-size European businesses lost 700,000 jobs, small businesses posted a gain of 2 million.[3] In addition, experts agree that small businesses will be important in the emerging economies of countries like Russia and Vietnam.

The contribution of small business can be measured in terms of its effects on key aspects of an economic system: In the United States, these aspects include *job creation*, *innovation*, and *importance to big business*.

Small Business Administration (SBA) Federal agency charged with assisting small businesses

small business Independently owned and managed business that does not dominate its market

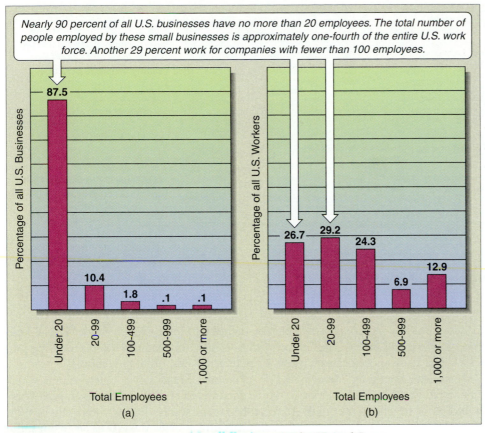

FIGURE 8.1 ◆ **The Importance of Small Business in the United States**

Job Creation In the early 1980s, David Birch of the Massachusetts Institute of Technology claimed that small businesses create eight out of every ten new jobs in the United States. Birch's claim generated considerable interest in the fostering of small business as a matter of public policy. As we will see, Birch's figures are no longer regarded as very accurate. The fact remains, however, that small business—especially in certain industries—is an important source of new (and often well-paid) jobs in this country. Small high-technology businesses are indeed creating new jobs at a much faster rate than older, larger businesses—at least in the manufacturing sector. Dell Computer, for instance, started in Austin, Texas, with one full-time and two part-time employees. The firm now has almost 10,000 employees and adds hundreds each year.

Adjusting the Myth: The Big Business Job Machine. While small businesses create many new jobs each year, the importance of big businesses in job creation should not be overlooked.[4] The large-scale layoffs and cutbacks of the late 1980s and early 1990s have contributed to an impression that jobs in all big businesses were on the decline. In reality, many large businesses have been creating thousands of new jobs every year. Figure 8.2, for example, details the increase in jobs at eight large U.S. companies between 1992 and 1994. As you can see, Wal-Mart alone created 182,000 new jobs during that period. Moreover, the other firms on the list span the spectrum of business areas from manufacturing to service.

At least one message is clear: business success, more than business size, accounts for most new job creation. In 1993, for example, while struggling retail chains like Sears and Woolworth eliminated 80,000 jobs, Wal-Mart more than made up the difference

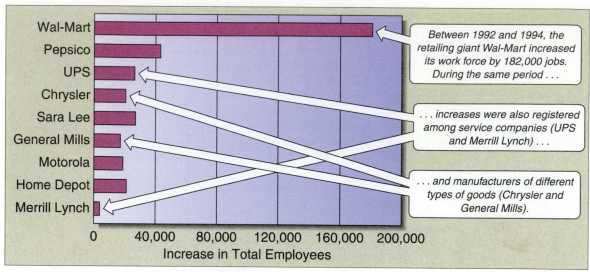

FIGURE 8.2 ◆ Big Business and Job Creation

by adding 85,000. Other successful chains, including Home Depot, Toys "Я" Us, Federated Department Stores, and Dayton Hudson, not only added 400,000 retailing jobs in 1993 but also announced expansion plans that will add thousands more.

"Size isn't the issue," reports M.I.T. economist Frank Levy. "The issue is which firms are adding jobs." Jobs are created by companies of all sizes, all of which hire workers and all of which lay them off. Admittedly, recent studies by Levy and others show that, *relative to their total employment*, small firms hire at twice the rate as large ones. But they also eliminate jobs at a far higher rate. Small firms are the first to hire in times of economic recovery, large firms the last. Big companies, however, are also the last to lay off workers during economic downswings.

> ## "Size isn't the issue. The issue is which firms are adding jobs."
>
> —Frank Levy
> *Economist at M.I.T.*

Innovation   History has shown that major innovations are as likely to come from small businesses (or individuals) as from big businesses. For example, small firms and individuals invented the personal computer and the stainless-steel razor blade, the transistor radio and the photocopying machine, the jet engine and the self-developing photograph. They also gave us the helicopter and power steering, automatic transmissions and air conditioning, cellophane, and the $.19 ballpoint pen.

Not surprisingly, history is repeating itself much more rapidly in the age of computers and high-tech communications. Since it was founded in 1983, for example, a small firm called Maxim Integrated Products has introduced more than 600 semiconductor chips for use in computers, telecommunications, and high-tech instruments. Maxim, which is located in Sunnyvale, California, specializes in the analog semiconductors needed to control such computerized functions as temperature, pressure, and sound. About half the company's revenues come from Europe and Asia.[5] ▶

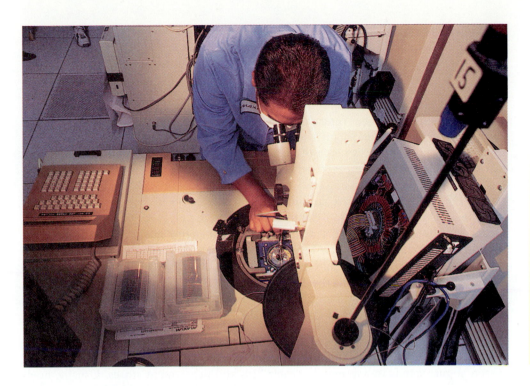

Barely more than a decade old, Maxim Integrated Products is already recognized as an industry leader in designing analog chips for such portable devices as laptop computers and cellular phones. The analog chip market is worth $10 billion per year, and Maxim targets the $2 billion-a-year high-performance segment. The company has found that this end of the market is highly profitable for the handful of U.S. specialty producers who have discovered a worldwide market for high-performance, high-margin products.

Importance to Big Business   Most of the products made by big manufacturers are sold to consumers by small businesses. For example, the majority of dealerships selling Fords, Chevrolets, Toyotas, and Volvos are independently owned and operated. Moreover, small businesses provide big businesses with many of the services, supplies, and raw materials they need. In Poway, California, for example, Norris Communications makes the EarPhone, a device designed by inventor Elwood G. "Woody" Norris to pick up the wearer's voice through the vibrations of bones in the skull. The EarPhone is a peanut-sized apparatus that combines a speaker and a microphone, and Apple Computer includes it in a hardware/software package that permits a Macintosh PC to dial phone calls, play voice mail, and send faxes.[6]

As suppliers, small businesses are almost always less expensive than large firms when volumes are low, close personal contact between seller and customer is needed, or—as in the case of the EarPhone—the product must meet buyers' unique needs or specifications.

Popular Forms of Small Business Enterprise

Small businesses are more common in some industries than in others. The four major small business industry groups are *services, retailing, wholesaling,* and *manufacturing.* Each group differs in its requirements for employees, money, materials, and machines. Remember: the more resources an industry requires, the harder it is to start a business and the less likely that the industry is dominated by small firms. Remember, too, that "small" is a relative term. The criteria—number of employees and total annual sales—differ from industry to industry and are often meaningful only when compared with businesses that are truly "large."

Finally, remember that, as a general rule, manufacturing businesses are the hardest to start and service businesses the easiest. To make sewing machines, for example, a manufacturer must invest not only in people but also in raw materials and machines. It must also develop a distribution network and advertise heavily. To prepare tax forms, however, an entrepreneur need invest only in an education and a few office supplies and reference books. The business can be run out of a storefront or a home.

Services   Partly because they require relatively few resources, service businesses are the largest—and fastest-growing—segment of small business enterprise. No other industry group offers a higher return on time invested. Services tend to appeal to the talent for innovation typified by many small enterprises.

Small business services range from shoeshine parlors to car rental agencies, from marriage counseling to computer software, from accounting and management consulting to professional dog walking. In Cambridge, Massachusetts, Marcia J. Radosevich started HPR Inc., a health care consultancy firm that assists health maintenance organizations (HMOs) spot medical claims that do not comply with company standards. HPR also offers a program that determines when patients are receiving insufficient care. In Atlantic Highlands, New Jersey, Maben Smith has started a business that provides information about small and mid-size businesses. Business Opportunities Online is an electronic database that provides listings for basic transactions—buying, selling, and even the criteria used by about 500 potential investors. It also collects information on about 500 franchisers and 350 professional consultants.[7]

Retailing   A *retail business* sells products manufactured by other firms directly to consumers. There are hundreds of different kinds of retailers, ranging from wig shops and frozen yogurt stands to automobile dealerships and department stores. Usually, however, small businesspeople favor specialty shops—say, big men's clothing or gourmet coffee stores—that let them focus limited resources on narrow market segments.

An interesting path to retailing growth is the one followed by Gymboree, a California-based company that sells clothes for young children. Gymboree started in 1976 with play and exercise centers for kids and their parents. In 1986, however, it shifted gears: it expanded its sideline business of kids' clothing and focused its growth strategy on its retail outlets. ▼ Gymboree designs its own brightly colored cotton outfits, contracts most of its manufacturing to Asian firms, and operates more than 150 stores.[8]

Wholesaling   As with services and retailing, small businesspeople dominate wholesaling. A *wholesale business* buys products from manufacturers or other producers and then sells them to retailers. Wholesalers usually buy goods in bulk and store them in quantities and places convenient for retailers. For a given volume of business, therefore, they need fewer employees than do manufacturers, retailers, or service providers.

They also serve fewer customers than other providers—usually customers who repeatedly order large volumes of goods. For example, wholesalers in the grocery industry buy packaged food in bulk from companies like Del Monte and Campbell's and then sell it to large grocery chains and smaller independent grocers. Like retailing, the wholesaling industry has been affected by the increase in consumer demand for specialty products—a trend that has fueled the growth of firms like Central Garden & Pet, a warehousing firm located in Lafayette, California. Cen-

When current CEO Nancy J. Pedot first came aboard as head of merchandising in 1989, play centers were Gymboree's core business, with retail clothing little more than a sideline. By the end of 1994, however the company had added 40 stores for two consecutive years to a growing chain. Gymboree has also begun to move beyond the preschool market with shoes and clothing targeted for older children. Pedot now regards the company as a "child-based retailer" and has plans to sell learning videos and interactive products as well as ideas for cable-TV sales.

tral began by stocking and distributing garden and pool supplies made by firms like Ortho and Monsanto. In 1991, it bought out a distributor of pet supplies and diversified. In addition to pesticides, gopher traps, and garden hoses, Central now stocks shelves and manages inventory for pet supply retailers—the fastest-growing facet of its business.[9]

Manufacturing   More than any other industry group, manufacturing lends itself to big business—and for good reason. Because of the investment normally required in equipment, energy, and raw materials, a great deal of money is usually needed to start a manufacturing business. Automobile manufacturing, for example, calls for billions of dollars of investment and thousands of workers before the first automobile rolls off the assembly line. Obviously, such requirements shut out most individuals. Although Henry Ford began with $28,000, it has been a long time since anyone started a U.S. car company from scratch.

This is not to say, however, that no small businesspeople do well in manufacturing. For example, George Kappler founded a small contract sewing business in 1976. Today, Kappler Development Co. of Guntersville, Alabama, employs 1,400 people, has annual sales approaching $100 million, and does business around the globe. Chaparral Steel, the subject of our *Business Field Trip* feature, has also prospered in the heavy manufacturing sector while remaining a relatively small enterprise. It is not uncommon for small competitors to outperform big business in such innovative industries as chemistry, electronics, toys, and computer software.[10]

■ ENTREPRENEURSHIP

In the previous section, we discussed each of the popular forms of small business. We also described two firms that started small and grew larger (sometimes much larger). In each of these cases, growth was spurred by the imagination and skill of the entrepreneurs who operated those companies. Although the concepts of *entrepreneurship* and *small business* are closely related, in this section we will discuss some important, though often subtle, differences between them. Then we describe some of the key characteristics of entrepreneurial personalities and activities.

The Distinction between Entrepreneurship and Small Business

Many small businesspersons like to think of themselves as **entrepreneurs**—individuals who assume the risk of business ownership with the primary goal of growth and expansion. In reality, however, a person may be a small businessperson only, an entrepreneur only, or both. Consider an individual who starts a small pizza parlor with no plans other than to earn enough money from the restaurant to lead a comfortable life style. That individual is clearly a small businessperson. With no plans to grow and expand, however, he is not really an entrepreneur. In contrast, an entrepreneur may start with one pizza parlor and turn it into a national chain to rival Domino's or Little Caesar's. Although this individual may have started with a small business, the growth of the firm resulted from entrepreneurial vision and activity.

entrepreneur
Businessperson who accepts both the risks and the opportunities involved in creating and operating a new business venture

Entrepreneurial Characteristics

In general, most successful entrepreneurs have a set of characteristics that sets them apart from most other businesspeople—for example, resourcefulness and a concern for good, often personal, customer relations. Most successful entrepreneurs also have a strong desire to be their own bosses. Many express a need to "gain control over my life" or "build for the family" and believe that building successful businesses will help them do it. They can also handle the ambiguity of not knowing what tomorrow holds.[11]

Many successful entrepreneurs also enjoy taking risks and are not afraid of hard work. They tend to appreciate the time commitment required to make new ventures succeed and are prepared to work the necessary hours. Finally, most successful entrepreneurs report a strong need for personal freedom and opportunity and for the type of creative expression that often goes with owning and operating one's own business.

TRENDS & CHALLENGES
The Generation X Files

So-called "Generation Xers"—people in their twenties and early thirties—are often viewed by their elders as lacking direction and drive, particularly in business. But Generation Xers have already started their own companies. Generation Xers may be more business-oriented than anyone imagined. According to surveys conducted by Babson College professor Paul Reynolds, they are creating small businesses faster than any other demographic group. The result: 1 out of 10 Americans in the 25- to 34-year-old age group has already started a company—a rate three times higher than any other age group.

Nor surprisingly, Generation Xers are choosing to run their companies differently from how their parents might have done. Jennifer Kushell, president of the Young Entrepreneurs Network, explains why:

> We . . . grew up in the '80s with parents who were getting divorced. . . . They didn't do things that were true to their original goals. They got too wrapped up in money, in succeeding at any expense. This new generation is saying, wait a minute, we don't want to have to screw people over for money. We want to do things that are going to improve our environment, our families, our communities. Younger people have a different set of values because they grew up lacking them.

Thus, Generation X entrepreneurs tend to create companies that focus on doing good as well as making money. When Kristin Roach founded Kurvz Extremewear, a company that produces snowboarding apparel for women, her goal was twofold. "I'm doing this to make money," she readily admits, "but I also have a cause here—to support women in sports."

> ### "Younger people have a different set of values because they grew up lacking them."
> —Jennifer Kushell
> *President of the Young Entrepreneurs Network*

Generation X entrepreneurs are also more employee- and customer-centered than their elders. As a group, for instance, they try harder to work around employees' childcare needs by creating flexible schedules, and many encourage workers to bring their children—and even their pets—to the workplace for visits. Many generation members shun the bureaucratic hierarchies of traditional corporations in favor of companies with few organizational barriers. They like to foster environments that value ideas, no matter where they come from. Their goal is to recognize and reward people for the contributions they make rather than for their titles in the corporate hierarchy.

This disdain for traditional ways of doing business sometimes creates unique corporate cultures. For example, at Earth-link Network, a Pasadena, California, Internet service provider, Sky Dayton, the 25-year-old president, invites employees to play roller hockey or go snowboarding to brainstorm new ideas. "I don't have preconceived notions about running the company," says Dayton, who contends that employees are more willing to talk when they are doing something they enjoy.

Are these nonconventional techniques and values likely to last as Generation X entrepreneurs mature into middle age? Jennifer Kushell thinks they will. "It's not a passing phase," she believes. "We're instilling values that will continue for years to come. It was different in the '80s. The surge of wealth and greed caused us to rebel."

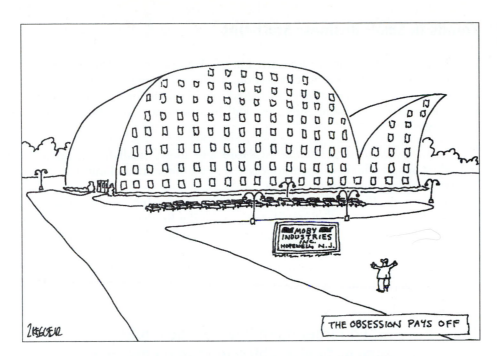

© 1998 Jack Ziegler *from* The Cartoon Bank,™ Inc.

■ FAILURE AND SUCCESS IN SMALL BUSINESS

For every Henry Ford, Walt Disney, or Bill Gates—people who transformed small businesses into major corporations—there are many small businesspeople and entrepreneurs who fail. Figure 8.3 illustrates recent trends in new business start-ups and failures. As you can see, new business start-ups have exceeded 800,000 a year since 1994. But although failures have declined recently, almost 100,000 firms fail each year. In this section, we look first at a few key trends in small business start-ups. Then we examine some of the main reasons for both failure and success in small business undertakings.

FIGURE 8.3 ◆ Start-Ups: Success and Failure

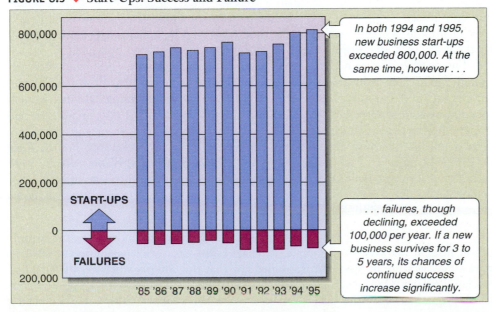

Trends in Small Business Start-Ups

Thousands of new businesses are started in the United States every year. Several factors account for this trend. In this section, we focus on four of them: entrepreneurs who cross over from big business, increased opportunities for minorities and women, new opportunities in global enterprise, and improved rates of survival among small businesses.

Crossovers from Big Business More and more, small businesses are being started by people who have opted to leave large corporations and put their experience and know-how to work for themselves.

For example, Ely Callaway left Burlington Industries Inc. after seventeen years to found Callaway Golf Co. Callaway developed the Big Bertha Metal Wood driver and a set of equally innovative irons that now enjoy the highest dollar sales of any golf clubs in the United States. Callaway credits his years at Burlington for making him the manager he is today. "I'd rather learn how to ride a bike on somebody else's bicycle," he says, "than on my own."[12]

"I'd rather learn how to ride a bike on somebody else's bicycle than on my own."

—Ely Callaway
Founder and CEO of Callaway Golf Co.

Opportunities for Minorities and Women In addition to big business expatriates, more small businesses are being started by minorities and women. Black-owned businesses, for example, are increasing two and one-half times as fast as all other types of start-ups. T. J. Walker and Carl Jones operate Threads 4 Life, a California-based fashion firm that makes and markets hip, inner-city designs—colorful T-shirts and outsized pants—for young black consumers.[13]

As you can see in Figure 8.4, the number of women entrepreneurs is also growing rapidly. Almost a third of all U.S. firms with fewer than 500 employees—some 6.5 million enterprises—are owned or controlled by women. These companies currently employ 11 million people—more than the total employed by the entire Fortune 500 list. By the year 2000, 40 percent of all U.S. businesses will be owned by women.[14]

The chart in Figure 8.4 also shows rates of increase between 1980 and 1990. Although the greatest gain was in services, the increase in the number of women-owned companies cuts across the business spectrum. In 1978, for example, Brenda French founded a small scarf-making business in a spare bedroom. In 1989, French learned about a new machine that can duplicate hand-knit quality with mass-production speed. Now a full-line clothing manufacturer emphasing mass customization, French Rags generates $5 million a year. ▶ In 1992, when Hillary Sterba and Nancy Novinc were laid off by Cleveland Twist Drill Co., they decided to pool 26 years worth of experience and contacts. They started S&N Engineering Services, which is now a successful competitor in the male-dominated field of tool engineering.[15]

Global Opportunities Many entrepreneurs today are also finding new opportunities in foreign markets. For example, Michael Giles left a well-paying job at IBM to start a new venture in South Africa. Giles saw that the country's black townships had few laundromats. One area, for example, had only four laundromats for 4.5 million people. Using a loan from the U.S. Overseas Private Investment Corp., Giles launched a

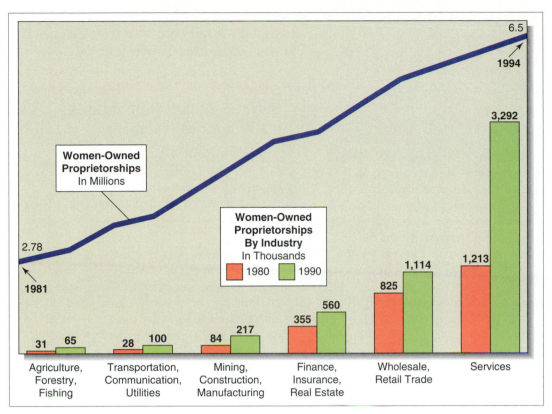

FIGURE 8.4 ◆ Women-Owned Businesses in the United States

chain of 108 coin-operated laundromats throughout the region's black townships. Other entrepreneurs have launched start-up newspapers, accounting firms, and communications companies throughout the world, especially in Eastern Europe.[16]

Better Survival Rates

More people are encouraged to test their skills as entrepreneurs because the failure rate among small businesses has been declining in recent years. During the 1960s and 1970s, for example, less than half of all new start-ups survived more than eighteen months; only one in five lasted ten years. Now, however, new businesses have a better chance of surviving. Of new businesses started in the 1980s, for instance, more than 77 percent remained in operation for at least three years.

When CEO Brenda French founded French Rags, a small scarf-making business, in 1978, her basic goal—and challenge—was to produce custom-made knitwear to be sold directly to customers. In addition to a sell-at-home distribution scheme, the means to meeting this challenge was technology. From Silicon Graphics, French first acquired a workstation for designing knitwear. Then partner Milé Rasic designed a software program for producing templates and loading yarn for fast and easy switching from garment to garment. New machines duplicate hand-knit quality with mass-production speed, and items that used to take a skilled craftsperson a day and a half can now be produced in less than an hour.

TRENDS & CHALLENGES

EASTERN MEETS EAST AND WEST AT SALAMI.COM

Eastern Meat Farms is known in Franklin Square, New York, for its delectable array of sweet sausages, fresh pastas, Crotonese cheese, and semolina bread. It is also known for its loyal customers, many of whom urged the store's owners to start a mail order operation so they could send its delicious bounty to relatives around the world. At first, Richard Lodico and Vinny Barbieri resisted the idea, believing there was little money in it.

Their attitude changed when someone suggested doing business on the Internet. The partners were sufficiently intrigued to set up a virtual shop on the World Wide Web, which they called salami.com. They had to wait more than a month for their first order, but when it finally came, it was from a Japanese customer who wanted $87 worth of pasta. Shipping charges nearly doubled the cost, but the customer didn't mind. Purchased in Japan, the same Italian delicacies would cost $150 more.

The experience of Eastern Meat Farms is not unique. Other small businesses are becoming international operations thanks to the Internet. Hot Hot Hot, a tiny Pasadena, California, store that specializes in 150 hot sauces, attracts about 1,500 visitors a day to its *hothothot.com*. Website. Among its customers are chili lovers from Brazil, New Zealand, and Switzerland. "Our 300-square-foot store," boasts co-owner Monica Lopez, "is now a global company."

On-line commerce gives small businesses the ability to reach a global market. Moreover, it helps to level the playing field for small companies by eliminating many of the costs associated with international marketing, distribution, and inventory storage. "On the Internet," explains Craig Dunuloff, president of a Seattle-based software developer, "Wal-Mart can't make much more of a fancier store than a general store can."

"Our 300-square-foot store is now a global company."

—Monica Lopez
*Owner of Hot Hot Hot
a Pasadena, California, company that does
business on the Internet*

A level playing field, of course, does not mean that doing business on the Internet is easy. For a small business to succeed in an environment in which worldwide comparison shopping is as simple as a click of the mouse, it must create a niche in the form of a specialized product or service, and it must learn how to build loyalty through electronic customer service. For example, when a customer places an order at salami.com, Eastern Meat immediately e-mails back a confirmation. This procedure requires a time commitment to servicing on-line accounts. At Hot Hot Hot, workers spend about ninety minutes a day on e-mail and calls generated by their Internet Website.

The most successful small businesses on the Internet realize the value of creating virtual communities—places where like-minded Web surfers can share information and opinions, make purchases, and come back for another visit a week or two later. Thus, Monica Lopez and her husband, Perry, encourage shoppers on hothothot.com to post reviews of their chili sauces.

Conducted correctly, on-line commerce can be profitable for small companies. After just nine months on line, for example, salami.com now generates about $8,000 a month in business. With monthly Web charges of about $1,800, the difference is meaningful profit. "It's a real moneymaker," says Richard Lodico. "It's really catching on."

Today the SBA estimates that slightly less than 40 percent of all new businesses can expect to survive for six years.[17]

Reasons for Failure

Unfortunately, 60 percent of all new businesses do not survive more than five years. Why do some succeed and others fail? Although there is no set pattern, there are some common causes of both failure and success.

Four general factors contribute to small business failure:

1. *Managerial incompetence or inexperience*. If managers do not know how to make basic business decisions, they are unlikely to be successful in the long run.

2. *Neglect*. Starting a small business requires an overwhelming time commitment.

3. *Weak control systems*. If control systems do not signal impending problems, managers may be in serious trouble before more visible difficulties alert them.

4. *Insufficient capital*. Here is a rule of thumb: a new business should have enough capital to operate at least six months without earning a profit.

Reasons for Success

Four basic factors are typically cited to explain small business success:

1. *Hard work, drive, and dedication*. Small business owners must be committed to succeeding and be willing to put in the time and effort to do so.

2. *Market demand for the products or services being provided*. Careful analysis of market conditions can help small businesspeople assess the probable reception of their products in the marketplace.

3. *Managerial competence*. Successful small businesspeople may acquire competence through training, experience, or by using the expertise of others.

4. *Luck*. Luck also plays a role in the success of some firms. For example, after Alan McKim started Clean Harbors, an environmental cleanup firm based in New England, he struggled to keep his business afloat. Then the U.S. government committed $1.6 billion to toxic waste clean-up, McKim's specialty. As a result, he was able to get several large government contracts and put his business on solid financial footing. Had the government fund not been created at just the right time, McKim's business may well have failed.

■ STARTING AND OPERATING A SMALL BUSINESS

Several other factors contribute to the success of a small business. In particular, most successful entrepreneurs make the right decisions when they start up their businesses. For example, they must decide precisely *how* to get into business. Should they buy an existing business or build from the ground up? In addition, would-be entrepreneurs must find appropriate sources of financing and decide when to seek the advice of experts.

Starting a Small Business

An old (and very famous) Chinese saying notes that "a journey of a thousand miles begins with but a single step." This is also true of a new business. The first step is the individual's commitment to becoming a small businessperson. Next is choosing the good or service to be offered—a process that means investigating the industry and market. Making this choice also requires that would-be entrepreneurs assess not only industry trends but also their own skills. Like the managers of big businesses, small businesspeople must also be sure that they understand the true nature of their chosen businesses.

Buying Out an Existing Business   After choosing a product and making sure that the choice fits his or her skills and interests, an entrepreneur must decide whether to buy an existing business or start from scratch. Consultants often recommend the first approach because the odds are better. A successful business has already proved its ability to draw customers at a profit. It has established working relationships with lenders, suppliers, and the community. Moreover, the track record of an existing business gives potential buyers a much clearer picture of what to expect than any estimate of a new business's prospects. About 30 percent of the new businesses started in the past decade were bought from someone else.

Starting from Scratch   Some people, however, seek the satisfaction that comes from planting an idea, nurturing it, and making it grow into a strong and sturdy business. There are also practical reasons to start a business from scratch. A new business, for example, does not suffer the ill effects of a prior owner's errors. The start-up owner is also free to choose lenders, equipment, inventories, locations, suppliers, and workers unbound by a predecessor's commitments and policies. Of the new businesses begun in the past decade, 64 percent were started from scratch. (The remaining 6 percent of all new businesses were inherited or created when one partner bought out another.)

Not surprisingly, the risks of starting a business from scratch are greater than those of buying an existing firm. Founders of new businesses can only make predictions and projections about their prospects. Success or failure thus depends heavily on identifying a genuine business opportunity—a product or service for which customers will pay but that is currently unavailable to them. To find openings, entrepreneurs must study their markets and answer the following questions:

- Who are my customers?
- Where are they?
- At what price will they buy my product?
- In what quantities will they buy?
- Who are my competitors?
- How will my product differ from that of my competitors?

Finding answers to these questions is a difficult task even for large, well-established firms. Where, then, can the small businessperson get the necessary information? Other sources of assistance are discussed later in this chapter, but we briefly describe three of the most accessible here:

- The best way to gain knowledge about a market is to work in it before going into business in it. For example, if you once worked in a bookstore and now plan to open one of your own, you probably already have some idea about the kinds of books people request and buy.
- A quick scan of the *Yellow Pages* or advertisements in trade journals will reveal many potential competitors. Visits to these establishments can help you understand their strengths and weaknesses.
- Studying magazines and books aimed specifically at small businesses can also be of help, as can hiring professionals to survey the market for you.

Financing the Small Business

Although the choice of how to start is important, it is meaningless unless a small businessperson can obtain the money to set up shop. As Figure 8.5 shows, a wide variety of monetary resources—both private and public—is available. Because the risks are better understood, lending institutions are more likely to help finance the purchase of an existing business than a new business. Individuals starting up new businesses must rely more on their personal resources.

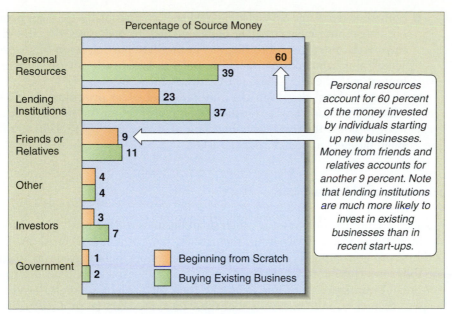

FIGURE 8.5 ◆ **Financing the Small Business**

According to a study by the National Federation of Independent Business, an owner's personal resources—not loans—are the most important source of finance. Including money borrowed from friends and relatives, personal resources account for more than two-thirds of all money invested in new small businesses and half of that invested in the purchase of existing businesses.

Although banks, independent investors, and government loans all provide much smaller portions of start-up funds than the personal resources of owners, they are important in many cases. Obtaining money from these sources, however, requires some extra effort. Banks and private investors, for instance, usually want to see formal business plans—detailed outlines of proposed businesses and markets, owners' backgrounds, and other sources of funding. Government loans have strict eligibility requirements.

Small Business Investment Companies   Created by the Small Business Investment Act of 1958, small business investment companies are federally licensed to borrow money from the SBA and to invest it in or loan it to small businesses. They are themselves investments for their shareholders. Beneficiaries of SBIC capital have included Apple Computer, Intel, and Federal Express. In addition, the government has recently begun to sponsor **minority enterprise small business investment companies (MESBICs).**

minority enterprise small business investment company (MESBIC)
Federally sponsored company that specializes in financing minority-owned and -operated businesses

SBA Financial Programs   Since its founding in 1953, the SBA has offered more than twenty financing programs to small businesses that meet its standards in terms of size and independence. Eligible firms must also be unable to get private financing at reasonable terms. Because of these and other restrictions, SBA loans have never been a major source of small business financing. In addition, budget cutbacks at the SBA have reduced the number of firms benefiting from loans. Several SBA programs, however, currently offer funds to qualified applicants:

■ Under the SBA's **guaranteed loans program,** small businesses can borrow from commercial lenders. The SBA guarantees to repay 75–85 percent of the loan amount, not to exceed $750,000. Under a related program, companies engaged in international trade can borrow up to $1.25 million. Such loans may be made for as long as fifteen years. Most SBA lending activity flows through this program.

guaranteed loans program
Program in which the SBA guarantees to repay 75–85 percent of small business commercial loans up to $750,000

immediate participation loans program
Program in which small businesses are loaned funds put up jointly by banks and the SBA

local development companies (LDCs) program
Program in which the SBA works with local for-profit or nonprofit organizations seeking to boost a community's economy

■ Sometimes bank and SBA-guaranteed loans are unavailable (perhaps because the business cannot meet stringent requirements). In such cases, the SBA may help finance the entrepreneur through its **immediate participation loans program.** Under this arrangement, the SBA and the bank each put up a share of the money, with the SBA's share not to exceed $150,000.

■ Under the **local development companies (LDCs) program,** the SBA works with a corporation (either for-profit or nonprofit) founded by local citizens who want to boost the local economy. The SBA can lend up to $500,000 for each small business to be helped by an LDC.

Sources of Management Advice

Financing is not the only area in which small businesses need help. Until World War II, the business world involved few regulations, few taxes, few records, few big competitors, and no computers. Since then, however, simplicity has given way to complexity. Today few entrepreneurs are equipped with all the business skills needed to survive.

Small businesspeople can no longer be their own troubleshooters, lawyers, bookkeepers, financiers, and tax experts. For these jobs, they rely on professional help. But to survive and grow, small businesses also need advice regarding management. This advice is usually available from four sources: *advisory boards*, *management consultants*, the *SBA*, and a process called *networking*.

Advisory Boards   All companies—even those that do not legally need boards of directors—can benefit from the problem-solving abilities of advisory boards. Thus, some small businesses create boards to provide advice and assistance. For example, an advisory board might help an entrepreneur determine the best way to finance a plant expansion or start exporting products to foreign markets.

management consultant
Independent outside specialist hired to help managers solve business problems

Management Consultants   Opinions vary widely about the value of **management consultants**—experts who charge fees to help managers solve problems. Because management consultants often specialize in one area, such as international business, small business, or manufacturing, they can bring objective and trained eyes to problems and provide logical recommendations. But consultants can be expensive. Some consultants, for example, charge $1,000 or more for one day of assistance.

Like other professionals, consultants should be chosen with care. They can be found, for example, through major corporations that have used their services and that can provide references and reports on their work. Not surprisingly, they are most effective when the client helps—for instance, by providing schedules and written proposals for work to be done.

The Small Business Administration   Even more important than its financing role is the SBA's role in helping small businesspeople improve their management skills. It is easy for entrepreneurs to spend money; SBA programs are designed to show them how to spend it wisely. The SBA offers small businesses four major management counseling programs at virtually no cost:

Service Corps of Retired Executives (SCORE)
SBA program in which retired executives work with small businesses on a volunteer basis

Active Corps of Executives (ACE)
SBA program in which currently employed executives work with small businesses on a volunteer basis

■ A small businessperson who needs help in starting a new business can receive free assistance through the **Service Corps of Retired Executives (SCORE).** All SCORE members are retired executives, and all are volunteers. Under this program, the SBA tries to match the expert to the need. For example, if a small businessperson needs help putting together a marketing plan, the SBA will send a SCORE counselor with marketing expertise.

■ Like SCORE, the **Active Corps of Executives (ACE)** program is designed to help small businesses that cannot afford consultants. The SBA recruits ACE volunteers from virtually every industry. All ACE volunteers are currently involved in successful activities, mostly as small businesspeople themselves.

Together SCORE and ACE have more than 12,000 counselors working out of 350 chapters throughout the United States. They provide assistance to some 140,000 small businesses each year.

- The talents and skills of students and instructors at colleges and universities are fundamental to the **Small Business Institute (SBI).** Under the guidance of seasoned professors of business administration, students seeking advanced degrees work closely with small businesspeople to help solve specific problems, such as sagging sales or rising costs. Students earn credit toward their degrees, with their grades depending on how well they handle a client's problems. Several hundred colleges and universities counsel thousands of small businesspeople through this program every year.

- The newest of the SBA's management counseling projects is its **Small Business Development Center (SBDC)** program. Begun in 1976, SBDCs are designed to consolidate information from various disciplines and institutions, including technical and professional schools. They then make this knowledge available to new and existing small businesses. In 1991, universities in forty-three states took part in the program.

Networking More and more, small businesspeople are discovering the value of **networking**—of meeting regularly with one another to discuss common problems and opportunities and, perhaps most important, pool resources. Businesspeople have long joined organizations like the local Chamber of Commerce and the National Federation of Independent Businesses (NFIB) to make such contacts.

Today organizations are springing up all over the United States to facilitate effective small business networking. One such organization, the Council of Smaller Enterprises of Cleveland, boasts a total membership of more than 9,000 small businesspeople—the largest number in the country. This organization offers its members not only networking possibilities but also educational programs and services tailored to their wants and needs. In a typical year, its 85 educational programs draw more than 8,500 small businesspeople.

In particular, women and minorities have found networking to be an effective problem-solving tool. For example, the Chief Executive Roundtable, a group of women business owners from across the United States, meets in a different major city every month to discuss and solve business problems. Topics range from dealing with late-paying customers to conflicts between partners over financing expansion. Sponsored by the New York–based American Women's Economic Development Corp., the Roundtable's members own and operate companies with annual sales of $1–$10 million.[18]

Small Business Institute (SBI)
SBA program in which college and university students and instructors work with small businesspeople to help solve specific problems

Small Business Development Center (SBDC)
SBA program designed to consolidate information from various disciplines and make it available to small businesses

networking
Interactions among businesspeople for the purpose of discussing mutual problems and opportunities and perhaps pooling resources

■ FRANCHISING

- When Louis Minella left his job as a store planner for Sears, he did the same thing as thousands of other managers who have voluntarily left—or been forced out of—big companies. After thirty-one years in the corporate world, Minella decided to join the ranks of more than a half million small business owners who run their own franchise stores. "It was time to do something different," says Minella, who adds, "I'm in reality now."

Minella chose Mail Boxes Inc., a San Diego–based company that serves at-home businesses, mobile workers, and large corporate accounts. For an upfront fee and a percentage of gross sales, Minella received rights to the Mail Boxes name, advertising support, and access to a variety of national accounts, such as Xerox and Panasonic, whose employees can contract to use his facility as a branch office for postal services like mailing, shipping, and faxing. To succeed in his new undertaking, then, Louis Minella had to master such nuts-and-bolts skills as sending faxes, making photocopies, and operating a cash register. Not everyone can make the transition, but Mail Boxes thinks corporate refugees are the best bet. They "tend to be better business people," says President Tony DeSio, who appreciates the fact that they perform the management basics, such as "checking their pricing and making sure costs are being controlled."[19]

franchise
Arrangement in which a buyer (franchisee) purchases the right to sell the good or service of the seller (franchiser)

As many people like Louis Minella have discovered, franchising agreements are an accessible doorway to entrepreneurship. A **franchise** is an arrangement that permits the *franchisee* (buyer) to sell the product of the *franchiser* (seller, or parent company). Franchisees can thus benefit from the selling corporation's experience and expertise. They can also draw upon the franchiser for managerial and financial help.

The franchiser, for example, may supply financing. It may pick the store location, negotiate the lease, design the store, and purchase necessary equipment. It may train the first set of employees and managers and provide standardized policies and procedures. Once the business is open, the franchiser may offer savings by allowing it to purchase from a central location. Marketing strategy (especially advertising) may also be handled by the franchiser. Finally, franchisees may benefit from continued management counseling. In short, franchisees receive—that is, invest in—not only their own ready-made businesses but expert help in running them.

Advantages and Disadvantages of Franchising

Franchises offer many advantages to both sellers and buyers. Franchisers, for example, benefit from the ability to grow rapidly by using the investment money provided by franchisees. This strategy has enabled giant franchisers like McDonald's and Baskin-Robbins to mushroom into billion-dollar concerns in a relatively brief time.

For the franchisee, the arrangement combines the incentive of owning a business with the advantage of access to big business management skills. Unlike the person who starts from scratch, the franchisee does not have to build a business step by step. Instead, the business is established virtually overnight. Moreover, because each franchise outlet is probably a carbon copy of every other link in the chain, the chances of failure are reduced. According to the U.S. Department of Commerce, only 5 percent of all franchises in the country were discontinued in 1990.

There are, of course, disadvantages as well. Perhaps the most significant is the start-up cost. Franchise prices vary widely. While Fantastic Sam's hair salon franchise fees are only $20,000, a Gingiss Formalwear franchise can run as high as $100,000. Extremely profitable or hard-to-get franchises are even more expensive. A McDonald's franchise costs $610,000 to $700,000, and a professional sports team can run to several million dollars. Franchisees may also have continued obligations to contribute percentages of sales to parent corporations.

Buying a franchise also entails less tangible costs. For one thing, the small businessperson sacrifices some independence. A McDonald's franchisee, for example, cannot change the way hamburgers or milkshakes are made. Nor can franchisees create individual identities in their communities; for all practical purposes, the McDonald's owner is anonymous. In addition, many franchise agreements are difficult to terminate.

Finally, while franchises minimize risks, they do not guarantee success. Many franchisees have seen their investments—and their dreams—disappear because of poor locations, rising costs, or lack of continued franchiser commitment. Moreover, figures on failure rates are artificially low because they do not include failing franchisees bought out by their franchising parent companies. An additional risk is that the chain itself could collapse. In any given year, dozens—sometimes hundreds—of franchisers close shop or stop selling franchises.

Continued from page 177

Value Lessons in the Doll-and-Book Niche

Toy Maker Prices the Fare to a Higher Plane

Demand for the Georgetown Collection's Magic Attic Club dolls is driven by the colorful catalogs in which the dolls are marketed and by the seventeen books published by Magic Attic Press. The stories center on the lives of four best friends—the doll characters Alison, Megan, Heather, and Keisha—who discover a trunk filled with elegant costumes and a magic mirror. When the girls don the costumes and look into the mirror, they are transported through time and space to encounter different adventures. "Each story," explains marketing VP Gretchen Springer, "leads the girls to a self-discovery, passing on to them a value lesson relating to something they are struggling with in real life."

Parents love the doll/book concept so much that 1.5 million books,

> "It's hard to maintain consistency and credibility with banks without a long track record, and it's hard to achieve a track record without adequate capital."
>
> —Jill S. Krutick
> *Analyst with Smith Barney*

priced at $5.95 each, are now in print. Says one mother, "I think it's great that my daughter is playing with these dolls so creatively. There isn't that much in the toy stores for girls. . . . Now suddenly the girls are into dressing up dolls, and it's so wonderfully old-fashioned."

Having found its marketing niche and overcome its 1995 production disaster, Georgetown's continuing challenge, according to Jill S. Krutick, an analyst with Smith Barney, is to attract the capital and resources that it needs to "take the business to a higher plane." But Georgetown, like many other small companies, finds itself in a chicken/egg situation. "It's hard to maintain consistency and credibility with banks without a long track record," admits Krutick, "and it's hard to achieve a track record without adequate capital." Assuming that Georgetown can find the capital it needs to expand, it is riding a crest in the toy industry—the phenomenal growth of the high-end doll-and-book category. "This category," reports one toy-industry consultant, "is very hot."

Case Questions

1. Why is Georgetown Collection Inc. an example of an entrepreneurial company?
2. What factors were responsible for Georgetown's problems in 1995, and how are these factors typical of those encountered by small businesses?
3. How do you assess Georgetown's chances for business success?
4. Why is an adequate financial cushion so important to a company like Georgetown? Your answer to this question should focus on both survival and growth.
5. What role have product and marketing innovation played in Georgetown's success so far?

SUMMARY OF LEARNING OBJECTIVES

1. **Define *small business* and explain its importance to the U.S. economy.** A *small business* is independently owned and managed and does not dominate its market. Small businesses are crucial to the economy because they create new jobs, foster *entrepreneurship* and *innovation*, and supply goods and services needed by larger businesses.

2. **Explain which *types of small business* best lend themselves to success.** Services are the easiest operations for small businesspeople to start because they require relatively low levels of resources. They also offer high returns on investment and tend to foster innovation. Retailing and wholesaling are more

difficult because they usually require some experience, but they are still attractive to many entrepreneurs. As the most resource-intensive area of the economy, manufacturing is the area least dominated by small firms.

3. **Define *entrepreneurship* and describe some basic *entrepreneurial characteristics*.** *Entrepreneurs* are small businesspeople who assume the risk of business ownership. Unlike many businesspeople, their primary goal is growth and expansion. Most successful entrepreneurs share a strong desire to be their own bosses and believe that building businesses will help them gain control over their lives and build for their families. Many also enjoy risk taking and committing themselves to the necessary time and work. Finally, most report that freedom and creative expression are important factors in the decision to own and operate their own businesses.

4. **Describe the *start-up decisions* made by small businesses and identify sources of *financial aid* and *management advice* available to such enterprises.** In deciding to go into business, the entrepreneur must choose between buying an existing business and starting from scratch. There are practical advantages and disadvantages to both approaches. A successful existing business, for example, has working relationships with other businesses and has already proved its ability to make a profit. New businesses allow owners to plan and work with clean slates, but it is hard to make projections abut the business's prospects. Small businesspeople generally draw heavily on their own resources for financing. The *Small Business Administration (SBA)* sponsors a variety of loan programs, including *small business investment companies*. Management advice is available from *advisory boards*, *management consultants*, the *SBA*, and the practice of *networking* (meeting regularly with people in related businesses to discuss problems and opportunities).

5. **Identify the advantages and disadvantages of *franchising*.** *Franchising* has become a popular form of small business ownership because the *franchiser* (parent company) supplies financial, managerial, and marketing assistance to the *franchisee*, who buys the right to sell the franchiser's product. Franchising also enables small businesses to grow rapidly. The risks in franchising are lower than those in opening a new business from scratch. However, the costs of purchasing a franchise can be high, and the franchisee sacrifices independence and creativity. In addition, franchises do not guarantee success.

STUDY QUESTIONS AND EXERCISES

Review

1. Why are small businesses important to the U.S. economy?
2. What factors typically contribute to the success and failure of small businesses?
3. Identify the primary sources of funding for small businesses and rank them in order of importance.
4. From the standpoint of the franchisee, what are the primary advantages and disadvantages of most franchise arrangements?

Analysis

5. If you were going to open a small business, what type would it be? Why?
6. Do you think you would be a successful entrepreneur? Why or why not?

7. Would you prefer to buy an existing business or start your own business from scratch? Why?

8. Would you prefer to open an independent business or enter into a franchise agreement? Why?

Application Exercises

9. Select a small local firm that has gone out of business recently. Identify as many factors as you can that led to the company's failure.

10. At the library, research the role of small business in another country.

BUILDING YOUR BUSINESS SKILLS

This exercise enhances the following SCANS workplace competencies: demonstrating basic skills, demonstrating thinking skills, exhibiting interpersonal skills, and working with information.

Goal

To encourage students to appreciate the value of networking to small business success and to develop a practical approach to finding and questioning networking sources

Situation

Suppose that you and three partners have just started a small publishing company specializing in ethnic cookbooks. All of you have publishing backgrounds, but none of you has ever owned a company or run a business. You decide that one of the best ways to learn what it takes to operate a successful small business is to seek the advice of others.

Method

Step 1: Suggest six different networking sources—including professional and community organizations—that might be of value to a start-up publishing company. Choose each source based on its ability to help you in a special way. For example, while one organization might place you in contact with qualified editorial workers, another might help you learn everything you need to know about running a company in your town. Make a list of the sources and describe their value to you.

Step 2: For each source, develop a list of questions, the answers to which might help your business in concrete ways. For example, in a networking meeting with the president of a professional editorial workers group, you might ask the following questions:

■ Can I find copy editors and proofreaders through your organization?

■ How much do they charge?

■ Can you recommend an excellent photo researcher?

Step 3: Now sit down with three or four other students in your class to compare and contrast your networking sources and questions.

Follow-Up

1. What is the most valuable networking source on your list and on the lists of other group members? Describe the reasons for your choices.

2. Sources of networking help can be long-term, short-term, or both. How would you classify each of the sources you identified?

3. What factors were responsible for the different approaches to networking that you found in your small group?

ONE OF THE MOST IMPORTANT CONTACTS FOR MOST SMALL BUSINESSPERSONS IS THE SMALL BUSINESS ADMINISTRATION (SBA). YOU CAN REACH THE SBA'S WEBSITE AT THE FOLLOWING ADDRESS:

http://www.sbaonline.sba.gov/textonly/

Begin by examining the sections on "Starting Your Business," "Financing Your Business," and "Expanding Your Business." After you have examined these features, consider the following questions:

1. Assume that you are planning to purchase an existing small business. In the areas identified above, what was the most important information that you could find? Identify other sections of the SBA site that might be relevant to you. What useful information did you find by browsing a few of these additional areas?

2. Assume that you are planning to start a new small business from scratch. Again, review the sections of the SBA site that might be most relevant, and report on the available information.

3. Assume that you are already operating a small business but are concerned about increasing competition. In what sections of its Website does the SBA offer material that might be helpful to you?

4. Use the SBA links to visit the Websites maintained by your U.S. representative and/or senator. What specific information on these sites, if any, might be most helpful to a small businessperson?

5. Overall, do you think the SBA site is likely to be more helpful for an existing business or for a new business just starting out? Why?

"If It's Not Fun, Why Do It?"
The Flavor of the Culture at Ben & Jerry's

Learning Objectives

The purpose of this video exercise is to help students:

1. Understand the relationships between a company's goals and strategies and its practical approach to everyday management
2. Appreciate the ways in which corporate culture affects both a company's approach to decision making and the decisions that it actually makes
3. Understand the responsibilities of a chief executive officer and the ways in which they reflect a company's particular goals and strategies

Background Information

If there is such a thing as a classic American success story, Ben & Jerry's Homemade Inc. may be it. The story opens in 1978, when Ben Cohen and Jerry Greenfield invested $12,000 to start a small ice cream company in Burlington, Vermont. In part, Ben & Jerry's success can be attributed to the co-founders' shared sense of social responsibility and environmental awareness. One instance of Ben & Jerry's socially conscious commitment to its employees is evident in such matters as its approach to compensation. At the outset, for example, policy stipulated that the highest-paid executive would receive only five times the compensation of the lowest-paid full-time employee. In 1990, the ratio was increased to 7 to 1.

This area of the company's so-called *economic mission* came into play during the partners' widely publicized 1994 search for a new CEO. In classic Ben & Jerry's style, the duo kicked off their executive search with an essay contest that gave interested persons a chance to explain why they should be the company's next CEO. Although the contest netted more than 22,000 entries, an executive recruiting firm ultimately led to management consultant Robert Holland, Jr. To persuade Holland to take the job, Ben & Jerry's board of directors had to make an exception to the 7-to-1 rule. Even so, Holland's base salary remained at the low end of the salary range for executives in mid-sized manufacturing firms.

Video Summary

Video Source. "Sharing Sweet Success," *20/20*, May 22, 1992, #1222. This video features an interview with Ben Cohen and Jerry Greenfield, founders of Ben & Jerry's Homemade Inc. The segment profiles an environmentally conscious company where the salaries of senior managers are only seven times higher than the wages of the lowest-paid employees.

Discussion Questions

1. Assess Ben & Jerry's success in terms of the criteria for small business success discussed in Chapter 8. Which factors do you think have been most important in the case of this well-known company?
2. Is Ben & Jerry's the type of company that you would like to work for? Why or why not?

3. In 1995, a Japanese supplier offered to distribute Ben & Jerry's products in Japan. CEO Holland favored the idea. Board Chairman Ben Cohen, however, did not and rejected the proposal for two reasons: (1) the Japanese company had no record of supporting socially conscious causes and (2) he believes that slower growth is needed to maintain the firm's current relations with its employees. If each of these two managers was called upon to explain his position directly to Ben & Jerry's employees, what do you think would be the best argument for each to make?

4. Consider these two facts about Ben & Jerry's:

   (1) By the end of 1995, Ben & Jerry's longstanding cap on executive salaries had been dropped, and the pay package of CEO Holland (who resigned in September 1996) equaled 14.5 times the salary of the company's lowest-paid employee.

   (2) When the company introduced its line of sorbets in 1996, it was extremely successful—but six months behind Häagen-Dazs. In addition, the company has had trouble expanding the sorbet line internationally because Cohen and others insist on using organic fruit, which is difficult to procure in large quantities.

   In light of such developments, how should management explain to employees the pressures on the organizational culture that Ben & Jerry's has been experiencing since 1994?

Follow-Up Assignment

Industry observers note that changes in product-labeling laws may draw consumer attention to the high fat content of Ben & Jerry's ice cream. Ultimately, suspect some experts, the new requirements will hurt sales. Go to the library and find out what this company and others are doing to maintain growth in an era of increasing health consciousness.

For Further Exploration

Ben & Jerry's can be contacted on the Internet at

http://www.benjerry.com

On the Web page, you will find a hyperlink to "The Library." Click there to gain access to what Ben & Jerry's calls "Vermont's Finest Reference Library." By accessing "Vermont's Finest Bibliography" and/or the "Instant Gratification Library," you may find yourself reading about social concerns the company considers important.

Also at the Web page you will find a hyperlink to a "Site Index." Here you'll find icons labeled "Take a Stand" and "Where in the World." By investigating these areas, you will be able to find which causes Ben & Jerry's is currently supporting and to learn about the company's progress in expanding globally. What sort of problems do you think Ben & Jerry's will have in implementing its socially conscious agenda in its various international locations?

> **"The level of complexity requires organizational, operational, and management expertise beyond what Ben and I can offer."**
>
> —Jerry Greenfield
> *Co-founder of Ben & Jerry's, 1994*

Planning in the Coming Home Division of Lands' End

How and When to Deploy a SWOT Team

Learning Objectives

The purpose of this video exercise is to help students:

1. Appreciate the process whereby marketing managers develop practical plans to carry out the strategic decisions they make
2. Understand the ways in which a specific company perceives its organizational strengths and uses them to seize marketplace opportunities
3. Understand the relationship between product development and marketing as interrelated management areas

Background Information

The *Coming Home* catalog, which specializes in products for bed and bath, was one of three specialty divisions launched by Lands' End in 1989. The decision to branch out into home textiles, says Managing Director Phil Young, came when marketers at Lands' End "recognized opportunity in the marketplace." Textile mills were either merging or closing, and those that stayed in business were stressing efficiency over quality. Lands' End thus saw an opportunity to enter the home-textiles market—especially in bedding—by introducing high-quality products backed by the company's unconditional guarantee and priced along its usual lines.

The process of developing such products as fitted sheets and folded baby blankets consists of several steps:

- The product development team identifies a need or opportunity in the marketplace.
- The strategy for designing the actual product reflects the company's mission—to develop the best product for the identified need.
- The competition is analyzed and the input of potential customers is collected.
- An appropriate supplier is selected.
- The product is tested, both in house and among customers.

Young characterizes this approach to strategic planning as *SWOT analysis:* matching internal organizational **s**trengths and **w**eaknesses with external **o**pportunities and **t**hreats.

The Video

Video Source. "Planning in the Coming Home Division at Lands' End," *Prentice Hall Presents: On Location at Lands' End.* The video focuses on the planning that underpins the product development process at the Coming Home division, which specializes in home textile products for bed and bath. Merchandising manager Rob Hayes discusses the approach that Lands' End marketers take to developing products that both meet carefully researched customer needs and satisfy the company's established quality standards.

Discussion Questions

1. How would you characterize the overall approach of Lands' End management to the concept of matching the organization with its environment? Does it take risks, for example, or is it conservative?

2. According to Phil Young, the division's approach to the "'sheet that fits' . . . provides an edge for all Coming Home products—meeting the needs of the customer." How might this goal be translated into an item in the company's mission statement? Does the product development process described in the video suggest any particular strategic goals that might have been set by Lands' End management?

3. Judging from the management approach to product development at the Coming Home division, what can you say about the nature of managerial responsibility and organizational structure at Lands' End? Judging from the video, what can you say about corporate culture at Lands' End?

Follow-Up Assignment

At the conclusion of the video, the narrator poses the following question: *How does Lands' End fight against competitors using its ideas, like "the sheet that fits"?* To address this question, secure a *Coming Home* catalog (phone, fax, or e-mail Lands' End). Next, consider the following comment made by Phil Young in 1996:

> One issue is always the "edge." Our just-completed SWOT analysis indicated that our competitors were catching up—chipping away at the "edge." So to identify all the elements of the edge, we listed the strengths and weaknesses that we have and what we *needed to do* to reinforce that edge. Then we set some specific goals in order to address everything we had to do in order to stay ahead of the competition.

Your instructor will divide you into groups of five or six people, with each group acting as a "product development team." Each team should examine the descriptions of several different products in the *Coming Home* catalog. Which products seem to be promoted most effectively? To which products would you attach an apparent marketing "edge"—some benefit or feature that, as a result of product development planning, looks as if it might help a given product to "stay ahead of the competition"? As a team, make recommendations for giving an "edge" to two or three products that seem to be in need of a competitive boost.

For Further Exploration

Visit Lands' End on the Internet at

http://www.landsend.com

On the Web page, scroll down to "The Company" and then down to the link to "The Company Inside and Out." To get a better idea of the areas in which the company tries to develop its organizational strengths, look at such features as "At Lands' End the Word 'Value' Rings True" and "Quality in the Apparel Business. . . ." According to Lands' End, in what ways does attention to quality furnish an "edge" in the development of its products? What role should "value" play in formulating a mission statement for Lands' End?

> **"Strategically, everything we do with our product, with our service, and in positioning the company relates to building an edge over our competition."**
>
> —Phil Young
> *Lands' End Managing Director*

9

CHAPTER

MOTIVATING, SATISFYING, AND LEADING EMPLOYEES

What Would Capitalism Be without "Bossy Bosses"?

THE CHICK-FIL-A APPROACH TO MOTIVATION

In the business environment of fast-food restaurants, company loyalty is virtually unheard of among hourly workers. Annual employee turnover rates in these businesses are as high as 300 percent. Chick-fil-A®, the Atlanta-based fast-food chicken chain, is different. It prides itself on a remarkably low annual turnover rate of 50 percent for hourly employees. And while other chains experience a 35-percent turnover in restaurant management, Chick-fil-A loses only about 5 percent of its operators each year.

A loyal work force has helped Chick-fil-A become the nation's third largest fast-food chicken company. With nearly $569.9 million in sales in 1996, the company is worth between $500 million and $1 billion (exact figures are not available because Chick-fil-A is a private company). At the core of the company's success is the conviction of company founder and chairman S. Truett Cathy that you can do right by employees and still do well—a credo that breeds loyalty among workers who are convinced that Cathy places people ahead of business. Cathy's business practices are based on his strongly held religious beliefs, which emphasize fair play, hard work, and a day of rest on

> **"We don't add a bunch of employees and then cut back a bunch."**
>
> —Huie Woods
> *Vice President for Human Resources at Chick-fil-A Inc.*

Sunday. "We don't expect every operator to be Christian," says Cathy, "but we tell them we do expect them to operate on Christian principles."

The loyalty that has contributed to Cathy's success in building a chain of 725 restaurants in 35 states, Canada, and South Africa, is linked to a number of factors. No single factor can fully explain the dedication of Chick-fil-A's workers. Taken together, however, the principles listed below add up to more than the sum of their parts in motivating people to work at their best.

- *A strong corporate culture.* Cathy's religious beliefs emphasize fair play and trust. They do not include close supervision of employees or store operators. "As long as you do your job, people are going to leave you alone," explains Huie Woods, Vice President for Human Resources. It is

Woods' conviction that the lack of "bossy bosses" is one of the most effective motivators of people.

- *A stable work environment.* In its more than 50-year history, Chick-fil-A has never laid off anyone. The company's record in this respect is a byproduct of its overall strategy. Instead of rapid expansion, management has pursued a strategy of gradual growth. As a result, explains Woods, "We don't add a bunch of employees and then cut back a bunch." Woods believes that workers who are free to do their jobs without fear of losing them do them better.

- *A good income.* The loyalty of Chick-fil-A's store operators stems from the deal that Cathy offers. Operators, who are not franchisees, pay the company a $5,000 commitment fee that is refundable. The company then builds a store and leases it to the operator in exchange for 15 percent of gross sales off the top, plus a 50–50 profit split. "Our deal offers operators a tremendous incentive," says Woods. In fact, this pay structure has allowed operators to earn about twice as much as operators at some other fast-food chains. They are guaranteed minimum incomes of $30,000, but many earn much more. Indeed, about 10 percent earn more than $100,000, and one operator of two shops earned $290,000 in a recent year.

■ *Attractive perks and benefits.* Cathy also motivates his workers with a package of attractive perks. Every February, for example, he takes the company's full-time headquarters staff, all store operators, and their spouses to a five-day meeting. In 1996, he took more than 1,300 people to Bermuda; in 1997, everyone (approximately 1,400) headed to Orlando. How do employees respond to such treatment? "The experience just blew us away," reports store operator David R. Roberts.

Cathy also gives cars to operators who increase store sales by 40 percent or meet predetermined sales for high-volume stores. In 1996, he gave away 25 cars (the highest ever was 46, in 1983). To further motivate high school and college students to stay in their jobs at Chick-fil-A, he offers $1,000 scholarships. Qualification is as simple as getting a recommendation from the store operator and supplying proof of enrollment in an accredited institution. So far, over $12 million in scholarships have been awarded.

Using this multifaceted approach, Chick-fil-A has been able to motivate its work force so that workers not only stay on the job but perform at the highest levels. The approach is successful because S. Truett Cathy seems to understand instinctively the complexity of human motivation. Consider, for example, the theme of an article on employee motivation that appeared recently in *HR Focus*, a publication of the American Management Association:

[People] are not purely economic animals. Nor are they purely political or psychological beings. Most people have a complex set of needs and desires—part material, part social, part emotional—that must be met if they are to be motivated. The answer is never as simple as "Give them more money" or "Give them more interesting work."

By focusing on the learning objectives of this chapter, you will better understand why employee morale and job satisfaction are important to all types of business organizations. You will also understand the role of leadership in motivating employees—or team members—to high levels of achievement.

After reading this chapter, you should be able to

1. Discuss the importance of *job satisfaction* and *employee morale* and summarize their roles in *human relations* in the workplace

2. Identify and summarize the most important theories of *employee motivation*

3. Describe some of the strategies used by organizations to improve job satisfaction and employee motivation

4. Discuss different managerial styles of *leadership* and their impact on human relations in the workplace

Continued on page 225

■ HUMAN RELATIONS IN THE WORKPLACE

human relations
Interactions between employers and employees and their attitudes toward one another

The foundation of good **human relations**—the interactions between employers and employees and their attitudes toward one another—is a satisfied work force. Although most people have a general idea what "job satisfaction" is, both job satisfaction and high morale can be elusive in the workplace. Because they are critical to an organization's success, we begin our discussion by explaining their importance.

The Importance of Satisfaction and Morale

job satisfaction
Degree of enjoyment that people derive from performing their jobs

morale
Overall attitude that employees have toward their workplace

Broadly speaking, **job satisfaction** is the degree of enjoyment that people derive from performing their jobs. If people enjoy their work, they are relatively satisfied; if they do not enjoy their work, they are relatively dissatisfied. In turn, satisfied employees are likely to have high **morale**—the overall attitude that employees have toward their workplace. Morale reflects the degree to which they perceive that their needs are being met by their jobs. It is determined by a variety of factors, including job satisfaction and satisfaction with such things as pay, benefits, co-workers, and promotion opportunities.[1]

Companies can improve employee morale and job satisfaction in a variety of ways. Some large firms, for example, have instituted companywide programs designed specifically to address employees' needs. Some, like Rockwell International, sponsor special career training programs for young students. These programs benefit both students and the sponsors, who ultimately benefit from a more highly educated and skilled—and committed—work force. Managers at Hyatt Hotels report that conducting frequent surveys of employee attitudes, soliciting employee input, and—most important—acting on that input gives their company an edge in recruiting and retaining productive workers. Managers of smaller businesses realize that the personal touch can reap big benefits in employee morale and even devotion. For example, First Tennessee, a midsize regional bank, believes that work and family are so closely related that family considerations should enter into job design. Thus it offers such benefits as on-site child care.[2] ▶

When workers are satisfied and morale is high, the organization benefits in many ways. Compared with dissatisfied workers, for example, satisfied employees are more committed and loyal. Such employees are more likely to work hard and to make useful contributions to the organization. In addition, they tend to have fewer grievances and engage in fewer negative behaviors (complaining, deliberately slowing their work pace, and so forth) than dissatisfied counterparts. Finally, satisfied workers tend not only to come to work every day but to remain with the organization. By promoting satisfaction and morale, then, management is working to ensure more efficient operations.

Conversely, the costs of dissatisfaction and poor morale are high. Dissatisfied workers are far more likely to be absent for minor illnesses, personal reasons, or a general disinclination to go to work. Low morale may also result in high turnover—the ratio of newly hired to currently employed workers. High levels of turnover have many negative consequences, including the disruption of production schedules, high retraining costs, and decreased productivity.

Recent Trends in Managing Satisfaction and Morale

Achieving high levels of job satisfaction and morale seems like a reasonable organizational goal. In fact, however, while many organizations work to meet it, some do not. Moreover, some that have tried have been unsuccessful. Reacting in large part to massive worker layoffs and downsizing programs, many workers in the late 1980s and early 1990s reported feeling unhappy with their work and concerned about their futures.

In the account reconcilement department of First Tennessee Bank's Alcoa branch, Constance Wembley balances work and family needs by doing her own scheduling and, if necessary, bringing her daughter into the office when she has to put in overtime. First Tennessee Bank also offers job-sharing and on-site child care. The rationale is that if family concerns affect productivity, helping to ease those concerns improves overall results.

More recently, however, downsizing programs have been completed, displaced workers have found new jobs, and job security has become a little more stable. Consequently, survey results suggest that satisfaction and morale in the United States have started to improve after several years of decline. Indeed, one recent survey found that most workers expressed positive attitudes about many different aspects of their work. The results compared very favorably with similar surveys of Canadian, Mexican, British, Japanese, and German workers.[3]

However, cutbacks and layoffs still continue in some organizations. For example, Nabisco recently announced plans to cut 4,200 jobs even as Conagra, another giant food products company, slashed 6,500 jobs. Apple Computer laid off 1,300 workers, and in one of the largest—and most widely publicized—downsizing programs, AT&T cut 40,000 jobs (2,000 in a single day).[4] ▶ Thus, although many workers may be more satisfied today, they do not necessarily feel secure. Even if they are satisfied with their own jobs, for example, many know other people—friends, relatives, or neighbors—who are losing their jobs. Others see similarities between their own employers and other firms that are downsizing. Still others experience drastically reduced morale in jobs they still hold. "I have a job," admits one AT&T employee who survived the company's cuts, "but I don't feel like I won the lottery. I was an AT&T man, but I don't feel like that anymore."[5]

> ## "I have a job, but I don't feel like I won the lottery. I was an AT&T man, but I don't feel like that anymore."
>
> —AT&T employee
> *who survived downsizing job cuts*

In January 1996, AT&T announced the cutting of 40,000 jobs over a three-year period. AT&T's action was part of the fallout from a so-called "jobs-creation" bill which, in theory, would create 3.6 million new jobs. The idea is to make local phone companies, long-distance carriers, and cable-TV operators more competitive by allowing them to enter each other's business. The tradeoff: they must learn to live without the regulations that have always protected them from competition. According to officials like those at AT&T, companies must drop the excess baggage—including payrolls bulging with too many traditional telecommunications jobs—that they've been carrying around for years.

Experts agree that a firm's best response to such concerns is announcing and implementing a solid plan for future growth. Management can also reassure employees by finding ways to avoid laying them off. Between 1990 and 1993, for example, Hewlett-Packard managed to reduce operating costs by more than 7 percent without laying off a single worker. Analysts also suggest, however, that when they can no longer provide job security, companies should assist employees in rethinking the nature of their roles in alternative organizational systems.

■ MOTIVATION IN THE WORKPLACE

motivation
The set of forces that cause people to behave in certain ways

Although job satisfaction and morale are important, employee motivation is even more critical to a firm's success. As we saw in Chapter 6, motivation is one part of the managerial function of directing. Broadly defined, **motivation** is the set of forces that cause people to behave in certain ways. One worker may be motivated to work hard to produce as much as possible, while another may be motivated to do just enough to get by. Managers must understand these differences in behavior and the reasons for them.

Over the years, a steady progression of theories and studies has attempted to address these issues. In this section, we survey the major studies and theories of employee motivation. In particular, we focus on three approaches to human relations in the workplace that reflect a basic chronology of thinking in the area: *classical theory* and *scientific management*, *behavior theory*, and *contemporary motivational theories*.

TRENDS & CHALLENGES

EMPLOYERS EMBRACE THE TWO Ls (LOYALTY AND LONGEVITY)

Loyalty. Sports fans have it in spades. Die-hard fans will wait years—even decades—for their team to win a World Series, a Super Bowl, or a Stanley Cup, and most of them never give up hope. But try applying the loyalty concept to business and you're likely to hear cat calls instead of cheers.

Until now. Battered by corporate layoffs and other downsides to downsizing, many workers today are looking for a new relationship with their bosses—namely, one based on the old-fashioned values of loyalty and commitment. Fortunately, at the same time an increasing number of companies are realizing that when employees feel secure—when they can go home at night knowing that they will have jobs the next morning—they are more productive.

According to Frederick Reichheld, a director of the Boston-based management consulting firm Bain & Co., today's most profitable companies succeed in inspiring loyalty from customers, investors, and employees. Companies with the lowest turnover in these key constituency groups earn the most money. Moreover, says Reichheld, when *employee* turnover is low, so is the turnover of *customers* and *investors*. Human Resources Consultant Patricia Milligan agrees. Employers, she says, are now convinced that they cannot "sustain performance without an engaged, committed work force. . . . Companies are saying, 'We have to rebuild employee commitment.'" Why? What is the connection between employee commitment and customer loyalty? Employees with long histories at the same companies, explains Milligan, know the best ways to do their jobs, reduce costs, and improve quality.

One company that values loyalty and that has worked for a long time to build employee commitment is State Farm Insurance. The average sales agent has worked for the company for about twenty years—a situation that encourages continuous customer service. At a time when most business relationships last minutes instead of years, it is not surprising that 95 percent of State Farm customers decide to stick with the company and that State Farm agents are 40 percent more productive than agents from competing firms.

> ## "Employers now believe that they can't sustain performance without an engaged, committed work force. Companies are saying, 'We have to rebuild employee commitment.'"
>
> —Patricia Milligan
> *Human Resources Consultant*

Keeping employees from jumping from one company to another often means spending heavily for training programs that provide continuing opportunities for job growth. Although no company can guarantee job security for every employee, training programs help workers acquire the flexibility that they need to adapt to changing workplaces. For example, Monsanto's Searle division in Skokie, Illinois, has expanded its in-house training function. Instead of offering only sales training, the program now helps employees learn the skills they need to cope with new tasks. Five years ago, reports Human Resources Official Sophia Capelli, management's attitude "was very much one that employees are disposable." Now, she says, the company "[recognizes] people as a critical renewable asset."

How do job seekers find companies that value loyalty, commitment, and longevity—and that are willing to make commitments of their own? One way is to ask tough questions about loyalty, employee turnover, and training during job interviews. If you are fortunate enough to locate a company that cares about loyalty, you may look back at your own career twenty years from now and realize that although your job description has changed dramatically since you were first hired, your company has not.

Classical Theory

According to the so-called **classical theory of motivation,** workers are motivated solely by money. In his seminal book *The Principles of Scientific Management* (1911), industrial engineer Frederick Taylor proposed a way for both companies and workers to benefit from this widely accepted view of life in the workplace.[6] If workers are

classical theory of motivation
Theory holding that workers are motivated solely by money

motivated by money, Taylor reasoned, then paying them more should prompt them to produce more. Meanwhile, the firm that analyzed jobs and found better ways to perform them would be able to produce goods more cheaply, make higher profits, and thus pay—and motivate—workers better than its competitors.

Behavior Theory: The Hawthorne Studies

In 1925, a group of Harvard researchers began a study at the Hawthorne Works of Western Electric outside Chicago. With an eye to increasing productivity, they wanted to examine the relationship between changes in the physical environment and worker output.

The results of the experiment were unexpected, even confusing. Not surprisingly, for example, increased lighting levels improved productivity. For some reason, however, so did lower lighting levels. Moreover, against all expectations, increased pay *failed* to increase productivity. Gradually, the researchers pieced together the puzzle. The explanation lay in the workers' response to the *attention that they were receiving*. The researchers concluded that productivity rose in response to almost any management action that workers interpreted as special attention. This finding, known widely today as the **Hawthorne effect,** had a major influence on human relations theory, although in many cases it amounted simply to convincing managers that they should pay more attention to employees.

Hawthorne effect
Tendency for productivity to increase when workers believe they are receiving special attention from management

Contemporary Motivational Theories

Following the Hawthorne studies, managers and researchers alike focused more attention on the importance of good human relations in motivating employee performance. Stressing the factors that cause, focus, and sustain workers' behavior, most motivation theorists are concerned with the ways in which management thinks about and treats employees. The major motivation theories include the *human resources model*, the *hierarchy of needs model*, *two-factor theory*, *expectancy theory*, *equity theory*, and *goal-setting theory*.

Human Resources Model: Theories X and Y   In an important study, behavioral scientist Douglas McGregor concluded that managers had radically different beliefs about how best to use the human resources at a firm's disposal. He classified these beliefs into sets of assumptions that he labeled "Theory X" and "Theory Y." The basic differences between these two theories are highlighted in Table 9.1.

Managers who subscribe to **Theory X** tend to believe that people are naturally lazy and uncooperative and must therefore be either punished or rewarded to be made pro-

Theory X
Theory of motivation holding that people are naturally irresponsible and uncooperative

TABLE 9.1 ◆ Theory X and Theory Y

Theory X	Theory Y
1. People are lazy.	1. People are energetic.
2. People lack ambition and dislike responsibility.	2. People are ambitious and seek responsibility.
3. People are self-centered.	3. People can be selfless.
4. People resist change.	4. People want to contribute to business growth and change.
5. People are gullible and not very bright.	5. People are intelligent.

ductive. Managers who incline to **Theory Y** tend to believe that people are naturally energetic, growth-oriented, self-motivated, and interested in being productive.

McGregor generally favored Theory Y beliefs. Thus, he argued that Theory Y managers are more likely to have satisfied, motivated employees. Of course, Theory X and Y distinctions are somewhat simplistic and offer little concrete basis for action. Their value lies primarily in their ability to highlight and classify the behavior of managers in light of their attitudes toward employees.

Maslow's Hierarchy of Needs Model   Psychologist Abraham Maslow's **hierarchy of human needs model** proposed that people have a number of different needs that they attempt to satisfy in their work. He classified these needs into five basic types and suggested that they are arranged in the hierarchy of importance shown in Figure 9.1. According to Maslow, needs are hierarchical because lower-level needs must be met before a person will try to satisfy higher-level needs.

Once a set of needs has been satisfied, it ceases to motivate behavior. This is the sense in which the hierarchical nature of lower- and higher-level needs affects employee motivation and satisfaction. For example, if you feel secure in your job, a new pension plan will probably be less important to you than the chance to make new friends and join an informal network among your co-workers. If, however, a lower-level need suddenly becomes unfulfilled, most people immediately refocus on that lower level. Suppose, for example, that you are seeking to meet your self-esteem needs by working as a divisional manager at a major company. If you learn that your division—and consequently your job—may be eliminated, you might very well find the promise of job security at a new firm as motivating as a promotion once would have been at your old company.

Maslow's theory recognizes that because different people have different needs, they are motivated by different things. Unfortunately, it provides few specific guidelines for action in the workplace. Furthermore, research has found that the hierarchy varies widely, not only for different people but across different cultures.

Two-Factor Theory   After studying a group of accountants and engineers, psychologist Frederick Herzberg concluded that job satisfaction and dissatisfaction depend on two factors: *hygiene factors*, such as working conditions, and *motivation factors*, such as recognition for a job well done.

> **Theory Y**
> Theory of motivation holding that people are naturally responsible, growth-oriented, self-motivated, and interested in being productive

> **hierarchy of human needs model**
> Theory of motivation describing five levels of human needs and arguing that basic needs must be fulfilled before people work to satisfy higher-level needs

FIGURE 9.1 ◆ Maslow's Hierarchy of Needs

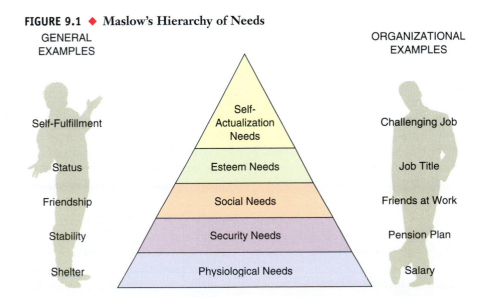

GENERAL EXAMPLES

ORGANIZATIONAL EXAMPLES

General Examples	Pyramid Level	Organizational Examples
Self-Fulfillment	Self-Actualization Needs	Challenging Job
Status	Esteem Needs	Job Title
Friendship	Social Needs	Friends at Work
Stability	Security Needs	Pension Plan
Shelter	Physiological Needs	Salary

"Phillip, I was going to thank you, but,
then, yours is a thankless job."

two-factor theory
Theory of motivation holding that job satisfaction depends on two types of factors, hygiene and motivation

According to the **two-factor theory,** hygiene factors affect motivation and satisfaction only if they are *absent* or *fail* to meet expectations. For example, workers will be dissatisfied if they believe that they have poor working conditions. If working conditions are improved, however, they will not necessarily become *satisfied;* they will simply be *not dissatisfied.* If workers receive no recognition for successful work, they may be neither dissatisfied nor satisfied. If recognition is provided, they will likely become more satisfied.

Figure 9.2 illustrates the two-factor theory. Note that motivation factors lie along a continuum from *satisfaction* to *no satisfaction.* Hygiene factors, in contrast, are likely to produce feelings that lie on a continuum from *dissatisfaction* to *no dissatisfaction.* While motivation factors are directly related to the work that employees actually perform, hygiene factors refer to the environment in which they perform it.

This theory thus suggests that managers should follow a two-step approach to enhancing motivation. First, they must ensure that hygiene factors—working conditions, clearly stated policies—are acceptable. This practice will result in an absence of dissatisfaction. Then they must offer motivation factors—recognition, added responsibility—as means of improving satisfaction and motivation.

Research suggests that although two-factor theory works in some professional settings, it is less effective in clerical and manufacturing settings. (Herzberg's research was limited to accountants and engineers.) In addition, one person's hygiene factor may be another person's motivation factor. For example, if money represents nothing more than pay for time worked, it may be a hygiene factor for one person. For another person, however, money may be a motivation factor because it represents recognition and achievement.

expectancy theory
Theory of motivation holding that people are motivated to work toward rewards that they want and that they believe they have a reasonable chance of obtaining

Expectancy Theory **Expectancy theory** suggests that people are motivated to work toward rewards that they want *and* that they believe they have a reasonable chance—or expectancy—of obtaining.[7] A reward that seems out of reach is likely to be undesirable even if it is intrinsically positive. Consider the case of an assistant department manager who learns that a division manager two levels above her in the organi-

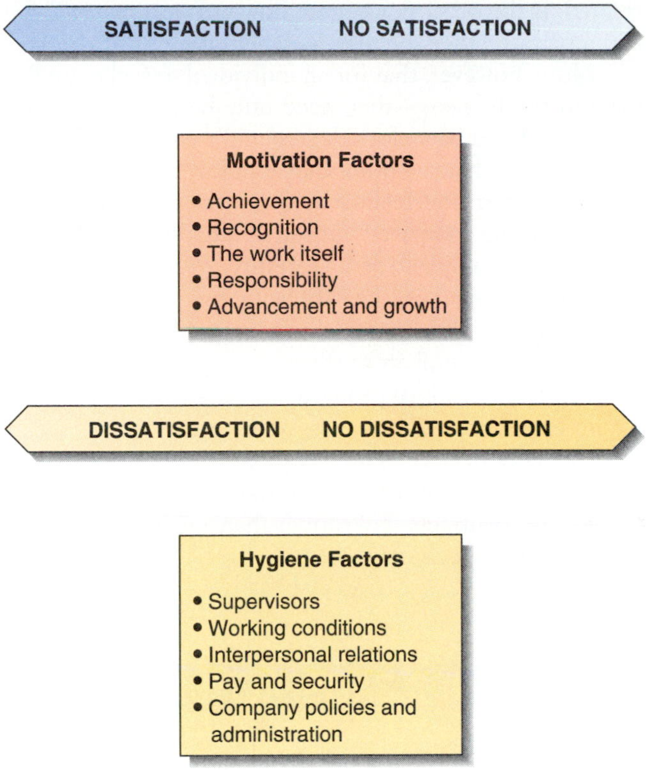

FIGURE 9.2 ◆ Two-Factor Theory of Motivation

zation has retired and that the firm is looking for a replacement. Even though she wants the job, she does not apply for it because she doubts that she will be selected. She also learns that the firm is looking for a production manager on a later shift. She thinks that she could get this job but does not apply because she does not want to change shifts. Finally, she learns of an opening one level higher—department manager—in her own division. She may well apply for this job because she both wants it and thinks that she has a good chance of getting it.

Expectancy theory helps explain why some people do not work as hard as they can when their salaries are based purely on seniority. Because they are paid the same whether they work very hard or just hard enough to get by, there is no financial incentive for them to work harder. In other words, they ask themselves, "If I work harder, will I get a pay raise?" and conclude that the answer is no. Similarly, if hard work will result in one or more *undesirable* outcomes—say, a transfer to another location or a promotion to a job that requires travel—employees will not be motivated to work hard.

Equity Theory   **Equity theory** focuses on social comparisons—people evaluating their treatment by the organization relative to the treatment of others. This approach holds that people begin by analyzing what they contribute to their jobs (time, effort, education, experience, and so forth) relative to what they receive in return (salary, benefits, recognition, security). The result is a ratio of contribution to return. They then compare their own ratios to those of other employees. Depending on their assessments, they experience feelings of equity or inequity.[8]

For example, suppose a new college graduate gets a starting job at a large manufacturing firm. His starting salary is $25,000 a year, he gets a compact company car, and he shares an office with another new employee. If he later learns that another new employee has received the same salary, car, and office arrangement, he will feel equitably

equity theory
Theory of motivation holding that people evaluate their treatment by employers relative to the treatment of others

treated. If the other newcomer, however, has received $30,000, a full-size company car, and a private office, he may feel inequity.

Note, however, that for an individual to feel equitably treated, the two ratios do not have to be the *same*—they need only be *fair*. Let's assume, for instance, that our new employee has a bachelor's degree and two years of work experience. Perhaps he learns subsequently that the other new employee has an advanced degree and ten years of experience. After first feeling inequity, the new employee may conclude that the person with whom he compared himself is actually contributing more to the organization. He or she is equitably entitled, therefore, to receive more in return.

When people feel they are being inequitably treated, they may do various things to restore fairness. For example, they may ask for raises, reduce their efforts, work shorter hours, or just complain to their bosses. They may also rationalize ("Management succumbed to pressure to promote a woman/Asian American"), find different people with whom to compare themselves, or leave their jobs.

Virtually perfect examples of equity theory at work can be found in professional sports. Each year, for example, rookies, sometimes fresh out of college, are often signed to lucrative contracts. No sooner than the ink is dry do veteran players start grumbling about raises or revised contracts.

■ STRATEGIES FOR ENHANCING JOB SATISFACTION AND MOTIVATION

Deciding what provides job satisfaction and motivates workers is only one part of human resource management. The other part is applying that knowledge. Experts have suggested—and many companies have implemented—a range of programs designed to make jobs more interesting and rewarding and to make the work environment more pleasant.

Reinforcement/Behavior Modification Theory

Many companies try to control—and even alter or modify—workers' behavior through systematic rewards and punishments for specific behaviors. In other words, they first try to define the specific behaviors that they want their employees to exhibit (working hard, being courteous to customers, stressing quality) and the specific behaviors they want to eliminate (wasting time, being rude to customers, ignoring quality). Then they try to shape employee behavior by linking reinforcement with desired behaviors and punishment with undesired behaviors.

reinforcement
Theory that behavior can be encouraged or discouraged by means of rewards or punishments

Reinforcement is used, for instance, when a company pays *piecework* rewards—that is, when workers are paid for each piece or product completed. In reinforcement strategies, *rewards* refer to all the positive things that people get for working—pay, praise, promotions, job security, and so forth. When rewards are tied directly to performance, they serve as *positive reinforcement*. For example, paying large cash bonuses to salespeople who exceed quotas prompts them to work even harder during the next selling period. John Deere has recently adopted a new reward system based on positive reinforcement. The firm now gives pay increases when its workers complete college courses and demonstrate mastery of new job skills.[9]

Punishment is designed to change behavior by presenting people with unpleasant consequences if they fail to change in desirable ways. Employees who are repeatedly late to work, for example, may be suspended or have their pay docked. Similarly, when the National Football League or Major League Baseball fines or suspends players found guilty of substance abuse, the organization is seeking to change players' behavior.

Extensive rewards work best when people are learning new behavior, new skills, or new jobs. As workers become more adept, rewards can be used less frequently. Because such actions contribute to positive employer–employee relationships, managers generally prefer giving rewards and placing positive value on performance. Conversely, most managers dislike meting out punishment, partly because workers may respond with anger, resentment, hostility, or even retaliation. To reduce this risk, many managers couple punishment with reward for good behavior.

Management by Objectives

Management by objectives (MBO) is a system of collaborative goal setting that extends from the top of an organization to the bottom. As a technique for managing the planning process, MBO is concerned mainly with helping managers implement and carry out their plans. As you can see from Figure 9.3, however, MBO involves both managers and subordinates in setting goals and evaluating progress. Once the program is set up, the first step is establishing overall organizational goals. It is also these goals that will ultimately be evaluated to determine the success of the program. At the same time, however, *collaborative activity*—communicating, meeting, controlling, and so forth—is the key to MBO. Therefore, it can also serve as a program for improving satisfaction and motivation. (Note, too, that MBO represents an effort to apply throughout an entire organization the goal-setting theory of motivation that we discussed earlier.)

Indeed, according to many experts, motivational impact is the biggest advantage of MBO. When employees sit down with managers to set upcoming goals, they learn more about companywide objectives, come to feel that they are an important part of a team, and see how they can improve companywide performance by reaching their own goals. If an MBO system is used properly, employees should leave meetings not only with an understanding of the value of their contributions, but with fair rewards for their performances. They should also accept and be committed to the moderately difficult and specific goals they have helped set for themselves.

Participative Management and Empowerment

In **participative management and empowerment**, employees are given a voice in how they do their jobs and how the company is managed—they become *empowered* to take greater responsibility for their own performance. Not surprisingly, participation

management by objectives (MBO)
Set of procedures involving both managers and subordinates in setting goals and evaluating progress

participative management and empowerment
Method of increasing job satisfaction by giving employees a voice in the management of their jobs and the company

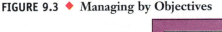

FIGURE 9.3 ◆ **Managing by Objectives**

and empowerment make employees feel more committed to organizational goals they have helped to shape.

Participation and empowerment can be used in large firms or small firms, with both managers and operating employees. For example, managers at General Electric who once needed higher-level approval for any expenditure over $5,000 now have the autonomy to make their own expense decisions up to as much as $50,000. At Adam Hat Co., a small firm that makes men's dress, military, and cowboy hats, workers who previously had to report all product defects to supervisors now have the freedom to correct problems themselves or even return products to the workers responsible for them.

Team Management   At one level, employees may be given decision-making responsibility for certain narrow activities, such as when to take lunch breaks or how to divide assignments with co-workers. On a broader level, employees are also being consulted on decisions like production scheduling, work procedures and schedules, and the hiring of new employees.

Although some employees thrive in participative programs, such programs are not for everyone. Many people will be frustrated by responsibilities they are not equipped to handle. Moreover, participative programs may actually result in dissatisfied employees if workers see the invitation to participate as more symbolic than substantive. One key, say most experts, is to invite participation only to the extent that employees want to have input and only if participation will have real value for an organization.[10]

Equally important, they say, is commitment from top management. Similarly, the line of responsibility between workers and their managers must be made very clear. Problems can beset even companies as experienced in innovative approaches as General Electric. For instance, when GE's medical systems division needed software for two new ultrasound devices, it assigned two teams of engineers. One team consisted of 13 designers in Hino, Japan, the other of 30 designers in Waukesha, Wisconsin. The U.S. team had expertise in software design, the Japanese experience in marketing ultrasound products in Asia. The idea, of course, was for the two groups to complement each other. Each team, however, reported to a different manager in its own country, and the results for two years were, perhaps, predictable. Local managers, for example, focused on features that appealed to their respective markets. In other areas, duplication wasted time and money. Eventually, GE assigned both teams to a single general manager with direct access to top management. The project is still in operation, with communications improved and a collaborative sensibility more in evidence.[11]

BUSINESS FIELD TRIP

"WE WANT EMPLOYEES TO THINK LIKE OWNERS"

Walk through the plant and adjacent facilities at Chaparral Steel Co. and you will see no time clocks, policy books, or assigned parking spaces. Their absence says a great deal about the company's human resource management philosophy: it is a philosophy—and a practice—designed to eliminate rather than create barriers between labor and management.

The attitude of top executives toward the company's 1,000-member work force emphasizes a number of explicit preferences:

- Teamwork over divisions
- Forward-looking goal setting over backward-looking performance appraisals
- Continuing education and broad job functions over limited repetitive tasks
- Pay for performance over rigid salary categories
- Profit sharing plus salary over salary alone

"We do everything we can," says Vice President for Administration Dennis Beach, "to eliminate the barriers that divide us from them."

MULTIFUNCTIONAL TRAINING. A key element in Chaparral's human resource management is a multifunctional training program designed to give every employee a wide range of production skills. At any given time, about eight out of ten production and maintenance workers are enrolled in some form of continuing education.

Chaparral's educational program involves both on-the-job and formal classroom training. The latter has 22 "modules," including courses on mathematics, hydraulics, blueprints, and metallurgy. As part of an apprenticeship program recognized by the Department of Labor, employees are given up to 3½ years to complete the classroom training needed to master specific jobs. "We allow a specific number of hours to become proficient in each task," explains Jeff Roesler, Chaparral's Manager of Human Resources. "Every six months, we review individual progress."

Although periodic reviews are part of the system, performance appraisals are not. "Performance appraisals," says Roesler, "tend to focus on the past, not the future. We work on goal setting. That's the thrust of what we do." Managers thus evaluate worker performance against stated goals, not according to their mistakes. Salary increases are discussed separately.

FINANCIAL INCENTIVES. Similarly, raises are tied to performance. "Once workers complete the apprenticeship program," explains Roesler, "they are considered senior operators. We rank them from top to bottom, and the best performers get the most money, the worst performers the least money." In addition, salaries of employees still in the apprenticeship program are tied to the pace of their progress. This scheme gives employees an incentive to learn skills and increase productivity as quickly as possible.

Another incentive is profit sharing. Chaparral's plan sets aside 8.5 percent of pretax profit, which is dispersed four times a year. "We want employees to think like owners and make decisions like owners," says Roesler. "In good times, everybody gets a piece of the pie; in bad times, we all have to buckle down." Thus, in the company's best year ever, some senior operators earned as much as 19.5 percent of their pay in the form of profit-sharing bonuses. Rewards, however, vary according to company earnings, and in some years, there have been no bonuses at all.

Encouraging greater employee commitment to ownership is a continuing management challenge. Jeff Roesler explains, "If we give an employee a pair of gloves and he throws them away in the parking lot on his way home, and we give him another pair the next day, that cost affects what comes out of his pocket. It is very hard to hit home runs from a cost standpoint; there are not that many out there. So much of what we do involves small, incremental steps that add up to big profits." ▼ How do managers convince workers that small savings are important? Roesler admits that, like many other human resource managers, he is still struggling with that question.

> **"We want employees to think like owners and make decisions like owners. In good times, everybody gets a piece of the pie; in bad times, we all have to buckle down."**
>
> **—Jeff Roesler**
> *Manager of Human Resources at Chaparral Steel Co.*

Safety consciousness at Chaparral is part of a program to encourage not only employee well-being but also a sense of how every cost-saving measure contributes ultimately to profits (and profit-sharing bonuses).

Given management's attitude toward the work force, it should be no surprise that Chaparral's human resource department is attached to the employee locker room. Executive offices are just one set of doors away. "We want to give our people every opportunity to shine," says Roesler, and this arrangement encourages open communication. It is also another tangible sign that traditional labor–management barriers are not part of Chaparral Steel's corporate culture.

Job Enrichment and Job Redesign

While MBO programs and empowerment can work in a variety of settings, *job enrichment* and *job redesign* programs are generally used to increase satisfaction in jobs significantly lacking in motivating factors.

job enrichment
Method of increasing job satisfaction by adding one or more motivating factors to job activities

Job Enrichment Programs
Job enrichment is designed to add one or more motivating factors to job activities. For example, *job rotation programs* expand growth opportunities by rotating employees through various positions in the same firm. Workers thus gain not only new skills but broader overviews of their work and their organization. Other programs focus on increasing responsibility or recognition. At Continental Airlines, for example, flight attendants now have more control over their own scheduling. The jobs of flight service managers were enriched when they were given more responsibility and authority for assigning tasks to flight-crew members.

Job Redesign Programs
Job redesign acknowledges that different people want different things from their jobs. By restructuring work to achieve a more satisfactory fit between workers and their jobs, **job redesign** can motivate individuals with strong needs for career growth or achievement. Job redesign is usually implemented in one of three ways: through *combining tasks*, *forming natural work groups*, or *establishing client relationships*.

job redesign
Method of increasing job satisfaction by designing a more satisfactory fit between workers and their jobs

Combining Tasks. *Combining tasks* means enlarging jobs and increasing their variety to make employees feel that their work is more meaningful. In turn, employees become more motivated. For example, the job done by a programmer who maintains computer systems might be redesigned to include some system design and system development work. While developing additional skills, then, the programmer also gets involved in the overall system package.

Forming Natural Work Groups. People who do different jobs on the same projects are candidates for *natural work groups*. These groups are formed to help employees see the place and importance of their jobs in the total structure of the firm. They are valuable to management because the people working on a project are usually the most knowledgeable about it—and thus the most capable problem solvers.

Establishing Client Relationships. Establishing client relationships means letting employees interact with customers. This approach increases job variety. It gives workers both a greater sense of control and more feedback about performance than they get when their jobs are not highly interactive.

For example, software writers at Microsoft watch test users work with programs and discuss problems with them directly rather than receive feedback from third-party researchers. In Fargo, North Dakota, Great Plains Software has employee turnover of less than 7 percent, compared with an average of 15–20 percent in the software industry. The company recruits and rewards in large part according to candidates' customer-service skills and their experience with customer needs and complaints.[12]

"Keeping customers always seemed like common sense to me," explains Doug Bergum (left), CEO of Great Plains Software. Bergum not only maintains personal contact wherever possible with customers like lumberyard owner Peter Simonson but also has compiled detailed profiles of 45,000 clients. Great Plains programs actually require users to contact the company after 50 transactions—whereupon they automatically receive personalized attention from specially trained consultants. In 1993, Great Plains induced an unheard-of 42 percent of users to update from one program to its newer version. When the new version proved to be flawed, Bergum personally mailed new disks to every buyer—and offered cash compensation to anyone whose business had suffered.

Modified Work Schedules

As another way of increasing job satisfaction, many companies are experimenting with *modified work schedules*—different approaches to working hours and the work week. The two most common forms of modified scheduling are *work share programs* and *flextime programs*, including *alternative workplace strategies*.

Work-Share Programs   At Steelcase Inc., the country's largest maker of office furnishings, two very talented women in the marketing division both wanted to work only part-time. The solution: they now share a single full-time job. With each working two and a half days a week, both got their wishes and the job gets done—and done well. In another situation, one person might work mornings and the other afternoons. The practice, known as **work sharing** (or **job sharing**), has "brought sanity back to our lives," according to at least one Steelcase employee.

work sharing (or job sharing) Method of increasing job satisfaction by allowing two or more people to share a single full-time job

> **"Job sharing has brought sanity back to our lives."**
> —Steelcase employee

Job sharing usually benefits both employees and employers. Employees, for instance, tend to appreciate the organization's attention to their personal needs. At the same time, the company can reduce turnover and save on the cost of benefits. On the negative side, job-share employees generally receive fewer benefits than their full-time counterparts and may be the first to be laid off when cutbacks are necessary.

Flextime Programs and Alternative Workplace Strategies   **Flextime programs** allow people to choose their working hours by adjusting a standard work schedule on a daily or weekly basis. There are, of course, limits. The Steelcase program, for instance, requires all employees to work certain core hours. This practice allows everyone to reach co-workers at a specified time of day. But employees can decide whether to make up the rest of the standard eight-hour day by coming in and leaving early (say, by working 6:00 A.M. to 2:00 P.M. or 7:00 A.M. to 3:00 P.M.) or late (9:00 A.M. to 5:00 P.M. or 10:00 A.M. to 6:00 P.M.).

flextime programs Method of increasing job satisfaction by allowing workers to adjust work schedules on a daily or weekly basis

Figure 9.4 shows a hypothetical flextime system that could be used by three different people. The office is open from 6:00 A.M. until 7:00 P.M. Core time is 9:00 A.M. to 11:00 A.M. and 1:00 P.M. to 3:00 P.M. Joe, an early riser, comes in at 6:00, takes an hour for lunch between 11:00 and noon, and finishes his day by 3:00. Sue, a working mother, prefers a later day. She comes in at 9:00, takes a long lunch from 11:00 to 1:00, and then works until 7:00. Pat works a more traditional 8-to-5 schedule.

In one variation, companies may also allow employees to choose four, five or six days on which to work each week. Some, for instance, may choose Monday through Thursday, others Tuesday through Friday. Still others may work Monday-Tuesday and Thursday-Friday and take Wednesday off. By working ten hours over four workdays, employees still complete 40-hour weeks.

Telecommuting and Virtual Offices.   Tammy Aultman sells computer systems for Hewlett-Packard, which is located in Mountain View, California. Aultman accepted the job even though she lives in Laguna Hills, 350 miles away. Her solution: she outfitted a room in her home with a modem-equipped personal computer and a fax machine and

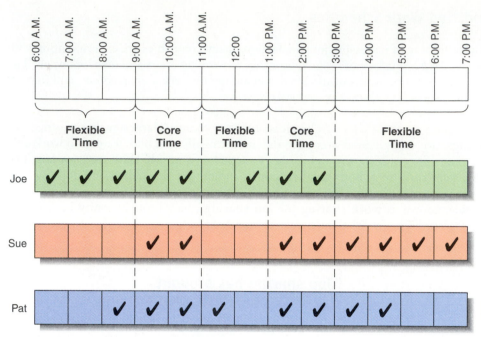

FIGURE 9.4 ◆ Sample Flextime Schedule

telecommuting
Form of flextime that allows people to perform some or all of a job away from standard office settings

now works comfortably out of Laguna Hills. Aultman is one of a rapidly growing number of U.S. workers who do a significant portion of their work by a relatively new version of flextime known as **telecommuting**—performing some or all of a job away from standard office settings. Among salaried employees, the telecommuter work force grew by 21.5 percent in 1994, to 7.6 million. By the year 2000, that number may reach 25 million. The key to telecommuting is technology. The availability of networked computers, fax machines, cellular telephones, and overnight-delivery services makes it possible for many professionals to work at home or while traveling.[13]

Other companies have experimented with so-called *virtual offices*. They have redesigned conventional office space to accommodate jobs and schedules that are far less dependent on assigned spaces and personal apparatus.[14] At the advertising firm of Chiat Day Mojo in Venice, California, only about a third of the salaried work force is in the office on any given day. The office building features informal work carrels or nooks and open areas available to every employee. "The work environment," explains Director of Operations Adelaide Horton, "was designed around the concept that one's best thinking isn't necessarily done at a desk or in an office. Sometimes it's done in a conference room with other people. Other times it's done on a ski slope or driving to a client's office."[15] ▶

"The work environment was designed around the concept that one's best thinking can be done on a ski slope or driving to a client's office."

—Adelaide Horton
Director of Operations at Chiat Day Mojo

*Nancy Allen (**left**) is Head of Human Resources at the advertising firm of Chiat Day Mojo, which prides itself on the interplay of creativity and productivity in its office design. Appropriated from carnival rides, for instance, colorful Tilt-a-Whirls now function as office furniture with built-in privacy. "I'm not tethered to a specific work area," says Allen. "As long as I get everything done, that's what counts. Ultimately, my productivity is greater and my job-satisfaction level is higher."*

■ MANAGERIAL STYLES AND LEADERSHIP

In trying to enhance morale, job satisfaction, and motivation, managers can use many different styles of leadership. **Leadership** is the process of motivating others to work to meet specific objectives. Leading is also one of the key aspects of a manager's job and an important component of the directing function.

leadership
Process of motivating others to work to meet specific objectives

■ Consider the experience of Jack Smith, whose leadership abilities were put to the test shortly after he became CEO of General Motors in November 1992. After losing $23.5 billion in 1991—the largest single-year net loss in U.S. corporate history—GM brought in Smith to turn things around. One of Smith's first moves as CEO was to close the executive dining room on the fourteenth floor of the company's corporate headquarters in Detroit. The dining room—a symbol of privilege and elitism that had survived war, recession, and the invasion of Japanese imports—could not survive Smith's determination to make GM more democratic. Symbols count, observes GM Executive Vice President William E. Hoglund. "Before," recalls Hoglund, "the big shooters went to the fourteenth floor, and the little people went somewhere else. [This] is a tiny step toward a company that moves and is responsive."

Since taking over GM, Smith has focused on five goals: developing a new product plan, reducing materials costs, aligning production capacity with demand, reducing the work force, and improving quality while reducing warranty expenses. Success in meeting these goals is important to everyone at GM, and Smith has introduced a management style that favors participation, delegation, and openness. Smith's style is also one of self-effacement. Close associates explain that he has been reluctant to take personal credit for improving GM's fortunes because he regards himself as part of a team.

Observers also attribute at least part of Jack Smith's success at GM to his concern for his work force. He believes in open communication—even with the United Auto Workers Union, whose top leaders have often locked horns with GM. After a recent meeting, for example, the leaders of several hundred UAW locals expressed approval of Smith's democratic approach even though they remained aware that tough times were still ahead. "He didn't use $600 words, and he was frank," reported Dick Long, President of UAW Local 653 in Pontiac, Michigan. "It's just refreshing."[16]

David E. Cole, Director of the Office for the Study of Automotive Transportation at the University of Michigan, summarizes the leadership style that Jack Smith has displayed at GM. "One of Smith's greatest attributes," says Cole, "is that he relies on people around him. He knows what he doesn't know, and a lot of people who are executives don't. He's not into picking car designs or second-guessing engineers. He's a good listener, but he's not afraid of making decisions." In this section, we begin by describing some of the basic features of and differences in managerial styles and then focus on an approach to managing and leading that, like Jack Smith's, understands those jobs as responses to a variety of complex situations.

> ### "Jack Smith knows what he doesn't know, and a lot of people who are executives don't."
> —David E. Cole
> *Director, Office for the Study of Automotive Transportation*
> *at the University of Michigan*

Managerial Styles

Early theories of leadership tried to identify specific "traits" associated with strong leaders. For example, physical appearance, intelligence, and public speaking skills were once thought to be "leadership traits." Indeed, it was once believed that taller people made better leaders than shorter people. The trait approach, however, proved to be a poor predictor of leadership potential. Ultimately, attention shifted from managers' traits to their behaviors, or **managerial styles**—patterns of behavior that a manager exhibits in dealing with subordinates. Managerial styles run the gamut from *autocratic* to *democratic* to *free-rein*. Naturally, most managers do not clearly conform to any one style. But these three major types of styles involve very different kinds of responses to human relations problems. Under different circumstances, any given style—or any combination of styles—may prove appropriate.

managerial style
Pattern of behavior that a manager exhibits in dealing with subordinates

autocratic style
Managerial style in which managers generally issue orders and expect them to be obeyed without question

democratic style
Managerial style in which managers generally ask for input from subordinates but retain final decision-making power

free-rein style
Managerial style in which managers typically serve as advisers to subordinates who are allowed to make decisions

■ Managers who adopt an **autocratic style** generally issue orders and expect them to be obeyed without question. The military commander prefers and usually needs the autocratic style on the battlefield. Because no one else is consulted, the autocratic style allows for rapid decision making. It may, therefore, be useful in situations testing a firm's effectiveness as a time-based competitor.

■ Managers who adopt a **democratic style** generally ask for input from subordinates before making decisions but retain final decision-making power. For example, the manager of a technical group may ask other group members to interview and offer opinions about job applicants. The manager, however, will ultimately make the hiring decision.

■ Managers who adopt a **free-rein** style typically serve as advisers to subordinates who are allowed to make decisions. The chairperson of a volunteer committee to raise funds for a new library may find a free-rein style most effective.

According to many observers, the free-rein style of leadership is currently giving rise to an approach that emphasizes broad-based employee input into decision making and the fostering of workplace environments in which employees increasingly determine what needs to be done and how.

- Consider the case of W. L. Gore, a Delaware-based maker of such products as waterproof fabrics for spacesuits. Founded in 1958 by a firm believer in McGregor's Theory Y, Gore now practices what it calls "unmanagement." There are no titles and no hierarchy, and new "associates" (not "employees") are hired when sponsored by current associates. "Product specialists" initiate projects by building teams from members recruited from all areas of the company. Large teams soon break up into smaller teams composed of people who can perform a variety of manufacturing tasks. Team members then commit themselves to specific tasks, and leaders emerge from a combination of group discussion and the willingness of others to follow. Compensation is determined not by leaders but by committees that depend heavily on the recommendations of associates.[17]

Regardless of theories about the ways in which leaders ought to lead, the relative effectiveness of any leadership style depends largely on the desire of subordinates to share input or to exercise creativity. While some people, for example, are frustrated, others prefer autocratic managers because they do not want a voice in making decisions. The democratic approach, meanwhile, can be disconcerting both to people who want decision-making responsibility and to those who do not. A free-rein style lends itself to employee creativity—and thus to creative solutions to pressing problems. This style also appeals to employees who like to plan their own work. Not all subordinates, however, have the necessary background or skills to make creative decisions. Others are not sufficiently self-motivated to work without supervision.

The Contingency Approach to Leadership

Because each managerial style has both strengths and weaknesses, most managers vary their responses to different situations. Flexibility, however, has not always characterized managerial style or responsiveness. For most of the twentieth century, in fact, managers tended to believe that all problems yielded to preconceived, pretested solutions. If raising pay reduced turnover in one plant, for example, it followed that the same tactic would work equally well in another.

More recently, however, managers have begun to adopt a **contingency approach** to managerial style. They have started to view appropriate managerial behavior in any situation as dependent, or contingent, on the elements unique to that situation. This change in outlook has resulted largely from an increasing appreciation of the complexity of managerial problems and solutions. For example, pay raises may reduce turnover when workers have been badly underpaid. The contingency approach, however, recognizes that raises will have little effect when workers feel adequately paid but ill-treated by management. This approach also recommends that training managers in human relations skills may be crucial to solving the problem in the second case.

The contingency approach also acknowledges that people in different cultures behave differently and expect different things from their managers. A certain managerial style, therefore, is more likely to be successful in some countries than in others. Japanese workers, for example, generally expect managers to be highly participative and to

contingency approach
Approach to managerial style holding that the appropriate behavior in any situation is dependent (contingent) on the unique elements of that situation

give them input in decision making. In contrast, many South American workers actually balk at participation and want take-charge leaders. The basic idea, then, is that managers will be more effective when they adapt their styles to the contingencies of the situations they face.[18]

Motivation and Leadership in the 1990s

Motivation and leadership remain critically important areas of organizational behavior. As times change, however, so do the ways managers motivate and lead their employees. From the motivational side, today's employees want rewards that are often very different from those that earlier generations desired. Money, for example, is no longer the prime motivator for most people. In addition, because businesses today cannot offer the degree of job security that many workers want, motivating employees to strive toward higher levels of performance requires skillful attention from managers.

Finally, as we will see in Chapter 10, the diversity inherent in today's work force also makes motivating behavior more complex for managers. The reasons for which people work reflect more goals than ever before, and the varying life styles of diverse workers means that managers must first pay closer attention to what their employees expect to get for their efforts and then try to link rewards with job performance.

Today's leaders are also finding it necessary to change their own behavior. As organizations become flatter and workers more empowered, managers naturally find it less acceptable to use the autocractic approach to leadership. Instead, many are becoming more democratic—functioning more as "coaches" than "bosses." Just as an athletic coach teaches athletes how to play and then steps back to let them take the field, many leaders now try to provide workers with the skills and resources to perform at their best before backing off to let them do their work with less supervision.

Continued from page 205

"Have You Ever Thought about This?"

What Some Companies Think about Motivation

Like Chick-fil-A, Dallas-based Southwest Airlines has an annual employee turnover rate that is the envy of its industry. At only 7.5 percent, Southwest's turnover rate is considered "amazingly low." Not surprisingly, Southwest can point to many of the same motivating factors as Chick-fil-A:

- *Job security and opportunities for growth.* Southwest's strategy of slow growth has allowed it to be the best—though not necessarily the biggest—airline in its markets. According to Sherry Phelps, Director of Corporate Employment, this strategy is linked to job security. "We won't staff up for peak and then furlough people once the peak season is over," Says Phelps. Many employees pass up higher-paying jobs with other airlines because they want the security that Southwest offers. Moreover, with job security comes opportunity for growth. Thus, employees who attend Southwest's "University for People" find opportunities for advancement when they acquire advanced skills.
- *Compensation.* Like Chick-fil-A, Southwest has devised a unique

> **"If people in the field have a great idea for something, they can go directly to that department head and say, 'Have you ever thought about this?'"**
>
> —Sherry Phelps
> *Director of Corporate Employment at Southwest Airlines*

compensation package that enables employees to earn more than they are likely to earn at comparable firms. The difference does not derive from salary or wages; 83 percent of Southwest's employees are covered by union contracts that are standard for the industry. Rather, the difference in earning power derives from motivation, and motivation comes in large part from employee involvement in Southwest's profit-sharing plan. Employees are vested in the plan after only five years, and because of the company's superior financial performance (Southwest has shown a profit for 24 straight years), many employees have become wealthy.

- *Perks.* Another incentive is free or discounted travel. Employees with perfect attendance and on-time records for just three months receive two free airline tickets to any city the airline serves (as long as there's an empty seat). "This is a very valuable incentive," observes Phelps. "It costs us nothing, because it's space available. But the value to our people is enormous."
- *A strong corporate culture.* Southwest's strong corporate culture deemphasizes hierarchy while encouraging employees to take the initiative in improving quality and performance. "If people in the field have a great idea for something," says Phelps, "they can go directly to that department head and say, 'Have you ever thought about this?'"

At both Chick-fil-A and Southwest Airlines, money is only one factor that motivates workers. Both companies attract and keep the workers they want by maintaining stable work environments with opportunities for growth, nurturing strong corporate cultures, and offering some extras that really matter.

Case Questions

1. Why do top managers at Chick-fil-A and Southwest Airlines believe that money is only one factor in motivating workers? Do you agree with their assessment?
2. What factors at these companies contribute to their extremely low employee-turnover rates?
3. Do you think that S. Truett Cathy would subscribe to Theory X or Theory Y? Explain your answer.
4. Applying what you know about equity theory, describe how you think employees at Chick-fil-A and Southwest Airlines would evaluate the way their companies treat them.
5. Knowing what you do about Cathy's management philosophy, what managerial style do you think he would be most comfortable following?

SUMMARY OF LEARNING OBJECTIVES

1. **Discuss the importance of *job satisfaction* and employee *morale* and summarize their roles in *human relations* in the workplace.**   Good *human relations*—the interactions between employers and employees and their attitudes toward one another—are important to business because they lead to high levels of *job satisfaction* (the degree of enjoyment that workers derive from their jobs) and *morale* (workers' overall attitude toward their workplace). Satisfied employees generally exhibit lower levels of absenteeism and turnover. They also have fewer grievances and engage in fewer negative behaviors.

2. **Identify and summarize the most important theories of employee *motivation*.**   Views of employee motivation have changed dramatically over the years. The *classical theory* holds that people are motivated solely by money. *Scientific management* tried to analyze jobs and increase production by finding better ways to perform tasks. The *Hawthorne studies* were the first to demonstrate the importance of making workers feel that attention is being paid to their needs. The *human resources model* identifies two kinds of managers—*Theory X managers*, who believe that people are inherently uncooperative and must be constantly punished or rewarded, and *Theory Y managers*, who believe that people are naturally responsible and self-motivated to be productive.

    Maslow's *hierarchy of needs model* proposes that people have a number of different needs (ranging from physiological to self-actualization) that they attempt to satisfy in their work. People must fulfill lower-level needs before seeking to fulfill higher-level needs. *Two-factor theory* suggests that if basic hygiene factors are not met, workers will be dissatisfied. Only by increasing more complex motivation factors can companies increase employees' performance.

    Expectancy theory holds that people will work hard if they believe that their efforts will lead to desired rewards. *Equity theory* says that motivation depends on the way employees evaluate their treatment by an organization relative to its treatment of other workers.

3. **Describe some of the strategies used by organizations to improve job satisfaction and employee motivation.**   Managers can use several strategies to increase employee satisfaction and motivation. The principle of *reinforcement*, or *behavior modification theory*, holds that reward and punishment can control behavior. *Rewards*, for example, are positive reinforcement when they are tied directly to desired or improved performance. *Punishment* (using unpleasant consequences to change undesirable behavior) is generally less effective.

    Management by objectives (a system of collaborative goal setting) and *participative management and empowerment* (techniques for giving employees a voice in management decisions) can improve human relations by making employees feel like part of a team. *Job enrichment*, *job redesign*, and *modified work schedules* (including *work share programs*, *flextime*, and *alternative workplace strategies*) can enhance job satisfaction by adding motivation factors to jobs in which they are normally lacking.

4. **Discuss different managerial styles of *leadership* and their impact on human relations in the workplace.**   Effective *leadership*—the process of motivating others to meet specific objectives—is an important determinant of employee satisfaction and motivation. Generally speaking, managers practice one of three basic managerial styles. *Autocratic managers* generally issue orders that they expect to be obeyed. *Democratic managers* generally seek subordinates' input into decisions. *Free-rein managers* are more likely to advise than to make

decisions. The *contingency approach* to leadership views appropriate managerial behavior in any situation as dependent on the elements of that situation. Managers thus need to assess situations carefully, especially to determine the desire of subordinates to share input or exercise creativity.

STUDY QUESTIONS AND EXERCISES

Review

1. Do you think most people are relatively satisfied or dissatisfied with their work? Why are they mainly satisfied or dissatisfied?

2. Compare and contrast Maslow's hierarchy of needs with the two-factor theory of motivation.

3. How can participative management programs enhance employee satisfaction and motivation?

Analysis

4. What managerial style do you think best describes your own approach to leadership?

5. Some evidence suggests that people fresh out of college show high levels of job satisfaction. Levels then drop dramatically as they reach their late twenties, only to increase gradually once they get older. What might account for this pattern?

6. As a manager, under what sort of circumstances might you apply each of the theories of motivation discussed in this chapter? Which would be easiest to use? Which would be hardest? Why?

7. Suppose you realize one day that you are dissatisfied with your job. Short of quitting, what might you do to improve your situation?

8. List five U.S. managers whom you think would also qualify as great leaders.

Application Exercises

9. At the library, research the manager or owner of a company in the early twentieth century and the manager or owner of a company in the 1990s. Compare and contrast the two in terms of their times, leadership styles, and views of employee motivation.

10. Interview the manager of a local manufacturing company. Identify as many different strategies for enhancing job satisfaction at that company as you can.

BUILDING YOUR BUSINESS SKILLS

This exercise enhances the following SCANS workplace competencies: demonstrating basic skills, demonstrating thinking skills, exhibiting interpersonal skills, and working with information.

Goal

To encourage students to think about the role that family-friendly strategies play in motivating workers

Situation

Business Week magazine, together with the Center on Work & Family at Boston University, recently published the results of a year-long study comparing the family-friendly strategies of some major U.S. corporations. Among strategies defined as family-friendly are flexible scheduling, telecommuting, job sharing, child care and elder care assistance, and employee help lines. As part of the study, *Business Week* surveyed 7,776 employees at 37 companies with established programs. The purpose of the study was to learn how employees perceive company policies and how these policies affect employees' ability to function both at work and at home.

Method

Step 1: Join with three or four other students in your class. Ask each person in the group to identify relatives and friends who are currently working and who would agree to answer several of the questions posed in the *Business Week* survey. Make a list of these workers, their positions, and the companies for which they work.

Step 2: Have each member of the group ask survey participants the following questions. Answers should fit into one of the categories listed below each question. The percentage that appears next to each answer reflects the response received in the *Business Week* survey.

■ What impact does your work have on your home life?

Negative impact	(42%)
Neutral	(26%)
Positive impact	(32%)

■ Does your company have high-quality programs for people who have to care for children or elder family members?

Not at all/Not much	(23%)
Somewhat	(26%)
Considerably/A great deal	(51%)

■ Can you have a good family life and still get ahead in your company?

Not at all/Not much	(22%)
Somewhat	(30%)
Considerably/A great deal	(48%)

■ Is your supervisor flexible when it comes to responding to your work/family needs?

Not at all/Not much	(8%)
Somewhat	(16%)
Considerably/A great deal	(76%)

Step 3: Meet as a group to analyze responses. Specifically, determine how the responses that your group gathered compare with those in the *Business Week* survey.

Follow-Up

1. How do family-friendly strategies affect employee motivation and productivity?

2. What do the responses to the *Business Week* survey tell you about the level of satisfaction or dissatisfaction people are experiencing at work as a result of their dual roles? Are workers satisfied that their companies are trying to help them balance their work/family responsibilities?

3. What do the differences and/or similarities in the responses reported by *Business Week* and those gathered by your own survey group tell you about the family-friendly strategies of the companies for which your survey subjects work?

Exploring the Net

THIS CHAPTER STRESSES THE FACT THAT EMPLOYEE SATISFACTION AND MORALE ARE IMPORTANT TO ANY ORGANIZATION. HOWEVER, IT IS ALSO QUITE DIFFICULT FOR MANAGERS TO KNOW FOR SURE JUST HOW SATISFIED AND MOTIVATED THEIR EMPLOYEES ACTUALLY ARE. IN MOST CASES, MANAGERS INTERESTED IN ASSESSING SATISFACTION AND/OR MORALE DO SO WITH SURVEYS. EMPLOYEES ARE ASKED TO RESPOND TO VARIOUS QUESTIONS ABOUT HOW THEY FEEL ABOUT THEIR WORK, AND THEIR RESPONSES ARE SCORED TO PROVIDE AN INDICATION OF THEIR SATISFACTION AND MORALE. TO EXAMINE SUCH A SURVEY, VISIT THIS WEBSITE:

http://www.fdgroup.co.uk/neo/djassoc/dj_jdq.html

After you have examined the satisfaction questionnaire at this site, consider the following questions:

1. For whose use is this questionnaire geared? After studying the explanatory headnote, can you identify two or three key principles of instruments like this one?

2. At face value, how valid does this survey instrument seem to be? Is it likely to meet the objectives outlined in the headnote?

3. Fill out the survey yourself, and then analyze your responses.

4. What appear to be the biggest strengths and weaknesses of this particular survey? Assuming this questionnaire to be typical, what would you judge to be the strengths and weaknesses of job satisfaction surveys in general?

5. Try writing a survey yourself. Focus it on job satisfaction in your present job, in a previous job, or in this class. What information do you most want to elicit? What aspect of this information is hardest to elicit? Why?

MANAGING HUMAN RESOURCES AND LABOR RELATIONS

Marriott Clears a Pathway to Productive Employment

PRIVATE-SECTOR SHOW FINDS ROLES FOR THOSE ON WELFARE

Human resources executives at Marriott International, the nation's fourth-largest hotel chain, heard President Clinton's message about welfare reform and took it seriously. After signing legislation requiring millions of welfare recipients to find work, the President told business leaders that the law would fail without their help. "We cannot create enough public service jobs to hire these folks," said the President, "so they have to be hired in the private sector. This basically has to be a private sector show."

Marriott's response, a program called Pathways to Independence, is viewed as a model for corporate participation in national welfare reform. The program has enrolled nearly 600 people at hotels in 15 cities and has shown that welfare recipients *can* work. Pathways teaches people with little or no work experience the skills

> ## "It makes bottom-line sense. If it didn't, we wouldn't do it."
>
> —J.W. Marriott Jr.
> *Chairman of Marriott International on the company's program for training welfare workers*

they need to hold a job. Over a six-week period, trainees learn everything from personal hygiene to punctuality. They learn how to talk out conflicts rather than start fights and how to juggle the needs of family with the needs of work. The demands placed on them are real, but then so is the help they get. Trainers, for example, make day-care arrangements. They help participants set up checking accounts and manage their money. And they attempt to instill

self-esteem by rewarding workers who finish the course with full-time jobs paying about $7 an hour.

Even with this help, nearly 20 percent of participants don't make it through the program. Marriott officials have found that for someone with no personal or family history of workplace success, a torn stocking is excuse enough for not showing up. "It's enough to drive you nuts," laments trainer Kenneth Tully.

The per-person cost to Marriott for putting workers through the Pathways program is about $5,500. With government funds covering all but $2,300 of it, the program makes good economic as well as social sense. Pathways graduates have a 13-percent turnover rate when placed in Marriott jobs, compared to a 37-percent turnover rate for average company workers. Moreover, 75 percent of graduates stay with the company more than 300 days.

"We're getting good employees for the long term," explains chairman J.W. Marriott Jr., "but we're also helping these communities. If we don't step up in these inner cities and provide work, they'll never pull out of it. But it also makes bottom-line sense. [If it didn't] we wouldn't do it." Bruce Reed, an advisor to President Clinton, agrees. "Companies should do this," he argues, "because it's in their interest, not just because it's the right thing to do."

The Pathways course has already changed lives. Former welfare recipient Sabrina McWhite now works in the kitchen at the Metro Center Marriott in Washington, D.C. She has dreams of becoming a chef and credits Pathways with teaching her "how to manage money correctly, how to always have backup for child care," and how to hope—and plan—for a better future.

This chapter discusses the nature of benefits in response to both chang-

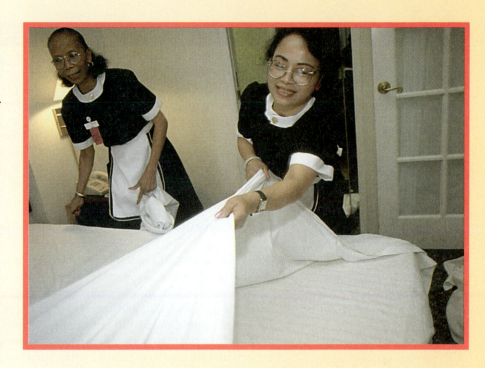

ing employee needs and changes in a company's external environment. By focusing on the learning objectives, you will better understand some of the formal systems that companies use to manage their employees, as well as some of the key issues in contemporary labor relations.

After reading this chapter, you should be able to

1. Define *human resource management* and explain how managers plan for human resources

2. Identify the steps involved in *staffing* a company

3. Explain how organizations can develop workers' skills and manage workers who do not perform well

4. Discuss the importance of *wages* and *salaries, incentives, and benefits programs* in attracting and keeping skilled workers

5. Describe some of the key legal and ethical issues involved in hiring

6. Describe the *major laws governing labor–management relations*

7. Identify the steps in the *collective bargaining process*

Continued on page 253

■ THE FOUNDATIONS OF HUMAN RESOURCE MANAGEMENT

human resource management
Development and administration of programs to enhance the quality and performance of a company's work force

human resource managers
Managers responsible for hiring, training, evaluating, and compensating employees

job relatedness
Principle that all employment decisions should be based on the requirements of the jobs in question

person-job matching
Process of matching the right person to the right job

job analysis
Evaluation of the duties and qualities required by a job

job description
Outline of the objectives, tasks, and responsibilities of a job

job specification
Description of the skills, education, and experience required by a job

Human resource management is the development and administration of programs to enhance the quality and performance of people working in an organization. **Human resource managers**—sometimes called *personnel managers*—are employed by all but the smallest firms. They recruit, train, and develop employees and set up evaluation, compensation, and benefits programs. In reality, however, all managers deal with human resources. Managers of accounting, finance, and marketing departments, for example, help select and train workers and evaluate their performances.[1] All managers must therefore understand the principles of *job relatedness* and *person-job matching*.

Job Relatedness and Person-Job Matching

Job relatedness, the foundation of effective human resource management, requires that all employment decisions be based on the requirements of a position. That is, the criteria used in hiring, evaluating, promoting, and rewarding people must be tied directly to the jobs being performed. For example, a policy that all office managers must be women would violate job relatedness because gender is irrelevant to the job. In contrast, hiring only young women to model clothing designed for teenage girls is job-related and thus reflects sound human resource management.

Central to the principle of job relatedness is **person–job matching**—the process of matching the right person to the right job. Good human resource managers match people's skills, interests, and temperaments with the requirements of their jobs. When people and jobs are well matched, the company benefits from high performance and employee satisfaction, high retention of effective workers, and low absenteeism.

Planning for Human Resources Like planning for future equipment or construction, planning for future human resource needs is crucial in any organization. Human resource planning starts with job analysis.

Job Analysis. **Job analysis** is the evaluation of the duties required by a particular job and the qualities required to perform it. For simple, repetitive jobs, managers may ask workers to create checklists of all the duties they perform and to identify the importance of each. In analyzing more complex jobs, they may also hold interviews to determine jobholders' exact duties. Managers may also observe workers to identify their duties.

From the job analysis, a manager develops a **job description**—a statement outlining the objectives, tasks, and responsibilities of a job. The job description also describes the conditions under which the job will be done, the ways in which it relates to other positions, and the skills needed to perform it. Managers also draw up **job specifications,** which describe the skills, education, and experience required by a job. Together, job analyses and descriptions serve as tools for filling specific positions, as guides in establishing training programs, and as comparative guidelines for setting wages. Most important, by objectively defining requirements, they allow managers to make employment decisions based on job relatedness.

■ STAFFING THE ORGANIZATION

Once managers have decided what positions they need to fill, they must find and hire qualified individuals. Staffing the organization is one of the most complex and important tasks of human resource management.[2] In this section, we describe both the process of acquiring staff from outside the company *(external staffing)* and the process of promoting staff from within *(internal staffing)*.

External Staffing

A new firm has little choice but to hire people from the outside. Established firms may also hire outsiders to fill positions for which there are no good internal candidates, to accommodate growth, or to attract fresh ideas. External staffing involves two processes:

■ *Recruitment.* The first step in hiring new workers is identifying and contacting a pool of applicants who are both interested in and qualified for available positions. Recruiters often visit high schools, vocational schools, colleges, and universities. Many companies advertise in newspapers or trade publications or seek the help of employment agencies. Unsolicited letters and résumés from job seekers can also produce the right person for a job.

■ *Selection.* After applicants have been attracted, the next step is to evaluate each individual and select the best candidate. Figure 10.1 shows the stages and possible outcomes of a typical selection process. Each organization develops its own mix of selection techniques and may use them in any order. The stages discussed on page 234 are common to most selection processes:

FIGURE 10.1 ◆ Sample Selection System

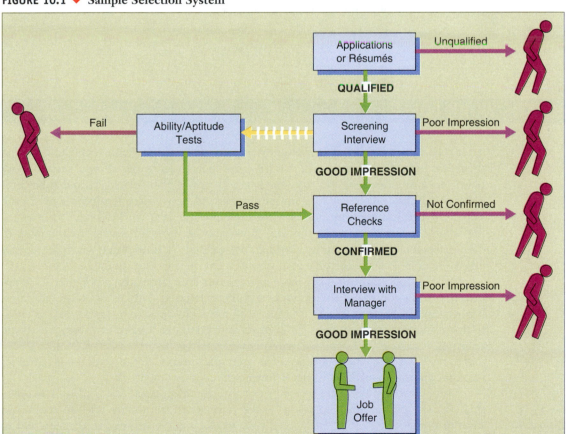

1. *Applications or résumés.* A job application is a standardized form that asks the applicant for such information as background, experience, and education. A *résumé* is a prepared statement of the applicant's qualifications and career goals.

2. *Screening interviews.* Companies often find themselves with several applications or résumés for every job opening. Managers thus narrow the field, first on the basis of applications and then by holding screening interviews to eliminate unqualified individuals. They then interview qualified applicants in greater depth.

3. *Ability and aptitude tests.* For some positions, ability or aptitude tests may be given. Such tests must meet two conditions. They must be job-related, and they must indicate clearly that top scorers are more likely to perform well in specified jobs.

Internal Staffing: Promotions

closed promotion system
System by which managers decide, often informally, which workers are considered for promotions

open promotion system
System by which employees apply, test, and interview for available jobs, requirements of which are posted

Many organizations prefer to hire from within. That is, they prefer whenever possible to promote or transfer existing employees to fill openings. Systems for promoting employees usually take one of two forms:

- In **closed promotion systems,** managers decide which workers will be considered for promotions. Decisions are usually made informally (and often subjectively) and tend to rely on the recommendations of immediate supervisors.
- In **open promotion systems,** available jobs and requirements are posted. Employees who feel they have the necessary qualifications fill out applications, take tests, and interview with managers.

■ DEVELOPING THE WORK FORCE

on-the-job training
Training, sometimes informal, conducted while an employee is at work

off-the-job-training
Training conducted in a controlled environment away from the work site

vestibule training
Off-the-job training conducted in a simulated environment

performance appraisal
Evaluation, often in writing, of an employee's job performance

After a company has hired new employees, it must acquaint them with the firm and their new jobs. This process, called *orientation*, focuses on simple things, such as work hours, parking priorities, and pay schedules. Typically, both managers and other employees will also take steps to train employees and help them develop necessary job skills. **On-the-job training** occurs while the employee is at work. Much of this training is informal, as when one employee shows another how to use the photocopier. In other cases, on-the-job training is formal. For example, a trainer may teach secretaries how to operate a new electronic mail system from their workstations.

Off-the-job training takes place at locations away from the work site. This approach offers a controlled environment and allows focused study without interruptions. For example, Chaparral Steel's training program includes four hours a week of classroom training in areas such as basic math and grammar. Other firms use **vestibule training**—training in simulated work environments—to make off-the-job training more realistic. American Airlines, for example, trains flight attendants through vestibule training, and AT&T uses it to train telephone operators.

Every company has some system for performance appraisal and feedback. In some small firms, "performance appraisal" takes place when the owner tells an employee, "You're doing a good job." In larger firms, **performance appraisals** are designed to

TRENDS & CHALLENGES

NEW LIFE ON THE HIGH-TECH LINE

In an economy in which manufacturing jobs are rapidly disappearing, there is considerable irony in the fact that high-technology manufacturers are scrambling to find qualified workers. High school graduates, for example, are often woefully unprepared to handle the technological demands of twenty-first century jobs. As a result, a company like APX International, a Michigan-based automotive designer, has more than 600 job openings it cannot fill. And when all the necessary jobs can't be performed, work and income must obviously be turned down. The downward spiral can be devastating.

To deal with this crisis, some manufacturers are creating high school apprenticeship programs to teach participants the skills they need to do actual jobs. The "Cadillac" of such programs is run by Siemens, the German manufacturer of high-tech industrial equipment. With 13,000 apprentices in 30 countries, it was a natural leap for Siemens to start a program in the United States. The Siemens program enrolls 337 apprentices, including 118 high school students and 219 community college students, in schools across the country.

One of these programs is run out of East Wake High School in Wendell, North Carolina. Along with their conventional studies, participants receive special training in math and physics. The apprentices also spend two hours a day working in a specially equipped shop filled with $250,000 worth of Siemens equipment. Apprentices learn to operate lathes and grinders, assemble electrical equipment, and navigate the Internet. The process is rigorous and leaves almost no room for error. Metal parts, for example, must be manufactured to an accuracy of 0.001 inch.

How have participants reacted to the program? Many consider it a new beginning. Says 18-year-old Josh Gifford: "When you're sitting in a regular class and watching a teacher teach, you don't know if that will be useful in your life. In the Siemens program, I knew everything I did was going to affect me after school."

> **"When you're sitting in a regular class and watching a teacher teach, you don't know if that will be useful in your life. In the Siemens program, I knew everything I did was going to affect me after school."**
>
> —Josh Gifford
> *Graduate of Siemens apprenticeship program*

Gifford signed on with Siemens right after graduation. His current job is attaching circuit breakers to metal panels in industrial motors. Already earning $10 an hour, he has plans to become an equipment tester. That's fine with management, which places no restrictions on the career paths that graduates take. Even the decision to join Siemens is voluntary. So far, however, Siemens has had considerable success in luring graduates into full-time jobs. After the first group of apprentices completed their training, 85 percent joined the company as field engineers for customer services, telecommunications technicians, precision tool-and-die makers, and assembly-line workers.

---

show more precisely how well workers are doing their jobs. Typically, the appraisal process involves a written assessment that is issued on a regular basis but that may represent only one part of a multistep process. This process begins when a manager defines performance standards for an employee. The manager then observes the employee's performance. If the standards are clear, the manager should have little difficulty comparing expectations with performance.

Written appraisals are especially important when a company must dismiss or demote employees. Most companies have step-by-step processes for dismissal. The first step might be a verbal warning about a particular problem—poor performance or attendance, for example. Many companies also require managers to give employees written warnings.

■ COMPENSATION AND BENEFITS

compensation system
Total package offered by a company to employees in return for their labor

People do not work for free. Providing workers with appropriate compensation for their time and talents is thus another important part of human resource management. Most workers today also expect certain benefits from their employers. Indeed, a major factor in retaining skilled workers is a company's **compensation system**—the total package that it offers employees in return for their labor.

Although wages and salaries are key parts of all compensation systems, most also include *incentives* and *employee benefits programs*. We discuss these and other types of employee benefits in this section. Finding the right *combination* of compensation elements is always complicated by the need to make employees feel valued while holding down company costs. Compensation systems differ widely, depending on the nature of the industry, the company, and the types of workers involved.[3]

Wages and Salaries

wages
Compensation in the form of money paid for time worked

salary
Compensation in the form of money paid for discharging the responsibilities of a job

Wages and salaries are the dollar amounts paid to employees for their labor. **Wages** are paid for time worked. Workers who are paid by the hour receive wages. A **salary** is paid for discharging the responsibilities of a job. A salaried executive earning $100,000 per year is paid to achieve results, even if that means working 5 hours one day and 15 the next. Salaries are usually expressed as an amount paid per year.

In setting wage and salary levels, a company may start by looking at its competitors' levels. A firm that pays less than its rivals knows that it runs the risk of losing valuable personnel. To attract top employees some companies pay more than their rivals. M&M/Mars, for example, pays managerial salaries about 10 percent above the average in the candy and snack food industry.

A firm must also decide how its internal wage and salary levels will compare for different jobs. Sears, for example, must determine the relative salaries of store managers, buyers, and advertising managers. In turn, managers must decide how much to pay individual workers within the company's wage and salary structure. Although two employees may do exactly the same job, the employee with more experience may earn more. Moreover, some union contracts specify differential wages based on experience.

Incentive Programs

incentive program
Special compensation program designed to motivate high performance

bonus
Individual performance incentive in the form of a special payment made over and above the employee's salary

merit salary system
Incentive program linking compensation to performance in nonsales jobs

Naturally, employees feel better about their companies when they believe they are being fairly compensated. Both studies and experience have shown, however, that beyond a certain point, more money will not produce better performance. Indeed, neither across-the-board nor cost-of-living wage increases cause people to work harder. Money motivates employees only if it is tied directly to performance. The most common method of establishing this link is the use of **incentive programs**—special pay programs designed to motivate high performance. Some programs are available to individuals, while others are distributed on a companywide basis.

Individual Incentives A sales bonus is a typical incentive. Employees receive **bonuses**—special payments over and above their salaries—when they sell a certain number or certain dollar amount of goods for the year. Employees who fail to reach this goal earn no bonuses. **Merit salary systems** link raises to performance levels in nonsales jobs. For example, many baseball players have contract clauses that pay them bonuses for hitting over .300, making the All-Star team, or being named Most Valuable Player.

Executives commonly receive stock options as incentives. Coca-Cola CEO Roberto C. Goizueta, for example, can buy several thousand shares of company stock each year at a predetermined price. If his managerial talent leads to higher profits and stock prices, he can buy the stock at a price lower than the market value—for which, in theory, he is largely responsible. He is then free to sell his shares at market price, keeping the difference for himself. In one recent year, $9.5 million out of Goizueta's total pay of $14.5 million came from the exercise of stock options.[4]

A relatively new incentive plan is called **pay-for-performance,** or **variable pay.** In essence, middle managers are rewarded for especially productive output—that is, for producing earnings that significantly exceed the cost of bonuses. Such incentives have long been common among top-level executives and factory workers, but variable pay goes to middle managers on the basis of companywide performance, business unit performance, personal record, or all three factors. At steel producer Nucor, for example, bonuses for plant managers are tied to companywide earnings. In 1992, for instance, Nucor managers topped a specified figure of $80 million in earnings by $30 million. At the Nucor mill in Norfolk, Nebraska, therefore, the plant manager pocketed an extra $80,000 in cash and $40,000 in stock.[5] ▶

Companywide Incentives   Some incentive programs apply to all the employees in a firm. Under **profit-sharing plans,** for example, profits earned above a certain level are distributed to employees. **Gain-sharing plans** distribute bonuses to employees when a company's costs are reduced through greater work efficiency. **Pay-for-knowledge plans** encourage workers to learn new skills and to become proficient at different jobs. Employees receive additional pay for each new skill or job they master.

Benefits Programs

A growing part of nearly every firm's compensation system is its benefits program. **Benefits**—compensation other than wages and salaries offered by a firm to its workers—make up a large percentage of most compensation budgets. Most companies are

pay-for-performance (or variable pay)
Individual incentive that rewards a manager for especially productive output

profit-sharing plan
Incentive program for distributing bonuses to employees for company profits above a certain level

gain-sharing plan
Incentive program for distributing bonuses to employees whose performances improve productivity

pay-for-knowledge plan
Incentive program to encourage employees to learn new skills or become proficient at different jobs

benefits
Compensation other than wages and salaries

© 1998 Bernhard Schoenbaum *from* The Cartoon Bank,™ Inc.

"It appears, Fredrick, since we instituted the merit system you owe us twenty-five-hundred dollars."

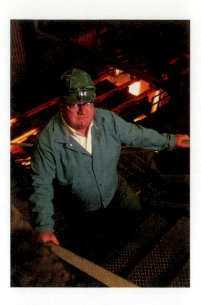

John A. Doherty runs a Nucor Steel mill in Norfolk, Nebraska. In one good year, bonuses totaling $120,000 almost doubled his salary. The catch: Doherty's bonus is tied to companywide performance—that is, to the achievements of other Nucor plant managers. Every year, therefore, plant managers and top Nucor executives get together to exchange sometimes blunt criticisms. "These bonuses aren't entitlements," explains Doherty. "We're running our own businesses, and we'd better perform."

worker's compensation insurance
Legally required insurance for compensating workers injured on the job

cafeteria benefits plan
Benefits plan that establishes dollar amount of benefits per employee and allows employees to choose from a variety of alternative benefits

required by law to provide social security retirement benefits and **workers' compensation insurance** (insurance for compensating workers injured on the job). Most businesses also voluntarily provide health, life, and disability insurance. Many also allow employees to use payroll deductions to buy stock at discounted prices. Another common benefit is paid time off for vacations and holidays. Counseling services for employees with alcohol, drug, or emotional problems are also becoming more common.

Retirement Plans   Retirement plans are an important—and sometimes controversial—benefit available to many employees. Most company-sponsored retirement plans are set up to pay pensions to workers when they retire. In some cases, the company contributes all the money to the pension fund. In others, contributions are made by both the company and employees. Currently, about 60 percent of U.S. workers are covered by pension plans of some kind.

Containing the Costs of Benefits   As the range of employee benefits has grown, so has concern about containing their costs. Many companies are thus experimenting with cost-cutting plans under which they can still attract and retain valuable employees. One approach is the **cafeteria benefits plan,** under which a certain dollar amount of benefits per employee is set aside and employees select from a variety of alternatives.

Another area of growing concern is health care costs. Medical procedures that once cost several hundred dollars now cost several thousand. Rising expenses have increased insurance premiums, which in turn have increased the cost to employers of maintaining benefits plans.

Many employers are thus looking for new ways to cut those costs. One increasingly popular approach is for organizations to create their own networks of health care providers. These providers agree to charge lower fees for services rendered to employees of member organizations. In return, they enjoy established relationships with large employers. Because they must make lower reimbursement payments, insurers also charge less to cover the employees of network members.

■ LEGAL AND ETHICAL ISSUES IN MANAGING PEOPLE

In the course of performing their jobs, human resource managers are confronted by a number of legal issues—issues that often have ethical implications as well. In this section, we discuss some of the basic principles that underlie human resource policies in U.S. business: *equal employment opportunity*, *equal pay* and *comparable worth*, and *occupational safety and health*.

Equal Employment Opportunity

For many years, white men dominated U.S. business, especially at the managerial and professional levels. In recent years, this situation has begun to change, partly as a result of changes in the legal environment. Title VII of the 1964 Civil Rights Act was the first major law to prohibit discrimination. It paved the way for more than three decades of change. The act also created the Equal Employment Opportunity Commission (EEOC), which is responsible for enforcing its provisions. Today, numerous federal and state laws, federal guidelines, presidential executive orders, and judicial decisions mandate **equal employment opportunity**—nondiscrimination in employment on the basis of race, color, creed, sex, or national origin.

Under the Equal Employment Opportunity Act of 1992, the EEOC can file civil suit in federal court on behalf of individuals who claim their rights have been violated. Remedies include reinstatement, back pay, and compensation for the victim's suffering. Because litigation can last for years, settlements can be huge. Recent awards include $2.3 million in back pay to three older employees of Federated Department Stores, $42.5 million to female and minority employees at General Motors, and $52.5 million to female employees at Northwest Airlines.[6]

Sexual Harassment Sexual harassment is a form of employer or management behavior that falls under the category of employment discrimination. Under the terms of the Equal Opportunity Act, any "'unwelcome' sexual attention, whether verbal or physical, that affects an employee's job conditions or creates a 'hostile' working environment" constitutes sexual harassment. When does "acceptable" behavior become "unacceptable"? The U.S. Supreme Court ruled in 1986 that behavior may be judged on the basis of what would offend a "reasonable woman."

In November 1993, the Court expanded its 1986 ruling and issued an even broader definition of sexual harassment in the workplace. The law is violated when—for a variety of reasons—"the environment would be reasonably perceived, and is perceived, as hostile or abusive."

Today most large corporations provide their employees with detailed information regarding what kinds of behavior are and are not acceptable. They also publish standard procedures for receiving and investigating reports of harassment. Some corporations, such as Du Pont and Corning, go even further: both require all employees to attend seminars in which participants role-play potential harassment situations.

Most companies today place a strong emphasis on a harassment-free workplace. The willingness to discipline offenders reflects a number of trends in modern business. Growing public outrage over sexual harassment, coupled with rising numbers of women in the work force, has had a significant impact. Any company that does not vigorously pursue all employee complaints of harassment may find itself being sued and paying huge settlements. Consider the repercussions for Mitsubishi Motors when a group of women complained that management took no action to curb sexual harassment at the company's Normal, Illinois, automobile plant. In April 1996, the EEOC filed charges on behalf of up to 700 women. In additional to statutory damages of $300,000 for each case, Mitsubishi would almost certainly face further losses in subsequent civil suits. Moreover, in May the National Organization of Women and other groups launched a boycott aimed not only at Mitsubishi's U.S. automotive dealerships but at products made by other companies owned by Mitsubishi (including Mitsubishi Electric, Nikon photographic equipment, and Kirin Brewing as well).[7] ▶

Affirmative Action Various executive orders spanning more than two decades have required many organizations to engage in affirmative action. Executive Order 11246, for example, mandates **affirmative action programs** to recruit qualified or qualifiable employees from racial, gender, and ethnic groups that are underrepresented in an organization. All organizations receiving more than $100,000 a year in government contracts must have written affirmative action plans. Many other businesses practice affirmative action on a voluntary basis. Legislation passed in 1991 reinforces the legal basis of affirmative action but specifically forbids organizations to set hiring quotas that might result in **reverse discrimination.** This practice can occur when an organization concentrates so much on hiring from some groups that other groups suffer discrimination.

equal employment opportunity
Legally mandated nondiscrimination in employment on the basis of race, creed, sex, or national origin

affirmative action program
Legally mandated program for recruiting qualified employees belonging to racial, gender, or ethnic groups that are underrepresented in an organization

reverse discrimination
Practice of discriminating against well-represented groups by overhiring members of underrepresented groups

When the EEOC filed sexual harassment charges at Mitsubishi Motors' Normal, Illinois, factory in April 1996, Jesse Jackson's Operation PUSH joined with the National Organization for Women to picket such sites as the carmaker's Illinois dealerships. Although the boycott itself had limited impact, automotive dealers and retailers of other Mitsubishi products wanted the parent company to resolve the issue. Matters only got worse, they claimed, when Mitsubishi instead sent 3,000 workers from the Normal plant to protest outside the EEOC's Chicago office.

Equal Pay and Comparable Worth

A special area of equal employment, employment opportunities for women, has given rise to one of the most controversial issues in compensation today. The Equal Pay Act of 1963 specifically forbids sex discrimination in pay. No company can legally pay men and women of equal experience differently for work that is performed under similar conditions and that requires equal skill, effort, and responsibility. Differing job titles alone cannot justify pay differences. Thus, if a woman whose job title is "senior secretary" performs essentially the same job as a man whose title is "administrative assistant," the two must face the same pay scales. As a result of the Equal Pay Act, many women have sued and received back pay and other adjustments from employers who discriminated on the basis of pay.[8]

The "Glass Ceiling"   Despite the Equal Pay Act, however, statistics show that women still earn less than men for performing similar jobs. Only in the last 20 or so years have large numbers of women sought professional careers. Thus, many women have less work experience than do men of the same age. A related issue is the "glass ceiling" phenomenon—the idea that an invisible but very real barrier keeps women and minorities from advancing to the highest levels in U.S. organizations.

In a series of hearings held between 1991 and 1994, a Congressional panel called the Glass Ceiling Commission gathered information and opinion for a report on the lack of progress in advancement by women and minorities. Findings show that despite the Civil Rights Act and women's rights activism, women comprise half the nation's work force but only 3–6 percent of its corporate officials. Minorities comprise only 1 percent. A survey released in 1996 also found several major companies that still have no female officers (that is, people holding the title of *chairman, chief executive, vice chairman, chief operating officer,* or *executive vice president*). For example, Exxon has 20 such positions, Compaq Computer 14, Texas Instruments 12, and Rockwell International 19. All are occupied by men—as are 97.6 percent of such jobs. Sheila W. Wellington, President of Catalyst, the nonprofit women's advocacy group that conducted the survey, interprets the numbers as "pathetic. It's darn hard to find a shred of daylight in this."[9]

"The numbers are pathetic. It's darn hard to find a shred of daylight in this."

—Sheila W. Wellington
*President of Catalyst on the fact that women occupy only
2.4 percent of the highest corporate jobs in America*

Progress toward "Comparable Worth"   Many experts agree that subtle and perhaps even unconscious discrimination still exists in many organizations. To combat this discrimination, some analysts have called for a policy of **comparable worth.** Women would receive the same wage for traditionally "female" jobs (such as secretary) as men do for traditional "male" jobs of the same worth to the company (such as mechanic).[10]

Both government statistics and working women confirm the suspicions of experts about lingering discrimination. For instance, figures show that in 1993, women earned 71 cents for every dollar earned by a man (up from 61 cents in 1978). As you can see from Table 10.1, part of the differential results from the fact that women are still concentrated in occupational categories that are traditionally low-paying, especially nursing, teaching, secretarial jobs, and retail sales.

comparable worth
Principle that women should receive the same pay for traditionally "female" jobs of the same worth to a company as traditionally "male" jobs

Occupational Safety and Health

Issues of worker safety on the job have also been addressed through legislation. The Occupational Safety and Health Act of 1970, which created the **Occupational Safety and Health Administration (OSHA),** is the most far-reaching piece of legislation in this area. The act covers all firms with one or more employees.

Occupational Safety and Health Administration (OSHA)
Federal agency that sets and enforces guidelines for protecting workers from unsafe conditions and potential health hazards in the workplace

TABLE 10.1 ◆ Women in Selected Occupational Categories

Occupational Category	Percentage of Women
Engineers	7.3
Lawyers and Judges	19.5
Librarians	85.4
Physicians	20.0
Dentists	9.3
Registered nurses	94.6
Elementary, secondary teachers	72.9
Managers, administrators	44.7
Sales workers, retail and personal service	68.6
Secretaries, stenographers, typists	98.2
Precision production, craft, and repair	8.7
Transportation and material moving	9.0
Food service workers	61.6
Private household (maids, servants)	96.3

OSHA sets numerous guidelines in two general areas. First, it protects employee safety by eliminating unsafe working conditions, such as dangerous machinery and unsafe ladders and scaffolding, that might lead to accidents. Second, it protects the health of workers from long-term exposure to health hazards ranging from excessive noise to cancer-causing chemicals. OSHA inspectors can investigate any complaint filed by a worker. They also spot-check companies in particularly hazardous industries. Plants failing to meet safety and/or health standards can be fined.

■ NEW CHALLENGES IN THE CHANGING WORKPLACE

As we have seen throughout this chapter, human resource managers face a number of ongoing challenges in their efforts to keep their organizations staffed with effective work forces. To complicate matters, new challenges arise as the economic and social environments of business change. Today's human resource managers must deal with work forces that are increasingly *diverse* and *contingent* in their makeup.

Managing Work Force Diversity

work force diversity
Range of workers' attitudes, values, and behaviors that differ by gender, race, and ethnicity

An extremely important set of human resource challenges centers on **work force diversity**—the range of workers' attitudes, values, beliefs, and behaviors that differ by gender, race, and ethnicity. The diverse work force is also characterized by individuals of different ages and physical abilities. In the past, organizations tended to work toward *homogenizing* their work forces—by getting everyone to think and behave in similar ways. Partly as a result of affirmative action efforts, however, many U.S. organizations are now creating work forces that are more diverse, embracing more women, more ethnic minorities, and more foreign-born employees than ever before.

The two graphs in this section will help to put the changing U.S. work force into perspective. Figure 10.2 shows changes in the percentages of different groups of workers—white men, white women, blacks, Hispanics, Asians, and others—in the work force in 1980, 1993, and 2005 (projected). Figure 10.3 shows the same changes among managerial and professional workers in the decade between 1983 and 1993. The first picture is one of increasing diversity. The second is one of a slower but still steady trend toward diversity. By the year 2005, says the Labor Department, half of all workers entering the labor force will be women, and more than a third will be nonwhite.[11]

FIGURE 10.2 ◆ Diversity: Total Work Force, 1980–2005

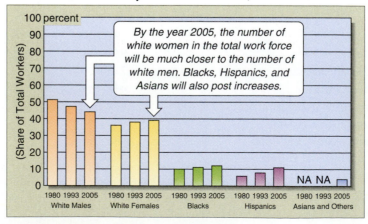

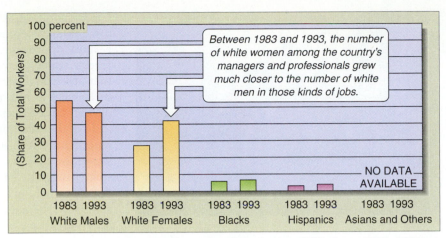

FIGURE 10.3 ◆ **Diversity: Managerial and Professional Workers, 1983–1993**

Diversity as a Competitive Advantage   Today many organizations are recognizing not only that they should treat everyone equitably, but that they should acknowledge the individuality of each person they employ. They are also recognizing that diversity can be a competitive advantage. For example, by hiring the best people available from every single group rather than hiring from just one or a few groups, a firm can develop a higher-quality work force. Similarly, a diverse work force can bring a wider array of information to bear upon problems and can provide insights on marketing products to a wider range of consumers. Says the head of work force diversity at IBM: "We think it is important for our customers to look inside and see people like them. If they can't . . . the prospect of them becoming or staying our customers declines."

> ## "We think it is important for our customers to look inside and see people like them."
>
> —Ted Childs
> *Director of work force diversity at IBM*

Not all American companies have worked equally hard to adjust their thinking and diversify their work forces. In fact, experts estimate that a mere 3–5 percent of U.S. corporations are diversifying with any effect. In a recent survey of executives at 1,405 participating firms, only 5 percent believed that they were doing a "very good job" of diversifying their human resources. Many others, however, have instituted—and, more important, maintained—diversity programs. The experience of these companies—including IBM, Xerox, Avon, AT&T, Burger King, Levi Strauss, and Hoechst Celanese—has made it possible to draw up some general guidelines for a successful work force diversity program:[12]

- *Make diversity a specific management goal.* ▶
- *Analyze compensation scales and be scrupulously fair in tracking individual careers.*
- *Continue to focus on diversity in the midst of downsizing.*
- *Respond to the concerns of white males.*

Diversity Training   Another guideline calls for companies to provide **diversity training**—programs designed to improve employees' awareness of differences in attitudes and behavior patterns among their co-workers. There is, however, no consensus yet on how to *conduct* such programs—or exactly what to "teach" and how to do it.

diversity training
Programs designed to improve employee awareness of differences in attitudes and behaviors of co-workers from different racial, ethnic, or gender groups

Ernest Drew, CEO of chemical giant Hoechst Celanese (shown here with a group of students), remembers a 1990 conference of the company's top 125 officers (most of them white males). Attendees were split into problem-solving teams and asked to address the impact of corporate culture on the company's business activities. Some groups were all male; others were mixed by race and gender. His eyes, says Drew, were opened wide: "It was so obvious that the diverse teams had the broader solutions. They had ideas I hadn't even thought of. For the first time, we realized that diversity is a strength as it relates to problem solving."

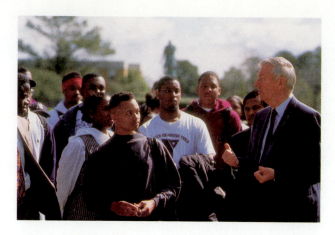

In addition, there are sometimes repercussions to certain approaches. Some recent studies have shown that focusing strictly on such issues as race and gender can arouse deep feelings and be almost as divisive as ignoring negative stereotyping in the first place. Other studies suggest that backlash occurs when participants appear to be either "winners" (say, black women) or "losers" (white men) as a result of the process. Many companies, therefore, try to go beyond mere awareness training. Du Pont, for example, offers a course for managers on how to seek and use more diverse input before making decisions. One consultant emphasizes that it is extremely important to integrate training into daily routines. "Diversity training," he says, "is like hearing a good sermon on Sunday. You must practice what you heard during the week."[13]

> ## "Diversity training is like hearing a good sermon on Sunday. You must practice what you heard during the week."
> —Richard Orange
> *Diversity Consultant*

The Contingency Work Force

contingent worker
Temporary employee hired to supplement an organization's permanent work force

Can you identify the largest private employer in the United States? Is it General Motors? Exxon? IBM? Actually, it is not a manufacturing company. Manpower Inc., the nation's largest supplier of temporary workers, has a payroll of nearly 600,000. (That is 200,000 more than GM and 340,000 more than IBM.) Firms like Manpower are products of dramatic changes in the U.S. work force.[14] For decades, businesses in all industries added new employees with regularity. In the 1980s and 1990s, however, cutbacks and retrenchments have caused many human resource managers to rethink their staffing philosophies. Rather than hiring permanent employees to fill all new jobs, many firms now use **contingent workers**—employees hired to supplement an organization's permanent work force. They include part-time employees, freelances, subcontractors, and temporary workers. ◄

Although most temp workers would prefer permanent jobs, some—especially those who are young—find that low-commitment work lets them sample a variety of jobs and explore career opportunities. This is the attitude of 23-year-old Jillian Perlberger, who earns $16 an hour in the secretarial pools at New York law firms. Temping, says one veteran, can be "wonderful, exhilarating, rewarding, and exciting. And it is also horrible, demeaning, thankless, and boring."

By most accounts, the number of contingent workers is on the rise. Figure 10.4, for example, shows the increase in daily temporary workers, from just over 400,000 in 1980 to 2.25 million in 1994. That number is projected to rise to 3.6 million by 2005.[15] According to a poll conducted by the research firm of Clark Martire & Bartolomeo, 44 percent of Fortune 500 CEOs said that they use more temps than they did 5 years ago; only 13 percent said they used fewer. Moreover, 44 percent indicated that they would be using more in the future. In the nearly 2 decades since 1983, 20 percent of the 20 million jobs created in the United States have been temporary or part-time. Some analysts predict that by the year 2000, half of all U.S. workers will be among the contingency workers supplied by agencies like Manpower. "Any worker still expecting to hold one job from cradle to grave," says Sara Lee CEO John Bryan, "will need to adjust his thinking."

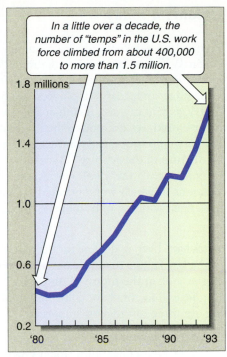

In a little over a decade, the number of "temps" in the U.S. work force climbed from about 400,000 to more than 1.5 million.

FIGURE 10.4 ◆ The Contingent Work Force, 1980–1993

> **"Any worker still expecting to hold one job from cradle to grave will need to adjust his thinking."**
>
> —John Bryan
> *CEO of Sara Lee*

■ DEALING WITH ORGANIZED LABOR

More than 2,000 years ago, the Greek poet Homer wrote, "There is a strength in the union even of very sorry men." There were, of course, no labor unions in Homer's time, but his comment effectively sums up the rationale for unions. A **labor union** is a group of individuals working together to achieve shared job-related goals, such as higher pay, shorter working hours, greater benefits, or better working conditions.

labor union
Group of individuals working together formally to achieve shared job-related goals

Collective Bargaining

Unions were organized to represent the interests of the workers. They ultimately prospered because they solved the worker's most serious problem. They forced management to listen to the complaints of all their workers rather than to just those few who were brave (or foolish) enough to speak out. The power of unions, then, comes from collective action. **Collective bargaining** is the process by which union leaders and managers negotiate common terms and conditions of employment for those workers represented by unions. Although collective bargaining does not often occur in small businesses, many midsize and larger businesses must engage in the process, which we discuss in more detail later in this chapter.

collective bargaining
Process by which labor and management negotiate conditions of employment for workers represented by the union

Unionism Today

Figure 10.5 shows trends in union membership as a percentage of the work force between 1977 and 1993. Since the mid-1950s, unions have experienced increasing difficulties in attracting members. Even as late as 1977, however, more than 26 percent of U.S. wage and salary employees (both private and public) still belonged to unions. Today, as you can see, less than 16 percent of workers are union members. If government employees are not counted, unions represent only about 11 percent of private-industry employees, and some experts suggest that this figure could drop to 4–5 percent by the turn of the century.[16] Workers at many plants are increasingly rejecting attempts to unionize. In the 1940s, 1950s, and 1960s, unions routinely won most certification elections in which workers voted on whether or not to unionize. In recent years, they have been winning only about 45 percent of those elections.

Factors in Declining Union Power   Despite occasional successes, union fortunes have been in decline for the past 40 years. In this section, we will first survey some of the key factors that have contributed to this reduction of union power. We then take a brief look at the future of American labor unions.

Several factors have contributed to the downward slide in union fortunes. Following are three of the most important:

- *Composition of the work force.* Traditionally, union members have been white men in blue-collar jobs. Today's work force, however, is increasingly composed of women and minorities. With a much weaker tradition of union affiliation, members of these groups are less likely to join unions when they enter the work force.

- *Antiunionization strategies.* Many nonunionized industries have developed strategies for avoiding unionization. Some companies, for example, have introduced new employee relations programs to keep facilities union free. Other employers have launched carefully managed campaigns to persuade workers to reject unions. Some firms have even relocated to states or countries in which unions are unpopular or difficult to install.

FIGURE 10.5 ◆ Union Membership as a Percentage of the Work Force

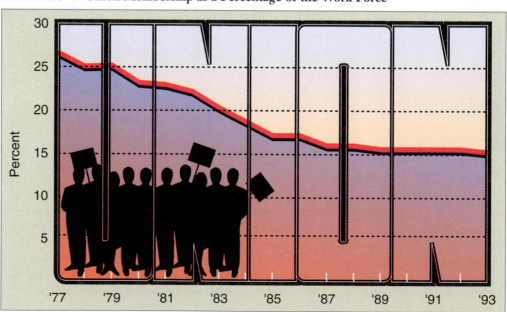

■ *Negotiated concessions.* Growing international competition in certain industries has led employers to demand unprecedented concessions. As a result, *givebacks*—or sacrifices of previously won rights and terms—have become commonplace.

As a result of such trends, many experts have observed that in the 1980s and 1990s, unions have altered the focus of the demands they make at the bargaining table. In recent talks, for example, the United Automobile Workers shifted its emphasis away from higher wages, fighting instead to prevent wage cuts, preserve health benefits, improve job security, and secure larger pensions.

The Future of Unions   Despite setbacks, however, labor unions remain a major factor in the U.S. business world. The 86 labor organizations in the AFL-CIO, as well as major independent unions like the Teamsters and the National Education Association, still play a major role in U.S. business.

Moreover, some unions still wield considerable power, especially in traditional strongholds in goods-producing industries. In March 1996, for example, 3,200 members of the United Automobile Workers struck General Motors' brake parts plant in Dayton, Ohio. The strike was prompted by GM's decision to buy certain parts from outside suppliers. Managers at GM argued that they could buy parts from nonunionized suppliers more cheaply than they could manufacture them—largely because the GM plant was paying higher, union-mandated wages. The UAW, meanwhile, was concerned that GM's decision threatened union jobs. Within two weeks, three-quarters of all GM plants had been shut down because of the parts shortage resulting from the strike at a single factory. When the strike was finally settled 17 days later, GM announced that its effects would include a 50-percent drop in anticipated profits for the first quarter of 1996.[17]

Labor and management in some industries—notably airlines and steel—are beginning to favor contracts that establish formal mechanisms for greater worker input into management decisions. Inland Steel, for instance, recently granted its major union the right to name a member to the board of directors. Union officers can also attend executive meetings.

The big question, however, remains: Will unions dwindle in power and perhaps disappear, or can they evolve, survive to face new challenges, and play a new role in U.S. business? Most likely, they will evolve to take on new roles and responsibilities. As we have already seen, more and more unions are asking for—and often getting—voices in management. In 1980, for example, as a part of the Chrysler bailout, UAW President Douglas Fraser became the first labor official appointed to the board of directors of a major corporation. Several other companies have since followed suit.

By the same token, unions are increasingly aware that they must cooperate with employers if both are to survive. Critics of unions contend that excessive wage rates won through years of strikes and hard-nosed negotiation are partly to blame for the demise of large employers like Eastern Airlines. Others argue that excessively tight work rules limit the productivity of businesses in many industries. More often, however, unions are working with organizations to create effective partnerships in which managers and workers share the same goals—profitability, growth, and effectiveness with equitable rewards for everyone.

■ LAWS GOVERNING LABOR–MANAGEMENT RELATIONS

Like almost every other aspect of labor–management relations today, the process of unionizing workers is governed by numerous laws, administrative interpretations, and judicial decisions. In fact, the growth and decline of unionism in the United States can be traced by following the history of labor laws.

TRENDS & CHALLENGES

SECURITY IS JOB 1

The United Auto Workers (UAW) union has been under siege since the mid-1970s. Although the union is still 400,000 workers strong, membership has dropped by half and conditions are not improving. One of the major problems facing the UAW in the late 1990s is *outsourcing*—the practice of using outside suppliers, instead of company employees, to complete essential work.

General Motors, Ford, and Chrysler have turned much of their auto parts business over to nonunionized companies, mainly because outsourcing is considerably cheaper than making the parts themselves. For example, while unionized employees at General Motor's anti-lock brake manufacturing plant in Dayton, Ohio, earn about $19 an hour, nonunion workers hired by ITT Industries in Asheville, North Carolina, earn $9.90 an hour to manufacture the same parts. Cost savings like these have left the Big Three automakers with little choice but to parcel out the parts business to nonunionized suppliers.

Competition with foreign automakers is largely responsible for this move. Management contends that it would be impossible to maintain high union wages in the auto parts sector and, at the same time, produce affordable cars. According to a recent study, Chrysler buys the most parts from low-cost outside suppliers and has a significant competitive advantage because of it. In fact, Chrysler's costs for auto parts are $600 lower per vehicle than the costs incurred by General Motors.

According to Chrysler president Robert A. Lutz, there is a connection between lower costs and higher market share. Automakers can increase market share, says Lutz, only "if we can continually reduce our costs and focus on the things that we do best, which is design engineering, fabricating bodies, painting them, trimming them, and doing transmissions and four-wheel-drive transfer cases and some axles—in other words, the core of the car."

With a great deal to lose and job security at stake, unions are fighting to stem the outsourcing tide. The battle has been uphill, even though outsourcing makes it harder for automakers to maintain quality control. Quality, it seems, is not always the single most important criterion for a car buyer. Because the public demands affordable cars, explains ITT president Timothy D. Leuliette, "fighting to defend higher-cost jobs ultimately can have little success."

> ### "Fighting to defend higher-cost jobs ultimately can have little success."
>
> **—Timothy D. Leuliette**
> *President of ITT Industries*

Organized labor achieved a modest success with the three-year settlement reached between the UAW and the Ford Motor Co. in 1996. To encourage Ford to stop shrinking its unionized work force from its current level of 105,000 employees, the UAW agreed to accept lower wages for workers involved in manufacturing parts that were previously purchased from outside suppliers. To the UAW, this compromise is a significant victory that saved thousands of jobs. In the long run, however, the agreement paves the way for potential tension between higher- and lower-paid unionized workers. Worse yet, it may represent little more than a temporary slowdown of the outsourcing trend.

For the first 150 years of U.S. independence, workers were judged to have little legal right to organize. Indeed, interpretation of the 1890 Sherman Antitrust Act classified labor unions as monopolies, thus making them illegal. During the first 30 years of the twentieth century, however, social activism and turmoil in the labor force changed the landscape of U.S. labor relations.

The Major Labor Laws

Five major federal laws—all enacted between 1932 and 1959—lay the groundwork for all the rules, regulations, and judicial decisions governing union activity in the United States. A number of more recent laws have dealt with specific groups and specific issues.[18]

Norris-LaGuardia Act   During the 1930s, labor leaders finally persuaded lawmakers that the legal environment discriminated against the collective efforts of workers to improve working conditions. Legislators responded with the **Norris-LaGuardia Act** in 1932. This act imposed severe limitations on the ability of the courts to issue injunctions prohibiting certain union activities, including strikes.

National Labor Relations (Wagner) Act   In 1935, Congress passed the **National Labor Relations Act** (also called the **Wagner Act**), the cornerstone of contemporary labor relations law. This act served to put labor unions on a more equal footing with management in terms of the rights of employees to organize and bargain:

- It gave most workers the right to form unions, to bargain collectively, and to engage in group activities (such as strikes) to reach their goals.
- It forced employers to bargain with duly elected union leaders and prohibited employer practices that unjustly restrict employees' rights (for example, discriminating against union members in hiring, promoting, and firing).

The Wagner Act also established the **National Labor Relations Board (NLRB)** to administer its provisions. Today the NLRB administers virtually all labor law in the United States.

Fair Labor Standards Act   Enacted in 1938, the **Fair Labor Standards Act** addressed issues of minimum wages and maximum work hours:

- It set a minimum wage (originally $.25 an hour) to be paid to workers. The minimum wage has been increased many times since 1938. In 1997 the minimum wage was $4.25 an hour.
- It set a maximum number of hours for the workweek (initially 44 hours a week, later 40 hours).
- It mandated pay of time and a half for those who worked beyond the legally stipulated number of hours.
- It outlawed child labor.

Taft-Hartley Act   Supported by the Norris-LaGuardia, Wagner, and Fair Labor Standards Acts, organized labor eventually grew into a powerful political and economic force. But a series of disruptive strikes in the immediate post–World War II years turned much public opinion against unions. Inconvenienced by strikes and the resulting shortages of goods and services, the public became openly critical of unions and pressured the government to take action. Congress responded by passing the **Labor-Management Relations Act** (more commonly known as the **Taft-Hartley Act**) in 1947.

Unfair and Illegal Union Practices.   The Taft-Hartley Act defined certain union practices as unfair and illegal. For example, it prohibited such practices as *featherbedding* (requiring extra workers solely in order to provide more jobs) and refusing to bargain in good faith. It also generally forbade the **closed shop**—a work place in which only workers already belonging to a union may be hired by an employer.

Injunctions and "Cooling-Off Periods."   Passed in the wake of crippling strikes in the steel industry, the Taft-Hartley Act also established procedures for resolving any strike deemed to pose a national emergency. Initially, the concept of "national emergency" was broadly interpreted. Today, however, the courts employ a more precise definition of "national emergency." A strike, for example, must affect a whole industry or most of it. The President may request an injunction requiring that workers restrain from striking for sixty days. During this "cooling-off period," labor and management must try to resolve their differences.

Enforced Resolution.   If differences are not resolved during the cooling-off period, the injunction may be extended for another 20 days. During this period, employees

---

Norris-LaGuardia Act (1932)
Federal law limiting the ability of courts to issue injunctions prohibiting certain union activities

National Labor Relations Act (Wagner Act) (1935)
Federal law protecting the rights of workers to form unions, bargain collectively, and engage in strikes to achieve their goals

National Labor Relations Board (NLRB)
Federal agency established by the National Labor Relations Act to enforce its provisions

Fair Labor Standards Act (1938)
Federal law setting minimum wage and maximum number of hours in the workweek

Labor-Management Relations Act (Taft-Hartley Act) (1947)
Federal law defining certain union practices as unfair and illegal

closed shop
Work place in which an employer may hire only workers already belonging to a union

must vote, in a secret-ballot election, on whether to accept or reject the employer's latest offer. If they accept the offer, the threat of strike is ended and the contract is signed. If they do not accept the offer, the President reports to Congress, and the workers may either be forced back to work under threat of criminal action or fired and replaced by nonunion employees.

Labor-Management Reporting and Disclosure Act (Landrum-Griffin Act) (1959)
Federal law imposing regulations on internal unions procedures, including elections of national leaders and filing of financial-disclosure statements

Landrum-Griffin Act   The National Labor Relations Act was further amended by the **Landrum-Griffin Act** in 1959. Officially titled the **Labor-Management Reporting and Disclosure Act,** this law resulted from congressional hearings that revealed unethical, illegal, and undemocratic union practices. The act thus imposed regulations on internal union procedures:

- It required the election of national union leaders at least once every five years.
- It gave union members the right to participate in various union affairs.
- It required unions to file annual financial-disclosure statements with the Department of Labor.

THE COLLECTIVE BARGAINING PROCESS

When a union has been legally certified, it assumes the role of official bargaining agent for the workers whom it represents. Collective bargaining is an ongoing process involving both the drafting and the administering of the terms of a labor contract.

Reaching Agreement on Contract Terms

The collective bargaining process begins when the union is recognized as the exclusive negotiator for its members. The bargaining cycle itself begins when union leaders meet with management representatives to agree on a contract. By law, both parties must sit down at the bargaining table and negotiate "in good faith."

Sometimes this process goes quite smoothly. At other times, however, the two sides cannot—or will not—agree. The speed and ease with which such an impasse is resolved depends in part on the nature of the contract issues, the willingness of each side to use certain tactics, and the prospects for mediation or arbitration.

Contract Issues

The labor contract itself can address an array of different issues. Most of these concern demands that unions make on behalf of their members. Most bargaining items generally fall into two categories:

- *Mandatory items* are matters over which both parties must negotiate if either side wants to. This category includes wages, working hours, and benefits.
- *Permissive items* may be negotiated if both parties agree. A union demand for veto power over the promotion of managerial personnel would be a permissive bargaining item.

Illegal items may not be brought to the table by either party. A management demand for a nonstrike clause would be an illegal item. The three issues that are typically most important to union negotiators are *compensation*, *benefits*, and *job security*.

Other possible issues include working hours, overtime policies, rest period arrangements, differential pay plans for shift employees, the use of temporary workers, grievance procedures, and allowable union activities (dues collection, union bulletin boards, and so forth).

Management Rights   Management wants to retain as much control as possible over hiring policies, work assignments, and so forth, while unions often try to limit management rights by specifying hiring, assignment, and other policies. At a Chrysler plant in Detroit, for example, the contract stipulates that three workers are needed to change fuses in robots: a machinist to open the robot, an electrician to change the fuse, and a supervisor to oversee the process. As in this case, contracts often bar workers in one job category from performing work that falls in the domain of another. Unions try to secure jobs by defining as many different categories as possible (the Chrysler plant has more than 100). Management resists the practice, which limits flexibility and makes it difficult to reassign workers.

When Bargaining Fails

An impasse occurs when, after a series of bargaining sessions, management and labor fail to agree on a new contract or a contract to replace an agreement that is about to expire. Although it is generally agreed that both parties suffer when an impasse is reached and action is taken, each side can employ several tactics to support its cause until the impasse is resolved.

Union Tactics   When their demands are not met, unions may bring a variety of tactics to the bargaining table. Chief among these is the *strike*, which may be supported by *pickets*, *boycotts*, or both.

The Strike.   A **strike** occurs when employees temporarily walk off the job and refuse to work. Most strikes in the United States are **economic strikes**—strikes triggered by stalemates over mandatory bargaining items, including such noneconomic issues as working hours. For example, flight attendants at American Airlines staged a brief strike in late 1993 demanding higher wages. They returned to work only when company management agreed to binding arbitration. Perhaps just as important as wage concessions in this strike was the position staked out by the airline's women employees, who make up the vast majority of its 21,000 flight attendants. They forced the airline to address the fact that women employees had long settled for less than male employees (including baggage handlers) in areas ranging from pay to weight codes to policies on how to behave nicely. American's agreement to arbitration was widely seen as a breakthrough for working women as well as a victory for organized labor.[19] ▶

Other Labor Actions.   To support a strike, a union faced with an impasse has recourse to additional legal activities:

- In **picketing,** workers march at the entrance to the employer's facility with signs explaining their reasons for striking.
- A **boycott** occurs when union members agree not to buy the products of a targeted employer. Workers may also urge consumers to boycott the firm's products.

Management Tactics   Like workers, management can respond forcefully to an impasse:

- **Lockouts** occur when employers deny employees access to the workplace. Lockouts are illegal if they are used as offensive weapons to give management a bargaining advantage. They are legal, however, if management has a legitimate business need—for instance, avoiding a buildup of perishable inventory. Although rare today, lockouts were used by baseball team owners in 1990 (without success).

---

strike
Labor action in which employees temporarily walk off the job and refuse to work

economic strike
Strike usually triggered by stalemate over one or more mandatory bargaining items

picketing
Labor action in which workers publicize their grievances at the entrance to an employer's facility

boycott
Labor action in which workers refuse to buy the products of a targeted employer

lockout
Management tactic whereby workers are denied access to their workplace

When President Clinton intervened to end a strike by American Airlines flight attendants in November 1993, labor analysts counted the outcome as a victory for the strikers. The airline had proposed radical changes in the schedules and procedures required of attendants, and American's 21,000 members of the Association of Professional Flight Attendants underscored management's miscalculation of employee resentment by rejecting the proposal, striking, and effectively shutting down the airline. American CEO Robert L. Crandall originally rejected the union's call for arbitration but relented when it became clear that the five-day strike would result in year-end losses for a company that had made money during only one of the previous four years.

strikebreaker
Worker hired as permanent or temporary replacement for a striking employee

mediation
Method of resolving a labor dispute in which a third party advises on, but does not impose, a settlement

voluntary arbitration
Method of resolving a labor dispute in which both parties agree to submit to the judgment of a neutral party

compulsory arbitration
Method of resolving a labor dispute in which both parties are legally required to accept the judgment of a neutral party

■ A firm can also hire temporary or permanent replacements for strikers called **strikebreakers.** The law, however, forbids the permanent replacement of workers who strike because of unfair practices. In some cases, an employer can also obtain legal injunctions that either prohibit workers from striking or prohibit a union from interfering with its efforts to use replacement workers.

Mediation and Arbitration   Rather than wield these weapons against one another, labor and management can agree to call in a third party to help resolve the dispute:

■ In **mediation,** the neutral third party (the mediator) can advise on but not impose a settlement.
■ In **voluntary arbitration,** the neutral third party (the arbitrator) dictates a settlement between the two sides, who have agreed to submit to outside judgment.
■ In some cases, arbitration is legally required to settle bargaining disputes. **Compulsory arbitration,** for example, is used to settle disputes between the government and some public employees, including firefighters and police officers.[20]

Continued from page 231

Speaking the Language of the Work Force

And Calculating the Cost of "Social Work"

How much do employers like Marriott International owe workers who lack the skills to succeed on their own? That's a question Marriott human resources executives are asking themselves as they move forward with the Pathways to Independence program. Their answer right now seems to be "a great deal"—as long as there is a bottom line return to the company.

As part of its effort, Marriott is helping employees overcome language barriers that stand in the way of communication. To help bridge the language gap that exists at hotels like the Seattle Marriott, where employees speak 17 languages, more than half of the Marriott hotels in the United States offer courses in English as a second language. In addition, employees who call headquarters for help with personal problems are offered advice in more than 100 languages. Marriott officials believe that by addressing employees in their native languages, they will save five

> **"Some managers spend 15 percent of their time doing social work. That's time not spent dealing with customer issues."**
>
> —Clifford J. Ehrlich
> *Senior Vice President
> for Human Resources
> at Marriott International*

times the $2 million program investment in the form of reduced turnover, absenteeism, and lateness.

Savings and increased productivity are the main reasons Marriott established the Pathways to Independence program. Although Marriott is doing the socially responsible thing by giving chances to workers who never held jobs, it is motivated largely by corporate self-interest. Few analysts would quibble with the observation that helping workers is good for

Marriott's bottom line. At the same time, however, some point out that there are also costs whose impact on the bottom line must also be calculated.

For many people, for example, Pathways is reminiscent of the kind of corporate paternalism that once molded and protected labor forces in towns dominated by single companies. After years of setting employees adrift on their own, notes Faith A. Wohl, Director for the U.S. General Services Administration's Office of Workplace Initiatives, Marriott and other employers "have returned full circle to a social contract with employees." According to Clifford J. Ehrlich, Marriott's Senior Vice President for Human Resources, this "contract" often involves taking on the role of social worker. Some Marriott managers, he reports, "spend 15 percent of their time doing social work. That's time not spent dealing with customer issues."

Case Questions

1. Is Marriott's Pathways to Independence program an example of corporate social responsibility, corporate self-interest, or both? Explain your answer.
2. In what ways is the Pathways to Independence program a unique approach to corporate staffing? Since normal selection techniques, such as interviews, résumés, and reference checks, cannot be used in this program, what standards can Marriott use to make sound hiring choices once participants have completed the program?
3. Is Pathways to Independence an example of a corporate training program? In what ways do you think the training is typical? In what ways do you think it is unique?
4. In an era of corporate downsizing, why do you think Marriott is making such a concerted effort to train and hire welfare recipients?
5. How does Pathways to Independence help Marriott increase the diversity of its work force?

SUMMARY OF LEARNING OBJECTIVES

1. **Define *human resource management* and explain how managers plan for human resources.**   *Human resource management* is the development, administration, and evaluation of programs to acquire new employees and enhance the quality and performance of people working in an organization. Planning for human resource needs entails several steps. Conducting a *job analysis* enables managers to create detailed, job-related *job descriptions* and *specifications*.

2. **Identify the steps involved in *staffing* a company.**   *External staffing*—hiring from outside the company—requires that a firm first *recruit* applicants and then *select* from among the applicants. The selection phase may include *interviewing*, and *testing*. When possible, however, many companies prefer the practice of *internal staffing*—that is, filling positions by *promoting* current employees.

3. **Explain how organizations can develop workers' skills and manage workers who do not perform well.**   If a company is to get the most out of its workers, it must develop those workers and their skills. Nearly all employees undergo some initial *orientation* process that introduces them to the company and to their new jobs. Many employees are given the opportunity to acquire new skills through *on-the-job* or *off-the-job training* and/or *management development programs*. *Performance appraisals* help managers decide who needs training and who should be promoted. Appraisals also tell employees how well they are meeting expectations.

4. **Discuss the importance of *wages* and *salaries, incentives,* and *benefits programs* in attracting and keeping skilled workers.**   Wages and salaries, incentives, and benefits packages may comprise a company's *compensation program*. By paying its workers as well as or better than competitors do, a business can attract and keep qualified personnel. Incentive programs—for example, *bonuses, gain sharing, profit sharing,* and *pay for knowledge*—can also motivate personnel to work more productively. However, while *benefits programs* may increase employee satisfaction, they are a major expense to business today.

5. **Describe some of the key legal and ethical issues involved in hiring, compensating, and managing workers in today's workplace.**   In hiring, compensating, and managing workers, managers must obey a variety of federally mandated laws. *Equal employment opportunity* and *equal pay laws* forbid discrimination except when based on legitimate job requirements. The concept of *comparable worth* holds that different jobs requiring equal levels of training and skills should pay the same. Firms are also required to provide employees with safe working environments, as set down by the guidelines of the *Occupational Safety and Health Administration*.

6. **Describe the major *laws governing labor–management relations*.**   Several significant laws affect labor–management relations. The *Norris-LaGuardia Act* and the *National Labor Relations (Wagner) Act* limited the ability of employers to keep unions out of the workplace. The *Fair Labor Standards Act* established a minimum wage and outlawed child labor. The *Taft-Hartley Act* and the *Landrum-Griffin Act* limited the power of unions and provided for the settlement of strikes in key industries.

7. **Identify the steps in the *collective bargaining process*.**   Once certified, the union engages in *collective bargaining* with the organization. The initial step in collective bargaining is reaching agreement on a *labor contract*. Contract demands usually involve wages, job security, and/or management rights.

Labor and management can use different tactics if negotiations break down. Unions may also attempt a *strike* or a *boycott*. Companies may hire replacement workers *(strikebreakers)* or lock out all workers. In extreme cases, *mediation* or *arbitration* may be used to settle disputes. Once a contract is agreed on, union and management representatives continue to interact to settle worker *grievances* and interpret the contract.

STUDY QUESTIONS AND EXERCISES

Review

1. What are the advantages and disadvantages of both internal and external staffing? Under what circumstances is each appropriate?
2. Why is the formal training of workers so important to most employers? Why don't most employers just let employees learn about their jobs as they perform them?
3. What are the different forms of compensation that firms typically use to attract and retain productive workers?
4. What is a cafeteria benefits plan? Compared with conventional plans, what are its advantages and disadvantages?

Analysis

5. Recall the most recent instance in which you applied for a job. Which selection techniques did the employer use to assess your qualifications? How well do you think each technique predicted your potential as an employee?
6. Have you or anyone you know ever suffered discrimination in a hiring decision? Did you or that person do anything about it?
7. Suppose that someone you know is interested in a career in human resources management. What advice might you give that person about applicable experience and preparation?
8. How much will benefit considerations affect your choice of an employer after graduation?

Application Exercises

9. Interview a human resource manager at a local company. Focus on a position for which the firm is currently recruiting applicants and identify the steps in the selection process.
10. Identify some journals in your library that might be useful to a human resource manager. What topics have been covered in recent features and cover stories?

BUILDING YOUR BUSINESS SKILLS

This exercise enhances the following SCANS workplace competencies: demonstrating basic skills, demonstrating thinking skills, exhibiting interpersonal skills, and working with information.

Goal

To aid students in understanding the complexity of writing human resources regulations that affect employee behavior in controversial areas

Situation

As the human resource director of a small manufacturing company with 400 employees, your mission is to revise sections of the employee handbook covering three of today's most important issues:

- sexual harassment
- diversity training
- drug testing of job candidates and current employees

Method

Step 1:   Work with three other students to research each of these areas. Through library research and interviews with human resources executives in local companies, try to find out as much as you can in each of the following areas:

- Current laws and regulatory requirements
- What other corporations are doing in each area
- How employees are responding to increasingly stringent rules

Step 2:   Working in groups, develop written guidelines for your company handbook. Try to be as specific as possible. Keep in mind that the handbook will be given to current employees and job candidates.

Step 3:   Compare your findings with those of other teams.

Follow-Up

1. Based on your research, which of the three areas poses the most difficulty for employers? For employees? Why?

2. Given what you know about the difficulty that many companies have in eliminating sexual harassment and discrimination in the workplace, do you think that education (in the form of clear employee guidelines and diversity training) or disciplinary action (perhaps even demotions and dismissals) is the key to change? Explain your answer.

3. Support the position that preemployment drug tests are fair to job candidates.

UNITED AIRLINES, FLIGHT ATTENDANT CAREER INFORMATION, AT
http://www.ualfltctr.com/docs/sw.html

MCDONALD'S, CAREERS, AT
http://www.mcdonalds.com./a_careersempopp

After you have read the material posted by these two companies, consider the following questions:

1. Do you qualify in terms of "Education/Work Experience" to apply to United's Flight Attendant training program? If you have had work experience that you consider relevant to United's "Work Experience" description, why do you think it would be an asset?

2. What part of United's training program do you think would be most challenging to you? Why?

3. What part of a flight attendant's job do you think you would enjoy the most? The least? Why?

4. Which of the skills listed by McDonald's would you list under your own strong points? Under your weak points? Which one or two skills do you think you need to focus on most conscientiously?

5. Why do you think McDonald's puts so much emphasis on career advancement within the company? Why does it put so much emphasis on the awards earned by the company's training program? In what respects are these important criteria for you?

6. What do you think the word "opportunities" should mean in a slogan like "McDonald's Means Opportunities"?

"You're Not Paid To Think—Just Do Your Job"

Or, When Is It Time to Make Productivity a Team Sport?

Learning Objectives

The purpose of this video exercise is to help students

1. Understand some of the ways in which U.S. companies are trying to enhance job satisfaction and motivation

2. Understand the ways in which different levels of employee participation and responsibility can affect productivity in a manufacturing workplace

3. Understand the relationship between organizational goals and the different ways in which employees can be encouraged to help meet them

Background Information

Pressed by foreign competitors, U.S. manufacturers in a wide range of industries are turning to teams in an effort to improve quality and cut costs. Employees, of course, face the challenge of abandoning traditional work environments while learning new roles in team-oriented cultures. Management, meanwhile, must come to grips with the task of turning over certain day-to-day operating responsibilities to line employees.

■ In Shelby, Mississippi, for example, G. Rives Neblett, owner of the Shelby Die Casting Co., has used the team approach to revitalize his manufacturing facility. In addition to being unprofitable, the Shelby plant was long plagued with poor employee morale and a high rate of wasted raw materials. Neblett thus invested in several books on total quality management (TQM) and proceeded to implement changes. Soon, the team approach began to pay off. Wastage, for example, fell from 35 percent to 8 percent, and the plant began showing a profit.

■ The story is much the same at the Square D Co. plant in Lexington, Kentucky, where the team concept has been a way of life for several years. Square D employees work in teams of 20 to 30 members each. Each team is responsible for a product from start to finish—a far cry from the days when employees performed a single task before an unfinished product continued down the assembly line. Now team members can make on-the-spot decisions without consulting management. Combined with the teamwork approach to quality control, independent decision making has cut the rejection rate by 75 percent, and the average time required to process a customer order has been cut from six weeks to three days.

■ In 1991, plant employees at the Frito-Lay factory in Lubbock, Texas, began working in teams with added responsibilities on the factory floor. Results of the new approach have been impressive in many areas. Double-digit annual cost reductions are the rule, and the number of managers at the Lubbock plant has been reduced by two-thirds. The plant has also climbed into the top six in terms of quality.

Video Summary

Video Source. "Assembly Line Teams Are Better Trained and More Efficient," *World News Tonight*, February 24, 1993. This segment of "The American Agenda" goes inside the Square D plant in Lexington, Kentucky, to investigate the results of the commitment to teamwork in manufacturing. Both line employees and managers are interviewed.

Discussion Questions

1. Do you think that manufacturing companies who use the team approach will find it easier to recruit and retain employees? Why or why not?
2. What is the biggest challenge to management in adjusting to a team approach? To employees?
3. Why do you think many companies currently invest only 1 percent of sales on employee training?

Follow-Up Assignment

This video focuses on the efforts of companies located in the United States to become more competitive in the face of global competition. Go to the library and conduct research to determine which foreign companies are also using the team approach to improve quality and cut costs. What are the major similarities and differences in teamwork practices in different countries?

For Further Exploration

You can contact Frito-Lay on the Internet at

http://www.fritolay.com

Click on the "Company Info" icon and then the "Career Opportunities" icon to find out how Frito-Lay describes the kinds of employees that will fit in with its corporate culture. How does the company characterize its "philosophy of 'Winning Together'"? What do you make of the reference to "Frito-Lay's Vision: To Own Fun Foods"?

> **"We never had meetings with employees.
> They were programmed to do what they were told."**
>
> —G. Rives Neblett
> *Owner of Shelby Die Casting Co.*

Some Secrets Of The Much-Envied Work Climate

Or, "If You Do What's Best for the Customer, You Won't Have to Worry about the Company"

Learning Objectives

The purpose of this video exercise is to help students

1. See how a specific company has implemented its human resources policies
2. Understand the relationship between a company's overall "culture" and its approach to human resources
3. Understand how specific strategies for enhancing job satisfaction and morale can affect the attitudes and performance of a company's employees
4. Appreciate the importance of training as an element in both job satisfaction and productivity

Background Information

According to Kelly Ritchie, Vice President for Human Resources at Lands' End,

> Turnover of our regular benefited group is in the single digits—very low for this industry. When people really like what they do, like who they do it with and for, work in facilities that are among the best around, and are fairly paid for their efforts, it would seem almost impossible not to be at least minimally satisfied.

In fact, Lands' End employees seem to be more than "minimally satisfied." Among the reasons is an 80,000-square-foot Activity Center that includes an Olympic-size swimming pool, a full-size gym, an indoor track, state-of-the-art exercise equipment, locker and shower rooms, and a not-for-profit cafeteria. The $8 million center was donated by founder Gary Comer in 1987.

Lands' End employees also seem to be happy about the way their input is solicited during monthly feedback meetings and about the way CEO Michael Smith openly shares company information during all-company quarterly meetings. For its part, Lands' End considers its employees' job satisfaction a key element in one of its most important competitive strategies—keeping customers satisfied. Thus, the emphasis on what Ritchie describes as "our commitment to continuous, proactive training. . . . By spending the money up front," she reports, "we have much happier employees, we don't have to spend nearly as much money . . . on quality checks, and, most importantly, we have satisfied customers."

The Video

Video Source. "The Establishing and Maintaining of a Much-Envied Work Climate," *Prentice Hall Presents: On Location at Lands' End.* The video focuses on three aspects of human resources at Lands' End: the importance of open communications, both top-down and bottom-up; the importance of the Activity Center in maintaining job satisfaction and morale; and the importance of job training in maintaining a high level of customer service. Participants include Human Resources Manager Kelly Ritchie, who describes company policy, and two veteran phone operators, who talk about the practical effect of company policy.

Discussion Questions

1. What strategies for enhancing motivation are evident at Lands' End? What strategies for enhancing job satisfaction and morale do you see at work?
2. Judging from the video, what can you say about the role played by human resources management in Lands' End's efforts to fulfill its organizational mission?
3. How would you describe the managerial style of CEO Michael Smith?
4. In what respect does the brand of human resources management practiced at Lands' End reflect thinking about motivation and leadership in the 1990s?

Follow-Up Assignment

At the end of the video, the narrator asks whether you think there might be "other tools" Lands' End could implement to improve its human resources "culture." To address this question, your instructor will divide the class into "advisory teams" of five or six students each. Each member of the team should use the Internet to contact the Office of the American Workplace (OAW) at

http://www.fed.org/uscompanies/labor/

Here you will find detailed reports on the "best practices" of several high-performance companies singled out by the OAW. Each member of the team should examine the report on a specific company and provide the team with a brief overview of its human resources practices. Each team should then prepare a descriptive list of those practices that might be useful as "other tools" for human resources managers at Lands' End. The team should prepare a brief report summarizing its recommendations.

For Further Exploration

To find out more about what Lands' End itself has to say about its people and about the relationship between its human resources philosophy and its corporate culture, contact the company on the Internet at

http://www.landsend.com

From the Home page, click on "The Library" to reach "In Persons," or click on "The Company" and then "The Company Inside" to reach "Out Our Way."

"We have discovered that by spending the money up front, we have much happier employees and, most importantly, we have satisfied customers."

—Kelly Ritchie
Vice President for Human Resources at Lands' End

11

CHAPTER

MANAGING PRODUCTION AND IMPROVING QUALITY

Crafty Brewers with a Marketing Angle

COOKING UP HOMESPUN RECIPES IN SOMEONE ELSE'S KITCHEN

Sometimes you can't blame the big guys for being annoyed at the little guys and wanting to set the record straight. Take, for example, the nation's large beer brewers, including Anheuser-Busch, who find themselves over the proverbial beer barrel because of production decisions made by such small "craft breweries" as the Boston Beer Co. (maker of Samuel Adams beers) and the Maui Beer Co. (maker of Aloha Lager). Anheuser-Busch's gripe is that although craft brewers market their products as specialty brews that have been manufactured with painstaking care in small batches—and charge premium prices for their distinctive alternatives to bland, mass-produced beers—many are really made by large beer companies putting excess capacity to use. In fact, about 10 percent of the 1,000 craft brewers in the United States do little or no manufacturing themselves. Rather, they pay other companies, known as "contract brewers," to make their beers according to their recipes.

> "If Julia Child comes to your kitchen, brings her own ingredients and makes dinner, but you own the kitchen, is it you or Julia Child who made dinner?"
>
> —James Koch
> *Founder of Boston Beer Co.*

"Crafty marketers are duping consumers," charges August Busch III, Vice President of Brand Management at his family's company. "If you're going to brew in somebody else's brewery, why don't you say so?" Boston Beer founder James Koch sees no reason to explain to anyone why Sam Adams beer is mass-produced in large factories. His reasoning: "If Julia Child comes to your kitchen, brings her own ingredients and makes dinner, but you own the kitchen, is it you or Julia Child who made dinner?"

Why is Anheuser-Busch making such a fuss over outsourcing in the specialty-brew business? After all, Anheuser-Busch controls a whopping 44 percent of the market—compared with only 2 percent for all craft breweries combined. To appreciate Anheuser-Busch's concern, we need to look at sales trends. At a time when overall beer sales are flat, sales of specialty brews have soared by 50 percent to 4 million barrels. That trend represents a real marketing threat, even to an industry giant. Anheuser-Busch takes that threat seriously because so much of the popularity of craft brews is linked to consumers' belief that they are made in small breweries. Not surprisingly, craft brewers do little to discourage this belief. James Koch has even promoted his product by suggesting out loud that "people will get more involved in beer as they realize that beer doesn't necessarily have to come from a big factory."

To perpetuate the small-factory myth Koch runs tours of a tiny run-down Boston facility owned by Boston Beer. Here beer lovers see rows of fermenting tanks; a brewermaster in rubber boots watches over two 10-barrel kettles. In fact, less than 1 percent of Samuel Adams beer is made in this plant. Much of the rest is manufactured 750 miles away at the Hudepohl-Schoenling Brewing Co. in Cincinnati, where the mix is brewed in 200-barrel steel tanks.

Koch is, however, willing to accommodate critics on some points. For example, he is rewriting the label of Samuel Adams beer to eliminate the phrase "brewed in small batches." Instead, the label will read "Crafted with care."

Anheuser-Busch, of course, is not likely to be content until the public realizes that many craft brews owe their success primarily to marketing rather than to superior production methods or quality breakthroughs. To give them their due, however, craft brewers have been smart enough to engage in sophisticated operations planning—planning that has taken into account both their own limited production capacity and the relatively unlimited capacity of contract brewers. They have also attempted to

maintain quality—and been largely successful—by ensuring that contract brewers follow recipes. By focusing on the learning objectives of this chapter, you will better understand the complexity of production processes for both goods and services.

After reading this chapter, you should be able to

1. **Identify the characteristics that distinguish *service operations* from *goods production* and explain the main differences in the service focus**

2. **Describe the three *ways of classifying operations processes***

3. **Describe the factors involved in *operations planning* and *scheduling***

4. **Explain some of the activities involved in *operations control*, including *materials management* and the use of certain *operations control tools***

5. **Identify some of the key tools for *total quality management*, including strategies for getting closer to the customer**

Continued on page 285

■ GOODS AND SERVICE OPERATIONS

Everywhere you go today, you encounter business activities that provide goods and services to their customers. You wake up in the morning, for example, to the sound of your favorite radio station. You stop at the corner newsstand for a newspaper on your way to the bus stop, where you catch the bus to work or school. Your instructors, the bus driver, the clerk at the 7-Eleven store, and the morning radio announcer are all examples of people who work in **service operations.** They provide you with tangible and intangible service products, such as entertainment, transportation, education, and food preparation. Firms that make tangible products—radios, newspapers, buses, textbooks—are engaged in **goods production.**

service operations
Business activities that provide tangible and intangible services

goods production
Business operations that create tangible products

Growth in the Goods and Service Sectors

Although the term "production" has historically referred almost exclusively to companies engaged in the production of goods, the concept of *production* now encompasses services as well. The abundance of services on which we rely—from fire protection and health care to mail delivery and fast food—are all produced by service operations. The production of services is receiving increased attention as the demand for services continues to grow. Despite the growth in the service section, however, the manufacturing base today still accounts for about 25 percent of all private sector jobs in the United States—just as it has for the past four decades. Nevertheless, the economic significance of manufacturing activity is rising. For example, real income from manufacturing has been rising steadily, increasing by more than 30 percent between 1986 and 1996. So effective are new manufacturing methods—and so committed are U.S. manufacturers to using them—that, in 1994, the United States surpassed Germany and Japan in manufactured exports, returning to the number-one spot for the first time in a decade.[1] "The near paralysis of the early 1980s," announces Blair LaCorte of Autodesk Inc., a software firm in Sausalito, California, "is long gone. We're seeing the beginnings of a revolution in American manufacturing." CEO Jack Welch of General Electric contends that the 1990s is "the decade of manufacturing."

> ### "The near paralysis of the early 1980s is long gone. We're seeing the beginnings of a revolution in American manufacturing."
>
> —Blair LaCorte
> *Director of Data Management Products for Autodesk Inc.*

Remember that although companies are often classified as either goods producers or service providers, the boundary is often blurred. All businesses are service operations to some extent. Consider the manufacturing giant General Motors. GM produces cars, but it also provides repairs and maintenance, warranty fulfillment, and installation advice. GM even lends money to people who want to buy its cars. Without its services operations, GM's automobile sales would plummet.

Some companies are now exploring the service sides of their traditional activities as if they were discovering entirely new markets for start-up businesses. Take Johnson Controls, a Milwaukee manufacturer of heating controls, batteries, and automobile seats established in 1883. Since 1989, Johnson has prospered by expanding its operations into services. It manages the lighting, security, and cleaning operations of office buildings. "It's a market worth tens of billions of dollars in the U.S. alone," says Vice President Terry Weaver. "It's a wave. It's a megatrend."▶

The Growth of Global Operations

Many countries have joined in the global competition that has reshaped production into a fast-paced, challenging business activity. Although the factory remains the centerpiece for manufacturing, it is virtually unrecognizable when compared with its counterpart of even just a decade ago. The smoke, grease, and danger have been replaced in many companies by glistening high-tech machines, computers, and "clean rooms" that are contaminant-free and carefully controlled for temperature.[2] ▼ Instead of the need to maintain continuous mass production, firms today face constant change. They must, for example, constantly develop new technologies to respond to ever-changing consumer demands. They must produce varieties of different products at high quality levels. They must strive to design new products, get them into production, and deliver them to customers faster than their competitors.

An old-line manufacturer for more than a century, Johnson Controls has discovered triple-digit growth in a service business that is actually an offshoot of its traditional operations: it services the heating, lighting, cleaning, and security operations of buildings like this one in Malvern, Pennsylvania, which belongs to mutual funds giant Vanguard Group. "Much of our growth," says CEO James Keyes quite simply, "has come from the fact that we do more for our customers."

This IBM plant in Charlotte, North Carolina, turns out products ranging from bar-code readers to medical equipment and satellite communicatins devices. Servicing each production team of about 12 workers are computers linked to the factory network. With computer screens displaying both up-to-the-minute lists of needed parts and detailed assembly instructions, teams can actually make 27 different IBM products simultaneously. This combination of computer networks, software, and highly trained human resources is called soft manufacturing. It typifies a technique originating in American factories that have committed to using human judgment in jobs for which robots and other technologies are not well suited.

■ CREATING VALUE THROUGH PRODUCTION

utility
A product's ability to satisfy a human want

To understand the production processes of a firm you need to understand the importance of products—both goods and services. Products provide businesses with economic results—profits, wages, and goods purchased from other companies. At the same time, they provide consumers with **utility**—that is, a product's ability to satisfy a human want. There are four basic kinds of production-based utility:

- When a company turns out ornaments in time for Christmas, it creates *time utility;* that is, it makes products available when consumers want them.
- When a department store opens its "Trim-a-Tree" department in the fall, it creates *place utility*. It makes products available where they are convenient for consumers.
- By making a product available for consumers to own and use, production creates *ownership* or *possession utility*, which customers enjoy when they buy boxes of ornaments and decorate their trees.
- Above all, however, production makes products available in the first place. By turning raw materials into finished goods, production creates *form utility*, as when an ornament maker combines glass, plastic, and other materials to create tree decorations.

**operations (or production)
management**
Systematic direction and control of the processes that transform resources into finished products

operations managers
Managers responsible for production, inventory, and quality control

Because the term *production* has historically been associated with manufacturing, it has been replaced in recent years by *operations*, a term that reflects both services and goods production. **Operations (or production) management** is the systematic direction and control of the processes that transform resources into finished goods and services.[3] Thus, production managers are ultimately responsible for creating utility for customers.

As Figure 11.1 shows, **operations managers** must draw up plans to transform resources into products. First, they must bring together basic resources—raw materials,

FIGURE 11.1 ◆ Operations Transformation Process

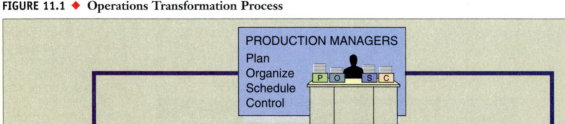

equipment, and labor. They must then put those resources to effective use in the production facility. As demand for a product increases, managers must schedule and control work to produce required amounts of products. Finally, they must control costs, quality levels, and inventory, and they must maintain their plant and equipment.

Although some production managers work in factories, others work in large and small offices and retail stores ranging from giant discount outlets to specialty shops. Farmers, too, are operations managers. They create utility by transforming soil, seeds, fuel, and other inputs into tobacco, soybeans, milk, and other outputs. As production managers, they may employ crews of workers to plant and harvest. Or they may opt for automated machinery or some combination of workers and machinery. These decisions affect costs, the role of buildings and equipment in their operations, and the quality and quantity of goods that they produce.

Operations Processes

Various types of production can be classified according to important differences in operations processes. These classifications help explain how managers determine the best strategies for managing operations in various settings.

Types of Goods Manufacturing Processes   Whether an independent businessperson or an employee of a multinational manufacturer, a production manager must control the process by which goods are produced. An **operations process** is the set of methods and technologies used in the production of a good or a service. All manufacturing processes can be classified by the type of *transformation technology* during transformation.

operations process
Set of methods and technologies used in the production of a good or service

Transformation Technology.   Manufacturers use the following types of processes to transform raw materials into finished goods:

■ In *chemical processes*, raw materials are chemically altered. Such techniques are common in the aluminum, steel, fertilizer, petroleum, and paint industries.
■ *Fabrication processes* mechanically alter the basic shape or form of a product. Fabrication occurs in the metal-forming, woodworking, and textile industries.
■ *Assembly processes* put together various components. These techniques are common in the electronics, appliance, and automotive industries.
■ In *transport processes*, goods acquire place utility by moving from one location to another. For example, goods are routinely trucked from manufacturing plants to consumers through warehouses and discount stores.
■ *Clerical processes* transform information. Combining data on employee absences and machine breakdowns into a productivity report is a clerical process. So is compiling inventory reports at a retail outlet.

Types of Service Processes: Extent of Customer Contact   One way of classifying services is to ask if a given service can be provided without the customer being part of the production system. In so doing, we classify services according to the extent of *customer contact.*

High-Contact Systems.   To consider the extent of customer contact in service operations, think about your local public transit system. The service provides transportation, and when you purchase transportation, you must board a bus or train. For example, the Bay Area Rapid Transit System (BART) connects San Francisco with many of its outlying suburbs. Like all public transportation systems, BART is a **high-contact system.** To receive the service, the customer must be a part of the system. For this reason, BART managers must worry, for example, about the cleanliness of the trains and the appearance of the stations. This is usually not the case in low-contact

high-contact system
Level of service-customer contact in which the customer receives the service as part of the system

systems: large industrial concerns that ship coal in freight trains are generally not concerned with the appearance of those trains.

Low-Contact Systems. In contrast to your public transit system, consider the check-processing operations at your bank. Workers sort the checks that have been cashed that day and dispatch them to the banks on which they were drawn. This operation is a **low-contact system.** Customers are not in contact with the bank while the service is performed. They receive the service—their funds are transferred to cover their checks—without ever setting foot in the check-processing center. Gas and electric utilities, auto repair shops, and lawn care services are also low-contact systems.

low-contact system
Level of service-customer contact in which the cutomer need not be a part of the system to receive the service

Differences in Service and Manufacturing Operations

Service and manufacturing operations share several important features. For example, both transform raw materials into finished products. In service production, however, the raw materials, or "inputs," are not glass or steel. Rather, they are people who choose among sellers because they have either unsatisfied needs or possessions for which they need some form of care or alteration. In service operations, then, "finished products" or "outputs" are people with needs met and possessions serviced.

In many ways, the focus of service operations is more complex than that of goods production. First, service operations feature a unique link between production and consumption—between process and outcome. Second, services are more *intangible* and *customized* and *less storable* than most products. Finally, quality considerations must be defined—and managed—differently in the service sector than in manufacturing operations.

Focus on Process and Outcome   As we saw earlier, manufacturing operations focus on the outcome of the production process. The products offered by most service operations, however, are actually combinations of goods and services. Services, therefore, must focus on both the transformation *process* and its outcome—both on making a pizza and on delivering it to the buyer. Service operations thus require different skills from manufacturing operations. For example, local gas company employees may need the interpersonal skills necessary to calm and reassure frightened customers who have reported gas leaks. The job, therefore, can mean more than just repairing defective pipes. Factory workers who install gas pipes while assembling mobile homes are far less likely to need such skills.

Focus on Service Characteristics   Service companies' transactions always reflect the fact that service products are characterized by three key qualities: *intangibility, customization,* and *unstorability*.

Intangibility. Often services cannot be touched, tasted, smelled, or seen. An important value, therefore, is the *intangible* value that the customer experiences in the form of pleasure, satisfaction, or a feeling of safety. For example, when you hire an attorney to resolve a problem, you purchase not only the intangible quality of legal expertise but the equally intangible reassurance that help is at hand. Although all services have some degree of intangibility, some provide tangible elements as well. Your attorney, for example, can draw up the living will that you want to keep in your safe deposit box.

Customization. When you visit a physician, you expect to be examined for your symptoms. Likewise, when you purchase insurance, get your pet groomed, or have your hair cut, you expect these services to be designed for your needs. Typically, therefore, services are *customized*.

Unstorability. Services like rubbish collection, transportation, child care, and house cleaning cannot be produced ahead of time and then stored. If a service is not used when available, it is usually wasted. Services, then, are typically characterized by a high degree of *unstorability*.

Focus on the Customer-Service Link Because they transform customers or their possessions, service operations often acknowledge the customer as part of the operations process itself. For example, to purchase a haircut you must usually go to the barbershop or beauty salon.

As part of the operations process, consumers of services have a unique ability to affect that process. In other words, as the customer, you expect the salon to be conveniently located, to be open for business at convenient times, to offer needed services at reasonable prices, and to extend prompt service. Accordingly, the manager adopts hours of operation, available services, and numbers of employees to meet the requirements of the customer.

Focus on Service-Quality Considerations Consumers use different criteria to judge services and goods. Service managers must understand that quality of work and quality of service are not necessarily synonymous. For example, although your car may have been flawlessly repaired, you might feel dissatisfied with the service if you were forced to pick it up a day later than promised.

■ OPERATIONS PLANNING

Managers from many departments contribute to decisions about operations management. As Figure 11.2 shows, however, no matter how many decision makers are involved, the process can be described as a series of logical steps. The success of any firm depends on the final result of this logical sequence of decisions.

The overall business plan and forecasts developed by a company's top executives guide operations planning. The business plan outlines the firm's goals and objectives, including the specific goods and services it will offer in the upcoming years. In this section, we survey the development of the major components of operations planning. We discuss the key planning activities that fall into one of five major categories: *capacity, location, layout, quality,* and *methods planning*.

Capacity Planning

The amount of a product that a company can produce under normal working conditions is its **capacity**. A firm's capacity depends on how many people it employs and the number and size of its facilities. Long-range planning must take into account both current and future capacity.

capacity
Amount of a product that a company can produce under normal working conditions

Capacity Planning for Producing Goods Capacity planning means ensuring that a firm's capacity just *slightly* exceeds the normal demand for its product. To see why this policy is best, consider the alternatives. If capacity is too small to meet demand, the company must turn away customers—a situation that not only cuts into profits but alienates both customers and salespeople. If capacity exceeds demand, the firm is wasting money by maintaining a plant that is too large, keeping excess machinery on line, or employing too many workers.

Capacity Planning for Producing Services Capacity in service operations depends on the number of people that a firm employs and the number and size of its

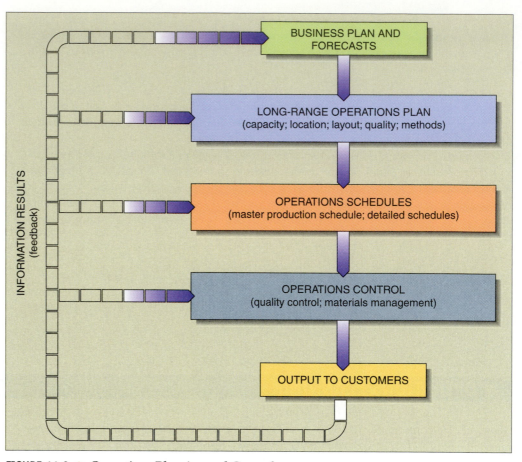

FIGURE 11.2 ◆ **Operations Planning and Control**

facilities. In low-contact systems, maintaining inventory lets managers set capacity at the level of *average demand*. For example, the J.C. Penney catalog sales warehouse may hire enough order fillers to handle 1,000 orders a day. When daily orders exceed this average demand, some are placed in inventory—set aside in a "to be done" file—to be processed on a day when fewer than 1,000 orders are received.

In high-contact systems, managers must plan capacity to meet *peak demand*. A supermarket, for instance, has more cash registers than it needs on an average day. But on a Saturday morning or during the three days before Thanksgiving, all registers are running full speed.

Location Planning

Because facility location affects production costs and flexibility, sound location planning is crucial. Depending on the site of its facility, a company may be capable of producing a low-cost product or find itself at an extreme cost disadvantage.

Location Planning for Producing Goods Managers in goods producing operations must consider many factors in location planning. Location attractiveness, for instance, is influenced by proximity to raw materials and markets, availability of labor, energy and transportation costs, local and state regulations and taxes, and community living conditions.

Location Planning for Producing Services   In planning low-contact services, companies can locate near resource supplies, labor, or transportation outlets. For example, the typical Wal-Mart distribution center is located near the hundreds of Wal-Mart stores that it supplies, not near the companies that supply the distribution center. Distribution managers regard Wal-Mart stores as their customers. To better serve them, distribution centers are located so that truckloads of merchandise flow quickly to them. To facilitate both outgoing and incoming transport, distribution centers are located near major roadways.

High-contact services are more restricted because they must locate near customers, who are a part of the system. Consider the following facts about the highest-volume sites of America's best-known fast food companies:

- The McDonald's restaurant on Interstate 95 near the New York–Connecticut border serves more customers each day than any other restaurant in the chain. Open 24 hours, this outlet serves 8,000 meals every day.
- The highest-volume KFC restaurant is located on the U.S. Army base at Fort Campbell, Kentucky. Although it serves as many as 2,000 customers a day, this outlet refuses to take its "captive" audience for granted. Promises Vice President for Operations Terry Rogers: "Employees who don't smile end up working in the kitchen." This KFC also features two drive-up lanes and home delivery.
- Located near the U.S. Marine Corps base in the Mojave Desert near Twenty-Nine Palms, California, the largest Domino's Pizza restaurant also thrives on military business. The restaurant's ovens can turn out 360 pies an hour, and the average order size is nearly $12.

The fundamental strategy is to establish outlets where the customers are. As prime sites for new restaurants become harder to find—and more expensive—fast food companies are setting up stands in malls, stadiums, convenience stores, and other non-traditional locations that already generate substantial customer traffic. "By the year 2000," predicts franchise attorney David J. Kaufmann, "many franchisers will have tens of thousands of retail locations of every species imaginable—as opposed to much smaller numbers of fixed-unit outlets." Wayne Norbitz, President of Nathan's Famous Hotdogs, agrees: "You used to open a restaurant, advertise, and ask people to come to you. Today the strategy is to find out where people already are and bring your product there."[4]

> **"You used to open a restaurant, advertise, and ask people to come to you. Today the strategy is to find out where people already are and bring your product there."**
>
> —Wayne Norbitz
> *President of Nathan's Famous Hotdogs*

Layout Planning

Once a site has been selected, managers must decide on plant layout. Layout determines if a company can respond quickly and efficiently to customer requests for more and different products or if it finds itself unable to match competitors' production speed or convenience of service.

Layout Planning for Producing Goods   In facilities that produce goods, layout must be planned for three different types of space:

1. *Productive facilities*, such as workstations and equipment for transforming raw materials
2. *Nonproductive facilities*, such as storage and maintenance areas
3. *Support facilities*, such as offices, restrooms, parking lots, and cafeterias

In this section, we focus on productive facilities. Alternatives include *process, product,* and *cellular layouts*.

Process Layouts.   In a **process layout,** equipment and people are grouped together according to function. In a custom cake bakery, for instance, the blending of batters is done in an area devoted to mixing, baking occurs in the oven area, and cakes are decorated on tables in a finishing area before boxing. Each task is performed in a specialized location. Machine, woodworking, and dry cleaning shops also feature process layouts.

Process layouts are well suited to *job shops*—firms that specialize in custom work. These companies perform a variety of jobs for different customers. They rely on general-purpose machinery and skilled labor to respond to the needs of individual customers. For example, your local bakery can accommodate both your request for a wedding cake and your friend's request for a birthday cake.

Product Layouts.   In a **product layout,** resources move through a fixed sequence of steps to become finished goods. Equipment and people are set up to produce only one type of good and are arranged according to its production requirements. Product layouts often use **assembly lines.** A partially finished product moves step by step through the plant on conveyer belts or other equipment, often in a straight line, until the product is completed. Automobile, food-processing, and computer assembly plants use product layouts.

Product layouts can be efficient and inexpensive because they simplify work tasks and use unskilled labor. They tend, however, to be inflexible because they require a heavy investment in specialized equipment that is hard to rearrange for new applications. In addition, workers are subject to boredom. Moreover, when workers at one end are absent or overworked, workers farther down the line cannot replace them.

Cellular Layouts.   A newer workplace arrangement for some applications is often called the **cellular layout.** Cellular layouts are used when families of products can follow similar flow paths. A clothing manufacturer, for example, may establish a "cell," or designated area, dedicated to making a family of clothing pockets—say, pockets for shirts, coats, blouses, trousers, and slacks. Although each type of pocket is unique in shape, size, and style, all go through the same production steps. Within the cell, therefore, various types of equipment (for cutting, trimming, sewing) are arranged close together in the appropriate sequence. All pockets pass, stage by stage, through the cell from beginning to end, in a nearly continuous flow. The cellular layout is similar to a product layout, except that product layouts are usually dedicated to single products rather than to families of products. Our clothing maker might also have cells for sleeves, collars, and so on. There may also be a separate area for final assembly.

Cellular layouts came into widescale use in the 1980s as an improvement over process layouts in some applications. They have several advantages. For example, because similar products require less machine adjustment, equipment set-up time is reduced. Because flow distances are usually shorter, materials handling and transit time are more efficient. Finally, inventories of goods in progress are lower—and paperwork is simpler—because materials flows are more orderly.[5]

Layout Planning for Producing Services   Service firms use some of the same layouts as goods-producing firms. In a low-contact system, for instance, the facility

---

process layout
Spatial arrangement of production activities that groups equipment and people according to function

product layout
Spatial arrangement of production activities designed to move resources through a smooth, fixed sequence of steps

assembly line
Product layout in which a product moves step-by-step through a plant on conveyor belts or other equipment until it is completed

cellular layout
Spatial arrangement of production facilities designed to move families of products through similar flow paths

should be arranged to enhance the production of the service. A mail-processing facility at UPS or Federal Express, therefore, looks very much like a product layout in a factory. Machines and people are arranged in the order in which they are used in the mass processing of mail. In contrast, Kinko's Copy Centers use *process layouts* for different custom jobs. Specific functions, such as photocopying, computing, binding, photography, and laminating, are each performed in specialized areas of the store.

High-contact systems should be arranged to meet customer needs and expectations.[6] For example, Piccadilly Cafeterias focus both layout and services on the groups that constitute their primary market—families and elderly people. As you can see in Figure 11.3 families enter to find an array of highchairs and rolling baby beds that make it convenient to wheel children through the line. Meanwhile, servers are willing to carry trays for elderly people and for those pushing strollers. Note, too, that customers must pass by the whole serving line before making selections. Not only does this layout help them make up their minds, but it also tempts them to select more.

Quality Planning

In planning production systems and facilities, managers must keep in mind the firm's quality goals. Thus, a complete operations plan today includes systems for ensuring that goods are produced to meet the firm's standards of quality. The American Society for Quality Control defines *quality* as follows:

> *The totality of features and characteristics of a product or service that bear on its ability to satisfy stated or implied needs.*[7]

In other words, **quality** means that operations processes must be geared to creating fitness for use—offering features that customers want. Such features may include a reasonable price and consistent performance in delivering the benefit that the product promises.

quality
A product's fitness for use; its success in offering features that consumers want

Methods Planning

In designing operations systems, managers must clearly identify every production step and the specific methods for performing them. They can then work to reduce waste and inefficiency by examining procedures on a step-by-step basis—an approach sometimes called *methods improvement.*

FIGURE 11.3 ◆ Layout of a Typical Piccadilly Cafeteria

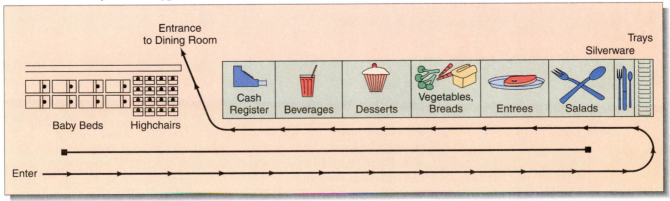

Improvement begins when a manager documents the current method. A detailed description, often using a diagram called the *process flow chart*, is usually helpful for organizing and recording all information. The process flow chart identifies the sequence of production activities, movements of materials, and work performed at each stage as the product flows through production. The flow can then be analyzed to identify wasteful activities, sources of delay in production flows, and other inefficiencies. The final step is implementing improvements.

Methods Improvement in Services In a low-contact system, the planning process may resemble process planning in a manufacturing operation. Methods improvements can be used to speed up services ranging from mowing lawns to filling prescriptions and drawing up legal documents. At First Chicago Bank, for example, the cash management unit collects accounts receivable for corporate clients. The sooner checks are collected and deposited, the sooner the client begins collecting interest. Delays—including the time required to check and adjust customer queries—are thus expensive, and speed and accuracy are of the essence. In First Chicago's methods planning, therefore, employees are not only trained to perform the specific requirements of their jobs but are also educated in the overall mission of the department so that they are prepared to make time- and money-saving judgments on their own.[8]

Design for Customer Contact in Services In a high-contact service, the demands on system designs are somewhat different. Managers must develop procedures that clearly spell out the ways in which workers interact with customers. These procedures must cover such activities as exchanging information or money, delivering and receiving materials, and even making physical contact. The next time you are at your dentist's office, for instance, notice the way dental hygienists "scrub up" and wear disposable gloves. They also scrub after patient contact, even if they intend to work on equipment or do paperwork, and they rescrub before working on the next patient. The high-contact system in a dental office, then, consists of very strict procedures designed to avoid contact that can transmit disease.

■ OPERATIONS SCHEDULING

Once plans identify needed resources and specify means of using them to reach a firm's goals, managers must develop timetables for acquiring resources. This aspect of operations is called *scheduling*.

Scheduling Goods Operations

Scheduling occurs on many levels. First, a *master production schedule* shows which products will be produced, when production will occur, and what resources will be used during specified time periods.

■ Consider the case of Logan Aluminum Inc. Logan produces coils of aluminum that its main customers, Atlantic Richfield and Alcan Aluminum, use to produce aluminum cans. Logan's master schedule extends out to 60 weeks and shows how many coils will be made each week. For various types of coils, the master schedule specifies how many of each width (coil widths can vary from 30 to 80 inches), alloy, and thickness will be produced. "We need this planning and scheduling system," says Materials Manager Candy McKenzie, "to determine how much of what product we can produce each and every month."[9]

This information, however, is not complete. For example, manufacturing personnel must also know the location of all coils on the plant floor and their various stages of production. Start-up and stop times must be assigned, and employees must be given scheduled work assignments. Short-term detailed schedules fill in these blanks on a daily basis. These schedules use incoming customer orders and information on current machine conditions to update the sizes and variety of coils to make each day.

Scheduling Service Operations

Service scheduling may involve both work and workers. In a low-contact service, work scheduling may be based either on desired completion dates or on the time of order arrivals. For example, several cars may be scheduled for repairs at a local garage. Thus, if your car is not scheduled for work until 3:30, it may sit idle for several hours even if it was the first to be dropped off. In such businesses, reservations and appointments systems can help smooth ups and downs in demand.

In contrast, if a hospital emergency room is overloaded, patients cannot be asked to make appointments and come back later. As we have seen, in high-contact services, the customer is part of the system and must be accommodated. Thus, precise scheduling of services may not be possible in high-contact systems.

In scheduling workers, managers must also consider efficiency and costs. McDonald's, for example, guarantees workers that they will be scheduled for at least four hours at a time. To accomplish this goal without having workers idle, McDonald's uses *overlapping shifts*—the ending hours for some employees overlap the beginning hours for others. The overlap provides maximum coverage during peak periods. McDonald's also trains employees to put off minor tasks, such as refilling napkin dispensers, until slow periods.

A 24-hour-a-day service operation, such as a hospital, can be an even greater scheduling challenge. Nurses, for example, must be on duty around the clock, seven days a week. Few nurses, however, want to work on weekends or during the wee hours of the morning. Similarly, although enough nurses must be scheduled to meet emergencies, most hospitals are on tight budgets and cannot afford to have too many on-duty nurses. Thus, incentives are often used to entice nurses to work at times they might not otherwise choose. For example, would you choose to work 12 hours a day, seven days a week? Probably not. But what if you were entitled to have every other week off in exchange for working such a schedule? A number of hospitals use just such a plan to attract nurses.

■ OPERATIONS CONTROL

Once long-range plans have been put into action and schedules have been drawn up, the production manager's task is to control operations activities so that they conform to plans. **Operations control** requires managers to monitor production performance, in part by comparing results with detailed plans and schedules. If schedules or quality standards are not met, corrective action is needed. *Follow-up*—checking to ensure that production decisions are being implemented—is an essential and ongoing facet of operations control.

Operations control involves *materials management* and *production process control*. Both activities seek to ensure that schedules are met and production goals are fulfilled, both in quantity and quality. In this section, we consider the nature of materials management and look at some important methods for process control.

operations control
Process of monitoring production performance by comparing results with plans

Materials Management

Both goods-producing and service companies use materials. For many manufacturing firms, materials costs account for 50–75 percent of total product costs. For goods whose production uses little labor, such as petroleum refining, this percentage is even higher. Companies thus have good reasons to emphasize materials management.

Materials management involves not just controlling but also planning and organizing the flow of materials. Even before production starts, materials management focuses on product design by emphasizing materials **standardization**—the use, where possible, of standard and uniform components rather than new or different components. Ford's engine plant in Romeo, Michigan, for instance, builds several different engine models. To save costs, the plant now uses common parts for several models rather than unique parts for each. One kind of piston, therefore, is now used in different engines. When components were standardized, the total number of different parts was reduced by 25 percent. Standardization also simplifies paperwork, reduces storage requirements, and eliminates unnecessary materials flows.

Once the product is designed, materials management purchases the necessary materials and monitors the production process through the distribution of finished goods. Of the four major areas of materials management, inventory control is a specialized and extremely important activity that we explain in a little more detail. The other three areas are *transportation*, *warehousing*, and *purchasing*:

- *Transportation* refers to the means of transporting resources to the company and finished goods to buyers.
- *Warehousing* refers to the storage of both incoming materials for production and finished goods for physical distribution to customers.
- *Purchasing* refers to the acquisition of all the raw materials (and services) that a company needs to produce its products. Most large firms have purchasing departments to buy proper materials in the amounts needed.

Inventory Control   **Inventory control** includes the receiving, storing, handling, and counting of all raw materials, partly finished goods, and finished goods. Inventory control of raw materials and finished goods is primarily a warehousing task. Production managers generally spend more time and effort controlling *materials inventory*—the stock of items needed during the production process, which might include such items

materials management
Planning, organizing, and controlling the flow of materials from design through distribution of finished goods

standardization
Use, where possible, of standard and uniform components in the production process

inventory control
Receiving, storing, handling, and counting of all raw materials, partly finished goods, and finished goods

© 1998 Robert Mankoff *from* The Cartoon Bank,™ Inc.

"Gentlemen, inventory is building up at an alarming rate."

as small components to be used in final assembly. Inventory control ensures that enough materials inventories are available to meet production schedules.

Tools for Operations Process Control

A number of tools assist managers in controlling operations. Chief among these are *just-in-time production systems*, *material requirements planning*, *quality control*, and *worker training*.

Just-in-Time Production Systems
To minimize excessive inventory costs, some managers use **just-in-time (JIT) production systems.** JIT brings together all the needed materials and parts at the precise moment that they are required for each production stage. Every item enters the process because it is time for it to be used. All resources, therefore, are continuously flowing—from the arrival of raw materials to subassembly, final completion, and shipment of finished products. JIT reduces to practically nothing the number of goods in process (that is, goods not yet finished) and saves money by replacing stop-and-go production with smooth movement. Once smooth movements become the norm, disruptions become more visible and thus get resolved more quickly. Finding and eliminating disruptions by continuous improvement of production is a major objective of JIT.[10]

Material Requirements Planning
Like JIT, **material requirements planning (MRP)** also seeks to deliver the right amounts of materials to the right place at the right time. MRP uses a *bill of materials* that is basically a "recipe" for the finished product. It specifies the necessary ingredients (raw materials and components), the order in which they should be combined, and the quantity of each ingredient needed to make one "batch" of the product (say, 2,000 finished telephones). The recipe is fed into a computer that controls inventory and schedules each stage of production. The result is fewer early arrivals, less frequent stock shortages, and lower storage costs. MRP is most popular among companies whose products require complicated assembly and fabrication activities, such as automobile manufacturers, appliance makers, and furniture companies.

Quality Control
Not all operations control tools focus on inventory control. Also important is **quality control**—the management of the production process so as to manufacture goods or supply services that meet specific quality standards. McDonald's, for example, has been a pioneer in quality control in the restaurant industry since the early 1950s. The company oversees everything from the farming of potatoes for French fries to the packing of meat for Big Macs. Quality assurance staffers even check standards for ketchup sweetness and French fry length.

In their quest for quality control, many U.S. businesses have adopted **quality improvement teams** (patterned after the Japanese concept of *quality circles*)—groups of employees from various work areas who define, analyze, and solve common production problems. Teams meet regularly to discuss problems and keep management informed of the group's progress in addressing various issues.

Frito-Lay Inc. has started such a program at its plant in Lubbock, Texas. Teams of ten hourly workers oversee activities ranging from potato processing to machine maintenance. Their primary job, however, is to cut costs while improving quality. Thus, workers now assume such "managerial" responsibilities as rejecting products that fail to meet quality standards and sending home employees who are unneeded (for example, when machines break down). They also schedule work crews and even interview prospective employees. Since 1990, the number of managers at the factory has dropped from 38 to 13, while the hourly work force has increased by 20 percent. From a place in the bottom 20 of Frito-Lay's 48 U.S. plants, the Lubbock operation has jumped into the top six in terms of quality.[11]▶

just-in-time (JIT) production system
Production method that brings together all materials and parts needed at each production stage at the precise moment at which they are required

material requirements planning (MRP)
Production control method in which a bill of materials is used to ensure that the right amounts of materials are delivered to the right place at the right time

quality control
Management of the production process designed to manufacture goods or supply services that meet specific quality standards

quality improvement team (or quality circle)
TQM tool in which groups of employees work together as a team to improve quality

Since Frito-Lay introduced work teams at its Lubbock, Texas, plant, the number of managers has dropped by more than half. Most of their work—including crew scheduling and interviewing potential employees—is now done by team members. To help them improve quality, teams receive weekly reports on costs and service performance, and each team is advised of its success in relation to corresponding teams at 22 other factories. At the Lubbock plant, the hourly work force has grown by 20 percent since 1990, but costs have gone down and quality has risen significantly during the same period.

Like Frito-Lay, many companies report that improvement teams have not only raised quality levels but also increased productivity and reduced costs. They have improved job satisfaction. But improvement teams also involve risks. Not all employees, for example, want to participate. Moreover, management cannot always adopt group recommendations, no matter how much careful thought, hard work, and enthusiasm went into them. The challenge for production managers, then, is to make wise decisions about when and how to use quality improvement teams.

Worker Training   Not surprisingly, customer satisfaction is closely linked to the employees who provide the service. As Bain & Co.'s Fred Reichheld puts it, "It's impossible to build a loyal book of customers without a loyal employee base."[12] Effective customer relationships do not come about by accident. Service workers can be trained and motivated in customer-oriented attitudes and behavior.

In service-product design, it is important to remember that most services are delivered by people. Service system employees are both the producers of the product and the salespeople. Human relations skills are vital in anyone who has contact with the public. Says Richard Bell-Irving, Vice President for Human Resources at Marriott: "We used to hire people who were good at the keyboard, good at processing information. Now we want associates who can look you in the eye, carry on a conversation, and work well under stress."[13] Like Bell-Irving, more and more human resource experts now realize that without employees trained in these skills, businesses like airlines, employment agencies, and hotels can lose customers to better-prepared competitors.

"We used to hire people who were good at processing information. Now we want associates who can look you in the eye and carry on a conversation."

—Richard Bell-Irving
Vice President for Human Resources at Marriott International

They realize how easily the wrong attitude expressed by service employees can reduce sales of services. Conversely, of course, the right attitude is a powerful sales tool. "You never know," says Disney employee trainer Robert Sias, "when something seemingly insignificant out in the workplace is going to have an enormous impact on a guest."[14]

In particular, the Disney organization does an excellent job of remembering that no matter what their jobs, service employees are all links to the public. Of the 35,000 employees at Disney World Resort in Buena Vista, Florida, some 20,000 have direct contact with guests. For example, Disney World has a team of sweepers constantly at work picking up bits of trash virtually as they fall to the ground. When visitors have questions about directions or time, they often ask one of the sweepers. Because their responses affect visitors' overall impressions of Disney World, sweepers are trained in appropriate ways to respond. Their work is evaluated and rewarded based on strict performance-appraisal standards.

In low-contact service operations, the technical skills of workers are more important than their human relations skills. As a consumer, you aren't terribly concerned about the charm of the individual who repairs your TV set. In high-contact service operations, however, human relations skills are more important. A student's counseling session can be made much more enjoyable by a cheerful, pleasant academic adviser. A pleased customer is more likely to return.

■ QUALITY IMPROVEMENT

It is not enough to measure production performance in terms of numbers of items produced. We must also take *quality* into account. For the past 50 years, the American Society for Quality Control (ASQC) has maintained standards for quality and provided services to assist U.S. industry's quality efforts.

Managing for Quality

Total quality management (TQM) (sometimes called **quality assurance**) includes any activity necessary for getting high-quality goods and services into the marketplace. Like all other management functions, TQM involves planning, organizing, directing, and controlling.

Planning for Quality   Planning for quality begins *before* products are designed or redesigned. To ensure that their needs are not overlooked, customers may be invited to participate in the planning process. In the predesign stage, managers must set goals for both performance quality and quality reliability. **Performance quality** refers to the *performance features* of a product. For example, Maytag gets premium prices for its appliances because they offer more advanced features and a longer life than competing brands. Through its advertising, the firm has made sure that consumers recognize the Maytag repairman as the world's loneliest service professional.

Performance quality, however, may or may not be related to a product's **quality reliability**—that is, the *consistency* of product quality from unit to unit. Toyotas, for example, enjoy high quality reliability—the firm has a reputation for producing very few "lemons." Consistency is achieved by controlling the quality of raw materials, by encouraging conscientious work, and by keeping equipment in good working order.

Some products offer both high quality reliability and high performance quality. Kellogg, for example, has a reputation for consistently producing cereals made of high

total quality management (TQM) (or quality assurance)
The sum of all activities involved in getting quality products into the marketplace

performance quality
The performance features offered by a product

quality reliability
Consistency of a product's quality from unit to unit

quality ingredients. As we saw earlier in this chapter, to ensure high quality, managers must plan for production processes—equipment, methods, worker skills, and materials—that will result in quality products.

Organizing for Quality   Perhaps most important to the quality concept is the belief that producing quality goods and services requires an effort from all parts of the organization. The old idea of a separate "quality control" department no longer holds. Everyone from the chairperson of the board to the part-time clerk—purchasers, engineers, janitors, marketers, machinists, and other personnel—must work to ensure quality. In Germany's Messerschmitt-Boelkow-Blohm aerospace company, for example, all employees are responsible for inspecting their own work. The overall goal is to reduce problems by making the product right from the beginning. The same principle extends to teamwork practice at Heinz Co., where teams of workers are assigned to inspect virtually every activity in the company. Heinz has realized substantial cost savings by eliminating waste and rework.

Although everyone in a company contributes to product quality, responsibility for specific aspects of total quality management is often assigned to specific departments and jobs. In fact, many companies have quality assurance, or quality control, departments staffed by quality experts. These people may be called in to help solve quality-related problems in any of the firm's other departments. They keep other departments informed of the latest developments in equipment and methods for maintaining quality. In addition, they monitor all quality control activities to identify areas for improvement.

Directing for Quality   Too often, firms fail to take the initiative in making quality happen. Directing for quality means that managers must motivate employees throughout the company to achieve quality goals. Managers throughout the company must help employees see how they affect quality and how quality affects both their jobs and the company. Chrysler CEO Robert J. Eaton, for example, observed poorly fitting interior trim and engine noise while test-driving the prototype Cirrus sedan in March 1994. He immediately postponed production until corrections could be made and launched a major program to increase the overall quality of Chrysler cars. Eaton's willingness to take fairly drastic action to ensure improvement was a visible display of a quality emphasis that had the added value of raising the quality consciousness of all Chrysler's employees.[15]

Like Eaton, leaders must continually find ways to foster a quality orientation by training employees, encouraging involvement, and tying compensation to work quality. Ideally, if managers succeed, employees will ultimately accept **quality ownership**—the idea that quality belongs to each person who creates it while performing a job.

quality ownership
Principle of total quality management that holds that quality belongs to each person who creates it while performing a job

Controlling for Quality   By monitoring its products and services, a company can detect mistakes and make corrections. First, however, managers must establish specific quality standards and measurements. For example, the control system for a bank's teller services might use the following procedure. Supervisors periodically observe the tellers' work and evaluate it according to a checklist. Specific aspects of each teller's work—appearance, courtesy, efficiency—are recorded. The results are reviewed with employees and either confirm proper performance or indicate changes needed to bring performance up to standards.

Tools for Quality Management

competitive product analysis
Process by which a company analyzes a competitor's products to identify desirable improvements in its own

Many companies rely on proven tools to manage for quality. Often, ideas for improving both the product and the production process come from **competitive product analysis.** Toshiba, for example, might take apart a Xerox copier and test each component. Test results then help managers decide which Toshiba product features are satis-

TRENDS & CHALLENGES

IF YOU THINK *YOU'RE* GOOD . . .

Former New York City mayor Edward I. Koch often asked his constituents this question: "How am I doing?" If Koch had been involved in a benchmarking program, he might have added, "in comparison to other mayors."

In business, companies that *benchmark* find, analyze, and apply the best practices of other companies—companies with whom they do not directly compete—to their own operations. Seeking to improve their competitive advantage, executives compare everything from strategic goals to day-to-day operations with those of companies considered the smartest, fastest, most flexible, and efficient. Their goal is to learn why—and *how*—other companies succeed.

For executives trying their best to do things right, the process of finding out what other companies do *better* can be disconcerting. But, says Robert Hiebeler, head of Arthur Andersen's global benchmarking group, there is no reason to despair. "The goal of identifying best practices," he explains, "is to disturb yourself in a positive way."

Over the years, certain companies have become favorite benchmarking targets because of their competitive excellence. Andersen Windows, Chrysler, Chevron, and MBNA (a Delaware-based credit card company) regularly attract pilgrimages to their head-quarters and factories, where visiting managers observe, listen, and gather information. However, although on-site benchmarking is considered the best way to gather firsthand information, it is not always possible to arrange needed visits. One alternative consists of report-based programs that gather benchmarking information on companies worldwide. One such program is Michigan State University's Global Procurement and Supply Chain Electronic Benchmarking Network, which monitors more than 200 companies worldwide and then issues written and electronic reports on how these firms are handling problems of supply chain management. Among the companies taking part in the program are Alcoa, Black & Decker, Compaq Computer, Johnson & Johnson, Kellogg, Rockwell International, Whirlpool, and Xerox.

> ## "The goal of identifying best practices is to disturb yourself in a positive way."
>
> —Robert Hiebeler
> *Partner in charge of Arthur Andersen's*
> *global benchmarking group*

No matter how benchmarking is done, applying lessons learned from companies can be difficult. Arun Maira, a Vice President at the Arthur D. Little consulting firm, believes that this final stage is the real challenge. "You can't just *impose* a best practice," he advises. "It has to be *adapted* to your company's own style." Fortunately, most companies that take the time to benchmark are also motivated to meet this challenge.

---

factory, which features should be upgraded, and which operations processes need improvement.

In this section, we survey three of the most important tools for total quality management: *statistical process control*, *quality/cost studies*, and various means of applying the principle of *getting closer to the customer*.

Statistical Process Control

Although every company would like complete uniformity in its output, the goal is unattainable. Every business experiences unit-to-unit variations in products and services. Firms can better control product quality, however, by understanding the sources of variation. **Statistical process control (SPC)** refers to methods by which employees can gather data and analyze variations in production activities to determine when adjustments are needed. The Glidden Co., for example, uses SPC to control paint-making processes more effectively. Litton Precision Gear uses SPC to ensure the quality of transmission gears installed in military helicopters. At Farbex, a plastics manufacturer, SPC analysts spot-check numerous standards—such as the weight of samples of plastic pellets—at several different points in the production

statistical process control (SPC)
Evaluation methods that allow managers to analyze variations in a company's production activities

process. Forty percent of all North American pulp and paper mills use SPC to reduce waste and increase productivity during production. One of the most common SPC methods is the use of control charts.

Control Charts.   Once a process is running properly, managers must still monitor the production process to prevent it from going astray. To detect the beginning of departures from normal conditions, managers can check production periodically and plot the results on a **control chart**. Three or four times a day, for example, a machine operator at Honey Nuggets might weigh several boxes of cereal together to determine the average weight. That average is then plotted on the control chart.

Figure 11.4 shows the control chart for Machine A at the Honey Nuggets plant. As you can see, the first five points are randomly scattered around the center line, indicating that the machine was operating well from 8 a.m. until noon. However, the points for samples 5 through 8 are all above the center line, indicating that something caused boxes to overfill. The last point falls outside the upper *control limit*, confirming that the process is out of control. At this point, the machine must be shut down so that an operator can investigate the cause of the problem. Control is completed when the problem is corrected and the process is restored to normal.

Quality/Cost Studies   Statistical process controls help keep operations up to existing capabilities. But in today's competitive environment, firms must consistently *raise* quality capabilities. However, any improvement in products or production processes means additional costs—for new facilities, equipment, training, or other changes. Managers thus face the challenge of identifying those improvements that offer the greatest promise. **Quality/cost studies** are useful because they not only identify a firm's current costs but also reveal areas with the largest cost-savings potential.

Quality costs are associated with making, finding, repairing, or preventing defective goods and services. All of these costs should be analyzed in a quality/cost study. For example, Honey Nuggets must determine its costs for *internal failures*. These are expenses—including the costs of overfilling boxes and the costs of sorting out bad boxes—incurred during production and before bad products leave the plant. Studies indicate that many U.S. manufacturers incur very high costs for internal failures—up to 50 percent of total costs.

control chart
Process control method that plots test sampling results on a diagram to determine when a process is beginning to depart from normal operating conditions

quality/cost study
Method of improving quality by identifying current costs and areas with the greatest cost-savings potential

FIGURE 11.4 ◆ Process Control Chart at Honey Nuggets Cereal

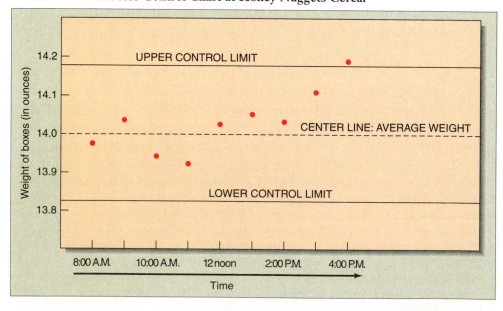

Despite quality-control procedures, however, some bad boxes may get out of the factory, reach the customer, and generate complaints from grocers and consumers. These are *external failures*, which occur outside the factory. The costs of correcting them—refunds to customers, transportation costs to return bad boxes to the factory, possible lawsuits, factory recalls—should also be tabulated in the quality/cost study.

The percentage of costs in the different categories varies widely from company to company. Thus, every firm must conduct systematic quality/cost studies to identify the most costly—and often the most vital—areas of its operations. Not surprisingly, these areas should be targets for improvement. Too often, however, firms substitute hunches and guesswork for data and analysis.

Getting Closer to the Customer   As one advocate of quality improvement puts it, "Customers are an economic asset. They're not on the balance sheet, but they should be."[16] One of the themes of this chapter has been that struggling companies have often lost sight of customers as the driving force for all business activity. Sometimes they waste resources designing products that customers do not want. Sometimes they ignore customer reactions to existing products or fail to keep up with changing consumer tastes. In contrast, the most successful businesses keep close to their customers and know what they want in the products they consume.

> ## "Customers are an economic asset. They're not on the balance sheet, but they should be."
>
> —Claess Fornell
> *Quality improvement advocate*

BUSINESS FIELD TRIP

"KEEP THE MILL RUNNING OR LOSE $10,000 AN HOUR"

It is fair to say that Chaparral Steel Co. sells steel. It is also fair to say that it sells production time. "Keep the mill running or lose $10,000 an hour," advises Jeff Werner, Senior Vice President for Structural Sales. The cost of electricity and fume control alone exceed $40 million annually.

STAGES OF PRODUCTION.   The process of producing about 1.5 million tons of steel a year takes place in two stages. The first occurs in the melt shop, where raw materials are melted down in 70-million-watt and 95-million-watt electric-arc furnaces at temperatures exceeding 3,000°. ▶ The process begins when steel is melted in a huge pot that produces 160 tons of molten metal. A huge ladle then pours the molten metal into a holding reservoir. The ladle continuously feeds the reservoir so that it always contains steel.

Chaparral's state-of-the-art electric-arc furnaces constitute the centerpiece of a production system whose hallmarks are speed and coordination. Production schedules, for instance, are worked out by both the production and marketing departments.

When the reservoir is filled, the liquid steel exits from the bottom of the reservoir into a copper mold. Cooling as it flows through, the steel retains the mold's shape. Located in a control room above the production floor, operators use sophisticated computers to cut the continuous strips into desired lengths. These lengths, known as "billets," constitute the raw material for the next production phase.

Stage two takes place in the rolling mills. While still hot, the billet is pushed through a series of processes that force it into its final shape. "It's similar to icing a cake," explains General Manager of Operations Duff Hunt. "The icing is forced through a nozzle that reduces its diameter and produces a continuous, uniform flow until all the icing is gone." As the billet flows through the rolling mill, it gradually gets longer and is reshaped into a specific product. For example, what entered as a 30- to 40-foot billet may leave the mill as a 300- to 400-foot I-beam.

Speed is crucial throughout the process. "The billets from the melt shop," says Hunt, "have to reach the rolling mill before they cool because rolling must be done while the metal is hot. Cool billets require reheating, which adds to energy and production costs. Getting the timing right takes a lot of coordination between the melt shop and rolling mill."

BUILDING A PRODUCTION SCHEDULE.
Based on sales forecasts, a sophisticated production schedule determines how much and when steel is produced. Working with the marketing department, the production department first analyzes annual demand in terms of different product sizes and shapes. It then schedules regular production runs for each item. For example, Chaparral's rebar and structural products are produced every six weeks in a steady, repeating production schedule.

Because the large variety of specialty products cannot be predicted in advance, SBQ products require more varied schedules. To determine the most efficient schedules, Chaparral tries to work directly with its customers. Thus, customer requirements enter the production game plan for the year in the form of scheduled blocks of time. Then, explains Duff Hunt, "we share these production plans with our customers so they can develop their own steel purchasing plans."

QUALITY ASSURANCE.
Closely linked to the production process at Chaparral is a sophisticated program of quality assurance. Quality standards are set by both internal customers (the company's employees) and external customers (the buyers of its products). Tom Harrington, who manages Chaparral's quality assurance department, explains how the process works. "A key function of the quality department is to review the specifications customers send us, including how they intend to use our material. Our initial review answers the question, 'Can we meet their technical requirements in terms of dimensions, hardness, chemistry of the steel, and internal cleanliness?' Our customers want us to certify that our manufacturing process will give the exact grade and type of steel they want. They may even audit our quality program, just as we audit our suppliers' programs."

> "Our customers want us to certify that our manufacturing process will give the exact grade and type of steel they want. They may even audit our quality program, just as we audit our suppliers' programs."
>
> —Tom Harrington
> *Head of the Quality Assurance Department at Chaparral Steel Co.*

Chaparral takes seriously its responsibility to analyze the quality of all incoming raw materials. For example, scrap vendors are given rigid specifications that define such characteristics as density, size, and cleanliness. To ensure that specifications are met, employees regularly inspect incoming scrap and audit suppliers' production processes. Naturally, Chaparral also monitors its own operations processes to ensure that temperature, water, and heat flow standards meet rigid specifications.

"A key principle at Chaparral," says Tom Harrington, "is that responsibility for the quality of the product resides with the production department, not with the quality assurance department. Production," he emphasizes, "does its own on-line inspection, controls the manufacturing process and equipment, and takes the lead in getting its equipment and processes improved. Production managers also make sure that their people are properly trained. The quality assurance department assists production in keeping quality standards high."

From automotive parts to highway guardrail posts, Chaparral Steel has gained the respect of fabricators, engineers, and architects around the world. In 1992, this respect earned CEO Gordon E. Forward the honor of being named U.S. Steelmaker of the Year—an award linked directly to the integrity and quality of the operations process at an executive's facilities.

Continued from page 263

A Case of Strange Bedfellows

The Campaign to Authenticate Entrepreneurs

Anheuser Busch is decidedly unhappy with the questionable marketing practices of craft brewers who pay other companies to brew their beer for them but claim that they produce "specialty" products under conditions of tight quality control. There are other unhappy parties as well, including more than 30 craft brewers who make every drop of their own beer in factories that they own and control. "What offends the real brewers," complains Paul Shipman, President of Redhook Brewing Co., in Seattle, "is when the contract brewers portray themselves as charming entrepreneurs who diligently brew their beers. In reality, they are pure marketing entities."

Part of their annoyance stems from the fact that it's extremely diffi-

> **"Contract brewers portray themselves as charming entrepreneurs who diligently brew their beers. In reality, they are pure marketing entities."**
>
> —Paul Shipman
> *President of Redhook Brewing Co.*

cult for craft brewers to make money. When Marcia King and her husband opened the New England Brewery Co. in 1989, they spent more than $2 million to buy the equipment they needed to brew their own beer in a converted Norwalk, Connecticut, warehouse. Among their expensive—

but in their opinion necessary—purchases were 50-barrel copper kettles from Germany. The cost of setting up the brewery and their manufacturing operation has left the Kings with little capital for advertising. Growth has thus been slow: after 7 years, they expect to brew only 7,000–10,000 barrels.

One proposal to distinguish brewers that make their own products from those that turn to contract companies is a seal of authenticity that would be included on bottle labels. This seal would let consumers know that while production practices are precisely what they're touted to be for certain brands, they're little more than smoke and mirrors for others.

Case Questions

1. Why do craft brewers emphasize their production methods in their marketing campaigns? What advantage do small, specialized production facilities have over larger facilities?
2. Do you agree with James Koch or August Busch about the ethics of using contract brewers without informing consumers? Explain your answer.
3. Is the use of contract brewers an example of smart capacity planning for both companies?
4. In your opinion, is it possible for contract brewers to maintain quality standards that are as high as those of craft brewers? Or does the personal touch truly make a difference?
5. What effect does the use of contract brewers have on inventory control?

SUMMARY OF LEARNING OBJECTIVES

1. **Identify the characteristics that distinguish *service operations* from *goods production*, and explain the main differences in the service focus.** Although the creation of both goods and services involves resources, transformations, and finished products, service operations differ from goods manufacturing in several important ways. In service production, the raw materials are people who choose among sellers because they have unsatisfied needs or possessions in need of care or alteration. While goods are typically produced, services are performed.

   In addition, services are largely *intangible*, more likely than physical goods to be *customized* to meet the purchaser's needs, and more *unstorable* than most products. Service businesses, therefore, focus explicitly on these characteristics of their products. Because services are intangible, for instance, providers work to ensure that customers receive value in the form of pleasure, satisfaction, or a feeling of safety. Often, they also focus on both the transformation process and the final product—say, making a pizza as well as the pizza itself. Finally, service providers typically focus on the customer service link, often acknowledging the customer as part of the operations process.

2. **Describe and explain the three *classifications of operations processes*.** Operations managers in manufacturing use one of two classifications to plan, organize, and control *operations processes*. Criteria include the type of *technology* used (*chemical, fabrication, assembly, transport,* or *clerical*) to transform raw materials into finished goods. Service operations are classified according to the extent of *customer contact*. In *high-contact systems*, the customer is part of the system. In *low-contact* systems, customers are not in contact with the service provider while the service is provided.

3. **Describe the factors involved in *operations planning* and *scheduling*.** *Operations planning* involves the analysis of five key factors. In *capacity planning*, the firm analyzes how much of a product it must be able to produce in order to stay ahead of normal demand. *Location planning* for goods involves analyzing proposed facility sites in terms of proximity to raw materials and markets, availability of labor, energy and transportation costs, regulations and taxes, and community living conditions. Location planning for high-contact services involves locating the service near customers.

   Layout planning involves designing a facility so as to enhance production efficiency. In *quality planning*, systems are developed to ensure that products meet a firm's quality standards. In *methods planning*, specific production steps and methods for performing them are identified. Once plans identify needed resources and specify means of using them, production timetables are developed in the form of schedules.

4. **Explain some of the activities involved in *operations control*, including *materials management* and the use of certain *operations control tools*.** *Materials management* refers to the planning, organizing, and controlling of the flow of materials. It focuses on the control of *transportation* (transporting resources to the manufacturer and products to customers), *warehousing* (storing both incoming raw materials and finished goods), *purchasing* (acquiring the raw materials and services that a manufacturer needs), and *inventory control*. To control inventory, operations managers use various methods. A *just-in-time (JIT) production system* brings together all materials and parts needed at each production stage at the precise moment that they are required. *Material requirements planning (MRP)* refers to a method for ensuring that the right amounts of materials are delivered to the right place at the right time. The use of *quality improvement teams* and worker training programs can assist in *quality control*—the management of the operations process so as to ensure products that meet specific quality standards.

5. **Identify some of the key tools for *total quality management*, including strategies for getting closer to the customer.** *Total quality management (TQM)* includes any activity for getting quality products to the marketplace. It involves all the key functions of management—planning, organizing, directing and controlling. It often begins with *competitive product analysis*—the process whereby a company analyzes a competitor's products to identify desirable improvements in its own.

TQM tools include *statistical process control (SPC)*—methods whereby employees gather data and analyze variations in production activities. The purpose of SPC is to identify needed adjustments. One SPC tool is the *control chart*, which plots test sampling results to identify when a process is beginning to depart from normal conditions. *Quality/cost studies* are useful because improvements in products or production processes always entail additional costs. This method helps manufacturers identify areas in which quality can be maintained with the greatest cost savings. Finally, an increasingly important area of quality improvement is the realization that heeding the needs and reactions of its customers is a good way of making the most cost-effective changes in a company's goods or services.

STUDY QUESTIONS AND EXERCISES

Review

1. What are the four different kinds of production-based utility?
2. What are the major differences between goods production operations and service operations?
3. What are the major differences between high-contact and low-contact service systems?
4. What are the five major categories of operations planning?
5. What activities are involved in total quality management?

Analysis

6. What are the resources and finished products of the following services?
   - Real estate firm
   - Child-care facility
   - Bank
   - City water department
   - Hotel
7. Analyze the layout of a local firm with which you do business—perhaps a restaurant or a supermarket. What problems do you see and what recommendations would you make to management?
8. Why is high quality in the service sector so difficult to achieve?

Application Exercises

9. Interview the owner of a local small manufacturing firm. Classify the firm's operations processes and then identify its major operations problems. Propose some solutions to these problems.
10. Using a local company as an example, show how you would conduct a quality/cost study. Identify the cost categories and give some examples of the costs in each category. Which categories do you expect to have the highest and lowest costs? Why?

BUILDING YOUR BUSINESS SKILLS

This exercise enhances the following SCANS workplace competencies: demonstrating basic skills, demonstrating thinking skills, exhibiting interpersonal skills, and working with information.

Goal

To encourage students to identify specific mechanisms for improving the service encounter in a high-contact service company

Situation

As the director of training at a regional airline, you decide to initiate a program for all employees who come in contact with the public. The goal of the program is to improve the quality of the service encounter.

Method

Step 1: Draft a memo to be distributed to all employees with customer contact. Your memo should outline the aims of your training program by addressing the following points:

- The implications of the high-contact nature of the airline business for customer service

- Specific procedures for improving the service encounter

- The "people" skills and attitudes that you want every employee to acquire

- The effects of technology on the nature of customer service

Step 2: Meet with three or four other students to compare your drafts. Analyze points of agreement and disagreement. Once you have negotiated a version that everyone can agree on, write a final draft.

Follow-Up

1. Identify the key points of your final draft, including the role played by employees in high-contact service businesses in improving the service encounter.

2. Would you have addressed the memo's key issues differently if you worked for a low-contact service business, such as a credit card company?

3. What steps can all service companies take to improve the quality of the service encounter? (Your answer should address the importance of employee training as well as other factors.)

AT A TIME WHEN RIGOROUS COMPETITION HAS DRIVEN MANY U.S. COMPANIES OUT OF THE STEEL-MAKING BUSINESS, CHAPARRAL STEEL HAS BECOME ONE OF THAT INDUSTRY'S MOST SUCCESSFUL FIRMS. TO LEARN MORE ABOUT PRODUCTION OPERATIONS IN A WORLD-CLASS COMPANY, LOG ON TO THE CHAPARRAL STEEL WEBSITE AT:

http://www.chaparralsteel.com

Browse the pages titled "Plant Tour," "Corporate & Financial," and "Products." Then consider the following questions:

1. How would you describe Chaparral's operations process? What type of transformation technology does it use?

2. What are the major inputs to the production process? What are its outputs?

3. What do you suspect are the biggest costs in Chaparral's production operations? Can you suggest some ideas for reducing those costs?

4. In the feature titled "Bar Products Business Unit," scroll down to "Products" and then to "Rolling Cycle." What do these cycle frequencies tell you about the production schedule for making bar products? How might this information be useful to Chaparral's customers?

5. According to the information in the feature entitled "Structural Products Business Unit," how many different products does Chaparral make? Do you expect that each product is made in large batches or in small batches? How does choice of batch size affect inventory levels for finished-goods storage?

6. Using specific information from Chaparral's Website, what can you conclude about this company's attitude on environmental issues? Are any environmental considerations evident in Chaparral's production activities?

7. Would you like to work at Chaparral? Which aspects of the company's practices and operations are most appealing to you? Which are least appealing?

12
CHAPTER

UNDERSTANDING ACCOUNTING AND INFORMATION SYSTEMS

There's No Business Like Show Business

THE SPECIAL EFFECTS OF NET PROFIT

When Ethel Merman belted out the famous refrain, "There's no business like show business," she wasn't singing about the business of accounting in Hollywood. But she probably should have been. That's because the accounting rules in Hollywood are like no other accounting rules in the world. According to critics, the rules make it difficult—if not impossible—for investors to determine the *real* financial condition of movie studios and their products.

Under existing rules, for example, studios can treat advertising costs as an *asset* (an economic resource) instead of an *expense*. This practice enables studios to inflate both assets and short-term profits. Studios can also choose to add to a film's costs millions in studio "overhead" charges and millions more in start-up costs of unrelated failed projects. Like advertising costs, these costs can be treated as assets and depreciated over a given number of years from the studio's balance sheet.

The following illustration (adapted from an article in *Business Week*) demonstrates how Hollywood's accounting system works. Using the unique system suggested above, studios manipulate balance sheet entries to paint a rosy financial picture that

> **"For most films, net profit participants don't receive anything."**
>
> —Philip Hacker
> *Consultant to plaintiffs in lawsuits against movie studios*

leaves investors in the dark about expenses and profits:

1. Let's say that Bigwig Pictures makes *Violent Death*, spending $50 million to acquire the story, hire actors, and film the movie.

2. The studio spends another $40 million to advertise and release *Violent Death*. This money is added to the movie's reported cost. This cost, moreover, climbs when Bigwig adds another $10 million to cover expenses from other films that were never released—plus costs related to everything from Bigwig salaries to paper clips. The total cost of *Violent Death* now stands at $100 million.

3. Now let's thicken the plot (albeit in a perfectly plausible way). Let's say that Bigwig is facing a depressed stock price and investor pressure to raise the value of shares by improving its performance. Bigwig management thus decides to project that *Violent Death*

will bring in $1 billion over the next 20 years. This revenue will come not only from the film's theatrical release, but from its release to home video, to pay and regular TV, and to laser disks, not to mention licensing in foreign markets. Because the studio states that *Violent Death* will be making money for 20 years, Bigwig can take the full two decades to subtract the film's bloated $100 million cost from its books.

4. Let's now say that *Violent Death* does well, taking in $200 million in box office and video revenue in the first year of its release. After deducting $20 million—that year's share of expenses—Bigwig shows an immediate profit of $180 million. Naturally, the studio's earnings—and stock price—jump. What about the remaining $80 million that the studio spent on the film? That sum remains on Bigwig's books for years—as an asset, not a liability.

Studios argue that this system makes sense. Because a movie has value that lasts long beyond the year in which it's made, it is reasonable to estimate profit margins *over the lifetime* of a movie. Profits, meanwhile, can be reported as such *as soon as box office dollars begin rolling in*. Why is this bookkeeping mechanism so important in the movie-making business? Studio executives point out that even a runaway hit has virtually no chance of making money *during its first distribution year.* In most cases, *first-year box office receipts* cannot cover the average $65 million cost required to make and market a Hollywood film. (For one thing, only 40 percent of the box office gross goes to the studio, with the remaining 60 percent going to theaters.)

However, this unique accounting system makes it extremely difficult for people with a so-called "net profit" interest in a movie to make any money from that interest. *Net profits* are the revenues that big studios agree to distribute among writers, actors, and others *after expenses, including salaries and distribution fees, have been paid.* Net profit arrangements are typically negotiated as part of individual contracts. Interesting, however, only 5–20 percent of all films pay any net profits. "For most films," charges Philip Hacker, a consultant to plaintiffs in lawsuits against studios, "net profit participants don't receive anything." Thus, even though the blockbuster hit *Forrest Gump* grossed approximately $650 million, it has paid no money to anyone with a net profit interest in the film. So, too, with such successful releases as *JFK, Coming to America,* and *Batman.*

The estate of Jim Garrison, the late New Orleans prosecutor whose book was the basis for the 1991 Warner Brothers movie *JFK,* has initiated a federal class-action suit over the net profit issue. Joining in the suit are thousands of people who signed net profits contracts with movie studios since 1988. All the studios involved, including Disney, Universal, Warner Brothers, 20th Century Fox, Paramount, Columbia–TriStar, and MGM–UA, use the same accounting practices. If successful, the Garrison-*JFK* suit could force payments of more than $1 billion and redefine Hollywood's approach to accounting.

It shouldn't be surprising that even the most successful superstars take crash courses in accounting—or, in most cases, hire an army of accountants and consultants to advise them on the financial intricacies of the deals they're offered. This chapter will introduce you to some of the concepts involved in this analysis, including the basic financial reports of economic activity that are the primary reason for accounting.

As you will also see in this chapter, accounting goes hand in hand with information management. In today's complex business environment, the need to manage information efficiently and quickly is crucial. Information, of course, can take many forms—information about expenses and assets, information about customers' locations and order patterns, information about supplies and finished goods on hand, information about workers' pay and productivity, information about products in development and information about competitors and customers.

After reading this chapter, you should be able to

1. Explain the role of *accountants* and the kinds of work done by *accountants*

2. Explain how the following three concepts are used in *record keeping: accounting equation, double-entry accounting,* and *T-accounts* for debits and credits

3. Describe two important *financial statements* and show how they reflect the activity and financial condition of a business

4. Explain how computing key *financial ratios* can help in analyzing the financial strengths of a business

5. Identify the role played in computer systems by *databases* and describe four important types of *business application programs*

6. List some trends in the application of technology to business information management

Continued on page 315

■ WHAT IS ACCOUNTING AND WHO USES ACCOUNTING INFORMATION?

accounting
Comprehensive system for collecting, analyzing, and communicating financial information

Accounting is a comprehensive system for collecting, analyzing, and communicating financial information. It is a system for measuring business performance and translating those measures into information for management decisions. Accounting also uses performance measures to prepare performance reports for owners, the public, and regulatory agencies. To meet these objectives, accountants keep records of such transactions as taxes paid, income received, and expenses incurred. They also analyze the effects of these transactions on particular business activities. By sorting, analyzing, and recording thousands of transactions, accountants can determine how well a business is being managed and how financially strong it is.[1]

bookkeeping
The recording of accounting transactions

Bookkeeping, a term that is sometimes confused with accounting, is just one phase of accounting—the recording of accounting transactions. Accounting is much more comprehensive than bookkeeping because accounting involves more than just the recording of information.

accounting system
Organized means by which financial information is identified, measured, recorded, and retained for use in accounting statements and management reports

Because businesses engage in many thousands of transactions, ensuring consistent, dependable financial information is mandatory. This is the job of the **accounting system**—an organized procedure for identifying, measuring, recording, and retaining financial information so that it can be used in accounting statements and management reports. The system includes all the people, reports, computers, procedures, and resources for compiling financial transactions.[2]

Users of Accounting Information

■ On December 14, 1994, General Mills announced plans to separate into two companies—the world's largest full-service restaurant company (which would operate Red Lobster, China Coast, and The Olive Garden) and a highly focused consumer foods company (including Betty Crocker, Cheerios, Wheaties, Yoplait, Gold Medal, and other brands). In preparation for the announcement, corporate officers relied on accounting to provide information for everyone who might be interested in the firm's activities. Issued to the public and stockholders, the *1995 Midyear Report* showed clearly how much each of the two segments contributed to General Mills's overall sales, expenses, and earnings. Current and potential stockholders were also told how the new stock shares would be distributed, and dividend policies for both companies were spelled out.[3]

General Mills accountants tabulated financial projections for the separation because stakeholders had important questions about the two companies. Do the business prospects for both indicate that they are good credit risks? As investments, will they pay sufficient financial returns to owners? Have adequate arrangements been made for employee retirement funds and benefits? Upon receiving accounting answers to questions like these, different information users—owners, employees, regulatory agencies, lenders, the public—are better prepared to make decisions for themselves and for their organizations.

As the General Mills example illustrates, there are numerous users of accounting information:

■ *Business managers* use accounting information to set goals, develop plans, create budgets, and evaluate future prospects.
■ *Employees and unions* use accounting information to get paid and to plan for and receive such benefits as health care, insurance, vacation time, and retirement pay.

- *Investors and creditors* use accounting information to estimate returns to stockholders, determine a company's growth prospects, and decide if a company is a good credit risk before investing or lending.
- *Tax authorities* use accounting information to plan for tax inflows, determine the tax liabilities of individuals and businesses, and ensure that correct amounts are paid on time.
- *Government regulatory agencies* rely on accounting information to fulfill their duties. The Securities and Exchange Commission, for example, requires firms to file financial disclosures so that potential investors have accurate information about a company's financial status.

■ WHO ARE ACCOUNTANTS AND WHAT DO THEY DO?

At the head of the accounting system is the controller, who manages all the firm's accounting activities. As chief accounting officer, the controller ensures that the accounting system provides the reports and statements needed for planning, controlling, and decision-making activities. This broad range of activities requires different types of accounting specialists. In this section, we begin by distinguishing between the two main fields of accounting, *financial* and *managerial.* We then discuss two of the most important services offered by accountants—*auditing* and *tax services.*

Financial versus Managerial Accounting

In any company, the two fields of accounting—financial and managerial—can be distinguished by the users they serve. As we have just seen, it is both convenient and accurate to classify users of accounting information as users outside the company and users inside the company. This same distinction allows us to categorize accounting systems as either *financial* or *managerial.*[4]

Financial Accounting   A firm's **financial accounting system** is concerned with external users of information—consumer groups, unions, stockholders, and government agencies. It prepares and publishes income statements and balance sheets, as well as other financial reports (such as the *General Mills 1997 Midyear Report*) at regular intervals. All of these documents focus on the activities of *the company as a whole, rather than on individual departments or divisions.*

financial accounting system Field of accounting concerned with external users of a company's financial information

Managerial Accounting   In contrast, **managerial** (or **management**) **accounting** serves *internal* users. Managers at all levels need information to make decisions for their departments, to monitor current projects, and to plan for future activities. Other employees also need accounting information. Engineers, for instance, want to know the costs of materials and production so that they can make product or operations improvements. To set performance goals, salespeople need data on past sales by geographic region. Purchasing agents use information on materials costs to negotiate terms with suppliers.

managerial (or **management**) **accounting** Field of accounting that serves internal users of a company's financial information

Accounting Services

Certified public accountants (CPAs) offer accounting services to the public. They are licensed at the state level after passing a three-day written exam prepared by the American Institute of Certified Public Accountants (AICPA). The AICPA also provides

certified public accountant (CPA) Accountant licensed by the state and offering services to the public

technical support to members and discipline in matters of professional ethics. Virtually all CPA firms—whether they consist of 10,000 employees in 100 nationwide offices or a single person in a small private facility—provide *auditing* and *tax services*. Larger firms earn 60–70 percent of their revenue from auditing services. Smaller firms typically earn most of their income from tax and management services.

audit
Systematic examination of a company's accounting system to determine whether its financial reports fairly present its operations

Auditing An **audit** examines a company's accounting system to determine whether its financial reports fairly present its operations. Companies must normally provide audit reports when applying for loans or selling stock. In 1996, for example, auditors from the accounting firm Deloitte & Touche disclosed that Baby Superstore Inc., a competitor of Toys "Я" Us, may have overstated cash reserves in its 1996 financial statements. An immediate result of the disclosure was a 29-percent plunge in the share price of Baby Superstore stock. Company officials hastened to report that the overstatement was a result of its accounting procedures, not of any illegal or improper management conduct.[5]

TRENDS & CHALLENGES
U.S. BUSINESS IS LOOKING FOR A FEW GOOD ACCOUNTANTS

Are college students learning the right things in their accounting courses? Not according to a report issued by the Institute of Management Accountants and the Financial Executives Institute. The report charges that "a preparation gap exists between the needs of today's lean, global, technologically savvy corporations and the accounting knowledge and skills of today's accounting graduates." Having surveyed hundreds of financial executives, Professor Gary Siegel, co-author of the report, states that "few college courses focus enough on business budgeting, cost accounting, and how to manage working capital, which is what companies need." Instead, says Siegel, too many college courses emphasize auditing, taxes, and other areas that would be most useful to someone preparing for a career with a public accounting firm. In reality, however, only about a third of accounting students end up working for such firms.

Steven R. Berlin, Senior Vice President of Finance at Citgo Petroleum Corp., agrees with Siegel. "Today's accounting students," he says, "don't hit the ground running. We need students who are more imaginative at seeing the strategic direction our business is taking." To deal with the problem, many firms are taking the initiative. At pharmaceutical giant Johnson & Johnson, for instance, newly hired accounting staffers are urged to take evening MBA courses or to study for the CPA exam. "Most accounting graduates," complains J&J finance executive Clark H. Johnson, "just aren't well prepared for business."

> **"Today's accounting students don't hit the ground running. We need students who are more imaginative at seeing the strategic direction our business is taking."**
>
> **—Steven R. Berlin**
> *Senior Vice President of Finance at Citgo Petroleum Corp.*

What, if anything, are colleges and universities doing to address the problem? Internships that provide students with real-world accounting experience can help. Another option is a seminar that requires each student to work with a local business to identify an actual accounting problem and propose a solution by semester's end. A graduate seminar at the University of Georgia focuses on corporate accounting policy. The objective, according to Professor James Don Edwards, "is to help students go beyond the traditional 'correct solution' mentality and acquire the multidimensional mindset that decision makers need when using financial statements." At California State University, emphasis is placed on coordinating accounting with other functional areas (such as marketing and information systems) and understanding the environmental factors that affect a business or industry.

The auditor must also ensure that the client's accounting system follows **generally accepted accounting principles (GAAP)**—rules and procedures governing the content and form of financial reports. The audit will also determine if a firm has controls to prevent errors and fraud. Ultimately, the auditor will certify whether or not the client's financial reports comply with GAAP.

Tax Services   Tax laws are immensely complex. Tax services thus include assistance not only with tax return preparation but also with tax planning. A CPA's advice, for example, can help a business structure (or restructure) operations and investments and perhaps save millions of dollars in taxes. In order to best serve their clients, accountants must stay abreast of changes in tax laws. This is no simple matter—legislators made more than 70 pages of technical corrections to the 1986 Tax Reform Act before it even became law.

generally accepted accounting principles (GAAP)
Accepted rules and procedures governing the content and form of financial reports

■ TOOLS OF THE ACCOUNTING TRADE

All accountants rely on record keeping to enter and track business transactions. Underlying all record-keeping procedures are the three key concepts of accounting: *the accounting equation, double-entry accounting,* and *T-accounts* for debits and credits.

Record Keeping with Journals and Ledgers

As Figure 12.1 shows, record keeping begins with initial records of a firm's financial transactions. These transactions include sales orders, invoices for incoming materials, employee time cards, and customer installment payments. Large companies receive and process tens of thousands of these documents every day. For example, before switching to credit cards with magnetic strips, Amoco Oil Co. received 650,000 sales receipts daily. Each receipt represented a transaction. Of course, few companies today are deluged with such tidal waves of paper, but even in the age of digitized information flows,

FIGURE 12.1 ◆ Accounting and Record Keeping

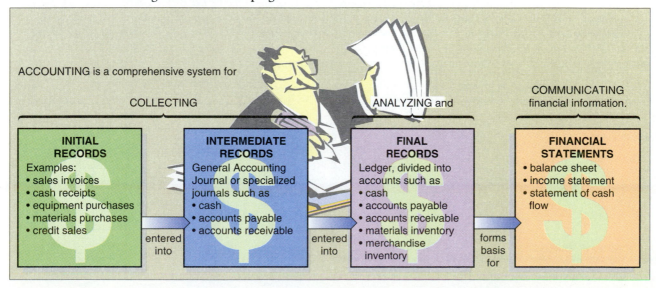

managers can track and control a company's progress only if its transactions are analyzed and classified in an orderly fashion.

Journals and Ledgers   As *initial records* are received, they are sorted and entered into a **journal**—a chronological record of financial transactions that includes a brief description of each. They are now *intermediate records*. Most companies keep specialized journals for different transactions, such as cash receipts, sales, and purchases.

Journal transactions are summarized, usually on a monthly basis, in a *final record* called the **ledger.** In the term *auditing the books*, the *book* is the ledger. Like specialized journals, the ledger is divided into *accounts*, such as *cash, inventories,* and *receivables.* The cash account, for example, is a detailed record of all the firm's changes in cash. Other accounts record changes in each type of asset and liability. Ledgers also feature an important column labeled "Balance," which shows the current total dollar amount in each account. If a balance in a given account is unexpectedly high or low, tracking backward to the corresponding journal entry should reveal the cause of the unexpected figure.

Financial Reports and the Fiscal Year   At the end of the year, all the accounts in the ledger are totaled, and the firm's financial status is assessed. This summation is the basis for annual financial reports. With the preparation of reports, the old accounting cycle ends and a new cycle begins. The timing of the annual accounting cycle is called the **fiscal year**—the 12-month period used for financial reporting purposes. Although most companies adopt the calendar year, many companies use 12-month periods that reflect the seasonal nature of their industries. For example, to close its fiscal year at the completion of harvesting, a fruit orchard may select the period from September 1, 1996, to August 31, 1997.

As an example of the record-keeping process, consider Figures 12.2 and 12.3, which illustrate a portion of the process for Perfect Posters Inc., a hypothetical wholesaler. In Figure 12.2, a check from Eye-Poppers (an initial record) is entered in Perfect Posters's General Accounting Journal (an intermediate record).

In Figure 12.3, this entry eventually turns up in Perfect Posters's General Ledger, where it becomes a final record showing a cash account balance of $98,808.43. In the next section, we will see how this entry is ultimately reflected in the financial reports that Perfect Posters submits to its stockholders and its bank.

---

journal
Chronological record of a firm's financial transactions, including a brief description of each

ledger
Record, divided into accounts and usually compiled on a monthly basis, containing summaries of all journal transactions

fiscal year
Twelve-month period designated for annual financial reporting purposes

---

FIGURE 12.2 ◆ Entering a Check in the General Journal. *The transaction begins when Perfect Posters receives a check from Eye-Poppers. Along with a brief explanation, the amount of the check is entered on the* debit *side of the Perfect Posters General Accounting Journal. Note that the amount—$245—has also been entered on Oct. 3 as an* account receivable. *The accountant has noted both a* decrease *in the company's assets (money owed Perfect Posters by Eye-Poppers) and an* increase *(money paid to Perfect Posters by Eye-Poppers). As we will see, these entries will be* balanced *in the firm's General Ledger (Figure 12.3).*

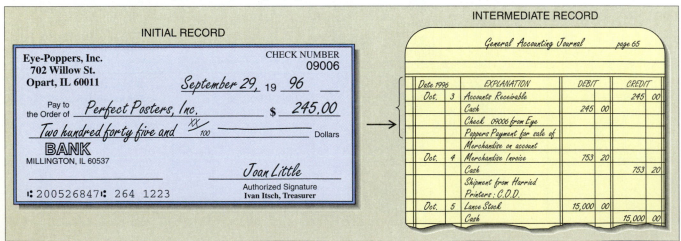

| General Ledger | | | | Page 19 |
| Accounts Receivable Account | | | | |

Date 1996		Debit	Credit	Balance
Sept.	30			7436 61
Sept.	30	No Blond Looks		324 46	4222 15
Oct.	3	Eye Poppers		245 00	3977 15
Oct.	6	Walls R Us	5131 32		9108 47
Oct.	10	Cover All		123 45	8985 02

| General Ledger | | | | |
| Cash Account | | | | |

Date 1996		Debit	Credit	Balance
Oct.	3				98,563 43
Oct.	3	Eye Poppers	245 00		98,808 43
Oct.	4	Harried Printers		753 20	98,055 23
Oct.	5	Lance		15,000 00	83,055 23
Oct.	5	Walls R Us		5,131 20	77,924 02

FIGURE 12.3 ◆ Entering a Check in the General Ledger. *Perfect Posters' accountant now transfers the entry from the General Journal to the General Ledger. The Ledger is divided into two* accounts—accounts receivable *and* cash. *Note that a new column—* balance—*also appears: Total dollar amounts for each type of account are entered here. As we will see, the accountant has used the* double-entry accounting system: *The $245 check from Eye-Poppers decreases Perfect Posters' accounts receivable account (it is no longer owed the money)* and *increases its cash account. On the company's Balance Sheet (Figure 12.5), both balances will appear as* current assets.

The Accounting Equation

At various points in the year, accountants use the following equation to balance the data in journals and ledgers:

$$\text{assets} = \text{liabilities} + \text{owners' equity}$$

To understand the importance of this equation, we must first understand the terms *assets*, *liabilities*, and *owners' equity*.

Assets and Liabilities   Charm and intelligence are often said to be "assets," and a nonswimmer is no doubt a "liability" on a canoeing trip. Accountants apply these same terms to items with quantifiable value. Thus, an **asset** is any economic resource that is expected to benefit a firm or individual who owns it. Assets include land, buildings, equipment, inventory, and payments due the company (accounts receivable). A **liability** is a debt that the firm owes to an outside organization or individual.

Owners' Equity   You may also have heard people speak of the "equity" they have in a home—that is, the amount of money that could be made by selling the house and paying off the mortgage. Similarly, **owners' equity** refers to the amount of money owners would receive if they sold all of a company's assets and paid all of its liabilities. We can rewrite the accounting equation to show this definition:

$$\text{assets} - \text{liabilities} = \text{owners' equity}$$

If a company's assets exceed its liabilities, owners' equity is *positive*—if the company goes out of business, the owners will receive some cash (a gain) after selling assets and paying off liabilities. If liabilities outweigh assets, however, owners' equity is *negative*—there are insufficient assets to pay off all debts. If the company goes out of business, the owners will get no cash and some creditors will not be paid. Owners' equity is a meaningful number to both investors and lenders. For example, before loaning money to owners, lenders want to know the amount of owners' equity existing in a business.

Owners' equity consists of two sources of capital:

- The amount that the owners originally invested
- Profits earned by and reinvested in the company

When a company operates profitably, its assets increase faster than its liabilities. Owners' equity, therefore, will increase if profits are retained in the business instead of paid

asset
Any economic resource expected to benefit a firm or individual who owns it

liability
Debt owed by a firm to an outside organization or individual

owners' equity
Amount of money owners would receive if they sold all of a firm's assets and paid all of its liabilities

out as dividends to stockholders. Owners' equity can also increase if owners invest more of their own money to increase assets. However, owners' equity can shrink if the company operates at a loss or if the owners withdraw assets.

Double-Entry Accounting

double-entry accounting system
Bookkeeping system that balances the accounting equation by recording the dual effects of every financial transaction

If your business purchases inventory with cash, you (1) decrease your cash and (2) increase your inventory. Similarly, if your business purchases supplies on credit, you (1) increase your supplies and (2) increase your accounts payable. If you invest more money in your business, you (1) increase the company's cash and (2) increase your owners' equity. In other words, *every transaction affects two accounts*. Accountants thus use a **double-entry accounting system** to record the dual effects of financial transactions.

Recording dual effects ensures that the accounting equation always balances. As the term implies, the double-entry system requires at least two bookkeeping entries for each transaction. This practice keeps the accounting equation in balance.

Debits and Credits: The T-Account

T-account
Bookkeeping format for recording transactions that takes the shape of a *T* whose vertical line divides the account into debits (left side) and credits (right side)

Another accounting tool uses debits and credits as a universal method for keeping accounting records. To understand debits and credits, we first need to understand the **T-account.** The format for recording transactions takes the shape of a **T** whose vertical line divides the account into two sides. As pictured below, for example, Perfect Posters' General Accounting Journal has the following **T** format:

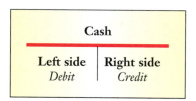

In bookkeeping, *debit* and *credit* refer to the side on which account information is to be entered. The left column of any T-account is called the *debit* side, and the right column is the *credit* side:

$$debit = left side$$

$$credit = right side$$

debit
Bookkeeping entry in a T-account that records increases in assets

credit
Bookkeeping entry in a T-account that records decreases in assets

When an asset increases, it is entered as a **debit.** When it decreases, it is entered as a **credit.** Thus, when Perfect Posters received payment from Eye-Poppers, it received more cash—an asset. It thus debited the General Accounting Journal (Figure 12.2) by placing $245 on the left side of the T-account.

Figure 12.4 shows how the rules of the T-account are consistent with the terms of the accounting equation. Debits and credits provide a system of checks and balances. Every debit entry in a journal must have an offsetting credit entry elsewhere (not shown here). If not, the books will not balance because some error (or deliberate deception) has been introduced in the record keeping. To ensure accurate financial records, accountants must find and correct such errors.

T-accounts and the double-entry system provide an important method of accounting control. At the end of the accounting cycle, debits and credits must balance—total debits must equal total credits in the account balances recorded in the General Ledger. An imbalance indicates improper accounting that must be corrected. "Balancing the books," then, is a control procedure to ensure that proper accounting has been used.

Accounting Equation	Assets		=	Liabilities		+	Owners' Equity	
Rules of the Account	Debit for Increase	Credit for Decrease		Debit for Decrease	Credit for Increase		Debit for Decrease	Credit for Increase

FIGURE 12.4 ◆ The T-Account and the Accounting Equation

■ FINANCIAL STATEMENTS

As we noted earlier, the primary purposes of accounting are to summarize the results of a firm's transactions and to issue reports to help managers make informed decisions. Among the most important reports are **financial statements,** which fall into two broad categories—*balance sheets* and *income statements*. In this section, we also explain the function of the *budget* as an internal financial statement.

financial statement
Any of several types of reports summarizing a company's financial status to aid in managerial decision making

Balance Sheets

Balance sheets supply detailed information about the accounting equation factors—assets, liabilities, and owners' equity. Because they also show a firm's financial condition at a point in time, balance sheets are sometimes called *statements of financial position.* Figure 12.5 shows the balance sheet for Perfect Posters.

balance sheet
Financial statement detailing a firm's assets, liabilities, and owners' equity

FIGURE 12.5 ◆ **Perfect Posters's balance sheet as of December 31, 1996.** *Perfect Posters' balance sheet shows clearly that the firm's total assets equal its total liabilities and owners' equality.*

□□□□□□□□□□ **Perfect Posters,** INC.
555 RIVERVIEW, CHICAGO, IL 60606

Perfect Posters, Inc.
Balance Sheet
As of December 31, 1996

Assets

Current Assets:			
Cash		$7,050	
Marketable securities		2,300	
Accounts receivable	$26,210		
Less: Allowance for doubtful accounts	(650)	25,560	
Merchandise inventory		21,250	
Prepaid expenses		1,050	
Total current assets			**$ 57,210**
Fixed Assets:			
Land		18,000	
Building	65,000		
Less: Accumulated depreciation	(22,500)	42,500	
Equipment	72,195		
Less: Accumulated depreciation	(24,815)	47,380	
Total fixed assets	.		**107,880**
Intangible assets:			
Patents		7,100	
Trademarks		900	
Total Intangible Assets			**8,000**
Total assets			**$173,090**

Liabilities and Owners' Equity

Current liabilities:			
Accounts payable		$16,315	
Wages payable		3,700	
Taxes payable		1,920	
Total current liabilities			**$ 21,935**
Long-term liabilities:			
Notes payable, 8% due 1998		10,000	
Bonds payable, 9% due 2000		30,000	
Total long-term liabilities			**40,000**
Total liabilities			**$ 61,935**
Owners' Equity			
Common stock, $5 par		40,000	
Additional paid-in capital		15,000	
Retained earnings		56,155	
Total owners' equity			**111,155**
Total liabilities and owners' equity			**$173,090**

Assets   As we have seen, an *asset* is any economic resource a company owns and from which it can expect to derive some future benefit. From an accounting standpoint, most companies have three types of assets—*current, fixed,* and *intangible.*

current asset
Asset that can be converted into cash within the following year

liquidity
Ease with which an asset can be converted into cash

Current Assets.   **Current assets** include cash and assets that can be converted into cash within the following year. They are normally listed in order of **liquidity**—the ease with which they can be converted into cash. Business debts, for example, can usually be satisfied only through payments of cash. A company that needs but cannot generate cash—in other words, a company that is not liquid—may thus be forced to sell assets at sacrifice prices or even go out of business.

By definition, cash is completely liquid. *Marketable securities*—purchased as short-term investments—are slightly less liquid but can be sold quickly if necessary. Marketable securities include stocks or bonds of other companies, government and municipal securities, and money market certificates. There are three other important nonliquid assets held by many companies—*accounts receivable, merchandise inventory,* and *prepaid expenses.*

accounts receivable
Amount due from a customer who has purchased goods on credit

ACCOUNTS RECEIVABLE.   **Accounts receivable** are amounts due from customers who have purchased goods on credit. Most businesses expect to receive payment within 30 days of a sale. In our hypothetical example, the entry labeled *Less: Allowance for doubtful accounts* in Figure 12.5 indicates $650 in receivables that Perfect Posters does not expect to collect. Total accounts receivable assets are reduced accordingly.

merchandise inventory
Cost of merchandise that has been acquired for sale to customers and that is still on hand

MERCHANDISE INVENTORY.   Following accounts receivable on the Perfect Posters balance sheet is **merchandise inventory**—the cost of merchandise that has been acquired for sale to customers and that is still on hand. Accounting for the value of inventories on the balance sheet is difficult because they are flowing in and out throughout the year. Assumptions, therefore, must be made about which items were sold and which remain in storage.

prepaid expense
Expense, such as prepaid rent, that is paid before the upcoming period in which it is due

PREPAID EXPENSES.   **Prepaid expenses** include supplies on hand and rent paid for the period to come. They are assets because they have been paid for and are available to the company. In all, Perfect Posters's current assets as of December 31, 1996, totaled $57,210.

fixed asset
Asset with long-term use or value, such as land, buildings, and equipment

depreciation
Process of distributing the cost of an asset over its life

Fixed Assets.   The next major classification on the balance sheet is usually **fixed assets.** Items in this category have long-term use or value—for example, land, buildings, and equipment. As buildings and equipment wear out or become obsolete, however, their value decreases. To reflect decreasing value, accountants use **depreciation** to spread the cost of an asset over the years of its useful life. Depreciation means calculating an asset's useful life in years, dividing its worth by that many years, and subtracting the resulting amount each year. Each year, therefore, the asset's remaining value decreases on the books. In Figure 12.5, Perfect Posters shows fixed assets of $107,880 *after depreciation.*

intangible asset
Nonphysical asset, such as a patent or trademark, that has economic value in the form of expected benefit

goodwill
Amount paid for an existing business above the value of its other assets

Intangible Assets.   Although their worth is hard to set, intangible assets have monetary value. **Intangible assets** usually include the cost of obtaining rights or privileges such as patents, trademarks, copyrights, and franchise fees. **Goodwill** is the amount paid for an existing business over and above the value of its other assets.

A purchased firm, for example, may have a particularly good reputation or location. In fact, a company's goodwill may be worth more than its tangible assets. For example, when Ford purchased Jaguar for $2.5 billion, $2 billion was recorded as goodwill. Similarly, when General Motors paid $5 billion for Hughes Aircraft, only $1 billion could be associated with assets on Hughes's balance sheet; the remaining $4 billion was paid for goodwill.

Perfect Posters has no goodwill assets. However, it does own trademarks and patents for specialized storage equipment. These are intangible assets worth $8,000. Larger companies, of course, have intangible assets that are worth much more.

Liabilities   Like assets, liabilities are often separated into different categories. **Current liabilities** are debts that must be paid within one year. These include **accounts payable**—unpaid bills to suppliers for materials—as well as wages and taxes that must be paid in the coming year. Perfect Posters has current liabilities of $21,935.

Long-term liabilities are debts that are not due for at least a year. These normally represent borrowed funds on which the company must pay interest. Perfect Posters' long-term liabilities are $40,000.

Owners' Equity   The final section of the balance sheet in Figure 12.5 shows owners' equity broken down into *common stock*, *paid-in capital*, and *retained earnings*. When Perfect Posters was formed, the declared legal value of its common stock was $5 per share. By law, this $40,000 ($5 × 8,000 shares) cannot be distributed as dividends. **Paid-in capital** is additional money invested in the firm by its owners. Perfect Posters has $15,000 in paid-in capital.

Retained earnings are net profits minus dividend payments to stockholders. Retained earnings accumulate when profits, which could have been distributed to stockholders, are kept instead for use by the company. At the close of 1996, Perfect Posters had retained earnings of $56,155.

Income Statements

The **income statement** is sometimes called a **profit-and-loss statement** because its description of revenues and expenses results in a figure showing the firm's annual profit or loss. In other words,

$$\text{revenues} - \text{expenses} = \text{profit (or loss)}$$

Popularly known as "the bottom line," profit or loss is probably the most important figure in any business enterprise. Figure 12.6 shows the 1996 income statement for Perfect Posters, whose bottom line that year was $12,585. Like the balance sheet, the income statement is divided into three major categories—*revenues*, *cost of goods sold*, and *operating expenses*.

Revenues   When a law firm receives $250 for preparing a will or a supermarket collects $65 from a customer buying groceries, both are receiving **revenues**—the funds that flow into a business from the sale of goods or services. In 1996, Perfect Posters reported revenues of $256,425 from the sale of art prints and other posters.

Cost of Goods Sold   In Perfect Posters' income statement, the category labeled **cost of goods sold** shows the costs of obtaining materials to make the products sold during the year. Perfect Posters began in 1996 with posters valued at $22,380. Over the year, it spent another $103,635 to purchase posters. During 1996, then, the company had $126,015 worth of merchandise available to sell. By the end of the year, it had sold all but $21,250 of those posters, which remained as "merchandise inventory." The cost of obtaining the goods sold by the firm was thus $104,765.

Gross Profit (or Gross Margin).   You subtract cost of goods sold from revenues to calculate **gross profit** (or **gross margin**). Perfect Posters' gross profit in 1996 was $151,660 ($256,425 − $104,765). Expressed as a percentage of sales, gross profit is 59.1 percent ($151,660/$256,425).

current liability
Debt that must be paid within the year

accounts payable
Current liabilities consisting of bills owed to suppliers, plus wages and taxes due within the upcoming year

long-term liability
Debt that is not due for at least a year

paid-in capital
Additional money, above proceeds from stock sale, paid directly to a firm by its owners

retained earnings
Earnings retained by a firm for its use rather than paid as dividends

income statement (or profit-and-loss statement)
Financial statement listing a firm's annual revenues, expenses, and profit or loss

revenues
Funds that flow into a business from the sale of goods or services

cost of goods sold
Total cost of obtaining materials for making the products sold by a firm during the year

gross profit (or gross margin)
Revenues from goods sold minus cost of goods sold

Perfect Posters, INC.
555 RIVERVIEW, CHICAGO, IL 60606

Perfect Posters, Inc.
Income Statement
Year Ended, December 31, 1996

Revenues (gross sales)			$256,425
Cost of goods sold:			
Merchandise inventory, January 1, 1996 .	$ 22,380		
Merchandise purchases during year	103,635		
Goods available for sale		$126,015	
Less: Merchandise inventory			
December 31, 1996		21,250	
Cost of goods sold			104,765
Gross profit			151,660
Operating expenses:			
Selling and repackaging expenses:			
Salaries and wages	49,750		
Advertising	6,380		
Depreciation—warehouse and repackaging			
equipment	3,350		
Total selling and repackaging expenses		59,480	
Administrative expenses:			
Salaries and wages	55,100		
Supplies	4,150		
Utilities	3,800		
Depreciation—office equipment	3,420		
Interest expense	2,900		
Miscellaneous expenses	1,835		
Total administrative expenses		71,205	
Total operating expenses			130,685
Operating income (income before taxes)			20,975
Income taxes			8,390
Net income			$ 12,585

FIGURE 12.6 ◆ Perfect Posters's income statement for year ended December 31, 1996. *The final entry on the income statement, the "bottom line," reports the firm's profit or loss.*

operating expenses
Costs, other than the cost of goods sold, incurred in producing a good or service

operating income
Gross profit minus operating expenses

net income (or net profit or net earnings)
Gross profit minus operating expenses and income taxes

Gross profit percentages vary widely across industries. In retailing, for instance, Safeway's gross profit percentage is 27 percent. In food processing, General Mills' gross profit is 48 percent. In the software industry, Microsoft's gross margin is 80 percent. For companies with low gross margins, product costs are a big expense. If a company has a high gross margin, it probably has low cost of goods sold but high selling and administrative expenses.

Operating Expenses In addition to costs directly related to acquiring goods, every company has general expenses, ranging from erasers to the president's salary. Like cost of goods sold, **operating expenses** are resources that must flow out of a company for it to earn revenues. As you can see from Figure 12.6, Perfect Posters had 1996 operating expenses of $130,685. This figure consists of $59,480 in selling and repackaging expenses and $71,205 in administrative expenses.

Selling expenses result from activities related to selling the firm's goods or services. These may include salaries for the sales force, delivery costs, and advertising expenses. *General and administrative expenses*, such as management salaries, insurance expenses, and maintenance costs, are expenses related to the general management of the company.

Operating and Net Income. Sometimes managers must determine **operating income,** which compares the gross profit from business operations against operating expenses. This calculation for Perfect Posters ($151,660 − $130,685) reveals an operating income, or *income before taxes*, of $20,975. Subtracting income taxes from operating income ($20,975 − $8,390), reveals **net income** (also called **net profit** or **net earnings**). In 1996, Perfect Posters's net income was $12,585.

■ ANALYZING FINANCIAL STATEMENTS

Financial statements present a great deal of information. But what does it all *mean?* How, for example, can statements help investors decide what stock to buy or help managers decide whether to extend credit? Statements provide data. These data can in turn be applied to various ratios—comparative numbers. These ratios can then be used to analyze the financial health of one or more companies. They can also be used to check a firm's progress by comparing current and past statements.

Ratios are normally grouped into three major classifications:

- **Solvency ratios,** both short- and long-term, estimate risk.
- **Profitability ratios** measure potential earnings.
- **Activity ratios** reflect management's use of assets.

Depending on the decisions to be made, a user may apply none, some, or all the ratios in a particular classification.

Short-Term Solvency Ratios

In the short run, a company's survival depends on its ability to pay its immediate debts. Such payments require cash. Short-term solvency ratios measure a company's relative liquidity—and thus its ability to pay immediate debts. The higher a firm's **liquidity ratios,** then, the lower the risk involved for investors.

Current Ratio   One commonly used measure of short-term solvency is the *current ratio*. The current ratio has been called the "bankers' ratio" because it reflects a firm's creditworthiness. The **current ratio** measures a company's ability to meet current obligations out of current assets. It thus reflects a firm's ability to generate cash to meet obligations through the normal, orderly process of selling inventories and collecting accounts receivable. It is calculated by dividing current assets by current liabilities.

As a rule of thumb, a current ratio is satisfactory if it is 2:1 or higher—that is, if current assets are more than double the amount of current liabilities. A lower ratio may indicate that a company will have difficulty paying its bills. Note, however, that a larger ratio may imply that assets are not being used productively and should be invested elsewhere.

How does Perfect Posters measure up? Look again at the balance sheet in Figure 12.5. Judging from its current assets and current liabilities at the end of 1996, we see that

$$\frac{\text{current assets}}{\text{current liabilities}} = \frac{\$57,210}{\$21,935} = 2.61$$

How does Perfect Posters's ratio compare with those of other companies? It is higher than Johnson & Johnson (1.83), Boeing (1.41), and Northeast Utilities (0.95). Although Perfect Posters may be holding too much uninvested cash, it looks like a good credit risk.

Long-Term Solvency Ratios

To survive in the long run, a company must be able to meet both its short-term (current) debts and its long-term liabilities. These latter debts usually involve interest payments. A firm that cannot meet them is in danger of collapse or takeover—a risk that makes creditors and investors quite cautious. Some large firms have failed in recent years, including Penn Square Bank, Ames Department Stores, and Eastern Airlines, because they could not meet their long-term cash obligations.

Debt-to-Owners' Equity Ratio   To measure the risk that a company may encounter this problem, we use the *long-term solvency ratios* called **debt ratios.** The most commonly used debt ratio is the **debt-to-owners' equity ratio** (or **debt-to-equity ratio**), which describes the extent to which a firm is financed through borrowed money. It is calculated by dividing **debt**—total liabilities—by owners' equity.

This ratio is commonly used to compare a given company's status with industry averages. For example, companies with debt-to-equity ratios higher than 1 are probably

solvency ratio
Financial ratio, both short- and long-term, for estimating the risk in investing in a firm

profitability ratio
Financial ratio for measuring a firm's potential earnings

activity ratio
Financial ratio for evaluating management's use of a firm's assets

liquidity ratio
Solvency ratio measuring a firm's ability to pay its immediate debts

current ratio
Solvency ratio that determines a firm's creditworthiness by measuring its ability to pay current liabilities

debt ratio
Solvency ratio measuring a firm's ability to meet its long-term debts

debt-to-owners' equity ratio (or debt-to-equity ratio)
Solvency ratio describing the extent to which a firm is financed through borrowing

debt
A firm's total liabilities

© 1998 Jack Ziegler *from* The Cartoon Bank,™ Inc.

"I realize, gentlemen, that thirty million dollars is a lot of money to spend. However, it's not real money and, of course, it's not our money either."

relying too much on debt. Such firms may find themselves owing so much debt that they lack the income needed to meet interest payments or repay borrowed money.

In the case of Perfect Posters, we can see from the balance sheet in Figure 12.5 that the debt-to-equity ratio works out as follows:

$$\frac{\text{debt}}{\text{owners' equity}} = \frac{\$61,935}{\$111,155} = 0.56$$

Because the ratio is well below 1, all creditors would be protected if the firm developed difficulties severe enough to force liquidation. Owners' equity, in other words, is more than sufficient to meet all debts.

Profitability Ratios

Although it is important to know that a company is solvent in both the long and the short term, safety or risk alone is not an adequate basis for investment decisions. Investors also want some measure of the returns they can expect. *Return on investment* and *earnings per share* are two commonly used *profitability ratios.*

Return on Investment   Owners are interested in the net income earned by a business for each dollar invested. **Return on investment** (sometimes called **return on equity**) measures this performance by dividing net income (recorded in the income statement, Figure 12.6) by total owners' equity (recorded in the balance sheet, Figure 12.5). For Perfect Posters, the return-on-investment ratio in 1996 can be calculated as follows:

$$\frac{\text{net income}}{\text{total owners' equity}} = \frac{\$12,585}{\$111,155} = 11.3\%$$

return on investment (or return on equity)
Profitability ratio measuring income earned for each dollar invested

Is this figure good or bad? There is no set answer. If Perfect Posters's ratio for 1996 is higher than in previous years, owners and investors should be encouraged. But if 11.3 percent is lower than the ratios of other companies in the same industry, they should be concerned.

Earnings per Share   Defined as net income divided by the number of shares of common stock outstanding, **earnings per share** determines the size of the dividend that a company can pay its shareholders. Investors use this ratio to decide whether to buy or sell a company's stock. As the ratio gets higher the stock value increases, since investors know that the firm can better afford to pay dividends. Naturally, stock will lose market value if the latest financial statements report a decline in earnings per share.

For Perfect Posters, we can use the net income total from the income statement in Figure 12.6 to calculate earnings per share as follows:

$$\frac{\text{net income}}{\text{number of common shares outstanding}} = \frac{\$12,585}{\$8,000} = \$1.57 \text{ per share}$$

As a baseline for comparison, Wal-Mart's recent earnings per share was $1.19.

earnings per share
Profitability ratio measuring the size of the dividend that a firm can pay shareholders

Activity Ratios

The efficiency with which a firm uses resources is linked to profitability. As a potential investor, then, you want to know which company "gets more mileage" from its resources. Activity ratios measure this efficiency. For example, say that two firms use the same amount of resources or assets. If Firm A generates greater profits or sales, it is more efficient and thus has a better activity ratio. By the same token, if a firm needs more resources to make profits comparable to its competitors', it has a worse activity ratio.

Inventory Turnover Ratio   Certain specific measures can be used to explain just how one firm earns greater profits than another. One of the most important is **inventory turnover ratio,** which measures the average number of times that inventory is sold and restocked during the year—that is, how quickly it is produced and sold. First, you need to know your *average inventory*—the "typical" amount of inventory on hand during the year. You can calculate average inventory by adding end-of-year inventory to beginning-of-year inventory and dividing by 2. You can now find your inventory turnover ratio, which is expressed as the cost of goods sold divided by average inventory:

inventory turnover ratio
Activity ratio measuring the average number of times that inventory is sold and restocked during the year

$$\frac{\text{cost of goods sold}}{\text{average inventory}} = \frac{\text{cost of goods sold}}{(\text{beginning inventory} + \text{ending inventory})/2}$$

A high inventory turnover ratio means efficient operations. Because a smaller amount of investment is tied up in inventory, the company's funds can be put to work elsewhere to earn greater returns. Inventory turnover, however, must be compared with both prior years and industry averages. An inventory turnover rate of 5, for example, might be excellent for an auto supply store, but it would be disastrous for a supermarket, where a rate of about 15 is common. Rates can also vary within a company that markets a variety of products. ▶

To calculate Perfect Posters inventory turnover ratio for 1996, we take the merchandise inventory figures from the income statement in Figure 12.6. The ratio can be expressed as follows:

$$\frac{\$104,765}{(\$22,380 + \$21,250)/2} = 4.8 \text{ times}$$

As a retailer of both toys and childcare products, Toys "Я" Us experiences a wide range of turnover rates. For example, seasonal toys turn over less than three times per year. On the other hand, baby formula and diapers turn over more than 12 times annually. The average for an entire store is about three times per year. The highest and lowest points? October 31 and January 31, respectively.

New merchandise replaces old merchandise every 76 days (365 days/4.8). The 4.8 ratio is below the average of 7 for comparable wholesaling operations, indicating that the business is slightly inefficient.

■ INFORMATION MANAGEMENT: AN OVERVIEW

Accounting information is a vital element in modern business. Business information, however, can take many forms in addition to the financial—information about customers' locations and order patterns, information about supplies and finished goods on hand, information about workers' pay and productivity, information about products in development, and information about competitors and customers, for example. Not surprisingly, the computer is at the forefront of contemporary information management. In this section, we explore the ways in which companies manage information with computers and related information technologies.

Businesspeople today are bombarded with facts and figures. Modern communications permit businesses to receive daily—even up-to-the-minute—information from remote plants, branches, and sales offices. To find the information that they need to make critical decisions, managers must often sift through a virtual avalanche of reports, memos, magazines, and phone calls. How can businesses get useful information to the right people at the right time?

Most businesses regard their information as a private resource—an asset that they plan, develop, and protect. It is not surprising, then, that companies have **information**

information managers
Managers responsible for designing and implementing systems to gather, organize, and distribute information

managers, just as they have production, marketing, and finance managers. Information management is an internal operation that determines business performance and outcomes. For example, the performance of Chaparral Steel—customer service, delivery times, sales, profits, and customer loyalty—has been boosted by an information system that gives customers fast access to listings of the steel products currently available in Chaparral's inventories for meeting their last-minute needs. The technology that allows customers to shop electronically through its storage yards gives Chaparral greater agility. Because it can respond more rapidly than its competitors, it generates more sales.

Data versus Information

Although businesspeople often complain that they get too much information, what they usually mean is that they get too many data. **Data** are raw facts and figures. **Information** is defined as the useful interpretation of data.

For example, consider the following data:

- There were 800 million tubes of toothpaste sold in the United States last year.
- There were 400 million tubes of toothpaste sold the year before last.
- The U.S. birth rate is rising.
- Advertising for toothpaste increased 17 percent last year.
- A major dentists' group recently came out in favor of brushing three times a day.

If all these data were put together in a meaningful way, they might produce information about what, in general, sells toothpaste and whether, in particular, toothpaste manufacturers should construct new plants to meet increasing demand. The challenge for businesses, then, is to turn a flood of data into manageable information.

data
Raw facts and figures

information
The useful interpretation of data

Management Information Systems

One response to this challenge has been the growth of **management information systems (MIS)**—systems for transmitting and transforming data into information that can be used in decision making. Those charged with running a company's MIS services must first determine what information will be needed. They then must gather the data and, finally, provide ways to convert data into desired information. They must also *control* the flow of information so that it goes only to the people who need it.[6]

Information supplied to employees and managers varies according to such factors as the functional areas in which they work (say, accounting or marketing) and the levels of management they occupy. The quality of the information transmitted to all levels depends increasingly on an organization's technological resources—and, of course, on the people who manage it. In this section, we discuss the technology that transmits information in today's organization.

management information system (MIS)
System for transforming data into information that can be used in decision making

DATABASES AND APPLICATIONS PROGRAMS

As we noted earlier, all computer processing is the processing of data. This processing is carried out by programs—instructions the computer reads and according to which it performs specified functions. In this section, we will begin by briefly describing the nature of computer data and databases. We then discuss a few of the specialized applications programs designed for business use.

Data and Databases

Computers convert data into information by organizing the data in some meaningful manner. Within a computer system, chunks of data—numbers, words, and sentences—are stored in a series of related collections called *fields*, *records*, and *files*. Taken together, these data files constitute a **database**—a centralized, organized collection of related data.[7]

database
Centralized, organized collection of related data

Processing   Once data are entered into the database, they can be processed—manipulated, sorted, combined, and/or compared. In **batch processing**, data are collected over some time period and then processed as groups or batches. Payrolls, for example, are usually run in batches. Because most employees get paid on either a weekly or a biweekly basis, the data (the hours worked) are accumulated over the pay periods and processed at one time.

batch processing
Method of collecting data over a period of time and then computer processing them as a group or batch

Batch processing was once the only type of computer processing. Although it is still widely used, companies today also use **real time** (or **on-line**) **processing,** in which data are entered and processed immediately. This system is always used when the results of each entry affect subsequent entries. For example, if you book seat F6 on Continental Flight 253 on December 23, the computer must thereafter keep other passengers from booking the same seat.

real-time (or **on-line**) **processing**
Method of entering data and computer processing them immediately

Application Programs

Increasingly inexpensive equipment and software have made computers an irresistible option for businesses of all types and sizes. Moreover, programs are available for a huge variety of business-related tasks. Some of these programs address such common, long-standing needs as accounting, payroll, and inventory control. Others have been developed for application to an endless variety of specialized needs. Most business application programs fall into one of four categories—*word processing, spreadsheets, database management*, and *graphics*.[8] Seventy percent of all PC software applications are designed for the first three types of programs.[9]

word-processing program
Application program that allows computers to store, edit, and print letters and numbers for documents created by users

Word Processing   Popular **word-processing programs,** such as Microsoft Word and WordPerfect, allow computers to store, edit, and print letters and numbers for documents created by users. Sentences or paragraphs can be added or deleted without retyping or restructuring an entire document, and mistakes are easily corrected. At *USA Today*, for example, hundreds of reporters and editors use word processing to write, edit, and store articles on computer terminals that are linked to a central system. Within minutes after stories are completed, the system sends typeset text via satellite to printing sites throughout the United States where the paper is printed and distributed to newsstands each day.

electronic spreadsheet
Application program with a row-and-column format that allows users to compare the effect of changes from one category to another

Spreadsheets   **Electronic spreadsheets** spread across and down the page in rows and columns. Users enter data, including formulas, at row and column intersections, and the computer automatically performs the necessary calculations. Payroll records, sales projections, and a host of other financial reports can be prepared in this manner.

Spreadsheets are also useful planning tools, because they allow managers to see how making a change in one item will affect related items. For example, a manager can insert various operating cost percentages, tax rates, or sales revenues into the spreadsheet. The computer will automatically recalculate all the other figures and determine net profit.

Because they are helpful for investigating the impact of possible changes, spreadsheets can be used in building decision support systems. Two popular spreadsheet packages are Lotus 1-2-3 and Excel.

Database Management   **Database management programs** can keep track of all of a firm's relevant data. They can then sort and search through data and integrate a single piece of data into several different files. Figure 12.7 illustrates a small database management program that might be used at a company called Artists' Frame Service. In this case, the program is integrating the file for customer orders with the company's inventory file. When sales to Jones and Smith are entered into the "Customer Orders File," the database system automatically adjusts the "Frame Inventory File." The "Quantities on Hand" of materials B5 and A3 are reduced because those materials were used in making the frames for Jones and Smith.

database management program
Application program for creating, storing, searching, and manipulating an organized collection of data

Graphics   **Computer graphics programs** convert numeric and character data into pictorial information, such as charts and graphs. These programs make computerized information easier to use and understand in two ways. First, graphs and charts summarize data and allow managers to detect problems, opportunities, and relationships more easily.[10]► Second, graphics are valuable in creating clearer and more persuasive reports and presentations.

computer graphics program
Application program that converts numeric and character data into pictorial information, such as graphs and charts

Some of the latest software for **desktop publishing** combines word-processing and graphics capability in producing typeset-quality text from personal computers. Quark XPress, for example, is able to manipulate text, graphics, and full-color photographs. Desktop publishing eliminates costly typesetting services for reports and proposals. Quark is also used by ad agencies, like J. Walter Thompson, where computer-generated design offers greater control over color and format.

desktop publishing
Process of combining word-processing and graphics capability to produce typeset-quality text from personal computers

Computer graphics capabilities extend beyond mere data presentation. They also include stand-alone programs for artists, designers, and special effects designers. Everything from simple drawings to fine art, television commercials, and motion picture special effects are now created by computer graphics software. The realism of the dinosaurs in *Jurassic Park* and the physical appearance of the legless Vietnam veteran in *Forrest Gump* are special effects created with computer graphics.[11]

FIGURE 12.7 ◆ Artists' Frame Service: Database Management Program

CUSTOMER ORDERS FILE			
Job Order Number	Customer Name	Quantity Ordered (inches)	Frame Material Number
12345	JONES, JOHN	42	B5
25974	SMITH, MARY	89	A3

FRAME INVENTORY FILE		
Frame Material Number	Description	Quantity on Hand
A3	ITALIAN OLIVE	500
B2	PLASTIC BLACK	010
B5	PLASTIC GREEN	272

Performing in seconds calculations that would take a human being working nonstop for 24,000 years, graphics workstations like this one at Ford's Studio 2000X in Dearborn, Michigan, add a new dimension (actually, several new dimensions) to computer-graphics imagery. Using programs from companies like Silicon Graphics and Evans & Sutherland, Ford engineers can transform a designer's sketched lines into rotating mathematical models of a vehicle's entire surface.

■ THE MARRIAGE OF INFORMATION AND COMMUNICATIONS TECHNOLOGY

The latest generation of computing is still being developed and includes such elements as *artificial intelligence, expert systems, office automation, data communications networks,* and *multimedia communications systems.* The most powerful vehicle for exploiting these elements is the marriage of computers to communications technologies. Thanks to lower-cost, higher-capacity networks, the joining of computers, communications, and the mass media is already in its first stages.

This marriage promises to change the future of business—indeed, of society itself. "Personal computing," observes Microsoft's Bill Gates, "was qualitatively a very, very different thing than the computing that came before. The advances in communication likewise will create new ways of using communication for learning, education, and commerce that go far beyond anything done to date." Thus, both independently and through joint ventures, companies like Microsoft, AT&T, Oracle Corp., and Telecommunications Inc. are pursuing such products as personal digital assistants, digital TVs, and devices for tapping into high-band-width networks, multimedia information, and on-line services.[12] In this section, we briefly discuss the progress of some of these projects.

"Personal computing was qualitatively a very, very different thing than the computing that came before. The advances in communication likewise will create new ways of using communication for learning, education, and commerce that go far beyond anything done to date."

—Bill Gates
CEO of Microsoft Corp.

Artificial Intelligence

Artificial intelligence (AI) can be defined as the construction and programming of computers to imitate human thought processes. In developing components and programs for artificial intelligence, computer scientists are trying to design computers capable of reasoning so that computers can perform useful activities.

Robotics is one category of AI. With their "reasoning" capabilities, robots can "learn" repetitive tasks such as painting, assembling components, and inserting screws. Furthermore, they avoid repeating mistakes by "remembering" the causes of past mistakes and, when those causes reappear, adjusting or stopping until adjustments are made.

Computer scientists are also designing AI systems with sensory capabilities. In addition, as machines become even more sophisticated in processing natural languages, humans will be able to give instructions and ask questions just by speaking to the computer.

artificial intelligence (AI) Construction and programming of computers to imitate human thought processes

Expert Systems

A special form of artificial intelligence programs, **expert systems** try to imitate the behavior of human experts in a particular field. Expert systems thus make available the rules that an expert applies to specific types of problems. In effect, they supply everyday users with "instant expertise."[13]

expert system Form of artificial intelligence that attempts to imitate the behavior of human experts in a particular field

Office Automation

Office automation refers to the computer-based devices and applications whose function is to enhance the performance of general office activities. In this section, we survey three of the most entrenched innovations in today's automated office—*fax machines, voice mail,* and *e-mail.*

Fax Machines   **Fax machines** (short for *facsimile transceiver machines*) can transmit text documents (and even drawings) over telephone lines in seconds, thus permitting written communication over long distances. Fax machines are popular with both large and small firms because of their speed and low cost.

fax machine Machine that can transmit copies of documents over telephone lines

Voice Mail   **Voice mail** is a computer-based system for receiving and delivering incoming telephone calls. Incoming calls are never missed, because a voice responds to the caller and stores a message. A company with voice mail has each employee's phone networked for receiving, storing, and forwarding calls.

voice mail Computer-based system for receiving and delivering incoming telephone calls

Voice mail software links the communications device (telephone) with a computer. The input from the telephone is sent to the computer, which digitizes the voice data and stores it on a disk. The employee can then call the voice mail center to retrieve from storage a recording of waiting calls and voice messages.

E-Mail   An **electronic mail** (or **e-mail**) system electronically transmits letters, reports, and other information between computers, whether in the same building or in another country. E-mail thus substitutes for the flood of paper and telephone calls that threatens to engulf many offices. A variety of e-mail services are available, some more expensive than others.

Data Communications Networks

Gaining popularity on both home and business computers are public and private **data communications networks**—global networks that permit users to send electronic messages, documents, and other forms of video and audio information quickly and economically. The most prominent networks, the *Internet* and the *World Wide Web*, have emerged as powerful communications technologies.[14]

The Internet   The **Internet** (or "the Net") is the largest public network, serving thousands of computers with information on business, science, and government and providing communications flows among certain private networks, including CompuServe and MCI Mail. Originally commissioned by the Pentagon as a communication tool for use during wartime, the Internet allows personal computers in virtually any location to be linked together by means of large computers known as network servers. The Net has gained in popularity because it makes available an immense wealth of academic, technical, and business information. Another major attraction is its capacity to transmit electronic mail, or e-mail. For thousands of businesses, therefore, the Net is joining—and even replacing—the telephone, the fax machine, and express mail as a standard means of communication.

In 1994, the number of Net users doubled to 15 million, with links to 138 countries. In 1995, more than 25 million people and 22,000 businesses had access to the Net.[15] The Net's power to change the way business is conducted has already been demonstrated. For example, Digital Equipment Corp. (DEC) is a heavy Internet user. With more than 31,000 computers connected to the network, DEC's monthly e-mail volume has jumped to an average of 700,000 messages.

The Net has also benefited small companies, especially as a means of expanding market research and improving customer service.[16] In Ann Arbor, Michigan, Grant's Flowers and Greenhouses has used the Net to establish an international presence. Owner Larry Grant reports that the Net now generates nearly as many orders as FTD. "We're getting orders from all over the country," he reports. "We even got an order from someone in Japan." "Basically," confirms Jon R. Zeef, the Internet service provider who put Grant's Flowers on the Net for a $28 monthly fee, "your small town store can suddenly have an international presence in a cost-effective manner."[17]

World Wide Web   Thanks to a subsystem of 7,000 computers known as the **World Wide Web** (WWW, or simply "the Web"), the Internet is easier to use than ever before. It has made the Internet usable to a general audience, rather than just to technical users. The Federal Express Website, for example, gives customers access to the FedEx package-tracking database. Every day up to 12,000 customers look through the FedEx Web pages to determine the status of their packages without any help from FedEx employees. This customer "self-help" saves FedEx up to $2 million a year.

The computers linked by the Web are known as "Web servers." They are owned by corporations, colleges, government agencies, and other large organizations. There

---

electronic mail (e-mail)
Computer system that electronically transmits information between computers

data communications network
Global network (such as the Internet) that permits users to send electronic messages and information quickly and economically

Internet
Global data communications network serving thousands of computers with information on a wide array of topics and providing communications flows among certain private networks

World Wide Web
Subsystem of computers providing access to the Internet and offering multimedia and linking capabilities

are now well over 200,000 such sites serving up about 20 million pages of publicly accessible information.[18] The individual user can connect to the Web by means of "browser" software (such as Netscape, Netcruiser, WebExplorer, and Mosaic). **Browsers** support the graphics and linking capabilities needed to navigate the Web. The user need only "point and click," and experts predict that as more people become familiar with "browsers," the number of Net users will grow by 10 to 15 percent a month. Netscape Navigator currently enjoys an 80-percent market share, although it is being challenged by new entries, including Microsoft Corp.'s Explorer.[19]

Among the most successful enterprises to take advantage of the Web are those that operate "search engines." Companies like InfoSeek and Lycos maintain free-to-use public directories of the Web's massive and ever-increasing content. These indexes constantly scan the Web to stay up to date. A search engine may respond to approximately 7 million inquiries a day. It is thus no surprise that search engines are packed with paid ads placed by companies such as Honda and AT&T.[20]

Intranets The success of the Internet has led some companies to extend the Net's technology internally for browsing remote internal Websites containing information throughout the firm. These private networks, or **intranets,** are accessible only to employees via entry through so-called electronic "fire walls"—software programs that allow employees access to both the Internet and the company's Intranet while barring entry by outsiders. At Compaq Computer Corp., the intranet allows employees to shuffle their retirement savings among various investment funds. Ford Motor Co.'s intranet, with linkages among design centers in Asia, Europe, and the United States, helped engineers design the 1996 Taurus. A major advantage of these intranets is their use of a more standardized electronic system for information storage and access. The revolutionary new information linkages were previously impossible between departments and offices separated by distance or by incompatible software, computers, and databases. The new technology uses a more standardized system based on the same structure used in the Internet.[21]

browser
Software supporting the graphics and linking capabilities necessary to navigate the World Wide Web

intranet
Private network of internal Websites and other sources of information available to a company's employees

---

BUSINESS FIELD TRIP

"Who Needs Paper Anyway?"

In the more than twenty years that Chaparral Steel has been in business, dramatic changes in computer technology have revolutionized the way the company processes information, the kind of information it handles, and the speed of its operations. Jack Loteryman, Chaparral's Manager of Information Systems, puts these changes into perspective. "Once upon a time, the only computer we had was a huge mainframe with limited data-processing capacity. Today we have vastly more powerful mainframes and PCs. In fact," says Loteryman, "our PCs are stronger than the mainframes we had

20 years ago, with the result that work is being done on desktops that used to be done on the mainframe. Information is now immediately available and in easy reach."

Loteryman also points out that Chaparral, like most large companies, has been an active participant in the software revolution. "Today," he observes, "the world is using mass-produced software, particularly on PCs. There is no longer any need to spend months writing software since so much of it is commercially available."

Chaparral relies on five major databases—manufacturing, accounting, sales, human resources, and purchasing—that contain both qualitative and quantitative information. Qualitative information includes production schedules, tonnage information, invoices, and similar data. Qualitative information concerns available inventory, customer shipment locations, and ten-day shipping histories.

THE MILLnet AND MILLfax SYSTEMS.

The lynchpin in Chaparral's state-of-the-art customer service system is the MILLnet and MILLfax PC-based software programs, which permit customers to review Chaparral's inventory as well as their own purchasing histories. ▼ To use the MILLfax system, a customer needs only a phone, a fax machine, and a customer identification number. "When a customer wants current information," explains Loteryman, "he dials our computer, which offers a selection list, similar to the kind used on a voice mail system. Option 1, for example, may provide the customer's ten-day shipping history; option 2, open purchase orders; option 3, items currently available for sale; and so on. When the customer presses these option buttons on his telephone, he automatically commands the computer to send him the requested information via fax."

The MILLnet system provides the same information over a computer-to-computer connection. MILLfax is an option designed to service smaller customers. "Although all our customers own faxes," says Loteryman, "some are small mom-and-pop operations and

Chaparral's customer-service systems, called MILLnet and MILLfax, are PC-based software programs designed to provide both large and small buyers with easy, immediate, up-to-date information about inventories and shipments.

don't have PCs." MILLfax, then, is typically the busier of the two systems. While 60 customers are connected to MILLnet, the MILLfax system transmits about 250 order- and inventory-related faxes each day. Until recently, the information available on the MILLfax and MILLnet systems was twenty-four hours old. Now, however, Chaparral can transmit "live" data from its mainframe computers. This information may be only ten minutes old.

To protect customer privacy, MILLfax/MILLnet will transmit a requested fax only to the customer registered in Chaparral's system. Loteryman explains, "Even if Customer A has Customer B's identification number—and is using it, for example, to learn Customer B's recent order history—the system automatically sends the fax to Customer B, who would then wonder why he received it and notify us."

A PAPERLESS WORKPLACE.

Chaparral's ultimate information management goal is to eliminate from company transactions all paperwork and the delays that come with it. Currently, there are no file cabinets in the accounting department, and information is stored as images on laser disks. Let's say, for instance, that a packing slip arrives from an outside vendor. It is scanned, indexed, and filed electronically. To call up the data, accounting managers can access the index from desktop PCs. In the same way, all documents generated from within the company are electronically transmitted from the mainframe to the scanning unit. "Our goal," says Loteryman, "is to have information flowing among departments so customer orders are processed faster. A sales order would flow at once to quality control, manufacturing, and engineering and would be immediately added to the general ledger."

Although the accounting department is leading the way in eliminating paperwork, the rest of the company is rapidly working in the same direction. "Who needs paper anyway?" asks Loteryman, tongue only slightly in cheek. "And, besides, every company wants to be 'green.'"

Continued from page 291

May the Task Force Be with You

A Little Dreamworks Adds Competitive Pressure

A task force reporting to the Financial Accounting Standard Board (FASB) is now taking a close look at the way Hollywood studios determine their balance sheets. Its goal is to reform many of the unorthodox practices that give investors a distorted view of studio finances. The toughest practice to change involves the capitalizing of advertising costs (treating them as assets rather than expenses). The FASB, which determines the accounting rules by which U.S. companies must generally live, objects to this practice. The movie industry, however, is determined to maintain the status quo.

> **"Most of us think that how we do the accounting makes sense."**
>
> —Peter Cyffka
> *Senior Vice-President of Finance at Twentieth Century Fox Film Corp.*

"Most of us think that how we do the accounting makes sense," says Peter Cyffka, a task force member and the Senior Vice-President of Finance at Twentieth Century Fox Film Corp.

Even if the task force succeeds in changing Hollywood's accounting practices, its reforms will not affect the disbursement of net profits to those who help create movies. Any change in the studios' net profit system must come from the studios themselves in the process of contracting with creative artists. Dreamworks, the production company founded by Steven Spielberg, Jeffrey Katzenberg, and David Geffen, was the first studio to initiate a change. Screenwriters, animators, and other artists working for Dreamworks now sign contracts guaranteeing that they will share in the success of the films they help create.

Case Questions

1. In your opinion, are Hollywood's current accounting practices fairer to investors?
2. What changes would you suggest to make Hollywood's accounting system fairer to both studios and investors?
3. Why is the contractual agreement to share in a film's net profits usually an empty agreement?
4. If you were a screenwriter, what accounting-related questions would you ask before agreeing to a movie deal?
5. Why is the Financial Accounting Standards Board involved in reforming Hollywood's accounting practices?

SUMMARY OF LEARNING OBJECTIVES

1. **Explain the role of accountants and describe the kinds of work they do.** By collecting, analyzing, and communicating financial information, accountants provide business managers and investors with an accurate picture of the firm's financial health. *Financial accounting* is concerned with external users of information; *managerial accounting* serves internal users. *Certified public accountants (CPAs)* are licensed professionals who provide auditing, tax, and management advisory services for other firms and individuals.

2. **Explain how the following three concepts are used in *record keeping*: the *accounting equation, double-entry accounting,* and *T-accounts* for *debits* and *credits*.** The *accounting equation* (assets = liabilities + owners' equity) is used to balance the data in both *journals* and *ledgers*. *Double-entry accounting* acknowledges the dual effects of financial transactions and ensures that the accounting equation always balances. Using the *T-account*, accountants record financial transactions in the shape of a *T*, with the vertical line dividing the account into *debit* and *credit* columns. These tools enable accountants to enter and track transactions.

3. **Describe two important *financial statements* and show how they reflect the activity and financial condition of a business.** The *balance sheet*, also called the *statement of financial condition*, summarizes a company's assets, liabilities, and owners' equity at a given point in time. The *income statement*, also known as the *profit-and-loss statement*, details revenues and expenses for a given period of time and identifies any profit or loss.

4. **Explain how computing key *financial ratios* can help in analyzing the financial strengths of a business.** Drawing upon data from financial statements, ratios can help creditors, investors, and managers assess a firm's finances. The *current ratio* measures short-term solvency—a firm's ability to pay its debt in the short run. The *debt-to-owners' equity ratio* measures long-term solvency. *Return on investment* and *earnings per share* both measure profitability. *Inventory turnover ratios* show how efficiently a firm is using its inventory funds.

5. **Identify the role played in computer systems by *databases* and describe four important types of *business application programs*.** Through computer sequences of instructions called *programs*, computers are able to process data and perform specific functions. Once *data* (raw facts and figures) are centralized and organized into meaningful *databases*, they can be manipulated, sorted, combined, and/or compared according to program instructions.

   Four major types of application programs for businesses are *word processing* (which allows computers to act like sophisticated typewriters), *electronic spreadsheets* (which enter data in rows and columns and perform calculations), *database management* (which organizes and retrieves a company's relevant data), and *graphics* (which convert numeric and character data into pictorial information).

6. **List some trends in the application of computer technology to business information management.** The latest generation of computers includes *artificial intelligence* (programming computers to imitate human thought processes), *expert systems* (which try to imitate the behavior of experts in a given field), *office automation* (which includes machine technology—fax machines, e-mail, and the like—that streamlines communications), and *data communications networks* (which permit users to send electronic messages and video and audio information quickly and economically). All of these technologies help businesspeople make decisions and solve problems.

STUDY QUESTIONS AND EXERCISES

Review

1. How does the double-entry system reduce the chances of mistakes or fraud in accounting?
2. What are the two basic financial statements and what major information items does each contain?
3. Identify the three major classifications of financial statement ratios and give an example of one ratio in each category.
4. Why does a business need to manage information as a resource?
5. How can an electronic-mailbox system increase office productivity and efficiency?

Analysis

6. Suppose that Inflatables Inc., makers of air mattresses for swimming pools, has the following transactions one week:

- Sale of three deluxe mattresses to Al Wett (paid $75 in cash) on 7/16
- Received check on 7/13 from Ima Flote in payment for mattresses bought on credit ($90) on 7/13
- Received new shipment of 200 mattresses from Airheads Mfg. (total cost, $2,000) on 7/17

Construct a journal for Inflatables, Inc.

7. Dasar Co. reports the following data in its September 30, 1996, financial statements:

- Gross sales $225,000
- Current assets   40,000
- Long-term assets   100,000
- Current liabilities   16,000
- Long-term liabilities   44,000
- Owners' equity   80,000
- Net income   7,200

Compute the following financial measures: current ratio, debt-to-equity ratio, and return on owners' equity.

8. Describe the types of work or activities for which a local department store might choose to use batch processing. Do the same for real-time processing.

Application Exercises

9. Interview the manager of a local retail or wholesale business about taking inventory. What is the firm's primary purpose in taking inventory? How often is it done?

10. Visit a small business in your community to investigate the ways it is presently using computers and the ways that it plans to use them in the future. Prepare a report for presentation in class.

BUILDING YOUR BUSINESS SKILLS

This exercise enhances the following SCANS workplace competencies: demonstrating basic skills, demonstrating thinking skills, exhibiting interpersonal skills, working with information, and applying systems knowledge.

Goal

To encourage students to think about the advantages and disadvantages of using an electronic system for handling accounts receivable and accounts payable

Method

Step 1: Study the illustration on the next page. The outside circle depicts the seven steps involved in the issuing of paper bills to customers, the payment of these bills by customers, and the handling by banks of debits and credits for the two accounts. The inside circle shows the same bill issuance and payment process handled electronically.

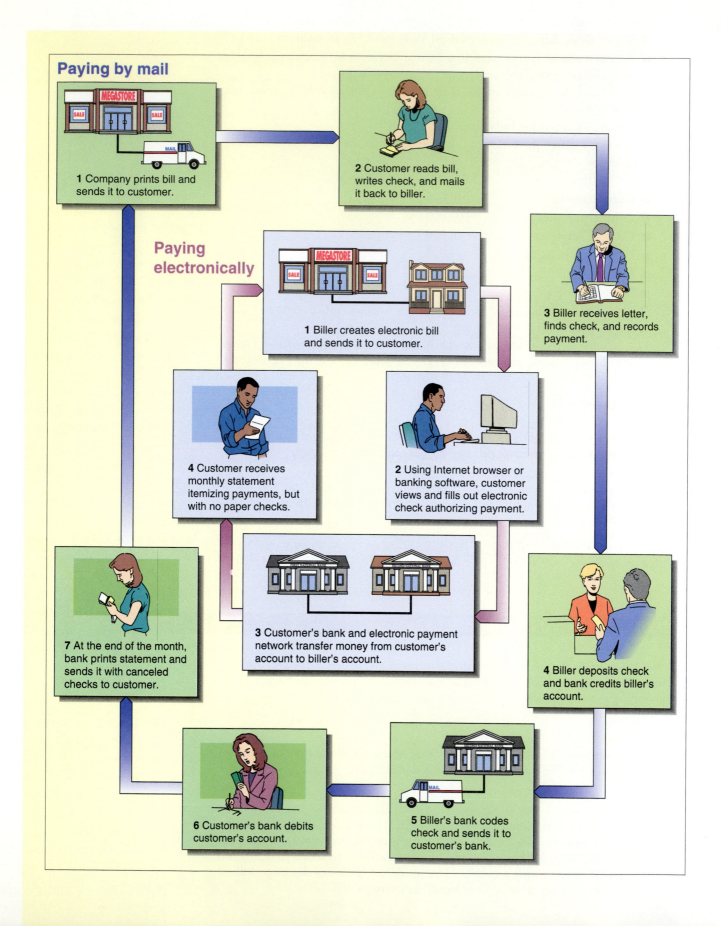

Paying by mail

1 Company prints bill and sends it to customer.

2 Customer reads bill, writes check, and mails it back to biller.

3 Biller receives letter, finds check, and records payment.

Paying electronically

1 Biller creates electronic bill and sends it to customer.

4 Customer receives monthly statement itemizing payments, but with no paper checks.

2 Using Internet browser or banking software, customer views and fills out electronic check authorizing payment.

7 At the end of the month, bank prints statement and sends it with canceled checks to customer.

3 Customer's bank and electronic payment network transfer money from customer's account to biller's account.

4 Biller deposits check and bank credits biller's account.

6 Customer's bank debits customer's account.

5 Biller's bank codes check and sends it to customer's bank.

Step 2: As the chief financial officer of a Midwestern utility company, you are analyzing the feasibility of switching from a paper to an electronic system of billing and bill payment. You decide to discuss the ramifications of the choice with four business associates (choose three fellow classmates to take on these roles). Your discussion requires that you research electronic payment systems now being developed. Specifically, using online and library research, you must find out as much as you can about the electronic bill-paying systems being developed by Visa International, Intuit, IBM, and the Checkfree Corporation. After you have researched this information, brainstorm the advantages and disadvantages of using an electronic bill-paying system in your company.

Follow-Up

1. What cost savings are inherent in the electronic system for both your company and its customers? In your answer, consider such costs as handling, postage, and paper.

2. What consequences would your decision to adopt an electronic system have on others with whom you do business, including manufacturers of check-sorting equipment, the U.S. Postal Service, and banks?

3. Switching to an electronic bill-paying system would require a large capital expenditure for new computers and computer software. How could analyzing the company's income statement help you justify this expenditure?

4. How are consumers likely to respond to paying bills electronically? Are you likely to get a different response from individuals and families than you get from business customers?

CCAS INC., CCAS FOR GOVERNMENT CONTRACTORS, AT
http://www.ccas.com/CCASDoc/ccasdoc0.html

Specifically, you are seeking access to the following features offered at the site:

■ Online User's Guide and Procedures Documentation
■ The CCAS Demo

You can gain access to the Demo without purchasing the software. You must, however, obtain a "UserID" and a "Password" by following the instructions at the Website. After obtaining the UserID and Password, you do not actually have to download the demo to perform this exercise. In order to view CCAS Online Documentation, select "Here" under "Downloading." A little patience will reward you with an informative adventure.

The purpose in examining this software demo is to see the contents of a real-world accounting software system, to recognize the wide range of accounting activities that it handles, to experience the detailed level of information required for such a system, and to appreciate how the various accounting activities are interrelated with one another within the system.

Begin by scrolling down to "User's Guide and Procedures Documentation: Table of Contents." From there, click on "CCAS Reports Available" and then on "Closing and Maintaining Your Books."

After examining the material in this section, consider the following questions:

1. On the page entitled "The CCAS and NewViews Relationship," a graphic is presented that "illustrates the CCAS concept." It shows "Accounting Transactions" as the input to the system and several reports that come out of the system. Based on this graphic and the various reports available from the system, would you classify CCAS as a *management accounting* system or as a *financial accounting* system? Why?

2. What information does the "Bank Accounts" report contain? How might that information be useful in managing a firm's activities?

3. What is the purpose of the "Fixed Asset Report"? What information does it contain?

4. How is the "Professional Time (PT)" report related to the "Payroll Records (PR)" report? What is the purpose of the flow of data between these two reports?

5. What is the function or purpose of the "ADDEMP" procedure? Explain how it relates to the "Payroll Records (PR)" report.

6. Explain the contents of the "PDIST—Payroll Distribution Entry" procedure. How does this procedure relate to the "Professional Time Report (PT)"?

7. How much time and effort do you suspect would be involved in first-time implementation of the CCAS system by a user company? What types of skills do you expect would be needed for system implementation?

The Sound of One Voice Talking
Or, Go Directly to Mail Jail

Learning Objectives

The purpose of this video exercise is to help students:

1. Appreciate some of the problems troubling the marriage of information and communications technology
2. Understand the relationship between technology and the performance of general activities in an office
3. Appreciate the need for businesses to balance the advantages and disadvantages of technology, especially in designing customer-service operations

Background Information

Today's demanding business environment continually forces companies to find ways not only to cut costs but to improve customer service at the same time. An increasingly popular means of achieving both goals is *voice mail*—a computer system capable of answering the telephone, directing calls to various destinations, and storing messages in individual "voice mailboxes." However, although voice messaging seems perfectly suited to the demands of contemporary business communications, it also seems to be capable of creating problems. Thus, communications experts suggest a number of ways for companies to ensure that voice-message technology does what it is supposed to do. Here are three of the most important:

■ Consultant Judith Cole notes that different callers have different needs. Thus, while a voice-messaging system might be appropriate for an accounting department, it would probably be an inappropriate system for taking customers complaints. "People calling a complaint center," she points out, "don't want to talk to a voice-mail system. They're already angry."

■ Similarly, if a company's telephone volume includes many callers from the general public or potential customers calling for the first time, its main telephone number should be answered by a person.

■ Finally, if customers are frustrated by unreturned calls, the fault probably does not lie with a company's technology. Experts stress the importance of basic telephone etiquette as a means of making voice-mail and other high-tech systems more people-friendly.

The Video

Video Source. "Voice Mail Jail," *Nightline*, May 9, 1994. In this segment, Bob Brown reports on the rapid growth of voice mail and voice-messaging technology, examining both the advantages and disadvantages offered by the new technology. While people who dislike voice mail express their frustrations about "talking to a machine," others extol its labor-saving virtues.

Discussion Questions

1. What experiences—positive or negative—have you had with voice-mail systems?

2. Besides those mentioned in the case, can you think of ways to improve voice-mail systems—and the ways they are used?

3. What benefits can voice-mail systems offer small businesses? Do you think the benefits outweigh the potential backlash from customers who react negatively to voice mail?

4. Although today's voice-mail systems are found mostly in businesses, experts predict that affordable home systems will soon be available. Compared to a standard answering machine, what advantages—indeed, what uses—might a home voice-mail system provide?

Follow-Up Assignment

Go to the library and investigate some other new communications and information technologies that will be available to businesses (and/or homes) in the future. What benefits and drawbacks do these technologies promise for both businesses and their customers?

"People calling a complaint center don't want to talk to a voice-mail system. They're already angry."

—Technology Consultant Judith Cole

From a Functional to a Team Approach at Lands' End
How to Reach a Consensus on Quality

Learning Objectives

The purpose of this video exercise is to help students:

1. Understand the purpose and function of formal teamwork within a larger organizational structure
2. Assess the ways in which organizational structure can affect employee attitudes and productivity
3. Appreciate some of the factors that affect a company's decisions about how to organize its operations

Background Information

In March 1994, certain key operations at Lands' End underwent a significant change. Up until then, different departments had been organized along *functional* lines: in other words, people who specialized in certain business functions—marketing, finance, quality control, and so on—were grouped with people performing "like" functions. But, says Joan Brown, Vice President for Quality Assurance, "while we were expected to work together as teams, it really wasn't working very well." Consequently, Lands' End changed the operations of its product development personnel. It shifted from a functional to a truly team-oriented approach.

Reorganization, of course, meant upheaval, both physical and psychological. Work space was reconfigured to accommodate the team concept, and team members had to adjust their attitudes toward both work space and privacy. Although the precise benefits in effectiveness and efficiency cannot yet be measured, the new team approach appears to be addressing the three main problems that it was designed to address. "Time to bring a new product to market has been reduced," reports Brown, "and communication has significantly improved. Even more importantly, everyone associated with the product now has the same goals."

The Video

Video Source. "Product Development at Lands' End: From a Functional to a Team Approach," *Prentice Hall Presents: On Location at Lands' End.* The video focuses on the sleepwear and swimwear team to show how teamwork has been integrated into product development operations at Lands' End. Members of the team recall the adjustments they had to make in order to adapt to the new form of organization and explain the advantages that it has brought to them in their jobs.

Discussion Questions

1. Briefly describe what you understand to be the key responsibility of each member of the sleepwear and swimwear team (copywriter, inventory manager, art director, quality assurance specialist, team manager, and team assistant).

2. In what ways does the change from functional to team approach probably affect each members' level of responsibility and authority?

3. Of the three types of organizational change—structural, technological, and people—people change is generally regarded as the hardest to implement. Judging from the video, how would you assess the effectiveness of this change at Lands' End?

4. In what ways does team organization probably contribute to quality planning and quality control? To inventory control? To improvements in system design? To worker motivation and quality of work life? To overall productivity?

Follow-Up Assignment

"None of our goals blended," recalls Joan Brown. "Inventory's goal, for example, was to get the product in the building and out the door to the customer. Quality, on the other hand, would stop anything from going out that did not meet its expectations—which ran headlong against the inventory manager's goal."

Your instructor will divide the class into product development teams like the one described in the video. First, each team will decide on the consumer product that it is developing; it can be anything that is of interest to everyone. On each team, members will assume the following roles: inventory manager, copywriter, art director, quality assurance specialist, and team manager. Your quality assurance specialist will meet briefly with your instructor to identify some quality control problem in the team's selected product; he or she will then explain the problem to the team. One team member should be appointed to take minutes. With all members contributing, the team will work to find a solution to its problem. Working from the minutes of its meeting, each team will report to the class on its meeting and its solution to its problem.

> **"Putting people on teams avoids those situations in which the quality person is miscommunicating with the merchandiser, who is miscommunicating with the vendor by sending out different information from what the inventory person wanted to communicate."**
>
> —Joan Brown
> *Vice President for Quality Assurance at Lands' End*

For Further Exploration

Visit Lands' End on the Internet at

http://www.landsend.com

Scroll down from the "Home" page to the link to "The Company." From there, take a trip to the "Internet Store," where you can select from such product categories as "Kids," "Men's Casual," and "Women's." To get a better idea of how teamwork is ultimately reflected in the copywriter's description of company products, browse the descriptions of several products. In what ways does the copywriter promote quality as a key function of a given Lands' End product?

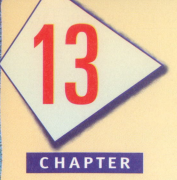

UNDERSTANDING MARKETING PROCESSES AND CONSUMER BEHAVIOR

Still Partying after All These Years?

THE SEIGE OF "FORT LIQUORDALE"

There's a certain irony in the struggle, but members of the Fort Lauderdale tourist industry aren't laughing about it. Charged with the mission of dispelling Fort Lauderdale's image as the destination of choice for party-going college students on spring break, tourism officials have the unenviable task of convincing baby-boomers that the new Fort Lauderdale is the ideal destination for family vacations. Unfortunately, the baby boomers the tourist industry hopes to attract to Fort Lauderdale's revitalized beaches, museums, performing arts center, and trendy shops are the party animals of old. Baby boomers, with a long collective memory, have adopted more sedate lifestyles and apparently refuse to believe that Fort Lauderdale has changed with them. Old impressions of Fort Lauderdale are dying hard—even among travel agents, who should know better. When Robert Poirier traveled to Chicago to promote his Fort Lauderdale hotel among travel agents, he repeatedly encountered a spring break mentality. "They still think we have students in Fort Lauderdale. It's terrible for the image to continue."

> **"They still think we have students in Fort Lauderdale. It's terrible for the image to continue."**
>
> **—Robert Poirier**
> *Fort Lauderdale hotel owner*

Fort Lauderdale's spring break image reached its peak during the mid-1980s, when the city attracted some 350,000 students. A 1986 *Time* magazine article about the phenomenon began this way:

Every year just before Easter, they flock to Florida's beaches, hundreds of thousands of them, bikinis and libidos at the ready. After a week of the unimaginable and the unmentionable (to parents), spending up to $300 million on their bacchanal, they return to their college campuses, survivors of spring break. Says Dave Mazur, a Canisius College freshman: "You have to make the trip [to Fort Lauderdale] at least once. It's what everybody says it is—beaches, beer, bikinis . . . , sand, surf, and sex."

Not surprisingly, this image of a mecca for debauchery drove families and upscale tourists away—a trend that cost the city hundreds of millions of dollars in lost tourist revenues. To attract an older, more sophisticated tourist population, city leaders spent nearly $300 million, including $26 million to modernize the beach front, and waged a variety of unsuccessful promotional campaigns to change public perception. But officials quickly learned that money—even combined with real changes—does not necessarily buy consumer acceptance. Informal polls of potential vacationers showed that ingrained perceptions tended to persist.

Realizing that they were stuck—at least temporarily—with the city's spring break image, Fort Lauderdale tourism officials finally accepted the fact that their best hope of changing public perceptions was to confront the problem head-on. Thus, in 1996 they launched a $1.65 million "Was/Is" advertising campaign designed to contrast the old and new images of the city. One ad in the campaign, for example, contrasts beer-guzzling spring breakers (yesterday's image) with well-dressed sophisticates enjoying cocktails at a beach-front restaurant (today's image). Stan Harris, president of the advertising agency that developed the new campaign, explains that its goal is "to say to people, if you're thinking about what was, you need to think about what is."

Like many for-profit organizations, the city of Fort Lauderdale turned to marketing to create a new image and encourage consumer acceptance. To change long-held negative perceptions, officials identified a target market, conducted promotional trips, developed new promotional strategies, and created advertising campaigns. By focusing on the learning objectives of this chapter, you will gain a better understanding of such marketing activities and the ways in which marketing influences consumer purchases.

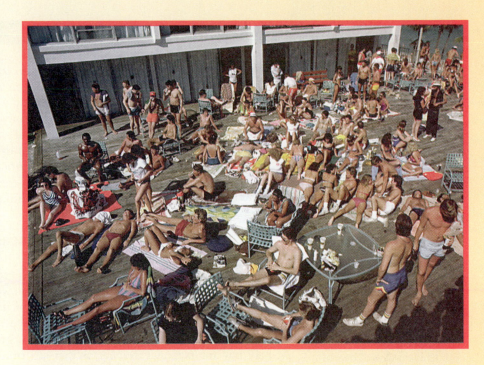

After reading this chapter, you should be able to

1. Define *marketing*

2. Describe the five forces that constitute the *external marketing environment*

3. Explain *market segmentation* and show how it is used in *target marketing*

4. Describe the key factors that influence the *consumer buying process*

5. Discuss the three categories of *organizational markets* and explain how *organizational buying behavior* differs from consumer buying behavior

Continued on page 349

■ WHAT IS MARKETING?

What do you think of when you think of *marketing?* Most people usually think of advertising for something like detergent or soft drinks. But marketing encompasses a much wider range of activities. The American Marketing Association has formally defined **marketing** as "the process of planning and executing the conception, pricing, promotion, and distribution of ideas, goods, and services to create exchanges that satisfy individual and organizational objectives."[1] In this section, we discuss the multifaceted activity of marketing by exploring this definition. We then explore the marketing environment and the development of marketing strategy. We focus on the four activities—developing, pricing, promoting, and placing products—that make up the *marketing mix*.

Marketing: Goods, Services, and Ideas

marketing
The process of planning and executing the conception, pricing, promotion, and distribution of ideas, goods, and services to create exchanges that satisfy individual and organizational objectives

The marketing of tangible goods is obvious in everyday life. You walk into a department store and a woman with a clipboard asks if you would like to try a new cologne. A pharmaceutical company proclaims the virtues of its new cold medicine. Your local auto dealer offers an economy car at an economy price. These products—the cologne, the cold medicine, and the car—are all **consumer goods:** products that you, the consumer, may buy for personal use. Firms that sell products to consumers for personal consumption are engaged in *consumer marketing*.

consumer goods
Products purchased by consumers for personal use

Marketing also applies to **industrial goods:** products used by companies to produce other products. Conveyors, surgical instruments, and earth movers are industrial goods, as are components and raw materials like transistors, integrated circuits, coal, steel, and unformed plastic. Firms that sell their products to other manufacturers are engaged in *industrial marketing*.

industrial goods
Products purchased by companies to produce other products

Marketing techniques can also be applied to **services:** intangible products, such as time, expertise or an activity that can be purchased. Service marketing has become a major area of growth in the U.S. Insurance companies, airlines, investment counselors, health clinics, and public accountants all engage in service marketing, either to individuals or to other companies.

services
Intangible products, such as time, expertise, or an activity, that can be purchased

Marketing can also be applied to ideas. For example, television advertising and other promotional activities have made the cartoon dog McGruff a symbol of crime prevention. Other advertisements stress the importance of driving only when sober and smoking.

Each of the advertisements in Figure 13.1 provides information about specific goods, services, or ideas—and, in some cases, combinations of all three. The ad for a Rolex watch, for example, "targets" a group of consumers whose needs are likely to be satisfied by a fine watch. The Visa Gold card offers a variety of travel-related services ranging from car rental upgrades to helicopter transport from the airport. The ad for the product works in conjunction with a marketing campaign conducted by the Monaco Government Tourist Office. The Public Broadcasting Service markets itself as a provider of services inspired by innovative ideas, such as social responsibility for making information and entertainment accessible to the hearing impaired.

Relationship Marketing   Although marketing often focuses on single transactions for products, services, or ideas, a longer-term perspective has become equally important for successful marketing. Rather than emphasizing a single transaction, **relationship marketing** emphasizes lasting relationships with customers and suppliers. Not surprisingly, stronger relationships—including stronger economic and social ties—can result in greater long-term satisfaction and retention of customers. Commercial banks, for example, feature "loyalty banking" programs that offer *economic* incentives to en-

relationship marketing
Marketing strategy that emphasizes lasting relationships with customers and suppliers

The legends who compete in the Senior Open prove that golf is truly a lifetime game.

When a golfer like Arnold Palmer plays the seventy-two holes that make up the championship, he's just as charged up as he was at Cherry Hills in 1960 when he won the U.S. Open.

In 1980, the United States Golf Association established the Senior Open, recognizing the growing popularity of senior golf both at the amateur and the professional level. Six hundred thirty-one players entered that first championship, which was played on the East Course of the famed Winged Foot Golf Club.

The champion was Roberto De Vicenzo, a national hero in his native Argentina and winner of the

Arnold Palmer, winner of the 1981 U.S. Senior Open.

Rolex and the Senior Open: The Classics Endure.

As "Arnie's Army" cheered from the sidelines, Palmer won a tense three-man play-off.

Today, the U.S. Senior Open ranks as one of golf's most anticipated events, both by the fans and by the players themselves. More than two thousand golfers are expected to enter this year's event. Like Palmer, players in the Senior Open have a classic style—they continue to delight fans year after year.

Thus it's not surprising that so many players wear a classic. Rolex.

Cherry Hills Country Club, site of the 1993 U.S. Senior Open.

1967 British Open. De Vicenzo finished with a one over par score of 285.

The second Senior Open was won by another national hero, Arnold Palmer.

ROLEX

Rolex Oyster Perpetual Day-Date Chronometer in 18kt gold with matching President bracelet.
Write for brochure. Rolex Watch U.S.A., Inc., Dept. RLX, Rolex Building, 665 Fifth Avenue, New York, N.Y. 10022-5383.
Rolex, ♛, Oyster Perpetual, Day-Date and President are trademarks.

FIGURE 13.1A ◆ Marketing: Goods, Services, and Ideas

courage longer-lasting relationships. Customers who purchase more of the bank's products—checking accounts, savings accounts, and loans—accumulate credits toward free or reduced-price services, such as free travelers checks or lower interest rates. Harley-Davidson offers *social* incentives through the Harley Owners Group (H.O.G.)—the largest motorcycle club in the world, with nearly 300,000 members and approximately 900 dealer-sponsored chapters worldwide. H.O.G., explain Harley marketers, "is dedicated to building customers for life. H.O.G. fosters long-term commitments to the sport of motorcycling by providing opportunities for our customers to bond with other riders and develop long-term friendships."[2]

The Marketing Environment

Marketing plans, decisions, and strategies are not determined unilaterally by any business—not even by marketers as experienced and influential as Coca-Cola and Procter & Gamble. Rather, they are strongly influenced by powerful outside forces. As you can

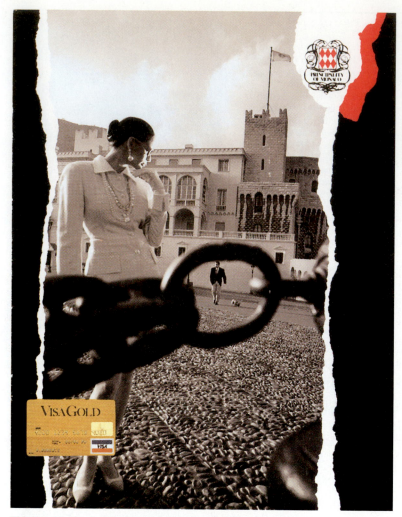

FIGURE 13.1B ◆ **Marketing Goods, Services, and Ideas**

external environment
Outside factors that influence marketing programs by posing opportunities or threats

see in Figure 13.2, any marketing program must recognize the outside factors that comprise a company's **external environment.** In this section, we describe five of these environmental factors: the *political/legal, social/cultural, technological, economic,* and *competitive environments.*

Political and Legal Environment

Political activities, both foreign and domestic, have profound effects on business. For example, Congressional hearings on tobacco, budgetary decisions on national defense expenditures, and enactment of the Clean Air Act have substantially determined the destinies of entire industries.

To help shape their companies' futures, marketing managers try to maintain favorable political/legal environments in several ways. For example, to gain public support for their products and activities, marketing uses advertising campaigns for public awareness on issues of local, regional, or national import. They also contribute to political candidates (although there are legal restrictions on how much they can contribute). Frequently, they support the activities of PACs, or political action committees, maintained by their respective industries. Such activities sometimes result in favorable laws and regulations and may even open up new international business opportunities.

Social and Cultural Environment

More women are entering the workforce, the number of single-parent families is increasing, food preferences and physical activities reflect the growing concern for healthful life styles, violent crimes are on the increase,

Millions of Americans watch us with their ears.

Secret Service agents swarmed. Crowds shivered. Cameras rolled. And the Governor of Arkansas took a presidential oath.

As expected, January 21, 1993 was filled with maximum media fanfare.

Only this inauguration was different. Because 6.5 million blind and visually-impaired people had the opportunity to experience the festivities live, on TV.

For the first time ever, a nationally-broadcast news event was made accessible to the blind. Brought to life exclusively through the Descriptive Video Services of Public Television.

A new TV format that provides added narration during pauses in dialogue.

Illuminating scene changes, actions and gestures. ("Mr. Clinton is now placing his hand on the Bible.")

Currently available to 58% of all households, DVS will soon roll out across the country. The latest in a series of innovations pioneered by Public Television on behalf of the underserved.

Innovations we started back in 1972, by introducing closed-captioning for the deaf and hearing-impaired.

Innovations we continue today — by offering second languages on select shows, so foreign-speaking viewers can also enjoy our programs.

Because no one in society should be left in the dark.

PUBLIC TELEVISION
Keep us in mind.

FIGURE 13.1C ◆ **Marketing: Goods, Services, and Ideas**

and the growing recognition of cultural diversity continues. These and other issues reflect the values, beliefs, and ideas that form the fabric of U.S. society today. These broad attitudes toward issues have direct effects on business. Today, for example, as we continue to insist on a "greener" America, we have seen the demise of freon in air conditioners and increased reliance on recycling materials in the goods we consume.

FIGURE 13.2 ◆ **The External Marketing Environment**

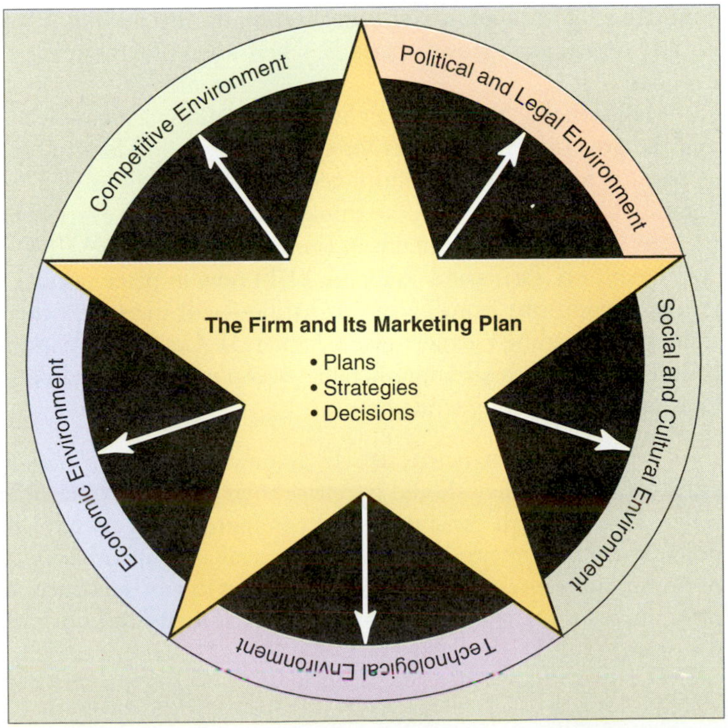

Competitive Environment

Political and Legal Environment

The Firm and Its Marketing Plan
• Plans
• Strategies
• Decisions

Economic Environment

Social and Cultural Environment

Technological Environment

By the same token, the need to recognize social values stimulates marketers to take fresh looks at the ways they conduct their business—developing and promoting new products for both consumers and industrial customers. For example, there are now more than 5 million female golfers spending nearly $170 million on equipment, most of which, up to now, has been modeled after men's gear. Responding to the growth in the number of female golfers, Spalding has introduced a line of golf gear designed specifically for women. Such equipment has entailed new methods for advertising, promoting, and distributing products to meet the emerging preferences of women golfers.[3]

Technological Environment Consider the phenomenon of DNA "fingerprinting." Just about everyone is aware of its availability to law enforcement officials. Bear in mind that it is part of a new industry that involves biological science and laboratory analysis and instrumentation as well as criminology. DNA fingerprinting, then, is a product. Along with its technical developments, therefore, it involves marketing decisions, like pricing and promotion. This has been the case with thousands of technological breakthroughs in such fields as genetics, electronics, aeronautics, medicine, information sciences, communications systems, and transportation.

New technologies affect marketing in several ways. They create new goods (the satellite dish) and services (home television shopping). New products, of course, make some existing products obsolete (compact discs are replacing audio tapes), and many of them change our values and lifestyles. In turn, they often stimulate new goods and services not directly related to the new technology itself. Cellular phones, for example, not only facilitate business communication but free up time for recreation and leisure.

Economic Environment Economic conditions determine spending patterns by consumers, businesses, and governments. They thus influence every marketer's plans for product offerings, pricing, and promotional strategies. Among the more significant economic variables, marketers are concerned with inflation, interest rates, recession, and recovery. In other words, they must monitor the general business cycle, which typically features a pattern of transition from periods of prosperity to recession to recovery (return to prosperity). Not surprisingly, consumer spending increases as "consumer confidence" in economic conditions grows during periods of prosperity. Spending decreases during low-growth periods, when unemployment rises and purchasing power declines.

Traditionally, analysis of economic conditions focused on the national economy and the government's policies for controlling or moderating it. Increasingly, however, as nations form more and more economic connections, the "global economy" is becoming more prominent in the thinking of marketers everywhere. With new pacts like the 1993 North American Free Trade Agreement (NAFTA) and the 1994 General Agreement on Tariffs and Trade (GATT) now in place, global economic conditions—indeed, conditions from nation to nation—will directly influence the economic fortunes of all trading partners (see Chapter 3). Certainly, marketers must now consider this new—and perhaps unpredictable—economic variable in developing both domestic and foreign marketing strategies.

Competitive Environment In a competitive environment, marketers must convince buyers that they should purchase their products rather than those of some other seller. Because both consumers and commercial buyers have limited resources, every dollar spent on one product is no longer available for other purchases. Each marketing program, therefore, seeks to make its product the most attractive. Theoretically, a failed program loses the buyer's dollar forever (or at least until it is time for the next purchase decision).

TRENDS & CHALLENGES

IN THE NEWS: "THE WORLD IS NOT GOING TO BE THE SAME IN 30 YEARS"

Over the years, we have learned to read business news with an eye toward nuances—small but significant differences. We have come to realize that an author's word choices can tell us a great deal about a situation and its broader impact. Consider, for example, a couple of recent articles—one in the *New York Times*, the other in the the *Wall Street Journal*—about the growth of both the Hispanic population and Hispanic-owned business in the United States. Wrote the *Times* article in its lead sentence (the italics are ours):

> Fueled by immigration and higher birth rates among Hispanic women, the United States is undergoing a *profound* demographic shift, and by the middle of the next century only about half of the population will be non-Hispanic whites, the Census Bureau predicted.

Four months later, the *Wall Street Journal* ran a story with the following lead (the italics are ours):

> The number of Hispanic-owned businesses in the U.S. *surged* 76% in five years, proliferating nearly three times as fast as businesses overall, the Commerce Department reported.

When publications known for normally noncommittal news coverage use adjectives like *profound* and verbs like *surged*, they are telling us that something important is going on. In this case, they are alerting us, among other things, to the opportunities to be found in doing business with Hispanic-owned small companies as we approach, enter, and become comfortably established in the twenty-first century.

According to the U.S. Department of the Census, the demographic shift in the population will be "profound" in the next 50 years. By 2050, Hispanics will make up 24.5 percent of the population, up from 10.2 percent in 1996. The annual growth rate of the Hispanic population is expected to be 2 percent through the year 2030. To put this growth in perspective, consider the fact that even at the height of the baby boom explosion in the late 1940s and early 1950s, the country's annual population increase never reached 2 percent. Demographers, it seems, are alerting us to the enormous importance of such change. Says Gregory Spencer, Director of the Census Bureau's Population Projections Branch, "The world is not going to be the same in thirty years as it is now."

Neither is the world of small business. The Commerce Department's report of a 76-percent surge in Hispanic-owned businesses is particularly striking. In the same five-year period, the total number of all U.S. businesses, excluding certain types of corporations, rose only 26 percent. By the end of 1992, the latest year for which data are available, there were 862,695 Hispanic-owned businesses in the United States, with receipts totalling $76.8 billion. Despite their surge in numbers, Hispanic-owned businesses remain relatively small—average annual receipts total only $94,000, as compared to $193,000 for all U.S. businesses (excluding certain types of corporations). Only 9,200 of these Hispanic-owned companies had revenues of $1 million or more.

Marketing successfully to Hispanic-owned businesses requires a targeted approach that identifies pockets of Hispanic business activity as well as the specific cultural ties of population subgroups. According to Commerce Department data, organizational marketers should focus their efforts in those states where Hispanic-owned businesses are prevalent, including California, Texas, and Florida. The data also show that the market of all Hispanic-owned businesses is divided into distinct ethnic segments, including ethnic Mexicans, ethnic Cubans, and ethnic Puerto Ricans, among others. Each group has its own cultural identity and should be approached with that identity in mind. Data show that the greatest marketing opportunity lies among ethnic Mexicans, who own more small businesses than any other Hispanic group. In 1992, for example, ethnic Mexicans owned nearly four times as many businesses as ethnic Cubans.

By studying the competition, marketers determine how best to position their own products for three specific types of competition:

substitute product
Product that is dissimilar to those of competitors but that can fulfill the same need

brand competition
Competitive marketing that appeals to consumer perceptions of similar products

international competition
Competitive marketing of domestic products against foreign products

■ **Substitute products** are dissimilar from those of competitors but can fulfill the same need. For example, your cholesterol level may be controlled with either a physical fitness program or a drug regimen. The fitness program and the drugs compete as substitute products.

■ **Brand competition** occurs between similar products, such as the auditing services provided by large accounting firms like Ernst & Young and KPMG Peat Marwick. The competition is based on buyers' perceptions of the benefits of products offered by particular companies.

■ **International competition** matches the products of domestic marketers against those of foreign competitors—a flight on Swissair versus Delta Airlines. The intensity of international competition has of course been heightened by the formation of alliances like the European Community and NAFTA.

The Marketing Mix

marketing mix
The combination of product, pricing, promotion, and distribution strategies used to market products

In planning and implementing strategies, marketing managers rely on four basic components. These elements, often called the "Four P's" of marketing, constitute the **marketing mix.** In this section, we describe each of the following activities:

■ Product
■ Pricing
■ Promotion
■ Place

Product   Marketing begins with a **product**—a good, a service, or an idea designed to fill a consumer need. Conceiving and developing new products is a constant challenge for marketers, who must always consider the factor of change. Marketers, for example, must consider changing technology, changing consumer wants and needs, and changing economic conditions.

Meeting consumer needs, then, often means changing existing products. In the clothing industry, for example, manufacturers must be alert to changes in fashion, which often occur rapidly and unpredictably. This is also true in electronics technology, where there are virtually constant advances.

■ Zebra Technologies Corp., for example, long enjoyed a reputation for manufacturing high-quality, top-of-the-line bar code printers. Zebra also saw sales potential in the low-end market but did not want to market a product that would tarnish its reputation or "cannibalize" sales from existing printers. Zebra thus developed a no-frills version, the new Stripes printer, to complement its faster, more versatile, more expensive model. Stripes was an immediate success in its own right—boosting sales by 47 percent the first year—and did not compete with Zebra's own high-end model.[4] ▼

Companies may also develop new products and enter markets in which they have not previously competed. For example, Daka International has an established winner with its Fuddruckers restaurants, which claim "the world's greatest hamburger." In 1988, Daka expanded into the food service business and now runs cafeterias and concession stands at more than 600 hospitals, universities, and corporations. With customers like the Smithsonian Institution and the University of Florida, revenues from its food service business have grown to 65 percent of Daka's total revenues.[5]

Product Differentiation. Often producers develop new or "improved" products for the sake of distinguishing them on the marketplace. **Product differentiation** is the creation of a product or product image that differs enough from existing products to attract consumers. For example, the popularity of Campbell's Soups is based, in part, on successful differentiation. In 1995, the company changed the packaging and ingredient mix for some of its classic soup lines, updating the time-honored red and white label with color pictures of what's inside. The label for condensed chicken noodle soup added a prominent announcement: "Now! 33% more chicken meat." In an even riskier move, Campbell's famous slogan

In developing a new bar-code printer, Zebra Technologies had to stress two elements of the marketing mix. First, because its main goal was a larger share of the lower end of the market, Zebra had to build a machine that would price for $500 less than its high-end model. Second, the new product had to be differentiated from the faster, more flexible model—without sacrificing the company's widely recognized level of quality. The result: the new Stripes printer is a high-quality printer minus a few top-of-the-line features. Moreover, because it cannot be upgraded, it cannot compete with Zebra's existing product.

336 PART 6 • UNDERSTANDING PRINCIPLES OF MARKETING

was changed from "M'm-m'm good" to "M'm-m'm better." The reasoning behind these changes? According to Marty Thrasher, the President of Campbell's United States soup business, "We needed to get noticed in a new way, and we needed to break through." Renewing the emphasis on the company's differentiated product line seemed to be the most logical strategy.[6]

> ## "We needed to get noticed in a new way, and we needed to break through."
>
> —Marty Thrasher
> *President of Campbell Soup's U.S. operations*
> *on the decision to stress product differentiation*

When successful, product differentiation always entails a change in the way customers respond to the product. For example, early kitchen and laundry appliances were available only in white. Frigidaire capitalized on this situation by offering comparably priced, equally efficient appliances in colors.

Services can also be sources of differentiation. For example, Weyerhauser Co. developed a computer system that allows customers at retail home centers and lumber yards to custom design decks and shelving. As a result, the company has differentiated its commodity two-by-fours by turning them into premium products.

Pricing *Pricing* a product—selecting the most appropriate price at which to sell it—is often a balancing act. On the one hand, prices must support a variety of costs—the organization's operating, administrative, and research costs as well as marketing costs, such as advertising and sales salaries. On the other hand, prices cannot be so high that consumers turn to competing products. Successful pricing means finding a profitable middle ground between these two requirements. For Chaparral Steel, for instance, price is actually a competitive weapon. Chaparral's sales volume is growing because the company provides a variety of steel products at prices lower than its competitors can offer.

Both low- and high-price strategies can be effective in different situations. Low prices, for example, generally lead to larger sales volumes. High prices usually limit market size, but they increase profits per unit. High prices may also attract customers by implying that a product is of especially high quality. We will discuss pricing in more detail in Chapter 14.

Promotion The most highly visible component of the marketing mix is no doubt *promotion*, which refers to techniques for communicating information about products. We will describe promotional activities more fully in Chapter 14. Here we briefly describe the most important promotional tools:

- *Advertising.* Advertising is any form of paid nonpersonal communication used by an identified sponsor to persuade or inform potential buyers about a product. For example, NationsBank, a financial adviser to corporations, reaches its customer audience by advertising its services in *Fortune* magazine.
- *Personal selling.* Many products—for example, insurance, clothing, and stereo equipment—are best promoted through personal selling, or person-to-person sales. Industrial goods, however, receive the bulk of personal selling. When companies buy from other companies, purchasing agents and others who need technical and detailed information are usually referred to the selling company's sales representatives.

- *Sales promotions.* Relatively inexpensive items are often marketed through sales promotions, which involve one-time direct inducements to buyers. Premiums (usually free gifts), coupons, and package inserts are all sales promotions meant to tempt consumers to buy products.
- *Public relations.* Public relations includes all communication efforts directed at building good will. It seeks to build favorable attitudes toward the organization and its products. Ronald McDonald Houses are a famous example of public relations. *Publicity* also refers to a firm's efforts to communicate to the public, usually through mass media. Publicity, however, is not paid for by the firm, nor does the firm control its content. Publicity, therefore, can sometimes hurt a business.

Place (Distribution)   In the marketing mix, *place* refers to **distribution.** Placing a product in the proper outlet—say, a retail store—requires decisions about a number of distribution activities, all of which are concerned with getting the product from the producer to the consumer. For example, transportation options include railroad, truck, air freight, and pipelines. Decisions about warehousing and inventory control are also distribution decisions.

distribution
Part of the marketing mix concerned with getting products from producers to consumers

Firms must also make decisions about the *channels* through which they distribute their products. Many manufacturers, for instance, sell to other companies that, in turn, distribute the goods to retailers. Del Monte, for example, produces canned foods that it sells to Evco Wholesale Foods and other distributors, who then sell the food to grocery stores. Other companies sell directly to major retailers like Sears, Wal-Mart, Kmart, and Safeway. Still others sell directly to final consumers. We will explain distribution decisions further in Chapter 15.

■ TARGET MARKETING AND MARKET SEGMENTATION

Marketers recognized long ago that products and services cannot be "all things to all people." Buyers have different tastes, interests, goals, lifestyles, and so on. Among other things, the emergence of the marketing concept and the recognition of consumer needs and wants led marketers to think in terms of *target marketing*. **Target markets** are groups of people with similar wants and needs. For most companies, selecting target markets is the first step in the marketing strategy.

target market
Group of people that has similar wants and needs and that can be expected to show interest in the same products

Target marketing clearly requires **market segmentation**—dividing a market into categories of customer types or "segments." Once they have identified market segments, companies may adopt a variety of strategies. Some firms try to market products to more than one segment of the population. For example, General Motors offers compact cars, vans, trucks, luxury cars, and sports cars with various features and at various price levels. GM's strategy is to provide an automobile for nearly every segment of the market.

market segmentation
Process of dividing a market into categories of customer types

In contrast, some businesses appeal to the optimal number of market segments by offering fewer products. *Reader's Digest* is an example of a single product that reaches several market segments (and is currently seeking to broaden its range). The *Digest*'s total audience of more than 50 million includes a younger-adults segment (25 percent of its readership), a computer owners segment (45 percent), a smaller brides-to-be segment (3 percent), and a segment consisting of professionals/managers (17 percent). To increase its readership, the magazine is trying to reach more younger people by experimenting with new advertisements, integrating more photographs and contemporary graphics, and incorporating highly visible biographies and photos of the *Digest*'s prominent contributing writers, many of whom are popular among families with parents under 50. This strategy, according to publisher Gary G. Coleman, means reaching so-called "misperceivers"—people who do not know what a typical issue of *Reader's Digest* currently offers. "It's very much on our radar screen," says Coleman, "to say, 'Let's do something about the people who really don't understand us.' So we're making painstaking efforts to listen to America. We must get a handle on what their thoughts are."[7]

> **"We're making painstaking efforts to listen to America. We must get a handle on what their thoughts are."**
>
> —Gary G. Coleman
> *Publisher of* Reader's Digest

Table 13.1 shows how the radio market might be segmented by a marketer of home electronics equipment. Note that segmentation is a strategy for analyzing consumers, not products. The analysis in Table 13.1, for example, identifies consumer users— joggers, commuters, travelers. Only indirectly, then, does it focus on the uses of the product itself. In marketing, the process of fixing, adapting, and communicating the nature of the product itself is called *positioning*.[8]

Identifying Market Segments

By definition, the members of a market segment must share some common traits that will affect their purchasing decisions. In identifying market segments, researchers look at a number of different influences on consumer behavior. Four of the most important are *geographic*, *demographic*, *psychographic*, and *product use variables*.

Geographic Variables   In many cases, buying decisions are affected by the places that people call home. The heavy rainfall in Washington State, for instance, means that inhabitants purchase more umbrellas than do people living in the Sun Belt. Urban res-

TABLE 13.1 ◆ **Possible Segmentation of the Radio Market**

Segmentation by	Product/Target Market
Age	Inexpensive, unbreakable, portable models for young children
	Inexpensive equipment—possibly portable—for teens
	Moderate-to-expensive equipment for adults
Consumer attitude	Sophisticated components for audio buffs
	All-in-one units in furniture cabinets for those concerned with room appearance
Product use	Miniature models for joggers and commuters
	"Boom box" portables for taking outdoors
	Car stereo systems for traveling
	Components and all-in-one units for home use
Location	Battery-powered models for use where electricity is unavailable
	AC current for North American users
	DC current for other users

idents have little use for four-wheel-drive vehicles, and sailboats sell better along the coasts than in the Great Plains. **Geographic variables** are the geographical units—from countries to neighborhoods—that may be considered in developing a segmentation strategy.

These patterns affect decisions about the marketing mix for a huge range of products. For example, consider a project to market down parkas in rural Minnesota. Demand will be high and price competition intense. Local newspaper advertising may be very effective, and the best retail location may be one that is easily reached from several small towns. Marketing the same parkas in downtown Honolulu would be considerably more challenging.

Although the marketability of some products is geographically sensitive, others benefit from nearly universal acceptance. Coca-Cola, for example, derives more than 80 percent of its income from international sales. Coke is the market leader in Great Britain, Germany, Japan, Brazil, and Spain. Pepsi's international sales equal only about 5 percent of Coke's. In fact, Coke's chief competitor in most countries is some local soft drink, not Pepsi, which earns 80 percent of its income at home.[9]

Clearly, marketers must keep track of changes in geographic patterns. The U.S. population, for instance, has been moving south and west for the past few decades. Revitalization of urban areas has also led to marketing changes, particularly in deciding where to locate stores.

Demographic Variables   **Demographic variables** describe populations, identifying such traits as age, income, gender, ethnic background, marital status, race, religion, and social class. Table 13.2 lists some possible demographic breakdowns. Depending on the marketer's purpose, a segment could be a single classification (*aged 20–34*) or a combination of categories (*aged 20–34, married with children, earning $25,000–$34,999*). For example, in its attempts to reach younger readers (the median age of its readers was 47 in 1996), *Reader's Digest's* targets advertising at specific demographic groups—especially families with parents under the age of 50 who have children at home and households with incomes of more than $75,000.[10]

geographic variables
Geographical units that may be considered in developing a segmentation strategy

demographic variables
Characteristics of populations that may be considered in developing a segmentation strategy

TABLE 13.2 ◆ Demographic Variables

Age	Under 5; 5–11; 12–19; 20–34; 35–49; 50–64; 65+
Education	Grade school or less; some high school; graduated high school; some college; college degree; advanced degree
Family life cycle	Young single; young married without children; young married with children; older married with children under 18; older married without children under 18; older single; other
Family size	1, 2–3, 4–5, 6+
Income	Under $9,000; $9,000–$14,999; $15,000–$24,999; $25,000–$34,999; $35,000–$45,000; over $45,000
Nationality	Including, but not limited to, African, American, Asian, British, Eastern European, French, German, Irish, Italian, Latin American, Middle Eastern, and Scandinavian
Race	Including, but not limited to, American Indian, Asian, black, and white
Religion	Including, but not limited to, Buddhist, Catholic, Hindu, Jewish, Moslem, and Protestant
Sex	Male, female

Naturally, demographics affect marketing decisions. For example, a number of general consumption characteristics can be attributed to certain age groups *(18–25, 26–35, 36–45,* and so on). Marketers can thus divide markets into age groups as they develop specific marketing plans.

In addition, marketers can use demographics to identify trends that might shape future spending patterns. Nursing care and funeral service companies, for example, are expanding offerings in response to projected changes in the U.S. population in the years 1995 to 2005. Those changes are shown in Figure 13.3. As you can see, the number of people between ages 60 and 89—and even the number of those in their 90s—is expected to rise. So-called "death care" companies, such as Stewart Enterprises and Service Corp. International, are preparing for the upturn by acquiring additional cemetary and funeral homes that give customers one-stop shopping.

Similar data indicate that the fastest-growing segment of America's population during the next decade will be aging baby boomers, the 45–60 age group. "You can see the trends working through the population," observes an economist at Merrill Lynch. "Fifteen years ago, openings at ski resorts and tennis courts were hard to come by. Now it's tee times at golf clubs." The resulting growth trends will be reflected in such industries as investment services, where boomers will be placing more of their savings in order to prepare for their retirement years. Similarly, mutual funds, financial services, insurance, and brokerage firms are expected to see greater demand for their products among this massive age group.[11]

> ### "Fifteen years ago, openings at ski resorts and tennis courts were hard to come by. Now it's tee times at golf clubs."
>
> —Donald Straszheim
> *Merrill Lynch Economist on the aging of the baby boom generation*

FIGURE 13.3 ◆ **Changes in the U.S. Population, 1995–2005**

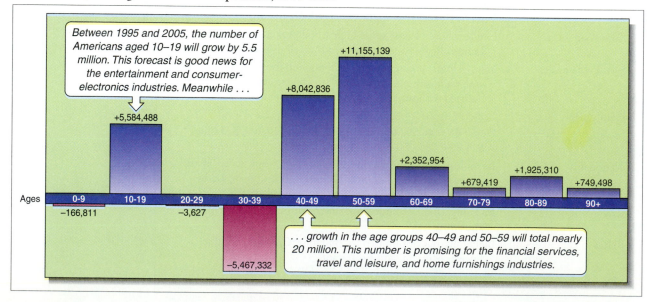

TRENDS & CHALLENGES

WHERE'S THE MARKET FOR SKINNY TIES AND SEE-THROUGH TRACK SHOES?

To the delight of marketers, today's teenagers are big spenders. In fact, they are spending more than teenagers ever have. The 29 million 12- to 19-year-olds in the United States made $109 billion in purchases in 1995, up from $99 billion in 1994.

In demographic terms, America's teen population started growing in 1992, following a 15-year period of stagnation and decline called the "baby bust." The U.S. Census Bureau now predicts that this segment will grow twice as fast as the overall population. When the growth wave peaks in 2010, there will be about 35 million teens. On a worldwide basis, the teenage population has grown to nearly 1 billion. This statistic, combined with the spending power, attitudes, and interests shared by today's teens, means that many companies are learning as much as they can about teenage buying habits.

What do marketers already know about today's teenagers? According to a recent survey of 25,000 adolescents in 41 countries, teenagers are comfortable enough with computers to be the primary force behind family technology purchases. They are also passionate about sports (especially basketball and soccer), watch about six hours of television a day, and love MTV and music videos. Companies like Levi Strauss and Procter & Gamble recognize MTV's extraordinary power in the teen market and consider it a perfect vehicle for reaching teens worldwide.

Apparel and related items (including athletic shoes) lead the way in attracting over $6 billion in annual sales. A survey conducted by Teenage Research Unlimited, a marketing research firm, reveals some additional facts about teenage spending:

- With the increase in single-parent and dual-income families, teenagers are playing a larger role than ever in household purchases. With 83 percent of all teens shopping for at least some family groceries, food manufacturers are now designing packages with teens in mind. According to Audrey Guskey, a Duquesne University marketing expert, "the packaging of supermarket products is being made brighter to catch the eye of young shoppers."

- Teens are attracted to expensive brands, including Tommy Hilfiger and Calvin Klein. Calvin Klein's success in this market was boosted by his controversial 1995 ads showing teenagers in provocative poses. Although many adults considered the ads virtually pornographic, teens liked them and paid greater attention to the Calvin Klein brand.
- With 42 percent of all surveyed teens calling Nike a "cool" brand, no company comes close to Nike's brand recognition.
- Teens pay for their purchases with their allowances and with the money they earn doing part-time work. With half of all 16- to 19-year-olds holding jobs, teens average an astounding $64 a week in income. Most teens spend 84 percent of their money on food, movies, and compact discs. They hoard their meager savings only until they can afford to buy such big ticket items as sound systems and rock concert tickets.

Companies that want to get in sync with teen tastes are conducting even more extensive market research to better understand what 13- to 19-year-olds want and need. For example, BSB Worldwide, a New York–based advertising agency, videotaped teenagers' bedrooms in 25 countries. Researchers reported remarkable similarities in what they found—Nike shoes, for instance, and Levi's jeans and Sega video games. Not surprisingly, marketing programs at companies in these industries reflect an intense interest in young people. For example, Reebok is trying to capitalize on teens' interest in sports, especially soccer. The company recently rolled out a line of soccer gear, with ads in Latin America and Europe featuring local soccer stars.

Marketers are also monitoring teen trendsetters to stay on the cutting edge of changing fashions. Corporate scouts are following teen trendsetters to rock concerts, clubs, and restaurants in an effort to spot products that are likely to sell to more mainstream buyers. "Now," admits one product director at Reebok, "we're watching kids, whereas we used to watch designers." According to Sputnik Inc., a New York–based market research company that specializes in the buying habits of teen trendsetters, the following trends are now considered cool:

- Girls in dominatrix clothing
- Bright skeleton prints
- Comic graphic T-shirts
- Reflective trim on field-sports shoes

- Hair sectioned into little wrapped ponytails that look like rockets projecting from the head
- Guys in vinyl skirts
- See-through track shoes
- Suspenders with African print shirts
- Military shoes or traditional Oxfords mixed with Malcolm X look
- Skinny ties, white shirts, basic black pants and jackets

At the same time, however, although marketers are increasingly targeting cutting-edge teen fashions, there is danger in assuming that all teens will embrace every trend. While the trendiest teens, according to one market researcher, may "experiment with ten trends, only one will cross over" to a mainstream market.

"Now we're watching kids, whereas we used to watch designers."

—Ruth A. Davis
Product Director at Reebok International

Psychographic Variables

psychographic variables
Consumer characteristics, such as lifestyles, opinions, interests, and attitudes, that may be considered in developing a segmentation strategy

Members of a market can also be segmented according to such **psychographic variables** as lifestyles, opinions, interests, and attitudes. One company that has combined demographic and psychographic variables to get a better picture of its market is Starbucks Coffee Co., which has expanded its original coffee bean shops into coffee bars. Among the trends observed by Starbucks, for example, is the nationwide push for sobriety. Young urbanites out for a night on the town are frequently looking for an alternative to alcohol. Starbucks fans enjoy the stylish coffee bars with lattes, mochas, and espresso drinks prepared by skilled "baristas."[12]

Psychographics are particularly important to marketers because, unlike demographics and geographics, they can sometimes be changed by marketing efforts. For example, many companies have succeeded in changing at least some consumers' opinions by running ads highlighting products that have been improved directly in response to consumer desires. For example, many companies in Poland have succeeded in overcoming consumer resistance by promoting the safety and desirability of using credit rather than depending solely on cash for family purchases. One product of such changing attitudes is a booming economy and the emergence of a growing and robust middle class. The increasing number of Polish households owning televisions, appliances, automobiles, and houses is fueling the status of Poland's middle class as the most stable in the former Soviet bloc.[13]

Product Use Variables

product use variables
Consumer characteristics based on the ways in which a product is used, the brand loyalty it enjoys, and the reasons for which it is purchased

Product use variables include the ways in which consumers use a product, their brand loyalty to it, and their reasons for purchasing it. A women's shoemaker, for example, might identify three segments—wearers of athletic, casual, and dress shoes. Each market segment is looking for different benefits in a shoe. A woman buying an athletic shoe, for instance, may not care much about its appearance but cares a great deal about arch support, sturdiness, and traction in the sole. A woman buying a casual shoe, however, will want it to look good and feel comfortable. A woman buying a dress shoe may require a specific color or style and may even accept some discomfort.

■ UNDERSTANDING CONSUMER BEHAVIOR

Although marketing managers can tell us what qualities people want in a new VCR, they cannot tell us *why* people buy VCRs. What desire are they fulfilling? Is there a psychological or sociological explanation for why consumers purchase one product and not another? These questions and many others are addressed in the area of marketing known as **consumer behavior**—the study of the decision process by which customers come to purchase and consume products.[14]

consumer behavior
Various facets of the decision process by which customers come to purchase and consume products

Influences on Consumer Behavior

According to the title of one classic study, we are "social animals." To understand consumer behavior, marketers draw heavily on the fields of psychology and sociology. The result is a focus on four major influences on consumer behavior: *psychological, personal, social,* and *cultural.* By identifying the four influences that are most active, marketers try to explain consumer choices and predict future purchasing behavior:

- *Psychological influences* include an individual's motivations, perceptions, ability to learn, and attitudes.
- *Personal influences* include lifestyle, personality, and economic status.
- *Social influences* include family, opinion leaders (people whose opinions are sought by others), and such reference groups as friends, co-workers, and professional associates.
- *Cultural influences* include culture (the "way of living" that distinguishes one large group from another), subculture (smaller groups, such as ethnic groups, with shared values), and social class (the cultural ranking of groups according to such criteria as background, occupation, and income).

All these factors can have a strong impact on the products that people purchase—often in complex ways. For example, many wealthy women wear real pearls for the prestige they represent. But Barbara Bush, the financially comfortable former First Lady, preferred to wear fake pearls. Personal influences thus outweighed social and cultural influences. The symbolism of real pearls did not match her self-image and social values.

The purchase of some products is influenced either very little or not at all by behavioral factors. Some consumers, for example, exhibit high *brand loyalty*—that is, they regularly purchase products because they are satisfied with their performance. Such people (say, users of Maytag appliances) are generally less subject to typical influences and stick with preferred brands. Closer to home, however, the clothes you wear and the food you eat often reflect social and psychological influences on your consuming behavior.

The Consumer Buying Process

Students of consumer behavior have constructed various models to help marketers understand how consumers come to purchase products. Figure 13.4 presents one such model. At the core of this and similar models is an awareness of the psychosocial influences that lead to consumption. Ultimately, marketers use this information to develop marketing plans.

Problem/Need Recognition   The buying process begins when the consumer recognizes a problem or need. After strenuous exercise, for example, you may realize that you are thirsty. After the birth of twins, you may find your one-bedroom apartment too small for comfort.

Need recognition also occurs when you have a chance to change your purchasing habits. For example, when you obtain your first job after graduation, your new income may let you purchase items that were once too expensive for you. You may also discover a need for professional clothing, apartment furnishings, and a car. American Express

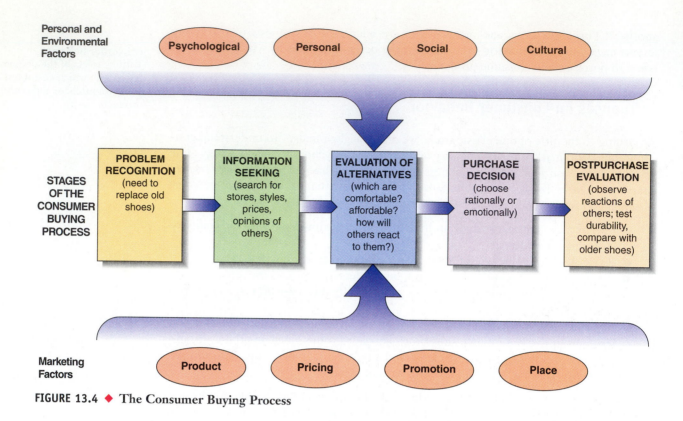

Personal and Environmental Factors

Psychological   Personal   Social   Cultural

STAGES OF THE CONSUMER BUYING PROCESS

PROBLEM RECOGNITION (need to replace old shoes)

INFORMATION SEEKING (search for stores, styles, prices, opinions of others)

EVALUATION OF ALTERNATIVES (which are comfortable? affordable? how will others react to them?)

PURCHASE DECISION (choose rationally or emotionally)

POSTPURCHASE EVALUATION (observe reactions of others; test durability, compare with older shoes)

Marketing Factors

Product   Pricing   Promotion   Place

FIGURE 13.4 ◆ **The Consumer Buying Process**

and Sears recognize this shift in typical needs when they market credit cards to college seniors.

Information Seeking   Once they have recognized a need, consumers often seek information. This search is not always extensive. If you are thirsty, for instance, you may simply ask someone to point you to a soft drink machine. At other times, you may simply rely on your memory for information.

Before making major purchases, however, most people seek information from personal sources, marketing sources, public sources, and experience. For example, if you move to a new town, you will want to identify the best dentist, physician, hair stylist, butcher, or pizza maker in your area. To get this information, you may check with personal sources, such as acquaintances, co-workers, and relatives. Before buying an exercise bike, you may go to the library and read the relevant issue of *Consumer Reports*. You may also question market sources such as sales clerks or rely on direct experience by test-riding several bikes before you buy.

Evaluation of Alternatives   If you are in the market for a set of skis, you probably have some idea of who makes skis and how they differ. You may have accumulated some of this knowledge during the information-seeking stage and combined it with what you knew before. By analyzing the product attributes that apply to a given product—color, taste, price, prestige, quality, service record—you will consider your choices and decide which product best meets your needs.

Purchase Decision   Ultimately, consumers must make purchase decisions. They may decide to defer a purchase until a later time or they may decide to buy now. "Buy" decisions are based on rational motives, emotional motives, or both. **Rational motives** involve the logical evaluation of product attributes: cost, quality, and usefulness. **Emotional motives** involve nonobjective factors and lead to "irrational" decisions. Al-

rational motives
Reasons for purchasing a product that are based on a logical evaluation of product attributes

emotional motives
Reasons for purchasing a product that are based on nonobjective factors

though not all irrational decisions are sudden, many spur-of-the-moment decisions are emotionally driven. Emotional motives include sociability, imitation of others, and aesthetics—motives that are common. For example, you might buy the same brand of jeans as your friends to feel comfortable among that group, not because your friends happen to have the good sense to prefer durable, comfortably priced jeans.

Irrational, therefore, does not mean wrong. It merely refers to a decision based on nonobjective factors. Such decisions can be either satisfying or, largely because they were not based on objective criteria, ill considered. We have all purchased items, taken them home, and then wondered, "Why in the world did I spend good money on this thing?"

Postpurchase Evaluations   Marketing does not stop with the sale of a product. It includes the process of consumption. What happens *after* the sale is important. Marketers want consumers to be happy after the consumption of products so that they are more likely to buy them again. Because consumers do not want to go through a complex decision process for every purchase, they often repurchase products they have used and liked.

Not all consumers are satisfied with their purchases, of course. Dissatisfied consumers may complain to sellers, criticize products publicly, or even file lawsuits. Dissatisfied consumers are not likely to purchase the same products again. Moreover, dissatisfied customers are much more likely to broadcast their experiences than are satisfied customers.

Although they can have a negative impact, dissatisfied customers are also potential sources of helpful information. At Hewlett-Packard, for example, every individual or corporate complaint is assigned to a specific employee. That person must check the H-P database to find out how frequent the problem is and what the company is doing about it, and then report back to the customer. One such complaint involved H-P's Perfview software, which is designed to monitor the speed of H-P networks. Customers pointed out that although Perfview did what it was supposed to do quite nicely, it did nothing else. The software was thus redesigned. It now tracks all the components of a network—even if they are manufactured by different companies.[15]

■ ORGANIZATIONAL MARKETING AND BUYING BEHAVIOR

Buying behavior is observable daily in the consumer market, where marketing activities, including buying and selling transactions, are visible to the public. Equally important, however, but far less visible, are *organizational* (or *commercial*) *markets*. Some 22 million organizations in the United States buy goods and services to be used in creating and delivering consumer products. As we will see in the following sections, marketing to these buyers must deal with different kinds of organizational markets and with buying behaviors that are different from those found in consumer markets.

Organizational Markets

Organizational or commercial markets fall into three categories—*industrial, reseller,* and *government/institutional markets*. Taken together, these three markets do about $6 *trillion* in business annually—approximately three times the business done in the consumer market.

Industrial Market   The **industrial market** includes businesses that buy goods to be converted into other products and goods that are used up during production. This market includes farmers, manufacturers, and some retailers. For example, Seth Thomas purchases electronics, metal components, and glass to make clocks for the consumer

industrial market
Organizational market consisting of firms that buy goods that are either converted into products or used during production

market. The company also buys office supplies, tools, and factory equipment—items never seen by clock buyers—to be used during production. Baskin-Robbins buys not only ingredients for ice cream but also paper bags and wrappers to package products for customers and freezer cabinets for storage.

reseller market
Organizational market consisting of intermediaries who buy and resell finished goods

Reseller Market   Before products reach consumers, they pass through a **reseller market** consisting of intermediaries, including wholesalers and retailers, who buy the finished goods and resell them (wholesalers and retailers are discussed in detail in Chapter 15). The Coast Distribution System, for example, is a leading distributor of parts and accessories for the pleasure boat market. It buys items like lights, steering wheels, and propellers and resells them to marinas and boat repair shops. On the products resold to their customers, 750,000 U.S. wholesalers have annual sales of $1.7 trillion. Some 3 million U.S. retailers purchase merchandise which, when resold to consumers, is valued at $1.9 trillion per year.[16] Retailers also buy such services as maintenance, housekeeping, and communications.

Government and Institutional Market   In addition to federal and state governments, there are more than 87,000 local governments (municipalities, counties, townships, and school districts) in the United States. State and local governments alone make annual purchases of $700 billion for durable goods, nondurables, purchased services, and construction.[17]

institutional market
Organizational market consisting of such nongovernmental buyers of goods and services as hospitals, churches, museums, and charitable organizations

The **institutional market** consists of nongovernment organizations, such as hospitals, churches, museums, and charitable organizations, that also comprise a substantial market for goods and services. Like organizations in other commercial markets, these institutions use supplies and equipment, as well as legal, accounting, and transportation services.

Organizational Buying Behavior

In many respects, organizational buying behavior bears little resemblance to consumer buying practices. Industrial product demand is stimulated by demand for consumer products and is less sensitive to price changes. Other differences include the buyers' purchasing skills and buyer–seller relationships.

Differences in Demand   Recall our definition of *demand* in Chapter 1—the willingness and ability of buyers to purchase a good or service. There are two major differences in demand between consumer and industrial products—*derived demand* and *inelasticity of demand.*

derived demand
Demand for industrial products that results from demand for consumer products

Derived Demand.   The term **derived demand** refers to the fact that demand for industrial products often results from demand for related consumer products (that is, industrial demand is frequently *derived from* consumer demand).

■ Consider the chain of industrial demand that was ignited when 3M realized how many consumers wanted the new Scotch-Brite Never Rust soap pads it launched in 1993. First, construction had already started in 1992 on a new plant in Prairie Du Chien, Wisconsin. This project required an array of services and such materials as structural steel, windows, bathroom fixtures, heating apparatus, and production equipment. In turn, these needs stimulated demand back up the supply chain. For example, in order to make the materials for the plant's construction, the steel supplier had to buy more scrap steel, carbon, and other raw materials from its suppliers. Once the 3M plant was complete (in 1993), there were new purchases of raw materials for production, including used plastic bottles and abrasives for coating the pads.[18]

Inelasticity of Demand. **Inelastic demand** is when a price change for a product does not have much affect on demand. Take, for instance, the demand for cardboard used to package products like file cabinets. Because cardboard packaging is such a small part of the manufacturer's overall cabinet cost, an increase in cardboard prices will not lessen the demand for cardboard. In turn, because cabinet buyers will see little price increase, demand for filing cabinets—and for their accompanying cardboard packaging—will remain at about the same level.

inelastic demand
Demand for industrial products that is not largely affected by price changes

Differences in Buyers   Unlike most consumers, organizational buyers are professional, specialized, and expert (or at least well informed):

- As *professionals*, organizational buyers are trained in arranging buyer–seller relationships and in methods for negotiating purchase terms. Once buyer–seller agreements have been reached, industrial buyers also arrange for formal contracts.
- As a rule, industrial buyers are company *specialists* in a line of items. As one of several buyers for a large bakery, for example, you may specialize in food ingredients like flour, yeast, butter, and so on. Another buyer may specialize in baking equipment (industrial ovens and mixers), while a third may purchase office equipment and supplies.
- Industrial buyers are often *experts* about the products they are buying. On a regular basis, organizational buyers learn about competing products and alternative suppliers by attending trade shows, reading trade magazines, and conducting technical discussions with sellers' representatives.

Differences in the Buyer–Seller Relationship   Consumer–seller relationships are often impersonal and fleeting—short-lived one-time interactions. In contrast, industrial situations often involve frequent, enduring buyer–seller relationships. Accordingly, industrial sellers emphasize personal selling by trained representatives who can better understand the needs of each customer.

■ THE INTERNATIONAL MARKETING MIX

Marketing products internationally means mounting a strategy to support global business operations—no easy task. Foreign customers, for example, differ from domestic buyers in language, customs, business practices, and consumer behavior. When they decide to go global, marketers must thus reconsider each element of the marketing mix—product, pricing, promotion, and place.[19]

International Products   Some products can be sold abroad with virtually no changes. Budweiser, Coca-Cola, and Marlboros are exactly the same in Peoria and Paris. In other cases, U.S. firms have been obliged to create products with built-in flexibility—for instance, electric shavers that adapt to either 115- or 230-volt outlets.

As we noted earlier, however, sometimes only a redesigned—or completely different—product will meet the needs of foreign buyers. To sell the Macintosh in Japan, for example, Apple had to develop a Japanese-language operating system. Nevertheless, more companies are designing products for universal application. Whether designed for unique or universal markets, the branding and labeling of products are especially important for communicating global messages about them. For example, KFC (formerly Kentucky Fried Chicken) boxes and Pepsi-Cola cans display universal logos that are instantly recognizable in many nations.

International Pricing   When pricing for international markets, marketers must handle all the considerations of domestic pricing while also considering the higher costs of transporting and selling products abroad. Bass Pro Shops, for example, sells outdoor sports equipment to customers in Europe at higher prices that cover the added costs of delivery. In contrast, major products like jet airplanes are priced the same worldwide because delivery costs are incidental; huge development and production costs are the major considerations regardless of customer location. Meanwhile, because of higher costs of buildings, rent, equipment, and imported meat, a McDonald's Big Mac that sells for $2 in the United States has a price tag of more than $10 in Japan.

International Promotion   Occasionally, a good advertising campaign here is a good advertising campaign just about everywhere else—it can be transported to another country virtually intact.[20] Quite often, however, standard U.S. promotional devices do not succeed in other countries. In fact, many Europeans believe that a product must be inherently shoddy if a company resorts to *any* advertising—particularly the American hard-sell variety.

International marketers must also be aware that cultural differences can cause negative reactions to products that are advertised improperly. Some Europeans, for example, are offended by television commercials that show weapons or violence. Advertising practices are regulated accordingly. Consequently, Dutch commercials for toys do not feature the guns and combat scenes that are commonplace on Saturday morning U.S. television.[21] Meanwhile, liquor and cigarette commercials that are banned from U.S. television are thriving in many Asian and European markets. Product promotions must be carefully matched to the customs and cultural values of each country.

International Distribution   International distribution presents several problems. In some industries, delays in starting new distribution networks can be costly. Therefore, companies with existing distribution systems often enjoy an advantage over new businesses. Similarly, several companies have gained advantages in time-based competition by buying existing businesses. Procter & Gamble, for example, saved three years of start-up time by buying Revlon's Max Factor and Betrix cosmetics, both of which are well established in foreign markets. P&G can thus immediately use these companies' distribution and marketing networks for selling its own U.S. brands in the United Kingdom, Germany, and Japan.

Given the need to adjust the marketing mix, success in international markets is hard won. Even experienced firms can err in marketing to other countries. International success requires flexibility and a willingness to adapt to the nuances of other cultures. Whether a firm markets in domestic or international markets, however, the basic principles of marketing still apply. It is only the implementation of those principles that changes.

Continued from page 327

Who Never Heard of "Spring Break"?

Tempting Tourists Back to Broward County

The goal of Fort Lauderdale's new "Was/Is" advertising campaign is to generate more tourist dollars than previous campaigns. To judge the success of the campaign, tourism officials compared the number of inquiries made to the toll-free phone numbers listed on the ads to the number of inquiries received the previous year. With fewer than 45,000 requests for tourist information, 1995 was a disappointing year. Officials were thus confidant that the new campaign would generate greater interest.

Part of the tourist board's strategy to develop this interest was to place print ads in the December issues of such upscale consumer travel magazines as *Condé Nast Traveler* and *Southern Living*. This tactic marked a change in the city's traditional approach of relying exclusively on television and newspaper ads. The 1996 strategy also included separate ad programs designed for Latin American and European publications. These ads highlighted Fort Lauderdale's beaches, weather, and shopping—and said nothing about spring break. Latin Americans and Europeans, it seems, have never heard of the concept.

Was the 1996 campaign successful? According to Andrea Fisher of the Broward County Convention and Visitors' Bureau, the response rate to its ads grew by 37 percent between October 1995 and June 1996, as measured against figures from the previous year. These results prompted officials to declare the campaign one of their most successful in five years.

Case Questions

1. How did changes in the social and cultural environment of the United States affect Fort Lauderdale's success—or lack of it—in appealing to its target tourist market?
2. Consider for a moment the fact that the city of Fort Lauderdale is the "product" in the marketing mix. How did city and tourism officials try to change their product in order to attract consumers? Could they have done more?
3. How do you evaluate Fort Lauderdale's 1996 advertising strategy? Why do you think tourism officials chose to advertise in upscale magazines?
4. What demographic and psychographic characteristics made baby boomers a more attractive market to Fort Lauderdale than spring breakers?
5. How do you explain the consumer behavior patterns that affect tourism?

SUMMARY OF LEARNING OBJECTIVES

1. **Define *marketing*.** According to the American Marketing Association, *marketing* is "the process of planning and executing the conception, pricing, promotion, and distribution of ideas, goods, and services to create exchanges that satisfy individual and organizational objectives."

2. **Describe the five forces that constitute *the external marketing environment*.** The *external environment* consists of the outside forces that influence marketing strategy and decision making. The *political/legal environment* includes laws and regulations, both domestic and foreign, that may define or constrain business activities. The *social/cultural environment* is the context within which people's values, beliefs, and ideas affect marketing decisions. The *technological environment* includes the technological developments that affect existing and new products. The *economic environment* consists of the factors, such as inflation, recession, and interest rates, that influence both consumer and organizational spending patterns. The *competitive environment* is the environment in which marketers must persuade buyers to purchase their products rather than their competitors'.

3. **Explain** *market segmentation* **and show how it is used in** *target marketing*. *Market segmentation* is the process of dividing markets into categories of customers. Businesses have learned that marketing is more successful when it is aimed at specific *target markets*—groups of consumers with similar wants and needs. Markets may be segmented by *geographic, demographic, psychographic,* or *product use variables*.

4. **Describe the key factors that influence the** *consumer buying process*. A number of personal and psychological considerations, along with various social and cultural influences, affect consumer behavior. When making buying decisions, consumers first determine or respond to a problem or need and then collect as much information as they think necessary before making a purchase. *Postpurchase evaluations* are also important to marketers because they influence future buying patterns.

5. **Discuss the three categories of** *organizational markets* **and explain how** *organizational buying behavior* **differs from consumer buying behavior.** The *industrial market* includes firms that buy (1) goods to be converted into other products and (2) goods that are used up during production. Farmers and manufacturers are members of the industrial market. Members of the *reseller market* (mostly wholesalers) are intermediaries who buy and resell finished goods. The *government and institutional market* includes governments and agencies at all levels, and nongovernment organizations such as hospitals, museums, and charities.

There are three main differences between consumer and organizational buying behavior. First, the nature of *demand* is different in organizational demands. It is often *derived* (resulting from related consumer demand), *inelastic* (largely unaffected by price changes), or both. Second, organizational buyers are typically professionals, specialists, or experts. Third, they often develop enduring buyer–seller relationships.

STUDY QUESTIONS AND EXERCISES

Review

1. What are the key similarities and differences between consumer buying behavior and organizational buying behavior?
2. Why and how is market segmentation used in target marketing?
3. What elements of the marketing mix may need to be adjusted to market a product internationally? Why?
4. How do the needs of organizations differ according to the different organizational markets of which they are members?

Analysis

5. Using examples of everyday products, explain why marketing plans must consider both the external marketing environment and the marketing mix.

6. Select an everyday product—books, dog food, or shoes, for example. Show how different versions of your chosen product are aimed toward different market segments. Explain how the marketing mix differs for each segment.

7. Select a second everyday product and describe the consumer buying process that typically goes into its purchase.

8. If you were starting your own small business—say, marketing a consumer good that you already know something about—which of the forces in the external marketing environment would you believe to have the greatest potential impact on your success?

Application Exercises

9. Interview the marketing manager of a local business. Identify the degree to which this person's job is oriented toward each element in the marketing mix.

10. Select a product made by a foreign company and sold in the United States. Compare it with a similar domestically made product in terms of product features, price, promotion, and distribution. Which of the two products do you believe is more successful with U.S. buyers? Why?

Extra Exercise

Break the class into small groups and assign each group a specific industry. Have each group discuss the marketing strategies that they believe important to the effective marketing of products in that industry.

BUILDING YOUR BUSINESS SKILLS

This exercise enhances the following SCANS workplace competencies: demonstrating basic skills, demonstrating thinking skills, exhibiting interpersonal skills, and working with information.

Goal

To encourage students to assess how their own buying behavior differs for major and minor purchases and to understand how their buying behavior compares with that of others

Method

Step 1: Keep a diary of the purchases you make during the next two weeks. Include both small purchases (a toothbrush, for example, or a can of tennis balls) and large ones (a computer, a mountain bike, a leather jacket).

If you make no major purchases during this period, think back to several purchases you have made recently (perhaps within the past six months). In thinking about each purchase, identify and describe the steps involved in each—recognizing a problem or need, seeking information about competing products, evaluating alternative products, making the decision to purchase a specific product, and evaluating the purchase after it has been made.

Step 2: Pair off with another student and take turns analyzing the five stages in each other's purchasing decisions.

Follow-Up

1. Looking at your own consumer buying process, how would you say that it differs for major and minor purchases? Conduct the same analysis for your partner's purchases.
2. List and explain the important differences between the ways you and your partner handle the consumer purchase process.
3. What factors influenced the different ways in which you and your partner approached consumer purchases? Analyze the effects of psychological, economic, social, and cultural differences.
4. For minor purchases—a new cap, for example—were the information-seeking and evaluation of alternatives steps always performed quickly? If not, analyze why they took longer than the purchase probably warranted.

GENERAL ELECTRIC COMPANY, WE BRING GOOD THINGS TO LIFE, AT
http://www.ge.com

After you have browsed the various pages and reports posted by General Electric (GE), think about the following questions pertaining to the company's marketing processes:

1. From a marketing perspective, why do you suppose GE separates its Website into two product/ service categories: "At Home with GE" and "In Business with GE"?

2. The feature entitled "Inside GE" contains information about the Elfun Society. Is this an example of "relationship marketing"? Explain why it is or is not. Is this a domestic activity or is it more international in scope? Explain your answer.

3. Identify some examples of *consumer goods marketing* at GE. What are the specific goods and services that you found?

4. Identify some examples of *industrial marketing* at GE? What are some of the specific goods and services that you found?

5. From the Website, can you identify any examples of *idea marketing* by GE?

6. Based on the full range of its products and customers, what challenges do you think GE's marketing managers face in their *political* and *legal* environments? In their *economic* environment? In their *social* and *cultural* environments?

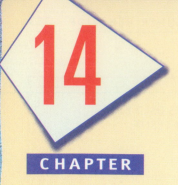

14

CHAPTER

DEVELOPING, PRICING, AND PROMOTING PRODUCTS

Charting the Air Jordan Route

NIKE GEARS FOR THE PREPLANNED SHORTAGE

With a 37-percent share of the nearly $7 billion worldwide sneaker market and 60 percent of footwear shelf space in U.S. stores, Nike is the clear winner in the race to dominate the athletic footwear market. Nowhere is Nike's dominance more evident than in the marketing strategy it uses to sell its biggest single product—Air Jordan sneakers. Endorsed by basketball superstar Michael Jordan, 12 different versions of Air Jordans have enjoyed the power of Nike's marketing muscle since 1985. The result, according to John G. Horan, Publisher of *Sporting Goods Intelligence*, is that "over time, there's been nothing even remotely close to the Air Jordan. It's that extra zing that Michael Jordan brings to the party."

Not surprisingly, the introduction of a new Air Jordan product has the power to ignite the action at athletic footwear retailers. Fueling this ignition is Nike's deliberate, carefully crafted marketing strategy: control

> **"It's that extra zing that Michael Jordan brings to the party."**
>
> —John G. Horan
> *Publisher of*
> Sporting Goods Intelligence

supply and increase demand while at the same time generating enough excitement among target customers—teenagers—to convince them to pay $115 a pair. Because of this strategy, customers are willing to pay for the Michael Jordan name—and, of course, state-of-the art sneakers with carbon-fiber spring plates, herringbone traction inserts, air insoles, and sixteen stitching-reinforced lace eyelets.

The strategy is implemented by means of hype, which begins when the company issues a release date for a new Air Jordan model. In Step 2, Nike deliberately manufactures too few shoes to meet expected demand.

Customers learn of the release date not through advertising, but through a word-of-mouth network that connects them with shoe salesmen. For example, 13-year-old Zaki O'Brien of Brooklyn, New York, found out when the Nike Air Jordan Low would be available by calling salesmen at Foot Locker and other local stores. The result of this combination of hype and operations control is a kind of self-perpetuating demand for Air Jordan sneakers. And make no mistake about it—demand issues from the star power of the Michael Jordan name. The Chicago Bulls superstar regularly wears the latest Air Jordan in one or two National Basketball Association play-off games, but Nike's advertising strategy is otherwise decidedly low key.

By stark contrast, there is nothing low key about the scene at stores on opening day for retail sales. Teenage customers arrive hours before the store opens, and many buy the latest Air Jordans even if they own six other Air Jordan models in good condition. Why? Because the sneakers are Jordans and because the shoes give them status among their peers.

On the day that Air Jordan Lows went on sale, it took the Foot Locker outlet in Brooklyn's Fulton Street Mall just 25 minutes to sell 30 pairs of sneakers. Latecomers found the stock depleted, and many made frantic phone calls to other stores in search of their sizes. Because Nike's marketing strategy does not include meeting current demand, the unlucky may have little choice but to wait for the next Air Jordan model and the next bout of hype and purchasing frenzy.

The way Nike markets Air Jordan sneakers provides insight into the unique requirements of developing, pricing, and promoting products. Developed for customers who want a high-quality, high-performance shoe, this marketing strategy was built around Nike's endorsement deal with Michael Jordan. Jordan's popularity among teenagers is so great that little advertising is necessary to promote new models. Instead, Nike carefullly

allocates a limited supply of product to keep prices high. As you will see in this chapter, it is the challenge of marketers to meet their strategic goals by making the right development, pricing, and promotional choices.

By focusing on the learning objectives of this chapter, you will better understand such activities as product development, pricing, and promotion.

After reading this chapter, you should be able to

1. Identify a *product* and distinguish between *consumer* and *industrial products*

2. Explain the importance of *branding and packaging*

3. Identify the various *pricing objectives* that govern *pricing decisions* and describe the *price-setting tools* used in making these decisions

4. Discuss *pricing strategies* and *tactics* for existing and new products

5. Identify the important objectives of *promotion* and discuss the considerations entailed in selecting a *promotional mix*

6. Describe the key *advertising media* available to marketing managers

7. Describe the various types of *sales promotions* and explain the uses of *publicity* and *public relations*

Continued on page 375

In Chapter 13, we introduced the four components of the marketing mix—product, price, promotion, and place (distribution). In this chapter, we look more closely at the first three of these components. Specifically, we examine the complex nature of products. Managers must keep these complexities in mind when developing, naming, packaging, labeling, and pricing both new and existing products.

■ WHAT IS A PRODUCT?

In developing the marketing mix for any products—whether ideas, goods, or services—marketers must consider what consumers really buy when they purchase products. Only then can they plan their strategies effectively. We begin this section by describing the major *classifications of products*, both consumer and industrial. Next we discuss the most important component in the offerings of any business—its *product mix*.

Classifying Goods and Services

One way to classify a product is according to expected buyers. Buyers fall into two groups—buyers of *consumer* products and buyers of *industrial* products. As we saw in Chapter 13, the consumer and industrial buying processes differ significantly. Not surprisingly, then, marketing products to consumers is vastly different from marketing them to other companies.

Classifying Consumer Products   Consumer products are commonly divided into three categories that reflect buyers' behavior:

convenience good/service
Relatively inexpensive product purchased and consumed rapidly and regularly

shopping good/service
Moderately expensive, infrequently purchased product

specialty good/service
Expensive, rarely purchased product

- **Convenience goods** (such as milk and newspapers) and **convenience services** (such as those offered by fast food restaurants) are consumed rapidly and regularly. They are relatively inexpensive and are purchased frequently and with little expenditure of time and effort.
- **Shopping goods** (such as stereos and tires) and **shopping services** (such as insurance) are more expensive and are purchased less frequently than convenience products. Consumers often compare brands, sometimes in different stores. They may also evaluate alternatives in terms of style, performance, color, price, and other criteria.
- **Specialty goods** (such as wedding gowns) and **specialty services** (such as catering for wedding receptions) are extremely important and expensive purchases. Consumers usually decide on precisely what they want and will accept no substitutes. They will often go from store to store, sometimes spending a great deal of money and time to get a specific product.

Classifying Industrial Products   Depending on how much they cost and how they will be used, industrial products can be divided into two categories:

expense item
Relatively inexpensive industrial product purchased and consumed rapidly and regularly

capital item
Expensive, durable, infrequently purchased industrial product, such as a building and machinery

- **Expense items** are any materials and services that are consumed within a year by firms producing other goods or supplying other services. The most obvious expense items are industrial goods used directly in the production process—for example, bulkloads of tea processed into tea bags.
- **Capital items** are "permanent"—that is, expensive and long lasting—goods and services. All these items have expected lives of more than a year—typically up to several years. Buildings (offices, factories), fixed equipment (water towers, baking ovens), and accessory equipment (computers, airplanes) are capital goods.

Capital services are those for which long-term commitments are made. These may include purchases for employee food services, building and equipment maintenance, or legal services.

The Product Mix

The group of products that a company makes available for sale—whether consumer or industrial or both—is its **product mix.** Black & Decker, for example, makes toasters, vacuum cleaners, electric drills, and a variety of other appliances and tools. The 3M Corp. makes everything from Post-it notes to laser optics.[1]

Many companies, of course, begin with a single product. Over time, however, they find that their initial products fail to suit all the consumers shopping for the product type. To meet market demand, therefore, they often introduce similar products designed to reach other consumers. For example, four different models of the Ford Escort now run the gamut from the three-door sport model to the five-door sedan at the same price. A group of similar products intended for a similar—but not identical—group of buyers who will use them in similar ways is a **product line.**

Companies may also extend their horizons and identify opportunities outside of existing product lines. The result—*multiple* (or *diversified*) *product lines*—is evident at firms like Procter & Gamble, which began by making soap but now also produces foods, coffee, and baby and paper products. Multiple product lines allow a company to grow more rapidly and can help minimize the consequences of slow sales in any one product line.

product mix
Group of products that a firm makes available for sale

product line
Group of similar products intended for a similar group of buyers that will use them in similar ways

■ NEW PRODUCTS AND THE PRODUCT LIFE CYCLE

To expand or diversify product lines—indeed, just to survive—firms must develop and successfully introduce streams of new products. Faced with competition and shifting consumer preferences, no firm can count on a single successful product to carry it forever. Even basic products that have been widely purchased for decades require nearly constant renewal. Consider the unassuming facial tissue. The white tissue in the low rectangular box has been joined (if not replaced) by tissues of many different colors and patterns. They arrive in boxes shaped and decorated for nearly every room in the house, and they are made to be placed or carried not only in the bathroom but in the purse, the briefcase, and the car.

The Product Life Cycle

A product that reaches the marketplace enters the **product life cycle (PLC),** a series of stages through which it passes during its profit-producing life. Depending on the product's ability to attract and keep customers over time, its PLC may be a matter of months, years, or decades. Strong products—Kellogg's Corn Flakes, Maxwell House coffee, H&R Block tax preparation—have had extremely long productive lives. In this section, we describe the various stages in the typical life cycle of most products.

product life cycle (PLC)
Series of stages in a product's profit-producing life

Stages in the Product Life Cycle   The product life cycle is a natural process in which products are born, grow in stature, mature, and finally decline and die.[2] Figure 14.1 shows the four stages of the cycle—not yet complete—for VCRs. The product was introduced in the late 1970s and is widely used today. (Note that profits lag behind sales because of the extensive costs of developing new products.) If the market becomes sat-

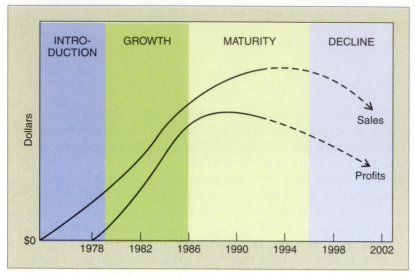

FIGURE 14.1 ◆ **The Product Life Cycle for VCRs**

urated, sales begin to decline. Sales will also fall if new products, such as Toshiba and Time Warner's new double-sided digital video disk, send the VCR the way of the eight-track audio player.[3]

1. *Introduction.* The introduction stage begins when the product reaches the marketplace. During this stage, marketers focus on making potential consumers aware of the product and its benefits. Extensive promotional and development costs mean that companies do not earn profits at this stage.

2. *Growth.* If the new product attracts and satisfies enough consumers, sales begin to climb rapidly. During this stage, the product begins to show a profit. Other firms in the industry move rapidly to introduce their own versions.

3. *Maturity.* Sales growth begins to slow. Although the product earns its highest profit level early in this stage, increased competition eventually leads to price cutting and lower profits. Toward the end of the stage, sales start to fall.

4. *Decline.* During this final stage, sales and profits continue to fall. New products in the introduction stage take away sales. Companies remove or reduce promotional support (ads and salespeople) but may let the product linger to provide some profits.

■ IDENTIFYING PRODUCTS

Developing a product's features is only part of a marketer's job. Marketers must also encourage consumers to identify products. Two important tools for accomplishing this task are *branding* and *packaging*.

Branding Products

Coca-Cola is the best-known brand in the world. In fact, the *name* "Coca-Cola" is so valuable that its executives like to say that if all of the company's other assets were obliterated, they could walk over to the bank and borrow $100 billion for rebuilding just on the strength of the brand name.[4] Brand names like *Coca-Cola* are symbols for characterizing products and distinguishing them from one another. They were originally introduced to simplify the process when consumers are faced with a wealth of purchase decisions. **Branding,** then, is really a process of using symbols to communicate the qualities of a particular product made by a particular producer. Brands are designed to signal uniform quality. Customers who try and like a product can return to it by remembering its name.

Types of Brand Names   Virtually every product has a brand name. Generally, the different types of brand names—*national, licensed,* and *private brands*—increase buyers' awareness of the nature and quality of products that must compete with any number of other products. When the consumer is satisfied with the quality of a recognizable product, marketers work to achieve brand loyalty among the largest possible segment of repeat buyers:

- **National brands** are produced by, widely distributed by, and carry the name of the manufacturer. These brands—say, Scotch tape or Scope mouthwash—are often widely recognized by consumers because of national advertising campaigns. Most national brand names, of course, are valuable assets that signal product recognition and uniform quality. As a rule, therefore, they rarely change. ▼[5]
- It has become increasingly common for nationally recognized companies (and even personalities) to sell the rights to place their names on products, which are thus known as **licensed brands.** Coca-Cola, Guns 'N Roses, and Hard Rock Cafe will all make millions on licensed apparel sales this year. Free advertising from licensed T-shirts and other clothing is just an added bonus. Tie-ins with movies and other entertainment vehicles are popular forms of licensing. In 1993, for example, marketers reported a record $66.6 billion in sales of licensed merchandise. Of that total, $15.8 billion was generated by entertainment properties.

    In 1994, the trend continued. The surprise movie hit *Forrest Gump,* for instance, climbed to number five on the all time box office list. In the process, it

branding
Process of using symbols to communicate the qualities of a product made by a particular producer

national brand
Brand-name product produced by, widely distributed by, and carrying the name of a manufacturer

licensed brand
Brand-name product for whose name the seller has purchased the right from an organization or individual

According to one of the company's marketing consultants, Xerox's new identity "is at the crossroads of the whole information age." No longer merely a maker of copiers, Xerox has diversified into printers, scanners, faxes, and a host of other high-tech communications instruments. The thrust of its transformation, says one expert in corporate identity projects, is to extend the term Document Company to "involve communications that use moving images, since that seems to be the direction in which communications are going."

Meridian Products Inc., which specializes in private-label seafood items, regarded Bubba Gump Shrimp as a licensing natural. "We realized," says the company's director of new product development, "that we could never create a brand and give it as much exposure as Bubba Gump has had." Publisher Oxmoor House more or less followed suit with The Bubba Shrimp Co. Cookbook. *The movie* Forrest Gump, *about an idiot savant from Alabama, generated almost 30 major licensing agreements for its owner, Viacom Inc., even though it was not a very likely candidate for successful merchandising. It was, for example, more of a drama than a comedy and appealed more to adults than to children. Moreover, it featured neither presold action figures like Batman nor images of cuddly cartoon characters like those in* The Lion King.

generated nearly 30 different licensing agreements, with products ranging from T-shirts and baseball caps to a line of shrimp foods from the Bubba Gump Seafood Co. The movie's owner, Viacom Inc., will be paid 5–12 percent of the wholesale price of every licensed item. As for the maker of Bubba Gump Shrimp, licensing is crucial to its new product pipeline. "We realized," says the company's director of new product development, "that we could never create a brand and give it as much exposure as Bubba Gump has had." ◄ 6

"We realized that we could never create a brand and give it as much exposure as Bubba Gump has had."

—Director of new product development at Meridian Products Inc., licensed marketer of Bubba Gump Shrimp

---

■ When a wholesaler or retailer develops a brand name and has the manufacturer place that name on the product, the resulting product name is a **private brand** (or **private label**). One of the best-known sellers of private brands is Sears, which carries such lines as Craftsman tools and Kenmore appliances.

**private brand
(or private label)**
Brand-name product that a wholesaler or retailer has commissioned from a manufacturer

Packaging Products

packaging
Physical container in which a product is sold, advertised, and/or protected

With a few exceptions—fresh fruits and vegetables, structural steel—products need some form of **packaging** in which to be sold. More important, a package also serves as an in-store advertisement that makes the product attractive, displays the brand name, and identifies features and benefits. It also reduces the risk of damage, breakage, or spoilage and increases the difficulty of stealing small products. Recent advances in both product usage and materials available for packaging have also created additional roles for packaging. For example, a paper-based material that can be used as a cooking container has made Budget Gourmet dinners a low-cost entry in the dinner entrée market. "No-drip spout" bottles have enhanced sales and brand loyalty for Clorox bleach.

■ DETERMINING PRICES

pricing
Process of determining what a company will receive in exchange for its products

In product development, managers decide what products the company will offer to customers. In **pricing**—the second major component of the marketing mix—managers decide what the company will receive in exchange for its products. In this section, we first discuss the objectives that influence a firm's pricing decisions. We then describe the major tools that companies use to meet those objectives.

Pricing to Meet Business Objectives

Companies often price products to maximize profits. But other **pricing objectives** refer to the variety of goals that sellers hope to attain in selling products. Some firms, for example, are more interested in dominating the market or securing high market share than in making the highest possible profits. Pricing decisions are also influenced by the need to survive in competitive marketplaces, by social and ethical concerns, and even by corporate image.

pricing objectives
Goals that producers hope to attain in pricing products for sale

Profit-Maximizing Objectives   Pricing to maximize profits is tricky. If prices are set too low, the company will probably sell many units of its product but may miss the opportunity to earn additional profits on each unit (and may indeed lose money on each exchange). Conversely, if prices are set too high, the company will make a large profit on each item but will sell fewer units. As a result, the firm may be left with excess inventory and may have to reduce or even close production operations. To avoid these problems, companies try to set prices to sell the number of units that will generate the highest possible total profits.

In calculating profits, managers weigh receipts against costs for materials and labor. However, they also consider the capital resources (plant and equipment) that the company must tie up to generate that level of profit. The costs of marketing (such as maintaining a large sales staff) can also be substantial. Concern over the efficient use of these resources has led many firms to set prices so as to achieve a targeted level of return on sales or capital investment.

Market Share Objectives   In the long run, of course, a business must make a profit to survive. Nevertheless, many companies initially set low prices for new products. They are willing to accept minimal profits—even losses—to get buyers to try products. They use pricing to establish **market share**—a company's percentage of the total market sales for a specific product type. Even with established products, market share may outweigh profits as a pricing objective. For a product like Philadelphia Brand Cream Cheese, dominating a market means that consumers are more likely to buy it because they are familiar with a well-known, highly visible product. Market domination means the continuous sales of more units—and thus higher profits even at a lower unit price.

market share
Sales of an individual company as a percentage of total sales in a particular market

Other Pricing Objectives   In some instances, neither profit maximizing nor capturing market share is the best objective. During difficult economic times, for instance, loss containment and survival may become a company's main objectives. Thus, in the mid-1980s, John Deere priced agricultural equipment low enough to ensure the company's survival in a severely depressed farm economy.

A still different objective might be to provide a benefit to customers. To introduce its services to industrial clients, for example, International Graffiti Control offered a *set-fee pricing system*—typically $60 a month per building—to owners who needed graffiti removed from building walls. This method shifted the risk from the customer to IGC. It appeals to customers who never know from day to day how much new graffiti will appear but who do know that removal is covered by a fixed fee.[7]

Price-Setting Tools

Whatever a company's objectives, managers must measure the potential impact before deciding on final prices. Two basic tools are frequently used for this purpose—*cost-oriented pricing* and *break-even analysis*. As a rule, these tools are combined to identify prices that will allow the company to reach its objectives.

Cost-Oriented Pricing   Cost-oriented pricing considers the firm's desire to make a profit and takes into account the need to cover production costs. A music store manager, for instance, would begin to price CDs by calculating the cost of making them available to shoppers. Included in this figure would be store rent, employee wages, utilities, product displays, insurance, and, of course, the cost of buying CDs from the manufacturer.

Let us assume that the cost from the manufacturer is $8.00 per CD. If the store sells CDs for this price, it will not make any profit. Nor will it make a profit if it sells CDs for $8.50 each—or even $10.00 or $11.00. The manager must account for product and other costs and stipulate a figure for profit. Together these figures constitute **mark-up.** In this case, a reasonable mark-up of $7.00 over costs would result in a $15.00 selling price.

Mark-up is usually stated as a percentage of selling price. Mark-up percentage is thus calculated as follows:

$$\text{mark-up percentage} = \frac{\text{mark-up}}{\text{sales price}}$$

In the case of our CD retailer, the markup percentage is 46.7:

$$\text{mark-up percentage} = \frac{\$7.00}{\$15.00} = 46.7\%$$

In other words, out of every dollar taken in, 46.7 cents will be gross profit for the store. From this profit, of course, the store must still pay rent, utilities, insurance, and all other costs.

Mark-up can also be expressed as a percentage of cost. The $7.00 markup is 87.5 percent of the $8.00 cost of a CD ($7.00/$8.00).

Break-Even Analysis: Cost-Volume-Profit Relationships   Using cost-oriented pricing, a firm will cover its **variable costs**—costs that change with the number of goods or services produced or sold. It will also make some money toward paying its **fixed costs**—costs that are unaffected by the number of goods or services produced or sold. But how many units must the company sell before all its fixed costs are covered and it begins to make a profit? To determine this figure, it needs a **break-even analysis.**

To continue our music store example, suppose again that the variable cost for each CD (in this case, the cost of buying the CD from the producer) is $8.00. This means that the store's annual variable costs depend on how many CDs are sold—the number of CDs sold times $8.00 cost for each CD. Say that fixed costs for keeping the store open for one year are $100,000. These costs are unaffected by the number of CDs sold. The costs of lighting, rent, insurance, and salaries remain the same whether the store sells no CDs, 100 CDs, or 100,000 CDs. Therefore, how many CDs must be sold to cover both fixed and variable costs and to generate some profit? The answer to that question is the **break-even point,** which is 14,286 CDs. We arrive at this number through the following equation:

$$\text{break-even point (in units)} = \frac{\text{total fixed costs}}{\text{price} - \text{variable cost}}$$

$$= \frac{\$100,000}{\$15.00 - \$8.00}$$

$$= 14,286 \text{ CDs}$$

Figure 14.2 shows the break-even point graphically. If the store sells fewer than 14,286 CDs, it loses money for the year. If sales exceed 14,286 CDs, profits grow by

---

mark-up
Amount added to a product's cost in order to sell it at a profit

variable cost
Cost that changes with the quantity of a product produced or sold

fixed cost
Cost unaffected by the quantity of a product produced or sold

break-even analysis
Assessment of the quantity of a product that must be sold before the seller makes a profit

break-even point
Quantity of a product that must be sold before the seller covers variable and fixed costs and makes a profit

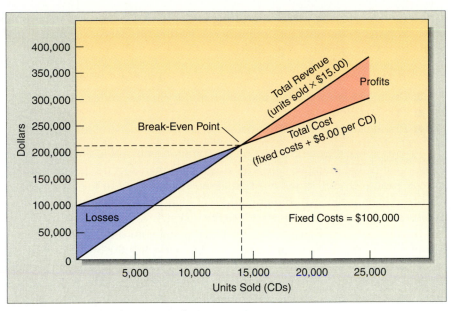

FIGURE 14.2 ◆ Break-Even Analysis

$7.00 for each CD sold. If the store sells exactly 14,286 CDs, it will cover all its costs but will earn zero profit.

Zero profitability at the break-even point can also be seen by using the profit equation (the answer is rounded to nearest whole CD):

profit = total revenue − (total fixed cost + total variable cost)

= [(14,286 CDs) × ($15)] − [$100,000 fixed cost

+ (14,286 CDs × $8.00 variable cost)]

$0 = $214,290 − [$100,000 + $114,288]

■ PRICING STRATEGIES AND TACTICS

The pricing tools discussed in the previous section are valuable in helping managers set prices on specific goods. They do not, however, help in setting pricing philosophies. In this section, we discuss *pricing strategy*—that is, pricing as a planning activity that affects the marketing mix. We then describe some basic *pricing tactics*—ways in which managers implement a firm's pricing strategies.

Pricing Strategies

Let's begin this section by addressing two questions. First, can a manager really identify a single "best" price for a product? The answer is, probably not. For example, a study of prices for popular nonaspirin pain relievers (such as Tylenol and Advil) found that some products sold for *twice* the price of other products with similar properties. Such wide price differences reflect differing brand images that attract different types of customers. In turn, these images reflect vastly different pricing philosophies and strategies.

This brings us to our second question. Just how important is pricing as an element in the marketing mix? Because pricing has a direct and visible impact on revenues, it is extremely important to overall marketing plans. In this section, we focus on the ways in which pricing strategies for both new and existing products can result in widely differing prices for very similar products.

Pricing Existing Products

A firm has three options for pricing existing products:

- Pricing above prevailing market prices for similar products
- Pricing below market prices
- Pricing at or near market prices

Pricing above the market plays on the common assumption that higher price means higher quality. For example, Curtis Mathes, which manufactures televisions, VCRs, and stereos, promotes itself as the most expensive television set in the United States—"but worth it." Companies like Bloomingdale's, Godiva chocolates, and Rolls-Royce have also succeeded with this pricing philosophy.

In contrast, both Budget and Dollar car rental companies promote themselves as low-priced alternatives to Hertz and Avis. Similarly, ads for Suave hair care products argue that "Suave does what theirs does—for a lot less." Pricing below prevailing market price can succeed if a firm can offer a product of acceptable quality while keeping costs below those of higher-priced competitors.

price leader
Dominant firm that establishes product prices that other companies follow

Finally, in some industries, a dominant firm called the **price leader** establishes product prices that other companies follow. This approach is called *market pricing*. When it prevails, there are fewer price wars in an industry. Moreover, follower companies avoid the trouble of determining prices that consumers are willing to pay—the price leader has already done that. (Do not confuse this approach with *price fixing*, which occurs when producers illegally agree on prices among themselves.) Companies often resort to market pricing when products differ little in quality from one firm to another (for example, structural steel, gasoline, and many processed foods). These companies generally compete through promotion, personal selling, and service—not through price.

Pricing New Products

Companies introducing new products must often choose between two pricing policy options—selecting very high prices or very low ones. The first option is called *price skimming*. The second is called *penetration pricing*.

FIGURE 14.3 ◆ Price Skimming on Cellular Phones, 1984–1994

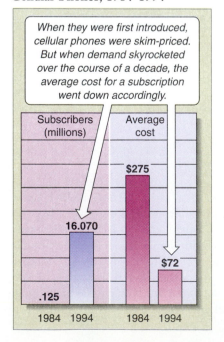

When they were first introduced, cellular phones were skim-priced. But when demand skyrocketed over the course of a decade, the average cost for a subscription went down accordingly.

Subscribers (millions) | Average cost
16.070 | $275
.125 | $72
1984   1994 | 1984   1994

price skimming
Setting the initial price high enough to cover new product costs and generate a profit

Price Skimming. **Price skimming** may allow a firm to earn a large profit on each item sold. The cash income is often needed to cover development and introduction costs. Skimming works, however, only if marketers can convince consumers that a product is truly different from those already on the market. Moreover, the initial high profits will eventually attract competition. Microwave ovens, calculators, video games, and video cameras were all introduced at comparatively high skim prices, but prices fell as soon as new companies entered the market. As you can see from Figure 14.3, the same is true of cellular phones. As the number of subscribers has skyrocketed in the last decade, the price has plummeted. The average monthly cost for a cellular subscription, skim-priced at $275 in 1984, is now just over $70.

penetration pricing
Setting the initial price low in order to establish a new product in the market

Penetration Pricing. In contrast, **penetration pricing** seeks to generate consumer interest and stimulate trial purchase of new products. For example, new food products—convenience foods, cookies, and snacks—are often promoted at special low prices to stimulate early sales. Penetration pricing provides for minimal (if any) profit. Thus, it can succeed only if sellers can raise prices as consumer acceptance grows. Increases, of course, must be carefully managed to avoid alienating customers.

Pricing Tactics

Regardless of its pricing strategy, a company may adopt one or more *pricing tactics*, such as *price lining* or *psychological pricing*. Managers must also decide whether to use *discounting tactics*.

Price Lining Companies selling multiple items in a product category often use **price lining**—offering all items in certain categories at a limited number of prices. A department store, for example, carries thousands of products. Setting separate prices for each brand and style of suit, glassware, or couch would take far too much time. With price lining, a store predetermines three or four *price points* at which a particular product will be sold. For men's suits, the price points might be $175, $250, and $400. That is, all men's suits in the store will be priced at one of these three points. The store's buyers, therefore, must select suits that can be purchased and sold profitably at one of these three prices.

> **price lining**
> Setting a limited number of prices for certain categories of products

Price lining means setting each price level with a specific type of customer in mind and then packaging and promoting products accordingly. For example, Sears offers three lines of power tools, batteries, and appliances. "Sears Good" is for novice or occasional users, "Sears Better" is for avid users, and "Sears Best" is for professionals.

Psychological Pricing Customers are not completely rational when making buying decisions, and **psychological pricing** takes advantage of this fact. For example, one type of psychological pricing, **odd-even pricing**, proposes that customers prefer prices that are not stated in even dollar amounts. That is, customers see prices of $1,000, $100, $50, and $10 as significantly higher than $999.95, $99.95, $49.95, and $9.95, respectively.

> **psychological pricing**
> Pricing tactic that takes advantage of the fact that consumers do not always respond rationally to stated prices
>
> **odd-even pricing**
> Psychological pricing tactic based on the premise that customers prefer prices not stated in even dollar amounts

Discounting The price that is eventually set for a product is not always the price at which it is sold. Often a seller must offer price reductions—**discounts**—to stimulate sales. Filene's Basement, a Boston-based retail chain, has built a reputation by discounting designer clothing by 20–60 percent. Analysts point out that this tactic accounts for Filene's success at a time when larger upscale stores like Macy's and Alexander's continue to suffer.

> **discount**
> Price reduction offered as an incentive to purchase

© 1998 Robert Mankoff *from* The Cartoon Bank,™ Inc.

"The manufacturer's suggested list price on this is sixty-seven thousand dollars, but, because of our low overhead, I can let you have it for thirty-nine ninety-five."

TRENDS & CHALLENGES

THE DEMISE AND RISE OF STICKER DICKERING

In the mid-1980s, the Saturn division of General Motors implemented a revolutionary pricing strategy. Saturn would take the hassle and heartache out of the dealer–consumer relationship by selling vehicles for a fixed low price that would make negotiation unnecessary. Pricing experts believed that this "no-haggle" approach to auto pricing would appeal to consumers who hated to dicker and who believed that traditional dealers maximized commissions by keeping prices high. Meanwhile, salespeople working for fixed-price dealers would be paid by the sale, not by a sliding scale commission linked to profit.

Anyone who has ever visited a traditional new car dealership knows how it operates. Dealers slash prices by hundreds, and sometimes thousands, of dollars for aggressive customers who know how to shop around and "haggle" but hold fast to the manufacturer's suggested retail price—the sticker price—for customers with few negotiating skills. In contrast, fixed-price dealers average what they would have earned from aggressive customers and unsophisticated buyers and then charge every customer the same price. By maintaining this average price, fixed-price dealers are also able to maintain their profit margins.

Unfortunately, not all good ideas work in the marketplace, and many auto dealers now believe that the fixed-price approach has some basic flaws. For example, although thousands of consumers have embraced the fixed-price concept, many more continue to seek dealers who are willing to negotiate price. "A bunch of us thought people would be willing to pay an extra hundred bucks" for the convenience of fixed prices, admits John B.T. Campbell, who recently sold his fixed-price Ford and Mazda dealerships in Santa Ana, California. "We found that didn't prove to be the case." Instead, says Campbell, he attracted customers who browsed at his showroom but bought elsewhere because they regarded his prices as higher than those that they could negotiate elsewhere.

In fact, according to a recent survey, 89 percent of customers who visit fixed-price dealers, rather than buying from them, use their quoted prices as starting points from which to negotiate with traditional dealers. This practice, of course, leaves fixed-price dealers with two types of customers—those who are too busy to shop around and want the convenience of one-stop shopping and those who know so little about car buying that they might have been willing to pay more than the averaged fixed price.

> ## "A bunch of us thought people would be willing to pay an extra hundred bucks for the convenience of fixed prices. That didn't prove to be the case."
>
> —John B.T. Campbell
> *Former owner of Ford and Mazda dealerships in Santa Ana, California*

Moreover, no-haggle dealers found themselves squeezed by competitors willing to undercut close-to-the-bone fixed prices in order to make sales and reduce inventories. The most aggressive competition is in cities where consumers routinely comparison shop at several dealers. Fixed-price dealers do best in areas—mostly rural—where they face few rivals. The reality, explains Chrysler CEO Robert J. Easton, is that "one price works better when you don't have dealerships selling the same product quite so close together."

A recent survey conducted by the marketing research firm of Dohring Co. found a sharp increase in the number of consumers who want to negotiate prices. According to Dohring's report, "Automotive consumers need to feel that they get a good deal when they purchase a vehicle, and, for most, the only way [to accomplish this] is through negotiation." As a result, the number of haggle-free new car dealerships has plummeted in recent years. From a total of nearly 2,000 in 1994, the number had dropped to fewer than 1,200 to 1996.

One alternative to the fixed-price strategy is *value pricing*—an approach that uses the economic pressure of auto makers to *encourage* dealers to set one price. One Oldsmobile dealer explains how the system works. "Olds did away will all rebates and all dealer incentives. They lowered their price and they lowered the dealers' margin. We used to make 14, 15, 16 percent on cars, and they lowered it to 8 or 9 percent . . . so we would be at the point where we could no longer reduce the prices." Although these slimmer profit margins leave dealers with less room to negotiate, they still give shoppers the option—and satisfaction—of negotiating final prices.

One retired executive at Procter & Gamble believes that if the company should ever erect a statue of former CEO Edwin L. Artzt "it would say: 'This SOB made us a truly global company.'" Artzt's push overseas went hand in hand with a revolution in P&G's pricing philosophy. In Brazil, for example, Pampers Uni is not quite the same quality diaper as the premium Pampers sold in the United States. It is, however, priced so that Brazilians can afford it, and it is good enough to generate confidence in Pampers as a product—perhaps enough confidence to prompt consumers to "trade up" the next time around. The pricing strategy is designed to create global volume rather than to recover typically high R&D costs as quickly as possible.

International Pricing

■ When Procter & Gamble reviewed the possibilities for marketing products in new overseas markets, it encountered an unsettling fact. Because it typically priced products to cover hefty R&D costs, profitably priced items were out of reach for too many foreign consumers. The solution was, in effect, to reverse the process. P&G now conducts research to find out what foreign buyers can afford and then develops products that they can buy. The strategy is to penetrate markets with lower-priced items and encourage customers to "trade up" as they become acquainted with—and can afford—higher-quality P&G products.[8] ▲

As P&G's experience shows, pricing products for sale in other countries becomes complicated because additional factors are involved. First, income and consumer spending trends must be analyzed. In addition, the number of middlemen varies from country to country, as does their effect on a product's cost. Exchange rates change daily (see Chapter 5), tariffs must be considered (Chapter 3), and different types of pricing agreements are permitted. P&G, for instance, discovered that per capita income affected cost-plus pricing. This strategy will also be affected by such costs as shipping and import tariffs. Jeep Cherokees are priced $12,000 higher in Japan than in the United States because of these two factors.

An alternate strategy calls for increasing foreign market share by pricing products below cost. As a result, a given product would be priced lower in a foreign market than in its domestic market. This practice is called *dumping*, which is regarded as both unfair and illegal. In recent years, for example, the U.S. International Trade Commission has agreed that motorcycles made by Honda and Kawasaki were being dumped on the U.S. market, as were computer memory chips. As a result, special U.S. tariffs were imposed on these products.

■ THE IMPORTANCE OF PROMOTION

Let's begin by looking at the way in which two well-known companies responded to an opportunity in their marketing environment:

■ In 1996, McDonald's and Disney announced a decade-long cross-promotional agreement with an estimated value of $1 billion. A major benefit of the marketing partnership to Disney is the attraction of more direct and faster customer attention to both its new movie and home video releases. McDonald's, meanwhile, stands to draw more restaurant customers who want popular tie-in toys from Disney movies. Other fast food restaurants, notably Burger King, had recently profited from year-to-year tie-ins with Disney. Burger King, for example, had conducted highly successful promotional campaigns with Disney's *Lion King, Pocahontas,* and *Hunchback of Notre Dame* movies. But McDonald's arrangement with Disney is a strategic long-term decision that paves the way for the development of new and lasting promotional relationships between family restaurants and family entertainment. The potential marketing benefits for both companies is evident in plans calling for McDonald's to be the "presenting sponsor" of the Dinoland attraction at the 1998 opening of Disney's Animal Kingdom at Walt Disney World in Orlando.[9]

promotion
Aspect of the marketing mix concerned with the most effective techniques for selling a product

As we noted in Chapter 13, **promotion** is any technique designed to sell a product. As part of the communications mixes designed for products, promotional techniques—especially advertising—must communicate the uses, features, and benefits of products. Sales promotions, however, also include various programs that add further value beyond the benefits inherent in the product. It is nice, for example, to get a high-quality product at a reasonable price but even better when the seller offers, say, a rebate or a bonus pack with "20 percent more FREE." In promoting products, then, marketers have an array of tools at their disposal.

Promotional Objectives

The ultimate objective of any promotion is to increase sales. In addition, however, marketers may use promotion to *communicate information, position products,* and *control sales volume.*

Communicating Information
Promotion is effective in communicating information from one person or organization to another. Consumers, of course, cannot buy products unless they have been informed about them. Information may thus advise customers that a product exists or educate them about its features. Information may be communicated in writing (in newspapers and magazines), verbally (in person or over the telephone), or visually (on television, matchbook covers, or billboards). Today, in fact, the communication of information about a company's goods or services is so important that marketers try to place it anywhere and everywhere consumers can be found. Experts estimate that the average consumer comes into contact with approximately 1,500 bits of promotional information each day.

positioning
Process of establishing an identifiable product image in the minds of consumers.

Positioning Products
As we saw in Chapter 13, **positioning** is the process of establishing an easily identifiable product image in the minds of consumers. Positioning a product is difficult because a company is trying to appeal to a specific segment of the market rather than to the market as a whole. First, therefore, it must identify which segments are likely to purchase its product and who its competitors are. Only then can it focus its strategy on differentiating its product from the competition's while still appealing to its target audience.

Controlling Sales Volume
Many companies, such as Hallmark Cards, experience seasonal sales patterns. By increasing promotional activities in slow periods, these firms

can achieve more stable sales volume throughout the year. They can thus keep production and distribution systems running evenly. Promotions can even turn slow seasons into peak sales periods. For example, greeting card companies and florists have done much to create Grandparents' Day. The result has been increased consumer demand for cards and flowers in the middle of what was once a slow season for both industries.

Promotional Strategies

Once its larger marketing objectives are clear, a firm must develop a promotional strategy to achieve them. Two fundamentally different strategies are often used:

- A **pull strategy** is designed to appeal directly to customers who will demand the product from retailers. In turn, retailers will demand the product from wholesalers. When publishing a Stephen King novel, for example, Doubleday directs its promotions at horror story fans. If a bookstore does not stock the book, requests from readers will prompt it to order copies from Doubleday.
- Using a **push strategy,** a firm aggressively markets its product to wholesalers and retailers who then persuade customers to buy it. Brunswick Corp., for instance, uses a push strategy to promote Bayliner boats, directing its promotions at dealers and persuading them to order more inventory. Dealers are then responsible for stimulating demand among boaters in their districts.

Many large firms, of course, use a combination of pull and push strategies. For example, General Foods uses advertising to create consumer demand (*pull*) for its cereals. At the same time, it pushes wholesalers and retailers to stock them.

The Promotional Mix

As we noted in Chapter 13, there are four types of promotional tools—*advertising, personal selling, sales promotions*, and *publicity* and *public relations*. The best combination of these tools—that is, the best **promotional mix**—depends on many factors. The company's product, the costs of different tools, and the characteristics of the target audience are all important.

Advertising Promotions Advertising is paid, nonpersonal communication used by an identified sponsor to inform an audience about a product. In 1994, U.S. firms spent $150 billion on advertising—with $43 billion of this amount spent by just 100 companies.[10] In this section, we describe each of the different types of *advertising media*, noting both advantages and limitations of each.

Advertising Media. Bombarded with thousands of advertisements, consumers tend to ignore the bulk of the ads they see or hear. Marketers, therefore, must find out who their customers are, which media they attend to, what message will appeal to them, and how to get their attention. Marketers use several different **advertising media**—that is, specific communication devices for carrying a seller's message to potential customers. IBM, for example, uses television ads to keep its name fresh in consumers' minds. It uses newspaper and magazine ads, however, to educate consumers on product features and trade publications to introduce new software. Each medium, of course, has its own advantages and disadvantages.[11] The combination of media that a company chooses to advertise its products is called its **media mix.** The following are the most common advertising media.

- *Newspapers* are the most widely used medium, accounting for about 25 percent of all advertising expenditures. Because each local market has at least one daily newspaper, newspapers provide excellent coverage. Each day, they reach more

pull strategy
Promotional strategy designed to appeal directly to customers, who will demand a product from retailers

push strategy
Promotional strategy designed to encourage wholesalers and/or retailers to market products to consumers

promotional mix
Combination of tools used to promote a product

advertising
Promotional tool consisting of paid, nonpersonal communication used by an identified sponsor to inform an audience about a product

advertising media
Variety of communication devices for carrying a seller's message to potential customers

media mix
Combination of advertising media chosen to carry messages about a product

than 113 million U.S. adults. The main advantage of newspaper advertising is flexible, rapid coverage—ads can easily be changed from day to day. However, newspapers are generally thrown out after one day, are usually not printed in color, and have poor reproduction quality. Moreover, newspapers do not usually allow advertisers to target audiences very well.

■ *Television* accounts for about 22 percent of all advertising outlays. Combining sight, sound, and motion, television appeals to a fuller complement of the viewer's senses. In addition, information on viewer demographics for a particular program allows advertisers to aim at target audiences. Finally, television reaches more people than any other medium. For example, recent Super Bowl games have consistently attracted more than 40 million households and 115 million viewers. Unfortunately, the fact that there are so many commercials on TV often causes viewers to confuse products. Television is also the most expensive medium in which to advertise. Companies like McDonald's, Pepsi, Frito-Lay, Anheuser-Busch, and Quaker State now pay about $1 million for 30–second commercials during the Super Bowl, with one 90-second Nike ad in 1995 becoming TV advertising's first $3 million spot. "If you're in the Super Bowl," reasoned one Nike executive, "you might as well give it your best shot."

"If you're in the Super Bowl, you might as well give it your best shot."

—Nike marketing executive
on the company's expenditure of $3 million for one 90-second Super Bowl ad

---

direct mail
Advertising medium in which messages are mailed directly to consumers

■ *Direct mail advertisements* account for 18 percent of all advertising outlays. **Direct mail** involves fliers or other types of printed advertisements mailed directly to consumers' homes or places of business. It allows the company to select its audience and personalize its message. In addition, although many people discard "junk mail," advertisers can predict in advance how many recipients will take a mailing seriously. These individuals have a stronger-than-average interest in the product advertised and are more likely than most to buy the promoted product.

■ About 7 percent of all advertising outlays are for *radio advertising*. More than 180 million people in the United States listen to the radio each day, and radio ads are relatively inexpensive. For example, a small business in a midwestern town of 100,000 people pays only about $20 for a 30-second local radio spot. (A television spot in the same area costs more than $250.) In addition, stations are usually segmented into categories, such as rock and roll, country and western, jazz, talk shows, news, and religious programming. Thus, their audiences are largely segmented. Unfortunately, radio ads, like television ads, are over quickly. Furthermore, they provide only audio presentations, and people tend to use the radio as "background" while doing other things.

■ *Magazine advertising* accounts for roughly 5 percent of all advertising. The huge variety of magazines provides a high level of ready market segmentation. Magazines also allow advertisers plenty of space for detailed product information. In addition, they allow for excellent reproduction of photographs and artwork. Finally, because magazines have long lives and tend to be passed from person to person, ads get constantly increased exposure. Ads must be submitted well in advance, however, and there is often no guarantee of where an ad will appear within a magazine.

- *Outdoor advertising*—billboards, signs, and advertisements on buses, taxis, and subways—makes up about 1 percent of all advertising. These ads are relatively inexpensive, face little competition for customers' attention, and are subject to high repeat exposure.
- *Other advertising channels.* A combination of many additional media, including catalogs, sidewalk handouts, *Yellow Pages*, skywriting, telephone calls, special events, and door-to-door communications, make up the remaining 22 percent of all U.S. advertising. The most recent of these channels is the Internet, where such well-known names as Burlington Coat Factory, Miller Genuine Draft, MCI Communications, and Reebok have all placed ads. Although Internet advertising is in its infancy and offers high potential, most marketers recognize that it also has limitations. In particular, consumers don't want to wade through electronic pages looking at details on hundreds of products. One expert offers the disappointing opinion that most of the commercial advertisements on the Internet may, in fact, never be read by anyone.[12]

Personal Selling Promotions In **personal selling,** a salesperson communicates one-to-one with potential customers to identify their needs and line them up with the seller's products. The oldest form of selling, it provides the personal link between seller and buyer and adds to a firm's credibility because it allows buyers to interact with and ask questions of the seller.

personal selling
Promotional tool in which a salesperson communicates one on one with potential customers

However, because it involves personal interaction, personal selling requires a certain level of trust between buyer and seller—a relationship that must often be established over time. Moreover, because presentations are generally made to only one or two individuals at a time, personal selling is the most expensive form of promotion per contact. Expenses may include salespeople's compensation and their overhead, usually travel, food, and lodging. Indeed, the median cost of a single industrial sales call has been estimated at approximately $250.[13]

Such high costs have prompted many companies to turn to *telemarketing*—using telephone solicitations to perform the personal selling process. Telemarketing can be used to handle any stage of the personal selling process or to set up appointments for outside salespeople. It saves the cost of personal sales visits to industrial customers. Each industrial buyer requires an average of nearly four visits to complete a sale. Some companies have thus realized savings in sales visits of $1,000 or more. Not surprisingly, such savings are stimulating the remarkable growth of telemarketing, which sold over $300 billion in goods and services in 1993. Experts expect nearly 5 million more people to be employed in telemarketing (for both retail and industrial sales) by the year 2000.[14]

Sales Promotions **Sales promotions** are short-term promotional activities designed to stimulate consumer buying or cooperation from distributors, sales agents, or other members of the trade. They are important because they increase the likelihood that buyers will try products. They also enhance product recognition and can increase purchase size and amount. For example, soap is sometimes bound in packages of four with the promotion "buy three, get one free."

sales promotion
Short-term promotional activity designed to stimulate consumer buying or cooperation from distributors and sales agents

To be successful, sales promotions must be convenient and accessible when the decision to purchase occurs. For instance, if Harley-Davidson has a one-week motorcycle promotion but you have no local dealer, the promotion is neither convenient nor accessible to you, and you will not buy. In contrast, if Folgers offers a $1-off coupon that you can save for use later, the promotion is both convenient and accessible.

Types of Sales Promotions. The best-known forms of promotions are coupons, point-of-purchase displays, various purchasing incentives (especially free samples and premiums), trade shows, and contests and sweepstakes.

BUSINESS FIELD TRIP

"OUR CUSTOMERS KNOW US AND WE KNOW THEM"

Can an industrial sales company be customer driven rather than product driven? At Chaparral Steel Co., the answer is a confident yes. The key, say Chaparral officials, is making customer satisfaction the company's number-one priority. "Our strategic advantage," says Jeff Werner, Senior Vice President for Structural Sales, "is to outservice the competition." Precisely what does service superiority mean for Chaparral managers? It means, says Werner, keeping 80 percent of the firm's products in stock at all times. It also means setting and meeting crucial goals—for instance, filling 80 percent of all inquiries within one to two weeks.

THE CUSTOMER SERVICE-INVENTORY LINK.

In large part, Chaparral delivers outstanding customer service because of inventory availability. For instance, 40 percent of its inventory is always available for customers who need steel in a hurry. The other 60 percent has been ordered between three weeks and three months in advance and is waiting to be shipped. With such an enormous commitment to immediate service, it is no surprise that Chaparral's 200,000-ton inventory is one of the largest at one site worldwide.

Chaparral believes so strongly in the connection between inventory availability and marketing success that it has assigned inventory "ownership" to its sales department. This practice gives the sales group responsibility for managing finished goods—a process that includes inventory, loading, shipping, and sales. "Having the sales group oversee inventory is not typical in this industry," admits Werner. "We do it because it helps us deliver product faster than traditional steel mills. It makes us market driven."

A "ONE-PRICE-FITS-ALL" PRICING STRATEGY.

With its emphasis on service and availability, Chaparral has chosen not to pursue an aggressive price-oriented marketing strategy. Even so, its prices are as low as its domestic and foreign competitors. "At one time," explains Jeff Werner, "our practice was to meet the prices of competitors, but when prices fell we had to change and take a chance. We switched to a 'one-price-fits-all' approach, regardless of location." What is the advantage of this practice? "It means that the customer pays a fixed price plus freight," says Werner, "and we no longer offer competitive or quantity discounts." Instead, Chaparral offers competitive prices, available inventory, and rapid shipment.

> ### "When prices fell, we had to take a chance. We switched to a 'one-price-fits-all' approach."
> —Jeff Werner
> *Senior Vice President for Structural Sales at Chaparral Steel Co.*

FLEXIBILITY AND QUICK RESPONSE.

Chaparral's marketing emphasis began in the early 1970s with the decision to build a minimill rather than a traditional steel mill. Guided by a competitive commitment to being an international producer of low-cost, high-quality products, its minimill operations give Chaparral the flexibility and speed to compete with larger traditional mills that are slow to improve production methods and even slower to respond to last-minute orders. The decision to locate near Dallas was also market driven. It positioned the company as a supplier situated at the center of a construction boom.

Chaparral's quick-response capability is particularly important in its relationships with building contractors, who are not always able to plan more than a few weeks in advance. It is not uncommon, for example, for a builder to order 500 tons of steel to be delivered in just two weeks. Vice President for Administration Dennis Beach stresses that its ability to meet such last-minute orders is a key factor in helping Chaparral build long-term relationships. "We establish long-term relationships with our customers in good times and bad that are based on competitive pricing, quality materials, service, and availability. Our customers know us and we know them. It's not an in and out type of business." ▶

WHO BUYS AND SELLS CHAPARRAL STEEL?

Chaparral services 1,200 industrial customers in three categories:

- Steel distributors, also called service centers, which purchase steel and keep it available for resale to their own end-user customers
- Intermediary manufacturers, known as metal processors, which convert Chaparral steel into products that are then sold to other manufacturers to make their own products

■ End users, who use steel to make parts for final products that are sold to other companies or to the public

Because building contractors can often plan only a few weeks in advance, Chaparral maintains a quick-response capability as one means of establishing close, long-term relationships with its customers.

"Most of our steel is sold to intermediaries," reports Dennis Beach, "not directly to companies that use the steel in final applications."

Although about 42 percent of product sales occur in Texas, Oklahoma, Louisiana, and Arkansas, Chaparral has expanded its marketing reach throughout North America, especially Canada and Mexico, as well as Europe and Asia. Its products are sold by a 30-person sales organization based at its Texas headquarters. Selling, including order processing, generally takes place over the telephone and via a state-of-the-art information system that gives customers immediate access to inventory and shipping information. With such timely, accurate data within immediate reach, Chaparral salespeople need to make in-person sales calls only about once every three months.

Although Chaparral owes a great deal of its success to its marketing strategy, it could not accomplish its goals without full cooperation from its production department. Indeed, it is the production department that supplies needed inventory and lowers costs through various economies of scale, including longer production runs. "Longer runs," explains Dennis Beach, "create real economic benefit. When we roll one size without stopping and starting, it's more cost effective." Chaparral maintains its competitive edge by passing these and other savings on to its customers.

■ A certificate that entitles the bearer to a stated savings off a regular price is a **coupon.** Coupons may be used to encourage customers to try new products, to attract customers away from competitors, or to induce current customers to buy more of a product. They appear in newspapers and magazines, are included with other products, and are often sent through direct mail.

■ To grab customers' attention as they walk through stores, some companies use **point-of-purchase (POP) displays.** Located at the ends of aisles or near checkout counters, POP displays make it easier for customers to find products and easier for sellers to eliminate competitors from consideration.

■ Free samples and premiums are *purchasing incentives*. Free samples allow customers to try products without risk. They may be given out at local retail outlets or sent by manufacturers to consumers by direct mail. **Premiums** are gifts, such as pens, pencils, calendars, and coffee mugs, that are given away to consumers in return for buying a specified product.

■ Periodically, industries sponsor **trade shows** for members and customers. Trade shows allow companies to rent booths to display and demonstrate products to customers who have a special interest in them or who are ready to buy.

■ Customers, distributors, and sales representatives may all be persuaded to increase sales by means of *contests*. For example, consumers may be asked to enter their cats in the Purina Cat Chow calendar contest by submitting entry blanks from the backs of cat food packages.

coupon
Sales promotion technique in which a certificate is issued entitling the buyer to a reduced price

point-of-purchase (POP) display
Sales promotion technique in which product displays are located in certain areas to stimulate purchase

premium
Sales promotion technique in which offers of free or reduced-price items are used to stimulate purchase

trade show
Sales promotion technique in which various members of an industry gather to display, demonstrate, and sell products

publicity
Promotional tool in which information about a company or product is transmitted by general mass media

public relations
Company-influenced publicity directed at building good relations with the public and dealing with unfavorable events

Publicity and Public Relations   Much to the delight of marketing managers with tight budgets, **publicity** is free. Moreover, because it is presented in a news format, consumers often see publicity as objective and highly believable. Thus, it is a very important part of the promotional mix.

Public relations is company-influenced publicity that seeks to build good relations with the public and to deal with the effects of unfavorable events.[15] It attempts to establish goodwill with customers (and potential customers) by performing and publicizing a company's public service activities. The McDonald's 1995 annual report, for example, proudly announces that there were 168 Ronald McDonald houses in 12 countries serving more than 2,500 away-from-home families with seriously ill children every night. Southwest Airlines gained favor with the flying public when it announced in 1996 it would spend $20 million to replace the flight data recorders ("black boxes") on its fleet of 737s—and that it would do so ahead of mandated improvements being considered by the Federal Aviation Administration. Southwest's plans were announced after two unexplained crashes of 737s operated by other airlines.[16]

Continued from page 355

The Swoosh of Air Jordan Sales

Nike Courts Another Championship Marketing Season

Riding high on the sale of Air Jordan sneakers and propelled by a marketing strategy that limits supply in the face of increasing demand, Nike's relationship with small, independent retailers is often strained. For one thing, these outlets receive their product shipments after national chains. Even so, they realize that they are getting an eminently salable product, and despite some frustration, many small retailers believe that late inventory shipments cost them relatively little in lost sales of Air Jordans. As one Brooklyn retailer explains, "I know I can sell them—

> ## "Nobody likes to be told that they can't maximize their business."
>
> ### —A small sporting goods retailer
>
> *on Nike's strict control over the allocation of its products*

before the [release] date or after." At the same time, however, Nike's practice of maintaining strict control over product allocation makes small retail-

ers nervous, especially when products not related to Jordan are involved. "Nobody," volunteers one store owner, "likes to be told that they can't maximize their business."

With its astounding success, of course, Nike has little reason to change its marketing strategy. "When we stop producing the best product and giving the best margins, then it will be the retailer's decision to stop selling Nike," says Nike President Tom Clarke. Until then, the marketing ball clearly remains in Nike's possession.

Case Questions

1. Air Jordan sneakers continue in the growth stage of the product life cycle. Is this trend likely to continue after Michael Jordan retires from basketball? Research the impact on sneaker sales during Jordan's temporary retirement in 1994–1995.
2. The latest Air Jordan model does not have the Nike *swoosh* symbol emblazoned on its side. How do you think the decision to remove it will affect brand recognition? Why do you think Nike decided to market a sneaker without the company's trademark symbol?
3. What are Nike's pricing objectives for the Air Jordan, and what specific pricing strategies are being used to achieve them?
4. Describe the elements in Nike's promotion of Air Jordan sneakers. Why is advertising such a small part of the promotional mix?
5. Why is Michael Jordan's endorsement so important to product success?

SUMMARY OF LEARNING OBJECTIVES

1. **Identify a *product* and distinguish between *consumer* and *industrial products*.** In developing products, firms must decide whether to produce *consumer goods* for direct sale to individual consumers or *industrial goods* for sale to other firms. Marketers must recognize that buyers will pay less for common, rapidly consumed *convenience goods* than for less frequently purchased *shopping* and *specialty goods*. In industrial markets, expense items are generally less expensive and more rapidly consumed than such capital items as buildings and equipment.
2. **Explain the importance of *branding and packaging*.** Each product is given an identity by its brand and the way it is packaged and labeled. The goal in developing *brands*—symbols to distinguish products and signal their uniform quality—is to increase the preference that consumers have for a product with a particular brand name. *National brands* refer to products that are produced and

widely distributed by the same manufacturer. *Licensed brands* are items for whose names sellers have bought the rights from organizations or individuals. *Private brands* are developed by wholesalers or retailers and commissioned from manufacturers. *Packaging* provides an attractive container and advertises a product's features and benefits. It also reduces the risk of damage, spoilage, and theft.

3. **Identify the various *pricing objectives* that govern *pricing decisions* and describe the *price-setting tools* used in making these decisions.**   A firm's *pricing decisions* reflect the *pricing objectives* set by its management. While these objectives vary, they all reflect the goals that a seller hopes to reach in selling a product. They include *profit maximizing* (pricing to sell the number of units that will generate the highest possible total profits) and meeting *market share goals* (ensuring continuous sales by maintaining a strong percentage of the total sales for a specific product type). Other considerations include the need to survive in a competitive marketplace, social and ethical concerns, and even a firm's image.

    Price-setting tools are chosen to meet a seller's pricing objectives. *Cost-oriented pricing* recognizes the need to cover the variable costs of producing a product (costs that change with the number of units produced or sold). In determining the price level at which profits will be generated, *break-even analysis* also considers *fixed costs* (costs, such as facilities and salaries, that are unaffected by the number of items produced or sold).

4. **Discuss *pricing strategies* and tactics for both existing and new products.**   Either a *price-skimming strategy* (pricing very high) or a *penetration-pricing strategy* (pricing very low) may be effective for new products. Depending on the other elements in the marketing mix, products may be priced at, above, or below prevailing prices for similar products. Guided by a firm's pricing strategies, managers set prices using tactics such as *price lining* (offering items in certain categories at a set number of prices), *psychological pricing* (appealing to buyers' perceptions of relative prices), and *discounting* (reducing prices to stimulate sales).

5. **Identify the important objectives of *promotion* and discuss the considerations entailed in selecting a *promotional mix*.**   Although the ultimate goal of a promotion is to increase sales, other goals include *communicating information*, *positioning a product*, and *controlling sales volume*. In deciding on the appropriate *promotional mix*, marketers must consider the good or service being offered, the cost of the various promotional tools, and the buyer decision process. Promotional mix strategies must also be balanced and usually change from stage to stage in the product's life cycle.

6. **Describe the key *advertising media* available to marketing managers.**   Marketing managers may use various *advertising media*, or specific communication devices, for transmitting a seller's message to potential buyers. The most common media—*newspapers, television, direct mail, radio, magazines,* and *outdoor advertising*—differ in their cost and their ability to segment target markets. The combination of media that a company chooses is called its *media mix*.

7. **Describe the various types of *sales promotions* and explain the uses of *publicity* and *public relations*.**   *Coupons* provide savings off the regular price of a product. *Point-of-purchase (POP) displays* are intended to grab attention and help customers find products in stores. *Purchasing incentives* include *samples* (which let customers try products without buying them) and *premiums* (rewards for buying products). At *trade shows*, sellers rent booths to display products to customers who already have an interest in buying. *Contests* and *sweepstakes* hope to increase sales by stimulating buyers' interest in products.

Publicity—general mass-media information about a company or a product—differs from other types of promotions in being free (though often uncontrollable). It is useful in ensuring the broad dissemination of a message. *Public relations* is company-influenced publicity whose purpose is to build good relations with the public and to deal with unfavorable events.

STUDY QUESTIONS AND EXERCISES

Review

1. What are the various classifications of consumer and industrial products? Give an example of a good and a service for each category other than those discussed in the text.
2. List the four stages in the product life cycle and discuss some of the ways a company can extend product life cycles.
3. How do cost-oriented pricing and break-even analysis help managers measure the potential impact of prices?
4. Explain the difference between pull and push strategies.
5. Compare and contrast the advantages and disadvantages of different advertising media.

Analysis

6. Suppose that a small publisher selling to book distributors has fixed operating costs of $600,000 each year and variable costs of $3.00 per book. How many books must the firm sell to break even if the selling price is $10.00? If the company expects to sell 50,000 books next year and decides on a 40-percent markup, what will the selling price be?
7. Suppose your company produces industrial products for other firms. How would you go about determining the prices of your products? Describe the method you would use to arrive at a pricing decision.
8. Find some examples of publicity about some business, either a local firm or a national company. Did the publicity have, or is it likely to have, positive or negative consequences for the business involved? Why?

Application Exercises

9. Select a product with which you are familiar and analyze various possible pricing objectives for it. What information would you want to have if you were to adopt a profit-maximizing objective? A market share objective? An image objective?
10. Select a product that is sold nationally. Identify as many of the media used in its promotion as you can. Which medium is used most? On the whole, do you think the campaign is effective? Why or why not?

BUILDING YOUR BUSINESS SKILLS

This exercise enhances the following SCANS workplace competencies: demonstrating basic skills, demonstrating thinking skills, exhibiting interpersonal skills, and working with information.

Goal

To encourage students to evaluate advertising from the standpoint of industry professionals

Situation

Bob Garfield is the advertising critic for *Advertising Age* magazine, which should be available in your college or local library. (An electronic edition can be found on Prodigy.) He discusses various advertising issues and evaluates new ads, awarding ratings that range from one star (★) to four stars (★★★★). Garfield has recently discussed ads for Magnavox (27-inch color TV infomercial), IBM ("Solutions for a Small Planet"), and Coors (Coors Light Channel).

Method

Step 1: Working individually or in small groups, identify one of the campaigns critiqued by Bob Garfield (your instructor may provide them for you, or you may get the information through library research).

Step 2: Evaluate and critique one or more ad campaigns individually or with a group. How would you rate a given ad?

Analysis

Compare your critique with Garfield's. What factors did you take into consideration when you evaluated the campaign? What was the rationale for your rating compared with Garfield's?

Follow-Up

1. In evaluating an ad, what issues appear to be most important to Garfield? How do they compare with the criteria you used in your evaluation?

2. Were you surprised by some of the information contained in Garfield's reviews, such as the size of the budgets for individual advertising campaigns? Why? Did such information prompt you to rethink your opinion about a campaign?

Exploring the Net

SHOPPING AT HOME BY MEANS OF ELECTRONIC MEDIA IS A RELATIVELY RECENT DEVELOPMENT. ELECTRONIC SHOPPING INVOLVES ALL ASPECTS OF MARKETING—STRATEGY, PRODUCT DEVELOPMENT, PRICING, PROMOTION, DISTRIBUTION—AIMED AT THE CONSUMER MARKET. TO FIND OUT MORE ABOUT MARKETING IN THE WORLD OF ELECTRONIC HOME SHOPPING, LOG ON TO THE FOLLOWING WEBSITE:

QVC INC., *i*QVC SHOP, AT
http://www.qvc.com

After you have explored the various pages and reports posted on the QVC Website, think about the various ways in which the principles of marketing apply to electronic shopping by considering the following questions:

1. How would you characterize the "product" being offered under the *i*QVC label?

2. What are the important *marketing variables* that had to be considered in designing the *i*QVC product?

3. At which stage of the *life cycle* is *i*QVC's product now situated? Explain your answer according to the information you obtained from this Website.

4. Can you identify any features in *i*QVC's Website that are designed to encourage *brand loyalty* for its product?

5. Compare *i*QVC's *price-setting* methods with those of its nonelectronic competitors. In what ways are they the same? In what ways do they differ?

6. Evaluate the *promotional methods* that *i*QVC uses at its Website. What are some of those methods, and how effective do you believe them to be? Can you offer any suggestions for making them more effective?

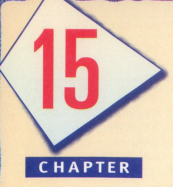

DISTRIBUTING PRODUCTS

The Battle Plan for Attacking Inventory at the Big Store

THE NEW LOGISTICS GENERAL AT SEARS

Retired General Norman Schwarzkopf has declared that William G. "Gus" Pagonis did a "magnificent" job for him during the Persian Gulf War. Then a three-star Army general, Pagonis managed the largest military logistics operation in history while fighting firestorms, extreme weather conditions, and cultural confusion. Operating under nearly impossible wartime demands, Pagonis was in charge of distributing 122 million meals, 1.3 billion gallons of fuel, 12,000 tanks and other combat vehicles, 800 million pounds of ammunition, and 32,000 tons of mail. As much as any single person, Pagonis made the U.S. war effort possible.

The remarkable logistics achievements of the Persian Gulf War convinced Arthur Martinez, CEO of Sears, Roebuck & Co., to offer the retired general a job as Sears' logistics czar—the person in charge of moving goods at the giant retailer from one place to another. Pagonis has now held this job for more than three years, and by all accounts, he has been as successful in retailing as he was in war. In 1993, skeptics doubted whether Pagonis' background had

> **"If I allow myself to concentrate on just one area, the stores suffer, the consumer suffers. I just don't let that happen. I always look at total systems."**
>
> —William G. "Gus" Pagonis
> *Senior Vice President in Charge of Logistics at Sears*

prepared him to handle the goods at Sears—7 billion pounds of merchandise a year carried by 600,000 truckload shipments from 160 warehouses and distribution centers to 800 stores. There are no longer any doubts. Indeed, at a critical time in Sears' history—with its customers deserting in droves and analysts dismissing it as a "dinosaur"—Pagonis cut in half the time it takes to move merchandise from suppliers to stores and cut overall logistics costs by $45 million a year. His efforts have helped turn the company around.

Once called "the stepchild of the retail industry," *logistics*—or distribu-

tion management—involves moving goods from supplier to warehouse to store to customer. It also entails managing the flow of supplies to increase efficiency and cut costs, and it means improving customer service. When Pagonis took charge at Sears, he found gross inefficiencies. Moreover, no single person was in charge—a fact that already disturbed Martinez. "It was very clear to me," the CEO recalls, "that getting costs out and getting a rational network could only happen if we had one executive in charge."

Pagonis attacked the status quo with military zeal. He reduced the number of channels used by store managers to order products from twelve to four and increased the average load carried by delivery trucks leaving Sears' distribution centers from 60 percent to 90 percent. Pagonis also coordinated the diverse operational functions. "You have to worry about all the elements working together," he explains. "Even in the Gulf War, if I had for a minute started worrying [only] about food, then nobody would have any tanks for the battlefield. . . . If I only thought about ammunition, what about the clothing? Some people say, no, I just want the ammunition. But what about the poor soldier? It was 140 degrees when we arrived. When we went to war, it was freezing. If we hadn't ordered more than 5 million sets of long underwear, our troops would have suffered. If I allow myself to concentrate on just one area, the stores suffer, the consumer suffers. I just don't let that happen. I always look at total systems."

Under Pagonis' leadership, distribution functions have changed in ways that are noticeable to customers. In many parts of the country, for example, consumers can now choose among morning, afternoon, and evening deliveries, and next-day delivery—even on Sunday—is possible in seven out of ten markets. The need for speed applies to everything from appliances to fashion merchandise. For instance, it now takes seven days instead of 14 to ship apparel from suppliers to stores. This increased speed is vital in a market that often gains momentum from sudden fashion trends. If merchandise is in the stores when customers look for it, sales are made.

Faster deliveries from suppliers to stores have enabled Sears to reduce inventories and thus lower inventory financing costs. With smaller inventories in each store, Sears has converted 800,000 square feet of store storage space into selling space and reduced inventory costs by $10 million.

As the success of Gus Pagonis shows, a rapid, efficient distribution system is vital to retailing success. Indeed, by cutting distribution costs, a company can gain an important competitive edge. Among domestic retailers, Sears now has one of the lowest ratios of general and administrative expenses as a percentage of domestic sales. Moreover, the $45 million in cost savings achieved by Pagonis has helped boost annual profits from continuing operations to $1.03 billion.

No firm can succeed without *placing* its products—that is, without getting them to its customers. As we saw in Chapter 13, *place* is the fourth *P* in the marketing mix. Choosing methods of distribution is a basic marketing decision. Should the company sell directly to customers? Would it reach more customers through retail stores? If so, at what types of outlets? Once stores are chosen, transportation methods must be selected. For example, how will merchandise be moved from factory to retailer? By focusing on the learning objectives of this chapter, you will consider questions like these and better understand the importance of distribution in the marketing process.

After reading this chapter, you should be able to

1. Identify the different *channels of distribution*

2. Explain the differences between *merchant wholesalers* and *agents/brokers*

3. Identify the different types of *retail stores*

4. Describe the major activities in the *physical distribution process*

5. Compare the five basic forms of *transportation* and identify the types of firms that provide them

Continued on page 402

■ THE DISTRIBUTION MIX

distribution mix
The combination of distribution channels by which a firm gets its products to end users

We have already seen that a company needs an appropriate product mix. But the success of any product also depends in part on its **distribution mix**—the combination of distribution channels that a firm selects to get a product to end users.[1] In this section, we consider some of the many factors that enter into the distribution mix. First, we look at the role of the target audience and explain the need for *intermediaries*. We then discuss the basic *distribution strategies*.

Intermediaries and Distribution Channels

intermediary
Individual or firm that helps to distribute a product

wholesaler
Intermediary that sells products to other businesses for resale to final consumers

retailer
Intermediary that sells products directly to consumers

Once called *middlemen*, **intermediaries** are the individuals and firms that help to distribute a producer's goods. They are generally classified as *wholesalers* or *retailers*. **Wholesalers** sell products to other businesses, which resell them to final consumers. **Retailers** sell products directly to consumers. While some firms rely on independent intermediaries, others employ their own distribution networks and sales forces. The decision normally hinges on three factors:

- The company's target markets
- The nature of its products
- The costs of maintaining distribution and sales networks

In this section, we examine these factors more closely by describing some of the distribution decisions that go into the marketing of consumer products.

distribution channel
Network of interdependent companies through which a product passes from producer to end user

Distribution of Consumer Products   A **distribution channel** is the path that a product follows from producer to end user. Figure 15.1 shows how the six primary distribution channels can be identified according to the kinds of channel members who participate in getting products to their ultimate destinations. As we move through this discussion, note that all channels begin with a manufacturer and end with a consumer or an industrial user. Channels 1 through 4 are most often used for the distribution of consumer goods and services.

direct channel
Distribution channel in which a product travels from producer to consumer without intermediaries

Channel 1: Direct Distribution of Consumer Products.   In a **direct channel,** the product travels from the producer to the consumer without intermediaries.

- Dell Computer Corp., for example, sells personal computers over the phone and customers receive their purchases by direct mail. Today Dell Computer is a $3.4-billion-a-year business and the fourth-largest PC maker in the United States. By selling direct, Dell and rival Gateway 2000 have captured about 20 percent of the $45 billion PC market. Dell runs a bare-bones operation in Austin, Texas, where workers assemble off-the-shelf components into finished PCs as orders are received. As the first entrepreneur to sell computers by mail, Michael Dell feels confident that he knows his market better than anyone else. However, Dell's experience has also taught him that direct sales is more difficult than it looks: "It's not as easy as a couple of 1-800 lines and a bunch of picnic tables," he warns.[2]

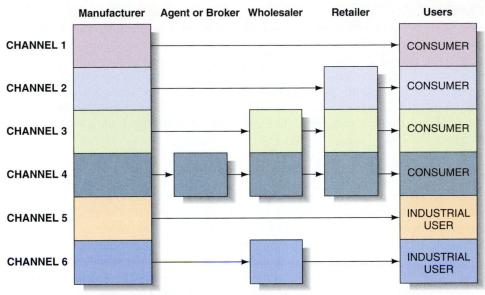

FIGURE 15.1 ◆ Channels of Distribution

"It's not as easy as a couple of 1-800 lines and a bunch of picnic tables."

—Computer entrepreneur Michael Dell
on the direct marketing venture

Channel 2: Retail Distribution of Consumer Products. In Channel 2, manufacturers distribute products through retailers. Companies like Goodyear and The Limited maintain their own systems of retail outlets. In contrast, Liz Claiborne relies on more than 9,300 retailers to sell its apparel worldwide. Similarly, most firms in the perfume and fragrance industry use sales forces to sell products to retailers, who then sell them over the counter to consumers.

Channel 3: Wholesale Distribution of Consumer Products. Until the mid-1960s, Channel 2 was the most widely used method of nondirect distribution. It requires a large amount of floor space, however, both for storing merchandise and for displaying it in retail stores. Faced with the rising cost of retail space, many retailers found that they could not afford both retail and storage space. Thus, wholesalers entered the distribution network to take over more and more of the storage service. An example of Channel 3 is combination convenience stores/gas stations. Approximately 90 percent of the space in these stores is needed for merchandise displays. Only about 10 percent is left for storage and/or office facilities.

At the same time, wholesale channels have always played a role in the distribution of some products. Many manufacturers, for example, distribute products only in large quantities. Thus, small businesses that cannot afford large-quantity purchases often rely on wholesalers to hold and supply inventories on short notice. For example, a family-owned grocery store that annually sells only 100 cases of canned spinach cannot afford a truckload order of 500 cases. Instead, it will order a few cases each month from a local wholesaler, which buys and stores large lots to resell in small quantities.

sales agent/broker
Independent intermediary that usually represents many manufacturers and sells to wholesalers, retailers, or both

Channel 4: Distribution through Sales Agents or Brokers. Channel 4 uses **sales agents,** or **brokers,** who represent manufacturers and sell to wholesalers, retailers, or both. They receive commissions based on the price of goods they sell. Agents generally deal in the related product lines of a few producers, serving as their sales representatives on a relatively permanent basis. Travel agents, for example, represent airlines, car rental companies, and hotels. In contrast, brokers are hired to assist in buying and selling temporarily, matching sellers and buyers as needed. This channel is often used in the food and clothing industries. The real estate industry also relies on brokers for matching buyers and sellers of property.

The Pros and Cons of Nondirect Distribution

Ultimately, of course, each link in the distribution chain makes a profit by charging a mark-up or commission. Thus, nondirect distribution channels mean higher prices for end users. The more members in the channel—the more intermediaries—the higher the final price. Mark-ups may vary widely, ranging from 10 to 40 percent for manufacturers, from 2 to 25 percent for wholesalers, and from 5 to 100 percent for retailers. The size of the mark-up depends on the particular industry and competitive conditions.

At the same time, however, intermediaries can save consumers both time and money. In doing so they provide *added value* for customers. Moreover, this *value-adding* activity continues and accumulates at each stage of the supply chain. In fact, if you recall our discussions of form, place, and time utility in Chapter 11, you will see that intermediaries can add value when they provide one or more types of utility by making the right products available where and when the customer needs them.[3] For example, consider Figure 15.2, which illustrates the problem of making chili without benefit of a common intermediary, the supermarket. You would obviously spend a lot more time, money, and mental energy if you tried to gather all the ingredients yourself. Moreover, if we eliminated intermediaries, we would not eliminate either their functions or the costs entailed by what they do. Intermediaries exist, then, because they perform necessary functions in cost-efficient ways.

industrial distribution
Network of channel members involved in the flow of manufactured goods to industrial customers

Distribution of Industrial Products

Industrial channels are important because every company is itself a customer that buys other companies' products. The Kellogg Co., for example, buys grain to make breakfast cereals. Lawless Container Corp. buys rolls of paper and vats of glue to make corrugated boxes. Humana, a nationwide chain of for-profit hospitals, buys medicines and other supplies to provide medical services. **Industrial distribution** refers to the network of channel members involved in the flow

FIGURE 15.2 ◆ The Value-Adding Intermediary

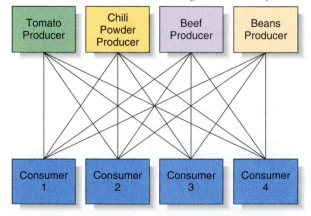

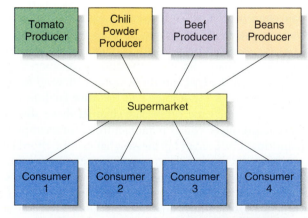

PURCHASE OF GOODS WITHOUT INTERMEDIARIES   PURCHASE OF GOODS WITH INTERMEDIARIES

of manufactured goods to industrial customers. Unlike consumer products, industrial products are traditionally distributed through Channels 5 or 6, shown in Figure 15.1.

Channel 5: Direct Distribution of Industrial Products. Most industrial goods are sold directly by the manufacturer to the industrial buyer. Lawless Container Corp., for instance, produces packaging containers that are sold directly to such customers as Fisher-Price (toys), Dirt Devil (hand vacuum cleaners), and Mr. Coffee (coffee makers). As contact points with their customers, manufacturers maintain **sales offices.** These offices provide all services for the company's customers and serve as headquarters for its salespeople.

Other products distributed through Channel 5 include steel, transistors, and conveyors. Intermediaries are often unnecessary because such goods are usually purchased in large quantities. In some cases, however, brokers or agents may enter the distribution chain between manufacturers and buyers.

sales office
Office maintained by a manufacturer as a contact point with its customers

Channel 6: Wholesale Distribution of Industrial Products. Wholesalers function as intermediaries between manufacturers and end users in only a very small percentage of industrial channels. Brokers and agents are even rarer. Channel 6 is most often used for accessory equipment (computer terminals, office equipment) and supplies (floppy disks, copier paper). While manufacturers produce these items in large quantities, companies buy them in small quantities. Few companies, for example, order truckloads of paper clips. As with consumer goods, then, intermediaries help end users by representing manufacturers or by breaking down large quantities into smaller sales units.

In some areas, however, relationships are changing. In the office products industry, for instance, Channel 6 is being displaced by the emergence of a new channel that looks very much like Channel 3 for consumer products. Instead of buying office supplies from wholesalers (Channel 6), many users are shopping at office discount stores like Staples, Office Depot, and Office Max.[4] ▼ All three warehouse-like superstores target small and midsize businesses, which generally buy supplies at retail stores, much as they target retail consumers. In these new "discount stores for industrial users," customers stroll down the aisles behind shopping carts, selecting from 7,000 items at prices 20 to 75 percent lower than manufacturers' suggested prices.

Retailers like Staples concentrate on dominant assortments of merchandise. Customers shopping for stationery or office equipment know beforehand that they will find what they are looking for. When such retailers maintain huge assortments in one product area, they complement wide selections with steep price discounts and are often called category killers. *Other well-known category killers include Home Depot, Crown Books, Sports-Mart, and Toys "Я" Us. What they are killing is the habit of one-stop shopping at stores like Wal-Mart and Kmart.*

CEO Bob Bennett of MicroFridge originally tried to distribute his product through independent sales representatives and distributors. "Theoretically," he says, "we had three-quarters of the country covered." Unfortunately, however, no one in Bennett's distribution channel had contacts at colleges or army bases—the kinds of places that need combination microwave/refrigerators that plug into standard outlets. S. Bennett changed his distribution strategy. He hired full-time sales reps to focus on college and army-base housing directors. Now he's using the same strategy to reach premium hotels and retirement communities.

Choosing an appropriate distribution channel is sometimes much more difficult than it seems, especially with new products:

■ An example is MicroFridge, a combination refrigerator-freezer and microwave oven for smaller housing units (apartments, dormitories, hotel rooms). CEO Bob Bennett chose some 17 established large-appliance distributors, covering most of the United States, to carry his new product. After five months of near business failure, he realized that these distributors had no idea how to move his product. They had no contacts at colleges or army bases— organizations with large concentrations of dormitories. Bennett thus replaced his distributors by hiring four full-time sales representatives who focused on college and army base housing directors. Today 75 percent of the company's sales are made through direct sales to colleges and military bases. The changeover to direct distribution (Channel 5) saved MicroFridge from financial disaster.[5] ▲

■ WHOLESALING

merchant wholesaler
Independent wholesaler that takes legal possession of goods produced by a variety of manufacturers and then resells them to other businesses

full-service merchant wholesaler
Merchant wholesaler that provides credit, marketing, and merchandising services in addition to traditional buying and selling services

limited-function merchant wholesaler
Merchant wholesaler that provides a limited range of services

drop shipper
Limited-function merchant wholesaler that receives customer orders, negotiates with producers, takes title to goods, and arranges for shipment to customers

Now that you know something about distribution channels, we can consider the role played by intermediaries in more detail. Wholesalers provide a variety of services to customers who are buying products for resale or business use. For example, in addition to storing and providing an assortment of products, wholesalers add value for customers by offering delivery, credit, and product information. Not all wholesalers, of course, perform all these functions. Services offered depend on the type of intermediary involved—*merchant wholesalers* or *agents/brokers*.

Merchant Wholesalers

Most wholesalers are independent operations that sell various consumer or business goods produced by a variety of manufacturers. **Merchant wholesalers,** the largest single group of wholesalers, play dual roles, buying products from manufacturers and selling them to other businesses. Merchant wholesalers purchase and own the goods they resell. Usually, they also provide storage and delivery. In the United States, the merchant wholesaling industry employs 5 million people and has an annual payroll of $140 billion.

A **full-service merchant wholesaler** also provides credit, marketing, and merchandising services. Approximately 80 percent of all merchant wholesalers are full-service wholesalers. **Limited-function merchant wholesalers** provide only a few services, sometimes merely storage. Their customers are normally small operations that pay cash and pick up their own goods. One such wholesaler, the **drop shipper,** does not even carry inventory or handle the product. Drop shippers receive orders from customers, negotiate with producers to supply goods, take title to them, and arrange for shipment to customers. The drop shipper bears the risks of the transaction until the customer takes title to the goods.

Other limited-function wholesalers, known as **rack jobbers,** market consumer goods—mostly nonfood items—directly to retail stores. Procter & Gamble, for example, uses rack jobbers to distribute products like Pampers diapers. After marking prices, setting up display racks, and displaying diapers in one store, the rack jobber moves on to another outlet to check inventories and shelve products.

rack jobber
Limited-function merchant wholesaler that sets up and maintains display racks in retail stores

Agents and Brokers

Agents and brokers serve as sales forces for various manufacturers. They are independent representatives of many companies' products. They work on commissions, usually about 4 to 5 percent of net sales. Unlike merchant wholesalers, they do not take title to—that is, they do not own—the merchandise they sell. Rather, they serve as sales and merchandising arms of manufacturers that do not have their own sales forces.

The value of agents and brokers lies primarily in their knowledge of markets and their merchandising expertise. They also provide a wide range of value-adding services, including shelf and display merchandising and advertising layout. Finally, they maintain product salability by removing open, torn, or dirty packages, arranging products neatly, and generally keeping them attractively displayed. Many supermarket products are handled through brokers.

■ A unique new brokerage service has emerged in the form of the "on-line" broker. CUC International, for example, has launched NetMarket shoppers advantage® on the Internet's World Wide Web. As an on-line broker, NetMarket offers a database displaying more than 250,000 discount products and takes customer orders and payments. Orders are passed along to distributors and manufacturers, which ship products directly to buyers. Because the electronic middleman has no need for expensive sales personnel, warehouses, inventories, or showrooms, an expected advantage for consumers is lower cost. "It's all leverage," explains one marketing researcher. "The brilliance is that they don't have to have a warehouse for just-in-time purchasing. It's the ideal middleman business."[6] ▶

"The brilliance is that they don't have to have a warehouse for just-in-time purchasing. It's the ideal middleman business."
—Marketing Researcher Gary Arlen
on "on-line broker" NetMarket shoppers advantage®

Trends in Intermediary–Customer Relationships

Like so many relationships in today's business environment, intermediary–customer relationships are undergoing a variety of changes. Two emerging trends are the use of more customer–supplier partnerships and fewer intermediaries.

In some industries, intermediaries are losing sales because customers with access to new information sources are locating new channels for the products they want. Travel

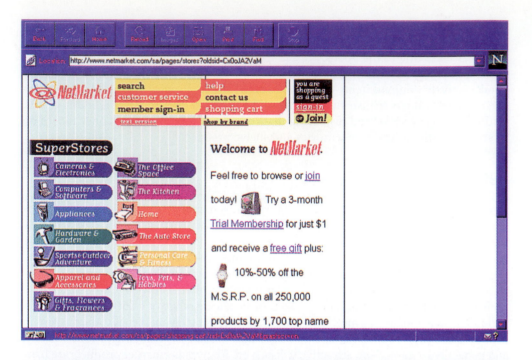

NetMarket shoppers advantage® is an on-line brokerage service. From a database of more than 250,000 brand-name, discount-priced products, the company uses an Internet Website to display products, take orders, and collect payment. The advantage of shopping this way is the elimination of the middleman's showroom, warehouse, inventory, and sales personnel. The on-line retailer can offer close-to-cost prices because orders are sent directly to manufacturers that, in turn, ship products directly to consumers. Currently, NetMarket features a huge array of consumer goods but will soon be joined by such services as Travel Advantage, Autoadvantage, and Premier Dining.

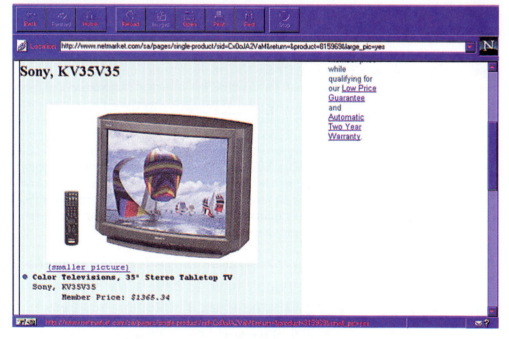

agents, for example, still sell about four-fifths of all U.S. air travel tickets (a service for which they are paid by the airlines). This service, however, is now threatened with displacement by consumers who have such services as Prodigy and CompuServe, which give them direct computer access to airline reservation systems.[7]

A variety of other products are also becoming available without intermediaries. Readers can order books direct from the publisher by fax or toll-free telephone. Similarly, telephone orders for Motorola pagers can be placed for made-to-order customers, as can computers at IBM's PC Direct operation in North Carolina.[8]

■ RETAILING

There are more than 2.5 million retail establishments in the United States. Most of them are small operations, often consisting of owners and part-time help. Indeed, over more than half of the nation's retailers account for less than 10 percent of all retail sales. Retailers also include huge retailing operations like Wal-Mart and Sears. Although there are large retailers in many other countries—Kaufhof in Germany, Carrefour in France, and Daiei in Japan—more of the world's largest retailers are based in the United States than in any other country.

In this section, we begin by describing in some depth the different types of outlets—both store and nonstore—that dot the U.S. retailing landscape. We also discuss some of the key factors involved in a company's retailing strategy, notably location and type of outlet.

Types of Retail Outlets

U.S. retail operations vary as widely by type as they do in size. They can be classified in various ways—by pricing strategies, location, range of services, or range of product lines.[9] Choosing the right types of retail outlet is a crucial aspect of every seller's distribution strategy. Consider, for instance, the experience of the Sara Lee Corp., whose name usually conjures up visions of cheesecake and chocolate brownies. The Sara Lee of the 1990s, however, has as much to do with pantyhose as it does with pies. To achieve broad distribution on its pantyhose line, Sara Lee had to design product lines that appealed to a variety of retailers. To appeal to food retailers, Sara Lee developed two inexpensive hosiery lines, L'Eggs and Just My Size. In this section, we describe U.S. retail stores by using two classifications—*product line retailers* and *bargain retailers*.

Product Line Retailers   Retailers that feature broad product lines include *department stores, supermarkets*, and *hypermarkets; specialty stores* are typified by narrow product lines.

Department Stores. As the name implies, **department stores** are organized into specialized departments—shoes, furniture, women's petite sizes, and so on. Department stores are usually large and handle a wide range of goods. In addition, they usually offer a variety of services, such as generous return policies, credit plans, and delivery. In the past, department stores have differentiated themselves by merchandising—by what they sold and by the prices they charged. Today, however, consumers report that ambiance and service levels differ more than merchandise—and thus drive buyer preferences among stores.[10]

> **department store**
> Large product-line retailer characterized by organization into specialized departments

Supermarkets. The shift from the small corner grocery to supermarkets began in the second half of the 1930s. Like department stores, **supermarkets** are divided into departments of related products—food products, household products, and so forth. The emphasis is on low prices, self-service, and wide selection. The largest supermarkets are chain stores like Safeway, Kroger, Lucky Stores, Winn-Dixie, A&P, and Albertson's.

> **supermarket**
> Large product-line retailer offering a variety of food and food-related items in specialized departments

Hypermarkets. A phenomenon begun in the late 1970s, **hypermarkets** are much larger than supermarkets (up to 200,000 square feet) and sell a much wider variety of products. They also practice **scrambled merchandising:** carrying any product—whether similar or dissimilar to the store's original product offering—that promises to sell. In Dallas, for example, Hypermart U.S.A. sells a wide range of food and grocery items, including specialty foods and fresh bakery goods. It also offers television sets, auto accessories, and dry cleaning services.

> **hypermarket**
> Very large product-line retailer carrying a wide variety of unrelated products
>
> **scrambled merchandising**
> Retail practice of carrying any product expected to sell well regardless of a store's original product offering

specialty store
Small retail store carrying one product line or category of related products

Specialty Stores. **Specialty stores** are small stores that carry one line of related products. They service clearly defined market segments by offering full product lines in narrow product fields and often feature knowledgeable sales personnel. Sunglass Hut International, for example, has 1,600 outlets carrying a deep selection of sunglasses at competitive prices. In the United States, Canada, Europe, and Australia, its stores are located in malls, airports, and anywhere else that is convenient for quick, one-stop shopping. "People's time," contends CEO Jack B. Chadsey, "is so limited, they don't want to walk through a maze of categories. If they're looking for electronics, they're going to go to an electronics speciality store. Sunglasses are no different."[11]

> **"People's time is so limited, they don't want to walk through a maze of categories."**
>
> —Jack B. Chadsey
> *CEO of Sunglasses Hut International*
> *on the growing strength of specialty stores*

Some specialty stores, such as Waldenbooks, are large nationwide chains of identical stores offering standardized product lines. Particularly in the apparel industry, the 1980s were the decade of the specialty store. Between 1980 and 1990, retailers like The Gap, The Limited, and Ann Taylor spearheaded the growth spurt of a $100 billion industry in stylish upscale clothing.[12]▼

bargain retailer
Retailer carrying a wide range of products at bargain prices

Bargain Retailers   **Bargain retailers** carry wide ranges of products and come in many forms. Included in this category are *discount houses, off-price stores, catalog showrooms, factory outlets, warehouse clubs,* and *convenience stores.*

In the 1980s, The Gap became the nation's second-largest apparel brand (behind Levi's). Then it got hit from both competitive ends as both discount and department stores started selling cheaper "knock offs" of the kinds of clothes in which The Gap had specialized. Now, with a new chain called the Old Navy Clothing Co., Gap Inc. is striking back. In an environment much like that of a discount store, customers at Old Navy outlets can get Gap quality and style plus a greater selection at lower prices. Old Navy targets shoppers who are slightly less affluent than those to whom the specialty stores of the 1980s had catered.

Discount Houses. After World War II, some U.S. retailers began offering discounts to certain customers. These first **discount houses** sold large numbers of items like televisions and other appliances by featuring substantial price reductions. As name-brand items became more plentiful in the early 1950s, discounters offered even better product assortments while still embracing a philosophy of cash only sales conducted in low-rent facilities. As they became more firmly entrenched, they began moving to better locations, improving decor, and selling better-quality merchandise at higher prices. They also began offering a few department store services, such as credit plans and non-cash sales.

Off-Price Stores. The 1980s witnessed the growth of the discount house variation commonly called the off-price store. **Off-price stores** buy the excess inventories of well-recognized high-quality manufacturers and sell them at prices up to 60 percent off regular department store prices. They are often prohibited from using manufacturers' names in their advertising because producers fear that a product's marketplace value and prestige will be compromised. One of the more successful off-price chains is Marshall's, which reduces prices on brand-name apparel for men, women, and children.

Catalog Showrooms. Another form of bargain store that has grown rapidly in recent years is the **catalog showroom**. These firms mail out catalogs with color pictures, product descriptions, and prices to attract customers into their showrooms. Once there, customers view display samples, place orders, and wait briefly while clerks retrieve orders from attached warehouses. Service Merchandise and LaBelle's are major catalog showroom retailers.

Factory Outlets. **Factory outlets** are manufacturer-owned stores that avoid wholesalers and retailers by selling merchandise directly from the factory to consumers. The first factory outlets featured apparel, linens, food, and furniture. Because they were usually located in warehouse-like facilities next to the factories, distribution costs were low. Lower costs were passed on to customers as lower prices.

Warehouse Clubs. The **warehouse club** (or **wholesale club**) offers large discounts on brand-name clothing, groceries, appliances, automotive supplies, and other merchandise. Unlike customers at discount houses and factory outlets, club customers pay annual membership fees. The first warehouse club, Price Club, opened in 1976. It merged with rival Costco in 1993 to form the second largest warehouse club in the nation (after Wal-Mart's Sam's Club).

---

discount house
Bargain retailer that generates large sales volume by offering goods at substantial price reductions

off-price store
Bargain retailer that buys excess inventories from high-quality manufacturers and sells them at discounted prices

catalog showroom
Bargain retailer in which customers place orders for catalog items to be picked up at on-premises warehouses

factory outlet
Bargain retailer owned by the manufacturer whose products it sells

warehouse club
(or wholesale club)
Bargain retailer offering large discounts on brand-name merchandise to customers who have paid annual membership fees

© 1998 Jack Ziegler *from* The Cartoon Bank,™ Inc.

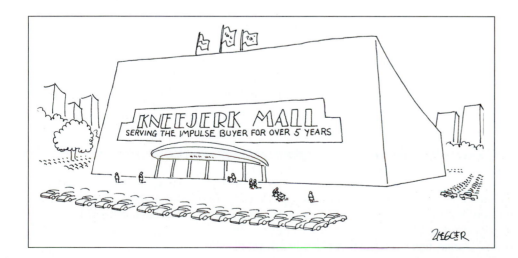

TRENDS & CHALLENGES

THE SPECIAL APPEAL OF AMERICAN RETAILERS

Europeans love things American, especially American fashions. After years of exposure to MTV and the omnipresent American tourist, Europeans crave the casual American look and are turning to American retailers to find it.

Increasingly, their search is just around the corner, as retailers like The Gap, Esprit de Corp., Levi Strauss, Foot Locker, and other American specialty chains set up shop in European cities and shopping malls. The Gap, a leader in the trans-Atlantic crossing of American retailers, entered Britain in 1987, and now has 71 stores in Britain, France, and Germany, with plans to expand into Spain and Italy. William Fisher, President of Gap International, explains the company's European success. "You can point to television, movies, or other media" as the source of Europeans' love affair with American fashion, he says. "The fact was there for everyone to see, and we took advantage of it." Other chains also spotted this trend and acted accordingly. Levi Strauss, for example, now has 278 stores in 11 countries; Foot Locker has 216 stores in 8 countries; and Esprit de Corp. has 121 stores in 13 countries.

The success of U.S. speciality chains can also be attributed to the American way of merchandising. Europeans, it seems, are enticed by merchandising techniques that restock stores with new designs every four to six weeks, compared to four or five times a year for Eu-

ropean retailers. Shoppers also like American bargains, including the slow-moving garments they find on sale racks whenever they enter the stores. In contrast, European retailers rely on seasonal sales.

> **"You can point to television, movies, or other media as the source of Europeans' love affair with American fashion."**
>
> —William Fisher
> *President of Gap International*

Not surprisingly, the invasion of American merchants has devastated many small European specialty stores. Ten years ago, independent retailers in France sold 50 percent of all women's clothing. Today their share is only about 33 percent. A similar story is being told in Italy, where the market share of independent retailers has dropped from 75 percent to 66 percent.

Traditionally located in city centers, European merchant retailers are also reeling as American-style malls draw shoppers into suburban centers. Progress in building these malls has been held back by antidevelopment pressures and the passage of laws to curb their construction in England, France, Italy, and Germany. However, when restrictions are surmounted and malls are built, the shoppers come. For example, the mall at Troyes, France, which opened in 1995, now attracts 2 million visitors a year to its 42 stores. Among these visitors are Parisians, who drive an hour and a half in search of Lee jeans, Reebok shoes, and Ralph Lauren fashions.

convenience store
Retail store offering easy accessibility, extended hours, and fast service

Convenience Stores.   Food retailers like 7-Eleven and Circle K stores are successful convenience store chains. As the name suggests, **convenience stores** offer ease of purchase. They stress easily accessible locations with parking, extended store hours (in many cases 24 hours), and speedy service. They differ from most bargain retailers in that they do not feature low prices. Like bargain retailers, however, they control prices by keeping in-store service levels to a minimum.

Nonstore Retailing

Of course, not all goods and services are sold in stores. In fact, some of the nation's largest retailers sell all or most of their products without stores. For example, certain types of consumer goods—soft drinks, candy, cigarettes—lend themselves to distribution in vending machines. Even at $30 billion a year, however, vending machine sales still represent less than 5 percent of all U.S. retail sales.

Major Types of Nonstore Selling   In this section, we survey a few of the more important forms of nonstore retailing. In particular, we will examine **direct response retailing**—selling in which firms make direct contact with customers both to inform them about products and to receive sales orders. This type *of retailing includes mail marketing, video marketing, telemarketing,* and *electronic shopping.* Another important form of nonstore retailing is *direct selling.*

direct response retailing
Nonstore retailing by direct interaction with customers to inform them of products and receive sales orders

Mail Marketing.   Direct mail and mail order marketing result in billions of sales dollars annually in both retail and industrial sales. In retailing, the world's largest mail order business is run by Otto Versand, a privately held company based in Hamburg, Germany. Company founder Werner Versand began in mail order back in 1950 by pasting pictures of shoes in handbound catalogs. Today, with annual sales topping $13 billion, Otto Versand has used mail order to build itself into one of the world's biggest multinational retailers. In addition to mail order companies in Hungary, Japan, Italy, France, Britain, and Germany, Otto Versand also owns 90 percent of Spiegel and its Eddie Bauer subsidiary in the United States.[13]

Direct mail is effective because it targets audiences that have been identified from research lists as likely to be interested in specific products. The single mailings sent by insurance companies, magazine and book publishers, and clothing and furniture stores are expensive direct mail promotions. These various pamphlets, letters, brochures, and convenient order forms result in high-response sales rates. Charities, too, rely on direct mail as a primary fundraising method. Although mail order responses are increasing at both for-profit and nonprofit organizations, the industry faces difficulties from increasing postal rates and a backlash against the accumulation of unwanted catalogs in customers' mailboxes.

MAIL ORDER (OR CATALOG MARKETING).   Firms that sell by **mail order** (or **catalog marketing**) typically send out splashy color catalogs describing a variety of merchandise. Currently, they garner sales of $45–$60 billion in the United States each year. L.L.Bean alone ships more than 10 million packages to mail order customers annually. As a whole, the brave new world of interactive commerce is an incredibly busy place. Each year, for example, AT&T's 800-line unit generates 13 *billion* calls. Competitors carry another 9 billion calls.[14]

mail order (or catalog marketing)
Nonstore retailing in which customers place orders for catalog merchandise received through the mail

Although mail order firms have existed for a long time, computer technology and telephone charge transactions have made this a booming industry in recent years. Advances in communications technologies are permitting U.S. mail order catalogers to expand by targeting overseas customers. Armed with 24-hour international toll-free phone lines, overnight delivery, inexpensive fax machines, and credit card offers, U.S.-based catalog marketing is now convenient and fast for consumers in Canada, Japan, Europe, and England. Japanese consumers can call a San Francisco outlet toll free around the clock, talk with a Japanese-speaking telemarketer, avoid import tariffs, and receive express mail delivery. Furthermore, they can buy U.S. mail order merchandise at lower prices—sometimes only a third the Japanese retailer's price—because Japan's multi-layered distribution system escalates in-store costs.[15]

Video Marketing.   More and more companies have begun using television to sell consumer commodities such as jewelry and kitchen accessories. Many cable systems now offer **video marketing** through home shopping channels that display and demonstrate products and allow viewers to phone in orders. On one weekend in 1993, for instance, Ivana Trump's appearance on the Home Shopping Club netted $2 million in orders for her high-fashion apparel. Phone traffic was so brisk that part of the scheduled two-day show had to be cut short because inventory had sold out.

video marketing
Nonstore retailing to consumers via standard and cable television

Meanwhile, QVC, another home shopping network, has entered agreements with British Sky Broadcasting to reach into England, Ireland, and parts of Europe and with Mexico's Grupo Telvisa to send live broadcasts to Mexico, Spain, Portugal, and South

America. Optimistic observers, including Microsoft's Bill Gates, believe that home shopping is finally prepared to launch itself into the digital, interactive, multimedia retailing future. Microsoft's Bill Gates is among them: "I can ignore geographical limits to my shopping," explains Gates. "It changes the nature of competition, which becomes pure because you can no longer benefit from customer ignorance. If you believe in markets—and I love markets—this is a good thing. It makes all markets work more efficiently."[16]

> ### "I can ignore geographical limits to my shopping. It changes the nature of competition. If you believe in markets—and I love markets—this is a good thing."
>
> —Bill Gates
> *Microsoft CEO on the prospects of high-tech shopping*

telemarketing
Nonstore retailing in which the telephone is used to sell directly to consumers

Telemarketing. **Telemarketing** is the use of the telephone to sell directly to consumers. WATS (Wide Area Telephone Service) lines can be used to receive toll-free calls from consumers responding to television and radio ads. Offering live or automated dialing, message delivery, and order taking, telemarketers can also use WATS lines to call consumers to promote products and services. Telemarketing is used not only for consumer goods but also for industrial goods and insurance and accounting services. Currently, telemarketing is experiencing exceptional growth in the United States, Canada, and Great Britain. With worldwide sales having topped $300 billion in 1992, the industry is expected to employ nearly 5 million additional people by the year 2000.[17]

electronic shopping
Nonstore retailing in which information about the seller's products and services is connected into consumers' computers allowing consumers to receive the information and purchase the products in the home

Electronic Shopping. **Electronic shopping** is made possible by computer information systems that allow sellers to connect into consumers' computers with information about products. With over a million members, Prodigy, a joint venture of IBM and Sears, is the largest of the home networks. The member's computer video display shows the available products, which range from airplane reservations to consumer goods. The viewer can examine detailed descriptions, compare brands, send for free information, or purchase by credit card—all at home.

direct selling
Form of nonstore retailing typified by door-to-door sales

Direct Selling. Possibly the oldest form of retailing, **direct selling** is still used by more than 600 U.S. companies that sell door to door or through home-selling parties. Some of us, for example, have attended Tupperware parties at friends' houses. Consider some current events at one of the world's best-known direct sellers:

■ For more than a century, Avon Products Inc. has prospered by marketing cosmetics to American women through a direct sales organization. Today even though most American consumers purchase cosmetics through such traditional retail channels as drugstores and department stores, Avon still rings up $4 billion in sales each year. In addition to its direct selling effort in the United States, Avon is also moving quickly to take advantage of growth opportunities in global markets. For example, even though low incomes limit expenditures on cosmetics and toiletries, sales in emerging countries like Brazil and Mexico now reach $1.3 billion a year. "Our distribution system," notes CEO James E. Preston, "is perfect for countries whose retail infrastructures are weak." In 1990, for example, Avon established a joint venture with Guangzhou Cosmetics Factory in the Chinese province of Old Canton. Avon thus became the first company officially permitted to sell door to door in China, and today its Chinese sales force numbers 25,000.► In 1993, sales reached $15 million. Avon has also moved into Germany, Hungary, and Czechoslovakia.[18]

> ### "Our distribution system is perfect for countries whose retail infrastructures are weak."
>
> —Avon CEO James E. Preston

Office-to-office direct selling is also common in the wholesaling of such industrial goods as commercial copying equipment. Although direct selling is convenient and gives customers one-on-one attention, prices are usually driven up by labor costs (salespeople often receive commissions of 40–50 percent). Even so, there are about 3.5

TRENDS & CHALLENGES

THE ALLURE OF ON-LINE COMMERCE

Although on-line retailing via the Internet is in its infancy, the infant is growing quickly. Of the $1.7 trillion that U.S. consumers spent in the retail industry during 1995, only $350 million was spent on line. But experts predict that annual on-line retail sales could reach $5 billion by the year 2000—and that's just the beginning. Hellene S. Runtagh, CEO of General Electric Information Services, believes that electronic commerce will also radically change wholesaling in the years ahead. "I really see the Internet as an explosion of electronic commerce," she says. "This is the most exciting sea change to hit commerce globally in the last 100 years."

> ### "I really see the Internet as an explosion of electronic commerce. This is the most exciting sea change to hit commerce globally in the last 100 years."
>
> —Hellene S. Runtagh
> *President and Chief Executive of*
> *General Electric Information Services*

Among the retail stores that have set up shop on the Internet is Amazon.Com Inc. (http://www.amazon.com), an on-line bookstore with more than a million titles. "You can't [have an inventory that large] with a physical store, and you can't do that with a paper catalog, which would be the size of seven Manhattan phone books," explains Jeffrey Bezos, the company's chief executive. With overhead less than half that of superstores like Barnes & Noble, Amazon.Com is able to discount 300,000 titles—more than twice as many as the superstores. And Amazon.Com is open 24 hours a day, 365 days a year.

The continued growth of on-line commerce depends on the industry's ability to clear several major hurdles. The first involves security. Many consumers fear that the credit card data they are asked to provide will be misused by cybercrooks with the technological know-how to steal card numbers from merchants' computer files. The second hurdle is speed. Doing business on the World Wide Web is so slow that many consumers become discouraged. Finally, consumers who are used to the marketing glitz and sophistication of traditional in-store and catalog retailers often find on-line commerce dull. Richard Fernandes of interactive services at CUC International Inc., a discount shopping club that does business via catalog, phone, and the Internet, admits that "today there's not enough compelling stuff out there to convince people to close a book, shut off their TV, and walk inside to turn on the computer."

As the sophistication of on-line retailers grows, however, so will sales. For now, consumers must accept retailers' growing pains and forgive many of them for playing the game of bait and switch—see us on the Internet, they tell consumers, but please do business with us by phone or fax.

Avon admits that since it entered the Chinese market in 1990, sales have grown slowly. Nevertheless, say company executives, it's a market with huge potential, and that's why Avon has a sales force of 25,000 there. Because Chinese consumers tend to be wary of door-to-door salespeople, Avon also maintains showrooms where interested buyers in large cities can sample products and consult with professional cosmeticians. The gamble on foreign markets is not hard to understand. While Avon's U.S. sales are flat, sales in emerging markets like China, Argentina, Mexico, and Poland were up nearly 20 percent in a recent year.

million direct salespeople in the United States, 80 percent of whom are women. Worldwide, 9 million direct salespeople generate annual retail sales of $35 billion. In Japan alone, for instance, 1.2 million distributors have made Amway Corp. second only to Coca-Cola as the most profitable foreign retailer.

■ PHYSICAL DISTRIBUTION

physical distribution
Movement of a product from manufacturer to consumer

Physical distribution refers to the activities needed to move products efficiently from manufacturer to consumer. The goals of physical distribution are to keep customers satisfied, to make goods available when and where consumers want them, and to keep costs low. Thus, physical distribution includes such activities as *warehousing* and *transporting operations*.

Warehousing Operations

warehousing
Physical distribution operation concerned with the storage of goods

Storing, or **warehousing**, products is a major part of distribution management. In selecting a strategy, managers must keep in mind the different characteristics and the costs of warehousing operations.

Types of Warehouses   There are two basic types of warehouses—*private* and *public*. Facilities can be further divided according to their use as *storage warehouses* or *distribution centers*.

private warehouse
Warehouse owned by and providing storage for a single company

Public and Private Warehouses.   **Private warehouses** are owned and used by a single manufacturer, wholesaler, or retailer. Most are operated by large firms that deal in mass quantities and need storage on a regular basis. J.C. Penney, for example, eases the movement of products to retail stores by maintaining its own warehouses.

Public warehouses are independently owned and operated. Companies rent only the space they need. Public warehouses are popular with firms that need storage only during peak periods. They are also used by manufacturers needing multiple storage locations to get products to numerous markets.

Storage Warehouses and Distribution Centers. **Storage warehouses** provide storage for extended periods of time. Producers of seasonal items, such as agricultural crops, use this type of warehouse. **Distribution centers** store products for which market demand is both constant and high. They are used by retail chains, wholesalers, and manufacturers that need to break down large quantities of merchandise into the smaller quantities that stores or customers demand.

Distribution centers are common in the grocery and food industry. Kellogg, for example, stores virtually no products at its plants. Instead, it ships cereals from factories directly to regional distribution centers. As wholesalers place orders for combinations of products, warehouses fill and ship them. Because warehouses are regional, wholesalers receive orders quickly.

Warehousing Costs Typical warehouse costs include such obvious expenses as storage space rental or mortgage payments (usually computed on a square-foot basis), insurance, and wages. They also include the costs of *inventory control* and *materials handling.*[19]

Inventory Control. **Inventory control** goes beyond keeping track of what is on hand at any time. It often involves the very tricky balancing act of ensuring that while an adequate supply of a product is in stock at all times, excessive supplies are avoided.

Materials Handling. Most warehouse personnel are employed in **materials handling**—the transportation, arrangement, and orderly retrieval of inventoried goods. Holding down materials-handling costs means developing a product storage strategy that takes into account product locations within the warehouse. Other considerations include packaging decisions, such as whether to store a product as individual units, in multiple packages, or in sealed containers.

One strategy for managing materials is *unitization*, which makes storage and handling more systematic by standardizing the weight and form of materials. For example, General Electric's Louisville, Kentucky, warehouse receives small refrigerators from Europe in containers holding 56 refrigerators. Using the huge containers rather than individual boxes not only makes handling easier but also reduces theft and damage. It also optimizes shipping space and allows for easier restocking.

Transportation Operations

The highest cost faced by many manufacturers is the cost of physically moving a product. Thus, cost is a major factor in choosing a transportation method. But manufacturers must also consider several other factors: the nature of the product, the distance it must travel, the speed with which it must be received, and, of course, customers' wants and needs.

Transportation Modes Figure 15.3 compares the relative strengths of the major transportation modes: *trucks, railroads, planes, water carriers,* and *pipelines.* Not surprisingly, differences in cost are most directly related to delivery speed.

Trucks. The advantages of trucks include flexibility, fast service, and dependability. Nearly all sections of the United States can be reached by truck. Because less breakage occurs than with railroad transport, trucked goods need less packing—a major cost

---

public warehouse
Independently owned and operated warehouse that stores goods for many firms

storage warehouse
Warehouse providing storage for extended periods of time

distribution center
Warehouse providing short-term storage of goods for which demand is both constant and high

inventory control
Warehouse operation that tracks inventory on hand and ensures that an adequate supply is in stock at all times

materials handling
Warehouse operation involving the transportation, arrangement, and orderly retrieval of goods in inventory

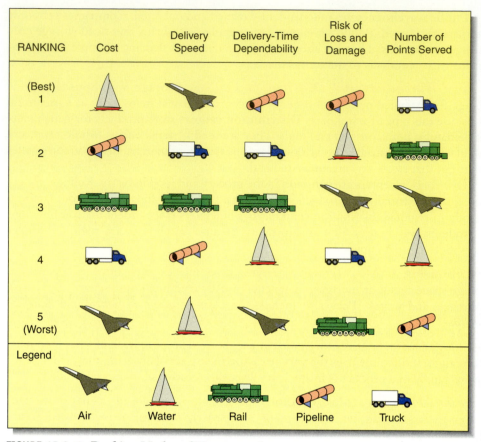

FIGURE 15.3 ◆ **Ranking Modes of Transportation**

savings. Trucks are a particularly good choice for short-distance distribution and for expensive products. They carry more freight than any other form of transport except rail carriers.

Railroads.   Railroads have been the backbone of the U.S. transportation system since the late 1800s. Until the 1960s, when trucking firms attracted many of their customers with lower rates, railroads were also fairly profitable. They are now used, however, primarily to transport heavy, bulky items like cars, steel, and coal. To regain market share, railroads have expanded services to include faster delivery times and so-called *piggyback service*, in which truck trailers are placed on railcars. This service alone can save shippers up to half the costs of shipping by truck.

Planes.   Air is the fastest mode of transportation. Other advantages include greatly reduced costs in handling and packing and unpacking compared with other modes. Inventory-carrying costs can also be reduced. Shipments of fresh fish, for example, can be picked up by restaurants each day, thus avoiding the risk of spoilage from packaging and storing. Air freight, however, is the most expensive form of transportation.

Water Carriers.   Of all transport modes, water is the least expensive. Modern networks of internal waterways, locks, rivers, and lakes allow water carriers to reach many areas in the United States and throughout the world. Unfortunately, water transport is also the slowest mode. Thus, ships and barges are used mostly for heavy, bulky materials and products (such as sand, gravel, oil, and steel) for which delivery speed is unimportant. Today, manufacturers use water carriers because many ships are now specially constructed to hold large standardized containers.

Pipelines. Like water transportation, pipelines are slow. Used to transport liquids and gases, pipelines are also inflexible. But pipelines do provide a constant flow of product and are unaffected by weather conditions. The Alaska Pipeline, for example, transports oil through Alaska on its route to the lower 48 states. Lack of adaptability to other products, however, makes pipelines a relatively unimportant transportation method for most industries.

Changes in Transportation Operations

For many years, U.S. transport companies specialized in one mode or another. Since deregulation in 1980, however, this pattern has changed. New developments in both cost-efficiency and competitiveness include *intermodal transportation*, *containerization*, and *information technology*.

Intermodal Transportation. **Intermodal transportation**—the combined use of different modes of transportation—has come into widespread use. Shipping by a combination of air and rail or truck is sometimes called "birdyback" transport. Large railroad companies, such as Burlington Northern and Union Pacific, are thus merging with trucking, air, and shipping lines. The goal is to offer simplified source-to-destination delivery by any necessary combination of methods.[20]

intermodal transportation Combined use of several different modes of transportation

Containerization. To make intermodal transport more efficient, **containerization** uses standardized heavy-duty containers in which many items are sealed at points of shipment and opened only at final destinations. On the trip, containers may be loaded onto ships for ocean transit, transferred onto trucks, loaded on railcars (piggyback service), and delivered to final destinations by other trucks. Sealed containers are then unloaded and returned for future use.

containerization Transportation method in which goods are sealed in containers at shipping sources and opened when they reach final destinations

Information Technology. Up-to-the-minute information about the location and progress of in-transit shipments can be just as important as the method of transportation. American President Cos., a large U.S.–based steamship and train operator, is an example. APC uses a high-tech computer system to monitor and guide transportation shipments for customers throughout the world. For example, containers of toys bound for Toys "Я" Us are tracked from suppliers in Asia until they reach regional distribution centers in the United States. APC keeps Toys "Я" Us headquarters informed electronically on where every container is and what's in it. The customer's managers know as much as two weeks in advance what product types, sizes, and colors are in each container and what their exact destinations are. They are also advised of potential delays. This enables the toy company to reorder missing products or divert cargo from one destination to another in order to keep store shelves adequately stocked.[21]

Companies Specializing in Transportation

The major modes of transport are available from four different types of companies:

- **Common carriers** transport merchandise for any shipper—manufacturers, wholesalers, retailers, and even individuals. They maintain regular schedules and charge competitive prices. Truck lines and railroads are common carriers.
- **Freight forwarders** are common carriers that lease bulk space from other carriers, such as railroads or airlines. They then resell parts of that space to smaller shippers. Once it has enough contracts to fill its leased bulk space, the freight forwarder picks up all merchandise to be shipped. It transports the goods to the bulk carrier, makes deliveries to specific destinations, and handles billing and inquiries.
- **Contract carriers** transport products for any firm for a contracted price and time period. They are usually self-employed operators who own their vehicles. When they have delivered contracted shipments, they generally try to locate

common carrier Transporting company, such as a truck line or railroad, that transports goods for any shipper

freight forwarder Transporting company that leases bulk space from other carriers to be resold to firms making smaller shipments

contract carrier Independent transporting company that usually owns the vehicles in which it transports products

another shipment (often with a different manufacturer) for the return trip. Contract carriers often tailor services for customers with special needs. Dairy tankers, for example, are often contract carriers with specialized equipment and skills.

■ A few manufacturers and retailers are **private carriers** that maintain their own transport systems—usually fleets of trucks—to carry their own products. These are usually very large manufacturers and retail chains, like Kraft General Foods and Kroger.

private carrier
Manufacturer or retailer that maintains its own transportation system

Distribution as a Marketing Strategy

Distribution is an increasingly important way of competing for sales. Instead of just offering advantages in product features and quality, price, and promotion, many firms have turned to distribution as a cornerstone of their business strategies. This approach means assessing and improving the entire stream of activities—wholesaling, warehousing, transportation—involved in getting products to customers. Its importance is illustrated at Compaq Computer, which registered a loss of nearly $1 billion in sales for 1994 because products were unavailable when and where customers wanted them. To correct the problem, Compaq has placed distribution at the top of its list as the competitive strategy for the future. This commitment entails reworking the company's whole supply chain of distributors and transportation.

The Use of Hubs   One approach to streamlining is the use of **hubs**—central distribution outlets that control all or most of a firm's distribution activities. Two contrasting strategies have emerged from this approach—*supply-side* and *"prestaging"* hubs on the one hand and *distribution-side hubs* on the other.

hub
Central distribution outlet that controls all or most of a firm's distribution activities

Supply-Side and "Prestaging" Hubs. *Supply-side hubs* make the most sense when large shipments of supplies flow regularly to a single industrial user, such as a large manufacturer. They are used, for example, by automobile factories, where thousands of incoming supplies can arrive by train, truck, and air. Supply-side hubs can create a nightmare of traffic jams, loading dock congestion, paperwork logjams, and huge storage-space requirements.

To clear this congestion, some firms operate "prestaging" hubs. Saturn, for example, maintains such a facility—managed by Ryder System—some two miles from its factory. All incoming transportation schedules and supplies are managed by Ryder to satisfy one requirement—meeting Saturn's production schedules. The long-haul tractors at the hub are disconnected from trailers and sent on their return trips to any of 339 suppliers located in 39 states. Responding to Saturn's up-to-the-minute needs, hub headquarters arranges the transport of presorted and preinspected materials to the factory by loading them onto specially designed shuttle tractors.

The chief job of the hub, then, is to coordinate the customer's materials needs with supply-chain transportation. If the hub is successful, the factory's inventories are virtually eliminated, storage space requirements are reduced, and long-haul trucks, instead of lining up at the customer's unloading dock, keep moving. By *outsourcing* distribution activities to its hub, Saturn can focus on what it does best—manufacturing. Meanwhile, Ryder, the nation's largest logistics management firm, is paid for its speciality—handling transportation flows.

Distribution-Side Hubs. While supply-side hubs are located near industrial customers, *distribution-side hubs* may be located much farther away—especially if customers are geographically dispersed:

■ National Semiconductor, one of the world's largest chipmakers, is an example. National's finished products, silicon microchips, are produced in plants throughout the world and shipped to customers like IBM, Toshiba, Siemens, Ford, and Compaq at factory locations around the globe. On the journey from producer to customer, chips originally sat waiting at one location after another—on factory floors, at customs, in distributors' facilities, and in customers' warehouses. Typically, they traveled 20,000 different routes on as many as 12 airlines, spending time in 10 warehouses before reaching their customers. National has streamlined its delivery system by shutting down six warehouses around the world. Now it airfreights microchips worldwide from a single distribution center in Singapore. All of its activities—storage, sorting, shipping—are run by Federal Express. As a result, distribution costs have fallen, delivery times have been reduced by half, and sales have increased.[22]

Continued from page 381

Some General Principles of Image

And the Logistics of Customer Service

Distribution management has everything to do with a retailer's image, and Sears' Gus Pagonis would be the first to explain the connection. "Logistics," he argues, "is concerned about image just as much as other parts of the team. If you walk into a Sears store, and if the hanging garments are wrinkled, [the store's image suffers]. We deliver those garments on hangers. They go right off the truck, right onto the floor. If you order a product and it's not delivered to your home properly or the guys walk in tracking mud—if those drivers are not courteous and concerned about the image of Sears, [then Sears loses]."

Pagonis' concern for image and customer service makes it natural for

---

"If you order a product and the guys walk in tracking mud, then Sears loses."

—William G. "Gus" Pagonis
Senior Vice President in Charge of Logistics at Sears

---

him to treat the 800 stores in the Sears chain as customers. Thus, when stores are in need of merchandise—when they are out of air conditioners in a heat wave, for example—Pagonis restocks store inventories within a day, not within the weeks that it used to take. To get an early jump on problems, for example, he started a system of "ghostbusters"—troubleshooters

who visit stores and distribution centers and ride trucks.

Pagonis' concern for the customer comes in part from the numerous moves he made during his military career. "I've moved 30 times in 29 years," he says. "So when I have a couple of scratches on an old table, that's normal. But when someone buys a new piece of furniture, they want it delivered to their home scratch-free, and that's understandable. We provide that service to them. So we work with the vendor to make sure the production line is good, that the product they're sending us is of quality, and then we have to make sure we don't damage it as we take it through the system."

Case Questions

1. What qualities made Gus Pagonis a superb candidate for the job of logistics czar at Sears?
2. Why is achieving a low ratio of general and administrative expenses as a percentage of domestic sales so important to Sears' management?
3. Why are retailers becoming increasingly dependent on rapid, efficient distribution?
4. How does distribution management affect inventory?
5. Is improving customer service and store image a "natural" function of distribution managers, or do you think that Gus Pagonis is unusual in his approach?

SUMMARY OF LEARNING OBJECTIVES

1. **Identify the different *channels of distribution*.** In selecting a *distribution mix*, a firm may use all or any of six distribution channels. The first four channels are aimed at getting products to consumers; the last two channels are aimed at getting products to industrial customers. Channel 1 involves direct sales to consumers. Channel 2 includes *retailers*. Channel 3 involves both a retailer and a *wholesaler*, while Channel 4 includes an *agent* or *broker* that enters the system before the wholesaler and a retailer. Channel 5 involves a direct sale to an industrial user. Channel 6, which is used infrequently, entails selling to industrial users through wholesalers.

2. **Explain the differences between *merchant wholesalers* and *agents/brokers*.** *Wholesalers* act as distribution intermediaries. They may extend credit as well as

store, repackage, and deliver products to other members of the channel. *Full-service* and *limited-function merchant wholesalers* differ in the number and types of distribution functions they offer. Unlike wholesalers, *agents* and *brokers* never take legal possession of products. Rather, they function as sales and merchandising arms of manufacturers that do not have their own sales forces. They may also provide such services as advertising and display merchandising.

3. **Identify the different types of *retail stores*.** Retailers can be described according to two classifications—product-line retailers and bargain retailers. *Product-line retailers* include department stores, supermarkets, hypermarkets, and specialty stores. *Bargain retailers* include discount houses, off-price stores, catalog showrooms, factory outlets, warehouse clubs, and convenience stores. These retailers differ in terms of size, products offered, and pricing. Some retailing also takes place without stores. *Nonstore retailing* may use direct mail catalogs, vending machines, video marketing, telemarketing, electronic shopping, and direct selling.

4. **Describe the major activities in the *physical distribution process*.** *Physical distribution* refers to all the activities needed to move products from manufacturer to consumer, including customer service, warehousing, and transporting products. *Warehouses* may be *public* or *private* and may function either as long-term *storage warehouses* or as *distribution centers*. In addition to storage, insurance, and wage-related costs, the cost of warehousing goods also includes *inventory control* (maintaining adequate but not excessive supplies) and *materials handling* (transporting, arranging, and retrieving supplies).

5. **Compare the five basic forms of *transportation* and identify the types of firms that provide them.** *Trucks, railroads, planes, water carriers* (ships and barges), and *pipelines* are the major transportation modes used in the distribution process. They differ in cost, availability, reliability of delivery, speed, and number of points served. Air is the fastest but most expensive mode; water carriers are the slowest but least expensive. Since transport companies were deregulated in 1980, they have become more cost-efficient and competitive by developing such innovations as *intermodal transportation* and *containerization*. Transportation in any form may be supplied by *common carriers, freight forwarders, contract carriers,* or *private carriers*.

STUDY QUESTIONS AND EXERCISES

Review

1. Discuss the advantages and disadvantages for manufacturers and end users of using intermediaries to distribute products.
2. Identify the six channels of distribution. In what key ways do the four channels used for consumer products differ from the two channels used for industrial products?
3. Identify and explain the differences between supply-side and distribution-side hubs.
4. Explain the different roles played by merchant wholesalers and agents/brokers.
5. Identify the five modes of transportation used in product distribution. What factors lead companies to choose one over the others to deliver products to end users?

Analysis

6. Give three examples (other than those in the chapter) of products that use full-service merchant wholesalers. Do the same for products that use agents and brokers. For which category was it easiest to find examples? Why?

7. Give examples of five products that typify the sort of products sold by video shopping networks. Explain why this form of nonstore retailing is effective for each of these different products.

8. If you could own a firm that transports products, would you prefer to operate an intermodal transportation business or one that specializes in a single mode of transportation (say, truck or air)? Explain your choice.

Application Exercises

9. Interview the manager of a local manufacturing firm. Identify the channels of distribution that the firm uses. Where applicable, describe the types of wholesalers or retail stores used to distribute the firm's products.

10. Choose any consumer item at your local supermarket and trace the chain of physical distribution activities that brought it to the store shelf.

BUILDING YOUR BUSINESS SKILLS

This exercise enhances the following SCANS workplace competencies: demonstrating basic skills, demonstrating thinking skills, exhibiting interpersonal skills, and working with information.

Goal

To encourage students to analyze the special requirements of catalog retailers

Situation

You and three partners have decided to go into business as catalog retailers of kitchen supplies. Included in your product line are dishes, cutlery, pots and pans, decorative china, and specialty kitchen appliances.

Method

Step 1:   Join with three other students and assume the roles of partners.

Step 2:   Choose one of two target markets for your catalog—either high-income consumers of gourmet products or low-budget, price-conscious shoppers. Then brainstorm ways of reaching your chosen market. Specifically, analyze how you would handle the following marketing issues:

■ *Catalog size and design.* How important is the look of the catalog to your company's success? Would you include photos and extra attractions, like specialty recipes, to increase its appeal?

- *Merchandise price levels.* Would you include top-of-the-line, moderate, or low-priced merchandise, or merchandise combinations?
- *Shipping policy.* How quickly will "normal" items be delivered? Will overnight shipping be an option?
- *Staffing of customer service lines.* How important is it for customers to receive rapid attention? What is the price of putting customers on hold?
- *Purchase of mailing lists.* When dealing with companies that sell mailing lists to catalog retailers, what criteria would you use to pinpoint your target market?
- *Returns policy.* How liberal will your returns policy be? Will the customer or retailer pay for return postage?

Step 3: Write up your analysis in the form of a working plan for your business. Make sure that each element of the plan is designed to help you reach your target market.

Follow-Up

1. Based on your analysis, identify and explain the most critical elements for reaching your target market.

2. Based on your analysis, how would each element of your plan change if your target market changed?

Exploring the Net ▶

TO COMPARE THE DISTRIBUTION STRATEGIES AND PRACTICES OF FIRMS IN DIFFERENT INDUSTRIES, ESPECIALLY DIFFERENCES IN THEIR CHOICES OF DISTRIBUTION CHANNELS AND THEIR PHYSICAL DISTRIBUTION METHODS, LOG ON TO THE FOLLOWING TWO WEBSITES:

QVC INC., *i*QVC SHOP, AT
http://www.qvc.com

CHAPARRAL STEEL COMPANY AT
http://www.chaparralsteel.com

After you have browsed both sites, consider the following questions:

1. Compare the channels of distribution for Chaparral Steel's products with the channels used for the merchandise offered by *i*QVC. How would you describe each of those channels? How do they differ?

2. Compare the physical distribution activities at Chaparral Steel and *i*QVC. What are their similarities and differences?

3. With respect to the geographic location of their target markets, how do the distribution strategies differ for Chaparral Steel and *i*QVC? What do you suspect are the reasons behind each firm's decision about geographic range?

4. How do these companies compare regarding the modes of transportation they use for getting products from producer to customer? Explain the reasons for each company's primary transportation mode.

5. Are intermediaries involved in the distribution mix for products sold by *i*QVC? For products sold by Chaparral Steel? If so, identify the types of intermediaries, describe the services they provide, and explain the value they add for each firm's customers.

6. Which of the two companies is likely to have the larger warehousing operation? Explain the rationale for your answer, including a description of the types of warehousing activities you would expect to see at *i*QVC and at Chaparral Steel.

"These May Not Be Clothes for the Street"

The Contemporary Theater of Fashion

Learning Objectives

The purpose of this video exercise is to help students:

1. Understand the uses and challenges of target marketing in a specific industry
2. Assess the development and use of the promotional mix in a specific industry
3. Understand international and cultural influences on the marketing strategies of both individual companies and the industries in which they operate
4. Understand the relationship between promotion and brand image

Background Information

Competing in an industry with annual sales estimated at tens of billions of dollars, Pierre Cardin, Ralph Lauren, and other designers have marshaled formidable marketing skills to create and sustain demand for stylish, sometimes flamboyant apparel, not only in the United States but in such far-off (and unlikely) places as Hong Kong, Bangkok, Kuala Lumpur, Bombay, and even Vietnam. Their target: consumers who must be convinced that they need new clothes—or rather, something new in clothes.

Today, however, designers are finding that walking the fine line between the outlandishly creative and the marketably expressive is more important than it has been in years. Why? Quite simply, aging U.S. baby boomers, long the chief consumers of the latest fashions, have other things to buy. To deal with such changes in its environment, the fashion industry has focused much of its energy on new and updated marketing strategies:

- Many designers, for instance, have turned to licensing. In fact, some now emphasize licensing over more costly and risky in-house production.
- Designers are turning to innovative forms of distribution, such as QVC, the home shopping television network.
- Designers have recognized the need for more effective advertising and public relations, particularly in an industry in which advertising and editorial coverage often go hand in hand in reaching both industry trendsetters and consumers.

The Video

Video Source. "The Tyranny of Fashion," *Nightline*, March 18, 1994. This segment focuses on how the fashion industry creates consumer demand through the marketing efforts of about 2,000 influential people engaged in designing fashion, evaluating what is "good" and "bad" fashion, or selling both concepts and products to consumers.

Discussion Questions

1. How successful do you think Western designers will be in "dressing" the world? Will their marketing techniques be as effective in, say, Vietnam as they have been in the United States and Western Europe?
2. Why are innovative marketing techniques in the fashion industry more important today than ever before?
3. How are changing consumer buying habits affecting fashion marketing?

Follow-Up Assignment

Go to the library and look up some current articles about fashion designers not mentioned in this case, such as Donna Karan, Tommy Hilfiger, or Jill Sander. How are they responding to the current marketing environment? What techniques are they using to maintain growth in the face of changing consumer buying habits? How do they gauge changing consumer tastes?

For Further Exploration

Contact *Fashion Internet* at

http://www.finy.com

This on-line magazine offers such departments as "Fashion," "Entertainment," "Features," and "Designer Showrooms." The icon labeled "Designer Showrooms" will take you to Websites for such designers as Bill Blass, Donna Karan, and Charles David. What can you tell about the current focus of each company's marketing strategy by browsing each company's site? The icon labeled "Features" will take you to articles and interviews about the fashion industry. What can you tell about the current relationship in the industry between advertising and publicity from browsing these features?

> **"These may not be clothes for the street, but fashion is about dreams as well as commerce."**
>
> —Pierre Cardin
> *Fashion designer*

Getting the Product Out at Lands' End

The Process from Receiving to Shipping

Learning Objectives

The purpose of this video exercise is to help students:

1. See how a specific company conducts its physical distribution operations
2. Understand the interaction of human and technological resources in the design and control of a company's distribution process
3. Appreciate the roles played by customer service and quality assurance in the design and control of a company's distribution process

Background Information

The flow chart accompanying this case outlines the operations that take place at Lands' End's distribution center. This process enables Lands' End to get products to customers in only two business days (or three if an order needs embroidering or monogramming). The key, according to Phil Schaecher, Senior Vice President for Operations, is the fact that "LE's distribution center is staffed by the best people available working together with some of the most sophisticated technology in the industry."

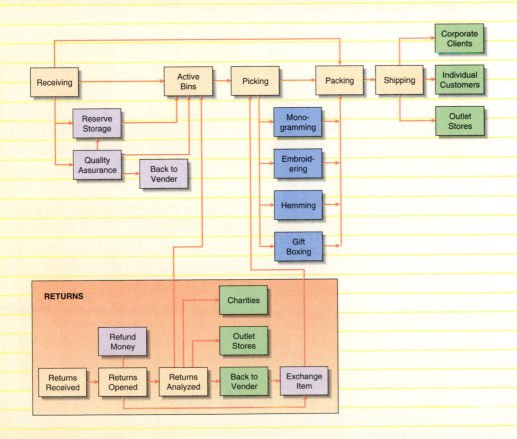

In each major step—receiving, active bins, picking, packing, and shipping—every item is tracked by a bar code prepared the night before it is received at the center. This bar code enables a computer system to track the item throughout the building. The computer, for example, uses data on current demand to direct merchandise to active bins, quality assurance, shipping, or (as in most cases) reserve storage. The computer also prints out the "pick tickets" used by order-fillers to take items from active bins, which store items that will be needed in the immediate future. Because the bar code on the pick ticket also serves as the packing ticket, all items destined for the same packing bin bear the same three-digit code and are thus delivered by the computer to the same packing bin.

The Video

Video Source. "Lands' End: Getting the Product Out," *Prentice Hall Presents: On Location at Lands' End.* The video describes in step-by-step detail the computerized operations that enable Lands' End to distribute products to customers within two days of receiving an order. The flow chart accompanying the case is followed carefully as each step in the company's distribution process is illustrated with scenes of the Dodgeville distribution center at work. Senior Vice President for Operations Phil Schaecher and veteran packer Bill Gantenbein explain how various steps in the system work.

Discussion Questions

1. Why is Lands' End's physical distribution process particularly appropriate for a mail order retailer?
2. In what areas do you see activities in the video that can be classified as operations management? As operations control?
3. Which activities depicted in the video pertain to the control of warehousing costs? To inventory control? To materials handling?
4. As the video shows, Lands' End attaches considerable importance to *order processing* (the filling of orders as they are received) and *order-cycle times* (the total time elapsed between the customer's placement and receipt of an order). In what respects does the Lands' End approach to these processes reflect its mission and competitive strategy?
5. In what ways is *total quality management* integrated into Lands' End's distribution operations?

Follow-Up Assignment

At the end of the video, the narrator asks, "With so much technology in place, why does Lands' End place such a high value on employees who work in the warehouse?" One way to address this question might be to find out exactly why other companies value employees as part of high-tech operations. Contact the Office of the American Workplace (OAW) at

http://www.fed.org/uscompanies/labor

Using the directories labeled "A–M" and "N–Z," go to the entries on one or more of the following companies:

- Davis Vision Inc.
- Motorola Inc.
- Rhino Foods
- White Storage and Retrieval Systems

By examining each company's description of its activities and goals under such headings as "Employee Participation," "Organizational Structure," "Product/Service Quality," and "Strategic Integration of Business," you should be in a position to draw up an informed answer to the question posed above.

For Further Exploration

Contact Lands' End at

http://www.landsend.com

At the Web page, scroll down to the icon labeled "Site Map." From here, you can access the company's description of the various "Services," including "Sizing," "Hemming Info," "Monogramming," "Gift Boxing," and "Care Info," that it offers between the "Picking" and "Packing" operations outlined in the flow chart above. In particular, the feature labeled "Let's Talk" might shed some light on the importance that Lands' End attaches to customer service operations as a component of its distribution process.

> **"When I worked for a mail order company in Baltimore, I honestly would have needed two people for every one I have here."**
>
> —Phil Schaecher
> *Sr. Vice President for Operations at Lands' End*

16

CHAPTER

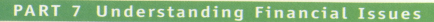

UNDERSTANDING MONEY AND BANKING

Accounting for South Africa's "Unbanked"

BANKERS TAKE AN INTEREST IN THE MIDDLE CLASS OF THE FUTURE

When South Africa's 35 million blacks experienced the miracle that ended apartheid, they witnessed a sea change in the politics of their nation that transferred control from a white minority government to a representative government headed by President Nelson Mandela and the African National Congress. They watched in amazement as world governments accepted South Africa back into the fold of nations after years of ostracism for its racist policies. Yet none of these monumental changes prepared South Africa's poor black population for a practice that nearly every American adult takes for granted—opening a personal bank account. "A bank here? I never dreamed of such a thing," exclaimed Mrs. Ntombizanele King, who recently opened an account at the E Bank affiliate of Standard Bank of South Africa, the country's second-largest bank.

King is in the forefront of a banking revolution that is attempting to reach the so-called "unbanked" of South Africa—impoverished, illiterate blacks who were virtually ignored as potential customers in the old South Africa. Today, E Bank, Peoples Bank (a division of Nedcor Bank), and

> ### "A bank here? I never dreamed of such a thing."
> —Mrs. Ntombizanele King
> *a new black South African banking customer*

other financial institutions see opportunity in serving this vast, untapped market, which represents approximately 80 percent of the country's entire population. "You cannot be a national bank and not bank the masses," explains E Bank general manager Bob Tucker, who believes that the poor black customers of today will become the middle-class savers of tomorrow.

Bankers like Tucker realize that although their institutions will earn little from each new account, there is money to be made by serving the *community* of customers. Collectively, the domestic workers, peddlers, and day laborers who make up South Africa's informal economy control millions of dollars in cash. These potential customers need basic services in the form of cash card debit-and-savings accounts that provide an easy way to deposit and withdraw money. E Bank thus offers an account that requires no

minimum balance and pays interest on average daily balances higher than the equivalent of about $60. Deposits are free, and cash withdrawals cost anywhere from a nickel to a quarter.

Having access to banking services offers poor South African blacks peace of mind. Gloria Mvunyiswa, a domestic worker who lives in a shack 20 miles east of Cape Town, has been robbed numerous times by knife-wielding thieves as she walked to the homes of relatives whom she helps to support. Now she deposits her wages in a bank ATM near her home, and her relatives withdraw what they need from the ATM in their own village. "It's much better now," she says, "because I draw only the money I need for the week's groceries and hide it in my bra until I get to the shop. The rest is safe in the bank."

By 1996, E Bank had 31 branches, serving 175,000 clients around South Africa. Two years earlier, there were probably no more than a few hundred blacks in all of South Africa with bank accounts. Moreover, as part of a five-year government program to move about a million families out of shacks and into houses, E Bank has begun reinvesting some of its new capital into home loans for poor black customers.

Not surprisingly, these changes have had important social consequences. As poor blacks open bank accounts for the first time, they are seen as individuals with money of their own. Says Henry Jackelen, an adviser with the United Nation's Development Program who helped E Bank develop its banking program: "It brings people into the institutional fabric of the society."

Whether in the United States or South Africa, meeting the money needs of an entire economy requires a complex system of financial institutions, especially banks. As the needs of the system change, so too does the structure of the financial industry that has grown up to service it. The theme of the South Africa banking story is the evolving nature of financial institutions that see opportunity in a changing environment. By focusing on the learning objectives of this chapter, you will better understand the environment for banking in the United States and the different kinds of institutions that conduct business in it.

After reading this chapter, you should be able to

1. Define *money* and identify the different forms that it takes in the nation's money supply

2. Describe the different kinds of *financial institutions* that make up the U.S. financial system and explain the services they offer

3. Explain how banks create money and describe the means by which they are regulated

4. Discuss the functions of the *Federal Reserve System* and describe the tools that it uses to control the money supply

5. Identify three important ways in which the financial industry is changing

Continued on page 435

■ WHAT IS MONEY?

When someone asks you how much money you have, do you count the dollar bills and coins in your pockets? Do you include your checking and savings accounts? What about stocks and bonds? Do you count your car? Taken together, the value of all these things is your "personal wealth." Not all of it, however, is "money." In this section, we consider more precisely what *money* is and does.

The Characteristics of Money

Modern money often takes the form of stamped metal or printed paper—U.S. dollars, British pounds, French francs, Japanese yen—issued by governments. Theoretically, however, just about any object can serve as **money** if it is *portable, divisible, durable,* and *stable*. To appreciate these qualities, imagine using something that lacks them—say, a 70-pound salmon:

money
Any object that is portable, divisible, durable, and stable and that serves as a medium of exchange, a store of value, and a unit of account

- *Portability*. Try lugging 70 pounds of fish from shop to shop. In contrast, modern currency is light and easy to handle.
- *Divisibility*. Suppose that you want to buy a hat, a book, and some milk from three different stores. How would you divide your fish-money? Is a pound of its head worth as much as, say, two gills? Modern currency is easily divisible into smaller parts, each with a fixed value. A dollar, for example, can be exchanged for four quarters. More important, units of money can be easily matched with the value of all goods.
- *Durability*. Whether or not you "spend" it, your salmon will lose value every day (in fact, it will eventually be too smelly to be worth anything). Modern currency, however, neither dies nor spoils, and if it wears out, it can be replaced. It is also hard to counterfeit it—certainly harder than catching more salmon.
- *Stability*. If salmon were in short supply, you might be able to make quite a deal for yourself. But in the middle of a salmon run, the market would be flooded with fish. Sellers of goods would soon have enough fish and would refuse to produce anything for which they could get only salmon. Goods would become scarcer, but the salmon would continue (or cease) running—regardless of the plenitude or scarcity of buyable goods. The value of our paper money also fluctuates, but it is considerably more stable than salmon. Its value is related to what we can buy with it.

© 1998 Robert Mankoff *from* The Cartoon Bank,™ Inc.

"Over there is the first dollar we ever made; next to that is the second dollar we ever made; next to that is the third dollar..."

The Functions of Money

Imagine a successful fisherman who needs a new sail for his boat. In a barter economy—one in which goods are exchanged directly for one another—he would have to find someone who not only needs fish but who is also willing to exchange a sail for it. If no sailmaker wants fish, the fisherman must find someone else—say, a shoemaker—who wants fish. Then the fisherman must hope that the sailmaker will trade for his new shoes. Clearly, barter is inefficient in comparison to money. In a money economy, the fisherman would sell his catch, receive money, and exchange the money for such goods as a new sail.

Money serves three functions:[1]

- *Medium of exchange.* Like the fisherman "trading" money for a new sail, we use money as a way of buying and selling things. Without money, we would be bogged down in a system of barter.
- *Store of value.* Pity the fisherman who catches a fish on Monday and wants to buy a few bars of candy on, say, the following Saturday, by which time the fish would have spoiled and lost its value. In the form of currency, however, money can be used for future purchases and so "stores" value.
- *Unit of account.* Money lets us measure the relative values of goods and services. It acts as a unit of account because all products can be valued and accounted for in terms of money. For example, the concepts of "$1,000 worth of clothes" or "$500 in labor costs" have universal meaning because everyone deals with money every day.

The Spendable Money Supply: M-1

For money to serve its basic functions, both buyers and sellers must agree on its value. That value depends in part on its *supply*—on how much money is in circulation. When the money supply is high, the value of money drops. When it is low, that value increases.

Unfortunately, it is not easy to measure the supply of money. One of the most commonly used measures, known widely as **M-1,** counts only the most liquid—that is, spendable—forms of money: *currency, demand deposits,* and other *checkable deposits.* These are all non-interest-bearing or low interest-bearing forms of money. In December 1995, M-1 in the United States was measured at just over $1.1 trillion.[2]

M-1
Measure of the money supply that includes only the most liquid (spendable) forms of money

Currency   **Currency** is the paper money and metal coins issued by the government. It is widely used for small exchanges. As the U.S. dollar bill states, currency is "legal tender for all debts, public and private"—that is, the law requires creditors to accept it in payment of debts. The average adult in the United States carries about $45 in currency. In late 1995, currency in circulation in the United States amounted to $373 billion, or about 33 percent of M-1. Traveler's checks, bank cashier's checks, and money orders, which are all accepted as currency, accounted for another $9 billion.

currency
Government-issued paper money and metal coins

Demand Deposits   A **check** is essentially an order instructing a bank to pay a given sum to a "payee." Checks permit buyers to make large purchases without having to carry large amounts of cash. Although not all sellers accept them as payment, many do. Checks are usually acceptable in place of cash because they are valuable only to specified payees and can be exchanged for cash. Checking accounts, which are known as **demand deposits,** are counted in M-1 because funds may be withdrawn at any time—"on demand." Eighty-four percent of all U.S. households have checking accounts. In December 1995, demand deposits accounted for $390 billion, or about 35 percent of M-1.

check
Demand deposit order instructing a bank to pay a given sum to a specified payee

demand deposit
Bank account funds that may be withdrawn at any time

TRENDS & CHALLENGES
WHAT THIS COUNTRY NEEDS IS A GOOD 20-MINUTE CIGAR

Since 1914, the federal government has printed the nation's money supply in the form of Federal Reserve notes, or dollars. For most of us, dollars are the only currency that we use as "legal tender for all debts, public and private." However, as the residents of about 30 U.S. cities and towns have discovered, dollars are not the nation's only *legal* currency. Community groups in these localities are printing and circulating their own money supply in order to boost local business.

In Ithaca, New York, for example, the local currency, known as "Ithaca Hours," has been used in addition to money since 1991. Ithaca Hours come in five denominations, each of which is based on the $10 value of the area's average hourly wage. Thus, there are bills worth $10 (one Ithaca Hour), $20 (two Ithaca Hours), portions of an Ithaca Hour (one-eighth of an Hour equals $1.25), and so on.

Hours are earned and spent locally to support home-grown commerce. According to Paul Glover, a self-styled "community economist" who dreamed up Ithaca's system, Ithaca Hours "stay in our region to help us hire each other." The total value of Ithaca Hours currently in circulation—about $57,000—is being earned and spent by some 1,500 people, including 300 businesses. Merchants who accept Ithaca Hours recirculate them for local purchases. Cooperating local businesses generally accept Hours as partial payment for bills owed, with the balance due in dollars.

When Glover first approached merchants with the idea of a local currency system, they were uncertain about its safety. Most did not want to carry more than 10 to 12 hours ($100–$120). "They were worried that the system was going to crash," explains James Cummins, owner of the Littletree Orchards, which accepts Hours as full payment for a sale. Now, says Cummins, "it's grown to a way of life in Ithaca. The chain has

enough people in it and it's unbroken. Virtually all professional services can be purchased with Hours." To keep the system safe, an advisory board meets regularly to oversee the money supply, replace damaged currency, and sell new bills. In the 5 years that Hours have been in circulation, they have been used to transact $1.5 million of local business in such places as movie theaters, restaurants, and barber shops.

For many residents, using Hours instead of dollars is an act of altruism. "You see the money's value coming around again and again," says Debby Thompson, who gets paid in Hours for private kayaking and weaving lessons while earning conventional currency at her regular job as a home health-care aide. The benefits of the system are especially clear when Hours are used to support local charities and as start-up loans to new businesses.

In a perverse kind of way, residents also delight in using Hours because the system has little to do with the federal government. Hours, says Carol Chernikoff, a local mortgage loan officer, are "backed by people you know, whose farms you've driven by, whose faces are familiar—rather than trillions of dollars of debt."

> **"Ithaca Hours are backed by people you know, whose farms you've driven by, whose faces are familiar—rather than trillions of dollars of debt."**
> —Carol Chernikoff
> *Mortgage loan officer in Ithaca, New York*

What does Uncle Sam think of local currencies? The government has no problem with them as long as the notes are smaller in size than Treasury notes and as they are reported as taxable income. Theoretically, then, every community could have its own currency, but Jesse Stiller, a historian in the Office of the Comptroller of the Currency, considers the consequences sobering: "I shudder to imagine the chaos that would ensue if dozens of communities followed Ithaca's example."

Other Checkable Deposits   Other checkable deposits—that is, deposits on which checks can be written—include automated teller machine (ATM) account balances and NOW accounts. *NOW (negotiable order of withdrawal)* accounts are interest-bearing accounts that can be held only in savings banks and savings and loan associations by individuals and nonprofit organizations. Checkable deposits exceeded $353 billion in December 1995, or 31 percent of M-1.

TRENDS & CHALLENGES

BEN FRANKLIN MOVES SLIGHTLY TO THE LEFT

The next time you have a $100 bill in your wallet, take some time to study it carefully. If it was minted after 1995, it will look different in a number of subtle ways from bills you are used to seeing. The differences reflect the first step in a U.S. Treasury Department currency-redesign program intended to thwart counterfeiting. Over the coming years, the $50 bill as well as other denominations will also be redesigned.

Counterfeiting has become a major problem all over the world, in large part because improved technology has made it easier for forgers to produce passable fakes. Using computer software, electronic digital scanners, color work stations, and sophisticated copiers and printers, forgers printed approximately $25 million in counterfeit U.S. currency in 1994. The government is determined to use its own technological arsenal to put counterfeiters out of business. According to Robert E. Rubin, Secretary of the Treasury in the Clinton Administration, "We must stay ahead of the technology curve in order to continue to have a safe currency."

Here are just some of the anticounterfeiting devices found on all new $100 bills:

- Ben Franklin's portrait is now larger and more detailed and appears to the left of center in order to create space for a watermark of the portrait, which is visible only when exposed to ultraviolet light.
- Special inks used in the numeral in the lower right-hand corner of the bill appear to change from green to black when viewed from different angles.
- Letters are printed in a smaller size to make it more difficult to duplicate them without blurring.

- The fine-line printing that circles the portrait of Ben Franklin is impossible to reproduce with traditional copying methods.
- Security threads, which are woven into the bill, are visible only when exposed to ultraviolet light.

As impressive as these changes are, however, they do not compare to the more than 20 anticounterfeiting features found on the newly designed 50-franc bill from Switzerland. The Swiss used state-of-the-art computer technology to resolve the bill's surface into 2.5 billion separate points, every one of which is accessible electronically. The result is the world's first digital bank note. In effect, the Swiss note is a chameleon that changes its appearance as its surface turns. Tilt it and a number in the upper left-hand corner appears and disappears. Tilt it again and a number in the center of the note moves from right to left. A reporter for the *New York Times* was impressed. "If the United States Bureau of Engraving and Printing . . . produced a jeep—a kind of a tough, all-terrain monetary vehicle," he observed, "the Swiss produced the Rolls-Royce of currencies."

> **"If the United States produced a jeep— a kind of a tough, all-terrain monetary vehicle—the Swiss produced the Rolls-Royce of currencies."**
> —*The* New York Times, *February 1996*

The engraving on the Swiss note is also so fine that it is impossible to reproduce it without blotching. Although the redesigned 50-franc note uses more sophisticated anti-counterfeiting technology than the new Ben Franklin, the Swiss government is spending more than five times as much as the U.S. government to produce each bill. While each new $100 bill costs the U.S. Treasury Department 4.7 cents, each new Swiss note costs the equivalent of 25 cents.

M-1 plus the Convertible Money Supply: M-2

M-2 includes everything in M-1 plus items that cannot be spent directly but that are easily converted to spendable forms. The major components of M-2 are M-1, *time deposits, money market mutual funds,* and *savings deposits.* Totaling nearly $3.7 trillion in December 1995, M-2 accounts for nearly all the nation's money supply. It thus measures the store of monetary value available for financial transactions. As this overall level of money increases, more is available for consumer purchases and business investment. When the supply is tightened, less money is available, and financial transactions, spending, and business activity thus slow down.

M-2
Measure of the money supply that includes all the components of M-1 plus forms of money that can easily be converted into spendable form

time deposit
Bank funds that cannot be withdrawn without notice or transferred by check

Time Deposits   Unlike demand deposits, **time deposits** require prior notice of withdrawal and cannot be transferred by check. However, time deposits pay higher interest rates. The supply of money in time deposits—such as *certificates of deposit (CDs)* and *savings certificates*—grew rapidly in the 1970s and 1980s after government ceilings on interest rates were removed. Depositors can now invest for both short and long periods of time. Time deposits in M-2 include only accounts of less than $100,000 that can be redeemed on demand with small penalties. Large time deposits, usually those made by businesses, cannot be redeemed early and are not included in M-2. In December 1995, U.S. time deposits amounted to nearly $938 billion—almost 26 percent of M-2.

money market mutual fund
Fund of short-term, low-risk financial securities purchased with the assets of investor-owners pooled by a nonbank institution

Money Market Mutual Funds   **Money market mutual funds** are operated by investment companies that bring together pools of assets from many investors. The fund buys a collection of short-term, low-risk financial securities. Ownership of and profits (or losses) from the sale of these securities are shared among the fund's investors.

Money market funds attracted many investors in the 1980s because they paid high rates and often allow investors to write checks against their shares. Why do mutual funds pay higher returns than most individuals can get on their own? There are two reasons:

1. Funds can buy into higher-paying securities that require larger investments than most individuals can afford.

2. They are managed by professionals who monitor changing investment opportunities.

Shortly after being introduced in 1974, money market mutual funds had attracted $1.7 billion. By December 1995, some $465 billion—nearly 13 percent of M-2—was invested in the funds.

Savings Deposits   In the wake of new, more attractive investments, traditional savings deposits, such as passbook savings accounts, have declined in popularity. Savings deposits represented 40 percent of M-2 in 1971 but only 31 percent by 1995.

Figure 16.1 shows how the two measures of money—M-1 and M-2—have grown since 1959. For many years, M-1 was the traditional measure of liquid money. Because it was closely related to gross domestic product, it served as a reliable predictor of the nation's economic health. This situation changed in the early 1980s, however, with the introduction of new types of investments and easier transfer of money among investment funds to gain higher interest returns. As a result, M-2 today is a more reliable measure than M-1 and is often used by economists for economic planning.

Credit Cards

Citicorp is the world's largest credit card issuer, with more than 38 million accounts among the 124 million U.S. cardholders who carry more than 1 billion cards. Spending with general purpose credit cards reached $731 billion in 1994 and is projected to reach $1.4 trillion—almost half of all transactions—by the year 2000.[3] Indeed, the use of cards—Visa, MasterCard, American Express, Discover, Diners Club—has become so widespread that many people refer to them as "plastic money."

Credit cards are big business for two basic reasons. First, they are convenient. Second, they are extremely profitable for issuing companies. Profits derive from two sources:

1. Some cards charge annual fees to holders. All charge interest on unpaid balances. Depending on the issuer—and on certain state regulations—cardholders pay interest rates ranging from 11 to 20 percent.

2. Merchants who accept credit cards pay fees to card issuers. Depending on the merchant's agreement with the issuer, 2 to 5 percent of total credit sales dollars goes to card issuers.

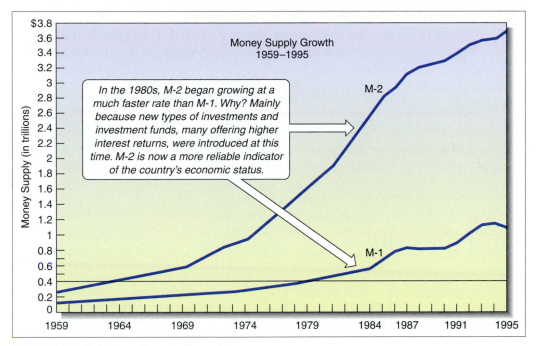

FIGURE 16.1 ◆ Money-Supply Growth

Credit card loans have been increasing at the rate of 20 percent per year since 1994. In 1995, for example, Citicorp issued $44.8 billion in credit card loans. Discover Card issued $27.8 billion in loans. By 1996, credit card debt issued by banks and by nonbank companies had reached 11 percent of commercial bank loan portfolios. Why are banks and other card issuers so willing to grant this kind of credit? Returns are up to three times higher than those from other forms of banking.[4]

THE U.S. FINANCIAL SYSTEM

Many forms of money—especially demand deposits and time deposits—depend on the existence of financial institutions to provide a broad spectrum of services to both individuals and businesses. Just how important are reliable financial institutions to both businesses and individuals? Try asking financial consumers in a country in which commercial banking can be an adventure:

■ In Russia, for example, there is almost no banking regulation and no way to distinguish qualified from unscrupulous bankers in the thousands of different financial institutions, large and small, that exist. The Moscow City Bank has no deposit insurance, no customer service desk, no loan officers, and no cash machine. Businesses need stable financial institutions to underwrite modernization and expansion, and individuals need them to handle currency. Imagine, then, the disappointment of Vladimir Shcherbakov, who needed to withdraw $500 from his account to buy a car but was turned away by a sign announcing that no withdrawals would be allowed for 10 days. "I'm resigned to losing my money," sighed Shcherbakov. "But if I do get it back, I'll change my rubles into dollars and hold on to it myself."[5]

"I'm resigned to losing my money. But if I do get it back, I'll change my rubles into dollars and hold on to it myself."

—Russian bank customer
lamenting the instability of the country's financial system

In the sections that follow, we describe the major types of financial institutions, explain how they work when they work as they are supposed to, and survey some of the special services that they offer. We also explain their role as creators of money and discuss the regulation of the U.S. banking system.

Financial Institutions

The main function of financial institutions is to ease the flow of money from sectors with surpluses to those with deficits. They do this by issuing claims against themselves and using the proceeds to buy the assets of—and thus invest in—other organizations. A bank, for instance, can issue financial claims against itself by making available funds for checking and savings accounts. In turn, its assets will be mostly loans invested in individuals and businesses and perhaps government securities.[6] In this section, we discuss each of the major types of financial institutions: *commercial banks*, *savings and loan associations*, *mutual savings banks*, *credit unions*, and various organizations known as *nondeposit institutions*.

commercial bank
Federal- or state-chartered financial institution accepting deposits that it uses to make loans and earn profits

state bank
Commercial bank chartered by an individual state

national bank
Commercial bank chartered by the federal government

Commercial Banks The United States today boasts more than 10,000 **commercial banks**—companies that accept deposits that they use to make loans and earn profits. Commercial banks range from the very largest institutions in New York, such as Citibank and Chase Manhattan, to tiny banks dotting the rural landscape. Bank liabilities include checking accounts and savings accounts. Assets consist of a wide variety of loans to individuals, businesses, and governments.

All commercial banks must be *chartered*. Until 1863, all banks were chartered by individual states. Today nearly 70 percent of all commercial banks remain **state banks.** Most of the largest U.S. banks, however, are **national banks,** chartered by the federal government. The nine largest U.S. commercial banks are all nationally chartered. In 1995, these nine institutions had combined profits of $16.2 billion. Taken together, all state and national banks hold $4.4 trillion in domestic assets and $2.3 trillion in loans.[7]

Diversification and Mergers. Many observers today believe that traditional banking has become a "mature" industry—one whose basic operations have expanded as broadly as they can. For instance, 1993 marked the first year in which the money invested in mutual funds—almost $2 trillion—equaled the amount deposited in U.S. banks. Thus, financial industry competitors in areas like mutual funds are growing, sometimes rapidly.

As consumers continue to look for alternatives to traditional banking services, commercial banks and savings and loan associations find themselves with a dwindling share of market. As you can see from Figure 16.2, nonbank competitors have increased their share of the market to nearly 70 percent. The investment bank Merrill Lynch, for example, has originated billions of dollars in commercial loans, formerly the province of commercial banks. Savers, too, are putting their savings into the money market funds, stocks, and bonds offered by companies like Charles Schwab instead of into the traditional savings accounts offered by banks. Many observers contend that in order to compete, banks, too, must diversify their offerings. The only way that banks can compete,

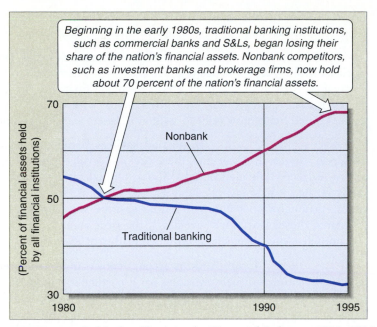

Beginning in the early 1980s, traditional banking institutions, such as commercial banks and S&Ls, began losing their share of the nation's financial assets. Nonbank competitors, such as investment banks and brokerage firms, now hold about 70 percent of the nation's financial assets.

FIGURE 16.2 ◆ **Market Share in the Financial Industry, 1980–1995**

says banking analyst Thomas Brown, "is to tranform themselves into successful retailers of financial services, which involves dramatic, not incremental change."[8]

"The only way that banks can compete is to transform themselves into successful retailers of financial services."

—Banking analyst Thomas Brown
on the dwindling market share of commercial banks

A related option seems to be to get bigger. In efforts to regain competitiveness, banks have been merging at a record-setting pace in the 1990s. In 1995, there were more than 400 mergers worth $60 billion—more than double the old record set in 1991.[9] BancOne, for example, which operates 62 separately chartered banks in 12 states, made 31 acquisitions between 1990 and 1994. One single merger in 1996 involved institutions with combined assets of $3 billion. Chase Manhattan Corp. became the largest U.S. bank when it merged with Chemical Banking Corp. The new company offers a wide range of services for both consumers and businesses, including private banking, credit card services, mortgages, and arranging loans. Mergers are the trend in U.S. banking, and fewer but larger banks are offering a wide range of financial products. The strategy streamlines operations to reduce costs and focuses on providing products that will win back customers.[10]

Commercial Interest Rates. Every bank receives a major portion of its income from interest paid on loans by borrowers. As long as terms and conditions are clearly revealed to borrowers, banks are allowed to set their own interest rates. Traditionally, the lowest rates were made available to the bank's most creditworthy commercial customers. That rate is called the **prime rate.** Most commercial loans are set at mark-ups over prime. However, the prime rate is no longer a strong force in setting loan rates. Borrowers can now get funds less expensively from other sources, including foreign banks

prime rate
Interest rate available to a bank's most creditworthy customers

that set lower interest rates. To remain competitive, therefore, U.S. banks now offer some commercial loans at rates below prime.

Savings and Loan Associations   Like commercial banks, **savings and loan associations (S&Ls)** accept deposits and make loans. They lend money primarily for home mortgages. Most S&Ls were created to provide financing for homes. Many of them, however, have ventured into other investments, with varying degrees of success. S&Ls in the United States now hold $1 trillion in assets and deposits of $737 billion.[11]

Mutual Savings Banks   In **mutual savings banks,** all depositors are considered owners of the bank. All profits, therefore, are divided proportionately among depositors, who receive dividends. Like S&Ls, mutual savings banks attract most of their funds in the form of savings deposits, and funds are loaned out in the form of mortgages. Although 90 percent of all mutual savings bank deposits are held in 5 northeastern states, these institutions have nearly the same volume of total assets as S&Ls. S&Ls and mutual savings banks had combined profits of $343 million in 1993.

Credit Unions   **Credit unions** accept deposits only from members who meet specific qualifications—usually working for a particular employer. Most universities, for example, run credit unions, as do the U.S. Navy and the Pentagon. Credit unions make loans for automobiles and home mortgages, as well as other types of personal loans. More than 12,000 credit unions now operate in the United States, nearly double the number operating in 1945. They hold $277 billion in savings and checking accounts.

Nondeposit Institutions   A variety of other organizations take in money, provide interest or other services, and make loans. Four of the most important are *pension funds*, *insurance companies*, *finance companies*, and *securities dealers*.

Pension Funds.   A **pension fund** is essentially a pool of funds managed to provide retirement income for its members. *Public pension funds* include Social Security and $1 trillion in retirement programs for state and local government employees. *Private pension funds*, operated by employers, unions, and other private groups, cover about 80 million people and have total assets of $2.4 trillion. The Teachers Insurance and Annuity Association (TIAA) operates the largest private fund in the United States, with assets of $113 billion in 1995.

Insurance Companies.   **Insurance companies** collect large pools of funds from the premiums charged for coverage. Funds are invested in stocks, real estate, and other assets. Earnings pay for insured losses, such as death benefits, automobile damage, and health care expenses (see Appendix I). At the end of 1994, insurance companies had total assets of more than $2.5 trillion.

Finance Companies.   **Finance companies** specialize in making loans to businesses and individuals. *Commercial finance companies* lend to businesses needing capital or long-term funds. They may, for instance, lend to a manufacturer that needs new assembly line equipment. *Consumer finance companies* devote most of their resources to small noncommercial loans to individuals. Consumer finance companies take greater risks and generally charge higher interest rates than banks. Most loans pay for such items as cars, appliances, medical bills, and vacations. By the end of 1994, U.S. finance companies had issued $742 billion of credit.

Securities Dealers.   **Securities investment dealers (brokers),** such as Merrill Lynch and A.G.Edwards & Sons, buy and sell stocks and bonds on the New York and other stock exchanges for client investors. They also invest in securities—that is, they buy stocks and bonds for their own accounts in hopes of reselling them later at a profit. These companies hold large sums of money for transfer between buyers and sellers. *Investment bankers* match buyers and sellers of newly issued securities and receive com-

---

savings and loan association (S&L)
Financial institution accepting deposits and making loans primarily for home mortgages

mutual savings bank
Financial institution whose depositors are owners sharing in its profits

credit union
Financial institution that accepts deposits from, and makes loans to, only its members, usually employees of a particular organization

pension fund
Nondeposit pool of funds managed to provide retirement income for its members

insurance company
Nondeposit institution that invests funds collected as premiums charged for insurance coverage

finance company
Nondeposit institution that specializes in making loans to businesses and consumers

securities investment dealer (broker)
Nondeposit institution that buys and sells stocks and bonds both for investors and for its own accounts

missions for the service. They, too, are thus financial intermediaries. At the end of 1993, U.S. investment dealers and investment bankers held $1.8 trillion in assets. (We will discuss the activities of brokers and investment bankers more fully in Chapter 17.)

Special Financial Services

The finance business today is a highly competitive industry. No longer is it enough for commercial banks to accept deposits and make loans. Most, for example, now offer bank-issued credit cards and safe-deposit boxes. In addition, many offer pension, trust, international, and brokerage services and financial advice. Most offer ATMs and electronic money transfer.

Pension Services   Most banks help customers establish savings plans for retirement. **Individual retirement accounts (IRAs)** are pension funds that wage earners and their spouses can set up to supplement other retirement funds. All wage earners can invest up to $2,000 of earned income annually in an IRA. IRAs offer a significant tax benefit: Under many circumstances, taxes on principal and earnings are deferred until funds are withdrawn upon retirement. Banks serve as financial intermediaries by receiving funds and investing them as directed by customers. They also provide customers with information on investment vehicles available for IRAs (deposit accounts, mutual funds, stocks, and so forth).

Banks also assist customers in establishing **Keogh plans.** Though similar to IRAs, Keogh plans can be opened only by self-employed people, such as doctors, small business owners, and consultants. Taxes on Keogh plans are always deferred until earners withdraw the funds. If a depositor needs to withdraw funds from a Keogh or an IRA before age 59 1/2, the Internal Revenue Service will impose a penalty of 10 percent on the withdrawn amount.[12]

Trust Services   Many commercial banks offer **trust services**—the management of funds left "in the bank's trust." In return for a fee, the trust department will perform such tasks as making your monthly bill payments and managing your investment portfolio. Trust departments also manage the estates of deceased persons.

International Services   The three main international services offered by banks are *currency exchange*, *letters of credit*, and *banker's acceptances*. Suppose, for example, that a U.S. company wants to buy a product from a French supplier. For a fee, it can use one or more of three services offered by its bank:

1. It can exchange U.S. dollars for French francs at a U.S. bank and then pay the French supplier in francs.

2. It can pay its bank to issue a **letter of credit**—a promise by the bank to pay the French firm a certain amount if specified conditions are met.

3. It can pay its bank to draw up a **banker's acceptance,** which promises that the bank will pay some specified amount at a future date.

A banker's acceptance requires payment by a particular date. Letters of credit are payable only after certain conditions are met. The French supplier, for example, may not be paid until shipping documents prove that the merchandise has been shipped from France.

Financial Advice and Brokerage Services   Many banks, both large and small, help their customers manage their money. Depending on the customer's situation, the bank may recommend different investment opportunities. The recommended mix might include CDs, mutual funds, stocks, and bonds. Many banks also serve as securities intermediaries, using their own stockbrokers to buy and sell securities and their

individual retirement account (IRA)
Tax-deferred pension fund with which wage earners supplement other retirement funds

Keogh plan
Tax-deferred pension plan for the self-employed

trust services
Bank management of an individual's investments, payments, or estate

letter of credit
Bank promise, issued for a buyer, to pay a designated firm a certain amount of money if specified conditions are met

banker's acceptance
Bank promise, issued for a buyer, to pay a designated firm a specified amount at a future date

own facilities to hold them. Bank advertisements often stress the role of banks as financial advisers.

Automated Teller Machines

automated teller machine (ATM)
Electronic machine that allows customers to conduct account-related activities 24 hours a day, seven days a week

Automated teller machines (ATMs) are electronic machines that allow customers to withdraw money and make deposits 24 hours a day, seven days a week. They also allow transfers of funds between accounts and provide information on account status. Some 109,000 machines are now located at bank buildings, grocery stores, airports, shopping malls, and other locations. Some banks offer cards that can be used in affiliated nationwide systems. U.S. bank customers conduct 8 billion ATM transactions a year, withdrawing an average of $50 per transaction.[13]

Increasingly, ATMs are also becoming global fixtures. In fact, among the world's 545,000 ATMs, 80 percent are located outside the United States. The world total is expected to reach nearly 950,000 machines by the year 2000. Many U.S. banks offer international ATM services. In China, for example, Citicorp installed Shanghai's first 24-hour ATM and is the first foreign bank to receive approval from the People's Bank of China to issue local currency through ATMs. Elsewhere Citibank machines feature touch screens that take instructions in any of ten languages.[14] ▼

Electronic Funds Transfer

electronic funds transfer (EFT)
Communication of fund transfer information over wire, cable, or microwave

ATMs are the most popular form of **electronic funds transfer (EFT).** EFT systems transfer many kinds of financial information via electrical impulses over wire, cable, or microwave. In addition to ATMs, EFT systems include automatic payroll deposit, bill payment, and automatic funds transfer. Such systems can help a business-person close an important business deal by transferring money from San Francisco to Miami within a few hours.

Banks as Creators of Money

In the course of their activities, financial institutions provide a special service to the economy—they create money. This is not to say that they mint bills and coins. Rather, by taking in deposits and making loans, they *expand the money supply*.

Citibank has realized a big payoff from its 20-year commitment to "consumer banking technology"—that is, to the world's most advanced ATM technology. In one recent year, for example, the consumer banking division earned more than all the bank's other divisions combined. That's why Citibank now has consumer banking outlets in 41 countries, where it strives to make its once specialized products universal. At this ATM machine in Budapest, Hungary, for example, Americans can access their U.S. accounts in English. Then, says Victor Meneszes, head of Citibank's U.S./Europe consumer banking operations, "they can withdraw cash and go across the street to McDonald's. They feel completely at home."

As Figure 16.3 shows, the money supply expands because banks are allowed to loan out most (although not all) of the money they take in from deposits. Suppose that you deposit $100 in your bank. If banks are allowed to loan out 90 percent of all their deposits, then your bank will hold $10 in reserve and loan $90 of your money to borrowers. (You, of course, still have $100 on deposit.) Meanwhile, borrowers—or the people they pay—will deposit the $90 loan in their own banks. Together, the *borrowers'* banks will then have $81 (90 percent of $90) available for new loans. Banks, therefore,

Deposit	Money Held in Reserve by Bank	Money to Lend	Total Supply
$100.00	$10.00	$90.00	$190.00
90.00	9.00	81.00	271.00
81.00	8.10	72.90	343.90
72.90	7.29	65.61	409.51
65.61	6.56	59.05	468.56

FIGURE 16.3 ◆ How Banks Create Money

have turned your original $100 into $271 ($100 + $90 + $81). The chain continues, with borrowings from one bank becoming deposits in the next.

Regulation of Commercial Banking

Because commercial banks are critical to the creation of money, the government regulates them to ensure a sound and competitive financial system. Later in this chapter, we will see how the Federal Reserve System regulates many aspects of U.S. banking. Other federal and state agencies also regulate banks to ensure that the failure of some banks as a result of competition will not cause the public to lose faith in the banking system itself.

Federal Deposit Insurance Corporation The **Federal Deposit Insurance Corporation (FDIC)** insures deposits in member banks. More than 99 percent of the nation's commercial banks pay fees for membership in the FDIC. In return, the FDIC guarantees, through its Bank Insurance Fund (BIF), the safety of all deposits up to the current maximum of $100,000. If a bank collapses, the FDIC promises to pay its depositors—through the BIF—for losses up to $100,000 per person. (A handful of the nation's 11,000-plus commercial banks are insured by states rather than by the BIF.)

Federal Deposit Insurance Corporation (FDIC)
Federal agency that guarantees the safety of bank deposits up to $100,000

■ THE FEDERAL RESERVE SYSTEM

Perched atop the U.S. financial system and regulating many aspects of its operation is the Federal Reserve System. Established by Congress in 1913, the **Federal Reserve System,** popularly called *the Fed,* is the nation's central bank. In this section, we describe the structure of the Fed, its functions, and the tools that it uses to control the nation's money supply.

Federal Reserve System (the Fed)
The central bank of the United States, which acts as the government's bank, services member commercial banks, and controls the nation's money supply

The Fed's Structure

The Federal Reserve System consists of a Board of Governors, a group of Reserve Banks, and member banks. As originally established by the Federal Reserve Act of 1913, the system consisted of twelve relatively autonomous banks and a seven-member committee whose powers were limited to coordinating their activities. By the 1930s, however, both the structure and function of the Fed had changed dramatically.

The Board of Governors   The Fed's Board of Governors consists of seven members appointed by the President for overlapping terms of 14 years. The chair of the board serves on major economic advisory committees and works actively with the administration to formulate economic policy. The board plays a large role in controlling the money supply. It alone determines the reserve requirements, within statutory limits, for depository institutions. It also works with other members of the Federal Reserve System to set discount rates and handle the Fed's sale and purchase of government securities.

Reserve Banks   There are 12 administrative areas and 12 banks in the Federal Reserve System. Each Federal Reserve Bank holds reserve deposits from and sets the discount rate for commercial banks in its region. Reserve Banks also play a major role in the nation's check-clearing process.

Member Banks   All nationally chartered commercial banks are members of the Federal Reserve System, as are some state-chartered banks. The accounts of all memberbank depositors are automatically covered by the FDIC/BIF. Although many state-chartered banks do not belong to the Federal Reserve System, most pay deposit insurance premiums and are covered by the FDIC.

The Functions of the Fed

In addition to chartering national banks, the Fed serves as the federal government's bank and the "bankers' bank," regulating a number of banking activities. Most importantly, however, it controls the money supply. In this section, we describe these functions in some detail.

The Government's Bank   Two of the Fed's activities are producing the nation's paper currency and lending money to the government. The Fed, for example, decides how many bills to produce and how many to destroy. To lend funds to the government, the Fed buys bonds issued by the Treasury Department. The borrowed money is then used to help finance the national deficit.

The Bankers' Bank   Individual banks that need money can borrow from the Federal Reserve and pay interest on the loans. In addition, the Fed provides storage for commercial banks, which are required to keep funds on reserve at a Federal Reserve Bank.

Check Clearing.   The Fed also *clears checks* for commercial banks. To understand the check-clearing process, imagine that you are a photographer living in New Orleans. To participate in a workshop in Detroit, you must send a check for $50 to the Detroit studio. Figure 16.4 traces your check through the clearing process:

   1. You send your check to the Detroit studio, which deposits it in its Detroit bank.
   2. The Detroit bank deposits the check in its own account at the Federal Reserve Bank of Chicago.
   3. The check is sent from Chicago to the Atlanta Federal Reserve Bank for collection because you, the check writer, live in the Atlanta district.
   4. Your New Orleans bank receives the check from Atlanta and deducts the $50 from your personal account.
   5. Your bank then has $50 deducted from its deposit account at the Atlanta Federal Reserve Bank.
   6. The $50 is shifted from Atlanta to the Chicago Federal Reserve Bank. The studio's Detroit bank gets credited, whereupon the studio's account is then credited $50. Your bank mails the canceled check back to you.

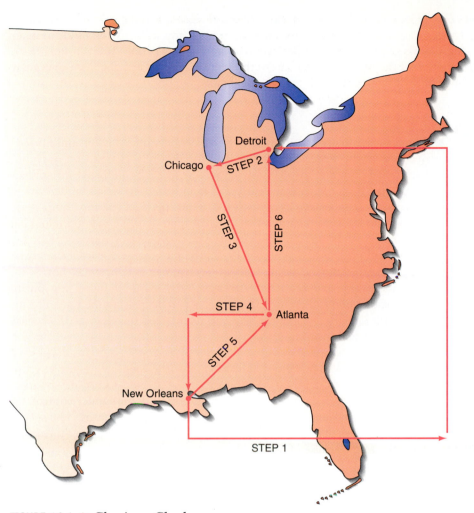

FIGURE 16.4 ◆ Clearing a Check

Depending on the number of banks and the distances between them, a check will clear in two to six days. Until the process is completed, the studio's Detroit bank cannot spend the $50 deposited there. Meanwhile, your bank's records will continue to show $50 in your account. Each day, approximately $1 billion in checks is processed by the system. The term **float** refers to all the checks in the process at any one time.

Overseeing the Banking Community   The Federal Reserve System is empowered to examine all banks in its system. In reality, however, it examines only the state banks because national banks are examined by the Comptroller of the Currency and the FDIC. Together these auditing efforts ensure the safety and stability of the state and national banks that are members of the Federal Reserve System.

Controlling the Money Supply   The Federal Reserve System is responsible for the conduct of U.S. **monetary policy**—the management of the nation's economic growth by managing money supply and interest rates. By controlling these two factors, the Fed influences the ability and willingness of banks throughout the country to loan money.

Inflation Management.   As we defined it in Chapter 1, *inflation* is a period of widespread price increases throughout an economic system. It occurs if the money supply

float
Amount of checks written but not yet cleared through the Federal Reserve

monetary policy
Policies by which the Federal Reserve manages the nation's money supply and interest rates

grows too large. Demand for goods and services increases, and the prices of everything rise. (In contrast, too little money means that an economy will lack the funds to maintain high levels of employment.) Because commercial banks are the main creators of money, much of the Fed's management of the money supply takes the form of regulating the supply of money through commercial banks.

■ Consider the following illustration from 1995. In July, the Fed announced a decrease in the Federal *funds rate*, the interest rate charged on overnight loans made among banks, from 6 percent to 5.75 percent. Inflationary trends had been easing since early 1994, and the step was intended *to keep the economy from slowing down too much*. Thus, the Fed's action completed a classical cycle of rate changes that it had begun in 1990, when the Fed had decreased interest *rates to stimulate the then recessionary economy*. The Fed steadily cut rates until September 1992, when it became apparent that its actions were having the desired effect—consumer and business borrowing were increasing and business activity showed signs of increasing during 1993. At that point, therefore, the Fed stopped decreasing the rate. The decision was effective. While the rate was unchanged throughout 1993, business activity continued to grow.

By 1994, however, the Fed perceived indications that the economy might be growing *too* quickly. It thus began gently increasing the interest rate to head off inflation. The first graph in Figure 16.5 shows that, in order to keep inflation under control, the central bank raised the funds rate seven times during the next 17 months. The second graph in Figure 16.5 shows that by early 1995 it was evident that the higher rates were having the desired effect. Because of higher interest rates, for example, consumer loans became more expensive. As consumers borrowed (and spent) less, overall economic activity slowed down. Inflationary pressures were under control. Finally, by mid-1995, there were indications that another economic slowdown might be under way. The Fed thus cut the rate for the first time since 1992.[15]

The Fed's Tools

According to the Fed's original charter, its primary duties were to supervise banking and to manage both the currency and commercial paper. The duties of the Fed evolved, however, along with a predominant philosophy of monetary policy. That policy includes an emphasis on the broad economic goals that we discussed in Chapter 1—stability, full employment, and growth. The Fed's role in controlling the nation's money supply stems from its role in setting policies to help reach these goals. To control the money supply, the Fed uses four primary tools: *reserve requirements*, *discount rate controls*, *open market operations*, and *selective credit controls*.

reserve requirement
Percentage of deposits a bank must hold in cash or on deposit with the Federal Reserve

discount rate
Interest rate at which member banks can borrow money from the Federal Reserve

Reserve Requirements   The **reserve requirement** is the percentage of its deposits a bank must hold, in cash or on deposit, with a Federal Reserve Bank. High requirements mean that banks have less money to lend. Thus, a high reserve requirement reduces the money supply. Conversely, low requirements permit the supply to expand. Because the Fed sets requirements for all depository institutions, it can adjust them to make changes in the overall supply of money to the economy.

Discount Rate Controls   As the "bankers' bank," the Fed loans money to banks. The interest rate on these loans is known as the **discount rate.** If the Fed wants to reduce the money supply, it increases the discount rate, making it more expensive for

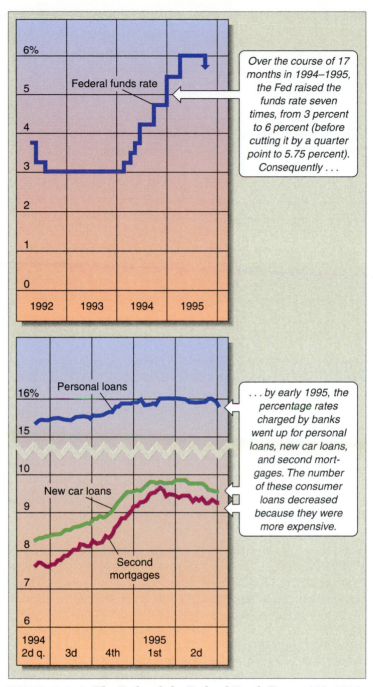

FIGURE 16.5 ◆ The Fed and the Federal Funds Rate, 1992–1995

banks to borrow money and less attractive for them to loan it. Conversely, low rates encourage borrowing and lending and expand the money supply.

Open-Market Operations   The third instrument for monetary control is probably the Fed's most important tool. **Open-market operations** refer to the Fed's sale and purchase of securities (usually U.S. Treasury notes and bonds) in the open market. Open-market operations are particularly effective because they act quickly and predictably on the money supply. How so? The Fed buys securities from dealers. Because the dealer's bank account is credited for the transaction, its bank has more money to

open-market operations
The Federal Reserve's sales and purchases of U.S. government securities in the open market

lend—and so expands the money supply. The opposite happens when the Fed sells securities.[16]

Selective Credit Controls The Federal Reserve can exert considerable influence on business activity by exercising **selective credit controls.** The Fed may set special requirements for consumer stock purchases and credit rules for other consumer purchases.

As we will see in Chapter 17, investors can set up credit accounts with stockbrokers to buy stocks and bonds. A *margin requirement* set by the Fed stipulates the amount of credit that the broker can extend to the customer. For example, a 60-percent margin rate means that approved customers can purchase stocks having $100,000 market value with $60,000 in cash (60 percent of $100,000) and $40,000 in loans from the dealer. If the Fed wants to increase securities transactions, it can lower the margin requirement. Customers can then borrow greater percentages of their purchase costs from dealers, thus increasing their purchasing power and the amount of securities that they can buy.

Within stipulated limits, the Fed is also permitted to specify the conditions of certain credit purchases. This authority extends to such conditions as allowable down payment percentages for appliance purchases and repayment periods on automobile loans. The Fed has chosen not to use these powers in recent years.

■ THE CHANGING MONEY AND BANKING SYSTEM

The U.S. money and banking systems have changed in recent years and continue to change today. Deregulation and interstate banking, for example, have increased competition not just among banks but between banks and other financial institutions. Electronic technologies affect not only how you obtain money but also how much interest you pay for it.

Deregulation

The Depository Institutions Deregulation and Monetary Control Act (DIDMCA) of 1980 brought many changes to the banking industry. Before its passage, there were clear distinctions between the types of services offered by different institutions. For example, although all institutions could offer savings accounts, only commercial banks could offer checking accounts, and S&Ls and mutual savings banks generally could not make consumer loans. The DIDMCA and subsequent laws sought to promote competition by eliminating many such restrictions.

Under deregulation, many banks were unable to survive in the new competitive environment. In the 1980s, more than 1,000 banks—1 more than 7 percent of the total—failed, as did 835 savings and loans.[17] Many economists, however, regard some bank closings as a beneficial weeding out of inefficient competitors.

Interstate Banking

The Interstate Banking Efficiency Act was passed into law in September 1994, thus allowing banks to enter (gradually) into interstate banking—the operation of banks or branches across state lines. It also mandates regulation by government agencies to ensure proper operation and competition. The key provisions in this act include the following:

- Limited nationwide banking is permitted, beginning in 1995. Bank holding companies can acquire subsidiaries in any state.
- The ultimate *size* of any company is limited. No one company can control more than 10 percent of nationwide insured deposits. No bank can control more than 30 percent of a state's deposits (each state is empowered to set its own limit).
- Beginning in 1995, banks can provide limited transactions for affiliated banks in other states. They can thus accept deposits, close loans, and accept loan payments on behalf of other affiliated banks. (They cannot, however, *originate* loans or *open* deposit accounts for affiliates.)
- Beginning in June 1997, banks can convert affiliates into full-fledged interstate branches.[18]

Interstate banking offers certain efficiencies. For example, it allows banks to consolidate services and eliminate duplicated activities. Opponents, however, remain concerned that some banks will gain undue influence, dominate other banks, and hinder competition.

The Impact of Electronic Technologies

Like so many other businesses, banks are increasingly investing in technology as a way to improve efficiency and customer-service levels. Many banks offer ATMs and EFT systems. Some offer TV banking, in which customers use television sets and terminals—or home computers—to make transactions. The age of electronic money has arrived. As the cartoon in Figure 16.6 suggests, ever since Western Union figured out, about 100 years ago, how to turn money into something that could be sent through wires, the days of currency have been numbered. Each business day, more than $2 trillion exists in and among banks and other financial institutions in purely electronic form. Digital money is replacing cash in stores, taxi cabs, subway systems, and vending machines.[19]

FIGURE 16.6 ◆ "Dead as a Dollar"

Debit Cards One of the most recent electronic offerings from the financial industry is the debit card. Unlike credit cards, **debit cards** allow only the transfer of money between accounts. They do not increase the funds at an individual's disposal. They can, however, be used to make retail purchases.

For example, in stores with **point-of-sale (POS) terminals,** customers insert cards that transmit to terminals information relevant to their purchases. The terminal relays the

debit card
Plastic card that allows an individual to transfer money between bank accounts

point-of-sale (POS) terminal
Electronic device that allows customers to pay for retail purchases with debit cards

information directly to the bank's computer system. The bank automatically transfers funds from the customer's account to the store's account.

smart card
Credit card-sized computer that can be programmed with "electronic money"

Smart Cards   The so-called **smart card** is a credit card–sized computer that can be programmed with "electronic money." Also known as "electronic purses" or "stored-value cards," smart cards have existed for nearly a decade. Shoppers in Europe and Asia are the most avid users, holding the majority of the 33 million cards in circulation at the beginning of 1995.[20]

Why are smart cards increasing in popularity today? For one thing, the cost of producing them has fallen dramatically—from as much as $10 to as little as $1. Convenience is equally important, notes Donald J. Gleason, President of Electronic Payment Services' Smart Card Enterprise division. "What consumers want," Gleason contends, "is convenience, and if you look at cash, it's really quite inconvenient."[21]

> ## "What consumers want is convenience, and if you look at cash, it's really quite inconvenient."
> —Donald J. Gleason
> *President of Smart Card Enterprise*

Smart cards can be loaded with money at ATM machines or, with special telephone hookups, even at home. After using your card to purchase an item, you can then check an electronic display to see how much money your card has left. Analysts predict that in the near future, smart cards will function as much more than electronic purses. For example, travel industry experts predict that people will soon book travel plans at home on personal computers and then transfer their reservations onto their smart cards. The cards will then serve as airline tickets and boarding passes. As an added benefit, they will allow travelers to avoid waiting in lines at car rental agencies and hotel front desks.

E-cash
Money that moves among consumers and businesses via digital electronic transmissions

E-Cash   A new, revolutionary world of electronic money has begun to emerge with the rapid growth of the Internet. Electronic money, known as **E-cash,** is money that moves along multiple channels of consumers and businesses via digital electronic transmissions. E-cash moves outside the established network of banks, checks, and paper currency overseen by the Federal Reserve. Companies as varied as new startup Mondex and giant Citicorp are developing their own forms of electronic money that allows consumers and businesses to spend money more conveniently, quickly, and cheaply than they can through the banking system. In fact, some observers predict that by the year 2005, as much as 20 percent of all household expenditures will take place on the Internet. "Banking," comments one investment banker, "is essential to the modern economy, but banks are not."

> ## "Banking is essential to the modern economy, but banks are not."
> —J. Richard Fredericks
> *Senior Managing Director at Montgomery Securities*

How does E-cash work? Traditional currency is used to buy electronic funds, which are downloaded over phone lines into a PC or a portable "electronic wallet" that can store and transmit E-cash. E-cash is purchased from any company that issues (sells) it, including companies such as Mondex, Citicorp, and banks. When shopping on-line—say, to purchase jewelry—a shopper sends digital money to the merchant instead of using traditional cash, checks, or credit cards. Businesses can purchase supplies and services electronically from any merchant that accepts E-cash. E-cash flows from the buyer's into the seller's E-cash funds, which are instantaneously updated and stored on a microchip. One system, operated by CyberCash, tallies all E-cash transactions in the customer's account and, at the end of the day, converts the E-cash balance back into dollars in the customer's conventional banking account.

Although E-cash transactions are cheaper than handling checks and the paper records involved with conventional money, there are some potential problems. Hackers, for example, may break into E-cash systems and drain them instantaneously. Moreover, if the issuer's computer system crashes, it is conceivable that money "banked" in memory may be lost forever. Finally, regulation and control of E-cash systems remains largely nonexistent; there is virtually none of the protection that covers government-controlled money systems.[22]

■ INTERNATIONAL BANKING AND FINANCE

Along with international banking networks, electronic technologies now permit nearly instantaneous financial transactions around the globe. The economic importance of international finance is evident from both the presence of foreign banks in the U.S. market and the sizes of certain banks around the world. In addition, each nation tries to influence its currency exchange rates for economic advantage in international trade. The subsequent country-to-country transactions result in an *international payments process* that moves money among buyers and sellers on different continents.

The International Payments Process

When transactions are made among buyers and sellers in different countries, exactly how are payments made? Payments are simplified through the services provided by their banks. For example, payments from buyers flow through a local bank that converts them from the local currency into the foreign currency of the seller. The local bank receives and converts incoming money from the banks of foreign buyers. The payments process is shown in Figure 16.7.[23]

> *Step 1.* A U.S. olive importer withdraws $1,000 from its checking account in order to buy olives from a Greek exporter. The local U.S. bank converts those dollars into Greek drachmas at the current exchange rate (230 drachmas per dollar).
> *Step 2.* The U.S. bank sends a check for 230,000 drachmas (230 × 1,000) to the exporter in Greece.
> *Steps 3 and 4.* The exporter sends olives to its U.S. customer and deposits the check in its local Greek bank. The exporter now has drachmas that can be spent in Greece, and the importer has olives to sell in the United States.

At the same time, a separate transaction is being made between a U.S. machine exporter and a Greek olive oil producer. This time, importer/exporter roles are reversed between the two countries: The Greek firm needs to import a $1,000 olive oil press from the United States.

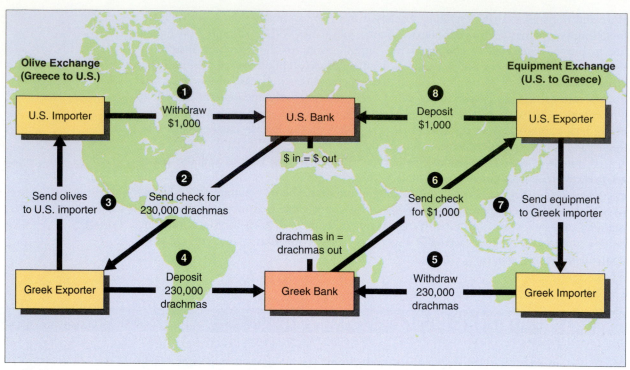

FIGURE 16.7 ◆ **The International Payments Process**

Steps 5 and 6. Drachmas (230,000) withdrawn from a local Greek bank account are converted into $1,000 U.S. dollars and sent via check to the U.S. exporter.

Steps 7 and 8. The olive oil press is sent to the Greek importer, and the importer's check is deposited in the U.S. exporter's local bank account.

In this example, trade between the two countries is *in balance*. Money inflows and outflows are equal for both countries. When such a balance occurs, *money does not actually have to flow between the two countries*. Within each bank, the dollars spent by local importers offset the dollars received by local exporters. In effect, therefore, the dollars have simply flowed from U.S. importers to U.S. exporters. Similarly, the drachmas have moved from Greek exporters to Greek importers.

Continued from page 413

The Challenge of Automating the Illiterate

Smoothing Out the Ironies of State-of-the-Art Technology

With the illiteracy rate among black South Africans at about 55 percent, South Africa's E Bank had to find a way to serve a market of unsophisticated banking customers while still making money. The bank pinned its hopes on technology—specifically, on automated teller machines.

Bank clerks who speak native dialects help new customers fill out simple computerized account applications. An ATM card is then issued and the customer watches the clerk insert the card into the slot. Using a numeric keyboard, the clerk punches in account information and then instructs the customer to make a choice—to deposit or withdraw money. This process is time consuming but necessary. "We will help cus-

> **"We will help customers as long as they need it. But the whole purpose is to try to educate our customers to help themselves."**
>
> Loyiso Maggaza
> *Area Manager for Standard Bank's E Bank operation*

tomers as long as they need it," explains Loyiso Maggaza, Area Manager for Standard Bank's E Bank operation. "But the whole purpose is to try to educate our customers to help themselves."

With labor being the bank's largest single operating cost, ATM

technology promises to keep expenses down. E Bank is also trying out more advanced technologies that may be even easier for illiterate customers to use. One device currently being tested reads the customer's fingerprints and foregoes the need to enter a secret code. After inserting the bank card, the customer places a thumb on the fingerprint reader and watches as account information pops onto the screen.

South African banks now realize that, ironically, technology gives them the ability to market to poorly educated consumers. They understand, too, that success depends on a simple approach. The key, according to E Bank general manager Bob Tucker, is the fact that "you can work our machines without even being able to read and write."

Case Questions

1. For poor South African blacks, what is the relationship between opening a bank account and becoming part of their nation's emerging economy?
2. Why are South African banks courting poor black consumers?
3. Why are banks relying on ATMs as their customer service centerpiece?
4. With so many black South African consumers now using ATM technology, do you think these same consumers would be willing to use debit cards at retail stores? What factors might stand in the way of implementing a debit card system?
5. Why do you think this population of banking customers shows little interest in checking accounts or investments like certificates of deposit?
6. What can U.S. banks learn from the experience of South African banks?

SUMMARY OF LEARNING OBJECTIVES

1. **Define *money* and identify the different forms that it takes in the nation's money supply.** Any item that is portable, divisible, durable, and stable satisfies the four basic characteristics of *money*. Money also serves three functions: it is a medium of exchange, a store of value, and a unit of account. The nation's money supply is often determined by two measures. *M-1* includes liquid (or spendable) forms of money: currency (bills and coins), demand deposits, and other checkable deposits (such as ATM account balances and NOW accounts).

M-2 includes M-1 plus items that cannot be directly spent but that can be easily converted to spendable forms, namely, time deposits, money market funds, savings deposits, and overnight transactions. *Credit* must also be considered as a factor in the money supply.

2. **Describe the different kinds of *financial institutions* that make up the U.S. financial system and explain the services they offer.**   The U.S. financial system includes federal- and state-chartered *commercial banks, savings and loan associations, mutual savings banks, credit unions,* and *nondeposit institutions,* such as pension funds and insurance companies. These institutions offer a variety of services, including pension, trust, and international services, financial advice and brokerage services, and convenient electronic funds transfer (EFT), including automated teller machines.

3. **Explain how banks create money and describe the means by which they are regulated.**   By taking in deposits and making loans, banks *expand the money supply.* The overall supply of money, however, is governed by several federal agencies. The *Federal Deposit Insurance Corporation (FDIC)* is the primary agency responsible for ensuring a sound, competitive financial system.

4. **Discuss the functions of the *Federal Reserve System* and describe the tools it uses to control the money supply.**   The *Federal Reserve System* (or the *Fed*) is the nation's central bank. As the government's bank, the Fed produces currency and lends money to the government. As the "bankers' bank," it lends money (at interest) to member banks, stores required *reserve funds* for banks, and clears checks for them. The Fed is empowered to audit member banks and sets U.S. *monetary policy* by controlling the country's money supply. To control the money supply, the Fed specifies *reserve requirements* (the percentage of deposits a bank must hold with the Fed). It sets the discount rate at which it loans money to banks and conducts *open-market operations* to buy and sell securities. It also exerts influence through *selective credit controls* (such as margin requirements governing the credit granted to buyers by securities brokers).

5. **Identify three important ways in which the financial industry is changing.** Many changes have affected the financial system in recent years. *Deregulation,* especially of interest rates, and the rise of *interstate banking* have increased competition. *Electronic technologies* offer a variety of new financial conveniences to customers. *Debit cards* are plastic cards that permit users to transfer money between bank accounts. *Smart cards* are credit card-sized computers that can be loaded with "electronic money" at ATMs or over special telephone hookups. *E-Cash* is money that can be moved among consumers and businesses via digital electronic transmissions.

STUDY QUESTIONS AND EXERCISES

Review

1. What are the components of M-1 and M-2?
2. Explain the roles of commercial banks, savings and loan associations, and nondeposit institutions in the U.S. financial system.
3. Explain the types of pension services that commercial banks provide for their customers.
4. Describe the structure of the Federal Reserve System.

5. Show how the Fed uses the federal funds rate to manage inflation in the U.S. economy.

Analysis

6. Do you think that credit cards should be counted in the money supply? Why or why not? Support your argument by using the definition of money.
7. Should commercial banks be regulated, or should market forces be allowed to determine the money supply? Why?
8. Identify a purchase made by you or a family member in which payment was made by check. Draw a diagram to trace the steps in the clearing process followed by that check.

Application Exercises

9. Start with a $1,000 deposit and assume a reserve requirement of 15 percent. Trace the amount of money created by the banking system after five lending cycles.
10. Interview the manager of a local commercial bank. Identify several ways in which the Fed either helps the bank or restricts its operations.

BUILDING YOUR BUSINESS SKILLS

This exercise enhances the following SCANS workplace competencies: demonstrating basic skills, demonstrating thinking skills, exhibiting interpersonal skills, and working with information.

Goal

To help students evaluate the risks and rewards associated with excessive credit card use

Situation

Suppose that you've been out of school for a year and are now working in your first job. Your annual $30,000 salary is enough to support your apartment, car, and the basic necessities of life, but the luxuries are still out of reach. You pay cash for everything until one day you get a preapproved credit card solicitation in the mail, which offers you a $1,500 line of credit. You decide to take the offer and begin charging purchases. Within a year, five other credit card companies have contacted you, and you accumulate a total credit line of $12,000.

Method

Step 1: Working with three or four classmates, evaluate the advantages and dangers inherent in this situation, both to the consumer and to credit card issuers. To address this issue, research the current percentage of credit card delinquencies and rate of personal bankruptcies. Find out, for example, how these rates compare with those in previous years. In addition, research the profitability of the credit card business.

Step 2: Evaluate the different methods that credit card companies use to attract new customers. Specifically, look at the following practices:

- Sending unsolicited, preapproved credit card applications to consumers with questionable and even poor credit

- Offering large credit lines to consumers who pay only monthly minimums

- Lowering interest rates on accounts as a way of encouraging revolving payments

- Charging penalties on accounts that are paid in full at the end of every billing cycle (research the GE Rewards MasterCard)

- Sending card holders catalogs of discounted gifts that can be purchased with their charge cards

- Linking credit card use to a program of rewards—say, frequent flier miles linked to amounts charged

Step 3: Compile your findings in the form of a set of guidelines designed for consumers receiving unsolicited credit card offers. Your guidelines should analyze the advantages and disadvantages of excessive credit card use.

Follow-Up

1. If you were the person in our hypothetical example, how would you handle your credit situation?

2. Why do you think credit card companies continue to offer cards to people who are financially overextended?

3. What criteria can you suggest to evaluate different credit card offers?

4. How do you know when you have enough credit?

Exploring the Net

TO OBTAIN INFORMATION ABOUT THE LATEST DEVELOPMENTS IN
ELECTRONIC BANKING, LOG ON TO THE FOLLOWING WEBSITE:

FLORIDA STATE UNIVERSITY, SOURCES OF FINANCIAL INFORMATION: BANKING AT
http://www.fsu.edu/~finance/bank/

From the main menu, select the feature entitled "On-line banking." From there, go into the lobby at Security First National Bank (SFNB). Select the customer window labeled "DEMO," and then browse the "Quick Demo" for information about SFNB's products and services. Now consider the following questions:

1. For a checking account, how does the electronic "Transaction Register" compare with the paper check register for keeping track of transactions?

   ■ Is the format convenient? Is it easy to understand and use? Does it contain useful information?
   ■ Are the electronic reports as accessible as paper reports? Are they as portable?

2. What advantages do you see to the "Quick Pay" feature in the electronic system?

3. How much saving in time and how much convenience would you gain from the "Select Bills to Pay" feature in the electronic system?

4. Suppose you want to transfer funds from a money market account into your checking account. Compare SFNB's electronic system with traditional methods for making such a transfer.

5. As a credit card customer, evaluate the conveniences/inconveniences of the "Account Statement" for a SFNB Visa account. How does it compare with a paper account statement?

6. What advantages and drawbacks would you expect to encounter in using the electronic transfer of funds in SFBN's credit card and checking accounts?

7. What is your assessment of the overall speed and accessibility of electronic banking information in the SFNB system?

17

UNDERSTANDING SECURITIES AND INVESTMENTS

Stories of Great Expectations in Hard Times

WHY WALL STREET DOESN'T SCARE THE DICKENS OUT OF EVERYONE

Statistics sometimes tell a story better than words alone. This is certainly the case when the story involves the phenomenal growth in popularity of the stock market among average Americans. According to the New York Stock Exchange, the number of Americans who own shares of stock in one form or another rose from 6 million in the early 1950s to well over 50 million today. By 1996, more than 37 percent of the adults in the United States were shareholders in American and international corporations.

More and more Americans are being drawn to the stock market because of its promise of financial growth during anxious economic times. As job insecurity increased, Americans watched the stock market soar to record levels—and they wanted a piece of the action for themselves. As a result, teachers, plumbers, postal workers, editors, university professors, and executives poured billions into equities and saw their net worth take off as the stock market rose 60 percent in just 19 months.

Today individuals are investing their discretionary income (available money over and above what is needed for a comfortable standard of living) as well as their retirement pensions in equities. With more and more companies shifting to self-directed 401(k)

> **"As African Americans we have always been told to put our money in the bank and save it for a rainy day, but because of inflation that just doesn't work. We've got to get involved in the stock market."**
>
> —Ricky Jack
> *Individual investor and member of the National Association of Investors Corp.*

pension plans—that is, plans giving employees the right to choose their own investment vehicles—stocks, often in the form of mutual funds, have been the vehicle of choice, despite the risk. "What we're seeing," explains Roger M. Kubarych, general manager of the investment firm Henry Kaufman & Co., "is the democratization of risk, and that has good and bad implications," On the upside, ordinary investors are building wealth as they take more responsibility for their financial futures. On the downside, the risk that a market crash or a bear (that is, a period of falling stock prices) market will diminish the value of their holdings is real.

Who are America's average investors? Here are three of them:

- Ricky Jack, a 32-year-old production manager with DuPont, began investing in the stock market 8 years ago and turned a modest investment into more than $200,000. Jack is a member of the Houston Council Board of Directors of the National Association of Investors Corp. (NAIC), a nonprofit group that boasts more than 22,000 investment clubs across the country. As an African American, he is committed to helping other African Americans learn to invest. "As African Americans," says Jack, "we have always been told to put our money in the bank and save it for a rainy day, but because of inflation that just doesn't work. We've got to get involved in the stock market."

- Janet Norris, a 43-year-old mother of two in Salinas, California, followed the stock market for 10 years, but owned only 50 shares of stock from her husband's employer, William Wrigley Jr. Co. Realizing that she and her husband faced the cost of college and retirement at the same time, she enrolled in an investment plan offered by her local NAIC club and began buying one share of stock at a time. "The time came," recalls Norris, "when I had to make a financial commitment myself." Her initial $250 investment went into five companies. To build her nest egg, she adds $25 a month to each stock and reinvests all dividends. In 1995, thanks to the success of one of her technology stocks, Norris's portfolio enjoyed a 30-percent annual return. If the market drops in value, Norris intends to increase her equity holdings. "Other than stock," she explains, "I don't see that I have any other options for retirement and college planning."

■ Although the ups and downs of the stock market "drive her crazy," Cyndi B. Moltz, a 29-year-old graphic artist from Denver, Colorado, has invested her $100,000 portfolio in individual stocks and mutual funds. She chose to invest $10,000 in T. Rowe Price's mutual funds because of convenience. "You don't have to baby sit your investment," says Moltz, who checks her account about once a week. With a goal of long-term growth, she is uncertain what will happen tomorrow but is confident about the future. She explains, "I watched *Friends* on television last night. One of the main characters put $100 in her first stock and she lost it all the next day. You can't invest today and expect to become a millionaire overnight."

Investors like Ricky Jack, Janet Norris, and Cyndi B. Moltz are changing the face of investing in America as they are making equities, purchased directly or through mutual funds, a pivotal part of their financial planning. Indeed, for the first time in decades, Federal Reserve data show that the value of stocks owned by members of a household was greater than the value of the equity in the family's home. A 1996 *Business Week*/Harris Poll shows that Americans will probably continue to look to the stock market for financial security. While 25 percent of those polled chose real estate as the single best investment they would likely make right now, 34 percent chose individual stocks and mutual funds.

As you will see in this chapter, investing in U.S. and international companies through the purchase of stocks and bonds is becoming part of the American Dream for acquiring and building wealth. Although both established and start-up companies are able to expand and prosper because of these investments, financial risk can affect the return for investors and corporations alike. By focusing on the learning objectives of this chapter, you will better understand the importance of the marketplaces in which securities are traded and the nature of such investment vehicles as stocks and bonds, mutual funds, and commodities.

After reading this chapter, you should be able to

1. Explain the difference between *primary* and *secondary securities markets*

2. Discuss the value to shareholders of *common* and *preferred stock* and describe the secondary market for each type of security

3. Distinguish among various types of *bonds* in terms of their issuers and safety

4. Describe the investment opportunities offered by *mutual funds* and *commodities*

5. Explain the process by which securities are bought and sold

6. Explain how securities markets are regulated

Continued on page 464

■ SECURITIES MARKETS

securities
Stocks and bonds representing secured, or asset-based, claims by investors against issuers

Stocks and bonds are known as **securities** because they represent *secured*, or *asset-based*, claims on the part of investors. In other words, holders of stocks and bonds have a stake in the business that issued them. As we saw in Chapter 2, stockholders have claims on some of a corporation's assets (and a say in how the company is run) because each share of stock represents part ownership.

In contrast, *bonds* represent strictly financial claims for money owed to holders by a company. Companies sell bonds to raise long-term funds. The markets in which stocks and bonds are sold are called *securities markets*.

Primary and Secondary Securities Markets

primary securities market
Market in which new stocks and bonds are bought and sold

In **primary securities markets,** new stocks and bonds are bought and sold by firms and governments.[1] Sometimes new securities are sold to single buyers or small groups of buyers. These so-called *private placements* are desirable because they allow issuers to keep their plans confidential.

In 1994, $101 billion in new private placements were purchased in the United States by large pension funds and other institutions that privately negotiated prices with sellers.[2] Because private placements cannot be resold in the open market, buyers generally demand higher returns from the issuers.

investment bank
Financial institution engaged in issuing and reselling new securities

Investment Banking   Most new stocks and some bonds are sold on the wider public market. To bring a new security to market, the issuing firm must get approval from the Securities and Exchange Commission—the government agency that regulates securities markets. It also needs the services of an **investment bank**—a financial institution that specializes in issuing and reselling new securities. Such investment banking firms as Merrill Lynch and Morgan Stanley provide three important services:

1. They advise companies on the timing and financial terms of new issues.
2. By *underwriting*—that is, buying—new securities, they bear some of the risks of issuing them.
3. They create the distribution networks for moving new securities through groups of other banks and brokers into the hands of individual investors.▶

secondary securities market
Market in which stocks and bonds are traded

In 1994, U.S. investment bankers brought to the market $60 billion in new corporate stocks and $365 billion in new corporate bonds.[3] New securities, however, represent only a very small portion of traded securities. Existing stocks and bonds are sold in the **secondary securities market,** which is handled by such familiar bodies as the New York Stock Exchange. We consider the activities of these markets later in this chapter.

■ STOCKS

Each year, financial managers, along with millions of individual investors, buy and sell the stocks of thousands of companies. This widespread ownership has become possible because of the availability of different types of stocks and because markets have been established for conveniently buying and selling them. In this section, we focus on the

You have to price three separate issues. And you only get one shot.

Get this done, and in a single transaction you save your company from burdensome debt and recapitalize it for a competitive future. The strategy is to repurchase high-coupon debt from bondholders, issue new debt with more favorable terms, and go public with an initial equity offering.

And this is the critical moment. You have to price all three elements — making each one attractive to investors but affordable for your company — simultaneously.

A tall order? This whole venture has been a tall order. First, there was the job of setting up the tender offer to bondholders — who had to be convinced that both the new debt issue and IPO would sell. Then there was the task of finding the right investors — ones who would support the strategy and make long-term commitments. There were negotiations, strategy sessions, and simultaneous road-shows for both the debt and equity markets. All this while running your company's day-to-day operations.

But you were prepared. You selected a global investment bank that could bring off this kind of multi-market transaction. They brought you scope, thinking, determination and, above all, credibility with investors.

While it hasn't been easy, and it isn't over yet, you feel confident these people will know how to price each issue so that you'll hit all three targets with one shot.

MORGAN STANLEY

Chicago   Frankfurt   Hong Kong   London   Los Angeles   Luxembourg   Madrid   Melbourne   Milan   New York   Paris   San Francisco   Seoul   Singapore   Taipei   Tokyo   Toronto   Zurich

Investment banks like Morgan Stanley Company Inc. may help an organization raise funds by issuing publicly traded securities or by arranging for private placements (that is, by finding single or small-group buyers for new securities). Banks like Morgan Stanley also serve large corporate and institutional investors by helping them to manage diversified global portfolios. The profits from such activities are substantial, and in recent years, other financial institutions, including commercial banks, insurance companies, and finance companies, have begun to compete with investment bankers for the business of corporate financial customers.

value of *common* and *preferred stock* as securities. We also describe the *stock exchanges* on which they are bought and sold.

Common Stock

Individuals and other companies purchase a firm's common stock in the hope that it will increase in value, provide dividend income, or both. But how is the *value* of a common stock determined? Stock values are expressed in three different ways—as *par*, *market*, and *book value*.

Par Value   **Par value** is the face value of a share of stock at the time it is originally issued. It is set by the issuing company's board of directors. In order to receive their corporate charters, all companies must declare par values for their stocks. Each company must preserve the par-value money in its retained earnings, and it cannot be distributed as dividends. However, because this procedural protection is largely a formality, par value usually bears no relationship to a stock's true value. In 1992, for example, the Coleman Co., which manufactures camping and outdoor recreational products, issued stock with a par value of only $0.01 a share. The firm proceeded to sell the stock to the public for $19.50 a share, a price that Coleman management believed investors would be willing to pay based on Coleman's assets and earnings potential.

par value
Face value of a share of stock, set by the issuing company's board of directors

Market Value   A stock's real value, then, is its **market value**—the current price of a share in the stock market. Coleman shares, for example, sold for up to $52 a share in 1996, indicating that investors value the stock at much more than the original $19.50. Market value, therefore, reflects buyers' willingness to invest in a company. It depends on a firm's history of dividend payments, its earnings potential, and on investors' expectations of **capital gains**—that is, profits to be made from selling the stock for more than it cost. Investors, then, are concerned primarily with market value.

market value
Current price of a share of stock in the stock market

capital gain
Profit earned by selling a share of stock for more than it cost

TRENDS & CHALLENGES

IPO CAPITALISM: THE MARKETPLACE FOR ENTREPRENEURIAL ZEAL

What do Netscape Communications Corp., Pixar Animation Studios, Borders Bookstores, and the Boston Brewing Company have in common? All were private companies that became public companies through *initial public offerings*, or *IPOs*.

IPOs provide entrepreneurs with the capital they need to expand innovative, small companies into large, thriving enterprises. Typically, entrepreneurs start with ideas and use their own money to build businesses. As the business grows, many turn to wealthy private investors or venture capitalists for needed capital. Entrepreneurs who identify a market for greater growth can either sell the company they have built to a corporate acquirer or sell stock to the public through an initial public offering. Those who want to maintain control of their businesses generally choose the IPO route.

In 1995 alone $30 billion was raised through IPOs. This money injected equity capital into new companies—money that was used to hire employees, build facilities, and conduct research and development. For example, at FPA Medical Management, a San Diego firm that assembles networks of doctors, an IPO raised $11.5 million in 1994. A year later, a subsequent offering raised $26 million. The company grew from 40 employees and $18 million in revenue to nearly 700 employees and $170 million in revenue within 18 months. "We owe that growth to public capital," says company chairman, Dr. Sol Lizerbram. "IPOs," adds Clifford Smith, Professor of Finance at the University of Rochester, "are critical for the market in allocating capital to new ventures and new products. IPOs are a big part of what makes the whole capital market process possible, allows the economy to tap into entrepreneurial zeal—and we're all the wealthier for it."

"IPOs are what allows the economy to tap into entrepreneurial zeal— and we're all the wealthier for it."

—Clifford Smith
Professor of Finance at the University of Rochester

Technology companies have been at the forefront of the most recent IPO boom, although the restaurant chain Planet Hollywood, the fashion house Donna Karan International, and the cosmetics company Revlon were also there. The stocks of these and other IPOs were quickly gobbled up by mutual fund managers looking for investment vehicles that would provide immediate, impressive results. "Companies [like these] can go public quickly," explains Dick Smith from Montgomery Securities, "because the market clamors for them."

Fund managers and corporate executives alike are often overwhelmed by just how impressive the results of an IPO can be. For example, when Pixar Animation, the computer-animation company controlled by Apple Computer co-founder Steven P. Jobs, went public, the stock price jumped from $22 to $39 on the first trading day. Netscape, a maker of Internet navigation software, went public at $28 a share in August 1995. By the first week of December, the price had skyrocketed to $171.

Ironically, the New York Stock Exchange waited until 1984 before it would accept new issues for trading. By then, the handwriting was on the wall for exchange officials: the IPO market was huge and would only get bigger. More than a decade later, the same can still be said. Moreover, the IPO market is the place where entrepreneurs dreams come true. "Without IPOs," maintains Netscape chairman James H. Clark, "you would not have any start-ups."

■ To get an idea of how perceptions about future performance can affect market value, consider the prices of AT&T, the nation's most widely held stock. On September 20, 1995, the stock gained 6⅛ points ($6.12) in one day with the announcement that AT&T would split into three companies. As you can see in Figure 17.1, this increase was followed by less dramatic ups and downs through June 1996. During this period, the company faced certain financial struggles with new business activities, such as wireless service, local service, and Internet access. In July, AT&T reported quarterly profits higher than those in the same quarter the previous year. Industry analysts, however, interpreted the numbers as relatively weak and not up to the the stronger earnings of competitors MCI Communications and Sprint Corp. As a result, AT&T's market price declined sharply. Then, on September 24, 1996, AT&T's market value fell nearly 10 percent ($9 billion in total value). The stock price plunged 5⅝ a share ($5.63) when the company announced that earnings for the rest of 1996 would be lower than previously expected. The stock price dropped because shareholders bid down the market price to reflect AT&T's lower future earnings power. Most analysts blamed AT&T's inability to keep pace with its competition. AT&T, suspects one investment banker, "was a bureaucratic, regulated beast asked to become a hard-charging competitor in a communications and information environment that's been totally unstable."[4]

"AT&T was a bureaucratic, regulated beast asked to become a hard-charging competitor in an environment that's been totally unstable."

—Wall Street analyst
on the 1996 drop in AT&T market value

Book Value   Recall from Chapter 12 our definition of *stockholders' equity*—the sum of a company's common stock par value, retained earnings, and additional paid-in capital. The **book value** of common stock represents stockholders' equity divided by the number of shares. In 1995, for example, Coleman had stockholders' equity of $292

book value
Value of a common stock expressed as total shareholders' equity divided by the number of shares of stock

FIGURE 17.1 ◆ **AT&T: Stock Price, September 1995–September 1996**

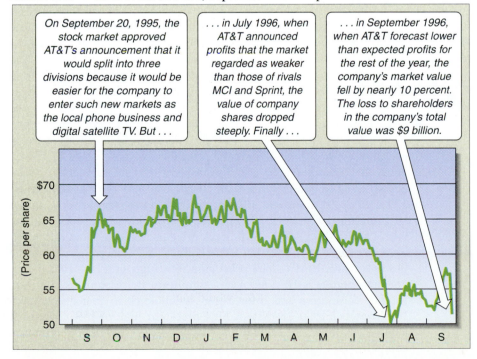

Although IBM's recent recovery owes much to renewed success in selling computers and information technology, the company is also focusing on ways to increase profits by building stronger long-term relationships with its customers. Because new systems are so complicated, and because technology evolves so quickly, many of its customers pay IBM to manage their purchases. With 35 percent of its earnings coming from such fees, IBM is sending many executives back to company-sponsored classrooms to hone their skills in selecting and assisting customers.

million. There were 26.6 million shares outstanding. Therefore, the book value of Coleman stock in 1995 was $10.98 per share ($292 ÷ 26.6).[5]

Book value is used as a comparison indicator because, for successful companies, the market value is usually greater than its book value. Thus, when market price falls to near book value, some investors buy the stock on the principle that it is underpriced and will increase in the future.

Investment Traits of Common Stock   Common stocks are among the riskiest of all securities. Uncertainties about the stock market itself, for instance, can quickly change a given stock's value. Furthermore, when companies have unprofitable years, they often cannot pay dividends. Shareholder income, therefore—and perhaps share price—drops.

■ Even companies with solid reputations sometimes have downturns. IBM is an example. IBM has paid cash dividends continuously to shareholders every year since 1916. Figure 17.2 traces the share price of IBM stock between December 1960 and November 1996. As you can see, revenues per share grew steadily from the 1970s to 1990 but began falling until 1993, when IBM showed a financial loss. Along with lower earnings per share during 1990–1993, IBM paid smaller dividends to shareholders each year. During this period, IBM's stock price fell steadily, from a 1990 high of $123 per share to a 1993 low of $41. By 1995, however, profits had again increased, and IBM's stock price rose to a high of $135. In 1996, things got even better, as IBM enjoyed a significant increase in its core business (selling computers and information technology to major corporations). In November 1996, IBM stock hit a nine-year high of 158½. "I wish I had kept more," sighs one mutual fund manager who sold at 90. "It's a changed company."[6] ▲

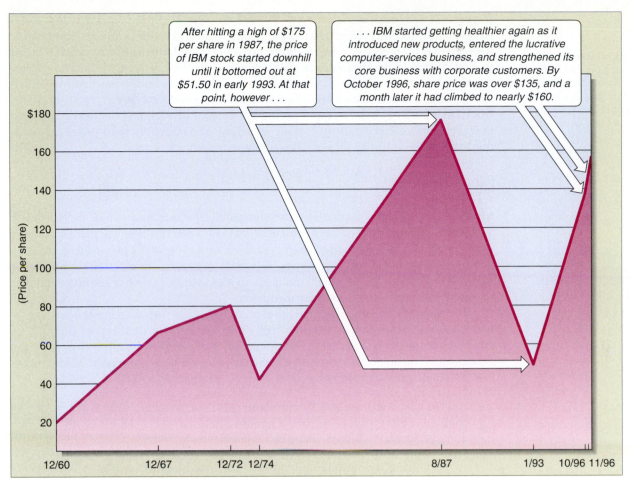

FIGURE 17.2 ◆ IBM: Stock Price, December 1960–November 1996

"I wish I had kept more."

—Mutual fund manager James Cramer,
who sold IBM stock at $90 per share, when it reached $158.50

At the same time, however, common stocks offer high growth potential. Naturally, the prospects for growth in various industries change from time to time, but the **blue chip stocks** of well-established, financially sound firms like Ralston Purina, Exxon, and many others have historically provided investors steady income through consistent dividend payouts.

Preferred Stock

Preferred stock is usually issued with a stated par value, and dividends are typically expressed as a percentage of par value. For example, if a preferred stock with a $100 par value pays a 6-percent dividend, holders will receive an annual dividend of $6 per share.

Some preferred stock is *callable*. The issuing firm can call in shares by requiring preferred stockholders to surrender them in exchange for cash payments. The amount of this payment—the *call price*—is specified in the purchase agreement between the firm and its preferred stockholders.

blue chip stock
Common stock issued by a well-established company with a sound financial history and a stable pattern of dividend payouts

Investment Traits of Preferred Stock   Because preferred stock has first rights to dividends, income is less risky than income from the same firm's common stock. Moreover, most preferred stock is **cumulative preferred stock,** which means that any missed dividend payments must be paid as soon as the firm is able to do so. In addition, the firm cannot pay any dividends to common stockholders until it has made up all late payments to preferred stockholders. Let's take the example of a firm with preferred stock having a $100 par value and paying a 6-percent dividend. If the firm fails to pay that dividend for 2 years, it must make up *arrears* of $12 per share to preferred stock-holders before it can pay dividends to common stockholders.

cumulative preferred stock
Preferred stock on which dividends not paid in the past must be paid to stockholders before dividends can be paid to common stockholders

Stock Exchanges

Most of the secondary market for stocks is handled by organized stock exchanges. In addition, a "dealer," or the over-the-counter (OTC) market, handles the exchange of some stocks. A **stock exchange** is an organization of individuals formed to provide an institutional setting in which stock can be bought and sold. The exchange enforces certain rules to govern its members' trading activities. Most exchanges are nonprofit corporations established to serve their members.

stock exchange
Organization of individuals formed to provide an institutional setting in which stock can be traded

To become a member, an individual must purchase one of a limited number of memberships, called *seats*, on the exchange. Only members (or their representatives) are allowed to trade on the exchange. In this sense, because all orders to buy or sell must flow through members, members of the exchange have a legal monopoly. Memberships can be bought and sold like other assets.

The Trading Floor   Each exchange regulates the places and times at which trading may occur. Trading is allowed only at an actual physical location called the *trading floor*. The floor is equipped with a vast array of electronic communications equipment for conveying buy and sell orders or confirming completed trades. A variety of news services furnish up-to-the-minute information about world events as well as business developments. Any change in these factors, then, may be swiftly reflected in share prices.

Brokers   Some of the people on the trading floor are employed by the exchange. Others are trading stocks for themselves. Many, however, are **brokers,** who receive and execute buy and sell orders from nonexchange members. Although they match buyers with sellers, brokers do not own the securities. They earn commissions from the individuals and organizations for whom they place orders.

broker
Individual or organization who receives and executes buy and sell orders on behalf of other people in return for commissions

As with many products, brokerage assistance can be purchased at either discount prices or at full-service prices:

■ Charles Schwab & Co., for example, a discount broker, offers well-informed individual investors a fast, low-cost way to participate in the market. Schwab's customers know what they want to buy or sell, and they usually make trades simply by using personal computers or Schwab's automated telephone order system without talking with a broker. Why are discount brokerage services low cost? For one thing, their sales personnel receive fees, not commissions. Unlike many full-service brokers, they offer no investment advice and hold no person-to-person sales conversations.

  The discount approach has filled a previously neglected niche among investors. At Schwab alone active accounts rose from about 1 million in 1988 to about 3 million in 1994. Why are investors coming to Schwab? The reason, at least according to Tom D. Seip, Schwab's Vice President for Branch Services, is fairly simple. "Many people come to us—it sounds sad, but it's true—after they have been shafted somewhere else." Today Schwab's competition includes other discount brokers, such as Fidelity Brokerage Services and National Discount, which have already undercut some of Schwab's fees.

There remains an important market for full-service brokerages to advise new, uninformed investors and for experienced investors who don't have time to keep up on the latest stock market developments. When you deal with busy people who want to invest successfully, says Joseph Grano of PaineWebber, "you can't do it through a telephone response system. In a world that's growing more and more complicated, the advice and counsel of a broker will be more important, not less important."[7]

"Many people come to us after they have been shafted somewhere else."

—Tom D. Seip
Vice President for Branch Services at Charles Schwab & Co.

The Major Exchanges and the OTC Market   There are two major stock exchanges in the United States—the New York and American Stock Exchanges. The New York Stock Exchange, the largest exchange in the United States, has recently begun to face stiff competition from both smaller regional U.S. exchanges and larger foreign exchanges, especially in London.

The New York Stock Exchange. For many people, "the stock market" means the New York Stock Exchange (NYSE). Founded in 1792 and located at the corner of Wall and Broad Streets in New York City, the largest of all U.S. exchanges is, in fact, the model for exchanges worldwide. An average of 346 million shares change hands each day; about 45 percent of all shares traded on U.S. exchanges are traded here.

Only firms meeting certain minimum requirements—earning power, total value of outstanding stock, and number of shareholders—are eligible for listing on the NYSE. Nearly 2,700 listings are traded on the NYSE with total market values of $3.1 trillion. Currently, Exxon Corp.'s common shares have the highest market value—$145 billion. NYSE trading volume in 1995 was over 87 billion shares.[8]

The American Stock Exchange. The second-largest U.S. exchange, the American Stock Exchange (AMEX), is also located in New York. It accounts for about 3 percent of all shares traded on U.S. exchanges. Like the NYSE, the AMEX has minimum requirements for listings. They are, however, less stringent. The minimum number of publicly held shares, for example, is 500,000, versus 1.1 million for the NYSE. The AMEX currently lists about 1,000 stocks of companies around the world. Indeed, in 1995, foreign stocks making up 20 percent of the total market value traded on the AMEX. As firms grow, they often transfer their listings from the AMEX to the NYSE. Well-known companies with stocks listed on the AMEX include Turner Broadcasting, TWA, and The New York Times Co.

Regional Stock Exchanges. Established long before the advent of modern communications, the seven regional stock exchanges were organized to serve investors in places other than New York. The largest regional exchanges are the Midwest Stock Exchange in Chicago and the Pacific Stock Exchange in Los Angeles and San Francisco. Other exchanges are located in Philadelphia, Boston, Cincinnati, and Spokane. Many corporations list their stocks both regionally and on either the NYSE or the AMEX.

Foreign Stock Exchanges. As recently as 1980, the U.S. market accounted for more than half the value of the world market in traded stocks. Indeed, as late as 1975, the equity of IBM alone was greater than the national market equities of all but four countries. Market activities, however, have shifted as the value of shares listed on foreign exchanges continues to grow. The annual dollar value of trades on exchanges in London, Tokyo, and other cities is in the trillions. In fact, the London exchange exceeds even the NYSE in number of stocks listed; in market value, transactions on U.S. exchanges are now second to those on Japanese exchanges. Relatively new exchanges are also beginning to flourish in cities from Shanghai to Warsaw.

Over-the-Counter Market: NASDAQ and NASD. The **over-the-counter (OTC) market** is so called because its original traders were somewhat like retailers. They kept supplies of shares on hand and sold them over the office counter to interested buyers as opportunities arose. Even today, the OTC market has no trading floor. Instead, it consists of many people in different locations linked by electronic communications, including the **National Association of Securities Dealers Automated Quotation (NASDAQ) system.**

Unlike brokers, NASDAQ members are *dealers* who own the securities they buy and sell, at their own risk. They must pass qualification exams and meet certain standards for financial soundness. The privilege of trading in the OTC market is granted by federal regulators and by the National Association of Securities Dealers (NASD), which has nearly 5,500 member firms. Currently, the NASD is working with officials in a growing number of countries, especially in Asia and Latin America, who want to replace the trading floors of traditional exchanges with electronic systems networks like NASDAQ.[9]

Nearly 5,000 companies are traded by Nasdaq. Newer firms are often listed here, including MCI Communications, Apple Computer, and Yellow Freight, along with many high-technology stocks in such industries as biotechnology, medical advancements, and electronics. Figure 17.3 shows rapid increases in market value of NASDAQ stocks during the 1990s, as reflected in the NASDAQ Composite Index. The index reached a record high of 1264 in November 1996. While the number of shares traded surpasses the New York Stock Exchange volume, the market value of NASDAQ stocks is only about one-fifth of those on the NYSE.[10] Figure 17.4 shows the number of shares traded on the various exchanges and the NASDAQ system.

over-the-counter (OTC) market
Organization of securities dealers formed to trade stock outside the formal institutional setting of the organized stock exchanges

National Association of Securities Dealers Automated Quotation (NASDAQ) system
Organization of over-the-counter dealers who own, buy, and sell their own securities over a network of electronic communications

FIGURE 17.3 ◆ **NASDAQ Composite Index, 1971–1995**

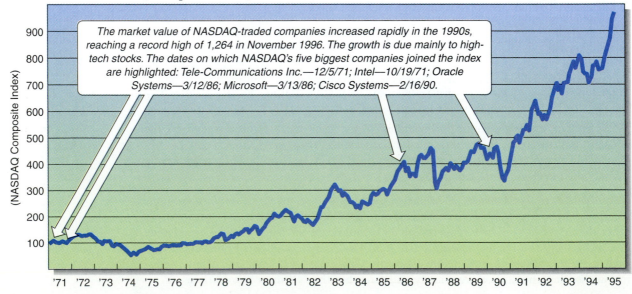

The market value of NASDAQ-traded companies increased rapidly in the 1990s, reaching a record high of 1,264 in November 1996. The growth is due mainly to high-tech stocks. The dates on which NASDAQ's five biggest companies joined the index are highlighted: Tele-Communications Inc.—12/5/71; Intel—10/19/71; Oracle Systems—3/12/86; Microsoft—3/13/86; Cisco Systems—2/16/90.

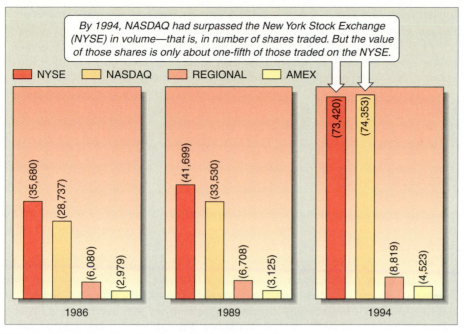

FIGURE 17.4 ◆ Trading Levels on U.S. Stock Exchanges

■ BONDS

A **bond** is an IOU—a promise by the issuer to pay the buyer a certain amount of money by a specified future date, usually with interest paid at regular intervals. The U.S. bond market is supplied by three major sources—the U.S. government, municipalities, and corporations. Bonds differ in terms of maturity dates, tax status, and level of risk versus potential yield.

To aid bond investors in making purchase decisions, several services rate the quality of bonds. Table 17.1, for example, shows the systems of two well-known services, Moody's and Standard & Poor's. Ratings measure default risk—that is, the chance that one or more promised payments will be deferred or missed altogether. The highest grades are *AAA* and *Aaa*, the lowest *C* and *D*. Low-grade bonds are usually called *junk bonds*.

bond
Security through which an issuer promises to pay the buyer a certain amount of money by a specified future date

U.S. Government Bonds

The U.S. government is the world's largest debtor. New federal borrowing from the public exceeded $349 billion in 1995, when the total U.S. debt reached $5 trillion.[11] To finance its debt, the federal government issues a variety of **government bonds.** The U.S. Treasury, for instance, issues Treasury bills (T-bills), Treasury notes, and Treasury

government bond
Bond issued by the federal government

TABLE 17.1 ◆ Bond Rating Systems

	High Grades	Medium Grades (Investment Grades)	Speculative	Poor Grades
Moody's	Aaa, Aa	A, Baa	Ba, B	Caa to C
Standard & Poor's	AAA, AA	A, BBB	BB, B	CCC to D

bonds (including U.S. savings bonds). Many government agencies (for example, the Federal Housing Administration) also issue bonds.

Government bonds are among the safest investments available. Securities with longer maturities are somewhat riskier than short-term issues because their longer lives expose them to more political, social, and economic changes. All federal bonds, however, are backed by the U.S. government. Government securities are sold in large blocks to institutional investors who buy them to ensure desired levels of safety in their portfolios. As investors' needs change, they may buy or sell government securities to other investors.

Municipal Bonds

municipal bond
Bond issued by a state or local government

State and local governments issue **municipal bonds** to finance school and transportation systems and a variety of other projects. In 1995, more than 7,000 new municipal bonds were issued at a value of more than $143 billion.

Some bonds, called *obligation bonds*, are backed by the issuer's taxing power. In 1994, for example, the Albany School District in Minnesota issued $15 million in obligation bonds to fund two new elementary schools and a junior high school. The issuer intends to retire the bonds from future tax revenues. In contrast, revenue bonds are backed only by the revenue generated by a specific project. Thus, Dade County Airport issued $142 million in revenue bonds in 1994 to expand aviation facilities. Operating revenues from building rentals and aviation fees will eventually pay both principal and interest.[12]

The most attractive feature of municipal bonds is the fact that investors do not pay taxes on interest received. Commercial banks invest in bonds nearing maturity because they are relatively safe, liquid investments. Pension funds, insurance companies, and even private citizens also make longer-term investments in municipals.

Corporate Bonds

corporate bond
Bond issued by a company as a source of long-term funding

Although the U.S. government and municipalities are heavy borrowers, corporate long-term borrowing is even greater. **Corporate bonds** issued by U.S. companies are a large source of financing, involving more money than government and municipal bonds combined. U.S. companies raised more than $500 billion from new bond issues in 1995. Bonds have traditionally been issued with maturities ranging from 20 to 30 years. In the 1980s, 10-year maturities came into wider use.

Like municipal bonds, longer-term corporate bonds are somewhat riskier than shorter-term bonds. To help investors evaluate risk, Standard & Poor's and Moody's rate both new and proposed issues on a weekly basis. Remember, however, that negative ratings do not necessarily keep issues from being successful. Rather, they raise the interest rates that issuers must offer. Corporate bonds may be categorized (1) in terms of the method of interest payment or (2) in terms of whether they are *secured* or *unsecured*.

registered bond
Bond bearing the name of the holder and registered with the issuing company

Interest Payment: Registered and Bearer Bonds   **Registered bonds** register the names of holders with the company, which simply mails out checks. Certificates are of value only to registered holders. **Bearer** (or **coupon**) **bonds** require bondholders to clip coupons from certificates and send them to the issuer in order to receive payment. Coupons can be redeemed by anyone, regardless of ownership.

bearer (or **coupon**) **bond**
Bond requiring the holder to clip and submit a coupon in order to receive an interest payment

Secured Bonds   With **secured bonds,** issuers can reduce the risk to holders by pledging assets in case of default. Bonds can be backed by first mortgages, other mortgages, or other specific assets. In 1994, for example, Union Pacific Railroad Co. issued $76 million in bonds to finance the purchase and renovation of equipment. Rated *Aaa* (prime) by Moody's and maturing in 2012, the bonds are secured by the newly pur-

secured bond
Bond backed by pledges of assets to the bondholders

chased and rehabilitated equipment itself—80 diesel locomotives, 1,300 hopper cars, and 450 auto-rack cars.[13]

Debentures Unsecured bonds are called **debentures.** No specific property is pledged as security. Rather, holders generally have claims against property not otherwise pledged in the company's other bonds. Thus, debentures are said to have "inferior claims" on a corporation's assets. Financially strong firms often use debentures. An example is Boeing's $175 million debenture issued in 1993, with maturity on April 15, 2043.[14] Similar issues by weaker companies often receive low ratings and may have trouble attracting investors.

debenture
Unsecured bond for which no specific property is pledged as security

Secondary Markets for Bonds

Nearly all secondary trading in bonds occurs in the over-the-counter market rather than on organized exchanges. Thus, precise statistics about annual trading volumes are not recorded. As with stocks, however, market values and prices change daily. The direction of bond prices moves *opposite* to interest rate changes. As interest rates move up, bond prices tend to go down. The prices of riskier bonds fluctuate more widely than those of higher-grade bonds.

■ OTHER INVESTMENTS

Stocks and bonds are not the only marketable securities available to businesses. Financial managers are also concerned with financial opportunities in *mutual funds* and *commodities.*

Mutual Funds

Companies called **mutual funds** pool investments from individuals and organizations to purchase a portfolio of stocks, bonds, and short-term securities. Investors are thus part owners of the portfolio. For example, if you invest $1,000 in a mutual fund with a portfolio worth $100,000, you own 1 percent of that portfolio. Investors in **no-load funds** are not charged sales commissions when they buy into or sell out of funds. Investors in **load funds** generally pay commissions of 2–8 percent.

Reasons for Investing The total assets invested in U.S. mutual funds has grown significantly every year since 1991, to a total of more than 6,000 different funds.[15] Why do investors find them so attractive? Remember first of all that mutual funds vary in their investment goals. Naturally, different funds are designed to appeal to the different motives and goals of investors. Funds stressing safety often include money market mutual funds and other safe issues offering immediate income. Investors seeking higher current income must generally sacrifice some safety. Typically, these people look to long-term municipal-bond, corporate-bond, and income-mutual funds that invest in common stocks with good dividend-paying records.

Mutual funds that stress growth include balanced mutual funds—portfolios of bonds and preferred and common stocks, especially the common stocks of established firms. Aggressive growth funds seek maximum capital appreciation. They sacrifice current income and safety and invest in stocks of new (and even troubled) companies and other high-risk securities. Figure 17.5 shows how total assets in mutual funds are divided among different types of mutual fund investments.[16] As you can see, the distribution of

mutual fund
Company that pools investments from individuals and organizations to purchase a portfolio of stocks, bonds, and short-term securities

no-load fund
Mutual fund in which investors pay no sales commissions when they buy in or sell out

load fund
Mutual fund in which investors are charged sales commissions when they buy in or sell out

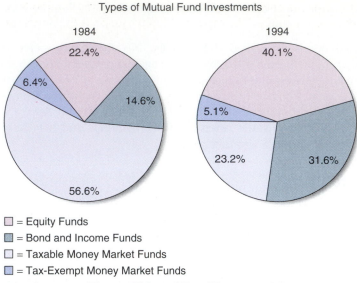

Types of Mutual Fund Investments

1984

22.4%
6.4%
14.6%
56.6%

1994

40.1%
5.1%
23.2%
31.6%

☐ = Equity Funds
☐ = Bond and Income Funds
☐ = Taxable Money Market Funds
☐ = Tax-Exempt Money Market Funds

FIGURE 17.5 ◆ **Types of Mutual Fund Investments**

assets has shifted since the early 1980s in order to meet changing investor goals and attitudes toward financial risk.

Commodities

futures contract
Agreement to purchase specified amounts of a commodity at a given price on a set future date

commodities market
Market in which futures contracts are traded

Individuals and businesses can buy and sell commodities as investments. **Futures contracts**—agreements to purchase specified amounts of commodities at given prices on set dates in the future—can be bought and sold in the **commodities market.** These contracts are available not only for stocks but also for commodities including coffee beans, hogs, propane, and platinum. Because selling prices reflect traders' estimates of future events and values, futures prices are volatile and trading is risky.

To clarify the workings of the commodities market, let's look at an example. On April 29, 1996, the price of gold on the open market was $392.40 per ounce. Futures contracts for October 1996 gold were selling for $397.10 per ounce. This price reflected investors' judgment that gold prices would be higher the following October. Now suppose that you purchased a 100-ounce gold futures contract in April for $39,710 ($397.10 × 100). If in June 1996 the October gold futures sold for $422.10, you could sell your contract for $42,210. Your profit after the two months would be $2,500.

margin
Percentage of the total sales price that a buyer must put up to place an order for stock or futures contracts

Margins   Usually, buyers of futures contracts need not put up the full purchase amount. Rather, the buyer posts a smaller amount—the **margin**—that may be as little as $3,000 for contracts up to $100,000. Let's look again at our gold futures example. As we saw, if you had posted a $3,000 margin for your October gold contract, you would have earned a $2,500 profit on that investment of $3,000 in only two months.

However, you also took a big risk involving two big *ifs:* if you had held on to your contract, and if gold had dropped (say, to $377) in October 1996, you would have lost $2,010. If you had posted a $3,000 margin to buy the contract, you would receive back only $990. In fact, between 75 and 90 percent of all small-time investors lose money in the futures market. For one thing, the action is fast and furious, with small investors trying to keep up with professionals ensconced in seats on the major exchanges. Although the profit potential is also exciting, experts recommend that most novices stick to safer stock markets. Of course, as one veteran financial planner puts it, commodities are tempting. "After trading commodities," he reports, "trading stocks is like watching the grass grow."[17]

> ### "After trading commodities, trading stocks is like watching the grass grow."
>
> —Rick Powers
> *Professional financial planner*

Most commodities investors have no intention of ever taking possession of the commodities in question. Some companies, however, buy futures to protect the prices of commodities important to their businesses. Hormel Meats, for example, trades in hog futures to protect the prices of pork and pork products.

■ BUYING AND SELLING SECURITIES

The process of buying and selling securities is complex. First, you need to find out about possible investments and match them to your investment objectives. Then you must select a broker and open an account. Only then can you place orders and make different types of transactions.

Financial Information Services

Have you ever looked at the financial section of your daily newspaper or seen stock transactions on TV and wondered what all those tables and numbers mean? It is a good idea to know how to read *stock* and *bond quotations* if you want to invest in issues. Fortunately, this skill is easily mastered.

Stock Quotations   Daily transactions for NYSE securities are reported in most city newspapers. Figure 17.6, for instance, shows part of a listing from the *Wall Street*

FIGURE 17.6 ◆ **Reading a Stock Quotation**

	①	②	③	④	⑤	⑥	⑦	⑧	⑨	⑩	⑪	⑫
	52 Weeks					Yld		Vol				Net
	High	Low	Stock	Sym	Div	%	PE	100s	High	Low	Close	Chg
s	$36\frac{1}{2}$	$20\frac{1}{2}$	Gap Inc	GPS	.30	1.0	21	11822	$30\frac{5}{8}$	30	$30\frac{1}{8}$	$+\frac{1}{4}$
▲	$28\frac{1}{4}$	$18\frac{3}{4}$	GaylrdEntn	GET	.36b	1.8	15	1352	$19\frac{7}{8}$	$19\frac{5}{8}$	$19\frac{3}{4}$	$-\frac{1}{8}$
	$27\frac{1}{4}$	$23\frac{3}{8}$	Geminill	GMI	.11e	.4	...	139	$27\frac{3}{4}$	$27\frac{3}{8}$	$27\frac{3}{4}$	$+\frac{1}{4}$
	$10\frac{3}{4}$	$9\frac{1}{2}$	Geminill pf		1.40	14.5	...	88	$9\frac{3}{4}$	$9\frac{5}{8}$	$9\frac{5}{8}$	$+\frac{1}{8}$
	17	$10\frac{1}{4}$	GenCorp	GY	.60	3.7	22	3287	$16\frac{3}{8}$	$15\frac{3}{4}$	$16\frac{3}{8}$	$+\frac{1}{2}$
	$55\frac{3}{8}$	$50\frac{3}{8}$	Genentech	GNE		...	49	460	$53\frac{7}{8}$	$53\frac{5}{8}$	$53\frac{7}{8}$	$+\frac{1}{4}$
	$23\frac{1}{2}$	$19\frac{1}{8}$	GenAmInv	GAM	.32e	1.4	...	201	$23\frac{1}{2}$	$23\frac{1}{4}$	$23\frac{1}{2}$	$+\frac{3}{8}$
n	21	$16\frac{5}{8}$	GenlChemGp	GCG	.08e	.4	...	555	19	$18\frac{3}{8}$	$18\frac{1}{2}$	$-\frac{1}{4}$
	$21\frac{7}{8}$	$9\frac{1}{8}$	GenData	GDC		...	dd	662	$10\frac{3}{4}$	$10\frac{1}{4}$	$10\frac{1}{2}$	$+\frac{1}{8}$
	72	$56\frac{3}{8}$	GenDynam	GD	1.64	2.4	15	2315	$67\frac{3}{4}$	$66\frac{3}{4}$	$67\frac{1}{4}$	$+\frac{1}{4}$
▲	$99\frac{3}{8}$	$63\frac{3}{8}$	GenElec	GE	1.84	1.8	24	27767	$101\frac{5}{8}$	$98\frac{5}{8}$	$101\frac{5}{8}$	$+2\frac{7}{8}$

Journal, with columns numbered 1 through 12. Let's analyze the listing for the company at the top, The Gap Inc.:

- The first two columns ("High" and "Low") show the highest and lowest prices paid for one share of The Gap stock *during the past year*. Note that stock prices throughout are expressed in *dollars per share*, with the smallest fraction of a dollar being ⅛, or 12½ cents. In the past year, then, The Gap's stock ranged in value from $36.50 to $20.50 per share. This range reveals a fairly volatile stock price.
- The third column ("Stock") is the abbreviated company name. (Sometimes the notation "pf" appears after the company's name to show that the stock is *preferred*, not common. The listing reveals that GeminiII offers both a preferred stock and a common stock.)
- The NYSE *symbol* for the stock is listed in column 4 ("Sym").
- The fifth column ("Div") indicates that The Gap pays an annual *cash dividend* of $.30 per share. This can be compared to payouts by other companies.
- Column 6 ("Yld %") is the *dividend yield* expressed as a percentage of the stock's current price (shown in column 11). The Gap's dividend yield is 1.0 percent (.30 ÷ 30.125, rounded). Potential buyers can compare this yield to returns they might get from alternative investments.

- Column 7 ("PE") shows the **price–earnings ratio**—the current price of the stock divided by the firm's current annual earnings per share. On this day, The Gap's PE is 21, meaning that investors are willing to pay $21 for each dollar of reported profits to own The Gap stock. This figure can be compared to PE ratios of other stocks to decide which is the best investment.
- The last five columns detail the day's trading. Column 8 ("Vol 100s") shows the *number of shares* (in hundreds) that were traded—in this case 11,822. Some investors interpret increases in trading volume as an indicator of forthcoming price changes in a stock.
- Column 9 ("High") shows the highest price paid *that day*—$30.625. Column 10 ("Low") shows the lowest price paid that day, $30.00.
- Column 11 ("Close") shows that The Gap's *last sale of the day* was for $30.125.
- The final column ("Net Chg") shows *the difference between the previous day's close and the close on the day being reported*. The closing price of The Gap stock is ¼ higher than it was on the previous business day. Day-to-day changes are indicators of recent price stability or volatility.

Finally, look back at the far-left column, which has no heading. This column reports unusual conditions of importance to investors. Note, for example, the "s" to the left of the "52-Week High" column for The Gap. This symbol indicates either a *stock split* (a division of stock that gives stockholders a greater number of shares but that does not change each individuals' proportionate share of ownership) or an *extra stock dividend* paid during the past 52 weeks. The "n" accompanying the General Chemical Group indicates that this stock was *newly issued* during the past 52 weeks. The dagger symbol (▲) indicates new 52-week highs in the prices of GeminiII and General Electric stocks.

Bond Quotations   Daily quotations on corporate bonds from the NYSE are also widely published. Bond quotations contain essentially the same type of information as stock quotations. One difference, however, is that the year in which it is going to mature is listed beside each bond.

OTC Quotations   Most OTC (NASDAQ) stock quotations are reported in the same format as listed stock quotations. Some OTC trades, however, are reported in terms of "bid" and "asked" quotations. For example, a quotation might show 7¼ as the bid price and 7¾ as the asked price. The **bid price** is the amount that the OTC dealer pays to obtain each share. The **asked price** is the amount the dealer charges clients to buy a share. The difference between bid and asked prices—in this case, ½—is the dealer's gain for making the transaction.

Market Indexes   Although they do not indicate the status of particular securities, **market indexes** provide useful summaries of trends, both in specific industries and in the stock market as a whole. Market indexes, for example, reveal bull and bear market trends. **Bull markets** are periods of rising stock prices. Periods of falling stock prices are called **bear markets.**

As Figure 17.7 shows, for example, the years 1981 to 1996 boasted a strong bull market, the longest in history. Inflation was under control as business flourished in a healthy economy. In contrast, the period 1972–1974 was characterized by a bear market. The Mideast oil embargo caused a business slowdown, and inflation was beginning to dampen economic growth. As you can see, the data that characterize such periods are drawn from two leading market indexes—the Dow Jones and Standard & Poor's.

The Dow and S&P.   The **Dow Jones Industrial Average** is the most widely cited U.S. index. The "Dow" is the sum of market prices for thirty of the largest industrial firms listed on the NYSE. By tradition, it is an indicator of blue chip stock price movements.

On February 23, 1995, the Dow topped 4,000 for the first time ever. On April 24, it went over 4,300—its third 100-point record in one month. On November 20, 1996, it broke the 6,400 barrier for the first time, and on February 13, 1997, it topped 7,000. Why such optimism on the part of investors? What does the Dow's performance say about attitudes toward the economy? Though unable to pinpoint one single reason for the Dow's performance, experts cite at least three factors in the surge:

- Continued (and surprising) growth in corporate profits
- Continued acquisition and merger activity among corporations
- Indications from the Federal Reserve that inflation is under control and that interest rates will remain at present levels

As you can see in Figure 17.8, the Dow's movement has generally been *opposite the trend for interest rates on long-term bonds.* Why is this so? As bond rates decrease, investors tend to become more interested in stocks as vehicles for higher financial

asked price
Price that an OTC broker charges for a share of stock

market index
Summary of price trends in a specific industry and/or the stock market as a whole

bull market
Period of rising stock prices

bear market
Period of falling stock prices

Dow Jones Industrial Average
Market index based on the prices of 30 of the largest industrial firms listed on the NYSE

© 1998 Dean Vietor *from* The Cartoon Bank,™ Inc.

FIGURE 17.7 ◆ **Bull and Bear Markets, 1972–1996**

returns. Furthermore, because lower interest rates mean cheaper borrowing for businesses, business expenses are reduced and businesses become more profitable. Thus, investor hopes for even greater profits continue. How high will the Dow reach before it begins to fall? No one knows. Says Jack Bogle, Chairman of the Vanguard Group, "Hope can turn to fear and greed pretty quickly. I think there's too much confidence in the market at these [1996] levels."[18]

Because it considers very few firms, the Dow is a limited gauge of the overall stock market. **Standard & Poor's Composite Index** is a broader report. It consists of 500 stocks, including 400 industrial firms, 40 utilities, 40 financial institutions, and 20 transportation companies. Interestingly, on the same day that the Dow topped 6,400, the S & P Index also jumped to a new record.

Placing Orders

After doing your own research and/or getting recommendations from your broker, you can choose to place several different types of orders:

- A **market order** requests that a broker buy or sell a certain security at the prevailing market price at the time of the order. For example, look again at Figure 17.6. On that day, your broker would have sold your Gap Inc. stock for between 30.00 and 30.625 per share.

  Note, however, that when you gave your order to sell, you did not know exactly what the market price would be. This situation can be avoided with *limit* and *stop orders*, which allow for buying and selling only if certain price conditions are met.

- A **limit order** authorizes the purchase of a stock only if its price is less than or equal to a specified limit. For example, an order to buy at $30 a share means that the broker is to buy if and only if the stock becomes available for a price of $30 or less. A **stop order** instructs the broker to sell if a stock price falls to a certain

Standard & Poor's Composite Index
Market index based on the performance of 400 industrial firms, 40 utilities, 40 financial institutions, and 20 transportation companies

market order
Order to buy or sell a security at the market price prevailing at the time the order is placed

limit order
Order authorizing the purchase of a stock only if its price is equal to or less than a specified amount

stop order
Order authorizing the sale of a stock if its price falls to or below a specified level

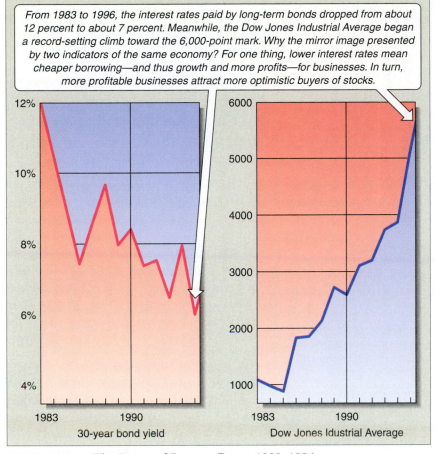

From 1983 to 1996, the interest rates paid by long-term bonds dropped from about 12 percent to about 7 percent. Meanwhile, the Dow Jones Industrial Average began a record-setting climb toward the 6,000-point mark. Why the mirror image presented by two indicators of the same economy? For one thing, lower interest rates mean cheaper borrowing—and thus growth and more profits—for businesses. In turn, more profitable businesses attract more optimistic buyers of stocks.

30-year bond yield

Dow Jones Idustrial Average

FIGURE 17.8 ◆ **The Dow and Interest Rates, 1983–1996**

level. For example, an order of $25 on a particular stock means that the broker is to sell that stock if and only if its price falls to $25 or below.

■ Orders also differ by size. An order for a **round lot** requests 100 shares of a particular stock or some multiple thereof. Fractions of round lots are called **odd lots.** Because an intermediary—an *odd-lot broker*—is often involved, odd-lot trading is usually more expensive than round-lot trading.

round lot
Purchase or sale of stock in units of 100 shares

odd lot
Purchase or sale of stock in fractions of round lots

Financing Purchases

When you place a buy order of any kind, you must tell your broker how you will pay for the purchase. You might, for example, maintain a cash account with your broker. As you buy and sell stocks, your broker adds proceeds to your account while deducting commissions and purchase costs. Like almost every product in today's economy, securities can also be purchased on credit.

Margin Trading Like futures contracts, stocks can be bought on *margin*—that is, the buyer can put down a portion of the stock's price. The rest is borrowed from the buyer's broker, who secures special-rate bank loans with stock.

Margin trading offers several advantages. For example, suppose you purchased $100,000 worth of stock in Dow Chemical. Let's also say that you paid $50,000 of your own money and borrowed the other $50,000 from your broker at 10-percent interest. Valued at its market price, your stock serves as your collateral. If, after one year, shares have risen in value to $115,000, you can sell them and pay your broker $55,000—

TRENDS & CHALLENGES

THE BRAVE NEW WORLD OF CYBERSPACE BROKERAGE

People who trade securities are in it to make money. Therefore, it should come as no surprise that thousands of computer-savvy investors are trying to maximize profits by doing business with discount brokers on the Internet. The following figures tell a story about how much investors can save by executing their own buys and sells in cyberspace:

- Merrill Lynch, a full-service broker offering extensive investment research, personal service, and order execution, charges $100–$1,100 to trade 100–5,000 shares of stock.

- Fidelity Investments, a traditional discount broker that executes orders over the phone but provides no research, charges between $55–$270 for the same trade.

- E*Trade Securities, an electronic discount broker that lets customers handle their own account activities, charges a flat $15–$20 for most trades.

Ed Harrison, a small investor from Santa Clarita, California, makes several trades a week on the Internet and sees cyberspace investing as an opportunity to save money. "My broker was so nice, but boy, he was robbing me," reports Harrison. "All he ever did was place my trades. I can do that for myself." And he can do it simply. "Anyone who feels comfortable picking up the phone and telling a broker, 'Buy me 100 shares of such and such' would find this just as easy," maintains Frederick Roehm, a Portland, Oregon, student.

Although investors are happy doing business with Internet-based discount brokers, full-service brokers are worried that this newest investment trend may undermine their customer base. As investors realize that they can tap into investment research sites on the Web, obtain stock quotes and mutual fund rankings, and execute orders via an Internet broker at any time of the day or night, they are likely to question whether full-service brokers are worth premium prices.

> ## "Anyone who feels comfortable picking up the phone and telling a broker, 'Buy me 100 shares of such and such' would find this just as easy."
>
> —Personal investor Frederick Roehm
> *on the ease of Internet discount brokerage*

This skepticism is likely to become more pronounced as Internet brokers add a variety of services to help guide investment decisions. Lombard Institutional Brokerage, for example, offers graphs showing the movement of stocks and options as well as a free quotation service that gives investors the ability to track, via their own computers, the movement of up to 50 stocks. By the middle of 1996, more than one million investors had visited Lombard's Website, and activity in the company's 7,000 Internet accounts tripled in a three-month period.

The pressure from Internet brokers is already changing traditional brokers. For the first time, Prudential is allowing customers to access their accounts on the Web, although trades are not yet permitted. Fidelity Investments will allow individuals to review their personal retirement accounts on the Web and plans to implement its own electronic trading system some time in the near future.

How do investors reach Web-based brokers? Here are three addresses:

- E*Trade
  http://www.etrade.com
- Lombard Institutional Brokerage Inc.
  http://www.lombard.com
- Pawws Financial Network
  http://www.pawws.com

$50,000 principal plus $5,000 interest. You will have $60,000 left over. Your original investment of $50,000, therefore, will have earned a 20-percent profit of $10,000. If you had paid the entire price out of your own pocket, you would have earned only a 15-percent return.

Brokers, meanwhile, benefit from margin trading in two ways:

1. Because it encourages more people to buy more stock, brokers earn more commissions.

2. Because they charge buyers higher interest rates than they pay banks, brokers earn profits on their loans.

Although investors often recognize possible profits to be made in margin trading, they sometimes fail to consider that losses, too, can be amplified:

■ Suppose, for example, that you decided on June 26, 1996, to buy 1,000 shares of Acme Electric, a producer of power conversion equipment, for $36 per share. You put up $18,000 of your own money and borrow $18,000 from your broker. As the stock rises, you reason, the loan will enable you to profit from twice as many shares. Now let's say that, shortly after you purchase your stock Acme's market price begins to fall. You decide to hold on until it recovers. By June 26, 1997, when the price has fallen to $8.50 a share, you give up hope and sell.

Now let's see how margin trading has amplified your losses. If you had invested your own $18,000, instead of borrowing it, you would recover $8,500 of your $36,000 investment (excluding commissions). Your loss, therefore, would be 76 percent ($27,500 loss/$36,000 invested). By trading on margin, however, even though you still recover $8,500 of your $18,000 investment, you must repay the $18,000 that you borrowed—plus $1,800 in loan interest (at a 10-percent annual rate). In this case, your losses total $29,300 ($37,800 in outlays less $8,500 recovered). The percentage loss is 163 percent of your investment ($29,300 loss/$18,000 investment)—much greater than the 76-percent loss you would have suffered without margin trading.[19]

Short Sales   In addition to lending money, brokerages also lend securities. A **short sale** begins when you borrow a security from your broker and sell it (one of the few times that it is legal to sell something that you do not own). At a given point in the future, you must restore an equal number of shares of that issue to the brokerage—along with a fee.

Let's go back to our Gap Inc. example. Suppose that in January, you believe the price of Gap stock will soon *fall*. You therefore order your broker to "sell short" 100 shares at the market price of $30.125 per share. Your broker will make the sale and credit $3,012.50 to your account. If The Gap's price falls to $25 per share in July, you can buy 100 shares for $2,500 and use them to repay your broker. You will have made a $512.50 profit (before commissions). Your risk, of course, is that The Gap's price will not fall. If it holds steady or rises, you will take a loss.

short sale
Stock sale in which an investor borrows securities from a broker to be sold and then replaced at a specified future date

■ SECURITIES MARKET REGULATION

One oft-cited cause of sudden market fluctuations is **program trading**—the purchase or sale of a group of stocks valued at $1 million or more, often triggered by computerized trading programs that can be launched without human supervision or control.[20] It works this way. As market values change and economic events transpire during the

program trading
Large purchase or sale of a group of stocks, often triggered by computerized trading programs that can be launched without human supervision or control

course of a day, computer programs are busy recalculating the future values of stocks. Once a calculated value reaches a critical point, the program automatically signals a buy or sell order. Because electronic trading could cause the market to spiral out of control, the NYSE has set up "circuit breakers" that suspend trading for a preset length of time (usually an hour). The interruption provides a "cooling-off" period that slows down trading activity and allows computer programs to be revised or shut down.

The Securities and Exchange Commission

Securities and Exchange Commission (SEC)
Federal agency that administers U.S. securities laws to protect the investing public and maintain smoothly functioning markets

prospectus
Registration statement filed with the SEC before the issuance of a new security

To protect the investing public and to maintain smoothly functioning markets, the **Securities and Exchange Commission (SEC)** oversees many phases in the process through which securities are issued. The SEC, for example, regulates the public offering of new securities by requiring that all companies file prospectuses before proposed offerings commence. To protect investors from fraudulent issues, a **prospectus** contains pertinent information about both the offered security and the issuing company. False statements are subject to criminal penalties.

Unfortunately, to ensure full disclosure, the typical prospectus is highly technical and not easily understod by most investors. To overcome this difficulty and to make the document more user friendly, the SEC is encouraging experimentation with a "profile prospectus." Currently this new abbreviated document is being tested by mutual fund companies. It contains summarized information about the fund's goals, risks, investment strategy, and past performance so investors can compare it with other funds. It also fits on one piece of paper instead of requiring an entitre booklet. At the very least, says A. Michael Lipper of Lipper Analytical Securities Corp., "This prospectus could save trees and lower costs to investors, and that's positive."[21]

> ### "This prospectus could save trees and lower costs to investors, and that's positive."
> —Investment Analyst A. Michael Lipper
> *on the one-page, user-friendly securities prospectus*

---

insider trading
Illegal practice of using special knowledge about a firm for profit or gain

The SEC also enforces laws against **insider trading**—the use of special knowledge about a firm for profit or gain. In May 1996, for example, the U.S. Attorney in Boston indicted a dentist on charges of lying to the SEC and gaining $140,000 in illegal profits by buying and selling shares of Purolator Products Co. The dentist allegedly had access to some advance, nonpublic information (a "tip"). Another company was preparing to purchase Purolator and, once the news became public, the price of Purolator shares would probably increase.

Along with the SEC's enforcement efforts, the stock exchanges cooperate in detecting and stopping insider action. In 1995, for example, NASD referred 113 cases to the SEC for possible insider trading. The New York Stock Exchange and the American Stock Exchange have spent millions on self-regulation. They use sophisticated surveillance methods that electronically monitor transactions to detect unusual trading patterns. In May 1996, for example, the Pacific Stock Exchange asked the SEC to investigate the trading patterns of several investors believed to have had ties to toymaker Hasbro Inc. The investigation began when the exchange observed a sudden rise in their trading of Hasbro stock just before Mattel Inc. announced its failed bid to purchase Hasbro. To stem the increase in illegal insider trading, the SEC is also using tougher enforcement, including criminal prosecution against offenders.[22]

State governments also regulate the sale of securities. For example, commenting that some promoters would sell stock "to the blue sky itself," one legislator's speech led to the phrase **blue sky laws** and the passage of statutes requiring securities to be registered with state officials. In addition, securities dealers must be registered and licensed by the states in which they do business. Finally, states may prosecute the sale of fraudulent securities.

blue sky laws
Laws requiring securities dealers to be licensed and registered with the states in which they do business

Continued from page 441

What Happens When Investors Stand Corrected?

Is There a Good Time to Panic?

Because stock market cycles are inevitable, individual investors may wake up one morning to find themselves in the midst of a market "correction" that has the potential to wipe out all or part of their hard-earned gains. How will they *react* if they see such a threat unfolding, especially when the value of their retirement dollars is linked to the market value of their investments? Because investors can react by shifting funds at computer keystroke or a telephone push button, this question is a practical one.

According to a recent *Business Week*/Harris Poll, nearly half of investors surveyed (48 percent) said that they would hold steady even if the market crashed. Ten percent said that they would regard a correction as an opportunity to buy more stocks. Although only 20 percent said that they would sell, experts wonder how in-

> **"There are a lot of stockholders out there who can abandon you at the drop of a hat."**
>
> —Louis Lowenstein
> *Professor at Columbia University Law School*

vestors would react to an actual crash, rather than to a hypothetical situation. With stocks representing an increasingly important share of family finances, many experts suspect that hordes of investors would panic as securities values dropped.

Ironically, mutual fund managers may abandon ship faster than individual investors. Known for judging stocks on the basis of short-term performance rather than long-term potential, fund managers have a well-

deserved reputation for lack of patience. "For corporations," explains Professor Louis Lowenstein of Columbia University Law School, "this means that there are a lot of holders out there who can abandon you at the drop of a hat. Individuals aren't performance-oriented the way institutions are, and they are certainly aren't focusing on returns from quarter to quarter."

How will this tendency affect corporations, which benefit when their stock value is high? As the market value of a stock drops, the cost to the company of raising capital increases. Thus, the up and down movement of the stock market affects established and start-up companies alike, because all companies need capital to innovate and take the risks needed to create jobs and spur economic growth.

Case Questions

1. Why does the stock market hold financial promise for so many Americans?
2. Why do you think more people are investing now than they did in the past?
3. Explain the risk and rewards of investing retirement income in securities.
4. How do companies benefit when the value of their stocks rise?
5. Why do fund managers tend to judge stocks on the basis of short-term performance, and how does this perspective affect the stock market, individual and fund investors, and corporations?
6. Why is it important for investors to be aware of market cycles?

SUMMARY OF LEARNING OBJECTIVES

1. **Explain the difference between *primary* and secondary *securities markets*.** *Primary securities markets* involve the buying and selling of new securities, either in public offerings or through *private placements* (sales to single buyers or small groups of buyers). *Investment bankers* specialize in issuing securities in primary markets. *Secondary markets* involve the trading of stocks and bonds through such familiar bodies as the New York and American Stock Exchanges.

2. **Discuss the value to shareholders of *common* and *preferred stock*, and describe the secondary market for each type of security.** *Common stock* af-

fords investors the prospect of *capital gains* and/or dividend income. Common stock values are expressed in three ways: as *par value* (the face value of a share when it is issued), *market value* (the current market price of a share), and *book value* (the value of shareholders' equity divided by the number of shares). Market value is most important to investors. *Preferred stock* is less risky. Cumulative preferred stock entitles holders to missed dividends as soon as the company is financially capable of paying. It also offers the prospect of steadier income. Shareholders of preferred stock must be paid dividends before shareholders of common stock.

Both common and preferred stock are traded on stock exchanges (institutions formed to conduct the trading of existing securities) and in *over-the-counter (OTC) markets* (dealer organizations formed to trade securities outside stock exchange settings). "Members" who hold seats on exchanges act as *brokers*—agents who execute buy and sell orders—for nonmembers. Exchanges include the New York, American, and regional and foreign exchanges. In the OTC market, licensed dealers serve functions similar to those of exchange members.

3. **Distinguish among various types of *bonds* in terms of their issuers and safety.** The issuer of a *bond* promises to pay the buyer a certain amount of money by a specified future date, usually with interest paid at regular intervals. U.S. *government bonds* are backed by government institutions and agencies such as the Treasury Department or the Federal Housing Administration. *Municipal bonds*, which are offered by state and local governments to finance a variety of projects, are also usually safe, and the interest is ordinarily tax-exempt. *Corporate bonds* are issued by companies to gain long-term funding. They may be secured (backed by pledges of the issuer's assets) or unsecured, and offer varying degrees of safety. The safety of bonds issued by various borrowers is rated by Moody's and Standard & Poor's.

4. **Describe the investment opportunities offered by *mutual funds* and *commodities*.** Like stocks and bonds, *mutual funds*—companies that pool investments to purchase portfolios of financial instruments—offer investors different levels of risk and growth potential. *Load funds* require investors to pay commissions of 2–8 percent. *No-load funds* do not charge commissions when investors buy in or out. *Futures contracts*—agreements to buy specified amounts of commodities at given prices on preset dates—are traded in the *commodities market*. Commodities traders often buy on margins—percentages of total sales prices that must be put up to order futures contracts.

5. **Explain the process by which securities are bought and sold.** Investors generally use such *financial information services* as newspaper stock, bond, and OTC quotations to learn about possible investments. *Market indexes* like the Dow Jones Industrial Average and Standard & Poor's Composite Index provide useful summaries of trends, both in specific industries and in the market as a whole. Investors can then place different types of orders. *Market orders* are orders to buy or sell at current prevailing prices. Because investors do not know exactly what prices will be when market orders are executed, they may issue *limit* or *stop orders* that are to be executed only if prices rise to or fall below specified levels. *Round lots* are purchased in multiples of 100 shares. Odd lots are purchased in fractions of round lots. Securities can be bought on margin or as part of *short sales*—sales in which investors sell securities that are borrowed from brokers and returned at a later date.

6. **Explain how securities markets are regulated.** To protect investors, the *Securities and Exchange Commission (SEC)* regulates the public offering of new securities and enforces laws against such practices as *insider trading* (using special

knowledge about a firm for profit or gain). To guard against fraudulent stock is-sues, the SEC lays down guidelines for *prospectuses*—statements of information about stocks and their issuers. Many state governments also prosecute the sale of fraudulent securities as well as enforce *blue sky laws*, which require dealers to be licensed and registered where they conduct business.

STUDY QUESTIONS AND EXERCISES

Review

1. What are the purposes of the primary and secondary markets for securities?
2. Which of the three measures of common stock value is most important? Why?
3. How do government, municipal, and corporate bonds differ from one an-other?
4. How might an investor lose money in a commodities trade?
5. How does the Securities and Exchange Commission regulate securities markets?

Analysis

6. What are your personal financial goals at this time? What types of stocks, bonds, or mutual funds would be best for meeting those goals? Why?
7. Which type of mutual fund would be most appropriate for your investment purposes at this time? Why?
8. Using a newspaper, select an example of a recent day's transactions for each of the following: a stock on the NYSE, a stock on the AMEX, an OTC stock, a bond on the NYSE. Explain the meaning of each element in the listing.

Application Exercises

9. Interview the financial manager of a local business or your school. What are the investment goals of this person's organization? What mix of securities does it use? What advantages and disadvantages do you see in its portfolio?
10. Either in person or through a toll-free number, contact a broker and request information about setting up a personal account for trading securities. Pre-pare a report on the broker's policies regarding the following: buy/sell or-ders, credit terms, cash account requirements, services available to investors, and commissions/fees schedules.

BUILDING YOUR BUSINESS SKILLS

This exercise enhances the following SCANS workplace competencies: demonstrating basic skills, demonstrating thinking skills, exhibiting interpersonal skills, and working with information.

Goal

To help students acquire the skills they need to evaluate companies or mutual funds that are considered socially responsible and to decide whether those companies are good investment vehicles

Situation

You have $5,000 to invest, and you want to invest it in socially responsible companies, specifically those that safeguard the environment. You would also consider purchasing a mutual fund made up of socially responsible companies. Your challenge is to compile a list of these companies and funds and then evaluate each for its investment value.

Method

Step 1: Working with three or four classmates, contact the following source for information on socially responsible companies:

> Social Investment Forum,
> 430 First Avenue N, Suite 290
> Minneapolis, MN 55401
> (612-333-8338)

Then, contact the following mutual funds specializing in socially responsible companies:

- Domini Social Index Trust (800-762-8814)
- Calvert Social Investment Fund (800-368-2748)
- Righttime Social Awareness Fund (800-242-1421)
- Pax World Fund (800-767-1729)

Step 2: Analyze the following sources for information about the companies and mutual funds that you are investigating:

- Corporate annual reports
- The prospectus from each mutual fund, which lists companies in the fund's portfolio
- Relevant articles in business publications, such as the Wall Street Journal and Barron's

The investor relations specialists employed by many corporations may also provide investment information.

Step 3: Analyze the information that you gather, both from an investor's point of view and from the point of view of someone concerned with the environment. Then choose a company or mutual fund in which to invest your $5,000. Base your decision on both the nature of the investment and on its prospects for future financial growth.

Follow-Up

1. Is a socially responsible company a good place to invest your money?

2. For each company or mutual fund that you chose, what factors are likely to influence its stock price over the coming year?

Exploring the Net

BECAUSE STOCK MARKET ACTION CAN BE FAST AND FURIOUS, UP-TO-DATE INFORMATION IS A MUST FOR MOST INVESTORS. CURRENT REGULATIONS ALLOW INFORMATION ABOUT SALES TO BECOME PUBLICLY AVAILABLE ONLY MINUTES AFTER TRANSACTIONS HAVE BEEN MADE ON THE STOCK MARKETS. TO SEE THE TYPES OF INFORMATION AVAILABLE ON THE INTERNET, ACCESS THE WEBSITE MAINTAINED BY NASDAQ AT THE FOLLOWING ADDRESS:

http://www.nasdaq.com

In order to observe the process and results of a day's actual trading activity, be sure to access the Website when the market is open. On the initial NASDAQ screen, examine both the "Glossary" and the "FAQ" (Frequently Asked Questions) sections for a good overview of the NASDAQ system and terminology. Now consider the following questions:

1. After reading data for the NASDAQ market on the initial screen of the Website, how would you characterize today's trend in the NASDAQ Composite Index? In the NASDAQ-100 Index? In the past year's Composite value and its volume of trading?

2. What is the NASDAQ Composite Index? How many and what types of companies are included in it? Compare it to the Dow Jones Industrial Average Index. Which of these indexes is more representative of overall market activity? Why?

3. Which are the ten most active and ten least active stocks in today's trading? Identify the ten most advanced stocks and the ten stocks that have declined the most. Select two or three stocks in each category and explain what the performance means to each company's stockholders.

4. The "Index Activity" option reveals eight business categories (Industrial, Telecommunication, Biotechnology, etc.). From each of four of those categories, select one or more companies. For each company, do a "Full Quote." What information did you obtain about each company?

5. Select the "News" option and explore some current news releases. How recently were these news items published? Why do you think NASDAQ displays these news releases at its Website?

6. Using the "News" option, can you find a news release that might influence investors to buy or sell the stock of a particular company? An item that might influence investors to trade the stocks of companies in a particular industry?

"Too Many Touts of Every Ilk"
The Ruble in The Rubble

Learning Objectives

The purpose of this video exercise is to help students:

1. Gain a better perspective on the nature and function of primary and secondary securities markets
2. Appreciate the role played by regulation in the operation of securities markets
3. Assess the reasons individuals invest in securities and understand attitudes toward investment risk

Background Information

In the brave new world of Russian capitalism, investment companies can play an important role. In particular, they can provide a means for individuals to pool their money in order to participate in the growth of a new sector consisting largely of privatized state companies. In the early 1990s, one investment company, known by the initials MMM, was particularly aggressive. In a national TV ad campaign featuring light-hearted rags-to-riches stories, MMM promised returns as high as *3,000 percent* a year. Investment money poured in from thousands of first-time investors.

In the West, of course, experienced investors (and, for that matter, most intelligent amateurs) have long understood at least one fundamental principle of the marketplace: if a sales pitch sounds too good to be true, it probably is. And sure enough, MMM turned out to be little more than a high-powered, high-profile *pyramid scheme*—an investment scheme in which payoffs are possible only so long as operators keep drawing in new investors. Thus, instead of buying assets in productive enterprises, executives at MMM were simply taking funds from new investors and paying them out (in part, of course) to earlier investors. The victims hardest hit were the latecomers, and MMM's promise of triple-digit *investment* returns was an empty one all around.

The Video

Video Source. "Moscow Investment Company Fraud," *World News Tonight*, July 28, 1994. The ABC News video is a segment in which the MMM story is covered on the evening newscast with Peter Jennings. The selection also includes a brief compilation of Russian TV ads for investment companies, including MMM. The ads were shown during the national news show *Vremya* ("Time"), which airs each evening at 9 P.M. Moscow time.

Discussion Questions

1. Could a scenario similar to the MMM story take place in the United States? Why or why not?

2. What are the primary differences between American and Russian attitudes toward investment risks?

3. When you compare Russian and American television advertising for financial services, what do you perceive to be the most obvious differences?

Follow-Up Assignment

Go to the library and find out what happened to MMM. In addition, research changes in the Russian economy and financial environment that have affected television advertising since the MMM scandal in mid-1994.

For Further Exploration

Visit the Securities and Exchange Commission Website at

http://www.sec.gov/

When you click on the link to "Investor Assistance and Complaints," you will find a department devoted to "Investor Protection: Tips from an SEC Insider." To what sort of activities does the SEC alert prospective investors? What steps is the SEC taking to deal with questionable or illegal activities? What kind of help does the SEC offer individual investors? You might also check out the department called "What Every Investor Should Know."

"Russians love to play roulette."

—Russian investor going back for a second try at the MMM pyramid scheme

■ APPENDIX I

Financial and Risk Management

The business activity known as **finance** (or **corporate finance**) typically entails four responsibilities:

- Determining a firm's long-term investments
- Obtaining funds to pay for those investments
- Conducting the firm's everyday financial activities
- Helping to manage the risks that the firm takes

As we saw in Chapter 11, production managers plan and control the output of goods and services. In Chapter 13, we saw that marketing managers plan and control the development and marketing of products. Similarly, **financial managers** plan and control the acquisition and dispersal of a firm's financial resources. In this section, we will see in some detail how those activities are channeled into specific plans for protecting—and enhancing—a firm's financial well-being.

Responsibilities of the Financial Manager

Financial managers collect funds, pay debts, establish trade credit, obtain loans, control cash balances, and plan for future financial needs. But a financial manager's overall objective is to increase a firm's value—and thus stockholders' wealth. Whereas accountants create data to reflect a firm's financial status, financial managers make decisions for improving that status. Financial managers, then, must ensure that a company's earnings exceed its costs—in other words, that it earns a profit. In sole proprietorships and partnerships, profits translate directly into increases in owners' wealth. In corporations, profits translate into an increase in the value of common stock.

The various responsibilities of the financial manager in increasing a firm's wealth fall into two general categories: *cash-flow management* and *financial planning*.

Cash-Flow Management   To increase a firm's value, financial managers must ensure that it always has enough funds on hand to purchase the materials and human resources that it needs to produce goods and services. At the same time, of course, there may be funds that are not needed immediately. These must be invested to earn more money for the firm. This activity—**cash-flow management**—requires careful planning. If excess cash balances are allowed to sit idle instead of being invested, a firm loses the cash returns that it could have earned.

How important to a business is the management of its idle cash? A study by Merrill Lynch has revealed that companies averaging $2 million in annual sales typically hold $40,000 in non-interest-bearing accounts. Larger companies hold even larger sums. More and more companies, however, are learning that these idle funds can become working funds. By locating idle cash and putting it to work, for instance, they can avoid borrowing from outside sources. The savings on interest payments can be substantial.[1]

---

finance (or **corporate finance**)
Activities concerned with determining a firm's long-term investments, obtaining the funds to pay for them, conducting the firm's everyday financial activities, and managing the firm's risks

financial manager
Manager responsible for planning and controlling the acquisition and dispersal of a firm's financial resources

cash-flow management
Management of cash inflows and outflows to ensure adequate funds for purchases and the productive use of excess funds

financial plan
A firm's strategies for reaching some future financial position

Financial Planning. The cornerstone of effective financial management is the development of a financial plan. A **financial plan** describes a firm's strategies for reaching some future financial position. In constructing the plan, a financial manager must ask several questions:

- What amount of funds does the company need to meet immediate needs?
- When will it need more funds?
- Where can it get the funds to meet both its short- and long-term needs?

To answer these questions, a financial manager must develop a clear picture of why a firm needs funds. Managers must also assess the relative costs and benefits of potential funding sources. In the sections that follow, we will examine the main reasons for which companies generate funds and describe the main sources of business funding, both for the short term and the long term.

WHY DO BUSINESSES NEED FUNDS?

Every company must spend money to survive: According to the simplest formula, funds that are spent on materials, wages, and buildings eventually lead to the creation of products, revenues, and profits. In planning for funding requirements, financial managers must distinguish between two different kinds of expenditures: *short-term (operating)* and *long-term (capital) expenditures.*

Short-Term (Operating) Expenditures

Short-term expenditures are incurred regularly in a firm's everyday business activities. To manage these outlays, managers must pay special attention to *accounts payable, accounts receivable,* and *inventories.* We will also describe the measures used by some firms in managing the funds known as *working capital.*

Accounts Payable   In Chapter 12, we defined *accounts payable* as unpaid bills owed to suppliers plus wages and taxes due within the upcoming year. For most companies, this is the largest single category of short-term debt. To plan for funding flows, financial managers want to know *in advance* the amounts of new accounts payable as well as when they must be repaid. For information about such obligations and needs—say, the quantity of supplies required by a certain department in an upcoming period—financial managers must rely on other managers.

Accounts Receivable   As we also saw in Chapter 12, *accounts receivable* consist of funds due from customers who have bought on credit. A sound financial plan requires financial managers to project accurately both how much and when buyers will make payments on these accounts. For example, managers at Kraft Foods must know how many dollars' worth of cheddar cheese Kroger's supermarkets will order each month; they must also know Kroger's payment schedule. Because they represent an investment in products for which a firm has not yet received payment, accounts receivable temporarily tie up its funds. Clearly, the seller wants to receive payment as quickly as possible.[2]

Inventories   Between the time a firm buys raw materials and the time it sells finished products, it ties up funds in **inventory**—materials and goods that it will sell within the year.

Failure to manage inventory can have grave financial consequences. Too little inventory of any kind can cost a firm sales. Too much inventory means tied-up funds that

inventory
Materials and goods which are held by a company but which will be sold within the year

cannot be used elsewhere. In extreme cases, a company may have to sell excess inventory at low profits simply to raise cash.

Working Capital   Basically, **working capital** consists of a firm's current assets on hand. It is a liquid asset out of which current debts can be paid. A company calculates its working capital by adding up the following:

- Inventories—that is, raw materials, work-in-process, and finished goods on hand
- Accounts receivable (minus accounts payable)

working capital
Liquid current assets out of which a firm can pay current debts

How much money is tied up in working capital? Fortune 500 companies typically devote 20 cents of every sales dollar—about $500 billion total—to working capital. What are the benefits of reducing these sums?[3] There are two very important pluses:

1. Every dollar that is not tied up in working capital becomes a dollar of more useful cash flow.
2. Reduction of working capital raises earnings permanently.

The second advantage results from the fact that money costs money (in interest payments and the like). Reducing working capital, therefore, means saving money.

Long-Term (Capital) Expenditures

In addition to needing funds for operating expenditures, companies need funds to cover long-term expenditures on fixed assets. As we saw in Chapter 12, *fixed assets* are items with long-term use or value, such as land, buildings, and machinery.

Long-term expenditures are usually more carefully planned than short-term outlays because they pose special problems. They differ from short-term outlays in the following ways, all of which influence the ways that long-term outlays are funded:

- Unlike inventories and other short-term assets, they are not normally sold or converted into cash.
- Their acquisition requires a very large investment.
- They represent a binding commitment of company funds that continues long into the future.

■ SOURCES OF SHORT-TERM FUNDS

Firms can call on many sources for the funds they need to finance day-to-day operations and to implement short-term plans. These sources include *trade credit and secured* and *unsecured loans*.

Trade Credit

Accounts payable are not merely expenditures. They also constitute a source of funds for the buying company. Until it pays its bill, the buyer has the use of *both* the purchased product *and* the price of the product. This situation results when the seller grants **trade credit,** which is effectively a short-term loan from one firm to another. The most common form of trade credit, **open-book credit,** is essentially a "gentlemen's agreement." Buyers receive merchandise along with invoices stating credit terms. Sellers ship products on faith that payment will be forthcoming.

trade credit
Granting of credit by one firm to another

open-book credit
Form of trade credit in which sellers ship merchandise on faith that payment will be forthcoming

Secured Short-Term Loans

secured loan
Loan for which the borrower must provide collateral

collateral
Borrower-pledged legal asset that may be seized by lenders in case of nonpayment

For most firms, bank loans are a very important source of short-term funding. Such loans almost always involve promissory notes in which the borrower promises to repay the loan plus interest. In **secured loans,** banks also require **collateral:** a legal interest in certain assets that can be seized if payments are not made as promised.

Secured loans allow borrowers to get funds when they might not qualify for unsecured credit. Moreover, they generally carry lower interest rates than unsecured loans. Collateral may be in the form of inventories or accounts receivable, and most businesses have other types of assets that can be pledged. Some, for instance, own marketable securities, such as stocks or bonds of other companies (see Chapter 17). Many more own fixed assets, such as land, buildings, or equipment. Fixed assets, however, are generally used to secure long-term rather than short-term loans. Most short-term business borrowing is secured by inventories and accounts receivable.

pledging accounts receivable
Using accounts receivable as loan collateral

When a loan is made with inventory as a collateral asset, the lender loans the borrower some portion of the stated value of the inventory. When accounts receivable are used as collateral, the process is called **pledging accounts receivable.** In the event of nonpayment, the lender may seize the receivables—that is, funds owed the borrower by its customers.

Unsecured Short-Term Loans

unsecured loan
Loan for which collateral is not required

With an **unsecured loan,** the borrower does not have to put up collateral. In many cases, however, the bank requires the borrower to maintain a *compensating balance:* the borrower must keep a portion of the loan amount on deposit with the bank in a non-interest-bearing account.

The terms of the loan—amount, duration, interest rate, and payment schedule—are negotiated between the bank and the borrower. To receive an unsecured loan, then, a firm must ordinarily have a good banking relationship with the lender. Once an agreement is made, a promissory note will be executed and the funds transferred to the borrower. Although some unsecured loans are one-time-only arrangements, many take the form of *lines of credit, revolving credit agreements,* or *commercial paper.*

line of credit
Standing arrangement in which a lender agrees to make available a specified amount of funds upon the borrower's request

A **line of credit** is a standing agreement between a bank and a business in which the bank promises to lend the firm a specified amount of funds on request. **Revolving credit agreements** are similar to consumer bank cards. A lender agrees to make some amount of funds available on demand and on a continuing basis. The lending institution guarantees that these funds will be available when sought by the borrower. In return for this guarantee, the bank charges the borrower a *commitment fee* for holding the line of credit open. This fee is payable even if the customer does not borrow any funds. It is often expressed as a percentage of the loan amount (usually one-half to one percent of the committed amount).

revolving credit agreement
Arrangement in which a lender agrees to make funds available on demand and on a continuing basis

commercial paper
Short-term securities, or notes, containing a borrower's promise to pay

Finally, some firms can raise short-term funds by issuing **commercial paper**—short-term securities, or notes, containing the borrower's promise to pay. Because it is backed solely by the issuing firm's promise to pay, commercial paper is an option for only the largest and most creditworthy firms.

How does commercial paper work? Corporations issue commercial paper with a certain face value. Buying companies pay *less* than that value. At the end of a specified period (usually 30 to 90 days, but legally up to 270 days), the issuing company buys back the paper—*at face value.* The difference between the price paid and the face value is the buyer's profit. For the issuing company, the cost is usually lower than prevailing interest rates on short-term loans.

■ SOURCES OF LONG-TERM FUNDS

Firms need long-term funding to finance expenditures on fixed assets: the buildings and equipment necessary for conducting their business. They may seek long-term funds through *debt financing* (that is, from outside the firm) or through *equity financing* (by drawing on internal sources). We will discuss both options in this section, as well as a middle ground called *hybrid financing*. We will also analyze some of the options that enter into decisions about long-term financing, as well as the role of the *risk-return relationship* in attracting investors to a firm.

Debt Financing

Long-term borrowing from sources outside the company—**debt financing**—is a major component of most firms' long-term financial planning. Long-term debts are obligations that are payable more than one year after they were originally issued. The two primary sources of such funding are *long-term loans* and the sale of *corporate bonds*.

debt financing
Long-term borrowing from sources outside a company

Long-Term Loans

Most corporations get long-term loans from commercial banks, usually those with which they have developed longstanding relationships. Credit companies (such as Household Finance Corp.), insurance companies, and pension funds also grant long-term business loans.

Long-term loans are attractive to borrowers for several reasons:

- Because the number of parties involved is limited, loans can often be arranged very quickly.
- The firm need not make public disclosure of its business plans or the purpose for which it is acquiring the loan. (In contrast, the issuance of corporate bonds requires such disclosure.)
- The duration of the loan can easily be matched to the borrower's needs.
- If the firm's needs change, loans usually contain clauses making it possible to change terms.

Long-term loans also have some disadvantages. Borrowers, for instance, may have trouble finding lenders to supply large sums. Long-term borrowers may also face restrictions as conditions of the loan. For example, they may have to pledge long-term assets as collateral or agree to take on no more debt until the loan is paid.

Corporate Bonds   As we saw in Chapter 17, a **corporate bond,** like commercial paper, is a contract—a promise by the issuer to pay the holder a certain amount of money on a specified date.[4] Unlike issuers of commercial paper, however, bond issuers do not pay off quickly. In many cases, bonds may not be redeemable for 30 years. Also, unlike commercial paper, most bonds pay bondholders a stipulated sum of annual or semiannual interest. If the company fails to make a bond payment, it is said to be *in default.*

Bonds are the major source of long-term debt financing for most corporations. They are attractive when firms need large amounts for long periods of time. The issuing company also gains access to large numbers of lenders through nationwide bond markets and stock exchanges. On the other hand, bonds entail high administrative and selling costs. They may also require stiff interest payments, especially if the issuing company has a poor credit rating.

Equity Financing

equity financing
Use of common stock and/or retained earnings to raise long-term funding

Although debt financing often has strong appeal, looking inside the company for long-term funding is sometimes preferable. In small companies, for example, founders may increase personal investments in their own firms. In most cases, **equity financing** means issuing common stock or retaining the firm's earnings. Both options involve putting the owners' capital to work.

Common Stock   People who purchase common stock seek profits in two forms—dividends and appreciation. Overall, shareholders hope for an increase in the market value of their stock (appreciation) because the firm has profited and grown. By issuing shares of stock, the company gets the funds it needs for buying land, buildings, and equipment.

Suppose, for example, that Sunshine Tanning's founders invested $10,000 by buying the original 500 shares of common stock (at $20 per share) in 1990. The company used these funds to buy equipment, and it succeeded financially. By 1996, then, it needed funds for expansion. A pattern of profitable operations and regularly paid dividends now allows Sunshine to raise $50,000 by selling 500 new shares of stock at $100 per share. This $50,000 would constitute *paid-in capital*—additional money, above the par value of its original stock sale, paid directly to a firm by its owners (see Chapter 12). As Table AI.1 shows, this additional paid-in capital would increase total stockholders' equity to $60,000.

Retained Earnings   Again, recall our discussion in Chapter 12, where we defined *retained earnings* as profits retained for the firm's use rather than paid out in dividends. If a company uses retained earnings as capital, it will not have to borrow money and pay interest. If a firm has a history of reaping profits by reinvesting retained earnings, it may be very attractive to some investors. Retained earnings, however, mean smaller dividends for shareholders. In this sense, then, the practice may decrease the demand for-and thus the price of-the company's stock.[5]

For example, if Sunshine Tanning had net earnings of $50,000 in 1996, it could pay a $50-per-share dividend on its 1,000 shares of common stock. Let's say, however, that Sunshine plans to remodel at a cost of $30,000, intending to retain $30,000 in earnings to finance the project. Only $20,000-$20 per share-will be available for shareholders.

TABLE AI.1 ◆ **Stockholders' Equity for Sunshine Tanning**

Common Stockholders' Equity, 1990:	
Initial common stock (500 shares issued @ $20 per share, 1990)	$10,000
Total stockholders' equity	$10,000
Common Stockholders' Equity, 1996	
Initial common stock (500 shares issued @ $20 per share, 1990)	$10,000
Additional paid-in capital (500 shares issued @ $100 per share, 1996)	50,000
Total stockholders' equity	$60,000

Hybrid Financing: Preferred Stock

A middle ground between debt financing and equity financing is the use of preferred stock (see Chapter 17). Preferred stock is a "hybrid" because it has some of the features of both corporate bonds and common stocks. As with bonds, for instance, payments on preferred stock are fixed amounts such as $6 per share per year. Unlike bonds, however, preferred stock never matures; like common stock, it can be held indefinitely. In addition, preferred stocks have first rights (over common stock) to dividends.

A major advantage to the issuer is the flexibility of preferred stock. Because preferred stockholders have no voting rights, the stock secures funds for the firm without jeopardizing corporate control of its management. Furthermore, corporations are not obligated to repay the principal and can withhold payment of dividends in lean times.

Choosing between Debt and Equity Financing

Needless to say, an aspect of financial planning is striking a balance between debt and equity financing. Because a firm relies on a mix of debt and equity to raise the cash needed for capital outlays, that mix is called its **capital structure.** Financial plans thus contain targets for capital structure; an example would be 40 percent debt and 60 percent equity. But choosing a target is not easy. A wide range of mixes is possible, and strategies range from conservative to risky.[6]

The most conservative strategy is all-equity financing and no debt: a company has no formal obligations to make financial payouts. As we have seen, however, equity is an expensive source of capital. The riskiest strategy is all-debt financing. Although less expensive than equity funding, indebtedness increases the risk that a firm will be unable to meet its obligations (and even go bankrupt). Somewhere between the two extremes, financial planners try to find mixes that will increase stockholders' wealth with a reasonable exposure to risk.

capital structure
Relative mix of a firm's debt and equity financing

The Risk-Return Relationship

While developing plans for raising capital, financial managers must be aware of the different motivations of individual investors. Why, for example, do some individuals and firms invest in stocks while others invest only in bonds? Investor motivations, of course, determine who is willing to buy a given company's stocks or bonds. Investors give money to firms and, in return, anticipate receiving future cash flows. Thus everyone who invests money is expressing a personal preference for safety versus risk.

In other words, some cash flows are more certain than others. Investors generally expect to receive higher payments for higher uncertainty. They do not generally expect large returns for secure investments like government-insured bonds. Each type of investment, then, has a **risk-return relationship** reflecting the principle that whereas safer investments tend to offer lower returns, riskier investments tend to offer higher returns.

Risk-return differences are recognized by financial planners, who try to gain access to the greatest funding at the lowest possible cost. By gauging investors' perceptions of their riskiness, a firm's managers can estimate how much they must pay to attract funds to their offerings. Over time, a company can reposition itself on the risk continuum by improving its record on dividends, interest payments, and debt repayment.

risk-return relationship
Principle that, whereas safer investments tend to offer lower returns, riskier investments tend to offer higher returns

■ FINANCIAL MANAGEMENT FOR SMALL BUSINESS

As we saw in Chapter 8, new business success and failure are often closely related to adequate or inadequate funding. For example, one study of nearly 3,000 new companies revealed a survival rate of 84 percent for new businesses with initial investments of at least $50,000. Unfortunately, those with less funding have a much lower survival rate. Why are so many start-ups underfunded? For one thing, entrepreneurs often underestimate the value of establishing *bank credit* as a source of funds and use trade credit ineffectively. In addition, they often fail to consider *venture capital* as a source of funding, and they are notorious for not planning *cash-flow needs* properly.

Establishing Bank and Trade Credit   Some banks have liberal credit policies and offer financial analysis, cash-flow planning, and suggestions based on experiences with other local firms. Some provide loans to small businesses in bad times and work to keep them going. Some, of course, do not. Obtaining credit, therefore, begins with finding a bank that can—and will—support a small firm's financial needs. Once a line of credit is obtained, the small business can seek more liberal credit policies from other businesses. Sometimes, for instance, suppliers give customers longer credit periods—say, 45 or 60 days rather than 30 days. Liberal trade credit terms with their suppliers let firms increase short-term funds and avoid additional borrowing from banks.

Long-Term Funding   Naturally, obtaining long-term loans is more difficult for new businesses than for established companies. With unproven repayment ability, start-up firms can expect to pay higher interest rates than older firms. If a new enterprise displays evidence of sound financial planning, however, the Small Business Administration (see Chapter 8) may support a guaranteed loan.

venture capital
Outside equity financing provided in return for part ownership of the borrowing firm

Venture Capital   Many newer businesses—especially those undergoing rapid growth—cannot get the funds they need through borrowing alone. They may, therefore, turn to **venture capital**: outside equity funding provided in return for part ownership of the borrowing firm. *Venture capital firms* actively seek chances to invest in new firms with rapid growth potential. Because failure rates are high, they typically demand high returns, which are now often 20 to 30 percent.[7]

Planning for Cash-Flow Requirements

Although all businesses should plan for their cash flows, this planning is especially important for small businesses. Success or failure may hinge on anticipating those times when either cash will be short or excess cash can be expected.[8]

Figure AI.1 shows possible cash inflows, cash outflows, and net cash position (inflows minus outflows) month by month for Slippery Fish Bait Supply—a highly seasonal business. As you can see, bait stores buy heavily from Slippery during the spring and summer months. Revenues outpace expenses, leaving surplus funds that can be invested. During the fall and winter, however, expenses exceed revenues. Slippery must borrow funds to keep going until revenues pick up again in the spring. Comparing predicted cash inflows from sales with outflows for expenses shows the firm's expected monthly cash flow position.

Such knowledge can be invaluable for the small business manager. By anticipating shortfalls, for example, a financial manager can seek funds in advance and minimize their cost. By anticipating excess cash, a manager can plan to put the funds to work in short-term, interest-earning investments.

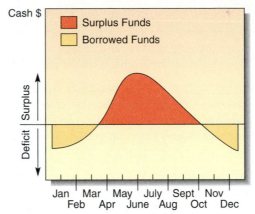

FIGURE AI.1 ◆ Projected Cash Flow for Slippery Fish Bait Supply Co.

■ RISK MANAGEMENT

Financial risks are not the only risks faced every day by companies (and individuals). In this section, we will describe various other types of risks that businesses face and analyze some of the ways in which they typically manage them.

Coping with Risk

Businesses constantly face two basic types of **risk**—that is, uncertainty about future events. **Speculative risks,** such as financial investments, involve the possibility of gain or loss. **Pure risks** involve only the possibility of loss or no loss. Designing and distributing a new product, for example, is a speculative risk. The product may fail, or it may succeed and earn high profits. In contrast, the chance of a warehouse fire is a pure risk.

For a company to survive and prosper, it must manage both types of risk in a cost-effective manner. We can thus define the process of **risk management** as "conserving the firm's earning power and assets by reducing the threat of losses due to uncontrollable events."[9] In every company, each manager must be alert for risks to the firm and their impact on profits. The risk management process usually entails five steps.

Step 1: Identify Risks and Potential Losses Managers analyze a firm's risks to identify potential losses. For example, a firm with a fleet of delivery trucks can expect that one of them will eventually be involved in an accident. The accident may cause bodily injury to the driver or others, may cause physical damage to the truck or other vehicles, or both.

Step 2: Measure the Frequency and Severity of Losses and Their Impact To measure the frequency and severity of losses, managers must consider both past history and current activities. How often can the firm expect the loss to occur? What is the likely size of the loss in dollars? For example, our firm with the fleet of delivery trucks may have had two accidents per year in the past. If it adds trucks, however, it may reasonably expect the frequency of accidents to increase.

Step 3: Evaluate Alternatives and Choose the Techniques That Will Best Handle the Losses Having identified and measured potential losses, managers are in a better position to decide how to handle them. With this third step, they generally have four choices: *risk avoidance, control, retention,* or *transfer.*

risk
Uncertainty about future events

speculative risk
Risk involving the possibility of gain or loss

pure risk
Risk involving only the possibility of loss or no loss

risk management
Process of conserving the firm's earning power and assets by reducing the threat of losses due to uncontrollable events

risk avoidance
Practice of avoiding risk by declining or ceasing to participate in an activity

risk control
Practice of minimizing the frequency or severity of losses from risky activities

risk retention
Practice of covering a firm's losses with its own funds

risk transfer
Practice of transferring a firm's risk to another firm

Risk Avoidance. A firm opts for **risk avoidance** by declining to enter or by ceasing to participate in a risky activity. For example, the firm with the delivery trucks could avoid any risk of physical damage or bodily injury by closing down its delivery service. Similarly, a pharmaceutical maker may withdraw a new drug for fear of liability suits.

Risk Control. When avoidance is not practical or desirable, firms can practice **risk control**—say, the use of loss-prevention techniques to minimize the frequency of losses. A delivery service, for instance, can prevent losses by training its drivers in defensive-driving techniques, mapping out safe routes, and conscientiously maintaining its trucks.

Risk Retention. When losses cannot be avoided or controlled, firms must cope with the consequences. When such losses are manageable and predictable, they may decide to cover them out of company funds. The firm is thus said to "assume" or "retain" the financial consequences of the loss: hence the practice known as **risk retention.** For example, our firm with the fleet of trucks may find that vehicles suffer vandalism totaling $100 to $500 per year. Depending on its coverage, the company may find it cheaper to pay for repairs out of pocket rather than to submit claims to its insurance company.

Risk Transfer. When the potential for large risks cannot be avoided or controlled, managers often opt for **risk transfer.** They transfer the risk to another firm-namely, an insurance company. In transferring risk to an insurance company, a firm pays a sum called a premium. In return, the insurance company issues an insurance policy—a formal agreement to pay the policyholder a specified amount in the event of certain losses. In some cases, the insured party must also pay a deductible—an agreed-upon amount of the loss that the insured must absorb prior to reimbursement. Thus, our hypothetical company may buy insurance to protect itself against theft, physical damage to trucks, and bodily injury to drivers and others involved in an accident.

Step 4: Implement the Risk-Management Program   The means of implementing risk-management decisions depends on both the technique chosen and the activity being managed. For example, risk avoidance for certain activities can be implemented by purchasing those activities from outside providers—say, hiring delivery services instead of operating delivery vehicles. Risk control might be implemented by training employees and designing new work methods and equipment for on-the-job safety. For situations in which risk retention is preferred, reserve funds can be set aside out of revenues. When risk transfer is needed, implementation means selecting an insurance company and buying the right policies.

Step 5: Monitor Results   Because risk management is an ongoing activity, follow-up is always essential. New types of risks, for example, emerge with changes in customers, facilities, employees, and products. Insurance regulations change, and new types of insurance become available. Consequently, managers must continually monitor a company's risks, reevaluate the methods used for handling them, and revise them as necessary.

Insurance as Risk Management

To deal with some risks, both businesses and individuals may choose to purchase one or more of the products offered by insurance companies. Buyers find insurance appealing for a very basic reason: in return for a relatively small sum of money, they are protected against certain losses, some of them potentially devastating. In this sense, buying insurance is a function of risk management. To define it as a management activity dealing with insurance, we can thus amplify our definition of *risk management* to say that it is "the logical development and implementation of a plan to deal with chance losses."[10]

With insurance, then, individuals and businesses share risks by contributing to a fund out of which those who suffer losses are paid. But why are insurance companies willing to accept these risks for other companies? Insurance companies make profits by taking in more **premiums** than they pay out to cover policyholders' losses. Quite simply, although many policyholders are paying for protection against the same type of loss, by no means all of them will suffer such a loss.

premium
Fee paid by a policyholder for insurance coverage

Insurable Versus Uninsurable Risks
Like every business, insurance companies must avoid certain risks. Insurers thus divide potential sources of loss into *insurable* and *uninsurable risks*. Obviously, they issue policies only for insurable risks. Although there are some exceptions, an insurable risk must meet the four criteria described in the following sections.

Predictability. The insurer must be able to use statistical tools to forecast the likelihood of a loss. For example, an auto insurer needs information about the number of car accidents in the past year to estimate the expected number of accidents for the following year. With this knowledge, the insurer can translate expected numbers and types of accidents into expected dollar losses. The same forecast, of course, also helps insurers determine premiums charged to policyholders.

Casualty. A loss must result from an accident, not from an intentional act by the policyholder. Obviously, insurers do not have to cover damages if a policyholder deliberately sets fire to corporate headquarters. To avoid paying in cases of fraud, insurers may refuse to cover losses when they cannot determine whether policyholders' actions contributed to them.

Unconnectedness. Potential losses must be random and must occur independently of other losses. No insurer can afford to write insurance when a large percentage of those who are exposed to a particular kind of loss are likely to suffer such a loss. One insurance company, for instance, would not want all the hurricane coverage in Miami or all the earthquake coverage in Los Angeles. By carefully choosing the risks that it will insure, an insurance company can reduce its chances of a large loss or even insolvency.

Verifiability. Finally, insured losses must be verifiable as to cause, time, place, and amount. Did an employee develop emphysema because of a chemical to which she was exposed or because she smoked 40 cigarettes a day for 30 years? Did the policyholder pay the renewal premium before the fire destroyed his factory? Were the goods stolen from company offices or from the president's home? What was the insurable value of the destroyed inventory? When all these points have been verified, payment by the insurer goes more smoothly.

The Insurance Product
Insurance companies are often distinguished by the types of insurance coverage they offer. Whereas some insurers offer only one area of coverage—life insurance, for example—others offer a broad range. In this section, we describe the four major categories of business insurance: *liability*, *property*, *life*, and *health*.

Liability Insurance. As we saw in Chapter 3, *liability* means responsibility for damages in case of accidental or deliberate harm to individuals or property. **Liability insurance** covers losses resulting from damage to people or property when the insured party is judged liable.[11]

liability insurance
Insurance covering losses resulting from damage to people or property when the insured is judged responsible

WORKERS' COMPENSATION. A business is liable for any injury to an employee when the injury arises from activities related to occupation. When workers are permanently or temporarily disabled by job-related accidents or disease, employers are required by law to provide **workers' compensation coverage** for medical expenses, loss of wages, and rehabilitation services. U.S. employers now pay out approximately $60 billion in workers' compensation premiums each year, much of it to public insurers.[12]

workers' compensation coverage
Coverage provided by a firm to employees for medical expenses, loss of wages, and rehabilitation costs resulting from job-related injuries or disease

property insurance
Insurance covering losses resulting from physical damage to or loss of the insured's real estate or personal property

business interruption insurance
Insurance covering income lost during times when a company is unable to conduct business

life insurance
Insurance paying benefits to the policyholder's survivors

group life insurance
Insurance underwritten for a group as a whole rather than for each individual in it

health insurance
Insurance covering losses resulting from medical and hospital expenses as well as income lost from injury or disease

disability income insurance
Insurance providing continuous income when disability keeps the insured from gainful employment

health maintenance organization (HMO)
Organized health care system providing comprehensive care in return for fixed membership fees

Property Insurance. Firms purchase **property insurance** to cover injuries to themselves resulting from physical damage to or loss of real estate or personal property. Property losses may result from fire, lightning, wind, hail, explosion, theft, vandalism, or other destructive forces. Losses from fire alone in the United States come to over $10 billion per year.

BUSINESS INTERRUPTION INSURANCE.   In some cases, loss to property is minimal in comparison to loss of income. A manufacturer, for example, may have to close down for an extended time while repairs to fire damage are being completed. During that time, of course, the company is not generating income. Even so, however, certain expenses—such as taxes, insurance premiums, and salaries for key personnel—may continue. To cover such losses, a firm may buy **business interruption insurance.**[13]

Life Insurance. Insurance can also protect a company's human assets. As part of their benefits packages, many businesses purchase **life insurance** for employees. Life insurance companies accept premiums in return for the promise to pay beneficiaries after the death of insured parties. A portion of the premium is used to cover the insurer's own expenses. The remainder is invested in various types of financial instruments such as corporate bonds and stocks.

GROUP LIFE INSURANCE.   Most companies buy **group life insurance,** which is underwritten for groups as a whole rather than for each individual member. The insurer's assessment of potential losses and its pricing of premiums are based on the characteristics of the whole group. Johnson & Johnson's benefit plan, for example, includes group life coverage with a standard program of protection and benefits—a master policy purchased by J & J—that applies equally to all employees.

Health Insurance. **Health insurance** covers losses resulting from medical and hospital expenses as well as income lost from injury or disease. It is, of course, no secret that the cost of health insurance has skyrocketed in recent years. In one recent year, for example, companies paid an average of $3,781 per employee on health insurance premiums to both commercial insurers like Prudential, Metropolitan, and Nationwide and special health insurance providers like Blue Cross/Blue Shield and other organizations called *health maintenance organizations* and *preferred provider organizations.*

DISABILITY INCOME INSURANCE.   **Disability income insurance** provides continuous income when disability keeps the insured from gainful employment. Many health insurance policies cover "short-term" disabilities, sometimes up to two years. Coverage for permanent disability furnishes some stated amount of weekly income—usually 50 to 70 percent of the insured's weekly wages—with payments beginning after a six-month waiting period. Group policies account for over 70 percent of all disability coverage in the United States.

SPECIAL HEALTH CARE PROVIDERS.   Instead of reimbursement for a health professional's services, Blue Cross/Blue Shield, which is made up of nonprofit health care membership groups, provides specific service benefits to its subscribers. Many other commercial insurers do the same. What is the advantage to the subscriber or policyholder? No matter what the service actually costs, the special health care provider will cover the cost. In contrast, when policies provide reimbursement for services received, the policyholder may pay for a portion of the expense if the policy limit is exceeded. Other important options include *HMOs* and *PPOs:*

■ A **health maintenance organization (HMO)** is an organized health care system providing comprehensive medical care to its members for a fixed, prepaid fee. In an HMO, all members agree that, except in emergencies, they will receive their health care through the organization.

■ A **preferred provider organization (PPO)** is an arrangement whereby selected hospitals and/or doctors agree to provide services at reduced rates and to accept thorough review of their recommendations for medical services. The objective of the PPO is to help control health care costs by encouraging the use of efficient providers' health care services.

Special Forms of Business Insurance   Many forms of insurance are attractive to both businesses and individuals. For example, homeowners are as concerned about insuring property from fire and theft as are businesses. Businesses, however, have some special insurable concerns. In this section, we will discuss two forms of insurance that apply to the departure or death of key employees or owners.

Key Person Insurance.   Many businesses choose to protect themselves against loss of the talents and skills of key employees. For example, if a salesperson who annually rings up $2.5 million dies or takes a new job, the firm will suffer loss. It will also incur recruitment costs to find a replacement and training expenses once a replacement is hired. **Key person insurance** is designed to offset both lost income and additional expenses.

Business Continuation Agreements.   Who takes control of a business when a partner or associate dies? Surviving partners are often faced with the possibility of having to accept an inexperienced heir as a management partner. This contingency can be handled in **business continuation agreements,** whereby owners make plans to buy the ownership interest of a deceased associate from his or her heirs. The value of the ownership interest is determined when the agreement is made. Special policies can also provide survivors with the funds needed to make the purchase.

preferred provider organization (PPO)
Arrangement whereby selected professional providers offer services at reduced rates and permit thorough review of their service recommendations

business continuation agreement
Special form of business insurance whereby owners arrange to buy the interests of deceased associates from their heirs

■ APPENDIX II

Business Careers and the Job Search

"What do you want to be?" Throughout your life, you have probably heard this question many times. Perhaps you already know the answer. But if you do not, you are not alone. Many people spend years searching for an answer.

Most experts agree that the people who are most likely to find an answer—and who have the most successful careers—are those who make efforts to plan a career. Just as a *career* is a lifelong progression, so career planning should not be limited to the search for your first job. Rather, it is a process that should occur throughout your working life. If you have not already begun to plan your career, now is probably the time to start.

Because the first step in any sound planning process is gathering of information, we will begin by looking at the *job market* that you will probably face when you graduate. Which fields are expanding and which are shrinking? Which regions of the country are growing—and thus hold the best employment prospects? After addressing these questions, we will look at specific ways to learn about job opportunities.

Next, we will survey the *tools* you will need to present yourself to prospective employers. We will examine in some detail both written tools—résumés and cover letters—and the oral communication tools necessary for effective employment interviews.

■ THE JOB OUTLOOK IN THE UNITED STATES

During the 1960s and 1970s, many U.S. businesses grew rapidly. They built new facilities, hired new employees, and expanded operations in many directions. In the 1980s, however, increased global competition forced many U.S. firms to reorganize—a trend that continued with the recession of the early 1990s. Virtually every industry was affected to some extent—airlines and retailers, computer manufacturers and car makers all felt the pinch. Many shut down plants and laid off workers. Even firms like Bell Laboratories, Digital Equipment, and IBM—organizations with longstanding "no-layoff" policies—found themselves with no alternative. As a result, college graduates in the late 1980s and early 1990s faced an especially tight job market. By the mid-1990s, however, many parts of the U.S. economy had bounced back, and many companies were hiring once again.

Job Prospects by Industry and Region

Despite this general upturn, there are important differences in job prospects related to particular *industries* and *regions* of the country.

Table AII.1 categorizes 25 industries that experienced the greatest job growth between 1991 and 1996. Average annual earnings in each industry is also listed. Table AII.2 (page 486) provides the same information for industries that experienced the greatest job loss.[1]

TABLE AII.1 ◆ Industries with the Highest Rate of Job Growth: 1991–1996

	Total Jobs in 1996 first quarter	Average annual growth rate	Average annual earnings in 1993
Business services	7,009 (in thousands)	6.7%	$22,499
Leisure	1,505	6.2	21,018
Nonbanking financial institutions	496	5.7	n.a.
Social services	2,370	5.6	15,320
Brokerage	531	4.9	96,497
Local transit	439	4.7	20,496
Transportation services	430	4.4	31,617
Motion pictures	516	4.4	31,692
Agricultural services	599	4.2	n.a.
Museum and zoos	83	4.0	19,514
Auto repair and parking	1,059	3.6	20,430
Furniture stores	950	3.4	21,208
Building materials stores	883	3.3	22,914
Health services	9,463	3.3	34,200
Trucking and warehousing	1,879	3.2	27,289
Engineering and management	2,849	3.1	33,709
Special trade contractors	3,334	3.1	26,443
Education	1,982	3.0	20,088
Eating and drinking places	7,419	2.8	11,920
Misc. services	44	2.5	n.a.
Auto dealers and service stations	2,234	2.2	25,433
Rubber and plastics	962	2.2	33,103
Air transportation	828	2.2	43,093
Lumber products	754	2.1	27,713
State and local government	16,584	1.5	28,859

Job prospects also differ from region to region. For a variety of reasons, some parts of the country are simply better than others as places to run a business. Normal business cycles, local business climates, tax rates, labor costs, the cost of living, and a host of other factors all affect the willingness and ability of companies to hire workers. Of course, these factors shift over time.

Using data from the U.S. Bureau of Labor Statistics, Regional Financial Associates, a Pennsylvania economic consulting firm, recently designated the following as the metropolitan areas with the fastest job growth between 1991 and 1996:[2]

1. Atlanta, Georgia
2. Chicago, Illinois
3. Phoenix, Arizona
4. Dallas, Texas
5. Detroit, Michigan
6. Minneapolis-St. Paul, Minnesota
7. Boston, Massachusetts
8. Houston, Texas
9. Denver, Colorado
10. Las Vegas, Nevada

The following metropolitan areas showed the most rapid job loss during the same period:

TABLE AII.2 ◆ Industries with the Highest Rate of Job Loss: 1991–1996

	Total Jobs in 1996 first quarter	Average annual growth rate	Average annual earnings in 1993
Legal services	926 (in thousands)	0.3%	$61,224
Stone, clay and glass	535	0.2	33,566
Food products	1,674	0.1	32,369
Paper products	682	0.1	42,178
Printing and publishing	1,532	–0.3	32,515
Primary metal industries	708	–0.7	47,020
Textile mills	642	–0.8	24,897
Chemicals	1,026	–0.9	56,289
Apparel and accessory stores	1,100	–1.1	13,971
Utility services	905	–1.2	55,722
Federal Government	2,781	–1.2	n.a.
Transportation equipment	1,747	–1.2	n.a.
Banks and savings institutions	2,022	–1.7	35,252
Metal mining	51	–2.3	56,964
Petroleum and coal	140	–2.4	67,996
Railroads	234	–2.7	55,707
Apparel and textile	868	–2.8	19,225
Tobacco	41	–3.4	55,983
Instruments	831	–3.4	45,795
Leather	99	–4.8	22,664
Oil and gas extraction	312	–5.0	36,011
Pipelines	14	–5.9	54,011
Coal mining	101	–6.4	62,044

1. Los Angeles, California
2. New York, New York
3. Hartford, Connecticut
4. San Francisco, California
5. Honolulu, Hawaii
6. Philadelphia, Pennsylvania
7. Binghamton, New York
8. Santa Barbara, California
9. Bakersfield, California
10. Bergen-Passaic, New Jersey

The Job Outlook for Business-Related Fields

In this text, we are naturally most concerned with the prospects for employment in the business sector. Table AII.3 lists some of the business jobs expected to experience the largest growth between 1992 and 2005. Some of these numbers reflect interesting—and not terribly surprising—trends. The demand for typists and word processors, for instance, is expected to drop by more than 26 percent as businesspeople at all levels use desktop computers and other technologies to produce their own documents.[3]

International Job Prospects

Part of the allure of an international job is the prospect of traveling to exotic countries, living in interesting places, and dealing with different kinds of people. However, an "international" job sometimes means nothing more than working—in the United States—

TABLE AII.3 ◆ Expected Growth in Selected Fields, 1992–2005

Job	Percentage of change, 1992–2005
Computer engineers and scientists	+112
Systems analysts	+110
Management analysts	+43
Bill and account collectors	+40
Marketing advertising, and public relations managers	+36
Personnel, training, and labor relations specialists	+36
Accountants and auditors	+32
Computer programmers	+30
Adjustment clerks	+27
Financial managers	+25
Clerical supervisors and managers	+24
Marketing and sales worker supervisors	+20
General managers and top executives	+13

for a foreign-owned firm like Sony, Nissan, MCA, or Lever Brothers. Indeed, most entry-level "international" jobs fall into this category.

If you are interested in an international career, however, openings are available. Moreover, the number of truly international jobs—those involving extensive travel or even relocation to other nations—is expected to rise in the decades to come. In general, entry-level jobs in this arena include sales positions and jobs for export brokers and import merchants (see Chapter 5). Senior managers in many areas of various firms are also candidates for international reassignment—usually after they have mastered another language in which to talk business.

■ LEARNING ABOUT SPECIFIC JOB OPPORTUNITIES

After analyzing employment trends, your next step is to locate actual job openings. Among the most valuable sources of information are college placement offices, employment agencies, help-wanted advertisements, and networking.

College Placement Offices

College placement offices list specific job opportunities and may hold job fairs for corporate recruiters. Many placement offices will also help you develop an effective résumé and provide personal career counseling. These services are offered to alumni as well as current students.

Employment Agencies

You can also learn about job openings by registering with *employment agencies. Private employment agencies* usually specialize in specific industries, such as banking, telecommunications, or retailing. You can locate the agency that is right for you by scanning the classified ads in your local paper, where undoubtedly you will see the same agency names repeated in different ads. Private employment agencies collect a fee for every job placement. Either the new employee or the hiring company will pay the fee, which is based on a percentage of first-year salary. Since this fee can be substantial, it is important to find out who is responsible for payment before you take the job.

Many workers seek short-term assignments through *temporary employment agencies*. These agencies may also deal with specialized fields such as accounting or data processing. As a temporary employee, you report to work at a company such as Motorola or General Foods, but your actual employer is the temporary agency. Although "temp" positions may be stopgap employment solutions, they often provide invaluable experience and may lead to permanent positions.

Help-Wanted Advertisements

Another valuable source for learning about actual job openings are *help-wanted advertisements*. Classified ads, as they are also known, appear in national and local newspapers, professional publications, and trade journals. An increasing number are also appearing on the Internet via commercial on-line services and the Internet home pages of such major corporations as IBM.

Linking employers and job seekers via the Internet is changing the nation's job market. Today, the Internet holds the most diverse database of job listings in the world. Whereas in 1994, there were only about 15,000 jobs on any given day listed in cyberspace, that figure jumped to about 500,000 in 1996. These jobs were included in the 15 leading on-line job banks.[4] Table AII.4 lists 10 popular on-line services, the number of jobs and résumés in their databases, and their Internet addresses.

Networking

Perhaps the best source of employment information is *networking*, the process of forming personal contacts through which you learn about job opportunities and meet peo-

TABLE AII.4 ◆ Job Hunting On-Line

Selected On-Line Services	No. of Jobs	No. of Résumés	Internet Address
America's Job Bank	300,000	n.a.	www.ajb.dni.us
Career Path	136,000	n.a.	www.careerpath.com
Online Career Center	32,000	27,000	www.occ.com
Career Mosaic	15,000	35,000	www.careermosaic.com
Help Wanted USA	15,000	8,000	iccweb.com
The Monster Board	15,000	45,000	www.monster.com
E-Span	12,000	10,000	www.espan.com
Career Magazine Database	12,000	5,000	www.careermag.com
Career City	5,000	n.a.	www.careercity.com
NationJob Network	4,000	n.a.	www.nationjob.com

Sources: Regional Financial Associations; Bureau of Labor Statistics

ple who make hiring decisions in major companies. Many of the jobs you learn about through networking are not advertised. This means that there is less competition for the position and a greater chance that your job search will be successful.

Networking contacts should include nearly everyone you know, including family, friends, neighbors, teachers, classmates, doctors, lawyers, and accountants. Talk with your contacts about your job objective and ask them if they have any information or advice that might help you find a job. Your inquiries should be low-key, and you should avoid asking for a job. Your purpose is to gather information, make a positive impression so that your contacts remember you if a job opportunity arises in the future, and get referrals to other networking sources. By extending your networking circle, you are likely to increase your knowledge about your chosen field and learn about actual job leads.

Whether you seek a job in the United States or a foreign country, you will need an effective résumé and cover letter to communicate your background and interests to prospective employers. We will examine these important employment communication tools next.

■ PREPARING A RÉSUMÉ AND COVER LETTER

Achieving good grades in school, acquiring real-world experience, and having a well-conceived career plan are important ingredients to landing a job, but they are usually not sufficient. Getting a job requires the ability to communicate your background and career goals to prospective employers through a résumé and cover letter.

Preparing an Effective Résumé

A résumé is probably the most important factor in landing an interview. Think of it as a sales tool that sells your background to prospective employers. Consider, for example, the sample résumé in Figure AII.1. lee Huan's résumé is only one page long because she understands that most employers get dozens of résumés and have little time to spend on each one. If your résumé is longer than a page, make sure that all the information you include is relevant to *the job that you are seeking.*

The sample shown here is a *chronological résumé*, which lists accomplishments in reverse chronological order within each category. In contrast, a *functional résumé* focuses on skills and career goals by highlighting between three and five functional headings, such as sales, accounting, and management. A *targeted résumé* highlights abilities and achievements that relate to a specific job goal. Many books are available in libraries and bookstores that illustrate a variety of sample résumé forms.

Most experts agree that your résumé should include the following information: *education, work experience, honors and activities.* (Academic honors can be listed under "Honors and Activities" or in the "Education" section.) They also recommend that you do *not* include a photo or information about your age, marital status, children, height and weight, or health. Opinion is divided on the inclusion of a career objective. A *career objective* identifies the particular position you are seeking—for example, "A sales position for a major pharmaceutical manufacturer." While specific career objectives can be valuable, vague statements designed to cover a variety of positions can do more harm than good. With today's sophisticated word processing software and laser printers, it is possible for job hunters to tailor their statement of career objective to different job opportunities.[5]

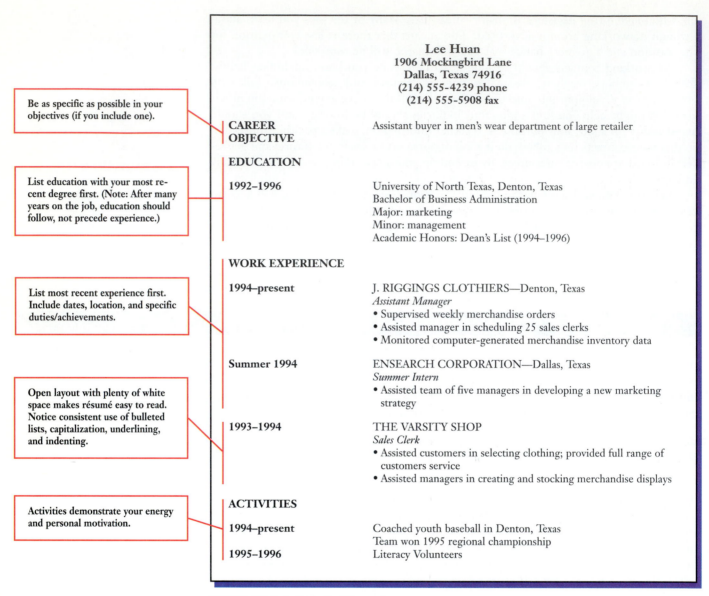

FIGURE AII.1 ◆ **Sample Résumé**

Using an Effective Résumé Writing Style The most effective résumés rely on concise, information-packed phrases, rather than complete sentences, to communicate value to employers. For example, do not write this:

"In my job as advertising manager, I was responsible for an ad campaign that turned my product around."

Rather, explain your contribution like this:

"Created $10 million broadcast and print ad campaign for Wonder Widgets that increased sales by 400 percent."

Action verbs that identify specific skills are critical in résumé writing. The following list contains examples of the kinds of words that employers respond to:

designed	negotiated	researched
forecasted	organized	sold
founded	planned	supervised
interviewed	reported	trained

Increasingly, companies are turning to optical character recognition software to scan key facts from the résumés they receive.[6] These facts are stored in the company's computerized employment database, which recruiters access when they have job openings. Computerized keyword searches that scan every résumé in the database link candidates with jobs.

Here are some suggestions for creating an effective scannable résumé. Your goal is to make key information about your background accessible during a keyword search:

- Use standard résumé headings: *objective, education, work experience, activities.*
- Describe your accomplishments in specific, rather than vague, language. Rely on the action verbs we just discussed.
- Use concrete nouns such as *creative director, compensation and benefits specialists, Tufts University, Ph.D.*
- Use standard typefaces in 10- to 14-point type, and use a laser printer to print your résumé. Avoid sending photocopies, especially if the quality is poor.

Creating an Accurate Résumé   Some people exaggerate their accomplishments to make themselves look better. *This tactic usually backfires.* For one thing, prospective employers generally verify the content of résumé before making offers. They do this by checking the job references you provide and by checking school transcripts. If they find misleading or downright false information, they will almost certainly reject the applicant. Thus, it is a mistake to identify yourself as "Warehouse and Distribution Manager" if your real job was carrying merchandise from the stockroom to the sales floor. On the other hand, don't hesitate to blow your own horn about your real accomplishments—if as advertising manager of your college newspaper, you tripled advertising income in a year, then say so.

Creating a Professional Résumé   Finally, be sure that your résumé looks professional. Most experts recommend that it be printed in black type on white or off-white paper and that it has an effective layout. Plenty of white space and indenting, headings that separate key sections, and bulleted lists will make your résumé easy to read. Be sure to use these elements consistently as shown in Figure AII.1 and to proofread your entire document; poor grammar and misspelled words make a bad impression.

Preparing a Cover Letter

You should always include a cover letter with your résumé. Your cover letter introduces you, indicates your intentions, refers the reader to your résumé, and suggests a course of action that the reader might take. Figure AII.2, the cover letter that Lee Huan sent along with her résumé, is structured in the following way:

- It begins with a brief mention of a mutual acquaintance. (Always be sure to say how you heard about a possible opening.)
- Next, Lee states her reason for writing. The letter then proceeds to note ways in which Lee (and her experience) may fit well into the employer's company. Be sure to phrase your description of that fit in terms of what you have to offer the organization.
- Lee concludes her letter by describing the action that might be taken next: either she will call the addressee or the recipient can contact her first. If you ask

September 2, 1997

Ms. Samantha Jacobs
Director of Buying–Men's Wear
Neiman Marcus Inc.
Main and Ervay Streets
Dallas, Texas 75201

Dear Ms. Jacobs:

Establish a connection with the addressee.

Edward Centric, an assistant in your department, told me about an entry-level opening in the men's wear buying department. I am interested in talking with you about this position and am enclosing a copy of my résumé for your consideration.

Sum up your assets and state how they would benefit the firm.

I have worked in retailing throughout college. My experience at J. Riggins Clothiers and The Varsity Shop taught me essential buying, merchandising, personnel-supervision, inventory-control, and customer-service skills. My extensive on-the-job experience reinforced the concepts I learned in college, where I studied marketing. Although I am a new college graduate, my work experience and education have given me the tools I need to succeed in an entry-level position in the buying department at Neiman Marcus.

State your business.

Be "proactive": outline a plan for follow-up.

I would appreciate the opportunity to discuss how I might apply my background in retailing to Neiman Marcus. I will call you next week to discuss the possibility of arranging an interview.

Sincerely,

Lee Huan

Lee Huan

FIGURE AII.2 ◆ Sample Cover Letter

the addressee to call you, you should have an answering machine or voice mail that takes calls when you are not there.

Cover letters should be brief. Unless you are responding to a "blind" ad—that is, one that does not indicate the name of the organization involved—your letters should always be addressed to a specific individual. Do not address applications to "Director of Human Resources" or (even worse) "To Whom It May Concern." Like your résumé, your cover letter should be proofread carefully.

Neither the greatest résumé nor the most persuasive cover letter will ensure that you get a job. Rather, the purpose of these documents is to get your foot in the door— that is, to get you an interview. Ultimately, the interview will determine whether or not you get the job.

■ THE EMPLOYMENT INTERVIEW

Interviewing for a job—whether your first or your twenty-first—is almost always a nerve-wracking experience. During an interview, recruiters and managers talk to you, ask you questions, listen to your answers, and answer questions you may have. They will then judge your qualifications. Because the interview is the basis on which most hiring decisions are made, it is crucial that you understand how to prepare for an interview, how to handle yourself during an interview, and what to do after an interview.

Preparing for an Interview

The first step is to learn all you can about the company with which you'll be interviewing. Get a copy of the firm's annual report. Research the company in business publications like *Fortune* and the *Wall Street Journal*. Visit the company's home page on the World Wide Web. In addition, learn all you can about the industry or market in which the company does business.

The next step is to practice answering the questions that you are likely to be asked. For example, know ahead of time what you will say about your prior experience, reasons for wanting a job change, reasons for wanting this job, ability to do this job, strengths, weaknesses, and future goals. Be prepared to answer these questions, but don't be complacent. If you interview with enough people, someone will ask you something you never dreamed of. For example:

- What is your personal work ethic?
- How have you helped co-workers improve their productivity?
- What work-related accomplishment are you most proud of?

The third step is to develop questions of your own to ask interviewers. These questions show your interest in the firm and help you decide whether you want to work there (assuming you are offered the job). Questions you might consider asking include these:

- Does the company offer training for new employees and opportunities for advancement?
- What skills and qualities do you believe are most important for this job?
- How would you describe a typical day in this job?
- What aspects of this job make it difficult to perform well?
- Do most supervisors or managers have advanced degrees?

Warning: Do not ask about salary, benefits, or retirement plans until you are offered the job. Interviewers may interpret your concern as a desire to be comfortable—not productive.

Finally, assemble the materials you need to take with you: a sample of your work (if appropriate), extra copies of your résumé, and written recommendations (if you have them). Contact the people whom you plan to use as references and let them know about your upcoming interview. They need to be prepared to answer questions about you.

Presenting Yourself at an Interview

When going to the interview, allow plenty of time to get there a few minutes early. Some experts suggest that you even do a "dry run" in advance so you can be sure how much time the trip will take.

Dress conservatively. A dark suit is your best bet for most professional jobs, regardless of your sex or age. However, if you are applying for a "creative" position—say, advertising copywriter—you may do better to dress with a bit more dash. What ever you wear, make it the best quality you can afford—it will pay off in the long run.

Handling Yourself during the Interview

When meeting the interviewer, try to project an air of competence and assurance. Relax. When the interviewer introduces himself or herself, state your own name and extend your hand. Speak clearly and directly.

The interviewer will usually start by asking a few general questions, both to set the tone and help you relax. Your answers should be honest, but politically smart. Never say that you did not get along with a previous boss. In fact, find something good to say about that person. If you were fired from a former job, admit it, but characterize the problem as a bad person-job fit—one from which you learned something. In general, try to present yourself as the right choice for the job—the person who has the needed skills, commitment and initiative to do the work as well as the personality to get along with others.

Make your answers to the point, but don't be too brief. Remember: your objective is to *convey some information* about yourself. If you are asked if you are the kind of person who would relocate for a job, simply saying "Certainly" is not enough. On the other hand, be careful not to talk too much. If asked whether you would relocate, don't launch into a 30-minute travelogue about all the cities that you have lived in. Strike a happy medium: indicate that you are willing to relocate and that you assume an occasional move may be necessary for advancement.

What if you are asked a question that you simply don't know how to answer? If you are at all uncertain, ask the interviewer to clarify the question. If you still don't know, admit it. Even more difficult is the situation in which an interviewer asks a question that is "out of bounds." Questions about age, ethnic background, religion, marital status, and personal life are illegal. Nonetheless, a surprising number of interviewers continue to ask them. What should you do? You have two options: to answer or not to answer.

If it doesn't make you uncomfortable, you may choose to answer. Or you may give a "nonanswer" that shifts the topic back to job-related issues. For example, if asked whether you have a boyfriend or girlfriend, you might say, "I have many friends here, but I consider myself very adaptable and wouldn't expect to have difficulty making new friends wherever I was located. Would the job call for relocating me after the initial training session?"

If you decide not to answer an illegal question and point out to the interviewer that the question is inappropriate, you risk losing the job. You can, of course, report the firm to the Equal Employment Opportunity Commission. However, you will need to prove that the purpose of the question was to discriminate against you—a difficult and time-consuming task at best.

Regardless of how you perceive the interview to be going, remain calm. And keep your sense of humor. Some interviewers may seem bored, others distant or even rude. These attitudes may have no bearing whatsoever on any assessment of you and your qualifications. The interviewer may be tired or cranky from traveling. Rudeness may just be his or her normal style. Frankly, some interviewers are simply not effective at what they do. Meanwhile, another interviewer may actually push you a bit just to see how you handle yourself under pressure. Remember that losing your temper will lose you the job for sure.

The interviewer will usually indicate when the interview is over. Rarely, however, will an interviewer tell you whether or not you will be offered the job. There may be several applicants for the job, or the interviewer may first need to discuss your qualifications with other managers. But the interviewer should explain what will happen next—when the company will contact you, what the next step will be if the company remains interested, and so forth. If this information is not offered, ask before you leave.

Following Up after the Interview

After each interview, be sure to write a letter to the person with whom you spoke. This letter is an opportunity not only to restate your interest and qualifications but to resolve one of life's common annoyances. Hours after an interview, almost everyone thinks of something he or she should have said. So here is your chance to say it.

If you have applied for a high-level position, you can expect more interviews before you get the job. You may be invited to the company's headquarters or regional office for more interviews with managers. When you are contacted for a second interview, remember that you did a good job the first time around and that you have to do it again.

Successful interviewing results in job offers. In the next section, we will examine ways to assess offers in order to maximize your chances of choosing a job that is right for you.

■ ASSESSING JOB OFFERS

When making your choice among several different job offers, there are six major considerations to take into account: *job responsibilities, person-job fit, employer image or quality, quality of training and development, career opportunities,* and *compensation and benefits.*

Job Responsibilities

Ask yourself which job you will enjoy most and which will best further your career objective. In general, try to choose a job that gives you a chance to use your existing skills while providing the opportunity to master new ones. The ideal assignment, then, is one with well-defined boundaries and an atmosphere in which you can get advice and assistance from others.

Person-Job Fit

You must also examine the fit between your own interests, aspirations, and preferences and the requirements and opportunities of the job that you are considering. For example, if you've always wanted a career in retailing, then you will probably have no trouble choosing Federal Department Stores over Westinghouse Electric.

The job itself, however, is only one part of the person-job fit story. Here are some other considerations:

- *Location.* Is one job in a big city and another in a small town?
- *Ambiance.* Did you feel more comfortable with the people and/or physical environment at one firm than you did at the other? (Remember: you will be spending between a quarter and a third of your life at work.)
- *Travel.* While some people look forward to the chance to travel, others prefer to stay close to home.
- *Family.* Relatives and friends may also influence your choice. You should consider the quality not only of the local schools but of the local job market for your spouse or significant other. It is hard to be happy at work—and to do your best work—if you are worrying about your home life.

Employer Image or Quality

In evaluating job offers, you should also consider the overall image or reputation of the organization for which you'll be working. Not surprisingly, most experts advise you to associate yourself with quality—a quality organization, quality people, quality products and services.

How do you go about making this assessment? Several resources are available, including the criteria from *Fortune* magazine's annual listing of the most admired corporations in the United States. Each January, the magazine surveys thousands of senior executives and evaluates firms on several grounds, including innovativeness, value, community and environmental responsibility, use of corporate assets, quality of management, quality of goods or services produced, financial soundness, and ability to attract, develop, and keep talented people.

For assessments of smaller firms, look at publications such as *Inc.*, *Black Enterprise*, and *Entrepreneur*. For information on firms in your area, check back issues of local newspapers. Above all, don't be afraid to ask any contacts you may have what they know—and feel—about a company that you are considering.

Quality of Training and Development

Throughout your career—but especially when choosing a first job—you should seriously weigh the value of the training and development that a firm offers its new employees. Your college education provides you with the fundamental information and skills that you'll need to succeed in the business world. But because each organization is unique—and because each values and expects different things from its employees— most large firms provide a systematic program to help them become more effective in performing their jobs.

Procter & Gamble, General Foods, IBM, and General Mills are all known to have outstanding training programs. Indeed, some firms actively seek people who have successfully completed these or similar programs. Although smaller firms do not generally offer structured programs, you may benefit greatly at these organizations from both the opportunity to work directly with upper-level management and exposure to many areas of a firm's operations.

Finally, be sure to weigh a company's attitudes toward further education. Some companies, for instance, pay all or part of tuition costs for employees who take technical and/or advanced college courses; they may also underwrite the costs of taking professional certification examinations.[7]

Career Opportunities

Clearly, career opportunities and prospects with each potential employer should play a major role in your decision. Where will you go in a firm that has just laid off hundreds of workers? Will you be subject to the same degree of job insecurity? On the other hand, if another firm is hiring hundreds of new people each year but provides advancement opportunities for only a few, what are your chances of succeeding?

Most large organizations have clearly formulated career paths to help people understand where they can expect to be at different points in their career. Be wary if a firm has not given consideration to these issues. But also be wary if career paths are highly programmed and regimented. Ideally, your new employer should offer several well-defined career paths while providing you with sufficient flexibility to pursue new opportunities.

Compensation and Benefits

Finally, carefully consider the compensation package that you are offered. You can get salary data for comparative purposes from campus placement offices, friends, and other sources. Because most firms know what competitors pay, there will probably be little variation in your salary offers. If you have excellent grades, a strong résumé, and solid references, you may be able to start at a somewhat higher salary than someone whose qualifications are weaker.

What if you like everything about the job—the fit, the location, the responsibilities, the prospects—except the pay? You can try to negotiate a higher salary, but you may not get far because most firms have predefined salary structures for new employees and may react negatively to requests for higher salaries. If your company of choice is offering less than other firms, you might subtly point out the differences and ask if there is any flexibility in the offer.

Finally, don't focus too narrowly on the starting salary itself. Factor in the value of benefits (insurance, retirement plans), perks (car, office), the cost of living where you will be working (Los Angeles versus Kansas City), and prospects for salary increases. Look at the whole package—and the whole job—before you say yes or no.

■ GLOSSARY

absolute advantage The ability to produce something more efficiently than any other country can [100]

accountability Liability of subordinates for accomplishing tasks assigned by managers [162]

accounting Comprehensive system for collecting, analyzing, and communicating financial information [292]

accounting system Organized means by which financial information is identified, measured, recorded, and retained for use in accounting statements and management reports [292]

accounts payable Current liabilities consisting of bills owed to suppliers, plus wages and taxes due within the upcoming year [301]

accounts receivable Amount due from a customer who has purchased goods on credit [300]

acquisition The purchase of one company by another [39]

Active Corps of Executives (ACE) SBA program in which currently employed executives work with small businesses on a volunteer basis [192]

activity ratio Financial ratio for evaluating management's use of a firm's assets [303]

advertising Promotional tool consisting of paid, nonpersonal communication used by an identified sponsor to inform an audience about a product [369]

advertising media Variety of communication devices for carrying a seller's message to potential customers [369]

affirmative action program Legally mandated program for recruiting qualified employees belonging to racial, gender, or ethnic groups that are underrepresented in an organization [239]

agent Individual or organization acting for, and in the name of, another party [65]

apparent authority Agent's authority, based on the principal's compliance, to bind a principal to a certain course of action [66]

appellate court Court that reviews case records of trials whose findings have been appealed [58]

articles of incorporation Document detailing the corporate governance of a company, including its name and address, its purpose, and the amount of stock it intends to issue [37]

artificial intelligence (AI) Construction and programming of computers to imitate human thought processes [311]

asked price Price that an OTC broker charges for a share of stock [457]

assembly line Product layout in which a product moves step-by-step through a plant on conveyor belts or other equipment until it is completed [272]

asset Any economic resource expected to benefit a firm or individual who owns it [297]

audit Systematic examination of a company's accounting system to determine whether its financial reports fairly present its operations [294]

authority Power to make the decisions necessary to complete a task [161]

autocratic style Managerial style in which managers generally issue orders and expect them to be obeyed without question [222]

automated teller machine (ATM) Electronic machine that allows customers to conduct account-related activities 24 hours a day, seven days a week [424]

balance of payments Flow of all money into or out of a country [101]

balance of trade Economic value of all products a country imports minus the economic value of all products it exports [101]

balance sheet Financial statement detailing a firm's assets, liabilities, and owners' equity [299]

banker's acceptance Bank promise, issued for a buyer, to pay a designated firm a specified amount at a future date [423]

bankruptcy Permission granted by the courts to individuals and organizations not to pay some or all of their debts [67]

bargain retailer Retailer carrying a wide range of products at bargain prices [390]

batch processing Method of collecting data over a period of time and then computer processing them as a group or batch [308]

bear market Period of falling stock prices [457]

bearer (or coupon) bond Bond requiring the holder to clip and submit a coupon in order to receive an interest payment [452]

benefits Compensation other than wages and salaries [237]

bid price Price that an OTC broker pays for a share of stock [456]

blue chip stock Common stock issued by a well-established company with a sound financial history and a stable pattern of dividend payouts [447]

blue sky laws Laws requiring securities dealers to be licensed and registered with the states in which they do business [463]

board of directors Governing body of a corporation, which reports to its shareholders and delegates power to run its day-to-day operations but remains responsible for sustaining its assets [38]

bond Security through which an issuer promises to pay the buyer a certain amount of money by a specified future date [451]

bonus Individual performance incentive in the form of a special payment made over and above the employee's salary [236]

book value Value of a common stock expressed as total shareholders' equity divided by the number of shares of stock [445]

bookkeeping The recording of accounting transactions [292]

boycott Labor action in which workers refuse to buy the products of a targeted employer [251]

branch office Foreign office set up by an international or multinational firm [109]

brand competition Competitive marketing that appeals to consumer perceptions of similar products [334]

branding Process of using symbols to communicate the qualities of a product made by a particular producer [359]

break-even analysis Assessment of the quantity of a product that must be sold before the seller makes a profit [362]

break-even point Quantity of a product that must be sold before the seller covers variable and fixed costs and makes a profit [362]

broker Individual or organization who receives and executes buy and sell orders on behalf of other people in return for commissions [448]

browser Software supporting the graphics and linking capbilities necessary to navigate the World Wide Web [313]

budget deficit Situation in which a government body spends more money than it takes in [16]

bull market Period of rising stock prices [457]

business An organization that provides goods or services in order to earn profits [2]

business continuation agreement Special form of business insurance whereby owners arrange to buy the interests of deceased associates from their heirs [483]

business interruption insurance Insurance covering income lost during times when a company is unable to conduct business [481]

business practice laws Laws or regulations governing business practices in given countries [115]

bylaws Document detailing corporate rules and regulations, including election and responsibilities of directors and procedures for issuing new stock [37]

cafeteria benefits plan Benefits plan that establishes dollar amounts of benefits per employee and allows employees to choose from a variety of alternative benefits [238]

capacity Amount of a product that a company can produce under normal working conditions [269]; competence required of individuals entering into a binding contract [59]

capital The funds needed to create and operate a business enterprise [2]

capital gain Profit earned by selling a share of stock for more than it cost [443]

capital item Expensive, durable, infrequently purchased industrial product, such as a building and machinery [356]

capital structure Relative mix of a firm's debt and equity financing [476]

capitalism Market economy that provides for private ownership of production and encourages entrepreneurship by offering profits as an incentive [4]

cartel Association of producers whose purpose is to control supply and prices [115]

cash-flow management Management of cash inflows and outflows to ensure adequate funds for purchases and the productive use of excess funds [471]

catalog showroom Bargain retailer in which customers place orders for catalog items to be picked up at on-premises warehouses [391]

cellular layout Spatial arrangement of production facilities designed to move families of products through similar flow paths [272]

centralized organization Organization in which most decision-making authority is held by upper-level management [162]

certified public accountant (CPA) Accountant licensed by the state and offering services to the public [293]

chain of command Reporting relationships within a company [156]

check Demand deposit order instructing a bank to pay a given sum to a specified payee [415]

check kiting Illegal practice of writing checks against money that has not yet been credited at the bank on which the checks are drawn [88]

chief executive officer (CEO) Top manager hired by the board of directors to run a corporation [39]

classical theory of motivation Theory holding that workers are motivated solely by money [209]

closed promotion system System by which managers decide, often informally, which workers are considered for promotions [234]

closed shop Work place in which an employer may hire only workers already belonging to a union [249]

collateral Borrower-pledged legal asset that may be seized by lenders in case of nonpayment [473]

collective bargaining Process by which labor and management negotiate conditions of employment for workers represented by the union [245]

collusion Illegal agreement between two or more companies to commit a wrongful act [83]

commercial bank Federal- or state-chartered financial institution accepting deposits that it uses to make loans and earn profits [420]

commercial paper Short-term securities, or notes, containing a borrower's promise to pay [474]

committee and team authority Authority granted to committees or work teams involved in a firm's daily operations [164]

commodities market Market in which futures contracts are traded [454]

common carrier Transporting company, such as a truck line or railroad, that transports goods for any shipper [399]

common law Body of decisions handed down by courts ruling on individual cases [54]

common stock Stock that pays dividends and guarantees corporate voting rights but offers last claims over assets [38]

comparable worth Principle that women should receive the same pay for traditionally "female" jobs of the same worth to a company as traditionally "male" jobs [241]

comparative advantage The ability to produce some products more efficiently than others [101]

compensation system Total package offered by a company to employees in return for their labor [236]

compensatory damages Monetary payments intended to redress injury actually suffered because of a tort [61]

competition Vying among businesses for the same resources or customers [9]

competitive product analysis Process by which a company analyzes a competitor's products to identify desirable improvements in its own [280]

compulsory arbitration Method of resolving a labor dispute in which both parties are legally required to accept the judgment of a neutral party [252]

computer graphics program Application program that converts numeric and character data into pictorial information, such as graphs and charts [309]

conceptual skills Abilities to think in the abstract, diagnose and analyze different situations, and see beyond the present situation [141]

consideration Any item of value exchanged between parties to create a valid contract [59]

consumer behavior Various facets of the decision process by which customers come to purchase and consume products [343]

consumer goods Products purchased by consumers for personal use [328]

consumerism Form of social activism dedicated to protecting the rights of consumers in their dealings with businesses [83]

containerization Transportation method in which goods are sealed in containers at shipping sources and opened when they reach final destinations [399]

contingency approach Approach to managerial style holding that the appropriate behavior in any situation is dependent (contingent) on the unique elements of that situation [223]

contingent worker Temporary employee hired to supplement an organization's permanent workforce [244]

contract Any agreement between two or more parties that is enforceable in court [59]

contract carrier Independent transporting company that usually owns the vehicles in which it transports products [399]

control chart Process control method that plots test-sampling results on a diagram to determine when a process is beginning to depart from normal operating conditions [282]

controlling Management process of monitoring an organization's performance to ensure that it is meeting its goals [137]

convenience good/service Relatively inexpensive product purchased and consumed rapidly and regularly [356]

convenience store Retail store offering easy accessibility, extended hours, and fast service [392]

copyright Exclusive ownership right belonging to the creator of a book, article, design, illustration, photo, film, or musical work [63]

corporate bond Bond issued by a company as a source of long-term funding [452]

corporate culture The shared experiences, stories, beliefs, and norms that characterize an organization [144]

corporate governance Roles of shareholders, directors, and other managers in corporate decision making [36]

corporation Business that is legally considered an entity separate from its owners and is liable for its own debts; owners' liability extends to the limits of their investments [35]

cost of goods sold Total cost of obtaining materials for making the products sold by a firm during the year [301]

coupon Sales promotion technique in which a certificate is issued entitling the buyer to a reduced price [373]

credit Bookkeeping entry in a T-account that records decreases in assets [298]

credit union Financial institution that accepts deposits from, and makes loans to, only its members, usually employees of a particular organization [422]

cumulative preferred stock Preferred stock on which dividends not paid in the past must be paid to stockholders before dividends can be paid to common stockholders [448]

currency Government-issued paper money and metal coins [415]

current asset Asset that can be converted into cash within the following year [300]

current liability Debt that must be paid within the year [301]

current ratio Solvency ratio that determines a firm's creditworthiness by measuring its ability to pay current liabilities [303]

customer departmentalization Departmentalization according to types of customers likely to buy a given product [158]

data Raw facts and figures [307]

data communications network Global network (such as the Internet) that permits users to send electronic messages and information quickly and economically [312]

database Centralized, organized collection of related data [308]

database management program Application program for creating, storing, searching, and manipulating an organized collection of data [309]

debenture Unsecured bond for which no specific property is pledged as security [453]

debit Bookkeeping entry in a T-account that records increases in assets [298]

debit card Plastic card that allows an individual to transfer money between bank accounts [431]

debt A firm's total liabilities [303]

debt financing Long-term borrowing from sources outside a company [474]

debt ratio Solvency ratio measuring a firm's ability to meet its long-term debts [303]

debt-to-owners' equity ratio (or debt-to-equity ratio) Solvency ratio describing the extent to which a firm is financed through borrowing [303]

decentralized organization Organization in which a great deal of decision-making authority is delegated to levels of management at points below the top [162]

decision-making skills Skills in defining problems and selecting the best courses of action [141]

delegation Assignment of a task, a responsibility, or authority by a manager to a subordinate [162]

demand The willingness and ability of buyers to purchase a good or service [5]

demand and supply schedule Assessment of the relationships between different levels of demand and supply at different price levels [6]

demand curve Graph showing how many units of a product will be demanded (bought) at different prices [6]

demand deposit Bank account funds that may be withdrawn at any time [415]

democratic style Managerial style in which managers generally ask for input from subordinates but retain final decision-making power [222]

demographic variables Characteristics of populations that may be considered in developing a segmentation strategy [339]

department store Large product-line retailer characterized by organization into specialized departments [389]

departmentalization Process of grouping jobs into logical units [157]

depreciation Process of distributing the cost of an asset over its life [300]

depression Particularly severe and long-lasting recession [12]

deregulation Elimination of administrative laws and rules that restrict business activity [55]

derived demand Demand for industrial products that results from demand for consumer products [346]

desktop publishing Process of combining word-processing and graphics capability to produce type-set-quality text from personal computers [309]

direct channel Distribution channel in which a product travels from producer to consumer without intermediaries [382]

direct investment Arrangement in which a firm buys or establishes tangible assets in another country [110]

direct mail Advertising medium in which messages are mailed directly to consumers [370]

direct selling Form of nonstore retailing typified by door-to-door sales [394]

direct response retailing Nonstore retailing by direct interaction with customers to inform them of products and receive sales orders [393]

directing Management process of guiding and motivating employees to meet an organization's objectives [137]

disability income insurance Insurance providing continuous income when disability keeps the insured from gainful employment [481]

discount Price reduction offered as an incentive to purchase [365]

discount house Bargain retailer that generates large sales volume by offering goods at substantial price reductions [391]

discount rate Interest rate at which member banks can borrow money from the Federal Reserve [482]

distribution Part of the marketing mix concerned with getting products from producers to consumers [337]

distribution center Warehouse providing short-term storage of goods for which demand is both constant and high [397]

distribution channel Network of interdependent companies through which a product passes from producer to end user [382]

distribution mix The combination of distribution channels by which a firm gets its products to end users [382]

diversity training Programs designed to improve employee awareness of differences in attitudes and behaviors of co-workers from different racial, ethnic, or gender groups [243]

division Department that resembles a separate business in producing and marketing its own products [167]

divisional organization Organizational structure in which corporate divisions operate as relatively autonomous businesses under the larger corporate umbrella [167]

double taxation Situation in which taxes may be payable both by a corporation on its profits and by shareholders on dividend incomes [36]

double-entry accounting system Bookkeeping system that balances the accounting equation by recording the dual effects of every financial transaction [298]

Dow Jones Industrial Average Market index based on the prices of 30 of the largest industrial firms listed on the NYSE [457]

drop shipper Limited-function merchant wholesaler that receives customer orders, negotiates with producers, takes title to goods, and arranges for shipment to customers [386]

dumping Practice of selling a product abroad for less than the cost of production [115]

E-cash Money that moves among consumers and businesses via digital electronic transmissions [432]

earnings per share Profitability ratio measuring the size of the dividend that a firm can pay shareholders [305]

economic strike Strike usually triggered by stalemate over one or more mandatory bargaining items [251]

economic system A nation's system for allocating its resources among its citizens [2]

electronic funds transfer (EFT) Communication of fund transfer information over wire, cable, or microwave [424]

electronic mail (e-mail) Computer system that electronically transmits information between computers [312]

electronic shopping Nonstore retailing in which information about the seller's products and services is connected into consumers' computers allowing consumers to receive the information and purchase the products in the home [394]

electronic spreadsheet Application program with a row-and-column format that allows users to compare the effect of changes from one category to another [308]

embargo Government order banning exportation and/or importation of a particular product or all products from a particular country [113]

eminent domain Governmental right to claim private land for public use after paying owners fair prices [65]

emotional motives Reasons for purchasing a product that are based on nonobjective factors [344]

employee stock ownership plan (ESOP) Arrangement in which a corporation holds its own stock in trust for its employees, who gradually receive ownership of the stock and control its voting rights [41]

entrepreneur Businessperson who accepts both the risks and the opportunities involved in creating and operating a new business venture [183]

environmental analysis Process of scanning the business environment for threats and opportunities [132]

equal employment opportunity Legally mandated nondiscrimination in employment on the basis of race, creed, sex, or national origin [239]

equity financing Use of common stock and/or retained earnings to raise long-term funding [475]

equity theory Theory of motivation holding that people evaluate their treatment by employers relative to the treatment of others [213]

ethical behavior Behavior conforming to generally accepted social norms concerning beneficial and harmful actions [77]

ethics Beliefs about what is right and wrong or good and bad in actions that affect others [77]

European Union (EU) Agreement among major Western European nations to eliminate or make uniform most trade barriers affecting group members [69]

exchange rate Rate at which the currency of one nation can be exchanged for the currency of another country [102]

expectancy theory Theory of motivation holding that people are motivated to work toward rewards that they want and that they believe they have a reasonable chance of obtaining [212]

expense item Relatively inexpensive industrial product purchased and consumed rapidly and regularly [356]

expert system Form of artificial intelligence that attempts to imitate the behavior of human experts in a particular field [311]

export Product made or grown domestically but shipped and sold abroad [98]

exporter Firm that distributes and sells products to one or more foreign countries [107]

express authority Agent's authority, derived from written agreement, to bind a principal to a certain course of action [66]

express warranty Warranty whose terms are specifically stated by the seller [66]

external environment Outside factors that influence marketing programs by posing opportunities or threats [330]

factors of production Resources used in the production of goods and services-natural resources, labor, capital, and entrepreneurs [2]

factory outlet Bargain retailer owned by the manufacturer whose products it sells [391]

Fair Labor Standards Act (1938) Federal law setting minimum wage and maximum number of hours in the workweek [249]

fax machine Machine that can transmit copies of documents over telephone lines [311]

Federal Deposit Insurance Corporation (FDIC) Federal agency that guarantees the safety of bank deposits up to $100,000 [425]

Federal Reserve System (the Fed) The central bank of the United States, which acts as the government's bank, services member commercial banks, and controls the nation's money supply [425]

finance (or corporate finance) Activities concerned with determining a firm's long-term investments, obtaining the funds to pay for them, conducting the firm's everyday financial activities, and managing the firm's risks [471]

finance company Nondeposit institution that specializes in making loans to businesses and consumers [422]

financial accounting system Field of accounting concerned with external users of a company's financial information [293]

financial manager Manager responsible for planning and controlling the acquisition and dispersal of a firm's financial resources [471]

financial plan A firm's strategies for reaching some future financial position [472]

financial statement Any of several types of reports summarizing a company's financial status to aid in managerial decision making [299]

first-line managers Managers responsible for supervising the work of employees [138]

fiscal policies Government economic policies that determine how the government collects and spends its revenues [17]

fiscal year Twelve-month period designated for annual financial reporting purposes [296]

fixed asset Asset with long-term use or value, such as land, buildings, and equipment [300]

fixed cost Cost unaffected by the quantity of a product produced or sold [362]

flextime programs Method of increasing job satisfaction by allowing workers to adjust work schedules on a daily or weekly basis [219]

float Amount of checks written but not yet cleared through the Federal Reserve [427]

franchise Arrangement in which a buyer (franchisee) purchases the right to sell the good or service of the seller (franchiser) [194]

free-rein style Managerial style in which managers typically serve as advisers to subordinates who are allowed to make decisions [222]

freight forwarder Transporting company that leases bulk space from other carriers to be resold to firms making smaller shipments [399]

full-service merchant wholesaler Merchant wholesaler that provides credit, marketing, and merchandising services in addition to traditional buying and selling services [386]

functional departmentalization Departmentalization according to functions or activities [159]

functional organization Form of business organization in which authority is determined by the relationships between group functions and activities [165]

futures contract Agreement to purchase specified amounts of a commodity at a given price on a set future date [454]

gain-sharing plan Incentive program for distributing bonuses to employees whose performances improve productivity [237]

General Agreement on Tariffs and Trade (GATT) International trade agreement to encourage the multilateral reduction or elimination of trade barriers [68]

general partnership Business with two or more owners who share in both the operation of the firm and in financial responsibility for its debts [32]

generally accepted accounting principles (GAAP) Accepted rules and procedures governing the content and form of financial reports [295]

geographic departmentalization Departmentalization according to areas served by a business [159]

geographic variables Geographical units that may be considered in developing a segmentation strategy [339]

globalization Process by which the world economy is becoming a single interdependent system [98]

goal Objective that a business hopes and plans to achieve [129]

goods production Business operations that create tangible products [264]

goodwill Amount paid for an existing business above the value of its other assets [300]

government bond Bond issued by the federal government [451]

gross domestic product (GDP) The value of all goods and services produced in a year by a nation's economy through domestic factors of production [14]

gross national product (GNP) The value of all goods and services produced by an economic system in one year regardless of when the factors of production are located [14]

gross profit (or gross margin) Revenues from goods sold minus cost of goods sold [301]

group life insurance Insurance underwritten for a group as a whole rather than for each individual in it [481]

growth Increase in the amount of goods and services produced by a nation's resources [12]

guaranteed loans program Program in which the SBA guarantees to repay 75–85 percent of small business commercial loans up to $750,000 [191]

Hawthorne effect Tendency for productivity to increase when workers believe they are receiving special attention from management [210]

health insurance Insurance covering losses resulting from medical and hospital expenses as well as income lost from injury or disease [481]

health maintenance organization (HMO) Organized health care system providing comprehensive care in return for fixed membership fees [482]

hierarchy of human needs model Theory of motivation describing five levels of human needs and arguing that basic needs must be fulfilled before people work to satisfy higher-level needs [211]

high-contact system Level of service-customer contact in which the customer receives the service as part of the system [267]

hub Central distribution outlet that controls all or most of a firm's distribution activities [400]

human relations Interactions between employers and employees and their attitudes toward one another [206]

human relations skills Skills in understanding and getting along with people [141]

human resource management Development and administration of programs to enhance the quality and performance of a company's workforce [232]

human resource managers Managers responsible for hiring, training, evaluating, and compensating employees [232]

hypermarket Very large product-line retailer carrying a wide variety of unrelated products [389]

immediate participation loans program Program in which small businesses are loaned funds put up jointly by banks and the SBA [192]

implied authority Agent's authority, derived from business custom, to bind a principal to a certain course of action [66]

implied warranty Warranty, dictated by law, based on the principle that products should fulfill advertised promises and serve the purposes for which they are manufactured and sold [67]

import Product made or grown abroad but sold domestically [98]

importer Firm that buys products in foreign markets and then imports them for resale in its home country [107]

incentive program Special compensation program designed to motivate high performance [236]

income statement (or profit-and-loss statement) Financial statement listing a firm's annual revenues, expenses, and profit or loss [301]

independent agent Foreign individual or organization that agrees to represent an exporter's interests [109]

individual retirement account (IRA) Tax-deferred pension fund with which wage earners supplement other retirement funds [423]

industrial distribution Network of channel members involved in the flow of manufactured goods to industrial customers [384]

industrial goods Products purchased by companies to produce other products [328]

industrial market Organizational market consisting of firms that buy goods that are either converted into products or used during production [345]

Industrial Revolution Major mid-eighteenth-century change in production characterized by a shift to the factory system, mass production, and the specialization of labor [28]

inelastic demand Demand for industrial products that is not largely affected by price changes [347]

inflation Phenomenon of widespread price increases throughout an economic system [11]

informal organization Network, unrelated to the firm's formal authority structure, of everyday social interactions among company employees [170]

information The useful interpretation of data [307]

information managers Managers responsible for designing and implementing systems to gather, organize, and distribute information [306]

insider trading Illegal practice of using special knowledge about a firm for profit or gain [462]

institutional investors Large investors, such as mutual funds and pension funds, that purchase large blocks of corporate stock [41]

institutional market Organizational market consisting of such nongovernmental buyers of goods and services as hospitals, churches, museums, and charitable organizations [346]

insurance company Nondeposit institution that invests funds collected as premiums charged for insurance coverage [422]

intangible asset Nonphysical asset, such as a patent or trademark, that has economic value in the form of expected benefit [300]

intangible personal property Property that cannot be seen but that exists by virtue of written documentation [63]

intellectual property Property created through a person's creative activities [63]

intentional tort Tort resulting from the deliberate actions of a party [60]

intermediary Individual or firm that helps to distribute a product [382]

intermediate goals Goals set for a period of one to five years into the future [131]

intermodal transportation Combined use of several different modes of transportation [399]

international competition Competitive marketing of domestic products against foreign products [334]

international firm Firm that conducts a significant portion of its business in foreign countries [108]

international law Set of cooperative agreements and guidelines established by countries to govern actions of individuals, businesses, and nations [68]

international organizational structures Approaches to organizational structure developed in response to the need to manufacture, purchase, and sell in global markets [169]

Internet Global data communications network serving thousands of computers with information on a wide array of topics and providing communications flows among certain private networks [312]

intranet Private network of internal Web sites and other sources of information available to a company's employees [313]

intrapreneuring Process of creating and maintaining the innovation and flexibility of a small business environment within the confines of a large organization [171]

inventory Materials and goods which are held by a company but which will be sold within the year [472]

inventory control In materials management, receiving, storing, handling, and counting of all raw materials, partly finished goods, and finished goods [276]; warehouse operation that tracks inventory on hand and ensures that an adequate supply is in stock at all times [397]

inventory turnover ratio Activity ratio measuring the average number of times that inventory is sold and restocked during the year [305]

investment bank Financial institution engaged in issuing and reselling new securities [442]

involuntary bankruptcy Bankruptcy proceedings initiated by the creditors of an indebted individual or organization [67]

job analysis Evaluation of the duties and qualities required by a job [232]

job description Outline of the objectives, tasks, and responsibilities of a job [232]

job enrichment Method of increasing job satisfaction by adding one or more motivating factors to job activities [218]

job redesign Method of increasing job satisfaction by designing a more satisfactory fit between workers and their jobs [218]

job relatedness Principle that all employment decisions should be based on the requirements of the jobs in question [232]

job satisfaction Degree of enjoyment that people derive from performing their jobs [206]

job specialization The process of identifying the specific jobs that need to be done and designating the people who will perform them [157]

job specification Description of the skills, education, and experience required by a job [232]

joint venture (or strategic alliance) Collaboration between two or more organizations on an enterprise [41]

journal Chronological record of a firm's financial transactions, including a brief description of each [296]

just-in-time (JIT) production system Production method that brings together all materials and parts needed at each production stage at the precise moment at which they are required [277]

Keogh plan Tax-deferred pension plan for the self-employed [423]

labor (or human resources) The physical and mental capabilities of people as they contribute to economic production [2]

labor union Group of individuals working together formally to achieve shared job-related goals [245]

Labor-Management Relations Act (Taft-Hartley Act) (1947) Federal law defining certain union practices as unfair and illegal [249]

Labor-Management Reporting and Disclosure Act (Landrum-Griffin Act) (1959) Federal law imposing regulations on internal unions procedures, including elections of national leaders and filing of financial-disclosure statements [250]

law of demand Principle that buyers will purchase (demand) more of a product as its price drops and less as its price increases [5]

law of supply Principle that producers will offer (supply) more of a product for sale as its price rises and less as its price drops [5]

laws Codified rules of behavior enforced by a society [54]

leadership Process of motivating others to work to meet specific objectives [221]

ledger Record, divided into accounts and usually compiled on a monthly basis, containing summaries of all journal transactions [296]

letter of credit Bank promise, issued for a buyer, to pay a designated firm a certain amount of money if specified conditions are met [423]

liability Debt owed by a firm to an outside organization or individual [297]

liability insurance Insurance covering losses resulting from damage to people or property when the insured is judged responsible [480]

licensed brand Brand-name product for whose name the seller has purchased the right from an organization or individual [359]

licensing arrangement Arrangement in which firms choose foreign individuals or organizations to manufacture or market their products in another country [109]

life insurance Insurance paying benefits to the policyholder's survivors [481]

limit order Order authorizing the purchase of a stock only if its price is equal to or less than a specified amount [459]

limited liability Legal principle holding investors liable for a firm's debts only to the limits of their personal investments in it [36]

limited-function merchant wholesaler Merchant wholesaler that provides a limited range of services [386]

line authority Organizational structure in which authority flows in a direct chain of command from the top of the company to the bottom [163]

line department Department directly linked to the production and sales of a specific product [163]

line of credit Standing arrangement in which a lender agrees to make available a specified amount of funds upon the borrower's request [163]

liquidity Ease with which an asset can be converted into cash [300]

liquidity ratio Solvency ratio measuring a firm's ability to pay its immediate debts [303]

load fund Mutual fund in which investors are charged sales commissions when they buy in or sell out [453]

local development companies (LDCs) program Program in which the SBA works with local for-profit or nonprofit organizations seeking to boost a community's economy [192]

local content law Law requiring that products sold in a particular country be at least partly made there [114]

lockout Management tactic whereby workers are denied access to their workplace [251]

long-term goals Goals set for extended periods of time, typically five years or more into the future [131]

long-term liability Debt that is not due for at least a year [301]

low-contact system Level of service-customer contact in which the customer need not be a part of the system to receive the service [268]

M-1 Measure of the money supply that includes only the most liquid (spendable) forms of money [415]

M-2 Measure of the money supply that includes all the components of M-1 plus forms of money that can easily be converted into spendable form [417]

mail order (or catalog marketing) Nonstore retailing in which customers place orders for catalog merchandise received through the mail [393]

management Process of planning, organizing, directing, and controlling an organization's resources in order to achieve its goals [136]

management by objectives (MBO) Set of procedures involving both managers and subordinates in setting goals and evaluating progress [215]

management consultant Independent outside specialist hired to help managers solve business problems [192]

management information system (MIS) System for transforming data into information that can be used in decision making [307]

managerial (or management) accounting Field of accounting that serves internal users of a company's financial information [293]

managerial style Pattern of behavior that a manager exhibits in dealing with subordinates [222]

margin Percentage of the total sales price that a buyer must put up to place an order for stock or futures contracts [454]

market Mechanism for exchange between buyers and sellers of a particular good or service [4]

market economy Economy in which individuals control production and allocation decisions through supply and demand [3]

market index Summary of price trends in a specific industry and/or the stock market as a whole [457]

market order Order to buy or sell a security at the market price prevailing at the time the order is placed [459]

market price (or equilibrium price) Profit-maximizing price at which the quantity of goods demanded and the quantity of goods supplied are equal [6]

market segmentation Process of dividing a market into categories of customer types [337]

market share Sales of an individual company as a percentage of total sales in a particular market [361]

market value Current price of a share of stock in the stock market [443]

marketing The process of planning and executing the conception, pricing, promotion, and distribution of ideas, goods, and services to create exchanges that satisfy individual and organizational objectives [328]

marketing concept Idea that a business must focus on identifying and satisfying consumer wants in order to be profitable [30]

marketing mix The combination of product, pricing, promotion, and distribution strategies used to market products [334]

mark-up Amount added to a product's cost in order to sell it at a profit [362]

material requirements planning (MRP) Production control method in which a bill of materials is used to ensure that the right amounts of materials are delivered to the right place at the right time [277]

materials handling Warehouse operation involving the transportation, arrangement, and orderly retrieval of goods in inventory [397]

materials management Planning, organizing, and controlling the flow of materials from design through distribution of finished goods [276]

matrix structure Organizational structure in which teams are formed and team members report to two or more managers [168]

media mix Combination of advertising media chosen to carry messages about a product [369]

mediation Method of resolving a labor dispute in which a third party advises on, but does not impose, a settlement [252]

merchandise inventory Cost of merchandise that has been acquired for sale to customers and that is still on hand [300]

merchant wholesaler Independent wholesaler that takes legal possession of goods produced by a variety of manufacturers and then resells them to other businesses [386]

merger The union of two corporations to form a new corporation [39]

merit salary system Incentive program linking compensation to performance in non sales jobs [236]

middle managers Managers responsible for implementing the strategies, policies, and decisions made by top managers [138]

minority enterprise small business investment company (MESBIC) Federally sponsored company that specializes in financing minority-owned and -operated businesses [191]

mission statement Organization's statement of how it will achieve its purpose in the environment in which it conducts its business [130]

mixed market economy Economic system featuring characteristics of both planned and market economies [4]

monetary policies Government economic policies that determine the size of a nation's money supply; policies by which the Federal Reserve manages the nation's money supply and interest rates [18]

money Any object that is portable, divisible, durable, and stable and that serves as a medium of exchange, a store of value, and a unit of account [414]

money market mutual fund Fund of short-term, low-risk financial securities purchased with the assets of investor-owners pooled by a nonbank institution [418]

monopolistic competition Market or industry characterized by a large number of buyers and a relatively large number of sellers trying to differentiate their products from those of competitors [10]

monopoly Market or industry in which there is only one producer, which can therefore set the prices of its products [10]

morale Overall attitude that employees have toward their workplace [206]

motivation The set of forces that cause people to behave in certain ways [208]

multinational firm Firm that designs, produces, and markets products in many nations [109]

municipal bond Bond issued by a state or local government [452]

mutual fund Company that pools investments from individuals and organizations to purchase a portfolio of stocks, bonds, and short-term securities [453]

mutual savings bank Financial institution whose depositors are owners sharing in its profits [422]

National Association of Securities Dealers Automated Quotation (NASDAQ) system Organization of over-the-counter dealers who own, buy, and sell their own securities over a network of electronic communications [450]

national bank Commercial bank chartered by the federal government [420]

national brand Brand-name product produced by, widely distributed by, and carrying the name of a manufacturer [359]

national debt Total amount that a nation owes its creditors [16]

National Labor Relations Act (Wagner Act) (1935) Federal law protecting the rights of workers to form unions, bargain collectively, and engage in strikes to achieve their goals [249]

National Labor Relations Board (NLRB) Federal agency established by the National Labor Relations Act to enforce its provisions [249]

natural monopoly Industry in which one company can most efficiently supply all needed goods or services [10]

natural resources Materials supplied by nature—for example, land, water, mineral deposits, and trees [3]

negligence Conduct falling below legal standards for protecting others against unreasonable risk [61]

net income (or net profit or net earnings) Gross profit minus operating expenses and income taxes [302]

networking Interactions among businesspeople for the purpose of discussing mutual problems and opportunities and perhaps pooling resources [193]

no-load fund Mutual fund in which investors pay no sales commissions when they buy in or sell out [453]

Norris-La Guardia Act (1932) Federal law limiting the ability of courts to issue injunctions prohibiting certain union activities [249]

North American Free Trade Agreement (NAFTA) Agreement to gradually eliminate tariffs and other trade barriers between the United States, Canada, and Mexico [68]

Occupational Safety and Health Administration (OSHA) Federal agency that sets and enforces guidelines for protecting workers from unsafe conditions and potential health hazards in the workplace [241]

odd lot Purchase or sale of stock in fractions of round lots [459]

odd-even pricing Psychological pricing tactic based on the premise that customers prefer prices not stated in even dollar amounts [365]

off-price store Bargain retailer that buys excess inventories from high-quality manufacturers and sells them at discounted prices [391]

off-the-job-training Training conducted in a controlled environment away from the work site [234]

oligopoly Market or industry characterized by a handful of (generally large) sellers with the power to influence the prices of their products [10]

on-the-job training Training, sometimes informal, conducted while an employee is at work [234]

open promotion system System by which employees apply, test, and interview for available jobs, requirements of which are posted [234]

open-book credit Form of trade credit in which sellers ship merchandise on faith that payment will be forthcoming [473]

open-market operations The Federal Reserve's sales and purchases of U.S. government securities in the open market [429]

operating expenses Costs, other than the cost of goods sold, incurred in producing a good or service [302]

operating income Gross profit minus operating expenses [302]

operational plans Plans setting short-term targets for daily, weekly, or monthly performance [135]

operations control Process of monitoring production performance by comparing results with plans [275]

operations (or production) management Systematic direction and control of the processes that transform resources into finished products [266]

operations managers Managers responsible for production, inventory, and quality control [266]

operations process Set of methods and technologies used in the production of a good or service [267]

organization chart Diagram depicting a company's structure and showing employees where they fit into its operations [156]

organizational analysis Process of analyzing a firm's strengths and weaknesses [133]

organizational structure Specification of the jobs to be done within an organization and the ways in which they relate to one another [154]

organizing Management process of determining how best to arrange an organization's resources and activities into a coherent structure [137]

over-the-counter (OTC) market Organization of securities dealers formed to trade stock outside the formal institutional setting of the organized stock exchanges [450]

owner's equity Amount of money that owners would receive if they sold all of a firm's assets and paid all of its liabilities [297]

packaging Physical container in which a product is sold, advertised, and/or protected [360]

paid-in capital Additional money, above proceeds from stock sale, paid directly to a firm by its owners [301]

par value Face value of a share of stock, set by the issuing company's board of directors [443]

participative management and empowerment Method of increasing job satisfaction by giving employees a voice in the management of their jobs and the company [215]

patent Exclusive legal right to use and license a manufactured item or substance, manufacturing process, or object design [65]

pay-for-knowledge plan Incentive program to encourage employees to learn new skills or become proficient at different jobs [237]

pay-for-performance (or variable pay) Individual incentive that rewards a manager for especially productive output [237]

penetration pricing Setting the initial price low in order to establish a new product in the market [364]

pension fund Nondeposit pool of funds managed to provide retirement income for its members [422]

performance appraisal Evaluation, often in writing, of an employee's job performance [234]

performance quality The performance features offered by a product [279]

person-job matching Process of matching the right person to the right job [232]

personal selling Promotional tool in which a salesperson communicates one on one with potential customers [371]

physical distribution Movement of a product from manufacturer to consumer [396]

picketing Labor action in which workers publicize their grievances at the entrance to an employer's facility [251]

planned economy Economy that relies on a centralized government to control all or most factors of production and to make all or most production and allocation decisions [3]

planning Management process of determining what an organization needs to do and how best to get it done [136]

pledging accounts receivable Using accounts receivable as loan collateral [474]

point-of-purchase (POP) display Sales promotion technique in which product displays are located in certain areas to stimulate purchase [373]

point-of-sale (POS) terminal Electronic device that allows customers to pay for retail purchases with debit cards [431]

positioning Process of establishing an identifiable product image in the minds of consumers [368]

preferred provider organization (PPO) Arrangement whereby selected professional providers offer services at reduced rates and permit thorough review of their service recommendations [482]

preferred stock Stock that guarantees its holders fixed dividends and priority claims over assets but no corporate voting rights [38]

premium Fee paid by a policyholder for insurance coverage [373]; sales promotion technique in which offers of free or reduced-price items are used to stimulate purchase [480]

prepaid expense Expense, such as prepaid rent, that is paid before the upcoming period in which it is due [300]

price leader Dominant firm that establishes product prices that other companies follow [364]

price lining Setting a limited number of prices for certain categories of products [365]

price skimming Setting the initial price high enough to cover new product costs and generate a profit [364]

price-earnings ratio Current price of a stock divided by the firm's current annual earnings per share [456]

pricing Process of determining what a company will receive in exchange for its products [360]

pricing objectives Goals that producers hope to attain in pricing products for sale [361]

primary securities market Market in which new stocks and bonds are bought and sold [442]

prime rate Interest rate available to a bank's most creditworthy customers [421]

principal Individual or organization authorizing an agent to act on its behalf [65]

private brand (or private label) Brand-name product that a wholesaler or retailer has commissioned from a manufacturer [360]

private carrier Manufacturer or retailer that maintains its own transportation system [400]

private corporation Corporation whose stock is held by only a few people and is not available for sale to the general public [35]

private enterprise Economic system that allows individuals to pursue their own interests without undue governmental restriction [8]

private property rights The right to buy, own, use, and sell almost any form of property [8]

private warehouse Warehouse owned by and providing storage for a single company [396]

privatization Process of converting government enterprises into privately owned companies [4]

process departmentalization Departmentalization according to production process used to create a good or service [159]

process layout Spatial arrangement of production activities that groups equipment and people according to function [272]

product Good, service, or idea that is marketed to fill consumer needs and wants [335]

product departmentalization Departmentalization according to products being created [158]

product differentiation Creation of a product or product image that differs enough from existing products to attract consumers [335]

product layout Spatial arrangement of production activities designed to move resources through a smooth, fixed sequence of steps [272]

product liability tort Tort in which a company is responsible for injuries caused by its products [62]

product life cycle (PLC) Series of stages in a product's profit-producing life [357]

product line Group of similar products intended for a similar group of buyers that will use them in similar ways [357]

product mix Group of products that a firm makes available for sale [357]

product use variables Consumer characteristics based on the ways in which a product is used, the brand loyalty it enjoys, and the reasons for which it is purchased [342]

production era Period during the early twentieth century in which U.S. business focused primarily on improving productivity and manufacturing efficiency [29]

productivity Measure of economic growth that compares how much a system produces with the resources needed to produce it [14]

profit center Separate company unit responsible for its own costs and profits [157]

profit-sharing plan Incentive program for distributing bonuses to employees for company for profits above a certain level [237]

profitability ratio Financial ratio for measuring a firm's potential earnings [303]

profits The difference between a business's revenues and its expenses [2]

program trading Large purchase or sale of a group of stocks, often triggered by computerized trading programs that can be launched without human supervision or control [461]

promotion Aspect of the marketing mix concerned with the most effective techniques for selling a product [368]

promotional mix Combination of tools used to promote a product [369]

property Anything of value to which a person or business has sole right of ownership [62]

property insurance Insurance covering losses resulting from physical damage to or loss of the insured's real estate or personal property [481]

prospectus Registration statement filed with the SEC before the issuance of a new security [462]

protectionism Practice of protecting domestic business against foreign competition [114]

proxy Authorization granted by a shareholder for someone else to vote his or her shares [38]

psychographic variables Consumer characteristics, such as lifestyles, opinions, interests, and attitudes, that may be considered in developing a segmentation strategy [342]

psychological pricing Pricing tactic that takes advantage of the fact that consumers do not always respond rationally to stated prices [365]

public corporation Corporation whose stock is widely held and available for sale to the general public [35]

public relations Company-influenced publicity directed at building good relations with the public and dealing with unfavorable events [374]

public warehouse Independently owned and operated warehouse that stores goods for many firms [397]

publicity Promotional tool in which information about a company or product is transmitted by general mass media [374]

pull strategy Promotional strategy designed to appeal directly to customers, who will demand a product from retailers [369]

punitive damages Fines imposed over and above any actual losses suffered by a plaintiff [61]

pure competition Market or industry characterized by a large number of small firms producing an identical product [9]

pure risk Risk involving only the possibility of loss or no loss [478]

push strategy Promotional strategy designed to encourage wholesalers and/or retailers to market products to consumers [369]

quality A product's fitness for use; its success in offering features that consumers want [273]

quality control Management of the production process designed to manufacture goods or supply services that meet specific quality standards [277]

quality improvement team (or quality circle) TQM tool in which groups of employees work together as a team to improve quality [277]

quality ownership Principle of total quality management that holds that quality belongs to each person who creates it while performing a job [280]

quality reliability Consistency of a product's quality from unit to unit [279]

quality/cost study Method of improving quality by identifying current costs and areas with the greatest cost-savings potential [282]

quota Restriction on the number of products of a certain type that can be imported into a country [113]

rack jobber Limited-function merchant wholesaler that sets up and maintains display racks in retail stores [387]

rational motives Reasons for purchasing a product that are based on a logical evaluation of product attributes [344]

real gross national product Gross national product adjusted for inflation and changes in the value of a country's currency [14]

real-time (or on-line) processing Method of entering data and computer-processing them immediately [308]

recession Period characterized by decreases in employment, income, and production [12]

registered bond Bond bearing the name of the holder and registered with the issuing company [452]

regulatory (or administrative) law Law made by the authority of administrative agencies [54]

reinforcement Theory that behavior can be encouraged or discouraged by means of rewards or punishments [214]

relationship marketing Marketing strategy that emphasizes lasting relationships with customers and suppliers [328]

reseller market Organizational market consisting of intermediaries who buy and resell finished goods [346]

reserve requirement Percentage of deposits a bank must hold in cash or on deposit with the Federal Reserve [428]

responsibility Duty to perform an assigned task [161]

retailer   Intermediary that sells products directly to consumers [382]

retained earnings   Earnings retained by a firm for its use rather than paid as dividends [301]

return on investment (or **return on equity**)   Profitability ratio measuring income earned for each dollar invested [304]

revenues   Funds that flow into a business from the sale of goods or services [301]

reverse discrimination   Practice of discriminating against well-represented groups by overhiring members of underrepresented groups [239]

revolving credit agreement   Arrangement in which a lender agrees to make funds available on demand and on a continuing basis [474]

risk   Uncertainty about future events [478]

risk avoidance   Practice of avoiding risk by declining or ceasing to participate in an activity [479]

risk control   Practice of minimizing the frequency or severity of losses from risky activities [479]

risk management   Process of conserving the firm's earning power and assets by reducing the threat of losses due to uncontrollable events [478]

risk retention   Practice of covering a firm's losses with its own funds [479]

risk transfer   Practice of transferring a firm's risk to another firm [479]

risk-return relationship   Principle that, whereas safer investments tend to offer lower returns, riskier investments tend to offer higher returns [477]

round lot   Purchase or sale of stock in units of 100 shares [459]

royalty   Payment made to a license holder in return for the right to market the licenser's product [109]

salary   Compensation in the form of money paid for discharging the responsibilities of a job [236]

sales agent/broker   Independent intermediary that usually represents many manufacturers and sells to wholesalers, retailers, or both [384]

sales office   Office maintained by a manufacturer as a contact point with its customers [385]

sales promotion   Short-term promotional activity designed to stimulate consumer buying or cooperation from distributors and sales agents [371]

savings and loan association (S&L)   Financial institution accepting deposits and making loans primarily for home mortgages [422]

scrambled merchandising   Retail practice of carrying any product expected to sell well regardless of a store's original product offering [389]

secondary securities market   Market in which stocks and bonds are traded [442]

secured bond   Bond backed by pledges of assets to the bondholders [452]

secured loan   Loan for which the borrower must provide collateral [473]

securities   Stocks and bonds representing secured, or asset-based, claims by investors against issuers [442]

Securities and Exchange Commission (SEC)   Federal agency that administers U.S. securities laws to protect the investing public and maintain smoothly functioning markets [462]

securities investment dealer (broker)   Nondeposit institution that buys and sells stocks and bonds both for investors and for its own accounts [422]

selective credit controls   Federal Reserve authority to set margin requirements for consumer stock purchases and credit rules for other consumer purchases [430]

Service Corps of Retired Executives (SCORE)   SBA program in which retired executives work with small businesses on a volunteer basis [192]

service operations   Business activities that provide tangible and intangible services [264]

services   Intangible products, such as time, expertise, or an activity, that can be purchased [328]

shopping good/service   Moderately expensive, infrequently purchased product [356]

short sale   Stock sale in which an investor borrows securities from a broker to be sold and then replaced at a specified future date [461]

short-term goals   Goals set for the very near future, typically less than one year [131]

shortage   Situation in which quantity demanded exceeds quantity supplied [8]

small business   Independently owned and managed business that does not dominate its market [178]

Small Business Administration (SBA)   Federal agency charged with assisting small businesses [178]

Small Business Development Center (SBDC)   SBA program designed to consolidate information from various disciplines and make it available to small businesses [193]

Small Business Institute (SBI)   SBA program in which college and university students and instructors work with small businesspeople to help solve specific problems [193]

smart card   Credit card-sized computer that can be programmed with "electronic money" [432]

social audit   Systematic analysis of a firm's success in using funds earmarked for meeting its social responsibility goals [90]

social responsibility   The attempt of a business to balance its commitments to groups and individuals in its environment, including customers, other businesses, employees, and investors [79]

social obligation approach   Approach to social responsibility by which a company meets only minimum legal requirements in its commitments to groups and individuals in its social environment [89]

social reaction approach   Approach to social responsibility by which a company, if specifically asked to do so, exceeds legal minimums in its commitments to groups and individuals in its social environment [89]

social response approach   Approach to social responsibility by which a company actively seeks opportunities to contribute to the well-being of groups and individuals in its social environment [89]

socialism   Planned economic system in which the government owns and operates only selected major sources of production [4]

sole proprietorship   Business owned and usually operated by one person who is responsible for all of its debts [31]

solvency ratio   Financial ratio, both short- and long-term, for estimating the risk in investing in a firm [303]

span of control   Number of people supervised by one manager [162]

specialty good/service   Expensive, rarely purchased product [356]

specialty store   Small retail store carrying one product line or category of related products [390]

speculative risk   Risk involving the possibility of gain or loss [478]

stability   Condition in which the balance between the money available in an economy and the goods produced in it are growing at about the same rate [11]

staff authority   Authority that is based on expertise and that usually involves advising line managers [164]

staff members   Advisers and counselors who aid line departments in making decisions but do not have the authority to make final decisions [164]

Standard & Poor's Composite Index   Market index based on the performance of 400 industrial firms, 40 utilities, 40 financial institutions, and 20 transportation companies [459]

standardization   Use, where possible, of standard and uniform components in the production process [276]

state bank   Commercial bank chartered by an individual state [420]

statistical process control (SPC)   Evaluation methods that allow managers to analyze variations in a company's production activities [281]

statutory law   Law created by constitutions or by federal, state, or local legislative acts [54]

stock   A share of ownership in a corporation [37]

stock exchange   Organization of individuals formed to provide an institutional setting in which stock can be traded [448]

stockholder (or **shareholder**)   An owner of shares of stock in a corporation [37]

stop order   Order authorizing the sale of a stock if its price falls to or below a specified level [459]

storage warehouse   Warehouse providing storage for extended periods of time [397]

strategic alliance (or **joint venture**)   Arrangement in which a company finds a foreign partner to contribute approximately half of the resources needed to establish and operate a new business in the partner's country [109]

strategic goals   Long-term goals derived directly from a firm's mission statement [132]

strategic plans   Plans reflecting decisions about resource allocations, company priorities, and steps needed to meet strategic goals [134]

strategy formulation   Creation of a broad program for defining and meeting an organization's goals [132]

strict product liability   Principle that liability can result not from a producer's negligence but from a defect in the product itself [62]

strike   Labor action in which employees temporarily walk off the job and refuse to work [251]

strikebreaker   Worker hired as permanent or temporary replacement for a striking employee [252]

subsidy   Government payment to help a domestic business compete with foreign firms [114]

substitute product   Product that is dissimilar to those of competitors but that can fulfill the same need [334]

supermarket   Large product-line retailer offering a variety of food and food-related items in specialized departments [389]

supply   The willingness and ability of producers to offer a good or service for sale [5]

supply curve   Graph showing how many units of a product will be supplied (offered for sale) at different prices [6]

surplus   Situation in which quantity supplied exceeds quantity demanded [8]

T-account   Bookkeeping format for recording transactions that takes the shape of a *T* whose vertical line divides the account into debits (left side) and credits (right side) [298]

tactical plans   Generally short-range plans concerned with implementing specific aspects of a company's strategic plans [135]

tangible personal property   Any movable item that can be owned, bought, sold, or leased [63]

tangible real property   Land and anything attached to it [62]

target market   Group of people that has similar wants and needs and that can be expected to show interest in the same products [337]

tariff   Tax levied on imported products [113]

technical skills   Skills needed to perform specialized tasks [140]

telecommuting   Form of flextime that allows people to perform some or all of a job away from standard office settings [220]

telemarketing   Nonstore retailing in which the telephone is used to sell directly to consumers [394]

Theory X   Theory of motivation holding that people are naturally irresponsible and uncooperative [210]

Theory Y   Theory of motivation holding that people are naturally responsible, growth-oriented, self-motivated, and interested in being productive [211]

time deposit   Bank funds that cannot be withdrawn without notice or transferred by check [418]

time-management skills   Skills associated with the productive use of time [142]

top managers   Managers responsible to the board of directors and stockholders for a firm's overall performance and effectiveness [138]

tort   Civil injury to people, property, or reputation for which compensation must be paid [60]

total quality management (TQM) (or quality assurance)   The sum of all activities involved in getting quality products into the marketplace [279]

trade credit   Granting of credit by one firm to another [473]

trade deficit   Situation in which a country's imports exceed its exports, creating a negative balance of trade [101]

trade show   Sales promotion technique in which various members of an industry gather to display, demonstrate, and sell products [373]

trade surplus   Situation in which a country's exports exceed its imports, creating a positive balance of trade [101]

trademark   Exclusive legal right to use a brand name or symbol [63]

transfer of title   Legal transfer of personal property

trial court   General court that hears cases not specifically assigned to another court [58]

trust services   Bank management of an individual's investments, payments, or estate [423]

two-factor theory   Theory of motivation holding that job satisfaction depends on two types of factors, hygiene and motivating [212]

unemployment   Level of joblessness among people actively seeking work [12]

Uniform Commercial Code (UCC)   Body of standardized laws governing the rights of buyers and sellers in transactions [66]

unlimited liability   Legal principle holding owners responsible for paying off all debts of a business [32]

unsecured loan   Loan for which collateral is not required [474]

utility   A product's ability to satisfy a human want [266]

variable cost   Cost that changes with the quantity of a product produced or sold [362]

venture capital   Outside equity financing provided in return for part ownership of the borrowing firm [471]

vestibule training   Off-the-job training conducted in a simulated environment [234]

video marketing   Nonstore retailing to consumers via standard and cable television [393]

voice mail   Computer-based system for receiving and delivering incoming telephone calls [311]

voluntary arbitration   Method of resolving a labor dispute in which both parties agree to submit to the judgment of a neutral party [252]

voluntary bankruptcy   Bankruptcy proceedings initiated by an indebted individual or organization [67]

wages   Compensation in the form of money paid for time worked [236]

warehouse club (or wholesale club)   Bargain retailer offering large discounts on brand-name merchandise to customers who have paid annual membership fees [391]

warehousing   Physical distribution operation concerned with the storage of goods [396]

warranty   Seller's promise to stand by its products or services if a problem occurs after the sale [66]

whistleblower   Employee who detects and tries to put an end to a company's unethical, illegal, or socially irresponsible actions by publicizing them [85]

wholesaler   Intermediary that sells products to other businesses for resale to final consumers [382]

word-processing program   Application program that allows computers to store, edit, and print letters and numbers for documents created by users [308]

work sharing (or job sharing)   Method of increasing job satisfaction by allowing two or more people to share a single full-time job [219]

work force diversity   Range of workers' attitudes, values, and behaviors that differ by gender, race, and ethnicity [242]

workers' compensation coverage   Coverage provided by a firm to employees for medical expenses, loss of wages, and rehabilitation costs resulting from job-related injuries or disease [481]

worker's compensation insurance   Legally required insurance for compensating workers injured on the job [238]

working capital   Liquid current assets out of which a firm can pay current debts [472]

World Wide Web   Subsystem of computers providing access to the Internet and offering multimedia and linking capabilities [312]

■ NOTES, SOURCES, AND CREDITS

Reference Notes

Chapter 1

[1]John Huey, "Waking Up to the New Economy," *Fortune*, June 27, 1994, 36–46.

[2]Carl E. Case and Ray C. Fair, *Principles of Economics*, 4th ed. (Upper Saddle River, NJ: Prentice Hall, 1996), 75.

[3]Howard W. French, "On the Street, Cubans Fondly Embrace Capitalism," *New York Times*, February 3, 1994, p. A4; Tim Golden, "Cubans Get a Taste of Capitalism," *New York Times*, September 26, 1994, A8.

[4]Joyce Barnathan et al., "Destination Vietnam," *Business Week*, February 14, 1994, 26–27; Seth Mydans, "Hanoi Seeks Western Cash but Not Consequences," *New York Times*, April 8, 1996, A3; Pete Engardio with Bruce Einhorn, "Rising from the Ashes," *Business Week*, May 23, 1994, 44–46+; Malcolm W. Browne, "First U.S. Trade Exhibit Is Held in Hanoi," *New York Times*, April 24, 1994, Sec. 3, 18.

[5]Nathaniel C. Nash, "Privatizing in Hungary: A Door Reopens," *New York Times*, October 17, 1995, D1, D6; Jane Perlez, "Post-Marxist Hungarian Bus Maker Takes to Capitalist Road," *New York Times*, August 10, 1995, D3.

[6]"Platinum Soars amid Signs of Demand by Auto Makers," *New York Times*, April 30, 1994, 49; Susan E. Kuhn, "Profiting from Platinum," *Fortune*, August 8, 1994, 30; Kenneth Gooding, "Platinum Price Hits 4 1/2-Year High," *Financial Times*, April 6, 1995, 27.

[7]Norman N. Scarborough and Thomas W. Zimmerer, *Effective Small Business Management*, 5th ed. (Upper Saddle River, NJ: Prentice Hall, 1996), 14.

[8]Christopher Farrell with Michael Mandel, "Why Are We So Afraid of Growth?" *Business Week*, May 16, 1994, 62–65+; Farrell, "The Triple Revolution," *Business Week*, November 18, 1994, 16–19+; Mike McNamee with Christopher Farrell, "The Great Growth Debate," *Business Week*, October 30, 1995, 160, 162; McNamee with Paul Magnusson, "Let's Get Growing," *Business Week*, July 8, 1996, 90–93+.

[9]Karen Pennar et al., "Economic Anxiety, *Business Week*, March 11, 1996, 50–53+; Louis Uchitelle, "The New Buzz: Growth Is Good," *New York Times*, June 18, 1996, D1, D22.

[10]E. Wayne Nafziger, *The Economics of Developing Countries*, 3rd ed. (Upper Saddle River, NJ: Prentice Hall, 1997), 12–21; Warren J. Keegan and F.H. Rolf Seringhaus, *Global Marketing Management* (Scarborough, Ontario: Prentice-Hall Canada, 1996), 69–80; Laxmi Nakarmi et al., "Global Hot Spots," *Business Week*, September 25, 1995, 116–120+.

[11]Case and Fair, *Principles of Economics*, 61–63, 570–71.

[12]Mike McNamee et al., "Dole's Gamble," *Business Week*, August 19, 1996, 28–34.

Chapter 2

[1]Thomas A. Stewart, "Welcome to the Revolution," *Fortune*, December 13, 1993, 66–68+.

[2]U.S. Bureau of the Census, *Statistical Abstract of the United States: 1995* (Washington, DC: 1995).

[3]See Norman N. Scarborough and Thomas W. Zimmerer, *Effective Small Business Management*, 5th ed. (Upper Saddle River, NJ: Prentice Hall, 1996), 123–127.

[4]Nancy K. Kubasek, Bartley A. Brennan, and M. Neil Browne, *The Legal Environment of Business: A Critical-Thinking Approach* (Upper Saddle River, NJ: Prentice Hall, 1996), 383.

[5]U.S. Bureau of the Census, *Statistical Abstract of the United States: 1995* (Washington, DC: 1995).

[6]*Fortune*, April 29, 1996, 260–264, F1–F19; Anne B. Fisher, "Creating Stockholder Wealth: Market Value Added," *Fortune*, December 11, 1995, 105–106.

[7]John W. Milligan, "The Rising Price of Shareholder Activism," *U.S. Banker*, June 1995, 28–31.

[8]Terence P. Paré, "The New Merger Boom," *Fortune*, November 28, 1994, 95–96+; Stephanie Strom, "Mergers for Year Approach Record," *New York Times*, October 31, 1995, A1, D4.

[9]Bill Carter, "Suddenly, at ABC, the Future Is Now," *New York Times*, August 1, 1995, D1; Michael Oneal, "Disney's Kingdom," *Business Week*, August 14, 1995, 30–34.

[10]Susan Antilla, "New Tactics in Takeovers: Rich Bids and Quick Closes," *New York Times*, June 15, 1995, D1, D12; Judith H. Dobrzynski, "The Art of the Hostile Deal," *New York Times*, June 22, 1995, D1, D28.

[11]Edith Updike with Laxmi Nakarmi, "A Movable Feast for Mitsubishi," *Business Week*, August 28, 1995, 50–51.

[12]Edmund L. Andrews with Geraldine Fabrikant, "MCI and Murdoch to Join in Venture for Global Media," *New York Times*, May 11, 1995, A1, D11; Ronald Grover et al., "Man Buys World," *Business Week*, May 29, 1995, 26–29.

[13]Louis Uchitelle, "Downsizing Comes to Employee-Owned America," *New York Times*, July 7, 1996, Sec. 3, 3.

Chapter 3

[1]See Henry R. Cheesman, *Contemporary Business Law*, 2nd ed. (Upper Saddle River, NJ: Prentice Hall, 1997), 2–9.

[2]This section is based on Cheesman, *Contemporary Business Law*, 2–3.

[3]Nancy A. Kubasek, Bartley A. Brennan, and M. Neil Browne, *The Legal Environment of Business: A Critical-Thinking Approach* (Upper Saddle River, NJ: Prentice Hall, 1996), 125–127.

[4]See David P. Baron, *Business and Its Environment*, 2nd ed. (Upper Saddle River, NJ: Prentice Hall, 1996), 269–276.

[5]Jeffrey Goldberg, "Next Target: Nicotine," *New York Times Magazine*, August 4, 1996, 22–29+; Peter T. Kilborn, "Clinton Approves a Series of Curbs on Cigarette Ads," *New York Times*, August 24, 1996, 1, 8; John Carey with Lori Bongiorno and Mike France, "The Fire This Time," *Business Week*, August 12, 1996, 67–68; David Greising, "The Race around the FDA," *Business Week*, September 9, 1996, 39–40.

[6]Edmund L. Andrews, "Congress Votes to Reshape Communications Industry, Ending a Four-Year Struggle," *New York Times*, February 2, 1996, A1, D6; Catherine Arnst, "The Coming Telescramble," *Business Week*, April 8, 1996, 64–66; Andrews, "Outlook '96: Giving Business a Chance to Test the Wings of Deregulation," *New York Times*, January 2, 1996, C1, C13; Mark Lewyn, "Showtime for the Watchdog," *Business Week*, April 8, 1996, 86–87; Andrew Kupfer, "The Telecom Wars," *Fortune*, March 3, 1997, 136–138+.

[7]Christopher Farrell with Michael Mandel, "Why Are We So Afraid of Growth?" *Business Week*, May 16, 1994, 62–65+.

[8]Cheesman, *Contemporary Business Law*, 176–177, 190–202.

[9]Charles Bullard, "Lawyer Tells Jury to Find for Couple," *The Des Moines (Iowa) Register*, September 13, 1994, 4M.

[10]Keith Schneider, "Exxon Is Ordered to Pay $5 Billion for Alaska Spill," *New York Times*, September 17, 1994, 1, 10; Schneider, "Tenacious Lawyer Turns Exxon Spill into Pollution Case for the Ages," *New York Times*, September 9, 1994, B7; Agis Salpukas, "Exxon Is Accused of 'Astonishing Ruse' in Oil-Spill Trial," *New York Times*, June 14, 1996, D4.

[11]Linda Himelstein, "Putting Science on Trial," *Business Week*, August 14, 1995, 76–77.

[12]Neil Gross with Dori Jones Yang and Julia Flynn, "Seasick in Cyberspace," *Business Week*, July 10, 1995, 110–111.

[13]Linda Himelstein with Peter Galuszka and Julia Flynn, "Who Owns the Smirnoff Name?" *Business Week*, January 15, 1996, 70–71.

[14]Cheesman, *Contemporary Business Law*, 109–110.

[15]Peter Coy with John Carey and Neil Gross, "The Global Patent Race Picks Up Speed," *Business Week*, August 9, 1993, 57–62; Gross, "New Patent Office Pending," *Business Week*, October 23, 1995, 130.

[16]Saul Hansell, "Personal Bankruptcies Surging as Economy Hums," *New York Times*, August 25, 1996, Sec. 1, 1, 38.

[17]Sylvia Nasar, "GATT's Big Payoff for the U.S.," *New York Times*, December 19, 1993, Sec. 3, 7; Louis S. Richman, "What's Next after GATT's Victory?" *Fortune*, January 10, 1994, 66–70.

[18]Douglas Harbrecht et al., "What Has NAFTA Wrought? Plenty of Trade," *Business Week*, November 21, 1994, 48–49.

Chapter 4

[1] Diana B. Henriques with Dean Baquet, "A Rice Exporter's Cozy Link to U.S. Agency Reaps Profit," *New York Times*, October 11, 1993, A1, D3. Data from U.S. Commodity Credit Corp.

[2] See David P. Baron, *Business and Its Environment*, 2nd ed. (Upper Saddle River, NJ: Prentice Hall, 1996), 601–606.

[3] Eric Schine, "Rockwell: Explosive Woes," *Business Week*, August 21, 1995, 70–71.

[4] Frank B. Cross and Roger LeRoy Miller, West's *Legal Environment of Business: Texts, Cases, Ethical and Regulatory Issues*, 2nd ed. (St. Paul, MN: West, 1995), 34–35.

[5] Baron, *Business and Its Environment*, 609–611.

[6] Fraser P. Seitel, *The Practice of Public Relations*, 6th ed. (Upper Saddle River, NJ: Prentice Hall, 1995), 122–124.

[7] Russell Mitchell, "Managing by Values," *Business Week*, August 1, 1994, 46–52; David Sheff, "Levi's Changes Everything," *Fast Company*, June/July 1996, 65–69+; G. Pascal Zachary, "Exporting Rights: Levi Tries to Make Sure Contract Plants in Asia Treat Workers Well," *Wall Street Journal*, July 28, 1994, A1, A6.

[8] Willy Stern, "Static in Cincinnati," *Business Week*, November 6, 1995, 170–172+.

[9] John Holusha, "Paper Maker Turns a Cleaner Page," *New York Times*, October 20, 1993, D1, D5; "Still Worst in U.S., California Air Is at Cleanest Level in 40 Years," *New York Times*, October 31, 1996, A20.

[10] B. Drummond Ayres, Jr., "California Smog Cloud Is Cleaning Up Its Act," *New York Times*, November 3, 1995, A14.

[11] John Holusha, "Recycled Material Is Finding a New and Lucrative Market," *New York Times*, October 8, 1994, 1, 41. Data from Browning-Ferris Industries.

[12] Joseph Weber with John Carey, "Did Denture Creams Put Users at Risk?" *Business Week*, April 22, 1996, 92, 94+.

[13] Thomas J. Lueck, "Illegal Price-Fixing Charged in Danbury Hospital Lawsuit," *New York Times*, September 14, 1995, B6.

[14] Baron, *Business and Its Environment*, 644–646.

[15] Mark Maremount, "Public Company, Private Fiefdom?" *Business Week*, October 25, 1993, 108–110.

[16] See Dan G. Stone, *April Fools: An Insider's Account of the Rise and Collapse of Drexel Burnham* (New York: Warner, 1991); James B. Stewart, *Den of Thieves* (New York: Simon & Schuster, 1991).

Chapter 5

[1] Alan Farnham, "Global—Or Just Globaloney?" *Fortune*, June 27, 1994, 97–98+.

[2] For an overview, see Ricky W. Griffin and Michael Pustay, *International Business: A Managerial Perspective* (Reading, MA: Addison-Wesley, 1996).

[3] Bill Saporito, "Where the Global Action Is," *Fortune*, Autumn/Winter 1993, 62–65.

[4] John Tagliabue, "Coca-Cola Reaches into Impoverished Albania," *New York Times*, May 20, 1994, D1, D3; Karen Lowry Miller and Frank J. Comes with Peggy Simpson, "Poland: Rising Star of Europe," *Business Week*, December 4, 1995, 64–66+; Louis Kraar, "Daewoo's Daring Drive into Europe," *Fortune*, May 13, 1996, 145–146+; Jane Perlez, "European Beachhead for Korean Ambition," *New York Times*, July 24, 1996, D1, D19.

[5] Brenton R. Schlender et al., "Special Report/Pacific Rim: The Battle for Asia," *Fortune*, November 1, 1993, 126–127+; William J. Holstein, "Building the New Asia," *Business Week*, November 28, 1994, 62–66+; Joyce Barnathan with Pete Engardio and John Wizenburg, "Asia's New Giants," *Business Week*, November 27, 1995, 64–67+; Edward A. Gargan, "A Boom in Malaysia Reaches for the Sky," *New York Times*, February 2, 1996, D1, D4.

[6] Karl E. Case and Ray C. Fair, *Principles of Economics*, 4th ed. (Upper Saddle River, NJ: Prentice Hall, 1996), 908–913.

[7] Jeffrey Taylor and Neil Behrmann, "Coffee Prices Surge after Frost Hits Brazil," *Wall Street Journal*, June 28, 1994, C1, C16; Dori Jones Yang with Bill Hinchberger, "Trouble Brewing at the Coffee Bar," *Business Week*, August 1, 1994, 62; "Coffee Surges on New Worries about Cold Weather in Brazil," *New York Times*, May 18, 1995, D15.

[8] Andrew Pollack, "Japan Trade Surplus Shrinks for the First Time in Five Years," *New York Times*, January 24, 1996, A1, D18; Amy Borus with Edith Hill Updike and Keith Naughton, "This Trade Gap Ain't What It Used to Be," *Business Week*, March 18, 1996, 50; Robert D. Hershey, Jr., "China Has Become Chief Contributor to U.S. Trade Gap," *New York Times*, August 21, 1996, A1, D4.

[9] James Bennett, "A Stronger Yen Is Hurting Sales of Japan's Cars," *New York Times*, November 5, 1993, A1, D2; John Rossant with Julia Flynn, "The Yanks Are Buying, the Yanks Are Buying," *Business Week*, October 11, 1993, 51.

[10] Andrew Pollack, "Shellshocked by Yen, Companies in Japan Still Find Ways to Cope," *New York Times*, April 18, 1995, A1, D8; Dean Foust et al., "The Strong Dollar Giveth . . ." *Business Week*, April 29, 1996, 34–35; Edith Updike et al., "Japan's Auto Shock," *Business Week*, May 29, 1995, 44–47; Kathleen Kerwin, "Detroit Is Getting Sideswiped by the Yen," *Business Week*, November 11, 1996, 54.

[11] Andrew Pollack, "Drop in Yen's Value Heartens Japanese Exporters," *New York Times*, August 18, 1995, D3; Keith Bradsher, "U.S. Auto Makers Fear Edge Strong Dollar Gives Japanese," *New York Times*, February 2, 1996, D1, D3; Richard W. Stevenson, "Dollar's Strength Has U.S. Executives Grumbling," *New York Times*, July 10, 1996, D1, D7; Bradsher with Pollack, "Falling Yen Puts Car Makers in Japan in the Driver's Seat," *New York Times*, July 15, 1996, A1, D10.

[12] Rob Norton, "Strategies for the New Export Boom," *Fortune*, August 22, 1994, 124–127+.

[13] Robert D. Hershey Jr., "China Has Become Chief Contributor to U.S. Trade Gap," A1, D4.

[14] Geraldine Fabrikant, "Blockbuster Seeks to Flex Its Muscles Abroad," *New York Times*, October 23, 1995, D7; Patricia Sellers, "Wal-Mart's Big Man Puts Blockbuster on Fast-Forward," *Fortune*, November 25, 1996, 111–113.

[15] John Rockwell, "The New Colossus: American Culture as Power Export," *New York Times*, January 30, 1994, Sec. 2, 1, 30.

[16] Anthony DePalma, "G.M. Gives Mexico Its Own 'Chevy,'" *New York Times*, May 12, 1994, D1, D6; James B. Treece et al., "New Worlds to Conquer," *Business Week*, February 28, 1994, 50–52.

[17] Norton, "Strategies for the New Export Boom," 124–126, 130.

[18] Paul Lewis, "Multinationals Raised '95 Investment in Third World 13%," *New York Times*, March 13, 1996, D5.

[19] Norton, "Strategies for the New Export Boom," 127, 129.

[20] Tim Smart et al., "GE's Brave New World," *Business Week*, November 8, 1993, 64–70; Emily Thornton, "Thailand: Japan vs. the U.S.," *Fortune*, November 1, 1993, 145–146+; Joyce Barnathan et al., "Behind the Great Wall," *Business Week*, October 25, 1993, 42–43.

[21] Peter Koenig, "If Europe Is Dead, Why Is GE Investing Billions There?" *Fortune*, September 9, 1996, 114–118.

[22] John Rossant et al., "Embargo? What Embargo?" *Business Week*, March 20, 1995, 30–31.

[23] Geri Smith, "NAFTA: A Green Light for Red Tape," *Business Week*, July 25, 1994, 48.

Chapter 6

[1] David Kirkpatrick, "Fast Times at Compaq," *Fortune*, April 1, 1996, 121–123.

[2] Patricia Sellers, "Women, Sex, and Power," *Fortune*, August 5, 1996, 42–46+.

[3] Adam Bryant, "The Candid Mr. Fix-It of the Skies," *New York Times*, November 12, 1996, D1, D22; Wendy Zellner, "Back to 'Coffee, Tea, or Milk?'" *Business Week*, July 3, 1995, 52, 56; Zellner, "The Right Place, the Right Time," *Business Week*, May 27, 1996, 74–75.

[4] Thomas A. Stewart, "3M Fights Back," *Fortune*, February 5, 1996, 94–99; Shawn Tully, "Why to Go for Stretch Targets," *Fortune*, November 14, 1994, 145–146.

[5] Mark Lewyn, "MCI: Attacking on All Fronts," *Business Week*, June 13, 1994, 76–79.

[6] See Charles W.L. Hill and Gareth Jones, *Strategic Management: An Analytic View*, 3rd ed. (Boston: Houghton Mifflin, 1995), 3–9.

[7] Gary McWilliams, "Compaq: All Things to All Networks?" *Business Week*, July 31, 1995, 79–80; McWilliams, "Compaq at the 'Crossroads,'" *Business Week*, July 22, 1996, 70–72.

[8] Stephen D. Solomon, "American Express Applies for a New Line of Credit," *New York Times Magazine*, July 30, 1995, 34–35+.

[9] Laurence Zuckerman, "I.B.M. Soars as It Beats Quarterly Expectations," *New York Times*, July 26, 1996, D1, D2; Brent Schlender, "Big Blue Is Betting on Big Iron Again," *Fortune*, April 29, 1996, 102–104; Ira Sager, "IBM's Parallel Power Rangers," *Business Week*, January 30, 1995, 81–82; Zuckerman, "After Another Climb, Whither I.B.M. Shares?" *New York Times*, September 30, 1996, D1, D3.

[10]Shawn Tully, "Super CFOs," *Fortune*, November 13, 1995, 160–164.

[11]See Kamal Fatehi, *International Management: A Cross-Cultural and Functional Perspective* (Upper Saddle River, NJ: Prentice Hall, 1996), 5–18, 153–164.

[12]Thomas A. Stewart, "Managing in a Wired World," *Fortune*, July 11, 1994, 44–47+; Robert D. Hof with Kathy Rebello and Peter Burrows, "Scott McNealy's Rising Sun," *Business Week*, January 22, 1996, 66–72.

[13]George Judson, "Egalitarianism Invades a Shrine of V.I.P. Privilege," *New York Times*, May 17, 1996, B1, B6.

[14]See Stratford Sherman, "A Master Class in Radical Change," *Fortune*, December 13, 1993, 82–84+.

Chapter 7

[1]Ira Sager with Amy E. Coretese, "Lou Gerstner Unveils His Battle Plan," *Business Week*, April 4, 1994, 96–98; Laurence Zuckerman, "I.B.M., in Its Dress Shoes, Chases Software Success," *New York Times*, May 6, 1996, D1, D8.

[2] See John A. Wagner III and John R. Hollenbeck, *Management of Organizational Behavior*, 2nd ed. (Englewood Cliffs, NJ: Prentice Hall, 1995), 494–495; Jay Heiser and Barry Render, *Production and Operations Management: Strategic and Tactical Decisions*, 4th ed. (Upper Saddle River, NJ: Prentice Hall, 1996), 483–484.

[3]Alan Deutschman, "How H-P Continues to Grow and Grow," *Fortune*, May 2, 1994, 99–100; Stratford Sherman, "Secrets of H-P's 'Muddled' Team," *Fortune*, March 18, 1996, 116–120.

[4]Jay Diamond and Gerald Pintel, *Retailing*, 6th ed. (Upper Saddle River, NJ: Prentice Hall, 1996), 83–84.

[5]Bart Ziegler, "IBM Plans to Revamp Sales Structure to Focus on Industries, Not Geography," *Wall Street Journal*, May 6, 1994, A3.

[6]Alex Taylor III, "GM Gets a Tune-Up," *Fortune*, November 29, 1993, 54–58; Taylor, "GM: Why They Might Break Up America's Biggest Company," *Fortune*, April 29, 1996, 78–82+.

[7]David Kirkpatrick, "Gerstner's New Vision for IBM," *Fortune*, November 15, 1993, 119–120; Ira Sager, "The View from IBM," *Business Week*, October 30, 1995, 142–146+; Brent Schlender, "Big Blue Is Betting on Big Iron Again," *Fortune*, April 29, 1996, 102–104+.

[8]Alessandra Bianchi, "What's Love Got to Do with It?" *Inc.*, May 1996, 76–79+.

[9]Noel M. Tichy, "Revolutionize Your Company," *Fortune*, December 13, 1993, 114–115+; Stephen P. Robbins and Mary Coulter, *Management*, 5th ed. (Upper Saddle River, NJ: Prentice Hall, 1996), 341.

[10]Donna Fenn, "The Buyers," *Inc.*, June 1996, 46–48+.

[11]Tim Smart, "UTC Gets a Lift from Its Smaller Engines," *Business Week*, December 20, 1993, 109–110.

[12]Brian Dumaine, "Payoff from the New Management," *Fortune*, December 13, 1993, 103–104+.

[13]Patrick Oster and John Rossant, "Call It Worldpool," *Business Week*, November 18, 1994, 98–99.

[14]Stanley Reed with Katherine Ann Miller, "Pearson May Be Poised for a Breakup," *Business Week*, September 2, 1996, 54–55.

[15]Byrne, "The Horizontal Corporation," 79.

[16]Thomas J. Peters and Robert H. Waterman Jr., *In Search of Excellence* (New York: Harper & Row, 1982).

[17] Shawn Tully, "Why to Go for Stretch Targets," *Fortune*, November 14, 1994, 145–146+; Larry Armstrong, "Nurturing an Employee's Brainchild," *Business Week*, Enterprise 1993, 196.

Chapter 8

[1]See Norman N. Scarborough and Thomas W. Zimmerer, *Effective Small Business Management*, 5th ed. (Upper Saddle River, NJ: Prentice Hall, 1996), 36.

[2]U.S. Department of Commerce, *Statistical Abstract of the United States* (Washington, DC: Bureau of the Census, 1995).

[3]Julia Flynn with Linda Bernier, "Springtime for Startups?" *Business Week*, May 22, 1995, 130D–130I.

[4]This section is based on Sylvia Nasar, "Myth: Small Business as Job Engine," *New York Times*, March 25, 1994, D1, D2.

[5]John Labate, "Companies to Watch: Maxim Integrated Products," *Fortune*, December 13, 1993, 172.

[6]Stephanie Losee et al., "Fortune Checks Out 25 Cool Companies," *Fortune*, July 11, 1994, 142, 144.

[7]Amy Barrett with Joseph Weber et al., "Hot Growth Companies," *Business Week*, May 27, 1996 113–114; Wilton Woods, "Products to Watch: On-Line Entrepreneuring," *Fortune*, May 30, 1994, 163.

[8]Amy Stone et al., "Hot Growth Companies," *Business Week*, May 23, 1994, 95; John Labate, "Companies to Watch: Gymboree," *Fortune*, February 7, 1994, 137.

[9]John Labate, "Companies to Watch: Central Garden & Pet," *Fortune*, February 7, 1994, 137.

[10]Martha E. Mangelsdorf, "The Startling Truth about Growth Companies," *Inc.*, The State of Small Business 1996, 84–85+.

[11]Michael Oneal, "Just What Is an Entrepreneur?" *Business Week*, Enterprise 1993, 104–105.

[12]Oneal, "Just What Is an Entrepreneur?" 105; Wilton Woods, "Products to Watch: Heavy Artillery," *Fortune*, May 30, 1994, 163; David Whitford, "Opposite Attraction," *Inc.*, December 1994, 60–64+.

[13]Brian Dumaine, "America's Smart Young Entrepreneurs," *Fortune*, March 21, 1994, 34–40+.

[14]Scarborough and Zimmerer, *Effective Small Business Management*, 21.

[15]Hal Plotkin, "Riches from Rags," *Inc. Technology*, Summer 1995, 62–64+; Wendy Zellner et al., "Women Entrepreneurs," *Business Week*, April 18, 1994, 104–108.

[16]William Echikson, "Young Americans Go Abroad to Strike It Rich," *Fortune*, October 17, 1994, 185–188+.

[17]See Scarborough and Zimmerer, *Effective Small Business Management*, 37.

[18]Barbara Presley Noble, "A Few Thousand Women, Networking," *New York Times*, March 27, 1994, Sec. 3, 4.

[19]Kirk Johnson, "Franchise Stores Lure Corporate Refugees," *New York Times*, May 13, 1994, A1, B5.

Chapter 9

[1]See Stephen P. Robbins, *Organizational Behavior: Concepts, Controversies, Applications*, 7th ed. (Englewood Cliffs, NJ: Prentice Hall, 1996), 193–197.

[2]Keith H. Hammonds, "Balancing Work and Family," *Business Week*, September 16, 1996, 74–78+.

[3]Jeffrey L. Seglin, "The Happiest Workers in the World," *Inc.*, The State of Small Business 1996, 62–64+.

[4]David Cay Johnston, "Nabisco to Eliminate 4,200 Jobs and Trim Product Line by 14%," *New York Times*, June 25, 1996, D1, D20; Lawrence M. Fisher, "Apple Plans 1,300 Layoffs and Takes Losses," *New York Times*, January 18, 1996, D1, D10; Edmund L. Andrews, "Job Cuts at AT&T Will Total 40,000, 13% of Its Staff," *New York Times*, January 3, 1996, A1, D2; Catherine Arnst, "The Bloodletting at AT&T Is Just the Beginning," *Business Week*, January 15, 1996, 30; Andrews, "Don't Go Away Mad, Just Go Away," *New York Times*, February 13, 1996, D1, D6; Louis D. Uchitelle and N.R. Kleinfield, "On the Battlefields of Bsiness, Millions of Casualties," *New York Times*, March 3, 1996, Sec. 1, 1, 26+.

[5]Robert Hanley, "New Jersey Hit Hard in Wave of Layoffs at AT&T," *New York Times*, January 17, 1996, B1, B5; Brian O'Reilly, "Ma Bell's Orphans," *Fortune*, April 1, 1996, 88–90+.

[6]See Jerald Greenberg and Robert A. Baron, *Behavior in Organizations: Understanding and Managing the Human Side of Work*, 6th ed. (Upper Saddle River, NJ: Prentice Hall, 1997), 11–12; Stephen P. Robbins and Mary Coulter, *Management*, 5th ed. (Upper Saddle River, NJ: Prentice Hall, 1996), 39–41.

[7]See Greenberg and Baron, *Behavior in Organizations*, 159–163; Robbins, *Organizational Behavior*, 230–233.

[8]See Greenberg and Baron, *Behavior in Organizations*, 154–159; Robbins, *Organizational Behavior*, 226–230.

[9]Kevin Kelly, "The New Soul of John Deere," *Business Week*, January 31, 1994, 64–65.

[10]Brian Dumaine, "The Trouble with Teams," *Fortune*, September 5, 1994, 86–88+.

[11]Aimee L. Stern, "Managing by Team Is Not Always as Easy as It Looks," *New York Times*, July 18, 1993, Sec. 3, 5.

[12]Patricia Sellers, "Keeping the Buyers You Already Have," *Fortune*, Autumn-Winter 1993, 56–58.

[13]Larry Armstron with Julie Tilsner, "'The Office Is a Terrible Place to Work,'" *Business Week*, December 27, 1993, 46d; Phil Patton, "The Virtual Office Becomes a Reality," *New York Times*, October 28, 1993, C1, C6; Kirk Johnson, "New Breed of High-Tech Nomads," *New York Times*, February 8, 1994, B1, B5.

[14]Joan O'C. Hamilton with Stephen Baker and Bill Vlasic, "The New Workplace," *Business Week*, April 29, 1996, 106–109+.

[15]Samuel Greengard, "Making the Virtual Office a Reality," *Personnel Journal*, September 1994,

66–68+; Ronald B. Lieber, "Cool Offices," *Fortune*, December 9, 1996, 204–206+.

[16]Brian S. Moskal, "Smith Freshens GM's Stale Air," *Industry Week*, October 4, 1993, 19–22; Joseph B. White, "GM's Overhaul of Corporate Culture Brings Results but Still Faces Hurdles," *Wall Street Journal*, February 13, 1993, A3, A4; White, "Metamorphosis at GM, in Style and Substance, May Be Taking Hold," *Wall Street Journal*, February 19, 1993, A1, A11.

[17]John Huey, "The New Post-Heroic Leadership," *Fortune*, February 21, 1994, 42–44.

[18]See Robbins, *Organizational Behavior*, 419–433; Greenberg and Baron, *Behavior in Organizations*, 450–462.

Chapter 10

[1]See Gary Dessler, *Human Resource Management*, 7th ed. (Upper Saddle River, NJ: Prentice Hall, 1997), 2–8; R. Wayne Mondy and Robert M. Noe, *Human Resource Management*, 6th ed. (Upper Saddle River, NJ: Prentice Hall, 1996), 4–6.

[2]See Dessler, *Human Resource Management*, Chaps. 4–6; Mondy and Noe, *Human Resource Management*, Chaps. 6–7.

[3]See Dessler, *Human Resources Management*, Chaps. 12–14; Mondy and Noe, *Human Resources Management*, Chaps. 12–13.

[4]John A. Byrne, "Their Cup Runneth Over—Again," *Business Week*, March 28, 1994, 26–27.

[5]Howard Gleckman et al., "Bonus Pay: Buzzword or Bonanza," *Business Week*, November 14, 1994, 62–64; Wendy Zellner et al., "Go-Go Goliaths," *Business Week*, February 13, 1995, 64–70.

[6]Nancy A. Kubasek, Bartley A. Brennan, and M. Neil Browne, *The Legal Environment of Business: A Critical Thinking Approach* (Upper Saddle River, NJ: Prentice Hall, 1996), 521–524; Robert N. Corley et al., *The Legal and Regulatory Environment of Business*, 9th ed. (New York: McGraw-Hill, 1993), 483.

[7]Robyn Meredith, "Few at Mitsubishi Are Silent over Accusations," *New York Times*, April 26, 1996, A20; Peter Elstrom with Edith Hill Updike, "Fear and Loathing at Mitsubishi," *Business Week*, May 6, 1996, 35; Elstrom with Steven V. Brill, "Mitsubishi's Morass," *Business Week*, June 3, 1996, 35.

[8]See Kubasek, Brennan, and Browne, *The Legal Environment of Business*, 506–508.

[9]Peter T. Kilborn, "Women and Minorities Still Face 'Glass Ceiling,'" *New York Times*, March 16, 1995, A22; Judith H. Dobrzynski, "Study Finds Few Women in Five Highest Company Jobs," *New York Times*, October 18, 1996, D4; Linda Himelstein with Stephanie Anderson Forest, "Breaking Through," *Business Week*, February 17, 1997, 64–68+.

[10]See Stephen P. Robbins, *Organizational Behavior: Concepts, Controversies, Applications* (Englewood Cliffs, NJ: Prentice Hall, 1996), 273–275; Dessler, *Human Resources Management*, 446–448.

[11]Michele Galen with Ann Therese Palmer, "White, Male, and Worried," *Business Week*, January 31, 1994, 50–55.

[12]This section is based on Faye Rice, "How to Make Diversity Pay," *Fortune*, August 8, 1994, 78–80+. For a series of profiles of companies that, according to the editors of *Fortune* magazine, "embrace diversity as a business imperative," see Amy Hilliard-Jones, "Diversity: A Global Success Strategy," *Fortune*, April 15, 1996.

[13]Kathleen Murray, "The Unfortunate Side Effects of 'Diversity Training,'" *New York Times*, August 1, 1993, Sec. 3, 5; Rice, "How to Make Diversity Pay," 84.

[14]This section is based on Jaclyn Fierman, "The Contingency Work Force," *Fortune*, January 24, 1994, 30–36; and Barnaby J. Feder, "Big Roles for Suppliers of Temporary Workers," *New York Times*, April 1, 1995, 37. See also Richard A. Melcher, "Manpower Upgrades Its Résumé," *Business Week*, June 10, 1996, 81–82.

[15]Fierman, "The Contingency Work Force," 32–33; Timothy Egan, "A Temporary Force to Be Reckoned With," *New York Times*, May 20, 1996, D1, D8.

[16]Aaron Bernstein, "Why America Needs Unions—But Not the Kind It Has Now," *Business Week*, May 23, 1994, 70–71+.

[17]Keith Bradsher, "G.M. Strikers Fear Threat to Way of Life," *New York Times*, March 21, 1996, D1, D8; Bradsher, "General Motors and Union Agree to End Walkout," *New York Times*, March 22, 1996, A1, D4; Bill Vlasic, "The Saginaw Solution," *Business Week*, July 15, 1996, 76–77; Bradsher, "Hurt by Strike, G.M.'s Profits Are Off by Half," *New York Times*, April 23, 1996, D1, D4.

[18]See M. Ali Raza and A. Janell Anderson, *Labor Relations and the Law* (Upper Saddle River, NJ: Prentice Hall, 1996), Chaps. 5, 7, 11.

[19]Peter T. Kilborn, "Strikers at American Airlines Say the Objective Is Respect," *New York Times*, November 22, 1993, A1, A9; Kilborn, "Strike Is Called Victory for Women, Not Unions," *New York Times*, November 24, 1993, A22.

[20]See Kubasek, Brennan, and Browne, *The Legal Environment of Business*, Chap. 6.

Chapter 11

[1]Gene Bylinsky, "The Digital Factory," Fortune, November 14, 1994, 92–96+.

[2]Bylinsky, "The Digital Factory," 92–93.

[3]See Jay Heizer and Barry Render, *Production and Operations Management: Strategic and Tactical Decisions*, 4th ed. (Upper Saddle River, NJ: Prentice Hall, 1996), 4.

[4]Jeffrey A. Tannenbaum, "Food Franchisers Expand by Pursuing Customers into Every Nook and Cranny," *Wall Street Journal*, October 26, 1994, B1.

[5]Richard J. Schonberger and Edward M. Knod Jr., *Operations Management*, 5th ed. (Burr Ridge, IL: Irwin, 1994), Chapter 11.

[6]See Roger W. Schmenner, *Service Operations Management* (Englewood Cliffs, NJ: Prentice Hall, 1995), 37–49.

[7]See Carol A. Reeves and David A. Bednar, "Defining Quality: Alternatives and Implications," *Academy of Management Review*, 19 (1994), 419–445.

[8]Myron Magnet, "Good News for the Service Economy," *Fortune*, May 3, 1993, 50–51.

[9]Robert Eade, "Untying the Scheduling and Control Knot," *APICS: The Performance Advantage*, October, 1994, pp. 75–77.

[10]See Heizer and Render, *Production and Operations Management*, 541–545; Louis W. Stern, Adel I. El-Ansary, and Anne T. Coughlan, *Marketing Channels*, 5th ed. (Upper Saddle River, NJ: Prentice Hall, 1996), 168–169.

[11]Geoffrey Smith et al., "The Rules of the Game in the New World of Work," *Business Week*, October 17, 1994, 94–100+.

[12]Ronald Henkoff, "Service Is Everybody's Business," *Fortune*, June 27, 1994, 48–50+.

[13]Ronald Henkoff, "Finding, Training, and Keeping the Best Service Workers," *Fortune*, October 3, 1994, pp. 110–113.

[14]Henkoff, "Finding, Training, and Keeping the Best Service Workers," 114.

[15]James R. Evans and William M. Lindsay, *The Management and Control of Quality*, 3rd ed. (Minneapolis/St. Paul: West, 1996), 186–187; David Woodruff, "Bug Control at Chrysler," *Business Week*, August 22, 1994, 26.

[16]David Greising, "Quality: How to Make It Pay," *Business Week*, August 8, 1994, 54–59.

Chapter 12

[1]See Charles T. Horngren, Walter T. Harrison Jr., and Michael A. Robinson, *Accounting*, 3rd ed. (Englewood Cliffs, NJ: Prentice Hall, 1996), 4–6.

[2]See Charles T. Horngren, George Foster, and Srikant M. Datar, *Cost Accounting: A Managerial Emphasis*, 9th ed. (Upper Saddle River, NJ: Prentice Hall, 1997), 2–3.

[3]General Mills Inc., *General Mills 1995 Midyear Report* (Minneapolis, 1995).

[4]See Charles T. Horngren, Gary L. Sundem, and William O. Stratton, *Introduction to Management Accounting*, 10th ed. (Upper Saddle River, NJ: Prentice Hall, 1996), 4–5.

[5]"Audit Raises Flag at Baby Superstore," *New York Times*, February 27, 1996, D10.

[6]See Kenneth C. Laudon and Jane Price Laudon, *Management Information Systems: Organization and Technology*, 4th ed. (Upper Saddle River, NJ: Prentice Hall, 1996), 24–26; Larry Long and Nancy Long, *Computers*, 4th ed. (Upper Saddle River, NJ: Prentice Hall, 1996), M13–M15.

[7]See James A. Senn, *Information Technology in Business: Principles, Practices, and Opportunities* (Englewood Cliffs, NJ: Prentice Hall, 1995), Chap. 6; Long and Long, *Computers*, P53–P61.

[8]See Senn, *Information Technology in Business*, 56–63; Laudon and Laudon, *Management Information Systems*, 247–251.

[9]Catherine Arnst et al., "The Information Appliance," *Business Week*, November 22, 1993, 98–102+.

[10]Stratford Sherman, "How to Bolster the Bottom Line," *Fortune*, Autumn 1993, 14–16+.

[11]Senn, *Information Technology in Business*, 281; Robert D. Hof with Neil Gross, "The Gee-Whiz Company," *Business Week*, July 18, 1994, 56–59.

[12]Richard Brandt, "Bill Gates's Vision," *Business Week*, June 27, 1994, 56–62.

13 See Long and Long, *Computers*, M18–M23; Senn, *Information Technology in Business*, 494–495; Laudon and Laudon, *Management Information Systems*, 646–651.

14 See Long and Long, *Computers*, Chap. 8; Laudon and Laudon, *Management Information Systems*, 349–358.

15 Amy Cortese et al., "The Software Revolution," *Business Week*, December 4, 1995, 78–83+; John W. Verity and Robert D. Hof, "The Internet: How It Will Change the Way You Do Business," *Business Week*, November 14, 1994, 80–86; Verity, "Everyone's Rushing to the Net," *Business Week*, June 5, 1995, 116, 118.

16 Phaedra Hise, "Getting Smart On-Line," *Inc. Technology*, No. 1 (1996), 59–60+.

17 Stephen D. Solomon, "Staking a Claim on the Internet," *Inc. Technology*, March 1995, 87–90+; Lewis, "Getting Down to Business on the Net," 1.

18 John W. Verity, "What Hath Yahoo Wrought?" *Business Week*, February 12, 1996, 88–90.

19 Robert D. Hof with Amy Cortese, "Browsing for a Bruising?" *Business Week*, March 11, 1996, 82, 84.

20 Verity, "What Hath Yahoo Wrought?" 88.

21 Amy Cortese, "Here Comes the Intranet," *Business Week*, February 26, 1996, 76–79+; Alison Sprout, "The Internet inside Your Company," *Fortune*, November 27, 1995, 161–162+.

Chapter 13

1 From "AMA Board Approves New Marketing Definition," *Marketing News*, March 31, 1985, 1. Published by the American Marketing Association.

2 *Harley-Davidson Inc.: 1995 Annual Report* (Milwaukee, WI: Harley-Davidson, 1995), 33. See Philip Kotler, *Marketing Management: Analysis, Planning, Implementation, and Control*, 9th ed. (Upper Saddle River, NJ: Prentice Hall, 1997), 12–13, 48–51.

3 Ricardo Sookdeo, "Golfing Gear for Women," *Fortune*, November 14, 1994, 257.

4 David Greising, "Quality: How to Make It Pay," *Business Week*, August 8, 1994, 58.

5 John Labate, "Companies to Watch: Daka International," *Fortune*, November 14, 1994, 258.

6 Glenn Collins, "Updating an Icon, Carefully," *New York Times*, November 17, 1995, D1, D4.

7 Robin Pogrebin, "A Magazine Only a Mother Could Love?" *New York Times*, July 22, 1996, D1, D8.

8 See Kotler, *Marketing Management*, 294–301.

9 Patricia Sellers, "How Coke Is Kicking Pepsi's Can," *Fortune*, October 28, 1996, 70–75+.

10 Pogrebin, "A Magazine Only a Mother Could Love?" D8.

11 Erick Schonfeld, "Betting on the Boomers," *Fortune*, December 25, 1995, 78–80+.

12 Dori Jones Yang, "The Starbucks Enterprise Shifts into Warp Speed," *Business Week*, October 24, 1994, 76–78; Alex Witchell, "By Way of Canarsie, One Large Hot Cup of Business Strategy," *New York Times*, December 14, 1994, C1, C8.

13 Jane Perlez, "A Bourgeoisie Blooms and Goes Shopping," *New York Times*, May 14, 1996, D1, D6.

14 See Michael R. Solomon, *Consumer Behavior: Buying, Having, and Being*, 3rd ed. (Englewood Cliffs, NJ: Prentice Hall, 1996), 7–9.

15 Terence P. Paré, "How to Find Out What They Want," *Fortune*, Autumn-Winter 1993, pp. 39–41.

16 *Statistical Abstract of the United States* (Washington, DC: U.S. Dept. of Commerce, 1994), 539.

17 *Statistical Abstract of the United States*, 295, 303.

18 Shawn Tully, "Why to Go for Stretch Targets," *Fortune*, November 14, 1994, 145–146+.

19 See Warren J. Keegan and Mark C. Green, *Principles of Global Marketing* (Upper Saddle River, NJ: Prentice Hall, 1997), Chaps. 13–16.

20 Zachary Schiller with Greg Burns and Karen Lowry Miller, "Make It Simple," *Business Week*, September 9, 1996, 96–99+.

21 John Rockwell, "The New Colossus: American Culture as Power Export," *New York Times*, January 30, 1994, Sec. 2, 1, 30.

Chapter 14

1 Shawn Tully, "Why to Go for Stretch Targets," *Fortune*, November 14, 1994, 145–148+.

2 See Philip Kotler and Gary Armstrong, *Principles of Marketing*, 7th ed. (Englewood Cliffs, NJ: Prentice Hall, 1996), 326–332.

3 Larry Holyoke and Larry Armstrong, "Video Warfare: How Toshiba Took the High Ground," *Business Week*, February 20, 1995, 64–66.

4 Betsy Morris, "The Brand's the Thing," *Fortune*, March 4, 1996, 72.

5 Glenn Collins, "Xerox Attempts a New Beginning by Making Its Name the Last Word in a Corporate Christening," *New York Times*, August 4, 1994, D17.

6 Stuart Elliott, "'Gump' Sells, to Viacom's Surprise," *New York Times*, October 7, 1994, D1, D16.

7 Sharon Nelton, "Cleaning Up by Cleaning Up," *Nation's Business*, January 1995, 14–15.

8 Bill Saporito, "Behind the Tumult at P&G," *Fortune*, March 17, 1994, 74–76+; Zachary Schiller, "Ed Artzt's Elbow Grease Has P&G Shining," *Business Week*, October 10, 1994, 84, 86.

9 Stuart Elliott, "Disney and McDonald's as Double Feature," *New York Times*, May 24, 1996, D1, D6; Michael McCarthy, "BK, 'LK' to Roar at X-Mas," *Brandweek*, September 5, 1994, 1; Ron Ruggless, "Burger King Scores TKO with Pocahontas Tie-In," *Nation's Restaurant News*, November 1994, 14.

10 R. Craig Endicott, "Top Marketers Snap Lull with Double-Digit Ad Hike," *Advertising Age*, September 27, 1995, 2, 62.

11 See William J. Donnelly, *Planning Media: Strategy and Imagination* (Upper Saddle River, NJ: Prentice Hall, 1996), Chap. 9.

12 Mary Kuntz, "Burma Shave Signs On the I-Way," *Business Week*, April 17, 1995, 102, 104; Ken Gofton, "Welcome to My Web," *Marketing*, April 11, 1996, xviii; Peter C. Elsworth, "Internet Advertising Growing Slowly," *New York Times*, February 24, 1997, D5.

13 Rolph Anderson, *Essentials of Personal Selling: The New Professionalism* (Englewood Cliffs, NJ: Prentice Hall, 1995), 48.

14 Ronald B. Marks, *Personal Selling: An Interactive Approach*, 5th ed. (Boston: Allyn and Bacon, 1994), 10–11.

15 See Fraser P. Seitel, *The Practice of Public Relations*, 6th ed. (Englewood Cliffs, NJ: Prentice Hall, 1995), 4–8.

16 Matthew L. Wald, "Southwest Is Changing Black Boxes," *New York Times*, August 17, 1996, D6.

Chapter 15

1 See Louis W. Stern, Adel I. El-Ansary, and Anne T. Coughlan, *Marketing Channels*, 5th ed. (Upper Saddle River, NJ: Prentice Hall, 1996), Chap. 1; Philip Kotler, *Marketing Management: Analysis, Planning, Implementation, and Control*, 9th ed. (Upper Saddle River, NJ: Prentice Hall, 1997), 530–542.

2 Stephanie Anderson Forest, "The Education of Michael Dell," *Business Week*, March 22, 1993, 82–86; Peter Burrows, "The Computer Is in the Mail—Really," *Business Week*, January 23, 1995, 76–77; Jennifer Steinhauer, "PC Shoppers Prove to Have Fickle Hearts," *New York Times*, January 8, 1997, D1, D2; Scott McCartney, "Michael Dell—and His Company—Grow Up," *Wall Street Journal*, January 31, 1994, B1, B2.

3 See Stern, El-Ansary, and Coughlan, *Marketing Channels*, 60–61.

4 Teri Lammers Prior, "Channel Surfers," *Inc.*, February 1995, 65–68.

5 Peter H. Lewis, "On-Line Middleman Opens for Business," *New York Times*, October 2, 1995, D5.

6 Zachary Schiller and Wendy Zellner, "Making the Middleman an Endangered Species," *Business Week*, June 6, 1994, 114–115.

7 Ronald Henkoff, "Delivering the Goods," *Fortune*, November 28, 1994, 64–66+; Gene Bylinsky, "The Digital Factory," *Fortune*, November 14, 1994, 92–95+.

8 See Jay Diamond and Gerald Pintel, *Retailing*, 6th ed. (Upper Saddle River, NJ: Prentice Hall, 1996), 5–19.

9 See Diamond and Pintel, *Retailing*, 86–92; Stephanie Strom, "Image and Attitude Are Department Stores' Draw," *New York Times*, August 12, 1993, D1.

10 Mary Kuntz et al., "Reinventing the Store," *Business Week*, November 27, 1995, 84–89+.

11 Susan Caminiti, "Will Old Navy Fill the Gap," *Fortune*, March 18, 1996, 59–62.

12 Karen Lowry Miller, Kevin Kelly, and Heidi Dawley, "Otto the Great Rules in Germany," *Business Week*, January 31, 1994, 70J, 70K.

13 John Huey, "Waking Up to the New Economy," *Fortune*, June 27, 1994, 36–38+.

14 Easy Klein, *D & B Reports*, 42:3 (May-June 1993), 20; Edith Hill Updike and Mary Kuntz, "Japan is Dialing 1 800 BuyAmerica," *Business Week*, June 12, 1995, 61, 64.

15 Laura Zinn et al., "Retailing Will Never Be the Same," *Business Week*, July 26, 1993, 54–60; Huey, "Waking Up to the New Economy," 38.

16 John Greenwald, "Sorry, Right Number," *Time*, September 13, 1993, 66.

17 Suein L. Hwang, "Ding Dong: Updating Avon Means Respecting History without Repeating It," *Wall Street Journal*, April 4, 1994, A1, A4; Claudia H. Deutsch, "Relighting the Fires at

Avon Products," *New York Times*, April 3, 1994, Sec. 3, 5; James Brooke, "Who Braves Piranha Waters? Your Avon Lady!" *New York Times*, July 7, 1995, A4.

[18] See Stern, El-Ansary, and Coughlan, *Marketing Channels*, 158–177.

[19] See Donald F. Wood and James C. Johnson, *Contemporary Transportation*, 5th ed. (Upper Saddle River, NJ: Prentice Hall, 1996), 244–269.

[20] Gregory L. Miles, "Marriages of Convenience," *International Business*, January 1995, 32–36.

[21] Henkoff, "Delivering the Goods," 76, 78.

Chapter 16

[1] See Karl E. Case and Ray C. Fair, *Principles of Economics*, 4th ed. (Upper Saddle River, NJ: Prentice Hall, 1996), 668–669; Michael G. Hadjimichalakis and Karma G. Hadjimichalakis, *Contemporary Money, Banking, and Financial Markets: Theory and Practice* (Chicago: Irwin, 1995), 3–6.

[2] The data in this section come from *Federal Reserve Bulletin* (Washington, DC: Board of Governors of the Federal Reserve System, September 1996), A13.

[3] *Standard & Poor's Stock Reports*, May 14, 1996, 537M; U.S. Dept. of Commerce, *Statistical Abstract of the United States* (Washington, DC: Bureau of the Census, 1995), 526.

[4] Mickey Meece, "Nonbanks Now Five of Top 10 Credit Card Issuers," *American Banker*, February 5, 1996, "The Cutting Edge," *The Economist*, July 27, 1996, 63–64.

[5] Richard W. Stevenson, "In New Economy, Russians Cannot Rely on Their Banks," *New York Times*, September 12, 1995, A1, A10.

[6] See Frank J. Fabozzi, Franco Modigliani, and Michael A. Ferri, *Foundations of Financial Markets and Institutions* (Englewood Cliffs, NJ: Prentice Hall, 1994), 21–24.

[7] "The Fortune Global 500," *Fortune*, August 5, 1996, F–1, F–10, F–17, F–19.

[8] Terence P Paré, "Clueless Bankers," *Fortune*, November 27, 1996, 151–152+.

[9] Paré, "Clueless Bankers," 151.

[10] Saul Hansell, "A New Chase Tries to Lead," *New York Times*, March 29, 1996, D1, D4; Stephanie Strom, "Kingpin of the Big-Time Loan," *New York Times*, August 11, 1995, D1, D4; Hansell, "Merger-Hungry Banks Find the Pickings Slim," *New York Times*, January 2, 1997, C22.

[11] Data in this and the following sections come from *Statistical Abstract of the United States*, 514, 522.

[12] See J. Kimball Dietrich, *Financial Services and Financial Institutions: Value Creation in Theory and Practice* (Upper Saddle River, NJ: Prentice Hall, 1996), 368–369; Peter Rose, *Commercial Bank Management*, 3rd ed. (Chicago: Irwin, 1996), 376–377.

[13] Data in this section come from *Statistical Abstract of the United States* (1994), 522; *Statistical Abstract of the United States* (1995), 526.

[14] Beth Piskora, "Trust Us, the U.S. Has Lots of ATMs," *American Banker*, November 30, 1994, 12; Mickey Meece, "Citicorp Launches First Shanghai ATMs," *American Banker*, October 7, 1994, 3; Saul Hansell, "The Ante Rises in East Asia," *New York Times*, July 14, 1996, Sec. 3, pp. 1, 12; Paré, "Clueless Bankers," 158.

[15] Keith Bradsher, "Federal Reserve Trims a Key Rate; First Cut since '92," *New York Times*, July 7, 1995, A1, D1, D4.

[16] See Case and Fair, *Principles of Economics*, 689–692.

[17] Koch, *Bank Management*, 370–371.

[18] Steve Cocheo, "Interstate Banking Law Gets a Low-Key Sendoff," *ABA Banking Journal*, November 1994, 7, 10+; Olad DeSenerpont Domis, "Loophole in Interstate Law Benefits Branching in '95," *American Banker*, December 14, 1994, 24.

[19] James Gleick, "Dead as a Dollar," *New York Times Magazine*, June 16, 1996, 26–30+.

[20] Russell Mitchell, "The Smart Money Is on Smart Cards," *Business Week*, August 14, 1995, 68–69; Nikhil Deogun, "The Smart Money Is on 'Smart Cards,' but Electronic Cash Seems Dumb to Some," *Wall Street Journal*, August 5, 1996, B1, B8.

[21] Kelly Holland and Greg Burns, "Plastic Talks," *Business Week*, February 14, 1994, 105–107; Saul Hansell, "An End to the 'Nightmare' of Cash," *New York Times*, September 6, 1994, D1, D5; Thomas McCarroll, "No Checks. No Cash. No Fuss?" *Time*, May 9, 1994, 60–62; Marla Matzer, "Plastic Mania," *Forbes*, October 24, 1994, 281–282.

[22] Kelly Holland and Amy Cortese, "The Future of Money," *Business Week*, June 12, 1995, 66–72+.

[23] See Robert J. Carbaugh, *International Economics*, 5th ed. (Cincinnati: South-Western, 1995), Chap. 11.

Chapter 17

[1] See George W. Gallinger and Jerry B. Poe, *Essentials of Finance: An Integrated Approach* (Englewood Cliffs, NJ: Prentice Hall, 1995), 190, 198–211.

[2] *Federal Reserve Bulletin* (Washington, DC: Board of Governors of the Federal Reserve, October 1996), A31.

[3] *Federal Reserve Bulletin*, October 1996, A31.

[4] Mark Landler, "AT&T Warns of a Drop in Earnings and Its Stock Plunges," *New York Times*, September 25, 1996, D1, D3; Landler, "Loss at AT&T Computer Unit Was $1 Billion over Estimates," *New York Times*, September 27, 1996, D1, D7; *The Wall Street Journal Index* (Ann Arbor, MI: UMI, July-September 1996), 23; Carol J. Loomis, "AT&T Has No Clothes," *Fortune*, February 5, 1996, 78–80; Andrew Kupfer, "AT&T: Ready to Run, Nowhere to Hide," *Fortune*, April 29, 1996, 116–118+.

[5] *Standard & Poor's NYSE Stock Reports*, August 1996, 564M.

[6] *The Value Line Investment Survey*, January 28, 1994, 1095; *Standard & Poor's NYSE Stock Reports*, August 1996, 1210M; Ira Sager, "How IBM Became a Growth Company Again," *Business Week*, December 9, 1996, 154–158+; Laurence Zuckerman, "I.B.M. Earnings Top Forecasts, but Stir Doubt on Stock Price," *New York Times*, January 22, 1997, D1, D9.

[7] Russell Mitchell, "The Schwab Revolution," *Business Week*, December 18, 1994, 88–91+; Ellyn E. Spragins, "Is Bigger Better?" *Business Week*, July 4, 1994, 54–55+.

[8] *NYSE Fact Book: 1995 Data* (New York: New York Stock Exchange, 1996), 7, 43.

[9] Michael Schroeder, "Babysitting the World's Emerging Bourses," *Business Week*, November 1, 1993, 112–114; William Glasgall with Dave Lindorff, "The Global Investor," *Business Week*, September 19, 1994, 96–102.

[10] Anthony Ramirez, "Nasdaq Index Flirts with 1,000, Perhaps Ahead of Its Time," *New York Times*, July 23, 1995, Sec. 3, 3.

[11] All data in this and the sections immediately following come from *Federal Reserve Bulletin*, October 1996, A27, A28, A31, A38.

[12] *Moody's Bond Survey*, July 4, 1994, 4932, and July 18, 1994, 4712.

[13] *Moody's Bond Survey*, July 11, 1994, 4811.

[14] *Moody's Bond Survey*, April 26, 1993, 5884.

[15] *Investment Companies Yearbook* 1996 (Rockville, MD: CDA/Wiesenberger), 13.

[16] The data in this section come from *Mutual Fund Fact Book* (Washington, DC: Investment Company Institute, 1995).

[17] Amey Stone, "Futures: Dare You Defy the Odds?" *Business Week*, February 28, 1994, 12–13.

[18] Susan E. Kuhn, "How Crazy Is This Market?" *Fortune*, April 15, 1996, 78–83; David Barboza, "Stocks Race Past New Milestone as Dow Breaks 7,000 Barrier," *New York Times*, February 14, 1997, A1, D6.

[19] This illustration is based on Bill Alpert, "The Times Are Risky, the Game Is Dangerous," *New York Times*, August 27, 1995, Sec. 3, 3.

[20] See George D. Kaufman, *The U.S. Financial System: Money, Markets, and Institutions*, 6th ed. (Englewood Cliffs, NJ: Prentice Hall, 1995), 432; Robert D. Hershey, Jr., "Nintendo Capitalism: Zapping the Markets," *New York Times*, May 28, 1996, D1, D4.

[21] Jeffrey M. Laderman, "The Prospectus Tries Plain Speaking," *Business Week*, August 14, 1995, 72.

[22] Michael Schroeder and Amy Barrett, "A Bigger Stick against Inside Traders," *Business Week*, May 27, 1996, 34–35.

Appendix I

[1] Shawn Tully, "Raiding a Company's Hidden Cash," *Fortune*, August 22, 1994, 82–87.

[2] See Walter T. Harrison, Jr., and Charles T. Horngren, *Financial Accounting*, 2nd ed. (Englewood Cliffs, NJ: Prentice Hall, 1995), 327–328; Timothy J. Gallagher and Joseph D. Andrew, Jr., *Financial Management: Principles and Practice* (Upper Saddle River, NJ: Prentice Hall, 1997), 453–456

[3] Shawn Tully, "Prophet of Zero Working Capital," *Fortune*, June 13, 1994, 113–114.

[4] See Nasser Arshadi and Gordon V. Karels, *Modern Financial Intermediaries and Markets* (Upper Saddle River, NJ: Prentice Hall, 1997), 296–301.

[5] See Harrison and Horngren, *Financial Accounting*, 557–559.

[6] See Gallagher and Andrew, *Financial Management*, 316–334.

[7] See Norman M. Scarborough and Thomas W. Zimmerer, *Effective Small Business Management*, 5th ed. (Upper Saddle River, NJ: Prentice Hall, 1996), 506–512.

[8] See Scarborough and Zimmerer, *Effective Small Business Management*, 315–332.

[9]Thomas P. Fitch, *Dictionary of Banking Terms*, 2nd ed. (Hauppauge, NY: Barron's, 1993), 531.

[10]Mark S. Dorfman, *Introduction to Risk Management and Insurance*, 5th ed. (Englewood Cliffs, NJ: Prentice Hall, 1994), 34.

[11]See S.S. Huebner, Kenneth Black, Jr., and Bernard L. Webb, *Property and Liability Insurance*, 4th ed. (Upper Saddle River, NJ: Prentice Hall, 1996), 369–372.

[12]Michael Quint, "Crackdown on Job Injury Costs," *New York Times*, March 16, 1995, D1, D7; see also Huebner, Black, and Webb, *Property and Liability Insurance*, 432–437.

[13]See Huebner, Black, and Webb, *Property and Liability Insurance*, 260–263.

Appendix II

[1]Judith H. Dobrzynski, "New Jobs: A Growing Number Are Good Ones," *New York Times*, July 21, 1996, Sec. 3, 1.

[2]Both of the following lists are reported in Dobrzynski, "New Jobs."

[3]Bureau of the Census, *Statistical Abstract of the United States* (Washington, DC: U.S. Dept. of Commerce, 1994), 410.

[4]Alex Markels, "Job Hunting Takes Off in Cyberspace," *Wall Street Journal*, September 20, 1996, B1.

[5]For more information on the value of business internships to the job-search process, see Douglas Martin, "Career Preview Also Works as Mirror for the Job Hunter," *New York Times*, August 23, 1993, D1.

[6]Information in this section comes from Resumix Inc. (Sunnyvale, CA), "Preparing the Ideal Scannable Résumé." It was posted on IBM's World Wide Web home page on June 4, 1996.

[7]For more information on the quality of job training and development, see Thomas Amirault, "Job Training: Who Needs It and Where They Get It," *Occupational Outlook Quarterly*, Winter 1992–1993, 18–31.

Source Notes

Chapter 1

Tired of Mickey Mouse Vacations? Lisa Bannon, "Disney Decides World Isn't So Small, Creating Education Resort for Boomers," *Wall Street Journal*, March 1, 1996, B1; "Celebrated Pro Gary Player to Design Golf Program at New Disney Institute," *Business Wire*, February 2, 1996; Greg Dawson, "Spirituality, Serenity? Spend a Day at Disney," *Orlando Sentinel*, March 10, 1996, B1; Leslie Doolittle, "Disney Executives Thinking Big—and Small—for Upcoming Asian Smalltrip," *Orlando Sentinel*, March 5, 1996, B1; Monika Guttman, "Facing the Facts of Life," *U.S. News & World Report*, April 22, 1996, 57–58; Kerry Hannon, "The Joys of a Working Vacation," *U.S. News & World Report*, June 10, 1996, 89–94; Dick Marlowe, "Will Institute Start Revolution?" *Orlando Sentinel*, July 24, 1995, 3; Christine Shenot, "Disney Breaks New Ground with Institute," *Orlando Sentinel*, February 7, 1996, A1; Shenot, "Disney Offers Alternative Vacation," *Orlando Sentinel*, December 18, 1995, 5. ***How Hollywood Blows Itself Out of Proportion*** Pat H. Broeske, "Movies: The Glory That Was Hollywood: It Cost $12 Million to Make 'Spartacus' in 1960," *The Los Angeles Times*, April 21, 1991, Home Edition, Calendar Section, 3; David R. Henderson, "Fun and Games with Inflation," *Fortune*, March 18, 1996, 35–36. **Building Your Business Skills** Barnaby J. Feder, "As the Cereal War Heats Up, Kellogg Reduces Prices," *New York Times*, June 11, 1996, D4; James P. Miller, "Cereal Makers Fight Bagels with Price Cuts," *Wall Street Journal*, June 20, 1996, B1. **Figures 1.3, 1.4, 1.5, 1.6, and 1.7** Christopher Farrell with Michael Mandell, "Why Are We So Afraid of Growth?" *Business Week*, May 16, 1994, 62–65+.

Chapter 2

Avis Tries Harder, Succeeds in Selling Out Jack Otter, "Big Payday: Avis Employees Reap Sweet Gains in HFS Buyout," New York *Newsday*, July 3, 1996, A61; Alan J. Wax, "Avis Sold for $800M," New York *Newsday*, July 2, 1996, A7; Edwin McDowell, "HFS Will Acquire Employee–Controlled Avis for $800 Million in Cash and Stock," *New York Times*, July 2, 1996, D6; Caitlin Liu, "For Employee-Owners of Avis, a Bittersweet Deal," *New York Times*, July 14, 1996, Sec. 3, 9; "Why Worker Owners Sell Out" (editorial), *New York Times*, July 7, 1996. Sec. 3, 8. ***The Trauma of Legal Separation*** Edward Felsenthal, "The Messiest Divorce That Jacoby & Meyers Ever Handled: It's Own," *Wall Street Journal*, January 23, 1996, A1; Scott Harris, "Their Best Argument Was with Each Other," *Los Angeles Times*, April 25, 1996, Metro section, 1. ***CalPERS Pressures Little Guys to Measure Up*** "CalPERS' Investments Power California Economy," *Business Wire*, December 15, 1995; "CalPERS Votes against Directors at Philip Morris," *Business Wire*, April 13, 1995; Judith H. Dobrzynski, "Small Companies, Big Problems," *New York Times*, February 6, 1996, D1. **Figure 2.1** Christopher Farrell with Michael Mandel, "Why Are We So Afraid of Growth?" *Business Week*, May 16, 1994, 72. **Figure 2.2** Data from U.S. Bureau of the Census, *Statistical Abstract of the United States: 1995* (Washington, DC: 1995).

Chapter 3

The Fine Line between Overseeing and Oversight Peter Cary and Stephen J. Hedges, "A Start–Up's Struggles," *U.S. News & World Report*, June 24, 1996, 50–52; Ronald B. Lieber, "Turns Out This Critter Can Fly," *Fortune*, November 27, 1995, 110–112; Howard Gleckman, "A Hard Truth about Deregulation," *Business Week*, July 15, 1996, 34; Marc Levinson and Anne Underwood, "A New Day at the FAA?" *Newsweek*, July 1, 1996, 46; Willy Stern, "A Greater Threat Than Terrorism?" *Business Week*, September 9, 1996, 86, 88–89; Matthew L. Wald, "Aviation Agency Seeks to Shift Its Mission, Focusing on Safety," *New York Times*, June 19, 1996, A1; Wald, "FAA Shuts Down ValuJet, Citing 'Serious Deficiencies,'" *New York Times*, June 18, 1996, A1; David Greising with Nicole Harris, "Up, Up, and a Ways to Go," *Business Week*, September 16, 1996, 86–87; Wald, "ValuJet, Grounded for Safety Problems, Is Cleared to Fly Again," *New York Times*, September 27, 1996, A24. ***Hooked on Telecommunications*** Catherine Arnst, "MCI Is Swarming over the Horizon," *Business Week*, February 19, 1996, 68–69; Bryan Gruley and Albert R. Karr, "Bill's Passage Represents Will of Both Parties," *Wall Street Journal*, February 2, 1996, B1; Brian O'Reilly, "First Blood in the Telecom Wars," *Fortune*, March 4, 1996, 124–136; "Telecom Vote Signals Competitive Free–for–All: Likely Mergers Herald an Era of Megacarriers," *Wall Street Journal*, February 2, 1996, B1. ***Scientists Search for the Missing Linkage*** Max Boot, "The Tort Case That Killed the Truth," *Wall Street Journal*, June 26, 1996, A16; Linda Himelstein with John Carey and Keith Naughton, "A Breast-Implant Deal Comes Down to the Wire," *Business Week*, September 4, 1995, 88–89+; John A. Byrne, "Informed Consent," *Business Week*, October 2, 1995, 104–116; Gina Kolata and Barry Meier, "Implant Lawsuits Create a Medical Rush to Cash In," *New York Times*, September 18, 1995, A1; Kolata, "Three Companies Agree to Settle Implant Cases," *New York Times*, November 14, 1995, A22; Meier, "As Thousands File Claims, Judge Revises Breast Implant Deal," *New York Times*, September 8, 1995, A17; "Still Fighting," *The Economist*, March 16, 1996, 67; Kolata, "Judge Rules Breast Implant Evidence Invalid," *New York Times*, December 19, 1996, A1, B17. **Building Your Business Skills** "Campus Fight Leads Reebok to Modify a Shoe Contract," *New York Times*, June 28, 1996, A16. **Figure 3.1** Center for the Study of American Business, Washington University.

Chapter 4

Mending Imperfections in the System Thomas Teal, "Not a Fool, Not a Saint," *Fortune*, November 11, 1996, 201–202+; Richard Jerome, "Holding the Line: After Fire Wrecked His Mill, Aaron Feuerstein Didn't Let His Workers Down," *People Weekly*, February 5, 1996, 122; "Malden Mills' President Aaron Feuerstein Assures Payment to Employees for Third Consecutive Month," *Business Wire*, February 9, 1996, 209–210; Steve Wulf, "The Glow from a Fire: a New England Textile Manufacturer Turns Tragedy into a Christmas Tale of Warmth for His Workers," *Time*, January 8, 1996, 49; Louis Uchitelle, "Chief Who Preserved Mill Jobs Is Now Cutting 450 Positions," *New York Times*, July 17, 1996, D6; Uchitelle, "The Risks of Keeping a Promise," *New York Times*, July 4, 1996, D1. ***What to Do in a Mad-Cow Crisis*** Lawrence

K. Altman, "U.S. Officials Confident That Mad Cow Disease of Britain Has Not Occurred Here," *New York Times*, March 27, 1996, A12; Gina Kolata, "Study Questions Top Theory on Cause of Mad Cow Disease," *New York Times*, January 17, 1997, A19; Patrick Barrett, "Beef Industry Takes Stock," *Marketing*, March 28, 1996, 14; John Darnton, "British Beef Banned in France and Belgium," *New York Times*, March 22, 1996, A8; Darnton, "For the British Beef War: A Truce but No Victory," *New York Times*, June 24, 1996, A9; Mary Kay Melvin, "Food Managers in England Report on Impact of Mad Cow Disease," *Amusement Business*, April 15, 1996, 16; Richard L. Papiernik, "U.S. Chains Switch Beef Sources in U.K.," *Nation's Restaurant News*, April 8, 1996, 1. ***Kathie Lee's Labor Pains*** Mark L. Clifford, "Pangs of Conscience," *Business Week*, July 29, 1996, 46–47; Rob Howe, "Labor Pains," *People Weekly*, June 10, 1996, 58; Larry Rohter, "To U.S. Critics, a Sweatshop; To Hondurans, a Better Life," *New York Times*, July 18, 1996, A1; Stephanie Strom, "A Sweetheart Becomes Suspect," *New York Times*, June 27, 1996, D1; George White, "Gifford to Help Reich in War on Sweatshops," *Los Angeles Times*, June 1, 1996, 2.

Chapter 5

For a Few Dollars More Marcus W. Brauchli, "The Outlook: China's Big Advantage Is a Young Population," *Wall Street Journal*, April 14, 1996, A1; Kathy Chen, "Young Chinese Loosen the Purse Strings," *Wall Street Journal*, July 15, 1996, A9; Pete Engardio, "Microsoft's Long March," *Business Week*, June 24, 1996, 52–54; Seth Faison, "U.S. and China Agree on Pact to Fight Piracy," *New York Times*, June 18, 1996, A6; David E. Sanger, "Software Pirates Growing in Number in China, U.S. Says," *New York Times*, May 8, 1996, A1, A9; Jarie H. Lii, "Boom–at–a–Glance," *New York Times Magazine*, February 16, 1996, 26–27. ***The Pitfalls of Marketing Murky Tea*** Norihiko Shirouzu, "Snapple in Japan: How a Splash Dried Up," *Wall Street Journal*, April 15, 1996, B1; Edith Hill Updike, "Is Cavalier Japanese for Edsel?" *Business Week*, June 24, 1996, 39. **Building Your Business Skills** See Edwart T. Hall, *The Silent Language* (Garden City, NY: Doubleday, 1959.) **Figure 5.1** Rob Norton, "Strategies for the New Export Boom," *Fortune*, August 22, 1994, 124–127. Data from *Fortune* magazine. **Figures 5.2 and 5.3** Robert D. Hershey Jr., "China Has Become Chief Contributor to U.S. Trade Gap," *New York Times*, August 21, 1996, A1, D4. Data from the U.S. Department of Commerce.

Video Exercise 2.1

Video Source "So Safe You Could Die: Overregulation by the FDA," *20/20*, August 12, 1994, #1432 **Additional Sources** Brent Bowers, "Safety First: How a Device to Aid in Breast Self-Exams Is Kept Off the Market," *Wall Street Journal*, April 12, 1994, A1, A11; Ron Winslow, "FDA Halts Test on Device That Shows Promise for Victims of Cardiac Arrest," *Wall Street Journal*, May 11, 1994, B7; John Carey with Joseph Weber and Joan O'C. Hamilton, "Is the FDA Hooked on Caution?" *Business Week*, January 30, 1995, 72–74; Laura Jereski, "Block That Innovation," *Forbes*, January 18, 1993, 48.

Chapter 6

If the Shoe Virtually Fits John Holusha, "Making the Shoe Fit, Perfectly," *New York Times*, March 20, 1996, D1; Peter Kafka, "Megamall Is Shoe Chains' First Local Step," *Minneapolis/St. Paul CityBusiness*, May 17, 1996; Dee Segel, "Custom Shoe Store Starts Out on Right Foot," *The Hartford (Connecticut) Courant*, March 22, 1996, F1; Isabelle Sender, "A Fitting Idea," *Footwear News*, February 12, 1996, 57; "A Shoe That Really Fits," *Forbes*, June 3, 1996, 104; "Shoemaker Steps into Database Marketing," *The Cowles Report on Database Marketing*, June 1996; Joan Verdon, "New Concept in Shoe Sales: Instep with the Times," *The Record*, July 23, 1996; Dan Woog, "If the Computer Fits, It Must Be Footgear," *Westport (Connecticut) News*, March 22, 1996, A21; Michelle Wong, "'Virtual Inventory,'" *Star Tribune (Minneapolis Edition)*, August 6, 1996, D1; "Computer Makes the Shoe More Likely to Fit," *The Record*, April 27, 1996; "The Custom Foot Offers a New Concept in Fitting Customers to Perfection" (press release). ***Booksellers at War*** Kirk Johnson, "A New Superstore of Books Enters the New York Fray," *New York Times*, September 4, 1996, B3; Patrick M. Reilly, "Where Borders Group and Barnes & Noble Compete, It's a War," *Wall Street Journal*, September 3, 1996, A1, A8. ***Culture Shock at Shoney's*** Dorothy J. Gaiter, "How Shoney's, Belted by a Lawsuit, Found the Path to Diversity," *Wall Street Journal*, April 16, 1996, A1, A6; Peter Romeo, "What Really Happened at Shoney's," *Restaurant Business*, May 1, 1993, 116–122; Rick Van Warner, "Shoney's Shakeup Raises New Cloud over Efforts to Embrace Minorities," *Nation's Restaurant News*, January 4, 1993, 21. **Figure 6.1** David Kirkpatrick, "Fast Times at Compaq," *Fortune*, April 1, 1996, 125. **Figure 6.2** Brent Schlender, "Big Blue Is Betting on Big Iron Again," *Fortune*, April 29, 1996, 108.

Chapter 7

United Gives Managers the Power to Manage Susan Chandler, "United We Own," *Business Week*, March 18, 1996, 96–100; Perry Flint, "The Buck Stops Lower," *Air Transport World*, September 1995, 28–32. ***What to Do When the Corporation Goes into Denial*** Larry Armstrong, "A Death in the Parsons Family," *Business Week*, April 22, 1996, 39; Joann S. Lublin, "Few Companies Plan Succession Past CEO Level," *Wall Street Journal*, April 8, 1996, B1, B6.

Chapter 8

Doll Maker Disarmed by Success Glenn Collins, "Growing Pains for a Doll Maker," *New York Times*, September 17, 1996, D1, D19; Sally Lodge, "Magic Attic Club Casts a Spell," *Publishers Weekly*, June 19, 1995, 23. ***The Generation X Files*** John Simons, "The Youth Movement," *U.S. News & World Report*, September 23, 1996, 65–68. ***Eastern Meets East and West at salami.com*** Jim Carlton, "Think Big," *Wall Street Journal*, June 17, 1996, R27; Kathy Rebello, "Making Money on the Net," *Business Week*, September 23, 1996, 104–105+. **Figure 8.1** U.S. Department of Commerce, *Statistical Abstract of the United States* (Washington, DC: Bureau of the Census, 1995). **Figure 8.2** Sylvia Nasar, "Myth: Small Business as Job Engine," *New York Times*, March 25, 1994, D1, D2. **Figure 8.3** Glenn Collins, "Growing Pains for a Doll Maker," *New York Times*, September 17, 1996, D1. Data from the Small Business Administration and Dun & Bradstreet. **Figure 8.4** Wendy Zellner et al., "Women Entrepreneurs," *Business Week*, April 18, 1994, 104–108+. **Figure 8.5** National Federation of Independent Business Research and Education Foundation, *Small Business in America* (1991).

Video Exercise 3.1

Video Source "Sharing Sweet Success," *20/20*, May 22, 1992, #1222. **Additional Sources** Claudia Dreifus, "Passing the Scoop: Ben & Jerry," *New York Times Magazine*, December 18, 1994, 38, 40–41; William M. Bulkeley and Joann S. Lublin, "Ben & Jerry's: New CEO Will Face Shrinking Sales and Growing Fears of Fat," *Wall Street Journal*, January 10, 1995, B1, B4; Paul C. Judge, "Is It Rainforest Crunch Time?" *Business Week*, July 15, 1996, 70–71; Jennifer J. Laabs, "Ben & Jerry's Caring Capitalism," *Personnel Journal*, November 1992, 50–57.

Chapter 9

What Would Capitalism Be without "Bossy Bosses"? Judith H. Dobrzynski, "Chicken Done to a Golden Rule," *New York Times*, April 3, 1996, D1, D4; Donald J. McNerney, "Employee Motivation: Creating a Motivated Workforce," *HR Focus*, August 1996, 1–4; Shelly Wolson, "Never on Sunday," *Restaurant Business*, May 1, 1992, 110–111. ***Employers Embrace the Two Ls (Loyalty and Longevity)*** Marshall Loeb, "Wouldn't It Be Better to Work for the Good Guys?" *Fortune*, October 14, 1996, 223–224; Joseph B. White and Joann S. Lublin, "Some Companies Try to Rebuild Loyalty," *Wall Street Journal*, September 27, 1996, B1, B6. **Building Your Business Skills** Keith H. Hammonds, "Balancing Work and Family," *Business Week*, September 26, 1996, 74–78+.

Chapter 10

Marriott Clears a Pathway to Productive Employment Dana Millbank, "Hiring Welfare People, Hotel Chain Finds, Is Tough but Rewarding," *Wall Street Journal*, October 31, 1996, A1, A10; Catherine Yang, "Low Wage Lessons," *Business Week*, November 11, 1996, 108–111+. ***New Life on the High-Tech Line*** Stephen Baker, "The New Factory Worker," *Business Week*, September 30, 1996, 59–61+; Glenn Burkins, "Good Jobs Go Unfilled amid Some Shortages of Skilled Workers," *Wall Street Journal*, November 27, 1996, A1, A6; Gene Bylinsky, "Creating Their Own Workforces," *Fortune*, October 14, 1996, 162A–162B+. ***Security Is Job 1*** Keith Bradsher, "Big Labor with a Smaller Agenda," *New York Times*, September 13, 1996, D1, D4; Bradsher, "GM Labor Cost for Parts Higher Than Rivals, Study Says," *New York Times*, June 25, 1996, D2; Bradsher, "Need to Cut Costs? Order Out," *New York Times*, April 11, 1996, D1, D4; Bradsher, "New Approach for Auto Union in Ford Accord," *New York Times*, September 18, 1996, A1, D6. **Figure 10.5** Aaron Bernstein, "Why America Needs Unions—But Not the Kind It Has Now," *Business Week*, May 23, 1994, 70–71.

Video Exercise 4.1

Video Source "Assembly Line Teams Are Better Trained and More Efficient," *World News Tonight*, February 24, 1993. **Additional Sources** Wendy

Zellner, "Team Player: No More 'Same–Ol'— Same–Ol'," *Business Week*, October 17, 1994, 95–96; Michael Barrier, "Adversity Brings Opportunity," *Nation's Business*, April 1993, 31–34; Dale E. Yeatts, Martha Hipstink, and Debra Barns, "Lessons Learned from Self–Managed Work Teams," Business Horizons, July–August 1994, 11–18.

Chapter 11
Crafty Brewers with a Marketing Angle Fred Bunz, "Microbrewers Feel Perfectly at Home with Do–It–Themselves Beer Makers," *Beverage World Periscope Edition*, July 31, 1995, 1–2; Yumiko Ono, "Who Really Makes That Cute Little Beer? You'd Be Surprised," *Wall Street Journal*, April 15, 1996, A1, A10. ***If You Think You're Good . . .*** Justin Martin, "Are You as Good as You Think You Are?" *Fortune*, September 30, 1996, 142–145+; James Morgan, "GEBN: Global Benchmarking Hits Its Stride," *Purchasing*, January 11, 1996, 102–107.

Chapter 12
There's No Business Like Show Business Reed Abelson, "The Shell Game of Hollywood 'Net Profits,'" *New York Times*, March 4, 1996, D1, D6; Elizabeth Lesly, "Fatal Subtraction?" *Business Week*, March 11, 1996, 66–68; Tim Carvell, "Accounting, Hollywood–Style," *Fortune*, November 11, 1996, 48. ***U.S. Business Is Looking for a Few Good Accountants*** Lee Burton, "College Courses on Accounting Get Poor Grades," *Wall Street Journal*, August 12, 1994, B1, B7; "Focus On: Accounting Education," *Journal of Accountancy*, June 1994, 44–45; Gary Siegel and James Sorenson, *What Corporate America Wants in Entry–Level Accountants* (New York: The Institute of Management Accountants, August 1994). **Building Your Business Skills** Saul Hansell, "Paying Bills without Any Litter," *New York Times*, July 5, 1996, D1, D3.

Video Exercise 5.1
Video Source "Voice Mail Jail," *Nightline*, May 9, 1994. **Additional Sources** William G. Flanagan and Toddi Gutner, "The Perils of Voice Mail," *Forbes*, January 17, 1994, 106–107; Gordon Brockhouse, "Operator, Gimme a Human!" *Canadian Business*, November 1992, 109–111+; Richard Shaffer, "Learn to Love Voice Mail," *Forbes*, October 26, 1992, 264; Patricia A. LaRosa, "Voice Messaging Is Quality 'Lip Service,'" *The Office*, May 1992, 10, 12; Gregg Keiser, "Press One for Gregg," *Compute*, August 1992, 73–75.

Chapter 13
Still Partying after All These Years? Martha Brannigan, "Florida Haven Still Has Taint of 'Liquordale,'" *Wall Street Journal*, March 22, 1996, B1, B6; Tracy Kolody, "Ad Campaign Realizes Lauderdale Can't Make Clean Break from Past," Fort Lauderdale *Sun Sentinal*, October 20, 1995, 1D; Kolody, "New Ads Will Tout Broward in Magazines," Fort Lauderdale *Sun Sentinel*, September 29, 1995, 1D; John S. DeMott, "Wreaking Havoc on Spring Break," *Time*, April 7, 1996, 29; phone interview (August 15, 1996) with representatives of the Broward County Convention and Visitors' Bureau. ***In the News: "The World Is Not Going to Be the Same in 30 Years"*** Steven A. Holmes, "Census Sees a Profound Ethnic Shift in U.S.," *New York Times*, March 14, 1996, A16; Jeffrey A. Tannen-

baum, "Number of Hispanic–Owned Businesses Jumped 76 Percent from '87 to '92, U.S. Says," *Wall Street Journal*, July 11, 1996, B1, B2. ***Where's the Market for Skinny Ties and See-Through Track Shoes?*** David Fischer, "Let the Good Times Roll," *U.S. News & World Report*, July 1, 1996, 51–52; David Leonhardt, "Like Totally Big Spenders," *Business Week*, June 3, 1996, 8; Shawn Tully, "Teens: The Most Global Market of All," *Fortune*, May 16, 1994, 90–94+; Laura Zinn, "Teens: Here Comes the Biggest Wave Yet," *Business Week*, April 11, 1994, 76–79+; John Greenwald, "Will Teens Buy It?" *Time*, May 30, 1994, 50–52; Jane L. Levere, "Advertising: A New Survey Charts the Habits of Teen–Agers around the World," *New York Times*, June 11, 1996, D8; Roger Ricklefs, "Marketers Seek Out Today's Coolest Kids to Plug into Tomorrow's Mall Trends," *Wall Street Journal*, July 11, 1996, B1, B2. **Figure 13.3** Erick Schonfield, "Betting on the Boomers," *Fortune*, December 25, 1995, 78–80+. Data from *Fortune* and U.S. Census Bureau estimates.

Chapter 14
Charting the Air Jordan Route Ian Fisher, "A New Jordan Sneaker Inspires a Frenetic Run," *New York Times*, July 4, 1996, B1, B4; Leigh Gallagher, "Industry Retailers See Swoosh as Double-Edged Sword," *Sporting Goods Business*, April 1996, 8; Robert McAllister, "Jordan Fever Is Heating Up Retailers," *Footwear News*, March 20, 1995, 2–3; Catherine Salfino, "Pro Name Game Gives Nike, Reebok Foothold in Apparel Arena," *Daily News Record*, February 28, 1996, 3. ***The Demise and Rise of Sticker Dickering*** Keith Bradsher, "Sticker Shock: Car Buyers Miss Haggling Ritual," *New York Times*, June 13, 1996, D1, D23; Bradley J. Fikes, "Haggling over Price Is No Longer Automatic," *San Diego Business Journal*, October 3, 1994, 17–18.

Chapter 15
The Battle Plan for Attacking Inventory at the Big Store Robert Berner, "Retired General Speeds Deliveries, Cuts Costs, Helps Sears Rebound," *Wall Street Journal*, July 16, 1996, A1, A7; June Carolyn Erlick, "Pagonis Takes Battle Plan to Sears," *HFD—The Weekly Home Furnishings Newspaper*, April 24, 1994, 12; "From Moving Tanks to Moving Merchandise," *Management Review*, June 1994, 30–32. ***The Special Appeal of American Retailers*** John Tagliabue, "Enticing Europe's Shoppers," *New York Times*, April 24, 1996, D1, D20; Tagliabue, "Europeans Agonize Over the Mall," *New York Times*, September 10, 1996, D1, D7. ***The Allure of On-Line Commerce*** Don Clark, "Virtual Safety," *Wall Street Journal*, June 17, 1996, R21, R25; Jared Sandberg, "Making the Sale," *Wall Street Journal*, June 17, 1996, R6; John W. Verity, "Invoice? What's an Invoice?" *Business Week*, June 10, 1996, 110–112; Kathy Rebello with Larry Armstrong and Amy Cortese, "Making Money on the Net," *Business Week*, September 23, 1996, 104–107+; Michael H. Martin, "The Next Big Thing: A Bookstore?" *Fortune*, December 9, 1996, 168–170; Rebello, "A Literary Hangout—Without the Latté," *Business Week*, September 23, 1996, 106.

Video Exercise 6.1
Video Source "The Tyranny of Fashion," *Nightline*, March 18, 1994. **Additional Sources** Martha

Duffy, "Fashion's Fall," *Time*, April 25, 1994, 76–80; Margot Hornblower, "Sowing His Label," *Time*, April 4, 1994, 72–73; Dan Graw, "Designing for Dollars: The Apparel Industry Struggles to Attract Price–Conscious Consumers," *U.S. News & World Report*, November 14, 1994, 103–106; Barbara Rudolph, "Skirting the Issues," *Time*, June 5, 1995, 58–62.

Chapter 16
Accounting for South Africa's "Unbanked" Ken Wells, "Its New ATMs in Place, a Bank Reaches Out to South Africa's Poor," *Wall Street Journal*, June 13, 1996, A1, A10; "Taking Microchips to Townships: South Africa's Banks Are Going Boldly Where Few Banks Have Gone Before," *The Economist*, July 8, 1995, 71–73 ***What This Country Needs Is a Good 20-Minute Cigar*** Ellen Graham, "Community Groups Print Local (and Legal) Currencies," *Wall Street Journal*, June 28, 1996, B1, B6. ***Ben Franklin Moves Slightly to the Left*** John Tagliabue, "A Bank Note, So Very Swiss and Computer–Drawn," *New York Times*, February 15, 1996, D6; "$100 Question: Will Ben's New Look Stop Counterfeits?" *New York Times*, September 28, 1995, D19; **Figure 16.2** Terence P. Paré, "Clueless Bankers," *Fortune*, November 27, 1995, 151. Data from the Federal Reserve. **Figure 16.5** Keith Bradsher, "Federal Reserve Trims a Key Rate; First Cut since '92," *New York Times*, July 7, 1995, A1, D1, D4. Data from Patrick J. Lyons/*New York Times*. **Figure 16.7** James Gleick, "Dead as a Dollar," *New York Times Magazine*, June 16, 1996, 27.

Chapter 17
Stories of Great Expectations in Hard Times Lloyd Gite, "Each One, Teach One: Educating African Americans about the Stock Market," *Black Enterprise*, February 1996, 60; Suzanne Woolley, "Our Love Affair With Stocks," *Business Week*, June 3, 1996, 91–93+. ***IPO Capitalism: The Marketplace for Entrepreneurial Zeal*** Judith Dobrzynski, "A Season of Opening Days," *New York Times*, April 19, 1996, D1, D4; Christopher Farrell, "The Boom in IPOs," *Business Week*, December 18, 1995, 64–69+; Robert A. Mamis, "No Tech, No Takers," *Inc.*, May 1996, p. 44–46+; John Wyatt, "America's Amazing IPO Bonanza," *Fortune*, May 27, 1996, 76–79. ***The Brave New World of Cyberspace Brokerage*** Vanessa O'Connell, "Stock Answer," *Wall Street Journal*, June 17, 1996, R8; "With the World Wide Web, Who Needs Wall Street?" *Business Week*, April 29, 1996, 120–121. **Figure 17.1** Mark Landler, "AT&T Warns of a Drop in Earnings and Its Stock Plunges," *New York Times*, September 25, 1996, D1, D3. Data from Datastream. **Figure 17.2** Ira Sager, "How IBM Became a Growth Company Again," *Business Week*, December 9, 1996, 154–158+. Data from IBM and Bloomberg Financial Markets. **Figure 17.3** Anthony Ramirez, "Nasdaq Index Flirts with 1000, Perhaps Ahead of Its Time," *New York Times*, July 23, 1995, Sec. 3, 3. **Figure 17.5** Data from *Mutual Fund Fact Book* (Washington, DC: Investment Company Institute, 1995). **Figure 17.8** Susan E. Kuhn, "How Crazy Is This Market?" *Fortune*, April 15, 1996, 78–83. Data from Smith Barney.

Video Exercise 7.1
Video Source "Moscow Investment Company Fraud," *World News Tonight*," July 28, 1994. **Addi-

tional Sources Adi Ignatius, "As 'Pyramid Scheme' in Russia Begins to Collapse, Rubble May Trap Many," *Wall Street Journal*, July 27, 1994, A10; Neela Banerjee, "While Many in Russia Decry MMM, Others Line Up to Buy More Shares," *Wall Street Journal*, August 1, 1994, A15; Banerjee, "Russian Police Raid the Home of MMM Chief," *Wall Street Journal*, August 5, 1994, A6; Claudia Rosett, "P.T. Barnum Missed a Mar-velous Thing: Russian Investments," *Wall Street Journal*, September 27, 1994, A1, A12; Steven Erlanger, "Risks of Russia's Young Markets," *New York Times*, August 5, 1994, D1, D2.

Appendix II
Tables AII.1, AII.2 Judith H. Dobrzynski, "The New Jobs: A Growing Number Are Good Ones," *New York Times*, July 21, 1996, Sec. 3, 1. Data from Regional Financial Associates: Bureau of Labor Statistics. **Table AII.4** Alex Markels, "Job Hunting Takes Off in Cyberspace," *Wall Street Journal*, September 20, 1996, B1.

Photo Credits

Preface
Page xvii: Stacie Ghali/Lands' End
Page xviii: Photographix

Chapter 1
Page 1: Jeffrey Macmillan Photography
Page 15: AP/Wide World Photos
Page 16 Ann States/SABA Press Photos, Inc.
Page 19: Photographix
Page 19: Photographix
Page 20: Photographix
Page 20: Photographix

Chapter 2
Page 27: Ed Bailey/AP/Wide World Photos
Page 32: Sears, Roebuck and Co.
Page 40: Porter Gifford/Gamma-Liaison, Inc.

Chapter 3
Page 53: Ken Hawkins/Sygma
Page 56: Ron Frehm/AP/Wide World Photos
Page 61: Anchorage Daily News/Gamma-Liaison, Inc.
Page 63: James King-Holmes/W Industries/Science Photo Library
Page 63: Churchill & Klehr Photography

Chapter 4
Page 75: Malden Mills Industries, Inc.
Page 78: Wendy Lamm/Los Angeles Times Syndicate
Page 79: Pablo Bartholomew/Gamma-Liaison, Inc.
Page 82: Anne Cusack/Los Angeles Times Syndicate
Page 87: Ed Bailey/AP/Wide World Photos
Page 91: Jeff Greenberg/Photo Edit

Chapter 5
Page 97: Greg Baker/AP/Wide World Photos
Page 100: Tomasz Tomaszewski Photography
Page 106: Jean-Pierre Arnel/Sygma
Page 111: Paul Lowe/Magnum Photo, Inc.
Page 113: Eric Bouvet/Agence Emoult Features

Chapter 6
Page 127: Edward Santalone Photography

Page 129: Daniel Simon/Gamma-Liaison, Inc.
Page 130: Chris Corsmeier Photography
Page 134: Reid Horn
Page 140: Chris Pizello/AP/Wide World Photos
Page 144: Marilynn K. Yee/New York Times Pictures

Chapter 7
Page 153: Ed Kashi
Page 158: Louis Psihoyos/Matrix International
Page 163: Silvia Otte
Page 165: Cliff Kucine/Kucine photo/Maine,
Page 167: John Abbott Photography
Page 169: James Schnepf Photography, Inc.

Chapter 8
Page 177: Ed Quinn
Page 181: John Harding/*Fortune*, 12/13/93, p.172
Page 182: Frederick Charles Photography/Fortune, 2/7/94, p.137
Page 187: Brian Leng Photography

Chapter 9
Page 205: Chick-fil-A® Restaurant, Inc.
Page 207: Tom Raymond/The Stock Shop, Inc./Medichrome
Page 208: Marty Lederhandler/AP/Wide World Photos
Page 217: Photographix
Page 218: Steve Woit
Page 221: Scott Montgomery Photography

Chapter 10
Page 231: Ann States/SABA Press Photos, Inc.
Page 238: John Nollendoris/*Fortune*, 11/1/93, p.84
Page 240: Frank Polich/AP/Wide World Photos
Page 244: Vincent J. Musi/*Fortune*, 8/8/94, pp. 78–79
Page 244: Ed Kashi/*Fortune*, 1/24/94, p.32
Page 252: AP/Wide World Photos

Chapter 11
Page 263: Per Eriksson/The Image Bank
Page 265: Top Fritz Hoffman/JB Pictures Ltd./The Image Works
Page 265: Bab Sacha Photography

Page 278: Frito-Lay, Inc.
Page 283: Chaparral Steel

Chapter 12
Page 291: Gamma-Liaison, Inc.
Page 306: Toys "Я" Us
Page 310: Louis Psihoyos/Matrix International
Page 314: Photographix

Chapter 13
Page 327: Gerald Davis/Contact Press Images
Page 329: Rolex Watch U.S.A., Inc.
Page 330: (c) 1994 VISA International Service Association, VISA and The Three Banks Design are Trademark of VISA International Service Association. All Rights Reserved
Page 331: Public Broadcasting Service
Page 335: Michael L. Abramson

Chapter 14
Page 355: Jean-Marc Giboux/Gamma-Liaison, Inc.
Page 367: Paulo Fridman/Sygma
Page 373: Photographix

Chapter 15
Page 381: Christopher Covey Photography
Page 385: Christopher Covey
Page 386: Brian Smith
Page 388: NetMarket is a service provided by CUC International, Inc. © 1997 CUC International, Inc.
Page 388: NetMarket is a service provided by CUC International, Inc. © 1997 CUC International, Inc.
Page 390: Churchill & Klehr Photography
Page 396: SABA Press Photos, Inc.

Chapter 16
Page 413: Laurence Hughes/The Image Bank
Page 424: Peter Korniss
Page 431: James McMullan, Inc.

Chapter 17
Page 441: Walter Hodges/Tony Stone Images
Page 443: Morgan Stanley and Company Inc.
Page 446: Porter Gifford/Gamma-Liaison, Inc.

■ INDEXES

Subject Index

Name, Company, and Product Index